NINTH EDITION

Health, Safety, and Nutrition *for the* Young Child

Lynn R. Marotz, RN, Ph.D.

University of Kansas

CENGAGE
Learning·

Australia • Brazil • Japan • Korea • Mexico • Singapore • Spain • United Kingdom • United States

Health, Safety, and Nutrition for the Young Child, Ninth Edition
Lynn R. Marotz

Senior Product Manager: Mark Kerr

Managing Development Editor: Lisa Mafrici

Content Developer: Kate Scheinman

Content Coordinator: Jessica Alderman

Product Assistant: Coco Bator

Media Developer: Renee Schaaf

Marketing Director: Jennifer Levanduski

Marketing Manager: Kara Kindstrom

Content Project Manager: Samen Iqbal

Senior Art Director: Jennifer Wahi

Manufacturing Planner: Doug Bertke

Rights Acquisitions Specialist:
Dean Dauphinais

Production Service: Teresa Christie, MPS

Photo Researcher: Jill Reichenbach

Text Researcher: Pablo D'Stair

Copy Editor: Cathy Albano

Designer: Diane Beasley

Cover Image: Ariel Skelley/Fotosearch

Compositor: MPS Limited

For product information and technology assistance, contact us at
Cengage Learning Customer & Sales Support, 1-800-354-9706

For permission to use material from this text or product,
submit all requests online at **www.cengage.com/permissions**
Further permissions questions can be e-mailed to
permissionrequest@cengage.com

Library of Congress Control Number: 2013938467

Student Edition
ISBN-13: 978-1-285-42733-1
ISBN-10: 1-285-42733-5

Cengage Learning
200 First Stamford Place, 4th Floor
Stamford, CT 06902
USA

Cengage Learning is a leading provider of customized learning solutions with office locations around the globe, including Singapore, the United Kingdom, Australia, Mexico, Brazil, and Japan. Locate your local office at **www.cengage.com/global**

Cengage Learning products are represented in Canada by Nelson Education, Ltd.

To learn more about Cengage Learning Solutions, visit **www.cengage.com**

Purchase any of our products at your local college store or at our preferred online store **www.cengagebrain.com**

Printed in the United States of America
2 3 4 5 6 7 17 16 15 14

Brief Contents

Contents

UNIT 2 Keeping Children Safe   167

Chapter 10 Maltreatment of Children: Abuse and Neglect 267

Chapter 11 Planning for Children's Health and Safety Education 292

Chapter 12 Nutrition Guidelines 320

Chapter 13 Nutrients That Provide Energy (Carbohydrates, Fats, and Proteins) 339

UNIT 4 Nutrition and the Young Child   379

Epilogue 507

Appendices 509

Glossary 524

Index 531

Preface

Children's state of wellness has an unquestionable effect on their development and ability to learn. Our understanding of the factors that shape and influence a child's well-being, including nutrition, environmental conditions, and emotional and social health, continues to improve as a result of ongoing research. In turn, this information has led to noteworthy changes in our views about health, approaches to health care, and the critical importance of addressing health education during the early years. It has also contributed to the development of numerous resources (e.g., National Health Education Standards, MyPlate, Healthy People 2020, NAEYC's Standards for Early Childhood Professional Preparation, National Health and Safety Performance Standards for Child Care) that currently guide personal and classroom practices. Additionally, our knowledge of wellness and the importance of promoting healthy lifestyle behaviors draw increasing attention to the pivotal role teachers play in identifying children's health needs, creating high-quality environments that are safe and support learning, and providing comprehensive health education in schools.

Health, Safety, and Nutrition for the Young Child, now in its ninth edition, has become the standard text in the early childhood field. Its comprehensive approach and well-documented student/teacher-oriented focus continue to make it the best-selling, full-color textbook about children's well-being. Most importantly, this book provides students and teachers with a functional understanding of children's health, safety, and nutrition needs and guides them in implementing effective classroom practices. It also emphasizes the importance of respecting and partnering with all families to help children establish healthy lifestyles and achieve their learning potential. *Health, Safety, and Nutrition for the Young Child* accomplishes this by addressing all three essential components of children's wellness in one book:

- promoting children's **health** through awareness, assessment, early identification of special health needs, and meaningful health education
- creating and maintaining **safe learning environments** and fostering children's understanding and development of protective behaviors
- meeting children's essential **nutrition needs** by planning healthy meals, providing safe and nutritious food, and educating children about consuming a nutritious diet.

Extensive resources, lesson plans, teacher checklists, video clips, references, and family education materials are also provided throughout the book to aid busy students and practicing teachers in making a difference in children's lives.

The Intended Audience

First and foremost, *Health, Safety, and Nutrition for the Young Child* is written on behalf of young children everywhere. Ultimately, it is the children who benefit from having families and teachers who know how to protect and promote their safety and well-being. The term *families* is used throughout the text in reference to the diverse caring environments in which children are currently being raised and that may or may not include their biological parents. The term *teachers* is used inclusively to describe all adults who care for and work with young children-including educators, therapists, coaches, camp leaders, administrators, health care providers, legislators, and concerned citizens, whether they work in early education centers, home-based programs, recreation activities, public or private schools, community agencies, or after-school programs. The term *teacher* acknowledges the important educational role that families play in their children's daily lives. Its use also recognizes the valuable contributions of the many educators who dedicate their lives to children.

Health, Safety, and Nutrition for the Young Child is written for several primary audiences:

▸ Students and preservice teachers who have chosen a career in early education
▸ Experienced teachers in community schools, home-based programs, early childhood centers, Head Start programs, agencies that serve young children, and before- and after-school programs
▸ Allied health professionals and child advocates who work in any role that touches children's lives
▸ Families, who are children's most important teachers!

Organization and Key Content

The ninth edition of *Health, Safety, and Nutrition for the Young Child* maintains its original purpose to focus attention on the three critical areas that influence children's well-being: promoting children's health (Unit 1); creating high-quality, safe environments (Unit 2); and, supporting children's nutrition (basic and applied), healthy eating behaviors, and nutrition education (Units 3 and 4). This arrangement maximizes student learning and offers instructors flexibility in designing their courses. However, the interrelatedness of these three subject areas must not be overlooked despite their artificial separation.

Chapter content is presented in a clear, concise, and thought-provoking manner. It reflects the latest research developments and applications regarding children and wellness within a diverse and family-oriented framework. Key topics, including national health initiatives, children's mental health, bullying, fostering resilience and social-emotional competence, brain development, childhood obesity, emergency and disaster preparedness, and food safety have been added and updated. More information about children with special health challenges and school-aged children has also been provided. Without a doubt, this comprehensive book is a resource that no teacher (new or experienced) should be without!

New Content and Special Features

The ninth edition continues to include numerous features, tables, and checklists designed to engage students, reinforce learning, and enhance their ability to apply the information in contemporary educational settings:

▸ **Chapter Content Linked to National Association for the Education of Young Children Professional Preparation Standards**—NAEYC standards, identified at the onset of each chapter, enable students to relate chapter content to the association's professional education framework.

▸ **New Learning Objectives**—correlated to the main sections in each chapter show students what they need to know to process and understand the content. After completing the chapter, students should be able to demonstrate how they can use and apply their new knowledge and skills.

▸ **New Digital Downloads**—include most of the Teacher Checklists presented in the textbook for students to download, often customize, and use in the classroom! Look for the Digital Downloads label that identifies these items.

▸ **New Did You Get It? quizzes**—allow students to measure their performance against the learning objectives in each chapter. One question for each learning objective is featured in the textbook to encourage students to go to CengageBrain.com, take the full quiz, and check their understanding.

▶ **New Chapters**—Several chapters have been rewritten, reorganized, and expanded to improve student learning. A new section, *Emergency and Disaster Preparedness*, has been added to Chapter 8. Former Chapters 14 and 15 have been combined into a new Chapter 14, *"Nutrients That Promote Growth and Regulate Body Functions (Proteins, Vitamins, Minerals, and Water."* Technical detail has been replaced with material that is easier for students to understand. Chapter 18, *"Food Safety,"* has been reorganized and new information added to draw attention to a serious health concern.

▶ **New Teach Source Video Connections**—feature footage from the classroom to help students relate key chapter content to real-life scenarios. Critical-thinking questions provide opportunities for in-class or online discussion and reflection.

▶ **New Partnering with Families**—is a feature designed to address the importance of family engagement and inclusion in children's health, safety, and nutrition education. Information on a variety of topics is provided in letter format for busy teachers to copy and send home or share with families in a newsletter, program handbook, website posting, parent conference, or bulletin board display.

▶ **Additional Teacher Checklists**—are a well-received feature that has been expanded in every chapter to provide teachers with quick, efficient access to critical information and best practices. Beginning practitioners will find these concise reference lists especially helpful in learning new material. Experienced teachers and administrators will appreciate their easy access for classroom use and staff training purposes. Most of the Teacher Checklists are also available as Digital Downloads.

▶ **New Connecting to Everyday Practice**—presents real-life situations that challenge students to resolve common dilemmas by applying chapter content. Thought-provoking questions encourage self-reflection and group discussion.

▶ **Classroom Corner Teacher Activities**—showcases lesson plans aligned with the National Health Education Standards. Learning objectives, materials lists, and step-by-step procedures are provided to save teachers preparation time and present children with meaningful learning experiences.

▶ **New Did You Know . . . ?**—offers interesting facts in a new marginal feature to increase student curiosity and interest in chapter content.

▶ **Monthly Calendar of National Health, Safety, and Nutrition Observances**—provides a month-by-month listing of national observances and related website resources that teachers can use when planning learning experiences for children. This information is located in Appendix B.

▶ **Children's Book List**—is an extensive, updated collection of children's books that can be used for teaching about health, safety, and nutrition while also encouraging literacy skills. This resource is located in Appendix D and includes titles that address topics such as dental health, mental health, self-care, safety, nutrition, special needs, and physical activity.

Chapter-by-Chapter Changes

Chapter 1 *Children's Well-Being: What It Is and How to Achieve It*

▶ *New* information on national health programs and initiatives, including National Health Education Standards, Coordinated School Health Program, Healthy People 2020, Children's Health Insurance Program, and Let's Move.
▶ Emphasis placed on health promotion and its effect on children's learning, development, and behavior.
▶ *New* information on early brain development, cultural influences on health, childhood stress, bullying, and cyber-bullying.
▶ *New TeachSource Video Connections* feature: "Infancy Brain Development."

Chapter 2 *Daily Health Observations*

- Additional *Teacher Checklists* highlighting key information for easy access.
- *New* references reinforcing teachers' role in early identification.
- *New TeachSource Video Connections* features: "Infants and Toddlers: Daily Health Checks" and "Communicating with Parents about Health in Early Childhood: A Parent-Teacher Meeting."

Chapter 3 *Assessing Children's Health*

- Greater emphasis placed on the teacher's role in identifying health problems (e.g., vision, hearing, language, nutrition) that affect learning.
- *New Teacher Checklists* for easy access to critical information.
- Additional content on childhood obesity and the short- and long-term consequences on health and learning.
- *New TeachSource Video Connections* features: "0–2 Years: Sensation and Perception, Vision in Infants and Toddlers" and "Students with Special Needs: The Referral and Evaluation Process."

Chapter 4 *Caring for Children with Special Medical Conditions*

- *New section* on inclusive classrooms and special education services, including a discussion of the Individuals with Disabilities Education Improvement Act (IDEA), Individualized Education Plans (IEPs), Individualized Family Service Plans (IFSPs), and Individualized Health Services Plans (IHSP).
- Updated information on the signs, symptoms, and management strategies for common chronic childhood diseases and medical conditions.
- *New TeachSource Video Connections* features: "Preschool: IEP and Transition Planning for a Young Child with Special Needs" and "Promoting Children's Health: Teacher Takes Care of Child With Asthma."

Chapter 5 *The Infectious Process and Environmental Control*

- The latest national childhood immunization recommendations (and chart).
- *New* information on classroom infection control practices, including hand washing and green cleaning products.
- *Newly issued warnings* and recommendations on mixing bleach solutions.
- *New TeachSource Video Connections* feature: "Promoting Children's Health: A Focus on Nutrition in Early Childhood Settings."

Chapter 6 *Childhood Illnesses: Identification and Management*

- *New* information on Sudden Infant Death Syndrome (SIDS).
- *New Teacher Checklists* highlighting critical information about childhood illnesses.
- *New TeachSource Video Connections* feature: "SIDS: Is There a Biological Cause?"

Chapter 7 *Creating High-Quality Environments*

- *New* information on safety features associated with high-quality environments, including outdoor play areas for children.
- More emphasis on the importance of outdoor play and physical activity in the prevention of childhood obesity, diabetes, and behavior problems.
- Field-based activities and a new case study reinforce application of chapter content to everyday practice.
- *New TeachSource Video Connections* features: "The Quality of Child Care" and "Creating a Safe Physical Environment for Toddlers."

Chapter 8 *Safety Management*

- *New* section on emergency and disaster preparedness, including strategies for helping children to cope following such an event.
- Additional information on school security.
- *New TeachSource Video Connections* feature: "Preschool Safety and Disaster Preparedness."

Chapter 9 *Management of Injuries and Acute Illness*

▸ *Updated* emergency and first aid techniques from the American Heart Association and Red Cross
▸ *New* information on initial injury assessment and assembling first aid kits.
▸ *New* section on anaphylaxis (life-threatening allergic reaction).
▸ *New TeachSource Video Connections* feature: "Working with Children Who Have Physical Disabilities."

Chapter 10 *Maltreatment of Children: Abuse and Neglect*

▸ *New* research-based information about the immediate and long-term emotional, cognitive, and economic effects maltreatment has on children's development.
▸ *New* information on vulnerable children, cultural implications, strategies for increasing resilience, and anger management.
▸ Updated booklist that teachers and families can use to address maltreatment with children and to build resilience.
▸ *New TeachSource Video Connections* feature: "0–2 Years: Observation Module for Infants and Toddlers."

Chapter 11 *Planning for Children's Health and Safety Education*

▸ Updated information on the National Health Education Standards and Health Education Curriculum Analysis Tool (HECAT).
▸ *New* lesson plan on "Yoga and Wellness."
▸ Additional teacher resources and children's book lists to use for lesson planning.

Chapter 12 *Nutrition Guidelines*

▸ *New* information on the Dietary Guidelines for Americans, Dietary Reference Intakes (DRIs), MyPlate, Healthy People 2020, and food labels.
▸ Emphasis placed on eating locally and the role of physical activity in health promotion.
▸ *New TeachSource Video Connections* feature: "Young Children's Stages of Play: An Illustrated Guide."

Chapter 13 *Nutrients that Provide Energy (Carbohydrates, Fats, and Proteins)*

▸ Additional information on childhood obesity, excess energy consumption, and weight management strategies for children.
▸ *New Teacher Checklists* highlighting key nutrient information.
▸ *New TeachSource Video Connections* feature: "Child Obesity and School Nutrition."

Chapter 14 *Nutrients that Promote Growth and Regulate Body Functions (Proteins, Vitamins, Minerals, and Water)*

▸ *New* chapter that combines Chapters 14 and 15 from the eighth edition. Content is presented in less technical terms and restructured to promote better understanding.
▸ *New* section on at-risk nutrients in children's diets.
▸ Additional information about vegetarian meal patterns.
▸ *New* case study challenges students to apply chapter content to real-life situations.
▸ *New TeachSource Video Connections* feature: "School-Age Children: Teaching about Nutrition."

Chapter 15 *Feeding Infants*

▸ *New* emphasis on the feeding relationship and its effect on infant biological, learning, and developmental needs.
▸ Additional information on nutrient contributions and early brain development.
▸ *New* tables on behavioral signs of hunger and fullness (satiety).
▸ *New* recommendations regarding vitamin D and fluoride supplementation.
▸ *New TeachSource Video Connections* feature: "Infants and Toddlers: Health and Nutrition."

Chapter 16 *Feeding Toddlers and Young Children*

▸ *New* guidelines for feeding preschool and school-age children aligned with the national standards.
▸ *New* information on safety considerations for children who have special feeding challenges and/or health problems.

- Additional information on increasing children's acceptance of unfamiliar foods and media influence on children's food preferences and eating habits.
- Updated information on feeding challenges and health problems (e.g., cardiovascular heart disease, diabetes, hypertension) related to children's dietary habits.
- *New TeachSource Video Connections* feature: "Technology and Media Use by Children and Adolescents."

Chapter 17 *Planning and Serving Nutritious and Economical Meals*

- *New* meal planning guidelines based on revised National School Lunch Program and Healthy Hunger-Free Kids Act standards.
- *New* resource tables and additional *Teacher Checklists*.
- Suggestions for incorporating more whole grain products, fresh produce, and ethnic foods into children's meals.
- *New TeachSource Video Connections* feature: "School-Age Children: Cooking Activities."

Chapter 18 *Food Safety*

- Reorganized content that reflects contemporary food safety concerns, research, and practices.
- *New* tables highlighting pesticide residues on fresh produce and safe cooking temperatures.
- *New* section added on national and international efforts to improve the safety of food supplies, including commercial food production practices.
- *New TeachSource Video Connections* feature: "Promoting Children's Health: A Focus on Nutrition in an Early Childhood Setting."

Chapter 19 *Nutrition Education: Rationale, Concepts, and Lessons*

- Greater emphasis placed on family engagement and educating children about healthy eating and physical activity.
- Lesson plans that include children's book lists.
- *New Teacher Checklists* highlighting key nutrient information.
- New *TeachSource Video Connections* feature: "Preschool: Cooking Activities."

Pedagogy and Learning Aids

Each chapter includes additional pedagogical features based on sound educational principles that encourage active student-centered learning, mastery, and application. The features also reflect student differences in learning needs, abilities, and styles.

- **Bulleted lists** are used extensively throughout the book to present important information in a concise, easy-to-access format.

- **Multicultural color photographs** taken on location at centers and schools show children as they work and play in developmentally appropriate settings.

- **Full-color illustrations** and tables reinforce and expand on important chapter content.

- A bulleted **Summary** concludes each chapter and recaps the main points of discussion.

- **Terms to Know** are highlighted in color throughout the chapters. Each term is defined on the page where it initially appears and also in a comprehensive glossary located at the end of the book.

- **Chapter Review** offers thought-provoking questions to reinforce student learning and comprehension. Questions can also be used for group discussion.

- **Case Studies** present real-life situations that require students to analyze and apply basic theory to solving everyday problems.

- **Application Activities** provide in-class and field projects that encourage students to practice and reinforce what they have learned in each chapter.

- **Helpful Web Resources** take advantage of technology to extend student learning beyond the pages of this book and to access valuable resource materials.

Ancillaries for Students

Early Childhood Education CourseMate

Cengage Learning's Early Childhood Education CourseMate brings course concepts to life with interactive learning, study, and exam preparation tools that support the printed textbook. Access the eBook, Did You Get It? quizzes, Digital Downloads, TeachSource Videos, flashcards, and more in your Education CourseMate. Go to CengageBrain.com to register or purchase access.

TeachSource Videos

The TeachSource videos feature footage from the classroom to help students relate key chapter content to real-life scenarios. Critical-thinking questions provide opportunities for in-class or online discussion and reflection.

Ancillaries for Instructors

Early Childhood Education CourseMate

Cengage Learning's Early Childhood Education CourseMate brings course concepts to life with interactive learning, study, and exam preparation tools that support the printed textbook. CourseMate includes the eBook, quizzes, Digital Downloads, TeachSource Video Cases, flashcards, and more—as well as EngagementTracker, a first-of-its-kind tool that monitors student engagement in the course. The accompanying instructor website, available through http://login.cengage.com, offers access to password-protected resources such as Microsoft® PowerPoint® lecture slides and the online Instructor's Manual with Test Bank. CourseMate can be bundled with the student text. Contact your Cengage sales representative for information on getting access to CourseMate.

Instructor's Manual

An online Instructor's Manual accompanies this book. It contains information to assist the instructor in course design, including sample syllabi, discussion questions, teaching and learning activities, field experiences, learning objectives, and additional online resources.

Online Test Bank

Extensive multiple choice, true/false, short answer, completion, and essay questions accompany each chapter and provide instructors with varied strategies for assessing student learning.

Online PowerPoint Slides

These vibrant PowerPoint lecture slides for each chapter assist you with your lecture by providing concept coverage using images, figures, and tables directly from the textbook!

Cengage Learner Testing Powered by Cognero

- Author, edit, and manage test bank content from multiple Cengage Learning solutions.
- Create multiple test versions in an instant.
- Deliver tests from your LMS, your classroom, or wherever you want.

Acknowledgments

A special thank you is extended to the instructors, students, and colleagues who use *Health, Safety, and Nutrition for the Young Child* in their classes and professional endeavors. Their suggestions continue to influence and improve each new edition. I would also like to recognize the contributions of dedicated teachers and families everywhere who strive to better children's lives.

I am grateful to have had the opportunity to again work with Lisa Mafrici, who has been my developmental editor on several book editions. Her professional expertise, insight, and encouragement have always been exceptional and led to a well-deserved promotion in the midst of this revision project. Although she will truly be missed, I wish her the very best! I also want to acknowledge and thank Kate Scheinman, who bravely stepped into an ongoing revision. She made the transition smooth, has been a pleasure to work with, and helped to produce another beautiful and improved edition. I would also like to extend my gratitude to Mark Kerr for his continued support, vision, and enthusiasm. The field is a better place because of his hard work and dedication. I thank Teresa, Catherine, and the production staff at Wadsworth Cengage Learning, who exercised their "Cinderella effect" and turned manuscript pages into a thing of worth and beauty! Thank you, too, to the many other behind-the-scenes individuals who contributed so much to making this book a success and to getting the word out!

Finally, I want to thank my husband and family for their patience and understanding during times when writing took precedence over times spent together.

I also offer my sincere appreciation to the following reviewers for sharing so many constructive suggestions:

Margaret Annunziata,
Davidson County Community College

Vella Black-Roberts,
Ohlone College

Dawn Burgess,
San Diego Community College

Cindy Calhoun,
Southern Union State Community College

Johnny Castro,
Brookhaven College

Mary Cordell,
Navarro College

Karan Demchak,
Allan Hancock College

Irene Den Bleyker,
University of New Mexico Gallup

Heather Flatness,
Wenatchee Valley College

Adrienne Gunn,
Santa Monica College

Marissa Happ,
Waubonsee Community College

Sharon Hirschy,
Collin County Community College

Bridget Ingram,
Clark State Community College

Sharon Little,
South Piedmont Community College

Rajone Lyman,
Houston Community College

Janelle Meyers,
St. Charles Community College

Dawn Munson,
Elgin Community College

Sandra Owen,
Cincinnati State Technical and Community College

Olivia Wagner Wakefield,
Central Carolina Community College

Janette Wetsel,
University of Central Oklahoma

Andrea Zarate,
Hartnell College

About the Author

Lynn R. Marotz received a Ph.D. from the University of Kansas, an M.Ed. from the University of Illinois, and a B.S. in nursing from the University of Wisconsin. She served as the health and safety coordinator and associate director of the Edna A. Hill Child Development Center (University of Kansas) for 35 years. She has worked closely with students in the Early Childhood teacher education program and taught undergraduate and graduate courses in the Department of Applied Behavioral Science, including issues in parenting, health/safety/nutrition for the young child, administration, and foundations of early childhood education. She provides frequent inservice training in first aid, children's safety, recognizing child abuse, childhood obesity, and identifying children's health problems for early childhood students and community educators.

Lynn has authored several invited chapters on children's health and development, nutrition, and environmental safety in national and international publications and law books. In addition, she is the co-author of *Developmental Profiles-Pre-Birth through Adolescence, Motivational Leadership*, and *By the Ages*. She has been interviewed for numerous articles about children's nutrition and well-being that have appeared in national trade magazines, and has served as a consultant for children's museums and training film productions. Her research activities focus on childhood obesity and children's health, safety, and nutrition. She has presented extensively at international, national, and state conferences and held appointments on national, state, and local committees and initiatives that advocate on children's and families' behalf. However, it is her daily interactions with children and their families, students, colleagues, and her beloved family that bring true insight, meaning, and balance to the material in this book.

Promoting Children's Health: Healthy Lifestyles and Health Concerns

chapter 1

Children's Well-Being: What It Is and How to Achieve It

naeyc **Standards Chapter Links**

▶ **#1 a and b:** Promoting child development and learning
▶ **#2 a, b, and c:** Building family and community relationships
▶ **#4 a, b, c, and d:** Using developmentally effective approaches to connect with children and families
▶ **#5 a, b, and c:** Using content knowledge to build a meaningful curriculum
▶ **#6 b, c, d, and e:** Becoming a professional
▶ Field Experience

Learning Objectives

After studying this chapter, you should be able to:

LO 1-1 Define the preventive health concept and describe several national programs that address children's health needs.

LO 1-2 Explain how health, safety, and nutrition are interrelated and discuss factors that influence the quality of each.

LO 1-3 Describe typical growth and developmental characteristics of infants, toddlers, preschool-age, and school-age children.

LO 1-4 Discuss ways that teachers can be proactive in promoting children's wellness in the areas of injury prevention, oral health, physical activity, and mental health.

Our ideas about health, disease, and the health care system are undergoing significant change. Individuals are beginning to realize that they must assume a more proactive role in maintaining personal health, and cannot continue to rely on the medical profession to always make them well. In part, this change is fueled by escalating medical costs, a lack of health insurance, and disabling conditions for which there are no current cures. In addition, and perhaps even more significant, are research findings that demonstrate positive health outcomes when people adapt healthy life-style behaviors (Maxwell et al., 2012; Daniels, Pratt, & Hayman, 2011).

1-1 The Preventive Health Concept

The concept of **preventive health** recognizes that individuals are able to reduce or eliminate many factors that threaten personal wellness (Figure 1–1). It implies that children and adults are able to make choices and engage in behaviors that improve the quality of life and lessen the risk of disease. This includes practices such as establishing healthful dietary habits (eating more fruits, vegetables, whole grains, and low-fat dairy products), implementing safety behaviors (wearing seat belts, limiting sun exposure), engaging in daily physical activity, and seeking early treatment for occasional illness and injury.

....

preventive health – *personal and social behaviors that promote and maintain well-being.*

FIGURE 1-1   **Examples of preventive health practices.**

A preventive health approach involves a combination of personal practices and national initiatives.

On a personal scale:

- eating a diet low in animal fats
- consuming a wide variety of fruits, vegetables, and grains
- engaging in aerobic and muscle-strengthening activities regularly
- practicing good oral hygiene
- using proper hand washing techniques
- avoiding substance abuse (e.g., alcohol, tobacco, drugs)
- keeping immunizations up-to-date

On a national scale:

- regulating vehicle emissions
- preventing chemical dumping
- establishing safety standard and inspecting food supplies
- measuring air pollution
- providing immunization programs
- fluoridating drinking water
- monitoring disease outbreaks

The early years are a critical time for children to establish preventive behaviors. Young children are typically more receptive to new ideas, curious, eager to learn, and have fewer unhealthy habits to overcome. Teachers, families, and health care providers can capitalize on these qualities and help children to develop practices that will foster a healthy, safe, and productive lifetime.

Although the preventive approach emphasizes an individual role in health promotion, it also implies a shared responsibility for addressing social and environmental issues that affect the quality of everyone's well-being, including:

- poverty and homelessness
- food insecurity
- inequitable access to medical and dental care
- adverse effects of media advertising
- substance abuse (e.g., alcohol, tobacco, drugs)
- food safety
- air and water pollution
- discrimination based on diversity
- unsafe neighborhoods

In addition to helping children learn about these complex issues, adults must also demonstrate their commitment by supporting social actions, policies, and programs that contribute to healthier environments and lifestyles for society as a whole.

1-1a National Health Initiatives

The positive health outcomes that are achievable through preventive practices continue to attract increased public interest, especially with respect to young children. Poor standards of health, safety, and nutrition have long been known to interfere with children's ability to learn and to ultimately become healthy, productive adults. As a result, a number of large-scale programs have been established to address children's health needs and to improve their access to preventive services. Descriptions of several initiatives follow; information about federal food programs for children is located in Appendix C.

Healthy People 2020 The nation's plan for improving the standard of health for its citizens is outlined in the *Healthy People 2020* initiative. It supports and strengthens the same underlying philosophy of health promotion and disease prevention presented in the original *Healthy People 2000 document*. It challenges communities to increase public health awareness and improve accessibility to preventive health services by encouraging better collaboration and coordination among agencies. It urges individuals to assume a more active role in achieving personal wellness, especially with regard to the prevention of heart disease, obesity, and diabetes. Many of the goals and objectives targeted in the *Healthy People 2020* plan also have direct application for schools and early childhood programs (Table 1–1). For example, teaching anger management skills, increasing outdoor play and physical activity in children's daily schedules, serving nutritious foods, providing more health and nutrition education, and creating safe learning environments reflect teachers' commitment to the *Healthy People 2020* ideals.

▼ **Early childhood is a prime time for teaching preventive health practices.**

© Cengage Learning

National Children's Agenda A similar Canadian proposal aimed at health promotion for children is outlined in a report entitled *A National Children's Agenda: Developing a Shared Vision*. This document presents a comprehensive agenda of goals and objectives for addressing children's health care and safety needs. It also embraces the importance of the early years and supports the vision of creating a unified approach to helping children achieve their full potential.

Children's Health Insurance Program The Children's Health Insurance Program (CHIP) provides low-cost health insurance to children in income-eligible families who don't qualify for Medicaid and cannot afford private coverage. The program is aimed at improving children's health and ability to learn through early identification and better access to preventive health care (Colby, Lipson, & Turchin, 2012). Services covered by the program include free or low-cost medical and dental care, immunizations, prescriptions, mental health treatment, and hospitalization.

CHIP is administered in each state through a combination of state and federal appropriations. Each state must submit a Child Health Plan describing how the program will be implemented, how eligibility will be determined, and how eligible children will be located. The Affordable Care Act extends reauthorization of the program through 2015 and expands service to an additional four million eligible children (Centers for Medicare & Medicaid Coverage, 2013).

TABLE 1–1　Healthy People 2020 Objectives

Areas targeted for improving children's health include the following:	
• physical activity and fitness	• immunizations and infectious diseases
• nutrition and weight status	• oral health
• substance abuse	• maternal, infant, and child health
• mental health	• access to health services
• sleep health	• health education
• environmental health	• vision, hearing, and communication disorders
• injury and violence prevention	

Source: Adapted from *Healthy People 2020*. (2012). U.S. Department of Health & Human Services.

Healthy Child Care America The primary objective of the Healthy Child Care America (HCCA) initiative is to foster high-quality improvements in out-of-home child care programs. HCCA, supported by the U.S. Department of Health and Human Services, the Child Care Bureau, and the Maternal and Child Health Bureau, was established in 1995 to coordinate the mutual interests of health professions, early education professionals, and families in addressing children's health and safety. The program is administered by the American Academy of Pediatrics (AAP) and has been instrumental in launching several large-scale educational campaigns, including Moving Kids Safely in Child Care, Tummy Time, Back to Sleep (for parents), Back to Sleep in Child Care Settings, and the Health Futures curriculum. Grant-supported offices, located in every state, have been established to evaluate and strengthen existing community infrastructure and to assist with new initiatives for improving children's health and safety in early childhood programs and access to preventive health care. Extensive resource information is available on their website (http://www .healthychildcare.org).

National Health and Safety Performance Standards for Child Care National concern for children's welfare led to a collaborative project among the American Academy of Pediatrics (AAP), the American Public Health Association (APHA), and the National Resource Center for Health and Safety in Child Care and Early Education (NRC) to develop health, safety, and nutrition guidelines for out-of-home child care settings. The resulting document, *Caring for Our Children: National Health and Safety Performance Standards: Guidelines for Out-of-Home Child Care* (3rd ed.), continues to identify quality standards and procedures for ensuring children's health and safety while they attend organized out-of-home care (Table 1–2) (AAP, APHA, & NRC, 2011). This document can be accessed at www.nrckids.org.

The current system allows individual states to establish their own child care licensing standards, which has resulted in significant differences in quality. The National Health and Safety Performance Standards attempt to address regulatory inconsistencies by proposing a uniform set of standards based on what research has identified as best practices. The National Association for the Education of Young Children (NAEYC) recently endorsed and aligned their accreditation criteria with the National Health and Safety Performance Standards (NAEYC, 2012).

TABLE 1–2   National Health and Safety Performance Standards

Comprehensive guidelines address the following areas of child care:

- staffing – child staff ratios, credentials, and training
- activities for healthy development – supervision, behavior management, partnerships with families, health education
- health promotion and protection – sanitation and hygiene practices, safe sleep, illness and medication management
- nutrition and food services – nutritional requirements, food safety, nutrition education
- facilities, supplies, equipment, and environmental health – space and equipment requirements, indoor/outdoor settings, maintenance
- playgrounds and transportation – space, water areas, toys, transportation safety
- infectious diseases – respiratory, blood-borne and skin conditions, immunizations
- children with special health care and disability needs – inclusion, eligibility for special services, facility modifications, assessment, service plans
- policies – health/safety, emergency plans, personnel, child records
- licensing and community action – regulatory agencies, teacher/caregiver support

Source: Adapted from AAP, APHA, & NRC. (2011). *Caring for our children: National health and safety performance standards* (3rd ed.). Elk Grove Village, IL: American Academy of Pediatrics; Washington, DC: American Public Health Association. Also available at http://nrckids.org.

No Child Left Behind The No Child Left Behind (NCLB) Act of 2001 authorized significant reforms of the K–12 educational system and strengthened partnerships with Head Start, Even Start, and early education programs in center- and home-based settings. It acknowledged families as children's first and most important teachers, the educational contributions of early childhood programs, and the importance of fostering early literacy skills (understanding and using language) to ensure children's readiness for, and success in, schools. The bill also provided funding to cover child care costs for low-income families, health care coverage for eligible children, and prenatal services for pregnant women. However, its main purpose was to improve educational outcomes for all children by holding educators more accountable. Several states were granted waivers in 2011 allowing them to opt out of the NCLB Act's required provisions if they agreed to establish their own performance standards.

Coordinated School Health Program In 1988, the Centers for Disease Control and Prevention (CDC) proposed a new school health services model called the Coordinated School Health program. At the time, teachers were being pressured to ensure children's success in school while studies demonstrated a strong association between children's health and academic outcomes. It became clear that traditional delivery methods were failing to address children's complex health needs and that a different approach was needed.

The Coordinated School Health program assumes a preventive health approach and emphasizes the collaborative involvement of teachers, administrators, staff, students, families, media, and community partners to promote children's well-being. Eight interactive standards and their corresponding performance indicators serve as curriculum guidelines for grades K–12 (Figure 1–2).

The National Children's Study One of the most comprehensive studies of children's health ever undertaken in the United States was authorized by the Children's Health Act of 2000. This longitudinal study is being led by the Eunice Kennedy Shriver National Institute of Child Health and Human Development (NICHD) and is currently following over 100,000 children from birth to age 21. The purpose of the study is to examine genetic and environmental effects on children's

FIGURE 1–2 Coordinated school health program components.

Health Education

Family/ Community Involvement

Physical Education

Health Promotion for Staff

Health Services

Healthy & Safe School Environment

Nutrition Services

Counseling, Psychological, & Social Services

©Dmitriy Shironosov/Shutterstock.com

Did You Get It?

The Children's Health Insurance Program provides healthcare coverage, and the Healthy Child Care America initiative focuses on the _____ of child care programs.

a. regulation
b. improvement
c. licensing
d. insuring

Take the full quiz on CourseMate.

health and their potential contributions to disease. It will eventually yield one of the most expansive information databases ever compiled about children's growth and development, differences in access to health care, and the incidence of disease. Data obtained from the study will also be used to improve children's health and well-being through future policy formulation, funding, and service interventions.

Let's Move! The *Let's Move!* initiative was established by First Lady Michelle Obama in 2010 to address the problem of childhood obesity in the United States. The program encourages children and their families to achieve a healthier lifestyle by improving eating habits and increasing physical activity. Schools are challenged to provide healthier meals for children, increase opportunities for physical activity, and incorporate more health and nutrition education into their curriculum. A companion initiative, *Let's Move! Child Care*, was launched the following year and challenges all child care providers to adapt similar improvement measures. Informational resources can be accessed on the initiatives' websites.

▼ **Active play is essential for children's health and development.**

© Cengage Learning

1-2 Health, Safety, and Nutrition: An Interdependent Relationship

Health, safety, and nutrition are closely intertwined and dependent on one another. The status of each has a direct effect on the quality of the others. For example, children who receive all essential nutrients from a healthful diet are more likely to reach their growth potential, benefit from learning opportunities, experience fewer illnesses, and have ample energy for play. In contrast, children whose diet lacks critical nutrients such as protein and iron may develop anemia, which can lead to fatigue, diminished alertness, growth and academic failure, and loss of appetite. When children lack interest in eating, their iron intake is further compromised. In other words, nutritional status has a direct effect on children's health and safety, and, in turn, influences the dietary requirements needed to restore and maintain well-being.

A nutritious diet also plays an important role in injury prevention. The child or adult who arrives at school having eaten little or no breakfast may experience low blood sugar, which can cause fatigue, decreased alertness, and slowed reaction times and, thus, increase an individual's risk of accidental injury. Similarly, overweight children and adults are more likely to sustain injuries due to excess weight, which may restrict physical activity, slow reaction times, and increase fatigue with exertion.

1-2a What Is Health?

Definitions of **health** are as numerous as the factors that affect it. In years past, the term referred strictly to an individual's physical well-being and the absence of illness. Contemporary

health – *a state of wellness. Complete physical, mental, social, and emotional well-being; the quality of one health element affects the state of the others.*

definitions view health from a broader perspective and recognize it as a state of physical, emotional, social, economic, cultural, and spiritual well-being. Each interactive component is assumed to make an equally important contribution to health and to affect the functional activity of the others. For example, a stressful home environment may be contributing to a child's asthma attacks, stomachaches, or headaches; in turn, a child's repeated illnesses or chronic disability can profoundly affect the family's emotional, financial, social, and physical stability and well-being.

The current health concept also recognizes that children and adults do not live in isolation, but are active participants in multiple groups, including family, peer, neighborhood, ethnic, cultural, recreational, religious, and community. Children's health, development, and opportunities for learning are directly influenced by the positive and negative experiences that occur in each setting. For example, children growing up in a poor, urban neighborhood may be at greater risk for becoming obese because they have fewer safe places for outdoor play and limited access to fresh fruits and vegetables. In other words, children's health and development must be considered in the context of their social and environmental conditions.

1-2b What Factors Influence Children's Health?

Health is a dynamic and complex state. It is a product of continuous interactions between an individual's genetic makeup, environmental conditions, and personal experiences (Figure 1–3). For example, an infant's immediate and long-term health is influenced by his or her mother's personal lifestyle practices during pregnancy: her diet; use or avoidance of alcohol, tobacco, and certain medications; routine prenatal care; and exposure to communicable illnesses or toxic stress. Mothers who fail to maintain a healthy lifestyle during pregnancy are more likely to give birth to infants who are born prematurely, have low birth weight, or experience a range of special challenges (McCormick et al., 2011). These children also face a significantly greater risk of developing chronic health problems and early death. In contrast, a child who is born healthy, raised in a nurturing family, consumes a nutritious diet, lives in a safe environment, and has numerous opportunities for learning and recreation is more likely to enjoy a healthy life.

Heredity Characteristics transmitted from biological parents to their children at the time of conception determine all of the genetic traits of a new, unique individual. **Heredity** sets the limits for growth, development, and health potential. It explains, in part, why children in one family are short while those from another family are tall or why some individuals have allergies or require glasses while others do not.

Understanding how heredity influences health can also be useful for assessing a possible inherited tendency, or **predisposition**, to certain health problems, such as heart disease, deafness, cancer, diabetes, lactose intolerance, or mental health disorders. Although a family history of heart disease or diabetes may increase one's risk, it does not imply that an individual will actually develop the condition. Many lifestyle factors, including physical activity, diet, sleep, and stress levels, interact with genetic material (genes) and can alter the child's chances of ultimately developing heart disease or any number of other chronic health diseases.

Environment Although heredity provides the basic building materials that predetermine the limits of one's health, environment

FIGURE 1–3   Health is an interactive and continuously changing state.

Physical • Mental • Economic • Social • Spiritual • Cultural

Health

---

heredity – *the transmission of certain genetic material and characteristics from biological parents to a child at the time of conception.*
predisposition – *having an increased chance or susceptibility.*

▼ **Heredity sets the limits for a child's growth, development, and health potentials.**

© Cengage Learning

plays an equally important role. Environment encompasses a combination of physical, psychological, social, economic, and cultural factors that collectively influence the way individuals perceive and respond to their surroundings. In turn, these experiences shape a person's behaviors and potential health outcomes. For example, two cyclists set off on a ride: One is wearing a helmet, the other is not. The choices each has made could potentially have quite different outcomes if they were to be involved in a serious collision. The helmet-wearing cyclist may suffer only minor scrapes and bruises while the cyclist without a helmet may sustain a serious head injury that could have significant health, economic, social, and psychological consequences.

Examples of several environmental factors that support and promote healthy outcomes include:

- making nutritious food choices
- participating in daily physical and recreational activities
- getting 8 to 9 hours of uninterrupted nighttime sleep
- having access to high-quality medical and dental care
- reducing stress levels
- residing in homes, child care facilities, schools, and workplaces that are clean and safe
- having friends and opportunities to form stable and meaningful relationships

There are also many environmental factors that have a negative effect on health. For example, exposure to chemicals and pollution, abuse, illness, obesity, prenatal alcohol exposure, **sedentary** lifestyles, poverty, acute and chronic stress, **food insecurity**, violence, or unhealthy dietary choices can interfere with children's optimal growth and development.

1-2c Safety

Safety refers to behaviors and measures taken to protect individuals from unnecessary harm. It is especially important that adults who work with young children view this responsibility seriously. Unintentional injuries are the leading cause of death among children from birth to 14 years in the United States and Canada and, sadly, many of these instances are avoidable (CDC, 2012; Safe Kids Canada, 2012). Young children are especially vulnerable to unexpected and serious injury because their developmental skills seldom match their level of enthusiasm and curiosity. Every adult who works with, or cares for, young children has a significant responsibility to maintain the highest standards of supervision and environmental safety.

Factors Affecting Children's Safety Protecting children's safety requires a keen awareness of their skills and abilities at each developmental stage (Marotz & Allen, 2013). For example, knowing that toddlers enjoy hand-to-mouth activities should alert teachers to continuously monitor the environment for small objects or poisonous substances that could be ingested. Understanding that preschoolers are spontaneous and exceedingly curious should cause adults to take extra precautions to prevent children from wandering away or straying into unsupervised water sources. Children who have developmental disabilities or sensory disorders are at increased risk of sustaining unintentional injury and must be monitored continuously (Cavalari & Romanczyk, 2012). In-depth discussions of environmental safety and safety management are presented in Chapters 7 and 8.

sedentary – *unusually slow or sluggish; a lifestyle that implies inactivity.*
food insecurity – *uncertain or limited access to a reliable source of food.*

1-2d Nutrition

The term *nutrition* refers to the science of food, its chemical components **nutrients**, and their relationship to health and disease. It includes all processes involved in obtaining nutrients from foods—from the ingestion, digestion, absorption, transportation, and utilization of nutrients to excretion of unused products. Nutrients are essential for life and have a direct effect on a child's nutritional status, behavior, health, and development.

Nutrients play critical roles in a variety of vital body functions, including:

- supplying energy
- promoting growth and development
- improving resistance to illness and infection
- building and repairing body tissue

A wide variety of foods must be consumed in the recommended amounts to meet the body's needs for essential nutrients. However, many family and environmental conditions, including financial resources, transportation, geographical location, cultural and religious preferences, convenience, and nutrition knowledge, can affect the quality of a child's diet. Most children in the United States live in a time and place where food is reasonably abundant. Yet, there is increasing concern about the number of children who may not be getting enough to eat or whose diets do not include the right foods (Okechukwu et al., 2012). Also, because many young children spend the majority of their waking hours in out-of-home child care programs or school classrooms, care must be taken to ensure that their nutrient needs are being met in these settings.

Nutrition's Effect on Children's Behavior, Learning, and Well-being Children's nutritional status has a significant effect on their behavior and cognitive development. Well-nourished children are typically more alert, attentive, physically active, and better able to benefit from learning experiences. Poorly nourished children may appear quiet and withdrawn, or exhibit hyperactive and disruptive behaviors in the classroom (Liu & Raine, 2011). They are also more prone to injury because of decreased alertness and slower reaction times. Children who are overweight also face a range of social, emotional, and physical challenges, including difficulty participating in physical activities, ridicule, emotional stress, and peer exclusion (Su & Aurelia, 2012). Additional information about children's specific nutrient needs and challenges associated with over- and under-consumption of foods is presented in Chapters 12 through 19.

Children's **resistance** to infection and illness is also directly influenced by their nutritional status (Weill, 2012). Well-nourished children experience fewer illnesses and recover more quickly when they are sick. Children who consume an unhealthy diet are more susceptible to infections and illness and often require longer time to recuperate. Frequent illness can interfere with a child's appetite, which may limit his or her intake of nutrients important for the recovery process. Thus, poor nutrition can create a cycle of increased susceptibility to illness and infection, nutritional deficiency, and prolonged recovery.

Teachers have an exceptional opportunity to protect and promote children's well-being. Their knowledge of children's development and health, safety, and nutritional needs can be applied when planning learning activities, classroom environments, meals and snacks, and supervision. In addition, teachers can implement sanitation and early identification practices to reduce children's unnecessary exposure to illness and infection. Furthermore, they can support the concept of preventive health by serving as positive role models and providing children with learning experiences that encourage a healthy lifestyle.

Did You Know...
that children who eat breakfast have better problem-solving skills, more energy, lower obesity rates, and feel more cheerful?

---

nutrients – *the chemical substances in food.*
resistance – *the ability to avoid infection or illness.*

▼ **Nutritional status also affects children's behavior.**

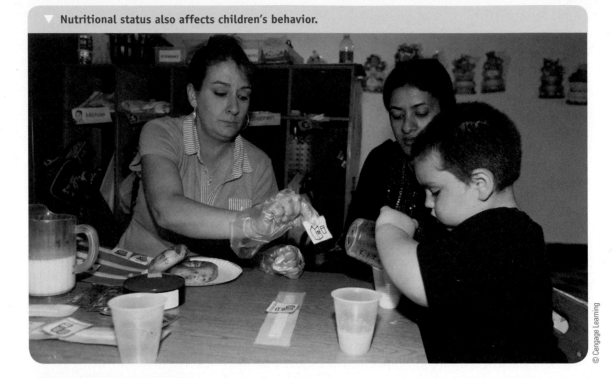

© Cengage Learning

Did You Get It?

What is the relationship between the roles of heredity and environment in determining an individual's health and well-being?
  a. They play equal, interrelated roles.
  b. They play unrelated roles.
  c. Heredity plays a greater role than environment.
  d. Environment plays a greater role than heredity.

Take the full quiz on CourseMate.

1-3 Children's Growth and Development

When teachers understand typical growth and developmental patterns, they are better able to identify and address children's diverse needs and to help children master critical skills. They can create learning experiences and set developmentally appropriate goals for children that foster positive self-esteem. They are able to design high-quality environments that are safe and encourage children's mastery of new skills. In addition, they are able to use this knowledge to promote children's well-being by identifying health problems and abnormal behaviors and teaching healthy practices.

The terms "average" or "normal" are often used to describe children's growth and development. However, such a child probably does not exist. Every child is a unique individual—a product of diverse experiences, environments, interactions, and heredity. Collectively, these factors can lead to significant differences in the rate at which children grow and acquire various skills and behaviors (Marotz & Allen, 2013).

Norms provide a useful reference for understanding, monitoring, and promoting children's growth and development. They represent the average or approximate age when the majority of children demonstrate a given skill or behavior. Thus, the term **normal** implies that although many children are able to perform a given skill by a specific age, some will be more advanced whereas others may take somewhat longer, yet they are still considered to be within the normal range.

norms – *an expression (e.g., weeks, months, years) of when a child is likely to demonstrate certain developmental skills.*
normal – *average; a characteristic or quality that is common to most individuals in a defined group.*

1-3a Growth

The term **growth** refers to the many physical changes that occur as a child matures. Although the growth process takes place without much conscious control, there are many factors that affect its quality and rate:

- genetic potential
- emotional stimulation and attachment
- cultural influences
- socioeconomic factors
- adequate nutrition
- parent responsiveness
- health status (i.e., illness)

Infants (0–12 months) The average newborn weighs approximately 7 to 8 pounds (3.2–3.6 kg) at birth and is approximately 20 inches (50.8 cm) in length. Growth is rapid during the first year; an infant's birth weight nearly doubles by the fifth month and triples by the end of the first year. For example, an infant who weighs 8 pounds (3.6 kg) at birth will weigh approximately 16 pounds (7.3 kg) at 5 months and 24 pounds (10.9 kg) at 12 months.

An infant's length increases by approximately 50 percent during the first year. Thus, an infant measuring 21 inches (53.3 cm) at birth should reach an approximate length of 31.5 inches (80 cm) by 12 months of age. A majority of this gain occurs during the first 6 months when an infant may grow as much as 1 inch (2.54 cm) per month.

An infant's head appears large in proportion to the rest of the body due to rapid brain growth. **Head circumference** is measured at regular intervals to ensure that brain growth is proceeding at a rate that is neither too fast nor too slow. Measurements should reflect a gradual increase in size so that by age 1, the head and chest circumferences are nearly equal.

Additional changes that occur during the first year include the growth of hair and eruption of teeth (four upper and four lower). The infant's eyes begin to focus and move together as a unit by the third month, and vision becomes more acute. Special health concerns for infants include the following:

- nutritional requirements
- adequate provisions for sleep
- **attachment**
- early brain development
- safety and injury prevention
- identification of birth defects and health impairments

At no other time in children's lives will they grow as much or as quickly as they do during the first year. A nutritious diet, adequate sleep, a nurturing environment, and responsive caregiving are especially important to foster growth during this critical period. (See Chapter 15.)

Toddlers (12–30 months) Toddlers continue to make steady gains in height and weight, but at a much slower rate than during infancy. Their weight increases an average of 6 to 7 pounds (2.7–3.2 kg) per year; by 2 years, toddlers have nearly quadrupled their birth weight. They also grow approximately 3 to 5 inches (7.6–12.7 cm) in height per year. Their body proportions begin to change and contribute to a more erect appearance.

Eruption of "baby teeth," or **deciduous teeth**, is complete by the end of the toddler period. (Deciduous teeth consist of a set of twenty temporary teeth.) Toddlers can begin learning how to brush their new teeth with close adult supervision. Special attention should also be paid to additional preventive measures such as providing foods that promote dental health; are colorful, appealing, and easily chewed; and, include all of the essential nutrients. Foods from all food groups—fruits,

growth – *increase in size of any body part or of the entire body.*
head circumference – *distance around the largest part of the head; used to monitor brain growth and development.*
attachment – *an emotional connection established between infants and their parents and/or primary caregivers.*
deciduous teeth – *a child's initial set of teeth; these teeth are temporary and gradually begin to fall out at around 5 years of age.*

▼ **Toddlers need plenty of sleep to meet their high energy demands.**

© Cengage Learning

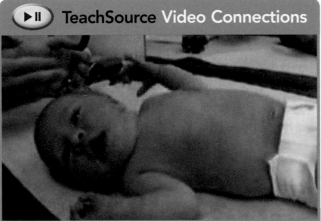

© 2015 Cengage Learning

▶❚❚ TeachSource Video Connections

Infancy Brain Development

You might be surprised to learn that infants have many more brain cells than you do! Discover why this occurs and what you can do to keep all of those you currently have. As you watch the learning video, *Infancy Brain Development*, consider to the following questions:

1. What enables neurons to communicate with one another?

2. What happens to neurons when they aren't used?

3. What functions are performed by the left side of the brain? What roles does the right side have?

4. How is brain size affected by environment and learning opportunities?

Watch on CourseMate.

vegetables, dairy, protein, whole-grains—should always be part of the toddler's daily meal pattern.

High activity levels make it essential for toddlers to get at least 10 to 12 hours of uninterrupted nighttime sleep and 1 to 2 hour-long naps each day. Insufficient sleep has been linked to an increase in learning and behavior problems, risk of injury, and a variety of health problems including obesity (Blunden, 2012). Safety awareness and injury prevention continue to be major concerns that demand close adult supervision.

Preschoolers/Early School-age (2 1/2–8 years) During the preschool and early school-age years, a child's appearance becomes more streamlined and adult-like in form. Head size remains relatively constant, while the child's trunk (body) and extremities (arms and legs) continue to grow. The head gradually appears to separate from the trunk as the neck lengthens. Legs grow longer and at a faster rate than the arms, adding extra inches to the child's height. The toddler's characteristic chubby body shape becomes more streamlined as muscle tone and strength increase and results in the preschoolers' flatter abdomen and straighter posture.

Gains in weight and height are relatively slow but steady throughout this period. By 3 years of age, children weigh approximately five times their birth weight. Ideally, preschoolers should gain no more than 4 to 5 pounds (1.8–2.3 kg) per year. They begin to grow taller during this period and gain an average of 2 to 2.5 inches (5.1–6.4 cm) in height per year. By 6 years, children have nearly doubled their original birth length (from approximately 20 inches to 40 inches [50.8–101.6 cm]). By age 7, girls are approximately 42 to 46 inches (106.7–116.8 cm) tall and weigh 38 to 47 pounds (17.2–21.3 kg); boys are 44 to 47 inches (111.8–119.4 cm) tall and weigh 42 to 49 pounds (19.1–22.2 kg). This combination of rapid growth and muscle development causes children to appear longer, thinner, and more adult-like.

It is important that preschool-age children continue to consume a nutritious diet. High activity levels replace the rapid growth of earlier years as the primary demand for calories. A general rule for estimating a child's daily caloric needs is to begin with a base of 1,000 calories and add an additional 100 calories per birthday. (For example, a 7-year-old would need approximately 1,700 calories). Adults should carefully monitor children's food intake and encourage healthy eating habits because decreased appetite, inconsistent eating habits, and considerable media influence are often evident during the preschool years.

Adequate sleep continues to be essential for children's optimal growth and development. When days are long and tiring or unusually stressful, children's need for sleep may be even greater. Most preschool and school-aged children require 8 to 12 hours of uninterrupted nighttime sleep in addition to daytime rest periods, although bedtime and afternoon naps often become a source of adult-child conflict. Preschool children often become so involved in play activities that they are reluctant to stop for sleep. Nevertheless, young children benefit from brief rest breaks during their normal daytime routine. Planned quiet times, with books, puzzles, quiet music, or a small toy, may be an adequate substitute for older children.

By the time children reach school-age, they begin to enjoy one of the healthiest periods of their lives. They generally experience fewer colds and upper respiratory infections. Children's visual acuity continues to improve, they grow taller at a fairly rapid rate, their muscle mass increases, hair becomes darker, and permanent teeth begin to erupt.

1-3b Development

In the span of 1 year, remarkable changes take place in the infant's **development**. The child progresses from a stage of complete dependency on adults to one marked by the acquisition of language and the formation of rather complex thought patterns. Infants also become more social and outgoing near the end of the first year, and seemingly enjoy and imitate the adults around them.

The toddler and preschool periods reflect a continued refinement of language, perceptual, motor, cognitive, and social achievements. Improved motor and verbal skills enable the toddler to explore, test, and interact with the environment for the purpose of determining personal identity, or autonomy.

Preschool-age children are becoming more self-sufficient and able to perform self-care and fine motor tasks with improved strength, speed, accuracy, control, and ease. Friends and friendships are increasingly important as preschool children expand their sphere of acquaintances beyond family members. Children are now able to participate in the socialization process as they begin to develop a conscience and learn emotional control.

A strong desire to achieve motivates 6-, 7-, and 8-year-olds. Participation in sports and other vigorous activities provides opportunities for children to practice and improve their motor skills. Adult approval and rewards continue to serve an important role in helping children build self-confidence and self-esteem. During this stage, children also begin to establish gender identity through meaningful social interactions.

A summary of major developmental achievements is presented in Table 1–3. It should be remembered that such a list represents accomplishments that a majority of children can perform at a given age. It should also be noted that not every child achieves all of these tasks. Many factors, including nutritional adequacy, opportunities for learning, access to appropriate medical and dental care, a nurturing environment, cultural expectations, and family support, exert a strong influence on children's skill acquisition.

Early Brain Development An infant's brain begins to form during the earliest weeks of a pregnancy. Its genetic composition is affected by various maternal practices (e.g., diet, sleep, prenatal care, physical activity, weight gain, smoking, alcohol or drug use, stress) prior to and during this period (O'Leary et al., 2013; Foltran et al., 2011). At birth, an infant's brain weighs approximately 25 percent of what their adult brain will eventually weigh and contains more

▼ **Preschoolers can manage most of their own self-care.**

© Cengage Learning

development – *commonly refers to the process of intellectual growth and change.*

TABLE 1–3   Major Developmental Achievements

Age	Achievements
2 months	• lifts head up when placed on stomach • follows moving person or object with eyes • imitates or responds to smiling person with occasional smiles • turns toward source of sound • begins to make simple sounds and noises • grasps objects with entire hand; not strong enough to hold on • enjoys being held and cuddled
4 months	• has good control of head • reaches for and grasps objects with both hands • laughs out loud; vocalizes with coos and giggles • waves arms about • holds head erect when supported in a sitting position • rolls over from side to back to stomach • recognizes familiar objects (e.g., bottle, toy)
6 months	• grasps objects with entire hand; transfers objects from one hand to the other and from hand to mouth • sits alone with minimal support • deliberately reaches for, grasps, and holds objects (e.g., rattles, bottle) • plays games and imitates (e.g., peek-a-boo) • shows signs of teeth beginning to erupt • prefers primary caregiver to strangers • babbles using different sounds • raises up and supports weight of upper body on arms
9 months	• sits alone; able to maintain balance while changing positions; picks up objects (e.g., bits of cracker, peas) with pincer grasp (first finger and thumb) • begins to crawl • attempts to say words such as "mama" and "dada" • hesitates when unfamiliar persons approach • explores new objects by chewing or placing them in mouth
12 months	• pulls up to a standing position • may "walk" by holding on to objects • stacks several objects one on top of the other • responds to simple commands and own name • babbles using jargon in sentence-like form • uses hands, eyes, and mouth to investigate new objects • can hold own eating utensils (e.g., cup, spoon)
18 months	• crawls up and down the stairs one at a time • walks unassisted; has difficulty avoiding obstacles in pathway • is less fearful of strangers • enjoys being read to; likes toys for pushing and pulling • has a vocabulary consisting of approximately 5–50 words, can name familiar objects • helps feed self; manages spoon and cup
2 years	• runs, walks with ease; can kick and throw a ball; jumps in place • speaks in two- to three-word sentences (e.g., "dada", "bye-bye"); asks simple questions; knows about 200 words • displays parallel play • achieves daytime toilet training • voices displeasure
3 years	• climbs stairs by using alternating feet • hops and balances on one foot • feeds self • helps dress and undress self; washes own hands and brushes teeth with help • is usually toilet trained • asks and answers questions; is quite curious • enjoys drawing, cutting with scissors, painting, clay, and make-believe

TABLE 1–3   Major Developmental Achievements (*continued*)

Age	Achievements
	• throws and bounces a ball • states name; recognizes self in pictures
4 years	• dresses and undresses self; helps with bathing; manages own tooth brushing • enjoys creative activities: paints, draws with detail, models with clay, builds imaginative structures with blocks • rides a tricycle with confidence, turns corners, maintains balance • climbs, runs, and hops with skill and vigor • enjoys friendships and playing with small groups of children • enjoys and seeks adult approval • understands simple concepts (e.g., shortest, longest, same)
5 years	• expresses ideas and questions clearly and with fluency • has vocabulary consisting of approximately 2,500–3,000 words • substitutes verbal for physical expressions of displeasure • dresses without supervision • seeks reassurance and recognition for achievements • engages in active and energetic play, especially outdoors • throws and catches a ball with relative accuracy • cuts with scissors along a straight line; draws in detail
6 years	• plays with enthusiasm and vigor • develops increasing interest in books and reading • displays greater independence from adults; makes fewer requests for help • forms close friendships with several peers • exhibits improved motor skills; can jump rope, hop and skip, ride a bicycle • enjoys conversation • sorts simple objects by color and shape
7 and 8 years	• enjoys friends; seeks their approval • shows increased curiosity and interest in exploration • develops greater clarity of gender identity • is motivated by a sense of achievement • begins to reveal a moral consciousness
9–12 years	• uses logic to reason and problem-solve • energetic; enjoys team activities, as well as individual projects • likes school and academic challenge, especially math • learns social customs and moral values • is able to think in abstract terms • enjoys eating any time of the day

Adapted from Marotz, L. R., & Allen, K. E., (2013). *Developmental profiles: Pre-birth through adolescence* (7th ed.). Belmont, CA: Wadsworth Cengage Learning.

than 100 billion brain cells or **neurons**. At this point, the brain is relatively unorganized and dysfunctional because few meaningful pathways have been established. This explains why young infants are not able to walk, talk, or care for themselves. Complex electrical connections begin to form between neurons in response to positive and negative experiences. Each time the same experience is repeated, the neural pathway becomes stronger (Figure 1–4). Connections and pathways that are seldom used undergo a process called pruning and gradually fade away. This process of adding and deleting neural connections reaches peak activity between the ages of 3 and 16 years and transforms the brain's architecture from an otherwise disorganized system into one capable of profound thought, emotions, and learning.

The majority of brain development occurs during the first 2 to 5 years of a child's life, when the brain's **plasticity** makes it more receptive to shaping and change. Note how quickly young children learn to speak another language and how adults often struggle to do the same, and you

neurons – *specialized cells that transmit electrical impulses or signals.*
plasticity – *the brain's ability to organize and reorganize neural pathways.*

FIGURE 1–4   Everyday experiences cause new neural connections to be formed and strengthened.

1 Month   2 Years   Adult

Did You Get It?

That most brain development occurs between ages 2 and 5 is most apparent when you observe the contrast between a young child and an adult attempting to master which task?

a. mathematics
b. inference and reasoning
c. learning a foreign language
d. reading skills

Take the full quiz on CourseMate.

will understand how this concept works. Researchers have also identified what they believe to be sensitive periods, or "windows of opportunity," during which neural connections in certain regions of the brain form more readily than they will later on. For example, vision and hearing connections peak between 2 and 4 months, whereas those governing emotional regulation begin to form months later. Sensory and learning pathways established during these sensitive periods are critical to the normal development of more advanced skills (Twardosz, 2012). For example, the visual system must be fully developed and functional before children are able to read or to play softball. An infant raised in a darkened room with few visual opportunities (e.g., mobiles, pictures, toys) will not form the network connections in the brain's sensory region that are conducive to the same quality of learning.

Neuroscientists have contributed significantly to our understanding of brain development and the practices that optimize its performance. Nutrition, especially during a mother's pregnancy and the first two years of a child's life, is of critical importance. Healthy brain and central nervous system development require specific proteins, minerals, and fats supplied in breast milk and formula. Malnutrition during infancy and toddlerhood can cause an irreversible decrease in brain cell production (and intelligence) and interfere with normal nervous system development. Poor nutrition also increases children's vulnerability to lead poisoning and affects brain function, behavior, and learning.

Although the brain's genetic foundation is in place at birth, it is the ongoing experiences in a child's environment that shape and determine how well the brain will ultimately perform. Safe, responsive caregiving helps infants to form strong attachments and neural connections that are important for learning and emotional regulation later on. Children's environments and the quality of available learning opportunities also exert a direct influence on brain development. When children are surrounded with language, encouraged to explore, play, and be creative, presented with varied and enriching experiences, and reinforced for their efforts, they are building strong neural pathways that are linked directly to cognitive development, self-esteem, and school success.

1-4 Promoting a Healthy Lifestyle

Today, concern for children's health and welfare is a shared vision. Changes in current lifestyles, family structures, cultural diversity, philosophies, and expectations have necessitated the collaborative efforts of families, teachers, and service providers to address children's well-being. Communities are also valued members of this partnership and must assume a proactive role in creating environments that are safe, enriching, and healthy places for children to live.

How can families and teachers determine whether or not children are healthy? What qualities or indicators are commonly associated with being a healthy or a **well child**? Growth and developmental norms always serve as a starting point. Again, it must be remembered that norms simply represent an average, not exact, age when most children are likely to achieve a given skill. Healthy children are more likely to exhibit characteristic behaviors and developmental skills appropriate for their age. They tend to be well-nourished, have energy to play, experience continued growth,

well child – *a child who enjoys a positive state of physical, mental, social, and emotional health.*

and have fewer illnesses. Developmental norms are also useful for anticipating and addressing children's special health needs, including injury prevention, body mechanics and physical activity, oral health, and mental well-being.

1-4a Injury Prevention

Unintentional injuries, especially those involving motor vehicles, pose the greatest threat to the lives of young children (Stewart de Ramirez et al., 2012). They are responsible for more than one-half of all deaths among children under 14 years of age in the United States. Each year an additional one million children sustain injuries that require medical attention, and many are left with permanent disabilities (Judy, 2011).

An understanding of normal growth and development is essential when planning for children's safety. Many characteristics that make children delightful to work with are the same qualities that make them prone to injury. Children's skills are seldom as well developed as their determination, and in their zealous approach to life, they often fail to recognize inherent dangers (Morrongiello et al., 2012). Their inability to judge time, distance, and speed accurately contributes to many injuries, especially those resulting from falls, as a pedestrian, or while riding a bike. Limited problem-solving abilities make it difficult for children to anticipate the consequences of their actions. This becomes an even greater challenge when infants or children with developmental disabilities are present. Adults have an obligation to provide continuous supervision and to maintain safe environments for all children at all times. Safety considerations and protective measures will be discussed in greater detail in Chapter 7.

▼ **Adults must supervise children closely to ensure their safety.**

© Cengage Learning

1-4b Body Mechanics and Physical Activity

Correct posture, balance, and proper body alignment are necessary for many physical activities that children engage in, such as walking, jumping, running, skipping, standing, and sitting. Teaching and modeling appropriate body mechanics can help children avoid problems related to poor posture that may develop later in life. The early recognition and treatment of ear infections is also important to address because they can affect children's balance and coordination.

Orthopedic problems (those relating to skeletal and muscular systems) are not common among young children. However, there are several conditions that warrant early diagnosis and treatment:

- birth injuries, such as hip dislocation, fractured collarbone
- abnormal or unusual walking patterns, such as limping or walking pigeon-toed
- bowed legs
- knock-knees
- flat feet
- unusual curvature of the spine
- unequal length of extremities (arms and legs)

Some irregularities of posture disappear spontaneously as young children mature. For example, it is not uncommon for infants and toddlers to have bowed legs or to walk slightly pigeon-toed. However, by age 3 or 4, these problems should correct themselves. If they do persist beyond the age of 4, children should be evaluated by a health professional to prevent permanent deformities.

Children's posture and body mechanics serve as excellent topics for classroom discussions, demonstrations, rhythm and movement activities, games, and art projects. Sharing this information in newsletters or posting it on bulletin boards or a website enables families to reinforce

▼ **Children should be discouraged from sitting in the "W" position.**

© Cengage Learning

correct practices at home. Children can begin to learn basic body mechanics, including:

▶ Sitting squarely in a chair, resting the back firmly against the chair back and with both feet flat on the floor.

▶ Sitting on the floor with legs crossed (in front) or with both legs extended straight ahead. Children should be discouraged from kneeling or sitting in a "W" position because this can place additional stress on developing joints. Have children sit in a chair with feet planted firmly on the ground or provide them with a small stool that can be straddled (one leg on each side); this eliminates adult nagging and forces children to sit in a correct position. Alternative seating supports may be required for children who have muscular or neurological disabilities.

▶ Standing with the shoulders square, the chin up, and the chest out. Body weight should be distributed evenly over both feet to avoid placing stress on one or the other hip joints.

▶ Lifting and carrying heavy objects by using the stronger muscles of the arms and legs rather than weaker back muscles. Standing close to an object that is to be lifted with feet spread slightly apart provides a wider support base. Stooping down to lift (with your legs); bending over at the waist when lifting places strain on back muscles and increases the risk of injury.

Correct posture and body mechanics are also important skills for parents and teachers to practice (Teacher Checklist 1-1). Because they perform many bending and lifting activities throughout the day, using proper technique can reduce chronic fatigue and work-related injury. Exercising regularly also improves muscle strength and makes demanding physical tasks easier to complete.

Vigorous physical activity should be an essential part of every child's day. It has a positive effect on children's growth, mental health, weight management, and behavior by relieving excess energy, stress, and boredom (Singh et al., 2012). Introducing children to a variety of sports, games, and other forms of physical activity also provides them with early opportunities

 TEACHER CHECKLIST 1-1

Proper Body Mechanics for Adults

- Use correct technique when lifting children; flex the knees and lift using leg muscles; avoid lifting with back muscles, which are weaker.
- Adjust the height of children's cribs and changing tables to avoid bending over.
- Provide children with step stools so they can reach water fountains and faucets without having to be lifted.
- Bend down by flexing the knees rather than bending over at the waist; this reduces strain on weaker back muscles and decreases the risk of possible injury.
- Sit in adult-sized furniture with feet resting comfortably on the floor to lessen strain on the back and knees.
- Transport children in strollers or wagons rather than carrying them.
- Exercise regularly to improve muscle strength, especially back muscles, and to relieve mental stress.
- Lift objects by keeping arms close to the body versus extended; this also reduces potential for back strain.

TeachSource Digital Download Download from CourseMate.

to discover those they enjoy and are likely to continue. Teachers should review classroom schedules and always look for ways to incorporate more physical activity into daily routines. Current guidelines recommend that children get a daily minimum of 180 cumulative minutes of aerobic activity (of any intensity), including at least 60 minutes that is of moderate intensity (CDC, 2011). It is important that families and teachers serve as positive role models for children by also participating in a variety of physical activities daily.

1-4c Oral Health

Children's oral health continues to be a major goal in the *Healthy People 2020* objectives. Yet, there are many children who seldom visit a dentist because their families cannot afford dental insurance or costly preventive care. Children from low-income and minority groups are twice as likely to experience tooth decay and to lack dental treatment (da Fonseca, 2012). Neglected dental care can result in painful cavities and infected teeth, interfere with concentration and academic performance, and affect children's behavior and self-esteem (Jackson et al., 2011). There are many adults who erroneously believe that "baby teeth," or deciduous teeth, do not require treatment because they will eventually fall out (Figure 1–5). This is an unfortunate assumption because children's temporary teeth are necessary for:

- chewing
- proper spacing for permanent teeth
- shaping the jaw bone
- speech development

Advancements in pediatric dentistry and educational efforts have resulted in significant improvements in children's dental health. Practices, such as consuming a nutritious diet during pregnancy, scheduling regular dental visits, the use of sealants, adding fluoride to drinking water supplies and toothpastes, and applying fluoride directly to teeth have collectively reduced the incidence of children's dental caries and gum disease.

Diet has an unquestionable effect on children's dental health. Proper tooth formation depends on an adequate intake of protein and minerals, particularly calcium and fluoride. Highly refined and sticky carbohydrates should be consumed in moderation to limit their negative effect on healthy teeth. They are commonly found in cakes, cookies, candies, gum, soft drinks, sweetened cereals, and dried fruits (e.g., raisins, dates, prunes). Replacing sweets in children's diet with fresh fruits and vegetables reduces the risk of dental caries and also promotes healthier eating habits. Children's medications and chewable vitamins are often sweetened with sugars so it is important that tooth brushing follow their ingestion.

Dietary practices also play an important role in the prevention of baby bottle tooth decay (BBTD). Extensive cavity development can occur when sugars in formula, breast milk, juices, and/or sweetened drinks come in frequent or extended contact with teeth. Practices that place a child at high risk for developing BBTD include putting an infant to bed with a bottle, lengthy breastfeeding at night, and allowing toddlers to carry around a sippy cup containing fruit juice, soda, or other sweetened drink.

Oral hygiene practices implemented early in children's lives also contribute to healthy tooth development. Food particles can be removed from an infant's gums and teeth by wiping them with a small, wet washcloth after feedings. A small, soft brush and water can be used for cleaning an older infant's teeth.

Most toddlers can begin to brush their own teeth with a soft brush and water at around 15 months of age (Teacher Checklist 1-2). However,

FIGURE 1–5   Approximate age when teeth erupt and are lost.

	Appears	Lost
Primary teeth		
Central incisor	8–12 mos.	6–7 yrs.
Lateral incisor	9–13 mos.	7–8 yrs.
Canine (cuspid)	16–22 mos.	10–12 yrs.
First molar	13–19 mos.	9–11 yrs.
Second molar	25–33 mos.	10–12 yrs.
Second molar	23–31 mos.	10–12 yrs.
First molar	14–18 mos.	9–11 yrs.
Canine (cuspid)	17–23 mos.	9–12 yrs.
Lateral incisor	10–16 mos.	7–8 yrs.
Central incisor	6–10 mos.	6–7 yrs.

TEACHER CHECKLIST 1-2

Promoting Children's Tooth Brushing

Make tooth brushing appealing and fun for children by:
- letting children pick out their favorite tooth brush (color and/or character) and label it with their name
- placing tooth brushes where they are accessible to children
- providing a footstool or chair so children can comfortably reach the sink
- demonstrating the correct tooth-brushing procedure and having children imitate; set a timer and brush your teeth together on occasions

⚠ CAUTION

Supervise children closely to prevent them from slipping or falling.

- recording a favorite song (e.g., "London Bridge," "Itsy Bitsy Spider," or "Wheels on the Bus") and play it while each child brushes his or her teeth. (Check the Internet for free downloads). This can make tooth brushing fun for children.
- making a habit of having children wash their hands and brush their teeth following a meal/snack
- designing a chart where children can place a check mark or sticker each time they brush.

TeachSource Digital Download   Download from CourseMate.

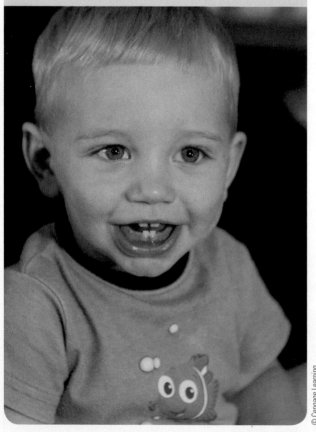

▼ **Improving children's oral health is a major goal of Healthy People 2020.**

© Cengage Learning

the use of toothpaste is not recommended before age 2; most toddlers do not like its taste and are unable to spit it out after brushing. When a child is first learning tooth brushing skills, an adult should brush over the teeth after at least one of the brushings each day to be sure all areas are clean. Teeth can also be kept clean between brushings by rinsing with water after meals and eating raw foods, such as apples, pears, and celery, that provide a natural cleansing action.

Preschool children are generally able to brush their teeth with minimal supervision, but it may still be advisable for an adult to provide a quick follow-up brushing. Although children's technique may not always be perfect, they are beginning to establish a lifelong tooth brushing habit. Proper brushing technique and fluoride-based toothpastes (pea-size application) have proven to be effective in reducing dental cavities. However, children must be supervised closely so they do not swallow the toothpaste. Ingesting too much fluoride over time can result in dental **fluorosis**, which causes white or brown spots to form on developing teeth (Kobayashi et al., 2011). The question of whether young children should learn to floss their teeth is best answered by the child's dentist. Although the practice is regarded as beneficial, much depends on the child's maturity and fine motor skills. Flossing is usually recommended once the permanent teeth begin to erupt and spaces between teeth disappear. Parents should assist children who are too young to manage this procedure by themselves.

---

fluorosis – *white or brown spots that form on children's teeth due to excessive fluoride intake.*

Routine dental checkups are also an important component of preventive health care, but they are not a substitute for daily oral hygiene practices and a healthful diet. Children's first visit to the dentist should be scheduled at around 12 to 15 months of age and every 6 to 12 months thereafter. Initial visits should be pleasant experiences that acquaint a child with the dentist, routine examinations, and cleanings without undergoing painful dental work. Children are more likely to maintain a favorable attitude toward dental care and to approach visits with less fear and anxiety if early experiences are positive.

During routine visits, dentists clean, apply a fluoride varnish, and inspect the child's teeth for potential problems. They also review the child's tooth brushing technique, diet, and personal habits, such as thumb sucking or grinding that may affect the teeth. The fluoridation of municipal water supplies and use of sealants (a plastic-like material applied to permanent molar groves) have also made significant contributions to a decline in childhood tooth decay.

1-4d Mental Health and Social-Emotional Competence

The wellness model recognizes a close relationship between a child's emotional and physical well-being. This association is receiving greater attention due to the increase in behavior problems, school dropout rates, substance abuse, violence, gang membership, depression, and child suicide. Approximately one in five children in the United States experiences mental health problems, and one in ten have disorders that seriously interfere with learning (Healthy People 2020, 2012). Children who live in dysfunctional or economically challenged families, or who have a disability, are at highest risk for developing mental health problems (Cushona et al., 2011).

A strong positive relationship exists between a child's mental health status and **self-concept**. Young children typically view themselves solely in terms of physical qualities, such as having brown hair, blue eyes, or being tall. By age 5 or 6, children begin to include social comparisons with peers as part of their self-definition; they can run faster than Tyshan, build higher towers than Mei, or draw flowers better than Abetzi. Nine- and 10-year-olds exhibit a higher order of self-evaluation that is more analytical: "I like to play baseball, but I don't field or hit the ball as well as Tori, so I probably won't be asked to play on a team."

A child's self-image and mental health are continuously being shaped and reshaped by complex interactions among biological (e.g., personality traits, physical well-being, illness, disability) and environmental factors (e.g., family structure, ethnicity, culture, poverty, household conditions). Each experience yields information that has a positive or negative influence on a child's outlook and behavior. For example, a child who has cerebral palsy and is teased because he doesn't walk like other children may withdraw from group activities and become depressed. In contrast, a child who is athletically talented and frequently befriended is likely to be confident and to have a positive self-concept.

Promoting Children's Social and Emotional Development Families and teachers play a major role in promoting children's social-emotional development. They improve children's chances for achieving positive outcomes by providing learning opportunities that build on individual strengths and interests. Children are more likely to experience success, take pride in their accomplishments, and feel good about themselves when adults set realistic goals and expectations. However, children's efforts should be acknowledged even when they have been unsuccessful. Failures and mistakes must be accepted as part of the learning process and should be viewed as occasions for offering guidance and positive support. In doing so, children begin to learn important lifelong lessons about initiative, risk-taking, problem-solving, and handling adversity. However, caution must be exercised never to judge children solely on their accomplishments (or failures) or to make comparisons with other children, but to recognize each child as a unique and valued individual.

Teachers occupy a strategic position for reinforcing children's development of social-emotional competence. They are able to create opportunities for children to acquire and practice effective communication, self-control, problem-solving, and decision-making skills in a supportive

self-concept – *a person's belief of who they are, how they are perceived by others, and how they fit into society.*

▼ **Teachers have many opportunities to promote children's mental health by teaching important social skills.**

environment (Willis & Schiller, 2011). Teachers also foster children's social-emotional competence by creating safe and respectful classrooms that convey positive attitudes, address children's individual needs, provide constructive feedback, and are conducive to learning. In addition, they play an integral role in:

- modeling positive mental health behaviors.
- implementing sound mental health principles by being accepting, responsive, and supportive.
- preventing emotional problems by teaching children effective social, communication, anger management, and problem-solving skills.
- identifying and referring children who may exhibit signs of emotional problems, such as excessive or uncontrollable frustration, aggressive behavior, or difficulty making and keeping friends.
- working collaboratively with families to locate community resources.
- advocating for community mental health services.

When children develop positive self-esteem and confidence in their own abilities, they are more likely to experience a trajectory of personal and academic success.

Teachers as Role Models Adults must never overlook their importance as role models for young children. Their personal behaviors and response styles exert a powerful and direct influence on children's social-emotional development.

Teachers must carefully examine their own emotional state if they are to be successful in helping children achieve positive **self-esteem**. They, too, must have a strong sense of self-worth and confidence in what they are doing. They should be aware of personal biases and prejudices, be able to accept constructive criticism, and recognize their strengths and limitations. They must have effective communication skills and be able to work collaboratively with families of diverse backgrounds, community service providers, health care professionals, and other members of the child's educational team.

....

self-esteem – *an individual's sense of value or confidence in himself or herself.*

If teachers are to serve as positive role models, they must also exercise the same control over their emotions that they expect of children. Personal problems and stressors must remain at home so that full attention can be focused on the children. Teachers must respect children as individuals—who they are, and not what they are able or not able to do—because every child has qualities that are endearing and worthy of recognition. Teachers must also be impartial in their treatment of children; favoritism cannot be tolerated.

Working with young children can be rewarding, but it can also be stressful and demanding in terms of the patience, energy, and stamina required. Noise, children's continuous requests, long hours, staff shortages, mediocre wages, and occasional conflicts with families or co-workers are everyday challenges. Physical demands and unresolved stress can gradually take their toll on teachers' health, commitment, and daily performance. Eventually, this can lead to job burnout and negative interactions with colleagues and children (Klassen & Chiu, 2012). For these reasons, it is important that teachers identify sources of stress in their jobs and take steps to address, reduce, or eliminate them to the extent possible (Marotz & Lawson, 2007). (See Teacher Checklist 1-3.)

Emotional Climate A classroom's emotional climate—the positive or negative feelings one senses—can have a significant impact on children's social-emotional development. Consider the following situations and decide which classroom you would find most inviting:

> Kate enters the classroom excited and eager to tell her teacher about the tooth she lost last night and the quarter she found under her pillow from the "tooth fairy." Without any greeting, the teacher hurries to check Kate in and informs her that she is too busy to talk right now, but maybe later. When the teacher is finished checking Kate she instructs her "to find something to do without getting into trouble." Kate quietly walks away to her cubbie.
>
> Ted arrives and seems reluctant to leave his mother for some reason this morning. The home provider immediately senses his distress and walks over to greet Ted and his mother. "Ted, I am so glad that you came today. We're going to learn about farm animals and build a farm with the wooden blocks. I know that blocks are one of your favorite activities. Perhaps you'd like to build something small for your mother before it's time for her to go home." Ted eagerly builds a barn with several "animals" in the yard around it and proudly looks to his mother for approval. When Ted's mother is ready to leave, he waves good-bye.

Clearly, the teacher's actions in the two examples created a classroom atmosphere that had a different effect on each child's behavior. Children are generally more receptive and responsive to teachers who are warm, nurturing, and sensitive to their needs. Exposure to negative adult responses, such as ridicule, sarcasm, or threats is harmful to children's emotional development and simply teaches inappropriate behaviors. However, an emotional climate that fosters mutual

TEACHER CHECKLIST 1-3
Strategies for Managing Teacher Stress

- Seek out training opportunities where you can learn new skills and improve your work effectiveness.
- Learn and practice time management techniques.
- Develop program policies and procedures that improve efficiency and reduce sources of tension and conflict.
- Join professional organizations; expand your contacts with other teachers, acquire new ideas, and advocate for young children.
- Take steps to improve your personal well-being—get plenty of sleep, eat a nutritious diet, and participate in some form of physical activity (outside of work) each day.
- Develop new interests, hobbies, and other outlets for releasing tension.
- Practice progressive relaxation techniques. Periodically, concentrate on making yourself relax and think about something pleasing.
- Plan time for yourself each day—read a good book, watch a movie or favorite TV program, go for a long walk, paint, go shopping, play golf, or participate in some activity that you enjoy.

cooperation, respect, trust, acceptance, and independence will promote children's social-emotional skill development.

A teacher's communication style and understanding of cultural differences also affect the emotional climate of a classroom. Treating all children as if they were the same is insensitive and can encourage failure, especially if a teacher's expectations are inconsistent or incompatible with the child's cultural background. For example, knowing that children in some Hispanic cultures are taught primarily through non-verbal instruction (modeling) may explain why a child who is only given verbal directives may not respond to this approach (Martins-Shannon & White, 2012). Some children are reluctant to participate in group activities or to answer a teacher's question because this is counter to the way they have been raised. Unless the teacher understands these cultural differences, such behaviors could easily be misinterpreted as defiance or inattention. When teachers make an effort to learn about individual children and their families, they are able to create a climate that supports learning and healthy social-emotional development.

The way in which the curriculum is planned and implemented also contributes to the emotional climate. Children's chances for achieving success are improved when learning activities are developmentally appropriate and matched to children's individual needs and interests.

Stress All children experience a host of stressful situations as they learn to master new skills, understand social convention, and/or encounter conflict. Developmental stress is a natural part of children's lives and can be healthy when it is used as a learning experience. It provides children with opportunities to acquire valuable coping and problem-solving skills if stress is experienced in a safe, secure, and supportive environment.

Scientists have increased their understanding of stress and its effects on children's physical and mental development. For example, it is now known that children's early exposure to intense, frequent, and/or chronic stress can actually damage genetic makeup (DNA) (Price et al., 2013).

▼ **The classroom atmosphere has a direct effect on children's behavior and development.**

© Cengage Learning

The term **toxic stress** has been used to describe situations that increase children's risk of serious physical and mental health disorders (Shonkoff & Garner, 2012). Toxic stressors include abusive treatment, neglect, poverty, chronic illness, violence, and war. Chronic food insecurity, maternal depression, and parental substance abuse have also been associated with children's long-term psychological problems (Church, Jaggers, & Taylor, 2012).

Some children feel overwhelmed and experience undue anxiety in response to everyday events, such as:

▸ separation from their families
▸ new experiences—for example, moving, enrolling in a new school, having a mother return to work, being left with a sitter, or the birth of a sibling
▸ chronic illness and hospitalization
▸ divorce of parents
▸ death of a pet, family member, or close friend
▸ conflict of ideas; confrontations with family, friends, or teachers
▸ overstimulation due to hectic schedules, participation in too many extracurricular activities
▸ learning problems

Children's immature brain development, limited experience and coping skills, and differences in temperament influence their ability to manage stress in a healthy manner. Sudden behavior changes are often an early indication that a child is experiencing significant tension or inner turmoil. Observable signs can range from less serious behaviors—nail biting, hair twisting, excessive fear, crying, prolonged sadness, and anxiety—to those that are of significant concern—repeated aggressiveness, destructiveness, withdrawal, depression, nightmares, psychosomatic illnesses, or poor performance in school. Brief episodes of these behaviors are usually not cause for concern, but children should be referred for professional evaluation if they persist.

Teachers can help children who are experiencing acute or chronic stress by showing additional patience, understanding, and support. Children also find comfort in knowing they are safe, secure, and able to count on teachers and parents to be accepting, even at times when their emotional control may fail. Additional coping strategies are outlined in Table 1–4.

Bullying   Most school-age children report that they have been subjected to occasional verbal or physical bullying by their peers. Bullying differs from occasional name-calling and social rejection in that it is usually intentional, repetitive, and ongoing. Girls are more likely to engage in verbal taunting directed toward another girl whereas boys tend to use physical aggression to intimidate other males.

Researchers have identified two types of bullies: those who are self-assured, impulsive, lacking empathy, angry, and controlling; and those who are passive and willing to join in once another

TABLE 1–4   Stress Management for Children

1. Encourage children to talk about what is causing them to feel tense or upset.
2. Empower children by helping them to identify and express feelings appropriately.
3. Nurture positive thinking and an "I know I can do this" attitude.
4. Prepare children for stressful events (e.g., doctor's visit, moving, flying for the first time, attending a new school) by role-playing or rehearsing what to expect. Practice "what if's": "What should you do if you get lost?", "What can you do if you're afraid?"
5. Maintain predictable schedules, including mealtimes and bedtimes as much as possible.
6. Make sure children are receiving a nutritious diet and engaging in brief periods of vigorous physical activity (an effective stress reliever).
7. Schedule unstructured play time when children are free to do what they want.

toxic stress – *stress over which children have no control or adult support; it is intense, frequent, and often prolonged.*

CONNECTING TO EVERYDAY PRACTICE

Children and Cyber-Bullying

Maddie was in tears when she finally decided to show her mother the message a friend's mother had posted on her Facebook page. The mother blamed Maddie for the low grade her daughter recently received on a group science project, and accused her of "not working as hard as the other team members" and "turning in sloppy work." Maddie was reluctant to let her mother see the posting despite the fact that it had been bothering her for several days. She fears that her mother will contact school authorities or the friend's mother now that she knows and worries about the repercussions.

School-age children have been quick to adopt **cyber-bullying** as a preferred method for harassing their peers. Access to cell phones, tablets, and computers has made it increasingly easy for children to reach their victims and to engage in non-confrontational bullying. They consider cyber-bullying to be reasonably anonymous, transparent, and unlikely to result in after-school detention. Although victims are spared physical injury, they often suffer significant humiliation, emotional trauma, and find it difficult to avoid unless they turn off all cell phones and computers.

Many administrators believe cyber-bullying is reaching crisis levels in their schools. School boards are establishing disciplinary policies in an effort to curb malicious postings and online harassment. State legislators have also begun to introduce bills that hold children and their parents, in some instances, responsible for engaging in cyber-bullying.

Think About This:

‣ Why do some children feel the need to bully others?

‣ What behavioral changes might a parent observe if their child was being harassed?

‣ Why not just tell children to turn off their cell phones and computers to avoid being bullied?

‣ Should children who engage in bullying be expelled from school? Why might this not be the best option?

‣ Should parents be held responsible when children engage in cyber-bullying? What are the pros and cons?

---

child initiates the bullying (Hong & Espelage, 2012). Children who bully are often from homes where poverty, domestic violence, inconsistent supervision, and lack of social support or parental concern are common. As a result, they have had limited opportunities to develop effective interpersonal skills, impulse control, and problem-solving abilities.

Children who are targeted by bullies may be singled out because they are perceived to be socially withdrawn or loners, passive and lacking in self-confidence, having a disability or special needs, not likely to stand up for themselves, and easily hurt (emotionally). They are more often from economically disadvantaged families, smaller in physical size than their peers, and seen as having fewer friends. Warning signs that a child is being victimized may include frequent complaints of health problems, change in eating and/or sleeping habits, reluctance to attend school, and declining academic performance.

Prevention programs have been implemented in many schools to reduce bullying behavior and to create environments where children feel safe. Educational efforts address both the victims and perpetrators and are designed to teach mutual respect, reinforce effective social and communication skills, reduce harassment, and improve children's self-esteem (Strohmeier & Noam, 2012). Children who are being bullied learn how to respond in these

cyber-bullying – *sending embarrassing or threatening messages to an individual via the Internet, electronic media, or cell phone.*

situations by avoiding bullies, walking away, practicing conflict resolution, and always informing a trusted adult.

Childhood Depression   Some children are unsuccessful or unable to cope with acute anxiety or chronic stress. They may develop a sense of persistent sadness and hopelessness that begins to affect the way they think, feel, and act. These may be early signs of childhood depression and can include:

- apathy or disinterest in activities or friends
- loss of appetite
- difficulty sleeping
- complaints of physical discomforts, such as headaches, stomachaches, vomiting, diarrhea, ulcers, repetitive tics (twitches), or difficulty breathing
- lack of energy or enthusiasm
- indecision
- poor self-esteem
- uncontrollable anger

Children who have learning and behavior disorders or a family history of mental health conditions are at an increased risk for developing depression. Children as young as 3 may begin showing early signs of depression particularly when their mothers also suffer from this condition (Hughes et al., 2013).

The onset of childhood depression may occur abruptly following a traumatic event, such as parental divorce, death of a close family member or friend, abusive treatment, or chronic illness. However, it can also develop slowly over time, making the early signs more difficult to notice. In either case, teachers must be knowledgeable about the behaviors commonly associated with childhood depression so children can be identified and referred for professional care. Depression requires early identification and treatment to avoid serious and debilitating effects on children's social, emotional, and cognitive development and to prevent long-term mental health disorders.

Childhood Fears   Most childhood fears and nightmares are a normal part of the developmental process and are eventually outgrown as children mature. Basic fears are relatively consistent across generations and cultures, although they vary somewhat from one developmental stage to the next. For example, a 3-month-old infant seldom displays any fear, whereas 3-year-olds often are fearful of "monsters under the bed." Fears that reflect real-life events, such as fire, kidnapping, thunderstorms, or homelessness, are more common among 5- and 6-year-olds, whereas 10- and 11-year-olds may express fears related to appearance and social rejection (Marotz & Allen, 2013). Some fears are unique to an individual child and may stem from personal experiences, such as witnessing a shooting, vicious dog attack, or being involved in a car accident.

Fears and nightmares are often accentuated during the preschool years, a time when children have a heightened imagination and are attempting to make sense of their world. Children's literal interpretation of the things they see and hear can also contribute to misunderstanding and fear. For example, children are likely to believe that an adult who says, "I'm going to give you away if you misbehave one more time" will actually do so.

It is important for adults to acknowledge children's fears and to accept that they are truly real to the child. Children need consistent adult reassurance and trust to overcome their fears, even though it may be difficult to remain patient and supportive when a child repeatedly awakens at 2:00 every morning! Children also find comfort in talking about things that frighten them and rehearsing what they might do, for example, if they were to become lost at the supermarket or if it began to thunder.

Poverty and Homelessness   Approximately 21.9 percent of all U.S. children currently live in families that fall below the national poverty level (U.S. Census Bureau, 2012). The adults in many of these families are either unemployed, working in low-wage jobs, recent immigrants, classified as minorities (especially Hispanic, Native American, and African American), or a single parent, usually a mother. Living in a single- versus a two-parent family places children at the highest economic risk for poverty. Children residing in rural areas also experience a high poverty rate, but they comprise an often overlooked group. Economic problems and high unemployment have forced many rural families into bankruptcy (Curtis, Voss, & Long, 2012). Collectively, these developments have caused families with young children to become the new majority of today's homeless population.

Poverty places additional burdens on the already challenging demands of parenting. Struggles to provide children with basic food, clothing, shelter, health care, and nurturing are often compromised by increased stress, fear, and conflict. Ultimately, these pressures can contribute to family tension, domestic violence, child maltreatment, and an inability to provide the love and support that children require.

The impact of poverty on children's growth and development has both immediate and long-term consequences. Children born into poverty experience a higher rate of birth defects, early death, and chronic illnesses, such as anemia, asthma, and lead poisoning (Reichman & Teitler, 2013). In addition, the quality of their diet, access to health and dental care, and mental health status are often compromised. Children living in poverty are also more likely to experience abuse or neglect, learning and behavior problems, teen pregnancy, substance abuse, high dropout rates, and reduced earning potential as adults. Ultimately, the cumulative effects of poverty can threaten children's chances of growing up to become healthy, educated, and productive adults.

Violence Children today live in a world where daily exposure to violence is not uncommon. The incidence of crime, substance abuse, gang activity, and access to guns tends to be greater in neighborhoods where poverty exists and can result in unhealthy urban environments where children's personal safety is at risk. Children living in these settings are also more likely to become victims of child abuse or to witness domestic violence. Their families exhibit a higher rate of dysfunctional parenting skills, are often less responsive and nurturing, and use discipline that is either lacking, inconsistent, or punitive and harsh (Burke et al., 2011). Parents in these situations are also less likely to be supportive of children's education or to assume an active role in their school activities. As a result, many children who grow up in poverty are at greater risk of experiencing learning problems, becoming violent adults, and developing serious mental health disorders. Teachers who understand this potential can be instrumental in helping children overcome adversity by reaching out and strengthening their resiliency skills as well as assisting families in locating supportive community resources. (See Teacher Checklist 1-4.)

Children growing up in violent and disadvantaged environments face challenges not only at home but also at school. Younger children are more likely to attend child care programs and schools that are of poorer quality than their counterparts in higher income neighborhoods (Burchinal et al., 2011). In addition, children of all ages often have fewer opportunities to engage in learning and enrichment experiences at home. Researchers have observed that children living in disadvantaged households typically have delayed language development and literacy skills due to a lower rate of parent-child interactions and lack of available reading materials (Nelson et al., 2011). This combination sets many children up for early school failure.

Media Violence Children are frequently exposed to sources of extreme violence and death in movies, video games, cartoons, on television, and on the Internet. Researchers have observed an increase in children's aggressive behaviors after they have witnessed violent media entertainment, but no direct link has been established with adult criminal activity (Gentile, Mathieson, & Crick, 2011). However, repeated exposure to media violence and death has been shown to desensitize children to their dysfunctional significance (Ferguson, 2011). Families are encouraged to limit children's media viewing to 1 or 2 hours daily, choose and monitor content carefully, and help children to understand media as a form of fantasy entertainment (AAP, 2011). Television and other media entertainment formats (e.g., CD movies, video games, smartphones, iPads) are not recommended for children under 2 years. Young children learn best through hands-on experience and have difficulty understanding abstract content viewed on an electronic screen.

TEACHER CHECKLIST 1-4

Strategies for Increasing Children's Resilient Behaviors

- Be a positive role model for children; demonstrate how you expect them to behave.
- Accept children unconditionally; avoid being judgmental.
- Help children develop and use effective communication skills.
- Listen carefully to children to show that you value their thoughts and ideas.
- Use discipline that is developmentally appropriate and based on natural or logical consequences.
- Use and enforce discipline consistently.
- Help children to understand and express their feelings; encourage them to have empathy for others.
- Avoid harsh physical punishment and angry outbursts.
- Help children establish realistic goals, set high expectations for themselves, and have a positive outlook.
- Promote problem-solving skills; help children make informed decisions.
- Reinforce children's efforts with praise and encouragement.
- Give children responsibility; assign household tasks and classroom duties.
- Involve children in activities outside of their home.
- Encourage children to believe in themselves, to feel confident rather than seeing themselves as failures or victims.

TeachSource Digital Download Download from CourseMate.

1-4e Resilient Children

Children face many challenges as they grow up in this complex world. Stress, violence, uncertainty, and negative encounters are everywhere. What makes some children more vulnerable to the negative effects of stress and aversive treatment or more likely to develop inappropriate behaviors? Many factors, including genetic predisposition, malnutrition, prenatal exposure to drugs or alcohol, poor attachment to primary caregivers, physical and/or learning disabilities, and/or an irritable personality, have been suggested as possible explanations. Researchers have also studied home environments and parenting styles that make it difficult for some children to achieve normal developmental tasks and positive self-esteem (Alegre, 2011).

Why are other children better able to overcome the negative effects of an impoverished, traumatic, violent, or stressful childhood? This question continues to be a focus of study as researchers attempt to learn what conditions or qualities enable some children to be more **resilient** in the face of adversity. Although much remains to be understood, several important protective factors have been identified. These include having certain personal characteristics (such as above-average intelligence, positive self-esteem, and effective social and problem-solving skills), having a strong and dependable relationship with a parent or parent substitute, and having a social support network outside of one's immediate family (such as a church group, organized sports, Boys and Girls clubs, or various youth groups).

Competent parenting is, beyond a doubt, one of the most important factors necessary for helping children to cope with and overcome adversity and its potentially damaging consequences (Hardaway, McLoyd, & Wood, 2012). Children who grow up in an environment where families are caring and emotionally responsive, provide meaningful supervision and discipline that is consistent and developmentally appropriate, offer encouragement and praise, and help children learn to solve problems in a peaceful way are more likely to demonstrate resilient behavior. Teachers, likewise, can promote resiliency by establishing classrooms where children feel accepted, respected, and supported in their efforts.

Management Strategies Understandably, all children undergo occasional periods of emotional instability or undesirable behavior. Short-term or one-time occurrences are usually not cause for

resilient – *the ability to withstand or resist difficulty.*

concern. However, when a child consistently demonstrates abnormal or antisocial behaviors, an intervention program or counseling therapy may be necessary.

At times, it may be difficult for families to recognize or acknowledge abnormal behaviors in their own children. Some emotional problems develop slowly over time and may therefore be difficult to distinguish from normal behaviors. Some families find it difficult to talk about or to admit that their child has an emotional disturbance. Others, unknowingly, may be contributing to their children's problems because of dysfunctional (e.g., abusive, unrealistic, inconsistent, or absent) parenting styles.

For whatever reasons, it may be teachers who first identify children's abnormal social and emotional behaviors based on their understanding of typical development, careful observations, and documentation of inappropriate conduct. They also play an instrumental role in promoting children's emotional health by providing stable and supportive environments that foster children's self-esteem and self-confidence. They model and help children develop socially appropriate behaviors. They teach conflict resolution, problem-solving, and communication skills so children will be able to cope effectively with daily problems. In addition, teachers can use their expertise to help families acknowledge children's problems, counsel them in positive behavior management techniques, strengthen parent-child relationships, and assist them in arranging professional counseling or other needed services. Although most families welcome an opportunity to improve their parenting skills, the benefit to high-risk or dysfunctional families may be even greater.

Did You Get It?

Children living in_____ families are at increased risk for developing mental health disorders.
- **a.** minority
- **b.** dysfunctional
- **c.** dual-earner
- **d.** inner-city

Take the full quiz on CourseMate.

PARTNERING with FAMILIES

Growing Your Child's Brain

Dear Families,

Your child's brain is much like a flower or plant in your garden. It requires daily nourishment and attention, especially in the beginning, and is affected by positive and negative conditions in the environment. There are many things you can do every day to encourage your child's healthy brain growth and development:

- Read, sing, and talk often to your infant or young child. Encourage your child to make up silly songs, rhymes, and stories. Read your child's favorite books over and over, have them turn the pages, point to pictures, and name objects.

- Provide nutritious meals and snacks to build healthy brain cells.

- Make sure your child gets sufficient sleep.

- Respond to your child's needs in a consistent, caring, and constructive manner. Harsh words, physical punishment, and abusive treatment can have a damaging effect on the brain's structure over time.

- Encourage your child to be physically active every day. Change an infant's position frequently so she uses different muscles and sees different things in the environment.

- Allow children time to try and solve their own problems; intervene only if they become overly frustrated and then help guide their solution by providing choices.

(continued)

PARTNERING with FAMILIES

Growing Your Child's Brain   *(continued)*

▶ Encourage your child's curiosity and provide safe learning opportunities for exploring and experimenting.

▶ Help your child learn to recognize and manage his feelings. Be a positive role model and show your child how to appropriately respond to difficult situations.

▶ Most importantly, tell and show your child often that he or she is loved.

CLASSROOM CORNER

Teacher Activities

The Importance of Friendship

(NHES PreK–2, National Health Education Standard 4.2.1)

Concept: Having fun with friends.

Learning Objectives

▶ Children will learn that there are many activities to do with friends.

▶ Children will learn that friendship requires sharing and turn-taking.

▶ Children will learn that working together can be a lot of fun.

Supplies

▶ a variety of colors of construction paper cut into large hearts (each heart should then be cut in half in a variety of ways so that the two heart pieces can be put back together to form a large heart); glue sticks; various art supplies (glitter, feathers, puff balls, foam shapes, etc.); adhesive tape; large piece of bulletin board paper (large enough to display all of the hearts)

Learning Activities

▶ Read and discuss one of the following books:
  * *What Is a Friend?* by Josie Firmin
  * *A Rainbow of Friends* by P.K. Hallinan
  * *Winnie the Pooh: Friendship Day* by Nancy Parent
  * *Pooh: Just Be Nice . . . to Your Little Friends!* by Caroline Kenneth

▶ Explain to the children that they are going to make a friendship quilt.
  * Have the children come up and pick a heart half. After they have all selected half of a heart, pair the two children together whose heart halves fit together. Provide art supplies and one glue stick per pair of children to encourage sharing and cooperation. When each pair of children has finished decorating their heart half, tape the two halves together. Label each heart set with the names of both children. Arrange the completed hearts on a large sheet of bulletin board paper to create a friendship quilt that can be hung up in your classroom.

▶ Talk about the experience, including what it means to work with a partner and to make a friendship quilt.

Evaluation

▶ Children will work together and take turns.

▶ Children will name activities they like to do with their friends.

Additional lesson plans for grades 3–5 are available on CourseMate.

Summary

▶ The concept of preventive health care:
- recognizes that health attitudes and practices are learned behaviors.
- encourages individuals to assume an active role in developing and maintaining practices that promote health.

▶ A child's health is determined by the interplay of genetic makeup and environment.
- Health is a dynamic state of physical, mental, and social well-being that is continuously changing as a result of lifestyle decisions.

▶ Children's growth and developmental potentials are determined, in part, by genetics, and the interactions of multiple health, safety, and nutrition factors.
- Health promotion begins with a sound understanding of children's growth and development.

▶ Several aspects of children's health require special adult attention: safety and injury prevention; body mechanics and physical activity promotion; oral health; and mental health, including fostering self-esteem, social-emotional competence, and resilience.

Terms to Know

preventive health *p. 3*	norms *p. 12*	plasticity *p. 17*
health *p. 8*	normal *p. 12*	well child *p. 18*
heredity *p. 9*	growth *p. 13*	fluorosis *p. 22*
predisposition *p. 9*	head circumference *p. 13*	self-concept *p. 23*
sedentary *p. 10*	attachment *p. 13*	self-esteem *p. 24*
food insecurity *p. 10*	deciduous teeth *p. 13*	toxic stress *p. 27*
nutrients *p. 11*	development *p. 15*	cyber-bullying *p. 28*
resistance *p. 11*	neurons *p. 17*	resilient *p. 31*

Chapter Review

A. By Yourself:

1. Define each of the *Terms to Know* listed at the end of this chapter.
2. Explain how genetics and environment influence the quality of a child's well-being.
3. Describe how singing, talking, and reading to an infant promote early brain development.
4. Explain why young children are at high risk for unintentional injury.
5. Identify several preventive practices that promote children's oral health.
6. Explain why children living in poverty may experience lower self-esteem.
7. Describe several ways that families can help children to build resilience.

B. As a Group:

1. Discuss how an individual's lifestyle decisions can have either a positive or negative effect on health.
2. Describe how teachers can use their knowledge of children's development for health promotion.
3. Explain why an abundant food supply does not always ensure a healthy diet.
4. Discuss why it is important to involve and include families in children's health education activities. What steps can a teacher take to be sure that children's cultural beliefs are respected?
5. Explain the benefits of physical activity for both children and teachers. Conduct several classroom observations with different age groups to identify ways that teachers can incorporate more aerobic activity into children's daily schedule. Describe how several of these activities could be modified for children who have limited vision or are in a wheelchair.

6. Define the term self-concept. Provide specific examples of things teachers might do that could have a positive and negative effect on children's self-esteem.

7. Discuss how a teacher's mental health state can potentially affect children.

Case Study

Jose, 7 years old, and his mother live alone in a one-bedroom apartment close to his school. Most afternoons Jose walks home alone, lets himself into their apartment, and watches television until his mother comes home from work. His favorite after-school snack consists of potato chips and a soda or fruit drink. For dinner, Jose's mother usually brings something home from a local fast food restaurant because she is "too tired to cook." She knows this isn't good for either one of them. Jose's mother is currently being treated for high blood pressure, and the pediatrician has expressed concern about Jose's continued weight gain. However, Jose's mother doesn't see how she can change anything given her work schedule and limited income.

1. How would you describe Jose's short- and long-term health potential?

2. What concerns would you have about Jose's safety?

3. What potential health problems is Jose likely to develop if his current behaviors do not change?

4. What environmental risk factors may be contributing to the family's health problems?

5. If you were working with this family, what suggestions would you have for improving their health?

Application Activities

1. Observe a small group of preschool-aged children for two 15-minute intervals during free-play or outdoor times. For each observation, select a different child and record the number of times that child engages in cooperative play. Repeat this observation procedure with a group of toddler or school-age children. Describe the differences.

2. Contact your local public health department. Arrange to observe several routine well-child visits. What preventive health information was given to families? Was it presented in a way that families could understand and use?

3. Select and read ten children's books from the Mental Health section in Appendix D. Prepare a brief annotation for each book, including the topic, theme, and recommendations. Describe how you would use each book to develop a learning activity that promotes children's social-emotional competence.

4. Research and read more about the national health initiatives described in this chapter. Find out if they are available in your area and what services are provided. Are the programs and services meeting the needs of children in your community? If not, what recommendations would you offer for improvement?

5. Develop a month-long series of classroom learning activities focused on children's oral health. Make arrangements to conduct several of your lessons with children in a local school and evaluate their effectiveness. What changes or improvements would you make the next time?

6. Modify the "Classroom Corner" activity on friendship to meet National Health Education Standard 4.5.3. (Demonstrate non-violent strategies to manage or resolve conflict.) Design and describe at least three classroom activities that would teach and reinforce positive resolution techniques.

Helpful Web Resources

American Institute of Stress	http://www.stress.org
Centers for Disease Control and Prevention: Coordinated School Health Program	http://www.cdc.gov/HealthyYouth/CSHP/

Council for Exceptional Children	http://www.cec.sped.org
Centers for Disease Control and Prevention: Adolescent and School Health	http://www.cdc.gov/HealthyYouth/
U.S. Department of Health and Human Services: Indian Health Service	http://www.ihs.gov
National Association for Child Development	http://www.nacd.org
Let's Move! Child Care	http://healthykidshealthyfuture.org
National Center for Children in Poverty	http://www.nccp.org
Mental Health America	http://www.mentalhealthamerica.net/go/children

Visit the Education CourseMate for this textbook to access the eBook, Did You Get It? quizzes, Digital Downloads, TeachSource Video Cases, flashcards, and more. Go to CengageBrain.com to log in, register, or purchase access.

References

Alegre, A. (2011). Parenting styles and children's emotional intelligence: What do we know? *The Family Journal*, 19(1), 56–62.

American Academy of Pediatrics (AAP). (2011). Media and children. Accessed on May 8, 2012 from http://www.aap.org/en-us/advocacy-and-policy/aap-health-initiatives/Pages/Media-and-Children.aspx.

American Academy of Pediatrics (AAP), American Public Health Association (APHA), & National Resource Center for Health and Safety in Child Care and Early Education (NRC). (2011). *Caring for our children: National health and safety performance standards: Guidelines for early care and education programs* (3rd ed.). Elk Grove Village, IL: American Academy of Pediatrics; Washington, DC: American Public Health Association.

Blunden, S. (2012). Behavioral sleep disorders across the developmental age span: An overview of causes, consequences, and treatment modalities, *Psychology*, 3(3), 249–256.

Burchinal, M., McCartney, K., Steinberg, L., Crosnoe, R., Friedman, S., McLoyd, V., & Pianta, R. (2011). Examining the black-white achievement gap among low-income children using the NICHD study of early child care and youth development, *Child Development*, 82(5), 1404–1420.

Burke, N., Hellman, J., Scott, B., Weems, C., & Carrion, V. (2011). The impact of adverse childhood experiences on an urban pediatric population, *Child Abuse & Neglect*, 35(6), 408–413.

Cavalari, R., & Romanczyk, R. (2012). Supervision of children with an autism spectrum disorder in the context of unintentional injury, *Research in Autism Spectrum Disorders*, 6(2), 618–627.

CDC. (2011). Physical activity for everyone. Accessed on April 28, 2012 from http://www.cdc.gov/physicalactivity/everyone/guidelines/children.html.

Centers for Disease Control & Prevention (CDC). (2012). Child injury. Accessed on April 15, 2012 from http://www.cdc.gov/vitalsigns/ChildInjury/index.html.

Centers for Medicare & Medicaid Coverage. (2013). Children's Health Insurance Program (CHIP). Accessed on April 5, 2013 from http://www.medicaid.gov.

Church, W., Jaggers, J., & Taylor, J. (2012). Neighborhood, poverty, and negative behavior: An examination of differential association and social control theory, *Children & Youth Services Review*, 34(5), 1035–1041.

Colby, M., Lipson, D., & Turchin, S. (2012). Value for the money spent? Exploring the relationship between expenditures, insurance adequacy, and access to care for publicly insured children, *Maternal & Child Health Journal*, 16(Suppl. 1), 51–60. DOI: 10.1007/s10995-012-0994-y.

Curtis, K., Voss, P., & Long, D. (2012). Spatial variation in poverty-generating processes: Child poverty in the U.S., *Social Science Research*, 41(1), 146–159.

Cushona, J., Vu, L., Janzen, B., & Muhajarine, N. (2011). Neighborhood poverty impacts children's physical health and well-being over time: Evidence from the Early Development Instrument, *Early Education & Development*, 22(2), 183–205.

da Fonseca, M. (2012). The effects of poverty on children's development and oral health, *Pediatric Dentistry*, 34(1), 32–38.

Daniels, S., Pratt, C., & Hayman, L. (2011). Reduction of risk for cardiovascular disease in children and adolescents, *Circulation*, 124, 1673–1686.

Ferguson, C. (2011). Video games and youth violence: A prospective analysis in adolescents, *Journal of Youth & Adolescents*, 40(4), 377–391.

Foltran, F., Gregori, D., Franchin, L., Verduci, E., & Giovannini, M. (2011). Effect of alcohol consumption in prenatal life, childhood, and adolescence on child development, *Nutrition Reviews*, 69(11), 642–659.

Gentile, D., Mathieson, L., & Crick, N. (2011). Media violence associations with the form and function of aggression among elementary school children, *Social Development*, 20(2), 213–232.

Hardaway, C., McLoyd, V., & Wood, D. (2012). Exposure to violence and socioemotional adjustment in low-income youth: An examination of protective factors, *American Journal of Community Psychology*, 49(1–2), 112–126.

Healthy People 2020. (2012). Mental health. Accessed on April 5, 2013 from http://www.healthypeople.gov/2020/LHI/mentalHealth.aspx.

Hong, J., & Espelage, D. (2012). A review of research on bullying and peer victimization in school: An ecological system analysis, *Aggression & Violent Behavior*, 17(4), 311–322.

Hughes, C., Roman, G., Hart, M., & Ensor, R. (2013). Does maternal depression predict young children's executive function?—A 4-year longitudinal study, *Journal of Child Psychology & Psychiatry*, 54(2), 169–177.

Jackson, S., Vann, W., Kotch, J., Pahel, B., & Lee, J. (2011). Impact of poor oral health on children's school attendance and performance, *American Journal of Public Health*, 101(10), 1900–1906.

Judy, K. (2011). Unintentional injuries in pediatrics, *Pediatrics in Review*, 32(10), 431–439.

Klassen, R., & Chiu, M. (2012). The occupational commitment and intention to quit of practicing and pre-service teachers: Influence of self-efficacy, job stress, and teaching context, *Contemporary Educational Psychology*, 36(2), 114–129.

Kobayashi, C., Belini, M., Italiani, F., Pauleto, A., Julianelli de Araújo, J., Tessarolli, V., Grizzo, L., Pessan, J., Machado, M., & Buzalaf, M. (2011). Factors influencing fluoride ingestion from dentifrice by children, *Community Dentistry & Oral Epidemiology*, 39(5), 426–432.

Liu J., & Raine, A. (2011). Malnutrition and externalizing behavior. In D. Benton (ed.), *Lifetime nutritional influences on cognition, behavior, and psychiatric illness*. Cambridge, UK: Woodhead Publishing.

Marotz, L.R., & Allen, K.E. (2013). *Developmental profiles: Pre-birth through adolescence* (7th ed.). Belmont, CA: Wadsworth Cengage Learning.

Marotz, L., & Lawson, A. (2007). *Motivational leadership*. Clifton Park, NY: Thomson Delmar Learning.

Martins-Shannon, J., & White, M. (2012). Support culturally responsive teaching!, *Kappa Delta Pi Record*, 48(1), 4–6.

Maxwell, M., Lemacks, J., Coccia, C., Ralston, P., & Ilich, J. (2012). A student-led pilot project to improve calcium intake and health lifestyle in African American communities, *Topics in Clinical Nutrition*, 27(1), 54–66.

McCormick, M., Litt, J., Smith, V., & Zupancic, J. (2011). Prematurity: An overview and public health implications, *Annual Review of Public Health*, 32, 367–379.

Morrongiello, B., Kane, A., McArthur, B., & Bell, M. (2012). Physical risk taking in elementary-school children: Measurement and emotion regulation issues, *Personality & Individual Differences*, 52(4), 492–496.

National Association for the Education of Young Children (NAEYC). (2012). NAEYC accreditation criteria. Accessed on April 15, 2012 from http://www.naeyc.org/files/academy/file/NewGuidanceOnNAEYCAccreditationCriteria EffectiveApril2012.pdf.

Nelson, K., Welsh, J., Trup, E., & Greenberg, M. (2011). Language delays of impoverished preschool children in relation to early academic and emotion recognition skills, *First Language*, 31(2), 164–194.

Okechukwu, C., El Ayadi, A., Tamers, S., Sabbath, E., & Berkman, L. (2012). Household food insufficiency, financial strain, work–family spillover, and depressive symptoms in the working class: The Work, Family, and Health Network Study, *American Journal of Public Health*, 102(1), 126–133.

O'Leary, C., Jacoby, P., Bartu, A., D'Antoine, H., & Bower, C. (2013). Maternal alcohol use and sudden infant death syndrome and infant mortality excluding SIDS, *Pediatrics*, 131(3), e770–e778.

Price, L., Hung-The, K., Burgers, D., Carpenter, L., & Tyrka, A. (2013). Telomeres and early-life stress: An overview, *Biological Psychiatry*, 73(1), 15–23.

Reichman, N., & Teitler, J. (2013). Lifecourse exposures and socioeconomic disparities in child health, *National Symposium on Family Issues*, 3, 107–134.

Safe Kids Canada. (2012). Safety information. Accessed on April 15, 2012, from http://www.safekidscanada.ca.

Shonkoff, J., & Garner, A.; Committee on Psychosocial Aspects of Child and Family Health; Committee on Early Childhood, Adoption, and Dependent Care; Section on Developmental and Behavioral Pediatrics. (2012). The lifelong effects of early childhood adversity and toxic stress, *Pediatrics*, 129(1), e232–246.

Singh, A., Uijtdewilligen, L., Twisk, J., van Mechelen, W., & Chinapaw, M. (2012). Physical activity and performance at school, *Archives of Pediatrics & Adolescent Medicine*, 166(1), 49–55.

Stewart de Ramirez, S., Hyder, A., Herbert, H., & Stevens, K. (2012). Unintentional injuries: Magnitude, prevention, and control, *Annual Review of Public Health*, 33, 175–191.

Strohmeier, D., & Noam, G. (2012). Bullying in schools: What is the problem, and how can educators solve it?, *New Directions for Youth Development*, 2012(133), 7–13.

Su, W., & Aurelia, D. (2012). Preschool children's perceptions of overweight peers, *Journal of Early Childhood Research*, 10(1), 19–31.

Twardosz, S. (2012). Effects of experience on the brain: The role of neuroscience in early development and education, *Early Education & Development*, 23(1), 96–119.

U.S. Census Bureau. (2012). Poverty. Accessed on September 17, 2012 from http://www.census.gov/hhes/www/poverty/about/overview.

Weill, J. (2012). Food insecurity in America: A call to action, *Journal of Applied Research on Children*, 3(1). Informing policy for children at risk, Article 1. Available at http://digitalcommons.library.tmc.edu/childrenatrisk/vol3/iss1/1/.

Willis, C.A., & Schiller, P. (2011). Preschoolers' social skills steer life success, *Young Children*, 66 (1), 50–54.

naeyc **Standards Chapter Links**

▶ **#1 a and b:** Promoting child development and learning
▶ **#2 a, b, and c:** Building family and community relationships
▶ **#3 a, b, c, and d:** Observing, documenting, and assessing to support young children and families
▶ **#6 b:** Becoming a professional
▶ Field Experience

Learning Objectives

After studying this chapter, you should be able to:

LO 2-1 Discuss several ways that teachers and programs can promote children's health.
LO 2-2 Explain why it is important to conduct daily health observations.
LO 2-3 Perform a daily health check.
LO 2-4 Discuss how teachers can involve children's families in the health appraisal process.
LO 2-5 Describe ways that teachers can incorporate health education into daily health checks.

The *Healthy People 2020* national initiative reinforces the important relationship that exists between children's health and their ability to learn (HHS, 2012). It also recognizes that not all children have equal access to medical and dental care or to environments that promote a healthy lifestyle. It underscores the collaborative effort necessary for ensuring children's health and educational success, and challenges professionals and communities to address these problems. Teachers and health care providers also play a critical role in implementing the *Healthy People 2020* goals to help children achieve their optimal health and development.

Only when children are healthy and well-nourished are they able to fully benefit from learning experiences. Acute and chronic illnesses, undetected health **impairments**, inadequate diet, maltreatment, and mental health problems can interfere with a child's level of interest, involvement, and performance in school. For example, a mild hearing loss may distort a child's perception of letter sounds, pronunciations, and responsiveness. If left undetected, it can have a profound and long-term effect on a child's language development and ability to learn. However, health problems do not have to be obvious or complex to have a negative effect. Even a simple cold, toothache, allergic reaction, or chronic tonsillitis will disrupt a child's energy level, cooperation, attention span, and learning enjoyment. Teachers are in an ideal position to monitor children's health, note early signs of problems that can hinder learning, and work with families to obtain the care children need to be successful.

....

impairments – *a condition or malfunction of a body part that interferes with optimal functioning.*

CONNECTING TO EVERYDAY PRACTICE

The Impact of Health on Learning

High drop-out rates among school-age children continue to attract national attention. According to several recent studies, many of these children have undiagnosed health problems, such as vision and hearing impairments, allergies, asthma, and anemia, which interfere with their ability to learn and to succeed in school. After years of struggle and failure, some children simply choose to abandon the source of their frustration.

The visionary founders of Head Start clearly understood the importance of early identification and treatment of health problems to ensure that children were ready and able to learn upon entering school. The same preventive philosophy is evident in the *Healthy People 2020* goals and reinforces the valuable role teachers play in assessing and promoting children's well-being.

Think About This:

▸ Should inservice and teacher education programs include more training about children's health care needs? Explain.

▸ In what ways do state child-care licensing regulations encourage teachers to be proactive in protecting children's health and safety?

▸ What right does a teacher have to insist that children receive treatment for their health problems? Explain.

▸ What health care options exist for children whose families cannot afford needed treatments?

Did You Get It?

Health impairments can have a profound effect on a student's ability to concentrate and learn successfully. The most critical step to overcoming these prospective barriers is
  a. accommodation.
  b. counseling.
  c. medical or behavioral intervention.
  d. detection.

Take the full quiz on CourseMate.

2-1 Promoting Children's Health

Schools and early childhood programs make significant contributions to children's wellness by providing on-site health care, educational programs, safe learning environments, and nutritious meals. High-quality programs also conduct teacher observations and daily health checks to monitor children's health and identify potential health problems. It is important that this process be ongoing because children's health status changes continuously, as illustrated in the following example:

> Braden, age 3, ran ahead of his mother so he could reach the classroom before she did. He greeted his friends with the usual, "Hey guys" and seemed fine when the teacher checked him in. However, later that morning she noted that Braden had refused snack and was lying in the book area with his blanket. When she touched his arm it felt warm and was covered with red, raised bumps. She immediately recognized the symptoms as a likely case of chickenpox and called Braden's mother to come and take him home.

When teachers remain alert to changes in children's appearance and behavior, they are often able to identify an impending illness or undiagnosed health condition when it is still in the early stages. This can be especially important for limiting the spread of a contagious disease or the negative impact of a disorder on a child's growth and development.

2-1a Gathering Information

Information about children's overall health can be obtained from a variety of resources, including:

- dietary assessment
- health histories
- results of medical examinations
- teacher observations and daily health checks
- dental examinations
- family interviews
- vision and hearing screenings
- speech evaluations
- psychological testing
- developmental evaluations

Several of these assessment tools can be administered by teachers or volunteers, whereas others require the skills of specially trained health professionals. Often, the process of identifying a specific health impairment requires the cooperative efforts of specialists from several different fields:

- pediatric medicine
- nursing
- speech
- dietetics
- dentistry
- psychology
- education
- ophthalmology
- social work
- audiology

Information about a child's health should always be collected from multiple sources before any final conclusions are reached. A single **health assessment** may present a biased and unreliable picture of the child's condition (Allen & Cowdery, 2012). Children may also behave or respond in **atypical** ways when faced with new surroundings or an unfamiliar adult examiner. However, the nature of a child's health problem and its impact on development and learning become more apparent when information is obtained from several evaluation procedures. For example, the need to refer a child to a hearing specialist may be confirmed when testing results are combined with teacher and family observations.

▼ **Changes in children's appearance and behavior may be early signs of an illness.**

© Cengage Learning

Did You Get It?

What describes the teacher's role in using health assessment screening tools?

a. Teachers can use some screening tools.

b. Teachers are forbidden by law to use screening tools.

c. Teachers can use some screening tools, but they should not use them.

d. Teachers can use all screening tools.

Take the full quiz on CourseMate.

2-2 Observation as a Screening Tool

Teachers are valuable members of a child's comprehensive health team. Their interactions with children in the classroom and knowledge of developmental patterns place them in an ideal position to note the early signs of health problems. They can use information obtained from daily **observations** to establish a baseline of typical behavior and appearance for each child. When this information is combined with an understanding of normal growth and development, teachers can be effective in detecting early changes and deviations.

health assessment – *the process of gathering and evaluating information about an individual's state of health.*
atypical – *unusual; different from what might commonly be expected.*
observation – *to inspect and take note of the appearance and behavior of other individuals.*

▼ **Teachers can observe and note children's health problems while they are engaged in daily classroom activities.**

© Cengage Learning

Health observations provide a simple and effective screening tool that is readily available to teachers. Many skills necessary for making objective health observations are already at their disposal. Sight, for example, is one of the most important senses; much can be learned about children's health by merely watching them in action. A simple touch can detect a fever or enlarged lymph glands. Odors may indicate lack of cleanliness or an infection. Careful listening may reveal breathing difficulties or changes in voice quality. Problems with peer relationships, eating habits, self-esteem, or abuse in the child's home may be detected during a conversation. Utilizing one's senses to the fullest—seeing children as they really are, hearing what they really have to say, and responding to their needs—is a skill that requires time, patience, and practice to perfect.

Conclusions drawn from teacher observations, as with any form of evaluation, should be made with caution. It must always be remembered that a wide range of normal behavior and skill attainment exists at each developmental stage. Norms merely represent the average age at which most children are able to perform a given skill. For example, many 3-year-olds can reproduce the shape of a circle, name and match primary colors, and walk across a balance beam. However, there will also be some 3-year-olds who will not be able to perform these tasks. This does not imply that they are not "normal." Some children simply take longer than others to master a particular skill. Developmental norms are useful for identifying children who may be experiencing health problems, as well as those who may simply require additional time and support in acquiring these skills. However, an abrupt change or prolonged delay in a child's developmental progress should be noted and prompt further evaluation.

Did You Get It?

The first step a teacher should take when using observation to monitor a child's health and development is to:

   a. note any and all changes
   b. note changes that have the potential to affect learning
   c. identify attainable goals
   d. establish a baseline for each child

Take the full quiz on CourseMate.

2-3 Daily Health Checks

Valuable information about health status and readiness to learn can be obtained by assessing children daily. Health checks require only a minute or two to complete and they enable teachers to detect the early signs and symptoms of common illnesses and health impairments. Daily health checks also help teachers to become familiar with each child's usual appearance and behavior so that changes are easily recognized. This is especially important in classrooms where children who have chronic conditions or other special health needs are present because their disorders can make them more susceptible to infectious illnesses (Forrest et al., 2011; Grier & Bradley-Klug, 2011). Teachers can minimize children's exposure by conducting daily health checks and identifying and removing any child who appears ill.

Parents should be encouraged to remain with their child until the health check has been completed. Children often find comfort in having a family member nearby. Families are also able to provide information about conditions or behaviors the teacher may observe. In addition, parents may feel less apprehensive if they have an opportunity to witness health checks firsthand and to ask their own questions. However, if a parent is unavailable, it may be advisable to have a second teacher witness the procedure to avoid any potential allegations of misconduct.

2-3a Method

A quiet area set aside in the classroom is ideal for performing health checks. A teacher may choose simply to sit on the floor with the children or provide a more structured setting with a table and chairs. Conducting health checks in the same designated area each day also helps children become familiar with the routine.

Performing health checks in a systematic manner improves the teacher's efficiency and ensures that the process will be consistent and thorough each time. Teacher Checklist 2-1 illustrates a simple observation tool that can be used for this purpose. It is organized so that observations are conducted from head to foot, first looking at the child's front and then back. However, this procedure can easily be modified to meet a program's unique needs in terms of the setting and children being served. For example, teachers who work with school-age children may prefer to use the information while simply observing children rather than for conducting a hands-on health check.

A teacher should begin daily health checks by observing children as they first enter the classroom. Clues about a child's well-being, such as personal cleanliness, weight change, signs of illness, facial expressions, posture, skin color, balance, and coordination can be noted at this time. The nature of parent-child interactions and their relationship with one another can also be observed and may help to explain why some children exhibit certain behaviors.

© 2015 Cengage Learning

▶❚❚ **TeachSource** Video Connections

Infants and Toddlers: Daily Health Checks

Children's ability to learn is affected by their state of well-being. Because young children are highly susceptible and prone to infectious illnesses, it is important that teachers conduct daily health checks. As you watch the learning video, *Infants and Toddlers: Daily Health Checks*, consider the following questions:

1. Why should health checks be conducted daily?
2. Why is it important that teachers spend time interacting with parents as part of their daily health checks?
3. What are the best times of the day to perform a daily health check on an infant or toddler?
4. What conditions should the teacher note during the health check?

Watch on CourseMate.

For example, does the parent have a tendency to do everything for the child—take off boots, hang up clothing, pick up items the child has dropped—or is the child encouraged to be independent? Is the child allowed to answer questions or does the parent always respond?

A flashlight is used to inspect the inside of the child's mouth and throat for unusual redness, swollen or infected tonsils, dental cavities, sores, or breath odors. The child's hair and face, including the eyes, ears, and nose, should also be closely observed for clues about general hygiene and signs of communicable illness.

Next, the child's clothing can be lifted and any rashes, unusual scratches, bumps or bruises, and skin color on the chest, abdomen, and arms noted. These areas should be carefully inspected as many rashes associated with communicable disease often first appear on the warmer areas of the body. Blue-gray discolorations, called **Mongolian spots**, may be visible on the lower back of children who are of Asian, Native American, and Middle Eastern ethnicities. These spots appear similar to bruises, but do not undergo the color changes typical of an injury. They also tend to gradually fade as children approach 8 or 9 years of age.

Finally, the child is asked to turn around so the head, hair, and back areas can be inspected. Teachers should continue to observe the child following the health check. For example, balance,

Mongolian spots – *patches of blue-gray skin located on the lower back; more common among children of Asian, Native American, and Middle Eastern ethnicities.*

TEACHER CHECKLIST 2-1

Health Observation Checklist

General appearance—note changes in weight (gain or loss), signs of fatigue or unusual excitability, skin tone (pallor or flushed), and size for age group.

Scalp—observe for signs of itching, head lice, sores, hair loss, and cleanliness.

Face—notice general expression (e.g., fear, anger, happiness, anxiety), skin tone, or any scratches, bruises, or rashes.

Eyes—look for redness, tearing, puffiness, sensitivity to light, frequent rubbing, sties, sores, drainage, or uncoordinated eye movements.

Ears—check for drainage, redness, and appropriate responses to sounds or verbal requests.

Nose—note any deformity, frequent rubbing, congestion, sneezing, or drainage.

Mouth—look inside and at the teeth; note cavities (brown or black spots), sores, red or swollen gums, mouth-breathing, or unusual breath odor.

Throat—observe for enlarged or red tonsils, red throat, drainage, or white patches on throat or tonsils.

Neck—feel for enlarged glands.

Chest—listen to the child's breathing and note any wheezing, rattles, shortness of breath, or coughing (with or without other symptoms).

Skin—observe the chest and back areas for color (pallor or redness), rashes, scratches, bumps, bruises, scars, or unusual warmth and perspiration.

Speech—listen for clarity, stuttering, nasality, mispronunciations, monotone voice, and appropriateness for age.

Extremities—observe posture, coordination; note conditions such as bowed legs, toeing-in, arms and legs of unequal length, or unusual gait.

Behavior and temperament—note any changes in activity level, alertness, cooperation, appetite, sleep patterns, toileting habits, irritability, or uncharacteristic restlessness.

TeachSource Digital Download   Download from CourseMate.

coordination, and posture can easily be noted as an infant crawls away or an older child walks over to join his or her friends. A child's aggressive tendencies or inability to play cooperatively with other children during outdoor play may provide important clues about social-emotional development and mental health. (See Teacher Checklist 2-2.)

TEACHER CHECKLIST 2-2

Warning Signs of Potential Mental Health Problems

Occasional responses to stress and change are to be expected. However, children who experience excessive or frequent episodes of the following behaviors may need to be referred for professional evaluation and treatment:

- *tearfulness or sadness*—cries easily; seldom appears happy
- *preference for being alone*—is withdrawn; reluctant to play with others
- *hostility or excessive anger*—overreacts to situations; has frequent tantrums
- *difficulty concentrating*—has trouble staying focused, remembering, or making decisions
- *aggressiveness*—initiates fights, hurts animals or others, destroys property
- *irritability*—seems anxious, restless, or overly worried; is continuously fidgeting
- *unexplained change in eating and/or sleeping habits*—refuses to eat or eats compulsively; has persistent nightmares and/or difficulty sleeping
- *excessive fear*—exhibits fear that is excessive or unwarranted
- *feelings of worthlessness*—is often self-critical; has undue fear of failure; is unwilling to try new things
- *refusal to go to school*—fails repeatedly to complete work; performs poorly in school
- *complains of physical ailments*—experiences frequent stomachaches, headaches, joint aches, or fatigue without any reasonable cause
- *engages in substance abuse (for older children)*—uses drugs and/or alcohol
- *talks about suicide*—is overly curious about death and suicide

TeachSource Digital Download   Download from CourseMate.

Teachers become skilled in conducting daily health checks and making insightful observations with practice. They are able to recognize the early signs and **symptoms** of various communicable illnesses and health conditions and know when it is necessary to refer a child for further evaluation.

2-3b Recording Observation Results

Information obtained during daily health checks should be recorded immediately following the procedure to ensure its accuracy. Checklists are ideal to use for this purpose because they enable teachers to conduct and record information systematically. Attendance records or a similar form developed for this purpose can also be used to record **anecdotal** information. These records should be placed in each child's permanent health file (electronic or hard copy) or a designated notebook. Any changes noted in a child's condition throughout the day, such as a seizure, uncontrollable coughing, or diarrhea, should also be documented on this form and reported to the family.

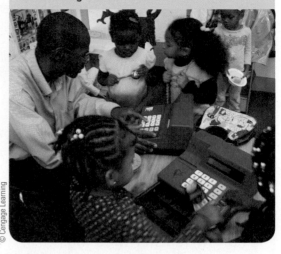

▼ **Valuable clues about children's health can be noted during teacher observations.**

© Cengage Learning

Observational information is only meaningful and useful to other teachers, administrators, and health care providers when it is recorded in clear, accurate, and precise terms. To say that a child "looks sick" is vague and open to individual interpretation. However, stating that a child is flushed, has a fever of 101°F (38.3°C), and is covered with a fine red rash on his torso is definitive and provides a functional description that can be shared with the child's family and physician (Weist et al., 2012).

2-3c Confidentiality of Health Information

Information obtained from daily health checks and teacher observations must be treated with utmost confidentiality. It should not be shared or made accessible to other families, staff, or service personnel. Additionally, this information must never be released to another individual or organization without first obtaining written permission

Did You Know...

that each year U.S. schools provide services for approximately 5.8 million children, 6 to 21 years, who have special health and disability needs?

▼ **Information in children's health records is confidential and should be shared only with certain school personnel.**

© Cengage Learning

Did You Know...

that the Family Education Rights and Privacy Act (Buckley Amendment) prohibits schools from releasing any information about a child under 18 years without written parental permission?

symptoms – *changes in the body or its functions that are experienced by the affected individual.*
anecdotal – *brief notes describing a person's observations.*

TeachSource Video Connections

© 2015 Cengage Learning

Communicating with Parents about Health in Early Childhood: A Parent-Teacher Meeting

Children ultimately benefit when schools establish meaningful partnerships with their families. Parents also gain from their involvement in children's educational programs. They may become more confident, have an improved understanding of what teachers are trying to accomplish, and develop a greater interest in children's learning. As you watch the learning video, *Communicating with Parents about Health in Early Childhood: A Parent-Teacher Meeting*, consider the following questions:

1. Why do you think it is important to schedule a parent-teacher meeting before a child begins to attend classes?

2. What did the teacher do to put the parent at ease and begin to establish a trusting partnership?

3. What communication skills (e.g., body language, checking for understanding, listening) did the teacher demonstrate during the meeting?

4. Was the teacher successful in communicating the program's health information to the parent? What suggestions would you offer to this teacher for improvement?

Watch on CourseMate.

from the child's parent or legal guardian (Johnson & Guthrie, 2012). Anecdotal records and health checklists should be kept in a notebook or folder to protect children's identity until the information can be transferred to their personal files. However, federal law guarantees families the right to access information in their child's health file at any time and to request the correction of any perceived errors (U.S. Department of Education, 2011).

2-3d Benefits of Health Observations

On-going monitoring of children's health status offers several distinct advantages. Teachers are able to fulfill their professional and moral obligations to protect the health of all children in a group setting. For example, a teacher may note changes in a child's appearance or behavior that signal the onset of a communicable illness. This information can then be used to determine if a child is too ill to remain in the classroom based on the program's exclusion policies. Sending a sick child home reduces the risk of exposing other children to an illness and often hastens the recuperation time.

Information gathered during daily observations is also useful to health care providers for diagnosing and treating a child's condition. Teachers are able to provide unique information that explains how a health problem, such as a hearing loss or allergies, is affecting the child's behavior and ability to perform in school. Their insights can hasten the diagnostic process and, thus, limit the negative effects an undetermined condition may otherwise have on a child's development.

> ⚠ **CAUTION**
>
> *Responsibility for interpreting signs and symptoms of an illness or health condition and establishing a final* **diagnosis** *always belongs to trained health care professionals.*

Daily health checks offer several additional benefits. They provide an opportunity for teachers to give children individualized attention and talk with them about a variety of health-related topics, such as why it is important to brush teeth, drink water, wash hands, or play outdoors. These one-on-one occasions convey a powerful message of caring and can empower children to begin developing a personal interest in their own well-being.

Patterns of illness or significant changes in a child's behavior may also be noted when daily health check information is examined. For example, knowing that several children have been exposed to chicken pox or that an outbreak of head lice has occurred in another classroom should alert teachers to be even more vigilant in the coming weeks.

diagnosis – *the process of identifying a disease, illness, or injury from its symptoms.*

Did You Get It?

Daily health checks are:

a. time consuming and tedious—weekly or biweekly health checks are far more practical

b. time consuming but necessary

c. brief and a source of invaluable information

d. best left to an attending school nurse

Take the full quiz on CourseMate.

2-4 Family Involvement

Health checks provide an ideal opportunity for involving families in children's health promotion. Teachers can create an atmosphere where families feel comfortable voicing concerns, asking questions, or seeking information about their child's health needs, behavior, or adjustment to school (Griffin, 2011). It is unrealistic to think that teachers will always be able to answer parents' question. However, they can begin to build a culturally responsive and trusting relationship with families by showing interest, encouraging their questions, and offering assistance in locating information and services (Edwards & Da Fonte, 2012; Grant & Ray, 2009).

▼ **Family-school collaboration is essential for addressing children's health care needs.**

© Cengage Learning

Teachers can also foster family involvement by sharing information about outbreaks of communicable illness, signs and symptoms to watch for, and effective preventive measures such as hand washing and good nutrition that can be taken. Parents may also be able to provide simple explanations for problems the teacher observes. For example, a child's fatigue or aggressiveness may be the result of a new puppy, a grandmother's visit, a new baby in the home, or a seizure the night before. Allergies or a red vitamin taken at breakfast may explain a questionable red throat. Without this direct sharing of information, such symptoms might otherwise be cause for concern.

2-4a The Family's Responsibility

Primary responsibility for a child's health care *always* belongs to the family. They are ultimately responsible for maintaining their child's well-being, following through with recommendations, and obtaining any necessary evaluations and medical treatments.

Often families are the first to sense that something is wrong with their child (Marotz & Allen, 2013). However, they may delay seeking professional advice, either denying that a problem exists or hoping the child will eventually outgrow it. Cultural differences in developmental expectations and the way children are raised may also explain why some families fail to take action. For example, a toddler's delayed walking may not be cause for concern in cultures where early walking is not encouraged. Parents may not understand that health problems can have negative consequences on children's development and learning potential or they may not know where to go for appropriate diagnosis and treatment. Some families fail to see the need for routine health care when a child appears to be healthy. Others simply cannot afford preventive care. However, cost must not discourage families from obtaining needed medical attention. In the United States, every state currently makes low-cost health insurance available to income-eligible children through the national Children's Health Insurance Program (CHIP). In addition, most communities offer a variety of free or low-cost health services for children through:

- Head Start
- Child Find screening programs
- Medicaid assistance
- Well-child clinics
- University-affiliated training centers and clinics
- Public health immunization centers
- Community centers
- Interagency coordinating councils

These agencies can generally be located in the telephone directory, on the Internet, or by contacting the local public health department. Teachers should also become familiar with community resources and assist families in securing appropriate health care services for children in need (Allen & Cowdery, 2012).

Did You Get It?

Although a variety of people and organizations are often involved in supporting children's well-being, the primary responsibility for a child's health and health care _____ lies with his or her family.

a. sometimes
b. always
c. ideally
d. most often

Take the full quiz on CourseMate.

2-5 Health Education

Daily health checks provide many informal opportunities for teaching children about health, safety, and nutrition. Teachers can encourage children's awareness and provide information about a range of healthy lifestyle practices, including oral hygiene, nutrition, physical activity, mental health, and sleep. For example:

- "Sandy, did you brush your teeth this morning? Brushing helps to keep teeth healthy and chases away the mean germs that cause cavities."
- "Mario, have you had a drink of water yet today? Bodies need water to grow and to stay healthy just like the plants in our classroom."
- "Harrison, what should you do if a stranger asks you to come with him or her?"

School-age children can be engaged in discussions that are more advanced. For example:

- "Yolanda, how many different fruits and vegetables have you eaten today? What vitamins and minerals does our body get from fruits and vegetables?"
- "Raja, did you put on sunscreen before playing outdoors? Why is this important? What else can we do to protect ourselves from the sun's harmful rays?"
- "Keiko, if someone teases or says hurtful things to you, who should you tell?"

When health education is linked to everyday situations, children are better able to comprehend its importance and application to their personal lives. They are also more likely to follow through and to implement what they have learned.

Including families in children's health education is also essential and improves the consistency of information and practices between school and the child's home. Teachers can utilize time during daily health checks to interact with families and to raise their awareness about a variety of children's health issues:

- new safety alerts and equipment recalls
- the importance of eating breakfast
- nutritious snack ideas
- ideas for increasing children's physical activity
- hand washing
- sun protection
- oral hygiene
- new vaccines
- home fire drills

Families are also more likely to support a school's health education goals when genuine efforts are made to reach out and to engage them in children's learning experiences.

Did You Get It?

Learning becomes more meaningful for children when it:
- **a.** is presented in the context of everyday experiences.
- **b.** addresses novel information.
- **c.** is provided during formal lessons.
- **d.** challenges children's curiosity.

Take the full quiz on CourseMate.

PARTNERING with FAMILIES

Children's Oral Health

Dear Families,

Oral health and a bright smile are important components of children's well-being. Teeth are essential for chewing, speech, maintaining proper space for permanent teeth, and appearance. Decay and infection can cause discomfort and make it difficult for children to focus on school. Unfortunately, tooth decay continues to affect many young children today despite increased public education and improved dental treatments. Practices that you can implement at home to promote children's oral health include:

- Keep an infant's gums clean by wiping them with a damp washcloth after each feeding.
- Dampen a soft toothbrush and use it twice daily to clean an infant's first teeth.
- Don't put infants to bed with a bottle containing juice, formula, or breast milk. These solutions can pool around gums and teeth and lead to early decay. Offer water if your infant takes a bottle to bed. Also, stop breastfeeding once he or she falls asleep.
- Apply a pea-sized dab of toothpaste to a soft brush and encourage toddlers to begin brushing their own teeth. Follow up their efforts by "going once around the block."
- Use fluoride toothpaste and drink fluoridated water (provided in most city water supplies) to reduce dental decay. Your child's dentist may prescribe fluoride drops or tablets if local water does not contain adequate fluoride.
- Continue to supervise preschool children's twice-daily tooth brushing. Discourage children from swallowing fluoride toothpaste because it can cause white or brown spots to form on permanent teeth.
- Monitor school-age children to make sure they brush and floss daily.
- Schedule your child's first routine dental check between 1 and 2 years of age. Older children should visit the dentist every six months. If you can't afford dental care, contact

(continued)

PARTNERING with FAMILIES

Children's Oral Health   *(continued)*

local public health personnel for information about free or low-cost options in your community. Reduced-cost dental insurance is also available to eligible families in some states.

▶ Serve nutritious meals and snacks. Include fresh fruits and vegetables, dairy products, whole-grain breads, crackers and cereals, and limit sugary foods and drinks.

▶ Offer children water when they are thirsty. Limit their consumption of carbonated beverages, fruit drinks, and sport drinks, which tend to be high in sugars.

CLASSROOM CORNER

Teacher Activities

Hear with My Ears . . .

(**NHES** PreK–2; National Health Education Standard 1.2.1)

Concept: You use your ears to hear sounds.

Learning Objectives

▶ Children will learn that ears are used for hearing sounds.

▶ Children will learn that there are many sounds all around.

Supplies

▶ various musical instruments (need two of each); a divider or a barrier

Learning Activities

▶ Read and discuss one of the following books:
  • *You Hear with Your Ears* by Melvin and Gilda Berger
  • *The Ear Book* by Al Perkins
  • *Hearing* (*The Five Senses*) by Maria Ruis, J. M. Parramon, & J. J. Puig
  • *The Listening Walk* by Paul Showers

▶ Explain to the children that their ears are for hearing sounds. Ask them some of the sounds that they hear each day.

▶ Place the musical instruments where the children can see them and play each one so they can become familiar with the sound each instrument makes.

▶ Next, place one of each instrument in front of the barrier/divider and one of each behind the barrier/divider.

▶ Call up one child to go behind the divider and pick an instrument to play. While that child is playing the instrument, call on another child to come up and pick the instrument that makes the matching sound to the instrument the child is playing behind the barrier.

▶ Continue until each child has had a turn, and then have the children play all the instruments at once.

▶ Talk about why it is important to take good care of our ears so we can hear.

Evaluation

▶ Children can name which body part is used for hearing.

▶ Children will name several different sounds in their environment.

▶ Children can match sounds.

Additional lesson plans for grades 3–5 are available on CourseMate.

Summary

◗ High-quality programs and schools understand that good health is essential to children's growth, development, and ability to learn.

- They promote wellness by monitoring and assessing children's health, making referrals, maintaining safe learning environments, providing health education, involving families, and serving nutritious food.

◗ Teachers' observations and health checks are an essential component of a school's health promotion efforts.

- They yield information that is useful for identifying changes in children's health status (physical, mental, social-emotional) and developmental problems.

◗ Daily health checks provide an efficient, effective, and cost-free method for monitoring children's health and development.

- Checklists can be used to ensure that observations are thorough and findings are recorded in meaningful terms.
- Information obtained from these sources must be treated with confidentiality and recorded immediately to retain its accuracy.

◗ Family involvement is essential for promoting children's wellness. Children benefit when there is mutual sharing of information between teachers and families. Teachers can make recommendations, but families are ultimately responsible for obtaining health care for children.

◗ Daily health checks provide teachers with valuable opportunities for educating children and their families about a variety of health-related topics.

Terms to Know

impairment *p. 39*
health assessment *p. 41*
atypical *p. 41*

observation *p. 41*
Mongolian spots *p. 43*
symptoms *p. 45*

anecdotal *p. 45*
diagnosis *p. 46*

Chapter Review

A. **By Yourself:**

1. Define each of the *Terms to Know* listed at the end of this chapter.

2. Explain how health status affects a child's ability to learn.

3. List the reasons why teachers should conduct daily health checks.

4. Describe how an elementary teacher might modify the health check procedure to use with school-age children.

5. Examine and describe your feelings about conducting daily health checks in a reflective journal entry. Do you think all beginning teachers have similar feelings? Outline several steps you might take to improve your observational skills and gain confidence in identifying children's health problems.

B. **As a Group:**

1. Describe the resources available to teachers for gathering information about a child's health.

2. Describe the health check routine. What common health problems/conditions should teachers look for?

3. Discuss how you might respond to a parent who objects to the daily health checks conducted by her child's teacher.

4. What benefits do daily health checks provide for children?

5. What suggestions would you have for a preschool teacher who says he is too busy to conduct daily health checks?

6. What are some things teachers can do to get families more involved in their child's preventive health care?

Case Study

Chris, the head teacher in the Sunflower classroom, has recently had some concerns about Lynette's vision. He has noticed that during group story time, Lynette quickly loses interest, often leaves her place in the circle, and crawls closer to him in an apparent effort to see the pictures in books he is holding up. Chris has also observed that when Lynette is working on puzzles, manipulatives, or an art project, she typically lowers her head close to the objects. Lynette's parents have also expressed concern about her clumsiness at home.

The results of two vision screening tests, administered by the school nurse on different days, suggest that Lynette's vision is not within normal limits. The nurse shared these findings during a conference with Lynette's parents, and encouraged them to arrange for a follow-up evaluation with an eye specialist. However, because Lynette's father was recently laid off from his job, they no longer have health insurance and cannot afford a doctor's visit at this time. The nurse continued to work closely with the family and helped them locate two reduced-fee health clinics in their community that provided the type of services Lynette required.

1. What behaviors did Lynette exhibit that made her teacher suspect some type of vision disorder?

2. Identify the sources from which information concerning Lynette's vision problem was obtained before she was referred to an eye specialist.

3. If the teacher suspected a vision problem, why didn't he just go ahead and recommend that Lynette get glasses?

4. What responsibilities do teachers have when they believe a child has a health impairment?

5. If you were the nurse advising Lynette's parents, what free or low-cost health service options could you recommend in your community?

Application Activities

1. Develop a health observation checklist. With another student, role-play the daily health check procedure. Use the checklist to record your findings, and discuss your reactions to the experience. What suggestions would you have for the "teacher" who conducted the observation?

2. Invite a public health nurse from a well-child clinic or a local pediatrician to speak to the class about preventive health care recommendations for children birth to 12 years.

3. Visit several early childhood programs in your community. Note whether health checks are conducted as children arrive. Describe the method you observed at each center. Also, briefly discuss how this information was recorded.

4. Develop a list of available resources in your state and local community for children who have vision or hearing impairments, speech problems, cerebral palsy, autism, and learning disabilities. Be

creative in your search; consider child care options, schools, special equipment needs, availability of special therapists, transportation requirements, family financial assistance, and so on.

5. Modify the "Classroom Corner" feature activity in this chapter so a child who is severely hearing impaired could participate.

Helpful Web Resources

Canadian Paediatric Society	http://www.caringforkids.cps.ca
Child Development Institute	http://childdevelopmentinfo.com
Early Head Start National Resource Center	http://www.ehsnrc.org
U.S. Department of Health & Human Services: Administration for Children & Families	http://www.acf.hhs.gov
Tufts University: Children and Family Web Guide	http://www.cfw.tufts.edu
National Center for Infants, Toddlers, and Families: Zero to Three	http://www.zerotothree.org

Visit the Education CourseMate for this textbook to access the eBook, Did You Get It? quizzes, Digital Downloads, TeachSource Video Cases, flashcards, and more. Go to CengageBrain.com to log in, register, or purchase access.

References

Allen, K. E., & Cowdery, G. (2012). *The exceptional child: Inclusion in early childhood education* (7th ed.). Belmont, CA: Wadsworth Cengage Learning.

Edwards, C., & Da Fonte, A. (2012). The 5-point plan: Fostering successful partnerships with families of students with disabilities, *Teaching Exceptional Children*, 44(3), 6–13.

Forrest, C., Bevans, K., Riley, A., Crespo, R., & Louis, T. (2011). School outcomes of children with special health care needs, *Pediatrics*, 128(2), 303–312.

Grant, K., & Ray, J. (2009). *Home, school, and community collaboration: Culturally responsive family involvement.* Thousand Oaks, CA: Sage Publications.

Grier, B., & Bradley-Klug, K. (2011). Collaborative consultation to support children with pediatric health issues: A review of the biopsychoeducational model, *Journal of Educational & Psychological Consultation*, 21(2), 88–105.

Griffin, D. (2011). Parent involvement with African American families in expanded school mental health practice, *Advances in School Mental Health Promotion*, 4(2), 16–26.

Johnson, K., & Guthrie, S. (2012). Harnessing the power of student health data, *NASN School Nurse*, 27(1), 26–33.

Marotz, L. R., & Allen, K. E. (2013). *Developmental profiles: Pre-birth through adolescence.* (7th ed.). Belmont, CA: Wadsworth Cengage Learning.

U.S. Department of Education. (2011). Family Educational Rights and Privacy Act (FERPA). *Federal Register*, 76(232). Accessed on March 30, 2012 from http://www.gpo.gov/fdsys/pkg/FR-2011-12-02/pdf/2011-30683.pdf.

U.S. Department of Health & Human Services (HHS). (2012). *Healthy People 2020.* Accessed April 2, 2012 from http://www.healthypeople.gov.

Weist, M., Mellin, E., Chambers, K., Lever, N., Haber, D., & Blaber, C. (2012). Challenges to collaboration in school mental health and strategies for overcoming them, *Journal of School Health*, 82(2), 97–105.

Assessing Children's Health

▸ **#1 a and b:** Promoting child development and learning
▸ **#2 a, b, and c:** Building family and community relationships
▸ **#3 a, b, c, and d:** Observing, documenting, and assessing to support young children and families
▸ **#4 a, b, and c:** Using developmentally effective approaches to connect with children and families
▸ **#5 b:** Using content knowledge to build meaningful curriculum
▸ **#6 b:** Becoming a professional
▸ Field Experience

Learning Objectives

After studying this chapter, you should be able to:

LO 3-1 Discuss how teachers can use information in health records to promote children's development and well-being.

LO 3-2 Describe five screening procedures and the common disorders they can be used to detect.

LO 3-3 Explain why it is important to follow up with families after making an initial referral.

Teachers understand that health problems can interfere with a child's ability to learn and that early detection improves the success of many interventions. They have access to screening tools for identifying children who may require further evaluation. When information is collected in an objective manner and from a combination of observations and screening procedures, it yields (1) reliable data for health promotion, (2) clues that aid in the early detection of conditions affecting children's growth and development, and (3) an opportunity to modify learning environments to meet a child's unique needs.

3-1 Health Records

Careful recordkeeping is not always a priority in many early childhood programs. However, when information in children's files is current and sufficiently detailed, it can be used to promote developmental progress and well-being (Table 3–1). The types of records schools are required to maintain are usually mandated by state departments of education. Child care licensing divisions in each state issue similar requirements for licensed centers and home-based programs. However, because these regulations typically reflect only minimal standards, programs may want to consider keeping additional types of documentation. Unlicensed programs are not obligated to maintain any records.

Forms and records should be designed to gather information that is consistent with a program's goals and philosophy and protects the legal rights of the children and staff. This information serves many purposes, including:

▸ determining children's health status
▸ identifying patterns and potential problem areas

TABLE 3–1   Children's Health Records

Children's permanent health records should include:
- child/family health history
- copy of a recent medical assessment (physical examination)
- immunization records
- emergency contact information
- record of dental examinations
- attendance data
- school-related injuries
- documentation of family conferences concerning the child's health
- screening results, e.g., vision, hearing, speech, developmental
- medications administered while the child is at school

- developing **intervention** programs
- evaluating the outcome of special services, e.g., speech therapy, occupational therapy
- coordinating services
- making referrals
- monitoring a child's progress
- research

Health records contain confidential information about children and their families. This information should be shared only with personnel who must know something specific about a child in order to work effectively with him or her. Personal details about a child or family must never serve as topics of conversation outside of the classroom. No portion of a child's health record should ever be released to another agency, school, health professional, or clinician until written permission has been obtained from the child's parent or legal guardian. A special release form, such as the one shown in Figure 3–1, can be used for this purpose. The form should clearly indicate the nature of information to be released and the agency or person to whom it is to be transferred. It must also be dated and signed by the parent or legal guardian, and a copy retained in the child's folder.

Recordkeeping is most efficient when one person is responsible for maintaining all health-related records. However, input from all members of the teaching team is important for determining how health problems may be affecting a child and for tracking children's progress. Health records are considered legal documents and should be retained for at least 5 years.

3-1a   Child Health Histories

The nature of information requested on health history forms varies from program to program. Unless a standardized form is required by a licensing agency or school district, programs may wish to develop their own. Sample forms can often be obtained from other programs or state agencies and modified to meet a program's specific needs. Health history questionnaires should be designed to gather basic information about:

- circumstances related to the child's birth
- family structure, such as siblings and their ages, family members, predominant language spoken, and legal custody issues
- major developmental milestones
- previous injuries, illnesses, surgeries, or hospitalizations
- daily habits, such as toileting, eating habits, and napping
- family concerns about the child, such as behavior problems, social development, and speech delays
- any special health conditions, such as allergies, asthma, seizures, diabetes, vision or hearing disorders, and prescribed medications

intervention – *practices or procedures implemented to modify or change a specific behavior or condition.*

FIGURE 3–1   **Sample information release form.**

INFORMATION RELEASE FORM

I understand the confidentiality of any personally identifiable information concerning my child shall be maintained in accordance with the Family Education Rights and Privacy Act (P.L.93–380), federal and state regulations, and used only for the educational benefit of my child. Personally identifiable information about my child will be released only with my written consent. With this information, I hereby grant the

_____
(Name of program, agency, or person)

permission to release the following types of information:

Medical information   _____
Assessment reports   _____
Child histories   _____
Progress reports   _____
Clinical reports   _____
(Other)   _____

to:_____
(Name of agency or person to whom information is to be sent)

regarding _____ _____ _____
    (Child's Name)   (Birthdate)   (Gender)

_____
Signature of Parent or Guardian

_____
Relationship of Representative

_____
Date

TeachSource Digital Download Download from CourseMate.

Families can complete a written health history form and provide a copy of the child's current immunization record at the time of enrollment. Alternatively, families may be asked to supply this information during a home visit or meeting with the program administrator. Information obtained from health history questionnaires enables teachers to better understand each child's uniqueness, including their family background, daily routines and preferences, health status, and developmental strengths and limitations. This information can be used to accommodate children's special needs, such as dietary restrictions, hearing loss, or mobility limitations and to establish developmentally appropriate learning goals. However, caution must be exercised not to base expectations for children on this information alone. A child's potential for learning must never be discounted until an impairment is confirmed and known to restrict performance. When goals are set too low, children may lack incentive and perform only to the level of adult expectations. In contrast, expectations that are unrealistic and beyond a child's capabilities may cause repeated failure and loss of motivation.

Child health histories also provide an indication of the medical supervision a child typically receives and the value a family places on preventive health care. This information can be especially beneficial for planning children's health education and making future referrals.

3-1b Medical and Dental Examinations

Most states require children to have a complete health assessment and current immunizations before they attend school or an early childhood program. Some states require an annual physical examination whereas others request it only at the time of admission. Health care providers recommend well-child checkups every 2 to 3 months for infants, every 6 months for 2- and 3-year-olds, and annually for children 4 and older. More frequent medical supervision may be necessary if children have existing health problems or new conditions develop.

Information about a child and his or her family is updated at each visit. Families may also be asked to complete a brief developmental questionnaire to better help medical personnel assess all aspects of the child's health. The child's immunization record is reviewed and additional doses are administered as indicated. The child's heart, lungs, eyes, ears, **skeletal** and **neurological** development, and gastrointestinal function (stomach and intestines) are also carefully examined. Head circumference is routinely measured on all infants and children until 3 years of age to be certain that head size continues to increase at an acceptable rate. Height, weight, and blood pressure readings (after age 3) are also recorded and compared to prior measurements to determine if a child's growth is progressing satisfactorily. Growth failure, especially in height, may be an indication of other health problems that need to be investigated. Specialized tests, such as blood tests for anemia, sickle cell disease, or lead poisoning, may be ordered to identify or rule out any of these conditions. Urinalysis, tuberculin testing, vision screening, and hearing evaluation may also be obtained.

Although dental examinations are seldom required for admission purposes, their benefits are unquestionable. Families should be encouraged to arrange routine dental checks and preventive care for children, including visual inspection of the teeth, cleaning, and fluoride applications, every 6 to 12 months.

Did You Get It?

The release of the health records for a child moving to a new school:

a. must be accompanied by a release form signed by the child's parent or legal guardian

b. can be processed after verbal permission has been obtained

c. can be done without consent if the child is moving to a school in the same state

d. can only be transferred with the consent of a court

Take the full quiz on CourseMate.

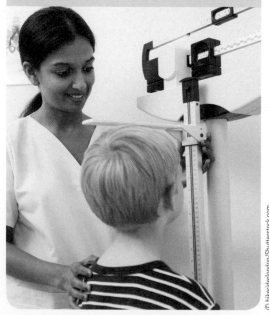

▼ **Height and weight measurements yield important information about children's health.**

© bikeriderlondon/Shutterstock.com

3-2 Screening Procedures

Screening tests are also an essential component of the comprehensive health assessment process. They support the preventive care philosophy through the early detection of health problems and impairments that could otherwise interfere with a child's ability to learn.

Most screening procedures are relatively quick, inexpensive, and efficient to administer to groups of young children. Some tests can be conducted by teachers whereas others require the services of professional clinicians. Screening tests are designed only to identify children who may have a condition that requires professional evaluation, *never* to diagnose or confirm a specific impairment. Test results simply provide additional information about a child that can be used in combination with family and teacher observations, assessments of growth and development, and daily health-check findings.

3-2a Height and Weight

The first 5 years of life are an important period of rapid growth. Increases in height and weight are most dramatic during infancy, and continue at a slower, but steady, rate throughout the preschool

---

skeletal – *pertaining to the bony framework that supports the body.*
neurological – *pertaining to the nervous system, which consists of the nerves, brain, and spinal column.*

and school-age years (Marotz & Allen, 2013). Height is the most reliable indicator of a child's general health and nutritional status. Because weight can fluctuate in response to recent illness, infection, emotional stress, or over- or undereating, it is not considered a dependable reflection of long-term health.

Teachers and families must understand that a child's growth potential is ultimately governed by genetics. This is especially important to remember when working with children from different cultures and ethnic backgrounds. The Centers for Disease Control and Prevention (CDC) has updated its standard growth charts to more accurately represent the diverse child population in the United States, although they still may not be appropriate for all ethnicities. The World Health Organization (WHO) has also published international Child Growth Standards for children birth to 19 years (www.who.int/childgrowth/en). Their charts include developmental milestones (Windows of Achievement) based on an extensive study of children birth to age 5 from around the world and may more accurately reflect the growth and developmental patterns typical of today's children.

Ideally, children's height and weight should be measured at 4- to 6-month intervals and recorded in their permanent health file. A single measurement is unlikely to identify the child who is experiencing a growth disturbance related to physical illness, dysfunctional parenting, or an eating disorder. Rather, what is most important is the pattern of change that occurs over time. Measurements recorded on standardized growth charts allow comparisons to be made with previous data and can be useful for determining if a child's growth is progressing satisfactorily. Growth charts are available from the Centers for Disease Control & Prevention (CDC) (http://www.cdc.gov/growthcharts).

3-2b Body Mass Index

The body mass index (BMI) is a relatively new screening tool that provides a height-for-weight ratio. It is appropriately used with children 2 years and older to determine their risk of being **underweight**, normal weight, **overweight**, or **obese**. Gender-specific charts for plotting children's BMI-for-age (2–20 years) can be accessed from the CDC (www.cdc.gov/healthyweight/assessing/BMI/index.html). Children who are underweight, overweight, or obese should be referred to a health care provider for further evaluation.

3-2c Vision

Most of what children learn during the early years is acquired through their senses, particularly vision and hearing (Basch, 2011). For this reason, it is important that these systems function properly to avoid disruptions in children's learning and development. Vision impairments affect approximately one in twenty preschoolers and one in four school-age children (Prevent Blindness America, 2010). Some conditions, such as cataracts or blindness, may be present at birth. Others can develop as the result of a head injury or infectious illness, such as meningitis. Vision problems are also more common in children who have other disabilities, such as cerebral palsy, Down syndrome, autism, or fetal alcohol syndrome (FAS) (Jackson, Krishnaswami, & McPheeters, 2011).

Early detection improves the success of medical treatments and a child's readiness for school (Morale et al., 2012). Permanent vision loss can often be avoided by examining an infant's eyes for abnormalities and muscle imbalance during routine well-child checkups. It is also recommended that all young children have a professional eye evaluation performed by an **ophthalmologist** or **optometrist** by age 2 years or

Did You Know...

that infants have extremely poor vision and are unable to see detail, such as facial features, until 3–4 months of age?

---

underweight – *a BMI of less than 18.5.*
overweight – *a BMI greater than 25.*
obese – *a BMI over 30.*
ophthalmologist – *a physician who specializes in diseases and abnormalities of the eye.*
optometrist – *a specialist (nonphysician) trained to examine eyes and prescribe glasses and eye exercises.*

▼ **Often it is the teacher who first notices signs of a child's vision problem.**

© Cengage Learning

at least before entering kindergarten. Undiagnosed vision problems may cause children to be inappropriately labeled as learning disabled or intellectually challenged when, in fact, they simply cannot see well enough to learn (Marotz & Allen, 2013). The following case study illustrates the point:

In many ways, Tina is a typical 4-year-old, although the teachers have been puzzled by some of her recent behaviors. Tina seems easily frustrated and unable to complete many of the pre-academic tasks that her peers enjoy, such as puzzles, tracing, threading beads, and simple object labeling. She trips over toys, runs into children, and is often reluctant to join her classmates in outdoor games. Tina's teachers are concerned that she may have a learning disability and have begun developmental testing. They also arranged with the school health consultant to have Tina's vision checked and were surprised to learn that it was only 20/100. Tina's mother was encouraged to make an appointment with an eye specialist and, after further testing, it was determined that Tina needed corrective glasses. The teachers are amazed by the changes that Tina's improved ability to see have made in her behavior, social interaction, and academic progress.

Assessment Methods Observing children carefully for specific behavioral indicators is an important first step in the early identification of vision problems (Teacher Checklist 3-1). For example, an infant's vision can be tested informally by holding an object, such as a rattle, 10 to 12 inches away and observing the infant's ability to focus on (fixation) and track (follow) the object as it is moved in a 180-degree arc around the child's head. The infant's eyes should also be observed for any uncoordinated movements as the object is brought closer to (convergence) and farther away from the face. In addition, the blink reflex (sweep hand quickly in front of the eyes; observe for blinking), and pupil response (shine a penlight, held 4 to 6 inches away, into the eye; pupil should become smaller) should also be checked. Infants exhibiting any abnormal responses should be referred for professional evaluation.

Teachers may be the first to notice clues in children's behavior that suggest a vision disorder. Young children are seldom aware or able to communicate to an adult that they are not seeing well, especially if their vision has never been normal. Some vision problems are also difficult to detect because they have no visible signs or symptoms. However, vision problems often become more

 TEACHER CHECKLIST 3-1

Early Signs of Visual Abnormalities in Infants and Toddlers

Observe the infant closely for:

- roving eye movements that are suggestive of blindness
- jerky or fluttering eye movements
- eyes that wander in opposite directions or are crossed (after age 3 months)
- inability to focus or follow a moving object (after age 3 months)
- pupil of one eye larger than the other
- absence of a blink reflex
- drooping of one or both lids
- cloudiness on the eyeball
- chronic tearing

TeachSource Digital Download Download from CourseMate.

TABLE 3-2 Examples of Acuity Tests for Preschool Children

- Denver Eye Screening Test (DEST)
- HOTV Symbols Visual Acuity Test
- Screening Test for Young Children and Retardates (STYCAR) (This test can be used with children who have developmental delays.)
- Snellen "Tumbling" E chart
- Allen Card Test
- Teller Acuity Cards
- Cover-Uncover Test
- Lea Symbols Visual Acuity Test
- Random Dot E Stereoacuity Test

apparent during the school years when children must complete academic work with greater detail and accuracy. Screening tests may confirm a teacher's observations and should be discussed with the child's family. It is also important to help families understand that children's vision problems are not outgrown, nor do they usually improve without treatment.

Teachers and volunteers can be trained by health professionals to administer many of the standardized visual acuity tests (Table 3–2). Printable versions of the Eye Tests for Children (HOTV charts for near and distance vision) can also be downloaded from the Prevent Blindness America website (www.preventblindness.org). Children's eyes should also be checked for:

- convergence
- depth perception (Titmus Fly test)
- binocular fusion (Worth 4-Dot test; Random Dot E)
- deviations in pupil position (Test by holding a penlight 12 inches from the child's face, direct light at the bridge of the nose; the light reflection should appear in the same position on both pupils; any discrepancy requires professional evaluation.)

Photoscreening is a relatively new screening tool that is increasingly being used with young children, especially those who are preverbal, nonverbal, or have developmental delays or disabilities that would make it difficult for them to complete conventional screening procedures (Longmuir et al., 2013). A special camera records a small beam of light as it reflects on the eyeball, and is an especially useful test for the early detection of amblyopia and strabismus. Although it is an efficient and effective screening technology, the equipment is relatively expensive and the test requires special training to administer.

It is important that children understand the instructions and expected response method before any screening test is administered or the results may be invalid. Children who fail an initial screening should be retested within 2 weeks. If a second screening is failed, testing results should be shared with the child's family and a referral made to a professional eye specialist for a comprehensive evaluation.

The early detection and treatment of vision impairments in children has been targeted as a major goal in the *Healthy People 2020* initiative. Efforts to increase public awareness and to reach children in medically underserved areas are aimed at combating unnecessary and irreversible vision loss. Information about the symptoms of common visual impairments, testing procedures, and treatments is available on many professional organization websites, including Prevent Blindness America (http://www.preventblindness.org), American Academy of Ophthalmology (http://www.aao.org), American Academy of Pediatrics (http://www.aap.org), and the American Association of Pediatric Ophthalmology and Strabismus (http://www.aapos.org).

▼ **Early detection and treatment of vision problems improves children's learning success.**

© Cengage Learning

TEACHER CHECKLIST 3-2

Signs of Visual Acuity Problems in Older Children

- rubs eyes frequently
- attempts to brush away blurs
- is irritable with close work
- is inattentive to distant tasks, e.g., watching a movie, catching a ball
- strains to see distant objects, squints, or screws up face
- blinks often when reading, holds books too close or far away
- is inattentive with close work, quits after a short time
- closes or covers one eye to see better
- tilts head to one side
- appears cross-eyed at times
- reverses letters, words
- stumbles over objects, runs into things
- complains of repeated headaches or double vision
- exhibits poor eye-hand coordination
- experiences repeated sties, redness, or watery eyes

TeachSource Digital Download | Download from CourseMate.

▶❚❚ **TeachSource Video Connections**

© 2015 Cengage Learning

0–2 Years: Sensation and Perception, Vision in Infants and Toddlers

Although infants see poorly at birth, their visual system matures rapidly in the months that follow. Improvements in the infant's ability to see are critical to learning and developments in other sensory systems. As you watch the learning video, *0–2 Years: Sensation and Perception, Vision in Infants and Toddlers*, consider the following questions:

1. Explain the term "tracking."
2. What does the infant's ability to track an object indicate?
3. What purpose does depth perception serve the infant?

Watch on CourseMate.

Common Disorders Vision screening programs are designed to detect three common disorders in young children, including:

- ▶ amblyopia
- ▶ strabismus
- ▶ myopia

Amblyopia, or "lazy eye," affects approximately 2 percent of all children younger than 10 years. Children born to mothers who smoke seem to be at higher risk for developing this and other vision disorders (Borchert et al., 2011). Amblyopia is caused by a muscle imbalance or childhood cataracts that result in blurred or double vision. The child's brain is confused by the distortion and begins to acknowledge only images received from the stronger eye while ignoring (suppressing) those from the weaker or "lazy" eye. Consequently, sight is gradually lost in the weaker eye as a result of disuse. This condition also causes a loss of depth perception, which requires comparable sight in both eyes.

Early identification and treatment of amblyopia is critical for preventing permanent vision loss. However, this condition is often overlooked and treatment delayed because there are no visible signs or abnormalities and children are seldom aware that anything is wrong with their vision. For these reasons, it is important that young children have periodic routine screenings and comprehensive eye examinations. A significant portion of the child's eyesight can often be restored if amblyopia is diagnosed before the age of 6 or 7. Even greater improvements

---

amblyopia – *a condition of the eye commonly referred to as "lazy eye"; vision gradually becomes blurred or distorted due to unequal balance of the eye muscles. There are no observable abnormalities of the eyes when a child has amblyopia.*

may be achieved when this condition is diagnosed and treated before the age of 2 years. However, research suggests that children as old as 12 may regain some lost sight with treatment (Gunton, 2013).

Several methods are used to treat amblyopia. One of the more common treatments involves patching the child's stronger (unaffected) eye for several hours each day until muscles in the weaker (affected) eye gradually become stronger. Other treatment methods include corrective glasses, eye drops, special eye exercises, and surgery. Teachers may be asked to administer treatments while children are in school. They must understand the importance of maintaining a child's treatment schedule and be supportive when children resist or are embarrassed by having to wear special glasses or a patch. Added safety precautions, such as clearing obstacles from pathways and guiding children through unfamiliar spaces, may need to be taken to avoid injury during treatments. Teachers can use these opportunities to help all children develop greater respect and acceptance of individuals who have special needs.

Strabismus, commonly referred to as crossed eyes, affects approximately 3 to 5 percent of young children (Optometrists Network, 2012). Strabismus causes an observable misalignment of the child's eyes (for example, both eyes may turn inward or one eye may turn inward or outward) that occurs intermittently or consistently. Because the eyes are not able to work together as one unit, children may experience symptoms similar to those of amblyopia, including double or blurred vision, images from the weaker eye being ignored by the brain, and gradual vision loss.

▼ **Strabismus interferes with children's ability to see properly.**

© Cengage Learning

Early recognition and treatment of strabismus is essential for restoring normal vision. Today, even infants are being treated aggressively for this condition. Although uncoordinated eye movements are common in very young infants, their eyes should begin moving together as a unit by 4 months of age. Treatments for strabismus include surgical correction, patching of the unaffected eye, and eye exercises.

Myopia, or nearsightedness, can affect young children, but is more common in school-aged children. A child who is nearsighted sees near objects clearly, but has poor distant vision. This condition is especially problematic for young children because they move about quickly and engage in play that involves running, jumping, and climbing. As a result, children who have myopia may appear clumsy, and repeatedly stumble or run into objects. Squinting is also common as children attempt to bring distant objects into focus. Teachers can be instrumental in noting these behaviors and referring children for comprehensive screening.

Farsightedness, or **hyperopia**, is thought to be a normal occurrence in children under the age of 5 due to a shortness of their eyeball (Tarczy-Hornoch, 2012). This condition often corrects itself as children mature and the eyeball enlarges and changes shape. Children who are farsighted see distant objects clearly but have difficulty focusing on near objects. Older children

strabismus – *a condition of the eyes in which one or both eyes appear to be turned inward (crossed) or outward (walleye).*
myopia – *nearsightedness; an individual has good near vision but poor distant vision.*
hyperopia – *farsightedness; a condition of the eyes in which an individual can see distant objects clearly but has poor close vision.*

may struggle academically, read poorly, have a short attention span, and complain of headaches, tired eyes, or blurred vision following periods of close work. Because hyperopia can be difficult to detect with most routinely administered screening procedures, teacher and parent observations may provide the best initial clues to this disorder. A child who exhibits signs of hyperopia should be referred to a professional eye specialist for evaluation.

Color blindness affects a small percentage of children and is generally limited to males. Females are carriers of this hereditary defect but are rarely affected. The most common form of color blindness involves the inability to discriminate between red and green. Testing young children for color blindness is difficult and often omitted because learning is not seriously affected and there is no corrective treatment.

Management When a vision problem is suspected, the child's family should be counseled and encouraged to arrange for professional evaluation. Teachers can assist families in locating services and reinforce the importance of following through with treatment recommendations. Vision testing can often be arranged through pediatricians' offices, "well-child" clinics, public health departments, professional eye doctors, and public schools. Local service organizations, such as the Lions Clubs, may assist qualified families with the costs of professional eye examinations and glasses.

Children who do not pass an initial vision screening should be retested. Failure to pass a second screening necessitates referral to a professional eye specialist for comprehensive evaluation and diagnosis. Results obtained from routine vision screening tests should be viewed with caution because they do not guarantee that a problem does or does not exist. Also, most routine screening procedures are not designed to detect all types of vision impairments. For these reasons, there will always be some over-referral of children who do not have a vision disorder, while other children may be missed. It is for this reason that teachers' and families' observations are extremely important. Children's visual acuity can also change over time, so it is important that adults be continuously vigilant of children's visual performance.

3-2d Hearing

Each year approximately 12,000 infants in the United States are born with a hearing loss (March of Dimes, 2011). Undetected hearing losses can have a profound effect on children's language acquisition, social interactions, emotional development, and learning abilities (Laws et al., 2012). When children do not hear properly, they may respond and behave in seemingly unacceptable ways. This can lead to incorrect labels such as slow learner, cognitively challenged, or behavior problem. The early diagnosis of hearing impairments or severe loss is, therefore, extremely critical.

Assessment Methods Inappropriate responses and behaviors may be the first indication that a child is not hearing properly. Signs of hearing loss can range from obvious problems to those that are subtle and difficult to identify (Teacher Checklist 3-3).

Hospitals in most states now comply with Universal Infant Hearing Screening recommendations (Deem, Diaz-Ordaz, & Shiner, 2012). Trained hospital personnel test infants' hearing shortly after birth to detect deafness so that early intervention services can be initiated. An interactive map listing state-by-state testing sites and services is available at the National Center for Hearing Assessment and Management (NCHAM) website (http://www.infanthearing.org/states/index.html).

An infant's hearing development should continue to be monitored by checking behavioral responses such as eye blinking or attempts to locate sounds (e.g., stop crying, turn head, interrupt sucking) (Teacher Checklist 3-4). Older infants and toddlers can be

Did You Know...

that over 5 million children and adolescents have permanent hearing loss caused by exposure to excessive noise levels?

TEACHER CHECKLIST 3-3

Behavioral Indicators of Children's Hearing Loss

Families and teachers may observe behaviors that suggest a possible hearing loss, such as:
- frequent mouth breathing
- failure to turn toward the direction of a sound
- delays in acquiring language; development of poor speech patterns
- difficulty understanding and following directions
- asking to have statements repeated
- rubbing or pulling at ears
- mumbling, shouting, or talking loudly
- reluctance to interact with others; quiet or withdrawn
- using gestures rather than words
- excelling in activities that do not depend on hearing
- imitating others at play
- responding to questions inappropriately
- mispronouncing many word sounds
- having an unusual voice quality—one that is extremely high, low, hoarse, or monotone
- failing to respond to normal sounds and voices

TeachSource Digital Download   Download from CourseMate.

assessed by observing as they search for sounds (often emitted through speakers in formal testing procedures), as well as by the appropriateness of their responses and language development. Although these procedures can be useful for identifying some children with hearing disorders, they are not effective for detecting all forms of hearing loss.

Children's hearing should be formally tested by a trained specialist, such as a nurse or **audiologist**, at least once during the preschool and school-age years and more often if a hearing problem is suspected. Hearing tests evaluate a child's ability to hear the normal range of tones used in everyday conversation.

Most children are able to complete routine hearing screenings with minimal instruction. However, an unfamiliar situation involving new people, instruments and equipment, a novel task, a lack of understanding, or failure to cooperate may occasionally interfere with a child's performance and yield unreliable test results. These factors must be taken into consideration if an initial screening is failed, and arrangements made to have the child retested at a later date to confirm or rule out the initial findings. Children who pass a hearing test yet continue to exhibit behaviors suggestive of a hearing loss should continue to be monitored.

TEACHER CHECKLIST 3-4

Early Signs of Hearing Loss in Infants and Toddlers

Observe the infant closely for:
- absence of a startle response to a loud noise
- failure to stop crying briefly when adult speaks to baby (3 months)
- failure to turn head in the direction of sound, such as a doorbell or a dog barking (4 months)
- absence of babbling or interest in imitating simple speech sounds (6–8 months)
- no response to adult commands, such as "no" or "come"

TeachSource Digital Download   Download from CourseMate.

audiologist – *a specially prepared clinician who uses nonmedical techniques to diagnose hearing impairments.*

▼ **Hearing screenings are conducted by an audiologist or specially trained personnel.**

© Brian Eichhorn/Shutterstock.com

Teachers and families should always prepare young children for hearing screenings so they know in advance what to expect. Play activities that require children to practice listening skills and wearing headphones (e.g., disk jockey, airplane pilot, musician) will help increase their comfort level with screening procedures. Teachers should also make an effort to determine what response method (such as raising one hand, pressing a button, pointing to pictures, or dropping a wooden block into an empty can) children will be expected to use during the screening and practice this activity in advance. If a special room is to be used for testing purposes, children should be given an opportunity to visit the facilities and equipment beforehand. This will help to reduce their anxiety and increase the reliability of test results.

Common Disorders Children who are born with any physical disability have an increased risk of also experiencing hearing problems (Marotz & Allen, 2013). Temporary and permanent hearing losses can affect one or both ears and are commonly associated with:

▶ a family history of hearing problems
▶ prenatal exposure to maternal infections, such as herpes, German measles, or cytomegalovirus
▶ prematurity, low birthweight
▶ bacterial meningitis, measles, mumps
▶ allergies
▶ frequent colds and ear infections (otitis media)
▶ birth defects, such as Down syndrome, fetal alcohol syndrome (FAS), cleft lip/cleft palate, cerebral palsy
▶ head injuries
▶ exposure to excessive or prolonged noise

Any parent who expresses concern about a child's hearing should always be acknowledged and encouraged to seek professional advice. The most common forms of childhood hearing loss are:

> **Did You Know...**
>
> that ears are important for maintaining balance and allow you to hear even when you are asleep?
>
> **?**

▶ **Conductive loss** affects the volume of word tones. For example, this child will be able to hear loud, but not soft, sounds. Conductive hearing loss occurs when sound waves are not transmitted properly from the external ear to structures in the middle ear (Figure 3–2). Foreign objects, excess wax, and fluid accumulation in the child's middle ear following an infection are common causes of conductive hearing loss.
▶ **Sensorineural loss** results when the structures of the inner ear (cochlea) or the auditory nerve (which connects to the brain) have been damaged or do not function properly. This type of hearing loss is permanent and affects a child's ability to understand speech and to hear sounds. Children who have a sensorineural loss are considered to have a learning disability that requires special educational management.
▶ **Mixed hearing loss** refers to a disorder that involves a combination of conductive and sensorineural hearing losses. Structures in both the outer or middle ear and the inner ear or auditory nerve have either been damaged or are no longer functional.

conductive loss – *affects the volume of word tones heard, so that loud sounds are more likely to be heard than soft sounds.*
sensorineural loss – *a type of loss that occurs when sound impulses cannot reach the brain due to damage of the auditory nerve, or cannot be interpreted because of prior brain damage.*
mixed hearing loss – *a disorder that involves a combination of conductive and sensorineural hearing losses.*

Management A child who experiences a sudden or gradual hearing loss should be referred to a health care provider for a medical diagnosis or to an audiologist for a comprehensive hearing evaluation. Families can arrange for this testing through the child's physician, a speech and hearing clinic, public health department, public school, or an audiologist.

Hearing loss can often be successfully treated if it is identified in the early stages. Treatment methods depend on the underlying cause and range from prescription ear drops and antibiotic therapy to surgery (Elloy & Marshall, 2012). Some children who experience permanent hearing loss benefit from hearing aids, whereas others may receive cochlear implants or eventually learn sign language.

Teachers who understand how various impairments affect children's ability to hear can take appropriate steps to improve communication and modify learning environments (Teacher Checklist 3-5). Additional information about hearing impairments, testing procedures, and resources for families can be accessed on the American Association of Speech-Language-Hearing Association website (http://www.asha.org).

FIGURE 3–2   Diagram of the ear.

Outer Ear   Middle Ear   Inner Ear

Auditory Nerve

Ear Canal

Cochlea

Ear Drum

3-2e Speech and Language

Throughout the early years, children make impressive gains in the number of words they understand (receptive vocabulary) and use to express themselves (expressive vocabulary) (Table 3–3). Children's receptive vocabulary develops earlier and is usually more extensive than their expressive vocabulary. For example, most toddlers understand and can follow simple directions long before they use words to verbalize their wants or needs. Children's language becomes increasingly fluent and complex with maturation and practice.

Although many factors influence children's **speech** and language development, the ability to hear is especially important during the early years when children are learning to imitate sounds,

TEACHER CHECKLIST 3-5

Strategies for Communicating with Children Who Are Hearing-Impaired

- Reduce background noises, such as musical tapes, radio, motors, or fans that can interfere with a child's limited ability to hear.
- Provide individualized versus group instructions.
- Face and stand near the child when speaking.
- Bend down to the child's level; this makes it easier for the child to hear and understand what is being said.
- Speak slowly and clearly.
- Use gestures or pictures to illustrate what is being said; for example, point to the door when it is time to go outside.
- Demonstrate what the child is expected to do; for example, pick up a bead and thread it on a shoestring.

TeachSource Digital Download   Download from CourseMate.

speech – *the process of using words to express one's thoughts and ideas.*

TABLE 3–3   Speech and Language Developmental Milestones

Infants	
birth–4 months	• turns to locate the source of sound • begins to coo and make babbling sounds: *baa, aah, ooh* • imitates own voice and sounds
4–8 months	• repeats syllables in a series: *ba, ba, ba* • "talks" to self • responds to simple commands: *no, come*
8–12 months	• recognizes labels for common objects: shoe, blanket, cup • "talks" in one word sentences to convey ideas or requests: *cookie* (meaning, "I want a cookie")

Toddlers	
12–24 months	• follows simple directions • knows and uses 10–30 words • points to pictures and body parts on request and asks frequently, "What's that?" "Why?" • enjoys being read to • understands 200–300 words • speaks in 2–3 word sentences • has speech that is 65–70 percent understandable
24–36 months	• refers to self as "me": "Me do it myself." • uses language to get desired attention or object • understands simple concepts when asked: "Find the small ball." • follows simple directions: "It's time to get dressed." • understands and uses 50–300 new words • has speech that is 70–80 percent understandable

Preschoolers	
3–6 years	• answers simple questions appropriately • describes objects, events, and experiences in fairly detailed terms • sings simple songs and recites nursery rhymes • carries on detailed telephone conversations • makes up and tells stories; acquires a vocabulary of approximately 10,000–14,000 words by age 6 • uses verb tenses and word order correctly

School-age	
6–8 years	• enjoys talking and conversing with adults • uses language, in place of physical aggression, to express feelings • tells jokes and riddles • understands complex statements and performs multistep requests • finds pleasure in writing stories, letters, and e-mail messages • expresses self fluently and in elaborate detail
9-12 years	• talks nonstop • understands grammatical sequences and uses them appropriately • speaks in longer, complex sentences • uses and understands irony and sarcasm • achieves mastery of language development • becomes a thoughtful listener

Adapted from Marotz L. R., & Allen, K. E. (2013). *Developmental profiles: Pre-birth through adolescence* (7th ed.). Belmont, CA: Wadsworth Cengage Learning.

words, and word patterns. Hearing disorders can jeopardize the normal acquisition of speech and language development and lead to long-term speech impairments. Whenever there is concern about the progress of a child's language development, a comprehensive hearing evaluation is always recommended.

It is also important to consider a child's home environment when evaluating language development. Families support children's language skills by reading aloud, engaging children in frequent conversation, and providing literacy-rich opportunities (e.g., books, singing, playing). Homes where these opportunities are lacking may limit children's ability to develop language, acquire vocabulary, and practice communication skills.

Young children also acquire early speech and language skills by imitating speech that is heard in their homes (Venuti et al., 2012). For example, children who have a parent with an unusual voice inflection or speech impairment are likely to exhibit similar qualities. Children who live in bilingual homes may take longer to acquire language skills because they must learn to think and speak in multiple languages (Dixon, Wu, & Daraghmeh, 2012). Cultural values and variations also exert a strong influence on children's language usage, style, and speech patterns.

Assessment Methods   Families are often aware of children's speech problems but may not know if action needs to be taken or where to go for help. Many adults also believe erroneously that children will eventually outgrow these disorders, so they take no action. Indeed, some children have developmentally appropriate **misarticulations** that will improve with time. For example, many 3-year-olds mispronounce "r" as "w" as in "wabbit" (rabbit) or "s" as "th" as in "thong" (song); by age 4 or 5 they are able to correctly pronounce these letter sounds. Nevertheless, children who demonstrate speech or speech patterns that are not developmentally appropriate should be referred to a speech therapist for evaluation (McQuiston & Kloczko, 2011). A hearing test should be included in this evaluation to rule out the possibility of a hearing loss that could be affecting the child's speech. Speech and hearing clinics are often affiliated with colleges and universities, medical centers, child development centers, public health departments, public schools, and Head Start programs. Certified speech and hearing specialists can also be located in telephone directories or Internet listings or by contacting local school districts or the American Speech, Language, and Hearing Association.

Common Disorders   The term *speech impairment* has many different meanings to persons working with children. For some, the term implies obvious problems, such as stuttering, lisping, or unintelligent speech patterns. For others, any deviation may be cause for concern, such as a monotone voice, nasality, improper pitch of the voice, a voice tone that is too high or too low, misarticulations, or omissions of certain letter sounds.

Delayed language development or abnormal speech patterns that persist for more than a few months should be evaluated and include:

- no speech by 2 years of age
- stuttering
- substitution of word sounds
- rate of speech that is too fast or unusually slow
- monotone voice
- no improvement in speech development
- speech by age 3 that is difficult to understand
- inattentive behavior or ignoring others

Management   Families and teachers serve as important role models and promote children's speech and language skills through frequent communication opportunities and experiences. Teachers can be instrumental in identifying and referring children who have speech and language patterns that are developmentally inappropriate or that interfere with effective communication. Significant improvements can often be achieved when these disorders are identified and treated in their earliest stages.

misarticulations – *improper pronunciations of words and word sounds.*

3-2f Nutritional Status

The quality of children's diets has an unquestionable effect on brain development, behavior, and health. However, rising costs and economic struggles have forced many families to sacrifice the quantity and nutritional value of foods they purchase and serve to children. Television advertising, fast food consumption, and increasing reliance on prepackaged and convenience foods have contributed to a further decline in children's nutrient intake at a time when obesity rates are climbing.

Valuable clues about a child's nutritional status can be obtained during daily health observations. Signs such as facial **pallor**, dry skin, bleeding gums, **lethargy**, or frequent illness may reflect poor eating habits. In contrast, a healthy, well-nourished child has:

- height appropriate for age
- weight appropriate for height
- bright, clear eyes—no puffiness, crusting, or paleness of inner lids
- clear skin—good color; no pallor or scaliness
- teeth—appropriate number for age; no caries or **mottling**
- gums—pink and firm; not puffy, dark red, or bleeding
- lips—soft, moist; no cracking at corner of mouth
- tongue—pink; no cracks, white patches, or bright red color

Assessment Methods Selecting an appropriate method for evaluating children's nutritional status depends upon the child's age, reason for concern, type of information desired, and available resources. Common methods include:

- dietary assessment—used to determine nutrient adequacy and areas of nutrient deficiencies in the child's eating patterns. Food intake is recorded for a specified time period (24 hours, 3 days, 1 week) (Figure 3–3). The data is then analyzed by using one of several methods, such as nutrient analysis software, Reference Daily Intakes (RDIs), or MyPlate. (See Chapter 12.)
- anthropometric assessment—based on height, weight, BMI, and head circumference measurements that are compared to standardized norms. **Skinfold** thickness and mid-arm circumference measurements may also be taken to estimate body fat percentage.
- clinical assessment—involves observing a child for signs of nutritional deficiency (Table 3–4). This is not considered a reliable method because of its subjective nature and the fact that physical symptoms typically do not appear until a deficiency is severe.
- biochemical assessment—involves laboratory testing of various body tissues and fluids, such as urinalysis or hemoglobin (testing for iron level) to validate concerns related to over- or underconsumption of nutrients. These tests must be ordered by a health care provider and performed by trained laboratory technicians.

Common Disorders—Malnutrition and Obesity Teachers and families should be alert to several nutritional problems that can have a significant effect on children's health and development. Malnutrition, for example, occurs when children's diets lack essential nutrients, especially protein, vitamins A and C, iron, and calcium for prolonged periods. Misinformation or inadequate nutrition knowledge, poverty, and food insufficiencies may leave children malnourished simply because they do not get enough to eat or are consuming unhealthy foods (Franklin et al., 2012). Long-term use of certain medications such as steroids, aspirin, antibiotics, and laxatives or the lack of exposure to sunshine can interfere with nutrient absorption and deplete children of essential vitamins and minerals. Malnourished children often fail to reach typical growth and developmental standards and are at greater risk for behavior and learning problems, communicable

pallor – *paleness.*
lethargy – *a state of inaction or indifference.*
mottling – *marked with spots of dense white or brown coloring.*
skinfold – *a measurement of the amount of fat under the skin; also referred to as fat-fold measurements.*

FIGURE 3–3   **Sample questionnaire for obtaining information about a child's eating habits.**

DIETARY ASSESSMENT

Dear Parent:

Nutrition is a very important part of our program. In order to plan appropriate nutrition-education activities and menus, we would like to know more about your child's eating patterns. Please take the time to fill out the questionnaire carefully.

CHILD'S NAME _____ AGE _____ DATE _____

1. How many days a week does your child eat the following meals or snacks?

   a morning meal _____ a midafternoon snack _____

   a lunch or midday meal _____ an evening snack _____

   an evening meal _____ snack during the night _____

   a midmorning snack _____

2. When is your child most hungry?

   morning _____

   noon _____

   evening _____

3. What are some of your child's favorite foods? _____

4. What foods does your child dislike?

   _____

5. Is your child on a special diet? Yes _____ No _____

   If yes, why? _____

   Describe diet _____

   Diet prescribed by whom? _____

6. Does your child eat things not usually considered food, e.g., paste, dirt, paper?_____

   If yes, what is eaten? _____

   How often? _____

7. Is your child taking a vitamin or mineral supplement?

   Yes _____ No _____ If yes, what kind? _____

8. Does your child have any dental problems that might create a problem when eating certain foods?_____

9. Does your child see a dentist regularly?_____

10. Does your child have any diet-related health problems?

    Diabetes _____ Allergies _____ Lactose Intolerance _____ Other _____

11. Is your child taking any medication for a diet-related health problem?

    _____

12. How much water does your child typically drink throughout the day?

    _____

13. Please list any foods that should be included or avoided for cultural or religious reasons.

    _____

14. Please list as accurately as possible what your child eats and drinks on a typical day. If yesterday was a typical day, you may use those foods and drinks.

TIME	PLACE	FOOD	AMOUNT

TABLE 3–4   Physical Signs of Malnutrition

Tissue	Sign	Cause
Face	Pallor	Niacin, iron deficiency
	Scaling of skin around nostrils	Riboflavin, B6 deficiency
Eyes	Hardening of cornea and lining: pale lining	Iron deficiency
	Foamy spots in cornea	Vitamin A deficiency
Lips	Redness; swelling of mouth and lips; cracking at corners of mouth	Riboflavin deficiency
Teeth	Decayed or missing	Excess sugar (or poor dental hygiene)
	Mottled enamel	Excess fluoride
Tongue	Red, raw, cracked, swollen	Niacin deficiency
	Magenta color	Riboflavin deficiency
	Pale	Iron deficiency
Gums	Spongy, red, bleeding	Vitamin C deficiency
Skin	Dry, flaking	Vitamin A deficiency
	Small underskin hemorrhages	Vitamin C deficiency
Nails	Brittle, ridged	Iron deficiency

illness, infection, chronic irritability, anemia, and fatigue. However, not all malnourished children are thin and emaciated. Some overweight children are also malnourished because their diets lack the proteins, vitamins, and minerals essential for healthy growth and development.

Obesity also presents a serious challenge to children's health. Approximately 33 percent of all children in the United States are considered obese or overweight for their age (AHA, 2012). Although the causes of childhood obesity are multiple and complex, the primary factors point to inactivity and unhealthy eating behaviors (Shi et al., 2013). Because these patterns are well-established during the early years and often persist throughout adulthood, it is important that corrective measures be taken while children are young. Children who are overweight or obese are at significantly greater risk for developing life-threatening health problems including heart disease, stroke, sleep apnea, asthma, and diabetes. They also experience a higher rate of bullying, psychological problems, and academic failure.

▼ **Increasing children's physical activity is an effective weight management strategy.**

© Cengage Learning

Management Obesity in young children cannot be ignored. Although prevention is always ideal, steps can be taken to help children of any age implement healthy eating and activity behaviors (Brotman et al., 2012). For maximum success, weight management approaches must include the collaborative efforts of the child, family, teachers, and health care personnel, and target:

- meal planning and establishing healthy eating habits
- strategies for increasing children's daily activity level (For example, children can be asked to run errands, walk a pet, help with daily household chores, or ride their bike to school.)
- acquainting children with new outside interests, hobbies, or activities, such as hiking, swimming, dancing, roller skating, neighborhood baseball, soccer, or learning to ride a bike (Involvement in fun activities can divert children's attention away from food.)
- finding ways to help children experience success and develop a positive self-image (For example, acknowledging children's efforts can boost self-esteem. For many children, positive adult attention replaces food as an important source of personal gratification.)

CONNECTING TO EVERYDAY PRACTICE

Children and Poverty

The U.S. Census Bureau redefined the term poverty so that it more accurately reflects today's economic standards (U.S. Census Bureau, 2011). However, current guidelines continue to exclude many families whose income is often not adequate to meet even minimal requirements for food, clothing, shelter, and health care. Race, ethnicity, immigrant status, and single-parenting place many children and their families at the highest risk for living in poverty (National Kids Count, 2012). Although a majority of adults in these families are employed, they often work in minimum wage jobs. Health care and insurance are luxuries that many cannot afford. Changes in eligibility guidelines for various government assistance programs (food, cash, medical care, housing, child care, and job training) have further reduced some families' access to resources that affect children's health. It is estimated that 1 in 4 children under 18 years (32 million) in the United States live in low-income or poverty families; children under 6 years account for nearly half of this number. Increased poverty has contributed to more homelessness and food insecurity (including obesity), especially among families with children—currently the fastest growing segment of the homeless population (NCTSN, 2011).

Think About This:

▶ Why is it important that teachers be aware of changes in national fiscal policy and federal programs?

▶ What effects would you expect poverty to have on children's early brain development?

▶ What physical and mental health problems might you anticipate if you were working with children who are economically disadvantaged?

▶ What steps can classroom teachers take to meet the special developmental and educational needs of children living in economically disadvantaged families?

▶ What resources are available in your community to assist low-income families with children?

Childhood obesity will be discussed throughout the book because of its current importance, complexity, and serious health consequences.

Long-term weight management is achieved by attending to all aspects of a child's well-being—physical, emotional, spiritual, and social. Placing children on weight reduction plans is not advisable unless they are under a doctor's or dietitian's supervision. Careful attention must be given to planning weight reduction programs that meet children's critical nutrient needs for sustained growth and development. Adults who model healthy eating and an active lifestyle are also in a position to have a positive influence on children's preferences and weight management behaviors. Additional ideas for healthy eating and physical activities will be addressed throughout the book and are also available on numerous websites, including the President's Council on Fitness, Sports & Nutrition (http://www.fitness.gov), the USDA's MyPlate for Kids (http://www.choosemyplate.gov), the CDC's Division of Adolescent and School Health (http://www.cdc.gov/healthyyouth/npao/index.htm), and the National Center for Physical Development and Outdoor Play (http://www.aahperd.org/headstartbodystart).

Did You Get It?

When working with children of varying _____, educators must be aware of the role that genetics plays in physical growth potential.

  a. cultures

  b. cultures, races, and ethnicities

  c. ethnicities

  d. socioeconomic backgrounds

Take the full quiz on CourseMate.

TeachSource Video Connections

Students with Special Needs: The Referral and Evaluation Process

Teachers play a central role in the early identification of children who may be experiencing developmental or academic challenges. They often initiate the evaluation process and meet with colleagues and families to discuss the child's special needs. As you watch the learning video, *Students with Special Needs: The Referral and Evaluation Process,* consider the following questions:

1. Why is it important to conduct a careful assessment before contacting the child's family?

2. What are the advantages of using a team approach for assessment?

3. Are there disadvantages to a team approach? Explain.

4. Why would it be important to include a vision and hearing screening in this assessment?

Watch on CourseMate.

3-3 Referrals

A **referral** is made by sharing observation and screening test results with a child's family and assisting them in identifying appropriate follow-up resources. Referrals are most successful when teachers have established cooperative and trusting partnerships with children's families. Knowing something about their beliefs, customs, values, and community resources improves a teacher's ability to make effective referrals. For example, mistrust of the medical profession, poverty, job conflicts, religious beliefs, a lack of transportation, or limited education may affect a family's ability and willingness to follow through with any recommendation.

Meeting with the child's family, or calling them on the telephone, is often the most effective method for making referrals:

Teacher: "I am concerned about Ryan's vision. On several occasions, I have noticed that his right eye turns inward more than the left eye and that he holds his head close to materials when he is working. Have you observed any of these behaviors at home?"

Parent: "Yes, but we didn't think it was anything to worry about. We thought he was just tired or trying to be funny."

Teacher: "I can't be sure that anything is wrong with Ryan's eyesight, but the behaviors I have observed may indicate a vision problem and should be evaluated by an eye specialist. I will provide a written copy of my observations that you can take along. Please let me know if I can be of assistance in locating a doctor, and the outcome of Ryan's evaluation."

Although a face-to-face meeting with the child's family is always preferable, a well-written letter may be the only way to reach some families. Copies of all screening test results should be given to families so they can be shared with the child's doctor. When medical personnel have access to this information, they are better able to understand how the child's behavior is being affected. Teachers can also alleviate some of the family's frustration by offering information about local resources, such as hospitals, clinics, health departments, medical specialists, public and private agencies, volunteer organizations, and funding sources where services can be obtained.

A follow-up contact should always be made after several days to determine if families have been successful in securing a professional evaluation. The occasion can also be used to learn about the child's diagnosis, treatment plan, and any instructional or environmental modifications that a teacher may need to make. It is also an ideal time to acknowledge the family's efforts in following through with recommendations and to convey the teacher's genuine interest in the child's well-being.

© 2015 Cengage Learning

....

referral – *directing an individual to other sources, usually for additional evaluation or treatment.*

PARTNERING with FAMILIES

Children's Eye Safety

Dear Families,

Each year, thousands of children sustain eye injuries as the result of hazardous conditions at home or school. The majority of these injuries are preventable through proper supervision, careful selection of toys and equipment, and use of appropriate eye protection. You play an important role in identifying potentially dangerous situations and taking steps to protect children from unnecessary exposure or risk. It is also important that you take similar precautions to protect your own eye safety and serve as a positive role model for children.

▶ Never shake an infant! Vigorous shaking can cause serious eye damage and blindness.

▶ Insist that children wear sunglasses whenever they play outdoors to limit exposure to ultraviolet (UV) light. Over time, UV exposure increases the risk of developing a number of serious eye conditions, including macular degeneration and cataracts. Purchase sunglasses that fit closely, wrap around the entire eye area, and provide UV-A and UV-B protection.

▶ Keep children indoors whenever mowing or edging the lawn. Stones, sticks, and small debris can become dangerous projectiles.

▶ Select toys and play equipment based on your child's age and abilities. Avoid toys with projectile parts, such as darts, slingshots, pellet guns, and missile-launching devices.

▶ Monitor children's access to items, such as stones, rubber bands, balls, wire coat hangers, and fish hooks that pose a serious eye danger.

▶ Supervise children closely whenever they are using a sharp item, such as a fork, pencil, toothpicks, wire, paperclips, scissors, or small wooden dowels.

▶ Keep children away from fireworks. Do not allow them to light fireworks or to be near anyone while they are doing so.

▶ Lock up household cleaners, sprays, paints, paint thinners, and chemicals such as garden fertilizers and pesticides that could injure children's eyes.

▶ Make sure children wear appropriate protective eyewear, such as goggles or a helmet with a face guard, when participating in sports.

▶ Don't allow children to shine a laser pointer or aim a squirt gun or spray nozzle toward anyone's eyes.

▶ Remind children to avoid touching their eyes with unwashed hands.

Teacher Activities

My Five Senses...

(NHES PreK–2; National Health Education Standard 1.2.2)

Concept: Seeing, hearing, tasting, touching, and smelling are your five senses.

Learning Objectives

▶ Children will learn to name all five senses.

▶ Children will learn which body parts go with which senses: see with eyes, hear with ears, taste with tongue, touch with fingers and skin, and smell with nose.

Supplies

▶ Small blanket; various objects (items that children can label—plastic foods, animals, people, and so on); small paper cups; tin foil; various scents or foods (vanilla, orange peel, ketchup, peppermint, chocolate, ranch dressing, green pepper, etc.); tape recording of children's and teachers' voices; feely box; various items with shapes that children can recognize (ball, pine cone, banana, block, plate, cup, and so on); salty (crackers), sweet (mandarin orange), sour (lemon), and bitter (unsweetened chocolate) items; hand wipes; plates; forks

Learning Activities

▶ Read and discuss the following books:

  ● *Your Five Senses* by Bobbi Katz

  ● *The Sense of Hearing* by Elaine Landau

  ● *You Smell with Your Nose* by Melvin Berger

  ● *You Touch with Your Fingers* by Melvin & Gilda Berger

▶ Each day discuss one of the senses and have the children participate in an activity.

▶ Seeing—Tell the children that you are going to play a game called "What's Missing?" This is a game that uses their sense of seeing. Place four to five objects out on the floor in front of the children. Name each item, and then line the items up in a way so that all the children can see them. Place the towel over the items. Remove one of the items and wrap it in the towel. Ask children to guess which item is missing. Call on children one at a time; if they name the missing item, they can come up and hide the next item. Continue until all children have had a turn. Vary the toys to keep children interested.

▶ Smelling—Tell the children that you are going to do an activity to learn about their sense of smell. Make "smelling cups": for liquid scents, put a few drops on a cotton ball and place it in the cup. Cover the cup with foil in which holes have been poked. Pass the cups around. Have children smell each cup and try to guess what the smell is. After each child has had a chance to smell each cup, remove the foil so they can see if they were correct.

▶ Hearing—Make a recording of the teachers and children while they are playing. On another day, tell the children that they will use their sense of hearing for this activity. Play the recording and see if the children can guess whose voices they are hearing on the tape.

▶ Feeling—Tell the children that this activity will involve using their sense of touch. Place various items in a feely box. Have each child reach in and use their sense of touch to determine what the object is.

(continued)

CLASSROOM CORNER

Teacher Activities   *(continued)*

▶ Tasting—Tell the children you are going to have them taste some different items to see if they are sweet, sour, salty, or bitter. Tell them that their tongue has little things called taste buds on it that help them know what a food tastes like. Next, have all the children wash their hands with a wipe. Place a cracker, a mandarin orange, a small piece of lemon, and bit of unsweetened chocolate on each plate, and set a plate in front of each child. Have the children taste one item at a time and talk about the different tastes.

Evaluation

▶ Children will name each of the five senses.

▶ Children will name which body parts are associated with each sense.

Additional lesson plans for grades 3–5 are available on CourseMate.

 **Summary**

▶ Teachers play an important role in the monitoring and assessing children's health

• Information about children's physical and mental health status can be obtained from a variety of sources, including teacher observations, health records, screening procedures, daily health checks, and interactions with families.

• Assessment information is used to identify children who require professional evaluation, make referrals, and modify children's learning environments to accommodate any special needs.

▶ Screening tools provide a relatively quick and inexpensive way to evaluate groups of children for a variety of conditions, including height/weight, BMI, vision and hearing disorders, speech and language problems, and nutritional status.

• The results of screening procedures are not diagnostic by themselves; they do not confirm that a child does or does not have an impairment. They do help to identify children who may have a potential problem that requires further evaluation.

▶ Teachers can initiate the referral process after gathering and evaluating information about a child's health from multiple sources.

• A follow-up contact should always be made with the child's family to learn about assessment outcomes, treatment recommendations, and any classroom modifications that may be needed.

Terms to Know

intervention *p. 56*
skeletal *p. 58*
neurological *p. 58*
underweight *p. 59*
overweight *p. 59*
obese *p. 59*
ophthalmologist *p. 59*
optometrist *p. 59*

amblyopia *p. 62*
strabismus *p. 63*
myopia *p. 63*
hyperopia *p. 63*
language *p.*
audiologist *p. 65*
conductive loss *p. 66*
sensorineural loss *p. 66*

mixed hearing loss *p. 66*
speech *p. 67*
misarticulations *p. 69*
pallor *p. 70*
lethargy *p. 70*
mottling *p. 70*
skinfold *p. 70*
referrals *p. 74*

Chapter Review

A. By Yourself:

1. Define each of the *Terms to Know* listed at the end of this chapter.

2. Select the screening test that is recommended for children with the following behaviors, signs, or symptoms. Place the appropriate code letter in each space for questions 1–15.

H	Hearing screening
V	Vision screening
D	Developmental screening
HW	Height and weight
Dt	Dental screening
S	Speech evaluation
N	Nutrition evaluation

_____ 1. blinks frequently; often closes one eye when reading

_____ 2. stutters whenever tense and in a hurry to speak

_____ 3. appears listless and very small for her chronological age

_____ 4. stumbles over objects in the classroom; frequently walks into play equipment in the play yard

_____ 5. has overlapping and missing teeth that make speech difficult to understand

_____ 6. ignores the teacher's requests; pushes and shouts at the other children to get their attention

_____ 7. is obese and experiences shortness of breath when running and playing

_____ 8. has trouble catching a ball, pedaling a bicycle, and cutting with scissors

_____ 9. appears to focus on objects with one eye while the other eye looks off in another direction

_____ 10. a toddler who has multiple cavities and refuses to chew solid foods

_____ 11. is extremely shy and withdrawn; spends the majority of his time playing alone and imitating other children's actions

_____ 12. seems extremely hungry at snack time; always asks for extra servings and takes food from other children's plates when the teacher isn't looking

_____ 13. becomes hoarse after shouting and yelling while playing outdoors

_____ 14. arrives at school each morning with potato chips, candy, or a cupcake and soda

_____ 15. a 4½-year-old who whines and has tantrums to get his own way

B. As a Group:

1. Identify and describe the vision disorders that are most common among young children. What behavioral indicators might a teacher observe? How is each typically treated?

2. Discuss how teachers might use information in health records to improve learning experiences for children with special sensory needs?

3. Discuss how the learning activities outlined in the Classroom Corner feature could be modified for a child who is blind or has low vision. How might they be adapted for a child with significant hearing loss?

4. Brainstorm ideas for ways that teachers can incorporate more physical activity into classroom routines to help children achieve the recommended 60 minutes of vigorous daily activity.

5. Debate whether or not teachers should calculate children's BMI and inform families if a child is overweight. Role-play how a teacher might share this information with an unreceptive parent and offer suggestions for improving the child's nutrition and physical activity. Critique each other's responses.

6. If a family asks you where they can get their 2-year-old's hearing tested, what resources in your community would you recommend?

◖◗ Case Study

A friend encouraged Mrs. Howard to take her son to the developmental screening clinic being held this week at the community recreation center. Parker is nearly 2 years old and speaks only a few words that are understandable. He has few opportunities to play with other children his age because he spends most days with his grandmother while his mother works at a nearby hospital. On the day of the developmental screening, team members checked Parker's height, weight, vision, hearing, speech, cognitive abilities, and motor skills. The team leader also read through the child history form that Mrs. Howard had completed and noted that Parker had several food allergies, as well as frequent upper respiratory and ear infections. All of Parker's screening results proved to be within normal limits, with the exception of his hearing tests, which revealed a significant loss in one ear and a moderate loss in the other.

1. Is Parker's speech development appropriate for his age? Explain.

2. What significance might Parker's ear infections have to his hearing loss? How might his food allergies be contributing to the loss?

3. Should the screening team's recommendation for Parker include a referral to his physician? Why?

4. What behavioral signs of hearing loss might you expect Parker to exhibit?

5. What strategies might the developmental team suggest to Parker's mother and grandmother for improving his speech development and communication skills?

◖◗ Application Activities

1. Locate and read instructions for administering the Snellen Tumbling E and one additional acuity screening test. Pair up with another student and practice testing each other. Alternatively, volunteer to conduct vision screening at a local early childhood program or shelter for homeless families. What advantages does each test offer? Disadvantages? Did you encounter any problems administering the test? How would you modify your instructions to a child based on this experience?

2. Devise a monitoring system that can be used in a group setting to record the daily food intakes of individual children. Be sure to address the following questions:

   a. What nutritional information do you want to collect? In what form?

   b. Who will be responsible for collecting this data?

   c. How can this information be obtained efficiently?

   d. How can teachers and families use this data to improve children's eating habits?

   e. What other ways might teachers use this information to promote children's health?

3. Collect samples of child history forms from several schools and early childhood programs in your area. Review the type of information that is most often requested. Design your own form and distribute it to several families for their comments and suggestions.

4. Attend a signing class. Learn to say "hello" and "good-bye" and 10 additional words in sign language.

5. Make arrangements with a local school or early childhood program to conduct a comparison study of children's growth. Measure and record the heights and weights of 15 children, ages

3 to 6 years, on the standard Growth Charts (download from the text's premium website). Then, determine each child's BMI and plot this information on the BMI-for-age charts. Which method provides the most accurate information about children's growth? What did you learn about the children's potential risk for becoming overweight? Learn more about the BMI measure and initiatives for preventing childhood obesity at the CDC website (http://www.cdc.gov).

6. Obtain an audiometer. Have a nurse or audiologist demonstrate the technique for testing a person's hearing. Practice administering the test with a partner. In what ways did this experience change your ideas about how to prepare children for testing?

7. Research the Internet or contact your local American Heart Association chapter to learn about their educational programs that target children's cardiovascular health. Are the materials/ programs developmentally appropriate? How is improvement measured?

Helpful Web Resources

American Speech, Language, and Hearing Association (ASHA)	http://www.asha.org
National Association of Parents with Children in Special Education	http://www.napcse.org
National Institutes of Health	http://www.health.nih.gov
Prevent Blindness America	http://www.preventblindness.org
Action for Healthy Children	http://www.actionforhealthykids.org

Visit the Education CourseMate for this textbook to access the eBook, Did You Get It? quizzes, Digital Downloads, TeachSource Video Cases, flashcards, and more. Go to CengageBrain.com to log in, register, or purchase access.

References

American Heart Association (AHA). (2012). Overweight in children. Accessed on April 10, 2012 from http://www.heart.org/HEARTORG/GettingHealthy/Overweight-in-Children_UCM_304054_Article.jsp#.T4SqhNmyEhA.

Basch, C. (2011). Vision and the achievement gap among urban minority youth, *Journal of School Health*, 81(10), 599–605.

Borchert, M., Varma, R., Cotter, S., Tarczy-Hornoch, K., McKean-Cowdin, R., Lin, J., Wen, G., Azen, S., Torres, M., Tielsch, J., Friedman, D., Repka, M., Katz, J., Ibironke, J., & Giordano, L. (2011). Risk factors for hyperopia and myopia in preschool children: The multi-ethnic pediatric eye disease and Baltimore pediatric eye disease studies, *Ophthalmology*, 118(10), 1966–1973.

Brotman, L., Dawson-McClure, S., Huang, K., Theise, R., Kamboukos, D., Wang, J., Petkova, E., & Ogedegbe, G. (2012). Early childhood family intervention and long-term obesity prevention among high-risk minority youth, *Pediatrics*, 129(3), e621–e628.

Deem, K., Diaz-Ordaz, E., & Shiner, B. (2012). Identifying quality improvement opportunities in a universal newborn hearing screening program, *Pediatrics*, 12(1), e157–e164.

Dixon, L., Wu, S., & Daraghmeh, A. (2012). Profiles in bilingualism: Factors influencing kindergartners' language proficiency, *Early Childhood Education Journal*, 40(1), 25–34.

Elloy, M., & Marshall, A. (2012). The management of hearing loss in children, *Paediatrics & Child Health*, 22(1), 13–18.

Franklin, B., Jones, A., Love, D., Puckett, S., Macklin, J., & White-Means, S. (2012). Exploring mediators of food insecurity and obesity: A review of recent literature, *Journal of Community Health*, 37(1), 253–264.

Gunton, K. (2013). Advances in amblyopia: What have we learned from PEDIG trials?, *Pediatrics*, 131(3), 540–547.

Jackson, K., Krishnaswami, S., & McPheeters, M. (2011). Unmet health care needs in children with cerebral palsy: A cross-sectional study, *Research in Developmental Disabilities*, 32(6), 2714–2723.

Laws, G., Bates, G., Feuerstein, M., Mason-Apps, E., & White, C. (2012). Peer acceptance of children with language and communication impairments in a mainstream primary school: Associations with type of language difficulty, problem behaviours, and a change in placement organization, *Child Language Teaching and Therapy*, 28(1), 73–86.

Longmuir, S., Boese, E., Pfeifer, W., Zimmerman, B., Short, L., & Scott, W. (2013). Practical community photoscreening in very young children, *Pediatrics*, 131(3), e764–e769.

March of Dimes. (2011). Newborn screening. Accessed on April 9, 2012 from http://www.marchofdimes.com/professionals/bringinghome_screening.html.

Marotz, L. R., & Allen, K. E. (2013). *Developmental profiles: Pre-birth through adolescence*. (7th ed.). Belmont, CA: Wadsworth Cengage Learning.

McQuiston, S., & Kloczko, N. (2011). Speech and language development: Monitoring process and problems, *Pediatrics in Review*, 32(6), 230–239.

Morale, S., Hughbanks-Wheaton, D., Cheng, C., Subramanian, V., O'Connor, A., & Birch, E. (2012). Visual acuity assessment of children with special needs, *American Orthoptic Journal*, 62, 90–98.

National Child Traumatic Stress Network (NCTSN). (2011). National Homeless Youth Awareness Month (November 2012). Accessed on April 10, 2012 from http://www.nctsnet.org/resources/public-awareness/national-homeless-youth-awareness-month.

National Kids Count. (2012). The Annie E. Casey Foundation. Accessed on May 4, 2012 from http://datacenter.kidscount.org.

Optometrists Network. (2012). Strabismus. Accessed on April 8, 2012, from http://www.strabismus.org.

Prevent Blindness America. (2010). Quick facts: Children's eye problems. Accessed April 9, 2012 from http://www.preventblindness.org/sites/default/files/national/documents/fact_sheets/MK03_QuickFactsChildren.pdf.

Shi, X., Tubb, L., Fingers, S., Chen, S., & Caffrey, J. (2013). Associations of physical activity and dietary behaviors with children's health and academic problems, *Journal of School Health*, 83(1), 1–7.

Tarczy-Hornoch, K. (2012). Accommodative lag and refractive error in infants and toddlers. Accessed on April 8, 2012 from http://dx.doi.org/10.1016/j.jaapos.2011.10.015.

U.S. Census Bureau. (2011). How the Census Bureau measures poverty. Accessed on April 10, 2012 from http://www.census.gov/hhes/www/poverty/about/overview/measure.html.

Venuti, P., de Falco, S., Esposito, G., Zaninelli, M., & Bornstein, M. (2012). Maternal functional speech to children: A comparison of autism spectrum disorder, Down syndrome, and typical development, *Research in Developmental Disabilities*, 33(2), 506–517.

chapter 4

Caring for Children with Special Medical Conditions

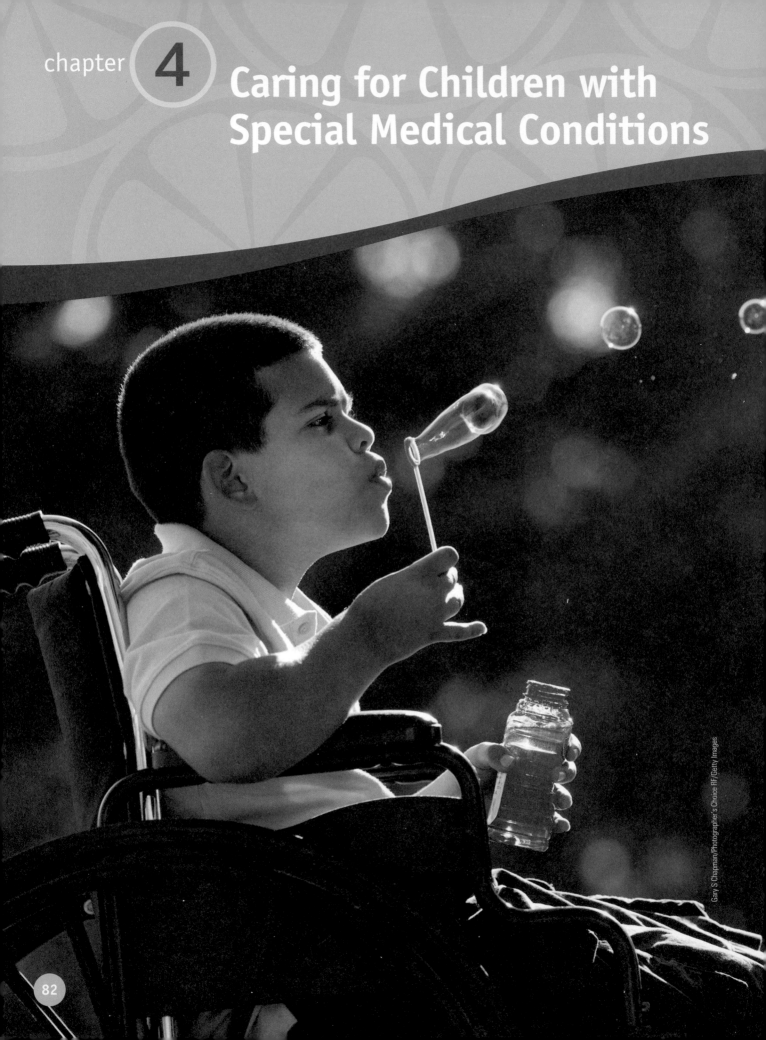

▶ **#1 a, b, and c:** Promoting child development and learning
▶ **#2 a, b, and c:** Building family and community relationships
▶ **#3 a, b, c, and d:** Observing, documenting, and assessing to support young children and families
▶ **#4 a, b, and c:** Using developmentally effective approaches to connect with children and families
▶ **#6 c:** Becoming a professional
▶ Field experiences

Learning Objectives

After studying this chapter, you should be able to:

LO 4-1 Describe how IDEA serves children who have special developmental and medical needs.

LO 4-2 Name and discuss the symptoms and management strategies for several common medical conditions addressed in this chapter.

Children who have disabilities, medical conditions, and chronic diseases are often present in early childhood and school-age classrooms. This means that teachers must be able to respond to children's educational, health, and medical needs. They also play an instrumental role in identifying children who may have undiagnosed conditions that require medical evaluation and treatment. Early identification, referral to appropriate professionals, and intervention strategies have proven successful in minimizing the negative effects that undiagnosed health conditions can have on children's developmental progress and ability to learn (Allen & Cowdery, 2012; Guralnick, 2012; Horn & Kang, 2012). The purpose of this chapter is to provide brief descriptions of several acute and chronic medical conditions and their management strategies to help prepare teachers for these important roles.

4-1 Inclusive Education: Supporting Children's Success

The practice of including and integrating children of varying abilities and limitations together in the same classroom is commonly referred to as **inclusion** or inclusive education. If teachers understand that all children are uniquely different, they are able to individualize instruction so that it supports and builds on each child's strengths. For example, some children may have recently immigrated and are learning a new language, others may be budding artists or creative thinkers, and still others may present troubling behaviors or special health conditions. However, all of these children are fundamentally similar and have the same basic needs (i.e., food, shelter, love, attention, dignity,

....

inclusion – *the practice of including and integrating children of all abilities in a classroom and individualizing instruction to meet each child's unique learning needs.*

respect) that must be met despite their individual differences. They must also have equal access to high quality educational experiences and opportunities if they are to achieve their fullest potential.

Prior to 2004, children who had physical or cognitive disabilities were often denied access to regular educational programs. However, passage of the Individuals with Disabilities Education (Improvement) Act (IDEA) now guarantees these children the same right to an appropriate education and the special services they need to succeed as their typically developing peers. IDEA is administered by the U.S. Department of Education in each state. The law's requirements strengthen the early identification process, the intervention services provided, and ensures family involvement in children's education. It also identifies specific health conditions that make a child eligible to receive needed services (Table 4–1).

Not all children who have a chronic or acute medical condition will qualify for special education services through IDEA. A child must first undergo a comprehensive evaluation to determine if a health disorder interferes with his or her developmental progress and educational performance. A child who is eligible to receive special services will have an educational plan formulated according to IDEA guidelines:

▶ Part B of IDEA provides services to children and youth ages 3 to 22 years. A multidisciplinary team creates an **individualized educational plan (IEP)** to meet children's developmental and academic needs. Learning goals are established, intervention services identified, and evaluation or outcome measures are noted.

▶ Part C of IDEA serves the needs of children 0 to 3 years of age and their families. An **individualized family service plan (IFSP)** is prepared in which specific developmental goals, and the intervention services a child needs to help achieve them, are outlined.

▶ **Individualized health services plans (IHSP)** are written for children who have health care needs (e.g., food allergies, medications, medical procedures, special equipment, or transportation needs) that must be addressed during school hours. Plans include safety and emergency considerations as well as ways to collaborate with health care professionals.

Children's successful inclusion requires that teachers partner with a variety of community specialists to meet children's health and educational requirements. They must also work closely with families to ensure that children's needs are being met, parents' concerns are addressed, and progress is being made.

An important point for teachers to remember when they work with children, especially children who may have a disease, physical disorder, or developmental difference, is the use of **person first language**. For example, instead of identifying a child as asthmatic, blind, or epileptic, the

TABLE 4–1   IDEA Disability Categories Eligible for Special Services

autism	multiple disabilities
deaf-blindness	orthopedic impairments
deafness	other health impairments
developmental delay	specific learning disabilities
emotional disturbance	speech or language impairment
hearing impairment	traumatic brain injury
intellectual disability	visual impairment, including blindness

Source: Individuals with Disabilities Education (Improvement) Act of 2004, U.S. Department of Education (http://www.idea.ed.gov).

individualized educational plan (IEP) – *a plan that identifies specific developmental and academic goals and intervention services for a child or youth 3 to 22 years of age who has special needs.*

individualized family service plan (IFSP) – *a plan that outlines specific goals and intervention services for children 0 to 3 years of age who have special needs and their families.*

individualized health services plan (IHSP) – *a plan that identifies and addresses a child's special health care needs during school hours.*

person first language – *a manner of addressing an individual first and then their disability; e.g., a child with autism.*

Did You Get It?

According to the Individuals with Disabilities Education (Improvement) Act (IDEA) guidelines, learning goals, intervention recommendations, evaluative documentation, and improvement outcomes for a 2-year-old child would be outlined in an individualized _____ plan.

a. health services

b. curriculum

c. family service

d. education

Take the full quiz on CourseMate.

teacher should refer to him or her as a child with asthma, a child who is blind, or a child who has epilepsy. When communications are framed in this manner, the child's individuality and contributions are acknowledged and attention is drawn away from existing limitations. Ideally, reference to a child's disease or disability should be avoided all together, unless it is essential to the conversation.

4-2 Common Chronic Diseases and Medical Conditions

Some chronic diseases such as anemia and diabetes may be difficult to recognize in children because they have been present since birth. Other conditions, such as allergies, asthma, and lead poisoning, may present few early symptoms and develop slowly over time so that even the child may not be aware that anything is wrong. This means that from time to time teachers are likely to encounter children who have chronic medical disorders that have not yet been diagnosed (Coker, Kaplan, & Chung, 2012).

When teachers have concerns about the possibility of an undiagnosed condition, an ideal starting point is to consider the child's environmental circumstances. Factors that may contribute to a child's health condition and also serve as barriers to treatment can include:

- location—living in an urban neighborhood, rural area, or being homeless
- family's financial situation—may affect dietary quality, living arrangement, and access to medical and dental care
- environmental pollutants—exposure to excessive noise, rodents, or chemicals in air or water
- toxic stress, maltreatment, or domestic violence
- family unit—divorce, parent death, dysfunctional parenting

TeachSource Video Connections

© 2015 Cengage Learning

Preschool: IEP and Transition Planning for a Young Child with Special Needs

Transitioning between schools and programs can be an unsettling experience for children and their families. Children are more likely to experience success when their current and new teachers meet to share information about an individual child's needs and developmental progress.

1. In what ways do teachers serve as children's advocates?

2. What steps did the preschool teacher take to put Mark's parents more at ease during the IEP transition meeting?

3. What is the purpose of a transition meeting? How do children benefit from these meetings?

Watch on CourseMate.

Teachers are not expected to be knowledgeable about the range of medical conditions and diseases that children may present in their classrooms. However, they have access to numerous resources where they can learn more about these disorders. Reliable information is available on professional websites and through local libraries. Community health care providers, such as public health nurses, are often willing to answer questions and to provide expert guidance. Health consultants may be available in some communities to train and work directly with classroom teachers. School nurses in public and some private schools provide similar assistance, and are often responsible for administering medications and medical procedures. Additional resources and support may also be available to teachers serving children who have an IEP, IFSP, or IHSP.

The remainder of this chapter is devoted to an overview of several common acute and chronic diseases and medical conditions that teachers may encounter in their classrooms. Note that developmental and genetic disabilities have not been included here because they are topics typically addressed in-depth in special education courses and specialized textbooks.

4-2a Allergic Diseases

Allergies are the leading cause of chronic disease among young children in the United States and may affect as many as one in every five children (AAFA, 2012). The incidence of allergic disease and the increasing number of substances to which children are reacting is raising significant concern. Although many allergic disorders can be successfully treated and controlled, it is estimated that more than 50 percent of children with symptoms remain undiagnosed (Coker, Kaplan, & Chung, 2012). Allergic reactions range in severity from mildly annoying symptoms to those that may severely restrict a child's activity or even result in unexpected death.

Signs and Symptoms   A substance capable of triggering an allergic reaction is called an *allergen*. An inherited error in the body's immune system causes it to overreact to otherwise harmless environmental substances such as dust, pollen, foods, chemicals, or medicines (Shah & Grammer, 2012).

Allergic reactions are generally classified according to the body site where contact with the allergen occurs and where symptoms most commonly develop:

▼ Allergies can cause a range of physical and behavioral symptoms.

© Cengage Learning

- ingestants—cause digestive upsets and respiratory problems. Common examples include foods such as milk, citrus fruits, eggs, wheat, chocolate, tree nuts, peanuts, and oral medications.
- inhalants—affect the respiratory system causing a runny nose, cough, wheezing, and itchy, watery eyes. Examples include pollens, molds, dust, particulate matter, animal dander, and chemicals such as perfumes and cleaning products.
- contactants—cause skin irritations, rashes, hives, and eczema. Common contactants include soaps, cosmetics, dyes, fibers, latex, topical medications, and some plants, such as poison ivy, poison oak, and grass.
- injectables—trigger respiratory, digestive, and skin disturbances. Examples of injectables include medications that are injected directly into the body and insect bites, especially those of bees, wasps, hornets, and spiders.

Children who have chronic allergies often experience irritability and malaise in addition to the discomfort that accompanies an acute reaction. To understand how allergies affect children on a day-to-day basis, consider the generalized fatigue and uneasiness that you experience at the onset of a cold. Certainly, children cannot benefit fully from learning when they are not feeling well. For these reasons, the possibility of an allergic disorder should be investigated because it could be contributing to a child's learning or behavior problems (e.g., fidgeting, disruptive behaviors, hyperactivity, fatigue, general disinterest, irritability, difficulty concentrating).

TEACHER CHECKLIST 4-1
✓✓✓ Cold or Allergy: How to Tell?

	Cold	Allergy
Time of year	More likely in fall and winter	Depends on what child is allergic to—may be year round or seasonal (fall, spring)
Nasal drainage	Begins clear; may turn color after 2–3 days	Remains clear
Fever	Common with infection	No fever
Cough	May become loose and productive	Usually not productive; nasal drainage irritates throat causing frequent throat clearing and shallow cough
Itchy eyes	No	Typical
Muscle aches	May be present during first 1–2 days	None
Length of illness	7–10 days	May last an entire season or year round

TeachSource Digital Download | Download from CourseMate.

Teachers can be instrumental in recognizing the early signs of children's allergic conditions. Daily observations and anecdotal records may reveal patterns of repetitious symptoms that may otherwise be overlooked (Teacher Checklist 4-1). Common signs and symptoms of allergic disorders include:

- frequent colds and ear infections
- chronic congestion, such as runny nose, cough, or throat clearing; mouth-breathing
- headaches
- frequent nosebleeds
- unexplained stomachaches
- hives, eczema, or other skin rashes
- wheezing or shortness of breath
- intermittent or permanent hearing losses
- reactions to foods or medications
- dark circles beneath the eyes
- mottled tongue
- frequent rubbing, twitching, or picking of the nose
- chronic redness of the throat
- red, itchy eyes; swollen eyelids
- irritability, restlessness, lack of energy or interest

Approximately 8 percent of all children have an inherited immune disorder that causes a true food allergy and is not outgrown (Gupta et al., 2011). However, many children experience unpleasant reactions to specific foods that parents commonly refer to as food allergies. This type of response is called a **food intolerance** or insensitivity and does not involve the immune system; gluten and lactose intolerances are examples. Unlike food allergies, the symptoms of food intolerances are usually not life-threatening and may eventually be outgrown (Turner & Kemp, 2012). Common symptoms of food allergies include:

- hives, skin rashes
- flushed or pale face
- cramps, vomiting, and diarrhea

. . . .

food intolerance – *unpleasant reactions to particular foods that do not involve an immune response and are usually outgrown.*

TABLE 4–2   **Common Food Allergens**

Foods that are most likely to trigger an allergic reaction include:

- eggs
- milk and milk products such as cheese and ice cream
- fish and shellfish
- peanuts
- tree nuts, such as almonds, cashews, and pecans
- wheat and wheat products
- soybeans

▮ runny nose, watery eyes, congestion, and wheezing
▮ itching or swelling around the lips, tongue, or mouth
▮ anxiousness, restlessness
▮ shock
▮ difficulty breathing

Symptoms of an allergic reaction can develop within minutes or several hours following the ingestion of an offending food. Foods that most commonly trigger allergic reactions are listed in Table 4–2. The Food Allergen Labeling & Consumer Protection Act (2004) requires manufacturers to clearly indicate on the food label if any of these substances are present in a product or if the product has been exposed to any of these ingredients during its preparation.

Some food allergies can be severe and potentially life-threatening. For this reason, school administrators and teachers must be prepared to implement safeguards that will protect the child's well-being (Figure 4–1) (Allen et al., 2012; Morris et al., 2011). They must work closely with the child's family to develop a plan of action in the event of an allergic reaction. A downloadable food allergy action plan is available in multiple languages from the Food Allergy Research & Education website (www.food-allergy.org). Extensive resource information about children's food allergies can also be accessed from this site. A program's action plan should include emergency telephone numbers and directives for the measures to be taken in an emergency. All staff members should be familiar with the child's plan and review it often; this step is especially important to address with new and substitute teachers. If injectable medications, such as an EpiPen® (epinephrine auto-injector), have been ordered by the child's physician, teachers should be trained to administer them properly.

Teachers must consider children's food allergies whenever planning lessons, celebrating holidays or special occasions, or taking field trips. It is also imperative that the cook read food labels carefully and avoid cross-contamination (with other children's food) when preparing the child's meals. Any special food items should be labeled with the child's name and stored away from other foods. A list of children and the foods to which they are allergic should be posted inside the classroom. One teacher should be responsible for monitoring, checking, and serving all foods to children who have known allergies to prevent mistakes from occurring. Everyone (adults and children) should wash their hands carefully following a meal or snack to avoid spreading potential food allergens. Teachers can use these opportunities to help children learn about allergies, explain why these precautions are necessary, and discuss why food items must not be exchanged.

FIGURE 4–1   **Precautions must be taken to protect children from known food allergies.**

© Cengage Learning

Management At present, there are no known cures for allergic conditions, only **symptomatic control**. In some cases, the substances to which a child is allergic may change over time. Although this gives the impression that an allergy has disappeared, it often redevelops at a later time or the child may become allergic to a different substance.

Symptoms and complications of allergies are generally less severe and easier to control if they are identified early. Treatment is aimed at limiting a child's exposure to troublesome allergens, and, in some cases, involves completely removing the substance(s) from the child's environment. For example, if a child is allergic to milk, all dairy products should be eliminated from the child's diet. If the pet dog is a source of a child's allergies, the dog should be kept outdoors or at least out of the child's bedroom and frequent hand washing practiced. In other cases, such as with dust or pollen allergies, it may be feasible to only control the amount of exposure (e.g., keeping doors and windows closed, dusting frequently, eliminating carpet). Smoking must always be avoided around children with respiratory allergies because it is known to aggravate and intensify breathing problems (Accordini et al., 2012). Left untreated, allergies can lead to more serious health problems, including chronic bronchitis, permanent hearing loss, sinusitis, asthma, and emphysema.

Antihistamines, decongestants, bronchodilators, and anti-inflammatory nasal sprays are commonly used to treat the symptoms of respiratory allergies. Many children also receive medication through aerosol breathing treatments. Although these medications provide effective control of symptoms, the relief is only temporary. Children taking antihistamines and decongestants often experience drowsiness, difficulty concentrating, and excessive thirst and should, therefore, be supervised closely, especially during outdoor times or when activities involve greater risk. Some children also experience restlessness or agitation from their medications. These side effects make it particularly difficult for children to pay attention and to learn, especially if the medications are prescribed for an extended period. Teachers must observe these children carefully and discuss any concerns about the medication's effectiveness or side effects with the child's family. Sometimes a different medication with fewer side effects can be prescribed.

 CAUTION

Teachers should always obtain approval from the child's physician and receive proper training before administering aerosol breathing treatments or any other form of medication therapy.

In some cases, allergy shots (desensitization therapy) are given when other treatments have been unsuccessful in controlling the child's symptoms. Although children may experience some improvement, the full effect can take 12 to 18 months to achieve.

Most allergic conditions are not considered to be life threatening. However, bee stings, medications, and certain foods can lead to a condition known as **anaphylaxis** in children who have a severe allergic reaction to these substances (Table 4–3)

 **CAUTION**

An ambulance should be called at once if anaphylaxis occurs.

TABLE 4–3 Symptoms of Anaphylaxis

Life-threatening symptoms can develop suddenly and include:
• wheezing or difficulty breathing
• swelling of the lips, tongue, throat, and/or eyelids
• itching and hives
• nausea, vomiting, and/or diarrhea
• anxiety and restlessness
• blue discoloration around the mouth and nail beds

symptomatic control – *treatment that controls symptoms but does not cure the condition.*
anaphylaxis – *a severe allergic reaction that may cause difficulty breathing, itching, unconsciousness, and possible death.*

FIGURE 4–2   An EpiPen auto-injector.

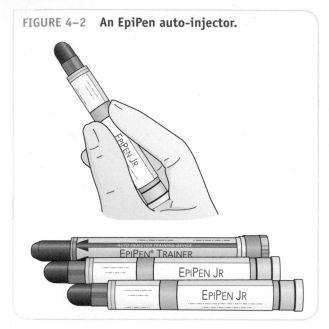

▶❚❚ **TeachSource** Video Connections

Promoting Children's Health: Teacher Takes Care of Child with Asthma

Many children struggle with allergen sensitivities and asthma. The smaller size of their airway makes breathing especially difficult during an attack, so it is important that teachers be prepared to respond. As you watch the learning video, *Promoting Children's Health: Teacher Takes Care of Child with Asthma*, consider the following questions:

1. What symptoms led the teacher to believe the child was experiencing an asthma attack?

2. What events may have triggered the attack?

3. Why didn't the teacher insist that the child use his medicated inhaler immediately?

4. What steps had the teacher taken to prepare herself in the event the child might experience an asthma attack?

Watch on CourseMate.

(Ercan et al., 2012). This life-threatening response requires urgent medical attention because it causes the body to go into shock and the air passages to swell closed.

Children who have a history of severe allergic reactions may keep an EpiPen at school. EpiPens are an auto-injecting device that administers a single dose of epinephrine when quickly pressed against the skin (usually the upper thigh) (Figure 4–2) (Nguyen et al., 2012). However, it is essential that emergency medical assistance also be summoned immediately because this medication provides only temporary relief.

The emotional effect that allergies can have on the quality of children's and families' lives cannot be overlooked. Families may overprotect children or subject them to frequent reminders to avoid offending allergens. Some children may also be sensitive about their appearance—frequent sneezing, runny nose, rashes, red and swollen eyes—along with feeling moody, irritable, or even depressed. In other cases, severe allergies may limit a child's participation in physical activity. Collectively, these feelings can lead to fear, withdrawal, poor self-esteem, and other maladjustment problems if children's allergies are not addressed in a positive manner.

It is also important that children not be allowed to use their allergies as a means for gaining attention or special privileges. Instead, adults can help children become more independent and self-confident in coping with their health problems. Teachers can often help children make simple adjustments in their daily lifestyles so they can lead a more normal, healthy life. Families may also need additional support and guidance. They may benefit from parenting classes, individual counseling, and community groups that will help them to understand the child's condition and ways to foster self-management and self-esteem. Local clinics and hospitals may also offer special classes to help families and children learn to cope with allergic disease.

4-2b Asthma

Asthma is both a chronic and acute respiratory disease that affects over seven million children and is a primary cause of school absenteeism (CDC, 2013a). It is a form of allergic response that is most often seen in children who also have other allergic conditions. Like allergies, asthma tends to be an inherited tendency that can become progressively worse without treatment. Children who are overweight or obese, especially males, are at increased risk for developing asthma. Excess weight further compromises their health and participation in physical activity (Yao et al., 2012).

Numerous theories are being investigated to determine why the incidence of asthma is increasing at such an alarming rate. Researchers are looking at multiple factors, including vitamin D deficiency, exposure to indoor and outdoor pollutants, early infant feeding practices, and stress (Bener et al., 2012). Mothers are encouraged to breastfeed and to withhold solid foods until infants reach 6 months of age to decrease the potential risk of food and respiratory allergies. Women are also being urged to not smoke during pregnancy or to expose infants to second-hand smoke after they are born; infants born to mothers who smoke are more likely to develop asthma (Accordini et al., 2012). Recent studies have also found the rate of asthma to be significantly higher among children of minority backgrounds and those living in poverty (Holt, Theall, & Rabito, 2013). Factors known to trigger acute asthma attacks include:

Did You Know...
that you breathe in approximately 6 teaspoons of airborne particles (e.g., formaldehyde and other organic chemicals, dust, smoke, mold spores, pet dander) every day?

- airborne allergens, such as pollen, animal dander, dust, molds, perfumes, cleaning chemicals, paint, ozone, cockroaches (Laumbach & Kipen, 2012)
- foods, such as nuts, wheat, milk, eggs
- second-hand cigarette smoke
- respiratory infections, such as colds and bronchitis
- stress (especially anger) and fatigue
- changes in temperature or weather, such as cold, rain, or wind
- vigorous exercise (Del Giacco, Carlsen, & Toit, 2012).

Signs and Symptoms   Acute asthma attacks are characterized by episodes of wheezing, coughing, and labored breathing (especially exhalation) caused by spasms, swelling, and excess mucus production in the respiratory tract (bronchial tubes) (Figure 4–3). As a result, the child may become anxious and develop a bluish discoloration around the lips and nail beds due to insufficient oxygen. Many children outgrow acute asthma attacks as the size of their air passageways increases with age.

Management   Asthma treatment is aimed at identifying and removing any substance(s) from the child's environment that are known to trigger an attack. In cases where complete removal is not feasible, as with dust or pollen, steps can be taken to limit the child's exposure. For example, it may be necessary to remove carpeting and to dust and vacuum a child's environment daily to address an airborne allergy. Replacing furnace filters on a regular basis or installing an electrostatic air purifier will also help to remove offending particles from the air. Adults should avoid smoking around children and limit the use of chemicals such as cleaning supplies, paints, and fragrances. Some families choose to enroll children who have asthma in smaller-sized early childhood programs where the environment can be monitored more closely and exposure to respiratory infections may be lower. Medications, such as anti-inflammatory drugs and bronchodilators, may be administered in the form of an inhaler or nebulizer breathing treatment to decrease swelling and open air passages.

A meeting should always be arranged with the family when a child with asthma is first enrolled. This enables the teacher to better understand the child's condition—what symptoms the child shows; what substances are likely to trigger an attack; what, when, and how medications are to be administered; and, what emergency actions are needed (Teacher Checklists 4-2 and 4-3). This information should be written down, posted where teachers can access it quickly, and reviewed frequently with the child's family to note any changes.

If weather triggers an attack, it may be advisable to keep a child indoors on days when abrupt temperature changes occur. However, children should be encouraged to participate in regular activities as much as their condition permits. If asthma attacks are caused by strenuous play, teachers should

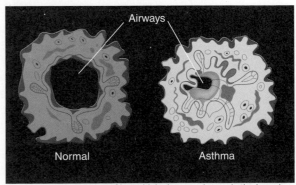

FIGURE 4–3   Swelling and excess mucus in the airways make breathing difficult during an asthma attack.

An artist's representation of bronchial tubes, or airways in the lung, in cross section. The normal airway, left, is open. The airway affected by asthma, right, is almost completely closed off. The allergic reaction characteristic of asthma causes swelling, excess mucus production, and muscle constriction in the airways, leading to coughing, wheezing, and difficult breathing.

From http://www.niaid.nih.gov

TEACHER CHECKLIST 4-2

Strategies for Managing Children's Asthma Attacks

- If you know that certain substances trigger a child's attack, remove the child from the environment (cold air, fumes).
- Encourage the child to remain quiet. Do not leave the child alone.
- Allow the child to assume a position that makes breathing easier; sitting upright is usually preferred.
- Administer any medications prescribed for the child.
- Offer small sips of room-temperature liquids (not cold).
- Contact the child's family if there is no relief from medications or if the family requests to be notified in the event of an attack.
- Do not delay calling for emergency medical assistance if the child shows any signs of struggling to breathe, fatigue, anxiety, restlessness, blue discoloration of the nail beds or lips, or loss of consciousness.
- Record your observations—child's condition prior to, during, and following an attack, factors that appeared to trigger the attack, medications administered, and that parents were contacted.
- Stay calm; this helps to put the child at ease and makes breathing easier.

TeachSource Digital Download   Download from CourseMate.

monitor children's activity level and encourage them to rest or to play quietly until the symptoms subside. In any event, teachers should always be prepared to respond quickly in the event that a child develops any difficulty breathing. (See Chapter 9.)

4-2c Anemia

Anemia is a common blood disorder that develops when too few red blood cells are available to deliver oxygen to the body's cells. This can be caused by a significant blood loss, decreased production of red blood cells, or their abnormal destruction. Approximately 15 percent of all children under age 5 years of age experience iron-deficiency anemia; however, this rate is greater than 22 percent among black children (CDC, 2012b). Insufficient food and unhealthy dietary patterns place many young children at risk for developing this disorder. Additional causes include:

- deficient nutrient intake (iron, folic acid, B-12)
- hereditary disorders, such as sickle cell disease
- chronic infections, such as hepatitis and HIV
- some forms of cancer, such as leukemia
- radiation, chemotherapy, and some medications
- chemical exposure, such as lead poisoning

TEACHER CHECKLIST 4-3

Children with Allergies and Asthma

- Be familiar with the symptoms of a child's allergic reaction.
- Keep children's emergency information located where it is readily accessible; make sure that others know where to find it.
- Post emergency telephone numbers next to the telephone.
- Know where emergency medications are stored and learn how to administer them.
- Review your program's emergency policies and procedures.
- Monitor all food or other allergen sources (e.g., animals, plants, lotions, cleaning supplies) that are brought into the classroom.
- Have the family review and update information about the child's condition periodically.

TeachSource Digital Download   Download from CourseMate.

It is important to understand that anemia is not itself a disease but a symptom of some other condition that requires medical attention. In the majority of cases, anemia is a temporary condition caused by nutrient deficiencies in the child's diet, especially iron intake, and is relatively easy to treat (Black et al., 2012).

Signs and Symptoms Excessive fatigue is a classic symptom of anemia and is caused by the lack of oxygen that cells receive. However, it may be difficult to recognize the signs of anemia because the body is often able to compensate for low oxygen levels in the early stages. Common signs that may be observed as anemia progresses include:

▼ Many children develop anemia due to food insufficiency or unhealthy eating habits.

© Cengage Learning

- pale skin color; blue discoloration of nail beds
- irritability
- complaints of feeling cold
- rapid heart beat
- dizziness or headache
- shortness of breath
- decline in school performance
- difficulty concentrating
- loss of appetite
- swollen or sore tongue
- failure to grow

Not every child will experience all of these signs and may present others depending on the underlying cause. Diagnosis requires a complete medical examination and blood tests to determine red blood cell count. For this reason, any concern about a child's health and vitality should be evaluated by a health care professional.

CONNECTING TO EVERYDAY PRACTICE

Childhood Asthma

It is 10 AM and six children are lined up on small plastic chairs in the director's office at the Wee Care 4 Kids Child Care Center. Steam hisses from clear plastic masks being held by older children over their noses and mouths while a teacher assists those who are still too young to manage the procedure alone. All of these children have one thing in common—asthma. Twice each day, teachers must administer nebulizer breathing treatments to increasing numbers of young children who suffer from frequent wheezing. Unfortunately, this scene is not uncommon in many schools today, as the reported incidence of childhood asthma continues to soar.

Think About This:

- What is asthma, and why are the numbers of children with this condition increasing?
- Why does the incidence of asthma appear to be higher among minorities and children living in poverty?
- Should teachers be responsible for administering medical procedures to children?
- What would you do if you observed a teacher administering a nebulizer treatment incorrectly?

Management Treatment for anemia is determined by the cause. If the child's diet is deficient, vitamin supplementation may be prescribed along with modifications in daily nutrient intake (Black et al., 2012). If the anemia is due to chronic infection, antibiotics may be prescribed. Anemia caused by lead toxicity is often successfully treated by eliminating exposure to lead sources and correcting the child's diet. Children with high lead levels may require additional medication therapy. In extreme cases, blood transfusion, surgery, or bone marrow transplant may be necessary.

It is important that families keep teachers informed about their child's condition and treatments so that similar adjustments can be made at school. Any special dietary requirements should be addressed during meal planning. Children may need to be given additional opportunities to rest during the day or to participate in less physically demanding activities. Because anemia reduces children's ability to resist infection, frequent hand washing and cleaning practices are important to implement. Teachers should also monitor children's play more closely, as fatigue, low energy, and lack of concentration may increase their vulnerability to unintentional injury.

4-2d Childhood Cancers

Childhood cancers are the leading cause of death from disease among children 0 to 14 years of age, with over 11,200 new cases diagnosed each year (National Cancer Institute, 2012). Young children (1–4 years) have the highest incidence of newly reported cases. Adolescents (15 to 19 years) experience the highest death rate due to leukemia, whereas children (5–9 years) have the highest death rate from brain tumors.

The term "childhood cancer" is used inclusively in reference to a broad range of cancer types. Most often, cancers target areas of children's bodies that are undergoing rapid growth, such as the circulatory (blood) system, brain, bones, and kidneys. Leukemia (a cancer of the blood and bone marrow) is more common in boys and accounts for approximately 34 percent of all childhood cancers, followed by brain and central nervous system tumors (American Cancer Society, 2012). Numerous causes, including environmental chemicals, radioactivity, and prenatal conditions, continue to be investigated although conclusive evidence remains limited to date. Some children appear to be at higher risk for developing cancer, especially those who have HIV infections, parents who smoke, or certain genetic disorders such as Down syndrome (Milne et al., 2012).

Signs and Symptoms Although childhood cancers are relatively rare, families should never hesitate to seek medical consultation if they have concerns. Many symptoms are unique to a specific form of cancer, while others are more general and easily mistaken for common infectious illnesses, such as the flu. Early warning signs can include:

- loss of appetite, unexplained weight loss
- excessive fatigue that doesn't improve with rest
- painful joints
- unusual bruising, bleeding gums, or small broken blood vessels under the skin
- night sweats or fever
- enlarged glands (in neck, armpits, or groin)
- frequent infections
- persistent headaches
- unexplained cough or difficult breathing
- lumps or masses
- unusual colored urine
- seizures

In most cases, children who present these symptoms will not have cancer. However, medical evaluation should be sought if symptoms appear suddenly or if they persist or cause the child unusual discomfort. Early diagnosis significantly improves recovery and survival.

Management Advances in diagnosis and treatment have resulted in dramatic improvements in children's survival rates. Many children are able to return to school after they have completed and recovered from their treatments. However, this transition requires careful planning and coordination between the child's family, doctors, and school personnel (Herrmann et al., 2011). Children may be sensitive about changes in their appearance, such as surgical scars or hair loss resulting from chemotherapy and radiation treatments. Weight loss or gain, fatigue, pain, and generalized weakness may make it difficult for children to participate fully in class activities. Extra precautions must be taken to protect children from communicable illnesses and other infectious conditions because their immune systems are often compromised by chemotherapy and radiation therapies. Children's hearing may also be affected by radiation treatments to the head or high doses of antibiotics that have been administered to fight infection.

▼ Children's return to school following treatment is an important step in their recovery process.

© Cengage Learning

Children's return to school is an important step in helping them to resume a near normal lifestyle. Peer interactions can also be beneficial for boosting children's morale and self-esteem. However, teachers must work closely with families to better understand the child's limitations and any adjustments that may be needed (Brown et al., 2011). If there are medications to be administered, proper forms and signatures must be obtained. In some cases, children may have an IEP, IFSP, or IHSP to assist with additional services and resources.

It is highly likely that teachers will encounter children who have, or are recovering from, cancer as treatment success rates continue to improve. Teachers can use these opportunities to better understand childhood cancers and, in turn, help all children learn about these conditions, accept children with differences, and discover ways to support their peers (Teacher Checklist 4-4). Initially, children may be apprehensive about a classmate whose appearance and/or ability to play may have changed. Preparing children in advance and encouraging them to talk about their concerns can reduce or even eliminate some of these feelings. The American Cancer Society (www.cancer.org) provides information with a user-friendly approach, designed to inform and assist families in their efforts to cope with this disease. Although the site is geared toward families, teachers will find much of the information useful. Visit the American Cancer Society's website and search for "Children diagnosed with cancer: Returning to school."

✓✓ TEACHER CHECKLIST 4-4

Children with Cancer

- Maintain close communication with the child's family. Ask what they want other children to know about their child's condition.
- Post children's emergency contact information in a designated location where it is readily accessible to school personnel.
- Determine what, if any, accommodations are needed when the child returns to school, such as dietary modifications, a place to rest, or a change in seating arrangement.
- Review and implement sanitation and hand washing practices.
- Adjust activities and expectations to acknowledge children's limitations, e.g., short attention span, memory problems, learning difficulties, and low energy.
- Secure any additional resources and services children may need to be successful.

TeachSource Digital Download Download from CourseMate.

4-2e Diabetes

Diabetes is a chronic disease that occurs when the body is unable to produce insulin or to use it efficiently. Insulin is a **hormone** required for the metabolism of carbohydrates (sugars and starches) and the storage and release of glucose (blood sugar) for energy. Type 1 diabetes is a chronic, incurable, and often hereditary condition that typically develops in young children when their pancreas fails to produce insulin. Type 2 diabetes, often referred to as adult-onset or insulin-resistant diabetes, results when an insufficient amount of insulin is produced or cells in the body are unable to use the insulin properly.

> **Did You Know...**
>
> that today's children will be the first generation to have a shorter life expectancy than their parents due to obesity and its associated health complications?

Approximately 1 out of every 400 children is diagnosed with diabetes, particularly type 2. However, this number is reaching epidemic proportions as childhood obesity rates continue to climb (Boney, 2012). At present, roughly 10 percent of children ages 2 to 5 years and 30 percent of children ages 6 to 17 are considered to be overweight (American Diabetes Association, 2011). Obesity and inactivity place children and adults at high risk for developing type 2 diabetes. Additional factors include having a family history of the disease, being born to a mother who experienced **gestational diabetes**, and ethnicity (Baptiste-Roberts, Nicholson, & Wang, 2012). Minority groups, particularly Native Americans, Hispanic/Latinos, and African Americans experience diabetes at a rate that is more than twice that of Caucasian populations (Gonzalez, 2012).

Signs and Symptoms It is important that teachers be familiar with the signs, symptoms, and treatment of diabetes because the number of children with diabetes continues to increase. Successful management of childhood diabetes requires careful monitoring and regulation, both of which can prove challenging given children's irregular eating habits, frequent respiratory infections, and unpredictable growth and activity levels (Hockenberry & Wilson, 2012).

When insulin is absent or the amount produced is insufficient, glucose continues to circulate freely in the bloodstream instead of being stored as glycogen in the liver. This causes a condition known as **hyperglycemia** and is responsible for the early signs associated with type 1 diabetes. If the condition is not identified and treated promptly, it can lead to serious complications including coma and death. The onset of type 1 diabetes in children is usually abrupt, and includes symptoms such as:

- rapid weight loss
- fatigue and/or weakness
- nausea or vomiting
- frequent urination
- **dehydration**
- excessive thirst and/or hunger
- dry, itchy skin
- blurred vision

Symptoms associated with type 2 diabetes are similar, but they tend to develop more slowly and over a longer period of time.

Management Teachers must be aware of each child's individualized situation and treatment regimen—whether the child has type 1 or type 2 diabetes, what dietary restrictions are

---

hormone – *special chemical substance produced by endocrine glands that influences and regulates certain body functions.*

gestational diabetes – *a form of diabetes that occurs only during pregnancy; affects the way the mother's body utilizes sugars in foods and increases health risks for the baby.*

hyperglycemia – *a condition characterized by an abnormally high level of sugar in the blood.*

dehydration – *a state in which there is an excessive loss of body fluids or extremely limited fluid intake. Symptoms may include loss of skin tone, sunken eyes, and mental confusion.*

required, and what medical treatments (urine testing, insulin injections, medications) must be administered. Children who have type 1 diabetes must be given insulin injections several times each day, have their glucose levels checked, and closely regulate their diet and activity. Insulin pumps are increasingly being used in children to replace the need for daily injections (Pickup, 2012). Children with type 2 diabetes are usually able to regulate their condition through careful dietary management and/or medications that help their bodies utilize glucose. Increasing children's activity level has proven effective in reducing the risk of developing type 2 diabetes and also in improving its management (Matyka & Annan, 2012). Teachers must also become familiar with the signs of complications associated with diabetes in addition to learning about children's treatment regimens. For example, a child who receives an insulin dose that is too large or too small will exhibit different symptoms and require quite different emergency care. (See the Teacher Checklist "Signs and Symptoms of Hyperglycemia and Hypoglycemia" in Chapter 9.)

Arrangements should be made to meet with the families of children who are diabetic before they begin to attend school or an out-of-home program. Families can provide teachers with valuable information about their child's condition and how to identify changes in behavior and appearance that may signal an impending complication (Perry, Engelke, & Swanson, 2012). Teachers should also be made aware of dietary restrictions and receive instructions on how to implement medical procedures while the child attends school. Plans for handling medical emergencies must also be worked out with families ahead of time and reviewed often.

▼ **Children with diabetes type 1 must follow special dietary restrictions.**

© Cengage Learning

When teachers are familiar with children's condition and management plans, they are better prepared to respond efficiently and effectively to diabetic emergencies (Teacher Checklist 4-5). This can be reassuring for families who may be reluctant to leave children in the care of others. Teachers are also in a unique position to help diabetic children accept and manage their condition and to help their peers learn more about diabetes (Table 4–4).

✔✔ *TEACHER CHECKLIST 4-5*

Children with Diabetes

- Meet with the family regularly to review the child's progress and treatment procedures.
- Be familiar with the symptoms of hypoglycemia (low blood sugar) and hyperglycemia (high blood sugar) and know how to respond.
- Keep children's emergency information where it is readily accessible; make sure others also know where to find this information.
- Post emergency numbers near the telephone.
- Know where emergency medications are stored and learn how to administer them. Also learn how to check children's blood sugar and train additional staff members to perform these tests.
- Be mindful of any changes in meal schedules, length of outdoor play, or impromptu field trips that might affect the child's insulin needs.
- Note signs of impending illness or infection and notify the child's family.
- Review your program's emergency policies and procedures.

TABLE 4–4   Coping Strategies for Children Who Have Diabetes

Teachers can be instrumental in helping children:

- learn about their diabetes in simple terms and not to be ashamed, afraid, or embarrassed about the condition
- maintain a nutritious diet and understand the critical relationship between healthy eating habits and well-being
- learn to enjoy a variety of physical activities
- assist with their own medical management, e.g., practice careful hand washing before glucose tests (finger sticks), cleansing the injection site, or caring for an injury
- participate in opportunities that build positive self-esteem.

4-2f Eczema

Eczema is a chronic inflammatory skin condition. Early symptoms usually appear in infants and children younger than 5, and affect 10 to12 percent of all children (Hockenberry & Wilson, 2012). Eczema often disappears or significantly improves between the ages of 5 and 15 years in approximately 50 percent of affected children.

Signs and Symptoms   Eczema is caused by an abnormal immune system response and is commonly associated with allergies, especially to certain foods (e.g., eggs, wheat, and milk) and substances that come in contact with the skin (e.g., wool, soaps, perfumes, disinfectants, and animal dander) (National Eczema Association, 2012). There is often a strong family history of allergy and similar skin problems.

Reddened patches of irritated skin may initially appear on an infant's or toddler's cheeks, forehead, scalp, or neck. Older children may develop dry, itchy, scaly areas on the knees, elbows, wrists, or back of hands. Repeated scratching of these areas can lead to open, weeping skin that is prone to infection. Weather changes can trigger an eczema flare-up or cause it to worsen, especially during summer heat or in winter cold when full-length clothing is likely to be worn. Older children may be self-conscious about their appearance and reluctant to wear short-sleeved clothing when warmer weather arrives.

Management   Eczema is not curable, but it can be controlled through a number of preventive measures. Eliminating environmental allergens is always the preferred and first line of defense. However, in some cases the offending substance may not yet be known. In other instances, the substance, such as dust or pollen, may be difficult to eliminate so that steps must be taken to reduce the child's exposure. Reminding children not to scratch irritated skin and keeping their skin moisturized, especially after bathing or washing, is also beneficial.

Avoiding exposure to extreme temperature changes can also be an effective measure for controlling eczema symptoms. Keeping children cool in warm weather prevents sweating, which can increase skin irritation. Reducing room temperatures, dressing infants and children in light clothing, and wiping warm areas of their body (creases in neck, elbow, knees, and face) with cool water can improve the child's comfort. Teachers may also be asked to administer antihistamines or topical cortisone ointments that the child's doctor has prescribed. Reducing children's exposure to stress and helping them to develop a healthy self-image are also important strategies for reducing flare-ups.

4-2g Excessive Fatigue

Most children enjoy an abundance of energy, stamina, enthusiasm, and curiosity for life. This state can be temporarily disrupted by growth spurts, delayed bedtimes, major family changes, recovery from a recent illness, or participation in too many activities that deprive children of essential sleep or increase the amount of sleep needed.

A small number of children experience periods of extreme daytime fatigue and listlessness due to existing health conditions or prolonged sleep disturbances (McCabe, 2011). Children who have developmental disabilities, including ADHD, autism, Down syndrome, and cerebral palsy experience a higher rate of disrupted or deficient sleep (Hatzinger et al., 2012). Sleep deprivation has been closely linked to a variety of learning problems, health conditions (obesity, heart disease, cancer), and unintentional injury (Knutson, 2012). The importance of sleep has been addressed in the *Healthy People 2020* initiative because it is so vital to an individual's well-being.

Signs and Symptoms Repeated or prolonged daytime fatigue is not considered a normal condition for young children and should be investigated because of its potentially negative effect on growth and development. Excessive or chronic fatigue may be an indication of other serious health problems, including:

- inadequate nutrition
- chronic infection, such as otitis media
- anemia
- **sleep apnea**
- allergies
- lead poisoning
- hepatitis
- **endocrine** (hormonal) disorders such as diabetes and thyroidism
- heart disorders
- anxiety

Management A thorough assessment of the child's personal habits and lifestyle may reveal an explanation for the undue fatigue. A complete medical examination may also be necessary to detect any existing health problems. If no specific medical cause can be identified, steps should be taken to improve the child's general well-being (Table 4–5). Often these measures can be incorporated into daily classroom routines and benefit all children.

4-2h Lead Poisoning

Lead poisoning continues to be a public health concern despite a continued decline in the numbers of children affected. Aggressive campaigns, legislation, and abatement programs have been successful in eliminating many common sources of lead contamination. The Centers for Disease Control and Prevention (CDC) estimates that approximately 500,000 U.S. children between 1 and 5 years of age have blood lead levels in excess of safety recommendations despite these efforts (CDC, 2013c). The CDC adopted new standards for lead poisoning in 2012 that significantly lowered acceptable blood levels from 10 to 5 micrograms (CDC, 2012a). Studies have shown that

---

TABLE 4–5 Strategies for Improving Excessive Fatigue in Children

- Help children develop healthy dietary habits.
- Encourage children to participate in moderate exercise, such as walking, swimming, playing ball, or riding bikes.
- Provide opportunities for improved sleep, such as earlier bedtimes, short daytime naps, or a quiet sleeping area away from activity.
- Arrange for alternating periods of active play and quiet times (e.g., reading a book, playing quietly with a favorite toy, listening to music).
- Reduce environmental stress.
- Help children build effective coping skills.

---

sleep apnea – *temporary interruptions or stoppages in breathing during sleep.*
endocrine – *refers to glands that produce substances called hormones that are secreted directly into the bloodstream.*

the old higher standard levels can interfere with children's health and cognitive development. The new guidelines will result in thousands of additional children who are likely to be identified as having lead poisoning.

Children living in poverty and inner city areas experience a high incidence of lead poisoning, although the condition is not limited exclusively to these populations. Many older houses and furniture pieces still contain lead-based paints, which legislation banned in 1978. Loose paint chips and paint dust released during house renovations can be inhaled or ingested when children put dirty hands into their mouths. Furthermore, many of these children consume unhealthy diets that actually increase lead absorption because they are high in fats and low in calcium, iron, and vitamin C (Khan, Ansari, & Khan, 2011). Inexpensive test kits can be obtained from local hardware stores to determine if lead-based paint is present on surfaces.

> ⚠️ **CAUTION**
>
> *Use care when purchasing used toys and furniture at garage sales, on the Internet, or from second-hand stores, as some of these items may contain lead-based paints.*

Signs and Symptoms Young children are especially vulnerable to lead poisoning. They frequently put toys and hands in their mouths, their bodies absorb lead more readily, and their developing brain and nervous systems are particularly sensitive to lead's harmful effects (Landrigan & Goldman, 2011). Lead accumulates in the child's bones, brain, tissues, and kidneys with repeated exposure, and is not eliminated.

Children with elevated levels of lead present a range of symptoms, including:

- irritability
- loss of appetite and nausea
- headaches
- unexplained abdominal pain, muscle aches
- constipation
- listlessness
- learning problems, short attention span, easily distracted, intellectual disabilities
- behavior problems, aggression, impulsivity

▼ **Children's nervous systems (including the brain) are especially vulnerable to the effects of lead poisoning.**

© Cengage Learning

Children younger than 6 years of age who are at risk for lead exposure should be tested if there is any concern about the symptoms they may be exhibiting.

Management Research has demonstrated that elevated levels of lead can lower a child's IQ by as much as 4 to 5 percent (Strayhorn & Strayhorn, 2012). Efforts to eliminate high blood lead concentrations in children continue to be a priority in the *Healthy People 2020* initiative. The CDC now recommends that all children, especially those at risk (including children who have immigrated to the United States), be screened for lead poisoning between 6 months and 6 years of age (CDC, 2013b). Teachers who have concerns about a child's physical complaints, behavior, or learning problems and believe there may be a risk of lead poisoning should encourage families to have their child tested.

Lead poisoning prevention requires that hazardous environmental sources be located and removed (Table 4–6). Early identification of children and their siblings who may also be affected by this condition is essential for halting further contamination, initiating treatment, and limiting lead's harmful effects on development. Children should be encouraged to practice frequent hand washing and to keep their hands and objects out of their mouths. Children who have significantly elevated blood lead levels may be treated with special medications and dietary modifications that increase their iron, calcium, and vitamin C intake. Unfortunately, there is little evidence to date suggesting that educational interventions can reverse or offer any improvement in children's behavior or learning problems if lead has already had damaging effects. Thus, public awareness and community education continue to be the most effective measures for combating this preventable condition.

4-2i Seizure Disorders

Many children in school settings experience **seizures**. At present, an estimated 325,000 children under age 15 have epilepsy (Epilepsy Foundation of America, 2012). Each year, an additional 120,000 children experience their first seizure, with more than half of these associated with high fever (febrile seizures). For some adults, the terms "seizures," "convulsions," or "epilepsy" cause feelings of considerable apprehension or fear. However, prior knowledge and planning can alleviate these feelings and enable teachers to respond with skill and confidence when caring for children who experience seizure disorders (Teacher Checklist 4-6).

Seizures are caused by a rush of abnormal electrical impulses in the brain that trigger involuntary or uncontrollable movements in different regions of the body. The intensity and location of this activity vary with the type of seizure involved. For example, some seizures result in only momentary attention lapses or interruptions of thought, while others may last several minutes and cause vigorous, spasmodic contractions involving the entire body. Temporary loss of consciousness, frothing, and loss of bowel and bladder control may also accompany some seizure types.

In many cases, a specific cause is never identified, although seizure disorders are more common in some families. Children who have certain developmental disabilities and genetic

TABLE 4–6 Common Sources of Environmental Lead

- old lead-based house paint (prior to 1978), including dust from remodeling projects
- soil contaminated by leaded gasoline emissions and old paint chips
- plastic mini blinds (manufactured before 1996, not made in the United States)
- contaminated drinking water (from lead solder in old water pipes)
- imported dishware and crystal
- folk remedies and medications
- imported toys and metallic trinkets; Mexican tamarind candies
- lead shot and fishing weights
- second-hand toys and furniture manufactured before 1978
- areas around lead smelters, oil drilling, and mining operations
- having a parent who works around motor vehicle batteries

seizures – *a temporary interruption of consciousness sometimes accompanied by convulsive movements.*

TEACHER CHECKLIST 4-6

Strategies for Working with Children Who Have a Seizure Disorder

1. Be aware of any children in the classroom who have a seizure disorder. Find out what the child's seizures are like, if medication is taken to control the seizures, and whether or not the child is limited in any way by the disorder.
2. Know emergency response measures. Develop guidelines for staff members to follow in the event that a child has a seizure; review the guidelines often.
3. Use the presence of a child with a seizure disorder as a learning opportunity for other children. Provide simple explanations about what seizures are; encourage children to ask questions and to express their feelings. Help children learn to accept others who have special conditions.
4. Gain a better understanding of epilepsy and seizure disorders. Read books and articles, view films, and talk with health professionals and families.
5. Obtain and read the following books and pamphlets written for children. Share them with children in the classroom.

   - Baltaro, E. (2010). *Karen's Epilepsy.*
   - Gosselin, K. (2002). *Taking Seizure Disorders to School: A Story about Epilepsy.*
   - Lears, L. (2002). *Becky the Brave: A Story about Epilepsy.*
   - Rocheford, D. (2009). *Mommy, I Feel Funny! A Child's Experience with Epilepsy.*
   - Zelenka, Y. (2008). *Let's Learn with Teddy about Epilepsy.*

TeachSource Digital Download Download from CourseMate.

syndromes are also at higher risk for developing seizures. Other conditions known to initiate seizure activity in young children include:

- fevers that are high or rise rapidly (especially in infants)
- brain damage
- infections that affect the central nervous system, such as meningitis or encephalitis
- tumors
- head injuries
- lead, mercury, and carbon monoxide poisoning
- hypoglycemia (low blood sugar)
- medication reactions

Signs and Symptoms Seizures are generally classified according to the pattern of symptoms a child presents, with the most common types being:

- febrile
- absence (previously known as petit mal)
- partial seizures (previously called focal)
- generalized or tonic-clonic (formerly called grand mal)

Approximately 3 to 5 percent of infants and children between the ages of 6 months and 5 years experience *febrile seizures,* with the majority of incidences occurring between 6 and 12 months of age (National Institute of Neurological Disorders & Stroke, 2012). Febrile seizures are thought to be triggered by a high fever, and may cause a child to temporarily lose consciousness and experience involuntary jerking movements involving the entire body. The child's seizures typically end once the fever subsides and, thus, are not thought to be serious or to result in any permanent damage.

Teachers may be the first to notice the subtle, abnormal behaviors exhibited by children with *absence seizures.* This type of seizure is characterized by momentary lapses of attention that may be observed as:

- repeated incidences of day dreaming
- staring off into space
- a blank appearance
- brief fluttering of the eyes

❱ temporary interruption of speech or activity
❱ twitching or dropping of objects

Absence seizures occur most commonly in children 4 to 10 years of age and cause a momentary loss of consciousness that lasts less than 20 seconds. Children may abruptly stop an activity and resume it almost as quickly once the seizure subsides. They also are unlikely to recall what has occurred. Teachers should report their observations to the family and encourage them to consult with the child's physician unless the condition has already been diagnosed.

Partial seizures, the most common form of seizure disorder, are characterized by involuntary movements that range from momentary muscle weakness to unusual behaviors such as lip smacking, arm waving, or hysterical laughter to convulsive tremors affecting the entire body. The child may or may not lose consciousness during the seizure and may have no recall of the event when it is over.

Rhythmic, jerky movements involving the entire body are characteristic of *generalized* or *tonic-clonic seizures*. Some children experience an aura or warning immediately before a seizure begins. This warning may be in the form of a specific sound, smell, taste, sensation, or visual cue. Sudden rigidity or stiffness (tonic phase) is followed by a loss of consciousness and uncontrollable muscular contractions or tremors (clonic phase). When the seizure ends, children may awaken briefly, appear confused, and complain of a headache or dizziness before falling asleep from exhaustion, but they will not remember the event.

Management Most seizures can be controlled with medication. It is vital that children take their medications every day, even after seizures are under control. Children may initially experience undesirable side effects to these drugs, such as drowsiness, nausea, and dizziness, but the problems tend to disappear with time. Children should be monitored closely by their physician to ensure that prescribed medications and dosages continue to be effective in controlling seizure activity and do not interfere with learning.

Whenever a child experiences a seizure, families should be notified. If the nature of the seizures changes, or if they begin to recur after having been under control, families should be encouraged to consult the child's physician. Teachers should also complete a brief, written report documenting their observations during the seizure and place it into the child's permanent health file (Teacher Checklist 4-7). This information may also be useful to the child's physician for diagnosing a seizure disorder and evaluating current medical treatments.

Teachers play an important role in facilitating the inclusion of children with seizure disorders in classrooms (West et al., 2013). They must work closely with families to develop a seizure action plan that includes information about the nature of children's seizures, medications, activity limitations, first aid measures to be taken (see Chapter 9), and when emergency medical personnel should be summoned. Careful attention should be given to arranging indoor and outdoor environments so they are safe and encourage children's full participation. Teachers can build

---

✓✓ *TEACHER CHECKLIST 4-7*

Information to Include in a Child's Seizure Report

- child's name
- date and time the seizure occurred
- events preceding the seizure
- how long the seizure lasted
- nature and location of convulsive movements (affected body parts)
- child's condition during the seizure, e.g., difficulty breathing, loss of bladder or bowel control, change in skin color (pallor, blue discoloration)
- child's condition following the seizure, e.g., any injuries, complaints of headache, difficulty with speech or memory, desire to sleep
- name of person who observed and who prepared the report

children's confidence and self-esteem by helping them to accept and to cope with their seizure disorder. They can also use the opportunity to teach all children about seizures and to encourage healthy attitudes toward people who may experience them. A teacher's own reactions and displays of genuine acceptance are especially important for teaching children about understanding and respect for persons with special health conditions.

4-2j Sickle Cell Disease

Sickle cell disease is an inherited disorder that interferes with the red blood cells' ability to carry oxygen (Hockenberry & Wilson, 2012). Approximately 1 in every 500 African-American infants and 1 in every 36,000 Hispanic-American infants will be born with this genetic disorder (SCDAA, 2012). Individuals of Mediterranean, Middle Eastern, and Latin American descent also have the sickle cell gene. Approximately 10 percent of African Americans have the trait for sickle cell disease but do not necessarily develop the disorder; these people are referred to as carriers. When both parents have the sickle cell trait, some of their children may be born with the actual disease, while others may be carriers.

Signs and Symptoms The abnormal formation of red blood cells in sickle cell anemia causes a range of chronic health problems for the child. Red blood cells develop in the shape of a comma or sickle rather than their characteristic round shape (Figure 4–4). As a result, blood flow slows throughout the body and occasionally becomes obstructed. Symptoms of the disease do not usually appear until sometime after the child's first birthday.

Clumping of deformed blood cells results in periods of acute illness called *crisis*. A crisis can be triggered by infection, injury, strenuous exercise, dehydration, exposure to temperature extremes (hot or cold) or, in some cases, for no known reason. Symptoms of a sickle cell crisis include fever, swelling of the hands or feet, severe abdominal and leg pain, vomiting, and ulcers (sores) on the arms and legs. Children are usually hospitalized during a crisis, but they may be free of acute symptoms between flare-ups. Children who have sickle cell disease are also at high risk for having a stroke, which is characterized by muscle weakness, difficulty speaking, and/or seizures (Gladwin & Sachdev, 2012). In addition, chronic infection and anemia may cause children to be small for their age, irritable, fatigued, and at risk for cognitive delays (Scantlebury et al., 2011). They are also more susceptible to infections, a fact that families should consider when placing young children in group care.

Management At present there is no known cure for sickle cell disease. Genetic counseling can assist prospective parents who are carriers in determining their probability of having a child with this condition. Hospitals in many states are beginning to screen newborns for the disease before they are sent home. Early diagnosis and medical intervention can help to lessen the frequency and severity of crises and also reduce mortality. Several new drugs are being tested for use with children but final approval has not yet been granted. Children may be given daily antibiotics to reduce the risk of infections, which are a common cause of death. Studies have also shown that frequent blood transfusions are helpful in preventing acute crises (Bruce & Adams, 2012).

Children who have sickle cell disease are living longer today as the result of improved diagnosis and treatments. Although children may appear to be perfectly normal between acute episodes, they often experience a high rate of absenteeism due to flare-ups, infections, and respiratory illnesses, which can interfere with their developmental and academic progress. Illness and pain may also disrupt children's intake of essential dietary nutrients. Children with sickle cell disease are eligible for special education services (under IDEA) and teachers can initiate the process. When teachers understand this disease and its effects on children's health, they can work collaboratively with families and intervention personnel to help children cope with the condition and continue to progress in school (Teacher Checklist 4-8).

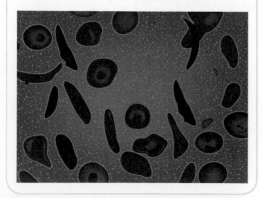

FIGURE 4–4 Normal and abnormal blood cells in sickle cell disease.

TEACHER CHECKLIST 4-8

Children with Sickle Cell Disease

- Meet with the family regularly to review the child's progress and treatment procedures.
- Be familiar with the symptoms of acute complications, such as fever, pain, difficulty breathing, or signs of a stroke (muscle weakness, difficulty speaking, or seizures).
- Keep children's emergency information in a place where it is readily accessible; make sure that others know where to find this information.
- Post emergency telephone numbers near the telephone.
- Collaborate with the child's family and provide learning materials that can be used at home.
- Maintain strict sanitation procedures (e.g., hand washing, sanitizing of surfaces and materials) in the classroom to protect children from unnecessary infections.
- Monitor the child's physical activity and provide frequent rest periods to avoid fatigue.
- Protect the child from temperature extremes (heat or cold); arrange for the child to stay indoors when conditions are not favorable.
- Encourage children to eat a nutritious diet and drink adequate fluids. (Allow them to use the restroom whenever necessary.)
- Review your program's emergency policies and procedures.

TeachSource Digital Download   Download from CourseMate.

Did You Get It?

Although accidents are the leading overall cause of child mortality, the majority of disease-related deaths among children are due to:

- **a.** heart disease
- **b.** infection
- **c.** cancer
- **d.** allergic reactions

Take the full quiz on CourseMate.

PARTNERING with FAMILIES

Children with Medical Conditions and Physical Activity

Dear Parents,

Participation in physical activity every day has untold benefits for children and adults. It provides significant health benefits and promotes children's motor development, problem-solving abilities, communication skills, socialization, and self-esteem. Daily activity also has positive effects on children's mental health and serves as an ideal outlet for releasing excess energy and frustration. Vigorous activity also improves children's appetite, sleep, weight control, and brain function by increasing blood flow and oxygen.

Children's diseases and medical conditions need not serve as barriers to participation in physical activity. In many cases, physical activity improves children's quality of life and treatment regimes. Talk with your child's doctor to determine what types of physical activity are appropriate and if there are any health restrictions. And, most importantly, do fun things together with your children.

- Encourage children to try a variety of different activities to find those they enjoy and are most likely to continue. Team activities provide opportunities for competition, whereas individual activities allow children to progress and experience challenge at their own pace.

- Be a positive role model. If you are active, children are more likely to follow your lead.

- Provide appropriate equipment; if necessary, modify equipment to children's functional abilities.

(continued)

PARTNERING with FAMILIES

Children with Medical Conditions and Physical Activity   *(continued)*

▶ Make sure play areas (especially public playgrounds) and equipment are safe for children's use.

▶ Monitor and supervise children's play closely; provide clear, simple instructions for playing safely and encourage their creativity.

▶ Know what limitations a child's health condition may present, and be prepared to respond if an emergency should occur.

▶ Continue to advocate for safe, accessible play grounds and public recreational facilities that are designed for all children.

CLASSROOM CORNER

Teacher Activities

Everyone Is Special

(PreK–2, National Health Education Standard 1.2.2)

Concept: People may be different, but everyone is special.

Learning Objectives

▶ Children will learn that people are more alike than different.

▶ Children will learn why it is important to show others respect.

Supplies: unbreakable mirror; sheets of white paper; crayons or markers; shoebox and magazine pictures of children (different ethnicities and abilities); ball of string or yarn

Learning Activities

▶ Read and discuss any of the following books about children who have special qualities:
  - *Taking Cerebral Palsy to School* by M. Anderson and T. Dineen (cerebral palsy)
  - *That's What Friends Do* by K. Cave (general)
  - *Someone Special, Just Like You* by Tricia Brown (general disabilities)
  - *Be Quiet, Marina!* by Kristen De Bear (cerebral palsy, Down syndrome)
  - *Listen for the Bus: David's Story* by P. McMahon (vision and hearing impaired)
  - *It's Okay to Be Different* by T. Parr (general)
  - *Russ and the Firehouse* by J. E. Rickert (Down syndrome)
  - *Mommy, I Feel Funny! A Child's Experience with Epilepsy* by D. Rocheford (epilepsy)
  - *A Book of Friends* by D. Ross (diversity)
  - *Andy and His Yellow Frisbee* by M. Thompson (autism)
  - *Susan Laughs* by Jeanne Willis (wheelchair)

Ask children to help you describe the word respect. Have them suggest other words that mean the same thing (e.g., being kind, treating a person kindly, doing things together, not making fun of a person).

▶ Have children sit in a circle. Give the first child a ball of string or yarn; ask him to name something special about the person sitting next to him. The first child should hold onto the end of the yarn and pass the ball to the person he has just described. Continue around the circle with each child describing something about the person sitting next to her and holding onto the string as it is passed to the next child. When everyone has had a turn, explain how the string illustrates that we are all connected by many of the same qualities and the things we need or like to do. (We are all different, but everyone is special.)

(continued)

CLASSROOM CORNER

Teacher Activities   *(continued)*

▶ As a group, make a list of things that everybody likes and needs (e.g., food, sleeping, playing, having friends).

▶ One at a time, have children look in a mirror and describe one quality that makes them special.

▶ Place the pictures of children in a shoebox. One at a time, have children pull a picture out of the box and describe why they think this person would be special.

Evaluation

▶ Children will name several different ways that people are the same and different.

▶ Children will explain why it is important to treat all people with respect and kindness.

 Additional lesson plans for grades 3-5 are available on CourseMate.

Summary

▶ Many children attending school and early childhood programs experience a range of chronic diseases and medical conditions.

- Teachers are important advocates for children and play a critical role in the early detection, referral, and management of their health needs in the classroom.
- The Individuals with Disabilities Education Improvement Act (IDEA) guarantees children with special needs the right to an accessible and appropriate education.
- First person language should always be used; it conveys respect and acceptance of people as individuals who may also have differing needs and abilities.

▶ Chronic diseases and medical conditions discussed in this chapter include:

- Allergies: are caused by an abnormal response to substances called allergens. Symptoms can include nasal congestion, headaches, eczema, rashes, asthma, and behavioral changes. Treatment is aimed at identifying offending substances and controlling symptoms.
- Asthma: involves an allergic response and is becoming increasingly more common for unknown reasons. Management is based on avoiding triggers (such as smoke, chemicals, infection) and administering medications during acute episodes.
- Anemia: occurs when there are too few red blood cells or they are unable to carry adequate oxygen to body cells. Treatment involves identifying and treating the underlying cause: infection, unhealthy diet, disease.
- Childhood cancers: are relatively uncommon. Symptoms and treatment vary according to the type of cancer involved; leukemia is the most common form experienced by children.
- Diabetes: is caused by an inadequate amount or lack of the hormone insulin. Early symptoms include weight loss, frequent urination, fatigue, and excessive thirst. Treatment includes daily insulin injections and careful regulation of diet and activity.
- Eczema: is an inflammatory skin condition commonly seen in children who have allergies; children sometimes outgrow it. Treatment is aimed at limiting exposure to offending substances and reducing skin irritation.
- Excessive fatigue: is not common among children, but can be caused by chronic infection, unhealthy diet, anemia, lead poisoning, and other serious conditions. Treatment is directed at eliminating the cause.

- Lead poisoning: is caused by lead ingested from contaminated objects; it continues to pose a threat to children's health. (See Table 4–6.) Elevated blood lead levels can result in impaired cognitive abilities, headaches, loss of appetite, fatigue, and behavior problems. Treatment is aimed at eliminating the source, correcting dietary deficiencies, and administering medication, if needed.
- Seizure disorders: are caused by abnormal electrical activity in the brain. Symptoms depend on the type of seizure and range from brief inattention to convulsive movements involving the entire body. Medication is usually prescribed to control seizure activity.
- Sickle cell disease: a genetic disease that affects certain ethnic groups; abnormally shaped red blood cells are unable to carry adequate oxygen to cells. Treatment involves avoiding infection and stress; blood transfusions may also be needed.

◖ Terms to Know

inclusion *p. 83*
individualized educational plan
  (IEP) *p. 84*
individualized family service plan
  (IFSP) *p. 84*
individualized health services plan
  (IHSP) *p. 84*

person first language *p. 84*
food intolerance *p. 87*
symptomatic control *p. 89*
anaphylaxis *p. 89*
hormone *p. 96*
gestational diabetes *p. 96*
hyperglycemia *p. 96*

dehydration *p. 96*
sleep apnea *p. 99*
endocrine *p. 99*
seizures *p. 101*

◖ Chapter Review

A. By Yourself:

1. Explain the process involved in securing intervention services for a child who you suspect may have a significant hearing impairment.

2. Explain why some chronic health conditions may be difficult to recognize.

3. Describe the ways in which febrile, absence, partial, and tonic-clonic seizures differ.

4. What are the early warning signs of diabetes? What resources are available in your community to help teachers improve their understanding of this condition and also learn how to administer injections?

5. Explain how you can determine if a child's symptoms are due to a cold or an allergy.

B. As a Group:

1. Divide into small groups. Each group should develop a case study to illustrate one of the chronic health conditions described in this chapter. The case study should include a description of the condition—its cause, symptoms, effects on the child and family, and classroom strategies for ensuring the child's successful inclusion. Have groups take turns reading, critiquing, and discussing each other's case studies.

2. Develop an emergency response plan for a child who has a seizure disorder and discuss how it would be implemented in the classroom.

3. Discuss factors that may be contributing to an increased incidence of childhood allergies and asthma.

4. Explain how a child's environment may contribute to the development and progression of chronic health conditions.

5. Discuss what teachers can do to support a child who has recently undergone cancer treatment and is ready to return to school.

Case Study

Mr. Lui arranged to take his first grade class on a field trip to a nearby nature park after they had spent several weeks learning about small mammals living in the wild. The day was warm and sunny, and the children were bubbling with excitement as they completed a short hike around the beaver ponds. As they headed back to the picnic shelter for lunch, one of the children who had run ahead let out a sudden shriek and fell to the ground. The teacher quickly ran to the child and observed that she was unconscious and her arms and legs were jerking violently. Mr. Lui sent one of the other children to get the park ranger, calmed the rest of the children down, and then used his cell phone to call 911 for emergency medical assistance. Within minutes, the seizure ended and the child regained consciousness. When the paramedics arrived, they checked the child over carefully and were satisfied that she required no additional treatment at the time. Mr. Lui contacted the child's family and learned that her doctor had recently prescribed a new seizure medication.

1.   What type of seizure was this child probably experiencing?

2.   What indication did the child give of a preceding aura?

3.   What signs, in addition to the jerky movements, might you expect to observe during and immediately following this type of seizure?

4.   Should Mr. Lui have called for emergency assistance? Would you expect his response to be different if he had known that the child was being treated for a seizure disorder?

5.   What steps should Mr. Lui take when the child's seizure ends?

6.   How can Mr. Lui turn this event into a learning experience for the other children?

Application Activities

1.   Locate and read at least eight children's books written about several of the chronic diseases and medical conditions discussed in this chapter.

2.   Interview teachers in three different educational settings. Inquire about the types of allergies they encounter most often and how they manage children's health needs in the classroom. Develop a simple, 5-day snack menu for a toddler who is allergic to milk and milk products, chocolate, and eggs.

3.   Locate and participate in several developmental screenings that are being conducted in your community. Evaluate the experience and identify things you thought could be improved.

4.   Design a poster for classroom teachers that illustrates, step-by-step, how to use an EpiPen.

5.   Visit the website *Bubbliboo* (http://www.bubbliboo.com) and click through each of the sections on childhood asthma. If you were a child, would you find the site attractive? Based on what you have learned in this chapter, is the information accurate and presented in a way that children would understand?

Helpful Web Resources

Asthma and Allergy Foundation of America	http://www.aafa.org
American Cancer Society	http://www.cancer.org
American Diabetes Association	http://www.diabetes.org
American Lung Association	http://www.lungusa.org
Canadian Paediatric Society	http://www.cps.ca

Centers for Disease Control and Prevention	http://www.cdc.gov
Center for Health and Health Care in Schools	http://www.healthinschools.org
CureSearch for Children's Cancer	http://www.curesearch.org
U.S. Department of Health and Human Services: Indian Health Service	http://www.ihs.gov
KidsHealth	http://www.kidshealth.org
National Diabetes Education Program	http://www.ndep.nih.gov

 Visit the Education CourseMate for this textbook to access the eBook, Did You Get It? quizzes, Digital Downloads, TeachSource Video Cases, flashcards, and more. Go to CengageBrain.com to log in, register, or purchase access.

References

Accordini, S., Janson, C., Svanes, C., & Jarvis, D. (2012). The role of smoking in allergy and asthma: Lessons from the ECRHS, *Current Allergy & Asthma Reports*, 12(3), 185–191.

Allen, K., Henselman, K., Laird, B., Quiñones, A., & Reutzel, T. (2012). Potential life-threatening events in schools involving rescue inhalers, epinephrine autoinjectors, and glucagon delivery devices: Reports from school nurses, *The Journal of School Nursing*, 28(1), 47–55.

Allen, K. E., & Cowdery, G. (2012). *The exceptional child: Inclusion in early childhood education* (7th ed.). Belmont, CA: Wadsworth Cengage Learning.

American Cancer Society. (2012). Cancer in children. Accessed on May 21, 2012 from http://www.cancer.org/Cancer/CancerinChildren/DetailedGuide/cancer-in-children-key-statistics.

American Diabetes Association. (2011). Diabetes statistics. Accessed on May18, 2012 from http://www.diabetes.org/diabetes-basics/diabetes-statistics.

Asthma and Allergy Foundation of America (AAFA). (2012). Asthma overview. Accessed on May 25, 2012 from http://www.aafa.org/asthma.html.

Baptiste-Roberts, K., Nicholson, W., & Wang, N. (2012). Gestational diabetes and subsequent growth patterns of offspring: The National Collaborative Perinatal Project, *Maternal & Child Health Journal*, 16(1), 125–132.

Bener, A., Ehlayel, M., Tulic, M., & Hamid, Q. (2012). Vitamin D deficiency as a strong predictor of asthma in children, *International Archives of Allergy & Immunology*, 157(2), 157–168.

Black, M., Quigg, A., Cook, J., Casey, P., Cutts, D., Chilton, M., Meyers, A., de Cuba, S., Heeren, T., Coleman, S., Rose-Jacobs, R., & Frank, D. (2012). WIC participation and attenuation of stress-related child health risks of household food insecurity and caregiver depressive symptoms, *Archives of Pediatric & Adolescent Medicine*, 166(5), 444–451.

Boney, C. (2012). Childhood onset and duration of obesity are significant risk factors for type 2 diabetes in adulthood, *Evidence Based Nursing*, 15(2), 38–39.

Brown, M., Bolen, L., Brinkman, T., Carreira, K., & Cole, S. (2011). A collaborative strategy with medical providers to improve training for teachers of children with cancer, *Journal of Educational & Psychological Consultation*, 21(2), 149–165.

Bruce, O., & Adams, R. (2012). Trends in comorbid sickle cell disease among stroke patients, *Journal of the Neurological Sciences*, 313(1–2), 86–91.

Centers for Disease Control and Prevention (CDC). (2013a). Asthma and schools. Accessed on April 21, 2013 from http://www.cdc.gov/HealthyYouth/asthma/.

CDC. (2013b). International adoption and prevention of lead poisoning. Accessed on April 20, 2013 from http://www.cdc.gov/nceh/lead/tips/adoption.

CDC. (2013c). Lead. Accessed on April 21, 2013 from http://www.cdc.gov/nceh/lead.

CDC. (2012a). What do parents need to know to protect their children? Accessed on April 21, 2013 from http://www.cdc.gov/nceh/lead/ACCLPP/blood_lead_levels.htm.

CDC. (2012b). 2011 Pediatric and pregnancy nutrition surveillance system: Pediatric data tables by health indicators. Accessed on April 21, 2013 from http://www.cdc.gov/pednss/pednss_tables/tables_health_indicators.htm.

Coker, T., Kaplan, R., & Chung, P. (2012). The association of health insurance and disease impairment with reported asthma prevalence in U.S. children, *Health Services Research*, 47(1), 431–445.

Del Giacco, S., Carlsen, K., & Toit, G. (2012). Allergy and sport in children, *Pediatric Allergy & Immunology*, 23(1), 11–20.

Epilepsy Foundation of America. (2012). Incidence and prevalence. Accessed on April 21, 2013 from http://www.epilepsyfoundation.org/aboutepilepsy/whatisepilepsy/statistics.cfm.

Ercan, H., Ozen, A., Karatepe, H., Berver, M., & Cengizlier, R. (2012). Primary school teacher's knowledge about and attitudes toward anaphylaxis, *Pediatric Allergy & Immunology*. Advanced online publication. DOI: 10.1111/j.1399-3038.2012.01307.x.

Gladwin, M., & Sachdev, V. (2012). Cardiovascular abnormalities in sickle cell disease, *Journal of the American College of Cardiology*, 59(13), 1123–1133.

Gonzalez, A. (2012). Vulnerable populations and diabetes, *Diabetes Spectrum*, 25(1), 6–7.

Gupta, R., Springston, E., Warrier, M., Smith, B., Kumar, R., Pongracic, J., & Holl, J. (2011). The prevalence, severity, and distribution of childhood food allergy in the United States, *Pediatrics*, 128(1), e9–e17.

Guralnick, M. (2012). Preventive interventions for preterm children: Effectiveness and developmental mechanisms, *Journal of Developmental & Behavioral Pediatrics*, 33(4), 352–364.

Hatzinger, M., Brand, S., Perren, S., von Wyl, A., Stadelmann, S., Klitzing, K., & Holsboer-Trachsler, E. (2012). Preschoolers suffering from psychiatric disorders show increased cortisol secretion and poor sleep compared to healthy controls, *Journal of Psychiatric Research*, 46(5), 590–599.

Herrmann, S., Thurber, J., Miles, K., & Gilbert, G. (2011). Childhood leukemia survivors and their return to school: A literature review, case study, and recommendations, *Journal of Applied School Psychology*, 27(3), 252–275.

Hockenberry, M., & Wilson, D. (2012). *Wong's essentials of pediatric nursing* (9th ed.). St Louis: Mosby.

Holt, E., Theall, K., & Rabito, F. (2013). Individual, housing, and neighborhood correlates of asthma among young urban children, *Journal of Urban Health*, 90(1), 116–129.

Horn, E., & Kang, J. (2012). Supporting young children with multiple disabilities. What do we know and what do we still need to learn?, *Topics in Early Childhood Special Education*, 31(4), 241–248.

Khan, D., Ansari, W., & Khan, F. (2011). Synergistic effects of iron deficiency and lead exposure on blood levels in children, *World Journal of Pediatrics*, 7(2), 150–154.

Knutson, K. (2012). Does inadequate sleep play a role in vulnerability to obesity?, *American Journal of Human Biology*, 24(3), 361–371.

Landrigan, P., & Goldman, L. (2011). Children's vulnerability to toxic chemicals: A challenge and opportunity to strengthen health and environmental policy, *Health Affairs*, 30(5), 842–850.

Laumbach, R., & Kipen, H. (2012). Respiratory health effects of air pollution: Update on biomass smoke and traffic pollution, *Journal of Allergy & Clinical Immunology*, 129(1), 3–11.

Matyka, K., & Annan, S. (2012). Physical activity in childhood diabetes. In I. Gallen (ed.), *Type 1 diabetes* (pp. 73–99), New York: Springer.

McCabe, M. (2011). Perceptions of school nurses and teachers of fatigue in children, *Pediatric Nursing*, 37(5), 244–252.

Milne, E., Grecnop, K., Scott, R., Bailey, H., Attia, J., Dalla-Pozza, L., de Klerk, N., & Armstrong, B. (2012). Parental smoking and risk of childhood acute lymphoblastic leukemia, *American Journal of Epidemiology*, 175(1), 43–53.

Morris, P., Baker, D., Belot, C., & Edwards, A. (2011). Preparedness for students and staff with anaphylaxis, *Journal of School Health*, 81(8), 471–476.

National Cancer Institute. (2012). Childhood cancers. Accessed on May 20, 2012 from http://www.cancer.gov/cancertopics/factsheet/Sites-Types/childhood.

National Eczema Association. (2012). Atopic dermatitis in children. Accessed on May 20, 2012 from http://www.nationaleczema.org/living-with-eczema/atopic-dermatitis-children.

National Institute of Neurological Disorders & Stroke. (2012). Febrile seizures fact sheet. Accessed on May 23, 2012 from http://www.ninds.nih.gov/disorders/febrile_seizures/detail_febrile_seizures.htm#1 20733111.

Nguyen, L., Cicutto, L., Soller, L., Joseph, L., Waserman, S., St-Pierre, Y., & Clarke, A. (2012). Management of anaphylaxis in schools: Evaluation of an epinephrine auto-injector (EpiPen®) use by school personnel and comparison of two approaches for soliciting participation, *Allergy, Asthma & Clinical Immunology*, 8(1), 4. Advanced online publication. DOI:10.1186/1710-1492-8-4.

Perry, A., Engelke, M., & Swanson, M. (2012). Parent and teacher perceptions of the impact of school nurse interventions on children's self-management of diabetes, *The Journal of School Nursing*, January 4, 2012. Advanced online publication. DOI: 10.1177/1059840511433860.

Pickup, J. (2012). Insulin pumps, *International Journal of Clinical Practice*, 66(Suppl. 175), 15–19.

Scantlebury, N., Mabbott, D., Janzen, L., Rockel, C., Widjaja, E., Jones, G., Kirby, M., & Odame, I. (2011). White matter integrity and core cognitive function in children diagnosed with sickle cell disease, *Journal of Pediatric & Hematology/Oncology*, 33(3), 163–171.

Shah, R., & Grammer, L. (2012). An overview of allergens, *Allergy & Asthma Proceedings*, 33(1), S2–S5(4).

Sickle Cell Disease Association of America (SCDAA). (2012). Sickle cell. Accessed on May 21, 2012 from http://www.sicklecelldisease.org.

Strayhorn, J., & Strayhorn, J. (2012). Lead exposure and the 2010 achievement test scores of children in New York counties, *Child & Adolescent Psychiatry & Mental Health*, 6, 4. DOI:10.1186/1753-2000-6-4.

Turner, P., & Kemp, A. (2012). Intolerance to food additives—Does it exist?, *Journal of Paediatrics & Child Health*, 48(2), e10–e14.

West, A., Denzer, A., Wildman, B., & Anhalt, K. (2013). Teacher perception of burden and willingness to accommodate children with chronic health conditions, *Advances in School Mental Health Promotion*, 6(1), 35–50.

Yao, T., Ou, L., Yeh, K., Lee, W., Chen, L., & Huang, J. (2012). Associations of age, gender, and BMI with prevalence of allergic diseases in children: PATCH study, *Journal of Asthma*, 48(5), 503–510.

chapter 5

The Infectious Process and Environmental Control

PhotoAlto/Laurence Mouton/Getty Images

naeyc **Standards Chapter Links**

▶ **#1 a, b, and c:** Promoting child development and learning
▶ **#3 a, c, and d:** Observing, documenting, and assessing to support young children and families
▶ Field Experience

Learning Objectives

After studying this chapter, you should be able to:

LO 5-1 Discuss why young children experience frequent communicable illness.

LO 5-2 Describe the components required for an illness to be communicable.

LO 5-3 Identify the four stages of a communicable illness.

LO 5-4 Name and discuss four control measures that teachers can use to reduce the transmission of communicable illnesses in the classroom.

Young children, especially those under 3 years of age, are highly susceptible to communicable illness. Frequent upper respiratory infections arc common, especially during a child's first experiences in group settings.

5-1 Risk Factors

Several factors contribute to the frequency of communicable illnesses that young children typically experience. First, children have had fewer opportunities to develop protective **antibodies** due to their limited prior exposures to infectious illnesses. Physical disabilities and chronic conditions, such as diabetes, sickle cell anemia, allergies, and asthma further reduce children's resistance and leave them more susceptible to communicable conditions.

Second, the immature development of children's body structures also contributes to a higher rate of illness. For example, shorter distances between an infant's or toddler's ears, nose, and throat make it easy for organisms to enter and infect these locations.

Third, group settings, such as home- and center-based early childhood programs and elementary school classrooms, are ideal environments for the rapid spread of illness (Vermeer et al., 2012). Children spend their days in close proximity and come in frequent contact with items, such as toys and furniture, that others have touched. They are also exposed to communicable illnesses in places wherever there are groups of people, including grocery stores, shopping centers, churches, libraries, and restaurants. Many of children's habits, such as sucking on fingers, mouthing toys, carelessness with bodily secretions (runny noses, drool, urine, stool), and an abundance of physical contact also encourage the rapid spread of communicable illness. For these reasons, every attempt must be made to establish and implement policies, practices, and learning experiences that will help protect young children from unnecessary exposure.

....

antibodies – *special substances produced by the body that help protect against disease.*

5-2 Communicable Illness

Communicable illnesses are infectious conditions that can be transmitted or spread from one person or animal to another. Three factors, all of which must be present at approximately the same time, are required for this process to occur (Figure 5–1).

- a pathogen
- a susceptible host
- a method of transmission

First, a **pathogen** or microorganism, such as a bacteria, virus, fungus, or parasite, must be present and available for transmission. These invisible germs are specific for each disease and are most commonly located in discharges from the respiratory (nose, throat, lungs) and intestinal tract of infected persons. They can also be found in the blood, urine, and discharges from the eyes and skin. Most pathogens require a living host (e.g., human, animal, insect) for their survival, with the exception of the organism that causes tetanus; it is able to survive in soil and dust for several years.

Second, there must be a **susceptible host** or person who is vulnerable to the disease-causing organism. Most communicable illnesses that children experience enter their new host through either a break in the skin, the **respiratory tract**, or digestive tract. The entry route is specific for each infectious disease.

Not every child who is exposed to a particular virus, bacteria, or other pathogen will become infected. Conditions must be favorable to allow an infectious organism to successfully avoid the body's defense systems, multiply, and establish itself. Children who are well rested, adequately nourished, **immunized**, and healthy are generally less susceptible to infectious organisms. Some children will have immunity as a result of having experienced a prior case of the same illness. However, the length of this protection varies with the illness and can range from several days to a lifetime. For example, a child who has had chickenpox will have permanent immunity against a recurrence of the

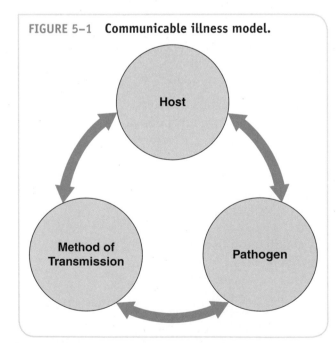

FIGURE 5–1 Communicable illness model.

Host

Method of Transmission

Pathogen

communicable – *capable of being spread or transmitted from one individual to another.*
pathogen – *a microorganism capable of producing illness or infection.*
susceptible host – *an individual who is capable of being infected by a pathogen.*
respiratory tract – *the nose, throat, trachea, and lungs.*
immunized – *a state of becoming resistant to a specific disease through the introduction of living or dead microorganisms into the body, which then stimulates the production of antibodies.*

disease, whereas immunity following a cold may last only a few days. Children who are carriers or who experience a mild case of some communicable diseases may also develop immunity without knowing that they have been infected.

Third, a method for transmitting the infectious agent from the original source to a new host is necessary to complete the communicable process. Infectious agents are most commonly spread via **airborne transmission** in school settings. Disease-causing pathogens are carried on tiny droplets of moisture that are expelled during coughs, sneezes, or while talking (Figure 5–2). Influenza, colds, meningitis, tuberculosis, and chickenpox are examples of infectious illnesses spread in this manner.

Fecal-oral transmission is the second-most common route by which infectious illnesses are spread in group settings, particularly when infants and toddlers in diapers are present. Teachers who fail to wash their hands properly after changing diapers or assisting children with toileting needs are often responsible for spreading disease-causing germs, especially if they also handle food. For this reason, it is advisable to assign diaper changing and food preparation responsibilities to different teachers. Children's hands should always be washed after diaper changes or after using the bathroom because their hands often end up in their mouths. Appropriate hand washing procedures should be taught and monitored closely to be sure children are washing correctly. Pinworms, hepatitis A, salmonella, and giardiasis are examples of illnesses transmitted by fecal-oral contamination.

A third common method of transmission involves **direct contact** with body fluids, such as blood or mucus, or an infected area on another person's body. The infectious organisms are transferred directly from the original source of infection to a new host. Ringworm, athlete's foot, impetigo, hepatitis B, and conjunctivitis (pinkeye) are a few of the conditions spread in this manner.

▼ **Communicable illnesses can be spread when children mouth toys and other objects.**

© Cengage Learning

Did You Know...

that children experience an average of 5-8 colds per year?

?

FIGURE 5–2   How infectious illnesses are spread.

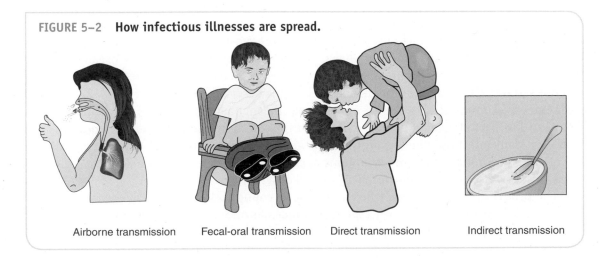

Airborne transmission   Fecal-oral transmission   Direct transmission   Indirect transmission

airborne transmission – *the process by which germs are expelled into the air through coughs and sneezes, and transmitted to another individual via tiny moisture drops.*

fecal-oral transmission – *the process in which germs are transferred to the mouth via hands contaminated with fecal material.*

direct contact – *coming in direct or immediate contact with infectious material.*

Communicable illnesses can also be transmitted through **indirect contact**. This method involves the transfer of infectious organisms from an infected individual to an intermediate object, such as water, milk, dust, food, toys, towels, eating utensils, animals, or insects, and finally to the new susceptible host. It is also possible to infect oneself with certain bacteria and viruses, such as those causing colds and influenza, simply by touching the moist linings of the eyes, nose, or mouth with contaminated hands. Several communicable illnesses, including conjunctivitis (pinkeye), cytomegalovirus (CMV), impetigo, scabies, and head lice can be transmitted through indirect and direct contact.

Eliminating any one of these factors (pathogen, host, or method of transmission) will interrupt the spread of a communicable illness. This is an important concept for families and teachers to understand when trying to control communicable illness, especially in group settings. It can also be beneficial for reducing the number of illnesses that teachers may experience or carry home to their families.

Did You Get It?

Which is not one of the three distinct factors that must be present for an illness to be transmitted from one child to another?
- **a.** A method of transmission.
- **b.** The child's age at the time of exposure.
- **c.** A pathogen.
- **d.** A host susceptible to a pathogen.

Take the full quiz on CourseMate.

5-3 Stages of Illness

Communicable illnesses generally develop in fairly predictable stages:

- incubation
- prodromal
- acute
- convalescence

The length of each stage is often different for each illness. In some cases, the stages may overlap and be difficult to identify when one begins and another ends.

The **incubation** stage includes the time between exposure to a pathogen and the appearance of the first signs or symptoms of illness. During this period, the infectious organisms enter the body and multiply rapidly in an attempt to establish themselves and overpower the body's defense systems. The length of the incubation stage is described in terms of hours or days and varies for each communicable disease. For example, the incubation period for chickenpox ranges from 2 to 3 weeks following exposure, whereas for the common cold it is thought to be only 12 to 72 hours. Many infectious illnesses are already communicable near the end of this stage. Children are often **contagious** before any symptoms appear, which can make some communicable illnesses difficult to control despite teachers' careful observations.

The **prodromal** stage begins when an infant or young child experiences the first nonspecific signs of infection and ends with the appearance of symptoms characteristic of a particular

---

indirect contact – *coming in contact with infectious material that is transmitted via surfaces, animals, or insects.*
incubation – *the interval of time between exposure to infection and the appearance of the first signs or symptoms of illness.*
contagious – *capable of being transmitted or passed from one person to another.*
prodromal – *the appearance of the first nonspecific signs of infection; this stage ends when the symptoms characteristic of a particular communicable illness begin to appear.*

communicable illness. This stage may last from several hours to several days. However, not all communicable diseases have a prodromal stage. Early symptoms commonly associated with the prodromal stage may include headache, unexplained fatigue, low-grade fever, a slight sore throat, and a general feeling of restlessness or irritability. Many complaints are so vague that they can easily go unnoticed. However, because children are highly contagious during this stage, teachers and parents must understand that these subtle changes may signal an impending illness.

During the **acute** stage there is no doubt that an infant or child is sick and highly contagious. The onset of this stage is marked by the appearance of symptoms characteristic of the illness and it ends as the child begins to recover. Early symptoms, such as fever, sore throat, cough, runny nose, rash, or enlarged lymph glands are common to many infectious diseases. However, they often develop in a characteristic pattern that can be useful for identifying the communicable illness involved.

The **convalescent** or recovery stage generally follows automatically unless complications develop. During this stage, symptoms gradually disappear and children begin to feel better.

> ### Did You Get It?
>
> A student who has been exposed to influenza, feels fine today, but will develop a high fever and stay home from school tomorrow is in the _____ stage.
>   **a.** prodromal
>   **b.** convalescent
>   **c.** incubation
>   **d.** acute
>
> Take the full quiz on CourseMate.

5-4 Control Measures

Teachers have an obligation and responsibility to help protect young children from communicable illnesses. Although many illnesses are simply an inconvenience, others can cause serious complications. Because classrooms are ideal settings for the rapid spread of many infectious conditions, control measures must be practiced diligently to limit their spread.

5-4a Observations

Teachers' daily health observations can be effective for identifying children in the early stages of a communicable illness. Removing children who are ill from classrooms eliminates a direct source of infection. However, it is important to remember that many illnesses are communicable before the characteristic symptoms appear, so not all spread can be avoided. For this reason it is important to continuously note changes in children's appearance and behavior patterns. This process is made easier by the fact that young children often look and behave differently when they are not feeling well. Their actions, facial expressions, skin color, sleep habits, appetite, and comments provide valuable warnings of impending illness. Additional signs may include:

- unusually pale or flushed skin
- red or sore throat
- enlarged **lymph glands**
- nausea, vomiting, or diarrhea
- rash, spots, or open lesions
- watery or red eyes
- headache or dizziness
- chills, fever, or achiness
- fatigue or loss of appetite

The appearance of these signs and symptoms does not always warrant concern in all children. For example, a teacher who knows that Tony's allergies often cause a red throat and cough

---

acute – *the stage of an illness or disease during which an individual is definitely sick and exhibits symptoms characteristic of a specific illness or disease.*

convalescent – *the stage of recovery from an illness or disease.*

lymph glands – *specialized groupings of tissue that produce and store white blood cells for protection against infection and illness.*

▼ **Changes in children's appearance and behavior can be early indications of an impending illness.**

© Cengage Learning

in the fall, or that Shadra's recent irritability is probably related to her mother's hospitalization, would not be alarmed by these observations. Teachers must be able to distinguish between children with potentially infectious illnesses and those with health problems that are explainable and not necessarily contagious. Knowing that some illnesses are more prevalent during certain times of the year or that a current outbreak exists in the community can also be useful for identifying children who may be infectious.

5-4b Policies

Written policies offer another important method for controlling infectious illnesses in group settings (Egger et al., 2012). Policies should be consistent with state regulations, and in place before a program begins to enroll children. They should be reviewed frequently so that staff members are familiar with the guidelines and more likely to enforce them consistently.

General health and exclusion policies should also be described in handbooks that are given to families. Collaborative partnerships are strengthened when families know in advance what to expect if their child does become ill. Exclusion and inclusion policies should establish clear guidelines for when children who are ill should be kept home, when they will be sent home due to illness, and when they are considered well enough to return (Figure 5–3).

Opinions differ on how restrictive exclusion policies should be. Some experts believe that children with mild illnesses can remain in group care, while others feel that children who exhibit symptoms should be sent home. Because many early signs of communicable illnesses are nonspecific, teachers and families may have difficulty distinguishing between conditions that warrant exclusion and medical attention and those that do not.

FIGURE 5–3   Sample exclusion policy.

EXCLUSION POLICY

Control of communicable illness among the children is a prime concern. Policies and guidelines related to outbreaks of communicable illness in this center have been developed with the help of the health department and local pediatricians. In order to protect the entire group of children, as well as your own child, we ask that families assist us by keeping children who are ill at home if they have experienced any of the following symptoms *within the past 24 hours:*

- fever over 100°F (37.8°C) orally or 99°F (37.2°C) axillary (under the arm)
- signs of a newly developing cold or uncontrollable coughing
- diarrhea, vomiting, or an upset stomach
- unusual or unexplained loss of appetite, fatigue, irritability, or headache
- any discharge or drainage from eyes, nose, ears, or open sores

Children who become ill with any of these symptoms will be sent home. We appreciate your cooperation with this policy. If you have any questions about whether or not your child is well enough to attend school or group care that day, please call *before* bringing your child.

FIGURE 5-4 **Sample letter notifying families of their child's exposure.**

Date_____

Dear Parent:

There is a possibility that your child has been exposed to impetigo. Please observe your child's skin closely for the next 2–10 days and look for:

- itchy rash that may develop blisters
- moist sores that are more likely to appear around the face, ears, nose, or arms
- sores that increase in size or spread to other parts of the body

Impetigo is highly contagious and requires careful hand washing to prevent it from infecting others. Please contact your child's health care provider for advice about treating the condition. Children may return to school after receiving medical care and all sores have healed over.

If you have any questions, please call before bringing your child to school. We appreciate your cooperation in helping us to protect children's well-being.

Consequently, programs may decide to set exclusion policies that are fairly restrictive unless they are prepared to care for sick children.

It is also important for programs to adopt policies about notifying families when children are exposed to communicable illnesses. This measure enables parents to watch for early symptoms and to keep sick children home (Figure 5–4). Immunization requirements, as well as actions the program will take if children are not in compliance, should also be addressed in a program's policies. Local public health authorities can provide useful information and guidance to programs when they are formulating new policies or are confronted with a communicable health problem about which they are unsure.

Guidelines for Teacher Illness Teachers are exposed to many infectious illnesses through their daily contact with young children. They often experience an increased frequency of illness—especially during the initial months of employment—that is similar to what young children experience when they enroll in a new program or school (Tak et al., 2011). However, over time, teachers gradually build up resistance to many of these illnesses. They can also take steps to minimize their risk by obtaining a pre-employment health assessment, having a tuberculin test, updating immunizations, following a healthy lifestyle, and practicing frequent hand washing. Teachers who are pregnant may want to temporarily reconsider working around young children because some communicable illnesses, such as cytomegalovirus (CMV) and German measles can affect the fetus, especially during the early months.

When teachers are ill and trying to decide whether or not they should go to work, they must follow the same exclusion guidelines that apply to sick children. Adults who do not feel well will not be able to meet the rigorous demands necessary for working with young children and also face an increased risk of sustaining personal injury. Programs should maintain a list of substitute teachers so that staff members do not feel pressured to work when they are ill.

Administration of Medication The administration of medicine to young children is a responsibility that must always be taken seriously. (See Teacher Checklist 5-1.) Policies and procedures for administering prescription and nonprescription medications, including ointments and creams; eye, ear, and nose drops; cough syrups; pain or fever-reducing medications; inhalers; and nebulizer breathing treatments should be developed in accordance with state licensing or school district regulations to safeguard children as well as teaching staff. These policies and procedures

TEACHER CHECKLIST 5-1

Administering Medications to Children

1. Always wash your hands before handling medications and after administering them.
2. Be honest when giving children medication! Do not use force or attempt to trick children into believing that medicines are candy. Instead, use the opportunity to help children understand the relationship between taking a medication and recovering from an illness or infection. Also, acknowledge the fact that the taste of medicine may be disagreeable or a treatment may be somewhat unpleasant; offer a small sip of juice or cracker to eliminate an unpleasant taste or read a favorite story as a reward for their cooperation.
3. Designate one individual to accept medication from families and administer it to children; this could be the director or the head teacher. This step will help minimize the opportunity for errors, such as omitting a dose or giving a dose twice.
4. When medication is accepted from a family, it should be in the original container and labeled with the child's name, the drug name, and the time and dose to be administered.

 CAUTION

NEVER give medicine from a container that has been prescribed for another individual.

5. Store all medicines in a locked cabinet. If it is necessary to refrigerate a medication, place it in a locked box and store it on a top shelf in the refrigerator.
6. Concentrate on what you are doing and do not talk with anyone until you are finished.
   a. Read the label on the bottle or container three times:
      • when removing it from the locked cabinet
      • before pouring it from the container
      • after pouring it from the container
   b. Administer medication on time, and give only the amount prescribed.
   c. Be sure you have the correct child! If the child is old enough to talk, ask "What is your name?" and have the child state his or her name.
7. Record and maintain a permanent record of each dose of medicine that is administered (Figure 5–5). Include the:
   • date and time the medicine was given
   • name of the teacher administering the medication
   • dose of medication given
   • any unusual physical changes or behaviors observed after the medicine was administered
8. Inform the child's family of the dosage(s) and time medication was given, as well as any unusual reactions that may have occurred.
9. NOTE: Adults should never take any medication in front of children.

TeachSource Digital Download   Download from CourseMate.

should be in writing, familiar to all staff members, filed in an accessible location, and distributed to every family (Figure 5–5).

When children are enrolled in part-day programs, families may be able to alter medication schedules and administer prescribed doses at times when children are home. However, this may not be an option for children who attend full-day school or early childhood programs. In these cases, families will need to make prior arrangements with the child's teachers or school nurse to have prescribed medications administered at the appropriate times.

Medications should never be given to children without their family's written consent and written instructions from a licensed physician. The label on a prescription drug is considered an acceptable physician's directive. In the case of nonprescription medicines, families should obtain written instructions from the physician stating the child's name, the medication to be given, the dose, frequency it is to be administered, potential reactions, and any special precautions that may be necessary. There are risks associated with giving children over-the-counter

FIGURE 5–5 **Sample medication recording form.**

ADMINISTRATION OF MEDICATION FORM

Child's name _____

Prescription number _____

Date of prescription _____

Doctor prescribing medicine _____

Medication being given for _____

Time medication is to be given by staff _____

Time medication last given by parent (guardian) _____

Amount to be given at each time (dosage): _____

I, _____ give my permission for the staff to administer the above prescription medication (according to the above guidelines) to _____ _____ . I understand that the staff cannot be held

(child's name)

responsible for allergic reactions or other complications resulting from administration of the above medication when given according to the directions.

Parent/guardian name (print) _____

Signature _____

Date _____

Staff Record

Staff member accepting medication and signing this form (print): _____

Is medication in its original container? _____

Is original label intact? _____

Is there written permission from the doctor attached (or the original prescription)? _____

Signature of accepting staff _____

Administration Record

DATE	TIME	AMOUNT GIVEN	STAFF ADMINISTERING	INITIALS

medications that have not been authorized by a physician. It is the physician's professional and legal responsibility to determine which medication and exact dosage is appropriate for an individual child. Teachers can protect themselves from potential liability by refusing to give medications without a doctor's order.

▼ **Immunizations protect children from many preventable childhood diseases.**

© Cengage Learning

5-4c Immunization

Immunization offers permanent protection against all preventable childhood diseases, including diphtheria, tetanus, whooping cough (pertussis), polio, measles, mumps, rubella, Haemophilus influenza, and chickenpox. However, outbreaks of some diseases continue to occur. Large-scale national, state, and local campaigns have successfully increased the number of children 19 to 35 months who have received all age-appropriate immunizations to approximately 90 percent (CDC, 2012). Yet, there are many adults and older children who are not current or fully immunized according to recommendations. Efforts to improve the immunization rates among all age groups remain a Healthy People 2020 priority (U.S. DHHS, 2012).

Why are some families so seemingly complacent about having their children immunized? Perhaps they do not realize that some communicable illnesses are still life-threatening and continue to pose a threat to children who are not protected. Recent outbreaks of mumps, measles, tuberculosis, and whooping cough, for example, have clearly demonstrated this potential (Luthy et al., 2013). Some families falsely believe that antibiotics are available to cure all infectious illness so they are willing to take a chance. Others have expressed concern about vaccine safety and the number of immunizations children must receive (Gidengil et al., 2012). Pharmaceutical companies continue to make strides in combining some vaccines to help reduce this number. Manufacturers have also eliminated questionable substances, such as thimerosal, from vaccines to improve their safety (Barile et al., 2012).

CONNECTING TO EVERYDAY PRACTICE

Hand Washing Compliance

It is easy to assume that everyone knows how to wash their hands and understands the importance of doing so. However, multiple studies have shown that even health care workers fail to follow recommended hand washing guidelines approximately 40 to 50 percent of the time (White et al., 2012; Fuller et al., 2011). Serious concerns have been raised about the lack of hand washing compliance in light of an increase in antibiotic-resistant infections. The use of hand sanitizing gels has proven beneficial for preventing the spread of some communicable illnesses, but they are not considered effective against all infectious organisms.

Because schools and early childhood programs provide ideal settings for the spread of communicable illnesses, it is especially important that teachers practice careful hand washing. However, hand washing is not always followed rigorously in these settings. As a result, researchers continue to look for ways to improve hand washing compliance in health care facilities, schools, and early childhood programs including the use of surveillance cameras, training videos, sanitizing gels, sink placement, and checklists (Armellino et al., 2012; Wilson, Jacob, & Powell, 2011).

Think About This:

▶ Why do you think teachers often fail to wash their hands at the necessary times?

▶ What are the barriers?

▶ What would motivate teachers to improve their hand hygiene compliance?

▶ Should schools resort to high tech methods (i.e., video cameras) to ensure compliance?

▶ How would you respond if you observed a teacher who served the children lunch without first washing his or her hands?

Most states require children's immunizations to be current when they enter school or enroll in early childhood programs. In states where immunization laws are lax, teachers must insist that every child be fully immunized unless families are opposed on religious or medical grounds. (Luthy et al., 2013; Gaudino & Robison, 2012). Teachers should also be diligent in keeping their own immunizations up-to-date.

Vaccines work by triggering the body's immune system to produce protective substances called antibodies. This process is similar to what occurs when a person becomes ill with certain infectious diseases. Infants are born with a limited supply of antibodies, acquired from their mothers, which protect them against some communicable illnesses. However, this maternal protection is only temporary and, therefore, the immunization process must be initiated early in an infant's life. The immunization schedule jointly recommended by the Centers for Disease Control and Protection (CDC), the American Academy of Pediatrics (AAP), and the American Academy of Family Physicians (AAFP) appears in Figure 5–6. Similar recommendations are available for Canadians and children in other countries (Public Health Agency of Canada, 2012).

Infants and young children, especially those in group care, are encouraged to be immunized against Haemophilus influenza Type b (Hib), an upper respiratory infection and common cause of

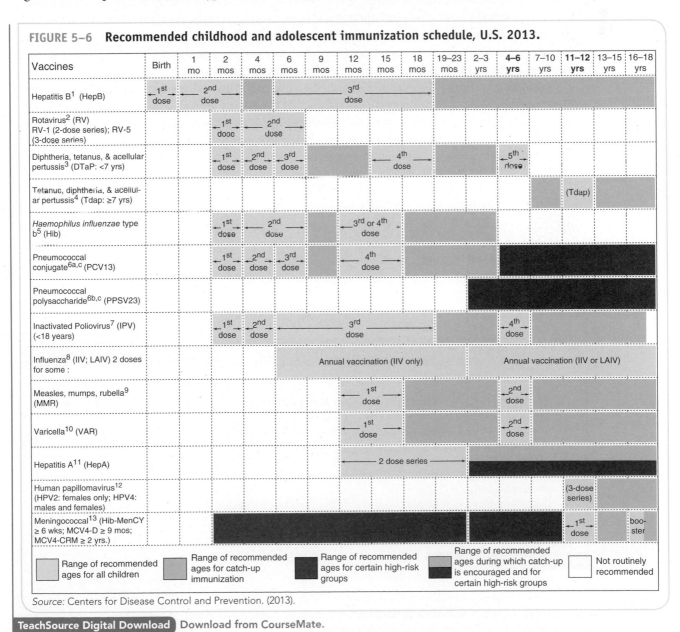

FIGURE 5–6   Recommended childhood and adolescent immunization schedule, U.S. 2013.

Source: Centers for Disease Control and Prevention. (2013).

meningitis. (See Figure 5–6.) Vaccines for chickenpox (varicella) and hepatitis B, a viral infection spread through contact with body secretions and feces, are also required in some states and recommended in others (Abrevaya & Mulligan, 2011). Children who have special health conditions are often more susceptible to communicable illnesses and should be immunized against these diseases as a precautionary measure even though they may not be required. Immunizations can be obtained from most health care providers, neighborhood health clinics, or public health departments where the cost is often reduced or free.

Programs that employ more than one teacher (including aides and substitutes) are required to offer free hepatitis B immunizations to employees during the first 10 days of employment or within 24 hours following exposure to blood or body fluids containing blood (OSHA, 2011). Teachers are at high risk for exposure to hepatitis B and should protect themselves by completing the immunization series.

5-4d Environmental Control

Communicable illnesses can also be controlled through a variety of effective environmental practices and modifications (Cannon et al., 2012; Stebbins, Downs, & Vukotich, 2011). Teachers should be familiar with these methods and understand how to implement them in their classrooms. Written procedures should be posted where they are visible and reviewed periodically with all employees. Teachers must also take personal precautions, such as wearing gloves and practicing frequent hand washing, to protect themselves from unnecessary exposure to contaminated materials.

Because respiratory illnesses are common in group settings where there are children, special attention should be given to control measures that limit their spread. For example, children can be taught to cough and sneeze into their elbow or a tissue, dispose of tissues properly, and then wash their hands. Children must also be reminded frequently to keep hands out of their mouth, nose, and eyes to prevent self-infection and the spread of infection to others.

Universal Infection Control Precautions The U.S. Department of Labor's Occupational Safety and Health Administration (OSHA) is responsible for protecting employees' safety by ensuring that workplace environments and practices meet federal guidelines. Regulations passed by OSHA require child care programs (except those without paid employees) to develop and practice **universal infection control precautions** for handling contaminated body fluids. (See Teacher Checklist 5-2.) In addition, schools must have a written exposure control plan for

TEACHER CHECKLIST 5-2

Universal Precautions for Handling Body Fluids

Whenever handling body fluids or items contaminated with body fluids, be sure to:

- Wear disposable gloves when you are likely to have contact with blood or other body fluids (e.g., vomitus, urine, feces, or saliva).
- Remove glove by grasping the cuff and pulling it off inside out.
- Wash hands thoroughly. (Lather for at least 30 seconds.)
- Dispose of contaminated materials properly. Seal soiled clothing in plastic bags to be laundered at home. Dispose of diapers by tying them securely in garbage bags. Place broken glass in a designated container.
- Clean all surfaces with an approved disinfectant or chlorine bleach solution (check product label and mix fresh daily).
- Subsidize the cost of hepatitis B immunizations for all employees.

TeachSource Digital Download Download from CourseMate.

universal infection control precautions – *special measures taken when handling bodily fluids, including careful hand washing, wearing disposable gloves, disinfecting surfaces, and proper disposal of contaminated objects.*

handling potentially infectious material, provide annual training for employees, and maintain records of any contact (OSHA, 2003).

Universal precautions are designed to protect teachers from accidental exposure to blood-borne pathogens, including hepatitis B and C and HIV/AIDS. All body fluids are considered potentially infectious and, therefore, should be treated as such. Any material that has been contaminated with blood or other body fluids that might possibly contain blood, such as urine, feces, saliva, and vomitus, must be handled with caution, regardless of whether or not a child is known to be ill.

Disposable gloves should always be accessible to teachers; non-latex gloves must be provided if a teacher or child has a latex sensitivity. They must always be worn whenever handling soiled objects or caring for children's injuries. Gloves should be removed by pulling them off inside out and carefully discarding them after use with an individual child. Thorough hand washing must follow to prevent any further spread of infection; *wearing gloves does not eliminate the need for washing one's hands.* Children's hands and skin should also be washed with soap and running water to remove any blood. Washable objects, such as rugs, pillows, or stuffed toys that have been contaminated with body fluids should be laundered separately from other items. Children's clothing should be rinsed out, sealed in a plastic bag, and sent home to be washed. Bloodstains on surfaces must be wiped up and disinfected with a commercial germicide or chlorine bleach solution.

Did You Know...

that hand washing can prevent more than 50 percent of all communicable illnesses?

NOTE: Manufacturers have recently changed the strength of their chlorine bleach products. Also, be aware that not all bleach products are designed for disinfecting purposes—some are simply laundry products. Read manufacturers' labels carefully and follow their instructions for appropriate dilution and use. Updated safety information and mixing guidelines are posted on the National Resource Center for Health and Safety in Child Care and Early Education (NRC) website, *Caring for Our Children* (3rd ed.), Appendix J (http://cfoc.nrckids.org/Bleach/Bleach.cfm) and can also be obtained from your state or local health department.

Hand Washing Hand washing is perhaps the single most effective control measure against the spread of communicable and infectious illness in child care and school environments (Schulte et al., 2012). (See Teacher Checklist 5-3.)

Infants and toddlers who are crawling on the floor, eating with their hands, or sucking their thumbs or fingers should have their hands washed frequently, and especially after diaper changes. Individual washcloths moistened with soap and water can be used for this purpose; however, infants and toddlers should also have their hands washed under running water several times a day. Preschoolers and adults should always wash with soap and running water. Children must be taught the correct procedure and supervised so that each step is followed carefully. School-age children should be given several opportunities during the day to wash their hands. In addition, children should wash their hands before and after eating or whenever they have blown their nose, used the bathroom, played outdoors or in sand, or touched animals. Although sanitizing hand gels are beneficial for limiting the spread

▶❚❚ **TeachSource Video Connections**

© 2015 Cengage Learning

Promoting Children's Health: A Focus on Nutrition in Early Childhood Settings

Young children often experience multiple episodes of communicable illness throughout the year. Although it is not reasonable to think that all communicable illness can be prevented, there are steps teachers can take to improve children's resistance. As you watch the learning video, *Promoting Children's Health: A Focus on Nutrition in Early Childhood Settings*, consider the following questions:

1. What role does nutrition education play in reducing the incidence of communicable illness?

2. What additional control measures did the teacher take to limit the potential spread of disease-causing organisms?

3. Why is it important that teachers wash their hands at appropriate times?

4. When should children wash their hands?

Watch on CourseMate.

TEACHER CHECKLIST 5-3
How and When to Wash Hands

Following proper hand washing technique is critical for controlling the spread of infectious illnesses:

- Pull down paper towel.
- Turn on the water; wet hands and wrists under warm, running water.
- Apply soap and lather hands to loosen dirt and bacteria.
- Rub hands and wrists vigorously for a minimum of 20 seconds. Friction helps to remove microorganisms and dirt. (Have children sing the entire ABC or similar song while rubbing their hands with soap.)
- Pay special attention to rubbing soap on the backs of hands, between fingers, and around finger nails.
- Rinse hands thoroughly under running water to remove dirt and soap. Hold hands higher than wrists to prevent recontamination. Leave the water running.
- Dry hand and arms carefully with paper towel.
- Use the paper towel to turn off water faucets. (This prevents hands from becoming contaminated again.)
- Open bathroom door with paper towel and discard it in an appropriate receptacle.

Correct hand washing technique should always be used:

- upon arrival or return to the classroom
- before handling food or food utensils
- before and after feeding children
- before and after administering medication
- after changing diapers or handling items contaminated with mucus, urine, feces, vomitus, or blood
- after personally using the restroom
- after cleaning up from snack or play activities, emptying garbage, handling pets, or using art materials such as clay and paint
- after touching animals or playing in sand and dirt

TeachSource Digital Download   Download from CourseMate.

▼ **Frequent hand washing reduces the risk of communicable illness.**

© Cengage Learning

of communicable illness, they are not considered a substitute for thorough hand washing and should be used only when running water is not available (Gerald et al., 2012; Nandrup-Bus, 2011).

Cleaning Frequent cleaning of furniture, toys, and surfaces is also an effective method for limiting the spread of communicable illness (APHA & AAP, 2011). Changing tables, mats, and potty chairs should be constructed of nonporous materials and free of any tears or cracks for ease of cleaning. They should be disinfected thoroughly after each use with an approved solution that has been mixed according to the manufacturer's directions. (Refer to new bleach solution guidelines.) Surfaces contaminated with blood or large amounts of urine, stool, or vomitus require special cleaning and disinfecting measures.

Toys that children have placed in their mouths should be removed for cleaning before they are used by another child. Items should be washed with soap and warm water, rinsed in a disinfecting solution, and allowed to air-dry. Some toys can be sanitized in the dishwasher. Washable cloth and stuffed objects should be laundered between use by other children. Surfaces, such as tables, gate tops, car seats, and crib rails that children mouth or drool on should be scrubbed daily with soap and water and disinfected. Desktops and equipment in school-age classrooms should also be wiped off with a mild disinfectant at least once a week, or daily during the cold and flu season.

TEACHER CHECKLIST 5-4
Sanitary Diapering Procedure

The consistent implementation of sanitary diapering procedures is important for reducing the spread of disease. Teachers should follow these steps:

- Organize and label all supplies.
- Have all items for diaper changing within reach.
- Place a disposable covering (paper towel, paper roll) over a firm changing surface. Do not change children on fabric chairs or sofas that could become soiled.
- If using gloves, put them on.
- Pick up the child, holding him away from your clothing to avoid contamination.
- Place the child on the paper surface; fasten security belt. Remove the child's clothing and shoes if necessary to prevent them from becoming soiled.
- Remove the soiled diaper. Place disposable diapers in a covered, plastic-lined receptacle designated for this purpose; seal cloth diapers in a plastic bag and send home to be laundered.
- Clean the child's bottom with a disposable wipe and place the wipe in receptacle; pat skin dry with a paper towel.
- Remove the paper lining from beneath the child and discard.
- Wash your hands or wipe with a clean disposable wipe and discard. *Never leave the child alone.*
- Wash the child's hands under running water.
- Diaper and redress the child. Return the child to a play area.
- Disinfect the changing surface and any supplies or equipment that was touched with a chlorine bleach solution or other approved disinfectant.
- Remove gloves (if worn) and wash your hands again.

TeachSource Digital Download   Download from CourseMate.

Diapering and Toileting Areas   Children who are not toilet-trained can spread infectious illnesses through urine and feces. Maintaining separate diapering and toileting areas can significantly reduce contamination and the spread of infection from one child to another. Careful adherence to sanitary diapering procedures, disinfection of surfaces (free of cracks), and thorough hand washing will further reduce this risk. (See Teacher Checklist 5-4.) Teachers may choose to wear disposable gloves when changing infants or handling soiled diapers, but this is not essential. Even if gloves are worn, meticulous hand washing must follow because they do not prevent contamination. Soiled diapers (disposable) should be placed in a covered waste container (lined with a plastic bag) that is not accessible to children. Cloth diapers must be sealed in a plastic bag and sent home for parents to launder. Infants' hands should be washed under running water following each diaper change.

Family preferences and cultural differences will influence when and how toilet training is initiated (Gonzalez-Mena & Eyer, 2011; Rowe & Casillas, 2011). When toddlers are ready to begin potty training, small, child-sized toilets should be made available. (See Teacher Checklist 5-5.)

TEACHER CHECKLIST 5-5
Readiness Indicators for Toilet Training

Successful toilet training requires that children have basic motor and cognitive skills:

- an ability to understand the concepts of wet and dry
- a regularity to patterns of elimination (at least during daytime)
- language to express the need for elimination
- an ability to pull clothing up and down

TeachSource Digital Download   Download from CourseMate.

Many states prohibit the use of shared potty-chairs in early childhood programs because they can spread infections if not properly disinfected. Families may wish to provide a chair for their child's sole use if the program's policy permits. However, teachers must still follow strict sanitizing procedures each time the chair is used. Any soiled material should first be removed with soap and water before spraying the surface with a disinfecting solution. Follow manufacturer's guidelines for mixing solutions and the length of time they must remain on surfaces to adequately disinfect. Teachers should wash their hands carefully after completing cleaning procedures and also be sure that children have washed their hands!

Room Arrangements Simple modifications in children's environments can also have a positive effect on the control of communicable illnesses. For example, room temperatures set at 68–70°F are less favorable for the spread of infectious illnesses and are often more comfortable for children. Their smaller body surfaces make children less sensitive than adults to cooler temperatures.

Rooms should be well ventilated to reduce the concentration of infectious organisms circulating within a given space. Doors and windows can be opened briefly, even on cool days, to introduce fresh air. Screens help to prevent disease-carrying flies and mosquitoes from coming indoors. Mechanical ventilating systems should undergo annual inspection and maintenance to improve air flow. Taking children outdoors, even in winter, also improves their resistance to illness.

The humidity level in rooms should also be checked periodically, especially in winter when rooms are heated. Extremely warm, dry air increases the risk of respiratory infection by causing the mucous linings in the mouth and nose to become dry and cracked. Moisture can be added to the air by installing a humidifier in the central heating system or placing a cool-mist vaporizer in individual rooms. Cool-mist units eliminate the risk of burns, but they must be emptied, washed out with soap and water, disinfected, and refilled with fresh distilled water each day to prevent bacterial growth. Plants or small dishes of water placed around a room also provide added humidity, but they can encourage the growth of mold spores, which may aggravate children's allergies and asthma (Nriagu et al., 2012).

The physical arrangement of a classroom also provides an effective method for controlling communicable and infectious illness. For example, separating older children from infants and toddlers who are not toilet-trained can significantly reduce the spread of intestinal illnesses. Surfaces such as floors, walls, counter tops, and furniture should be smooth and easy to clean. Laundry and food preparation areas should be separated from each other as well as from the classrooms. Pedal-operated sinks or faucets with infrared sensors encourage frequent hand washing and prevent recontamination.

Arranging children in small groups helps to limit close contact and enables teachers to more closely monitor behaviors that could potentially spread communicable illnesses. Children's rugs, cribs, and sleeping mats can be arranged in alternating directions, head to foot, to decrease talking, coughing, and breathing in each other's faces during naptimes. Individual lockers or storage spaces where children can store personal items, such as blankets, coats, hats, toys, and toothbrushes are also effective for reducing contact and transfer of infectious organisms.

Several additional areas of children's environments deserve special attention. Sandboxes should be covered to prevent contamination from animal feces. Water tables and wading pools need to be emptied and washed out daily to prevent bacterial growth and the spread of communicable disease; a water pH of 7.2–8.2 and chlorine level of 0.4–3.0 parts per million should be maintained in swimming pools at all times (as specified in commercial test kits). Items that children put on their heads, such as hats, wigs, and beauty parlor items can spread head lice and, therefore, may not be appropriate to use as play items in group settings unless they can be washed or disinfected. Play clothes should be laundered weekly or more often if communicable illnesses are present in the classroom.

▼ **Rearranging the environment can be an effective step in reducing the spread of communicable illness.**

© Cengage Learning

5-4e Education

Teachers also make a valuable contribution to the control of communicable illness through the health promotion lessons they design for children. Educational activities that teach children about personal wellness, physical activity, and nutritious diet play an important role in improving resistance to illness and shortening convalescence if they do become ill (Gleddie, 2012; Johnson, Weed, & Touger-Decker, 2012). Examples of topics that are of interest and value to young children include:

- hand washing (appropriate technique and times)
- proper method for covering coughs, blowing noses, and disposing of tissues
- not sharing personal items, such as drinking cups, toothbrushes, shoes, hats, towels, eating utensils
- germs and how they spread
- dressing appropriately for the weather
- growing and cooking nutritious foods
- the importance of sleep
- fun ways to be physically active (and how this makes a body healthy)
- staying safe around animals

Communicable illness outbreaks provide excellent opportunities for teachers to review important preventive health concepts and practices with children. Learning is more meaningful for children when it is associated with real-life experiences, such as when a classmate has chickenpox, a cold, or pinkeye. Teachers can use these opportunities to review correct hand washing procedures, reinforce the importance of eating nutritious foods, conduct simple experiments to illustrate how germs spread, and model sound health practices for children to imitate. Children are far more likely to remember what they have seen than what they have been told.

Families must be included in any educational program that is aimed at reducing the incidence of communicable illness. They should be informed of health practices and information that is being taught to the children. Teachers can also reinforce the importance of (1) serving nutritious meals and snacks at home, (2) making sure that children get sufficient sleep and physical activity, (3) obtaining immunizations for infants, toddlers, and older children, (4) eliminating water sources where mosquitos can breed, and (5) scheduling routine medical and dental supervision. Successful control of communicable illness and the promotion of children's well-being depend on schools and families working together.

Did You Get It?

What is/are considered the earliest visible symptoms of an impending illness?
- **a.** A drop in academic performance.
- **b.** Concrete symptoms such as fever, cough, and sneezing.
- **c.** Appearance and behavioral changes out of the ordinary for that child.
- **d.** Increased appetite.

Take the full quiz on CourseMate.

PARTNERING with FAMILIES

Giving Children Medication

Dear Families,

Special precautions should be taken whenever administering medication to children. Their smaller bodies are more sensitive to many medications, and they may respond differently than an adult. It is also easy to give children too much of a medication because their dosages are typically quite small.

(continued)

PARTNERING with FAMILIES

Giving Children Medication *(continued)*

Unattended medications may attract children's curiosity and must always be stored in a locked cabinet to prevent unintentional poisoning. Additional safety precautions that you can take include:

▶ Always check with your child's physician before giving over-the-counter medications, especially to children under 2 years.

▶ Read medication labels carefully. Be sure you are giving the correct medication to the right child at the appropriate time interval. Also, double-check the dose that has been prescribed, and administer only that amount. Make sure the medication is approved for children; many drugs are not advised for children younger than 12 years.

▶ Ask your pharmacist about potential drug interactions—with other medications or food—that should be avoided. Also, learn about possible reactions that should be noted before giving your child any new medication.

▶ Always follow the instructions for administering a medication and finish giving the full course that has been prescribed.

▶ Dispose of outdated medications. Old medications can lose their effectiveness and cause unexpected reactions. Always check with a pharmacist if in doubt.

▶ Store medications in their original container and according to instructions.

▶ Never tell children that medicines are "candy" and avoid taking medication in front of children.

CLASSROOM CORNER

Teacher Activities

Those Invisible Germs...

(**NHES** PreK–2, National Health Education Standard 1.2.3)

Concept: Germs are everywhere; germs are on the things we touch.

Learning Objectives

▶ Children will understand that germs are invisible and on most things we touch.

▶ Children will learn that correct hand washing removes germs.

Supplies

▶ Baby powder or glitter; small spray bottle with water; paper towel; hand lotion

Learning Activities

▶ Read and discuss one of the following books:

   ▶ *Germs Are Not for Sharing* by Elizabeth Verdick

   ▶ *Those Mean Nasty Dirty Downright Disgusting but . . . Invisible Germs* by Judith Rice

   ▶ *The Magic School Bus Inside Ralphie: A Book About Germs* (for older children) by Joanna Cole

   ▶ *The Berenstain Bears Come Clean for School* by Jan and Mike Berenstain

▶ Ask children if they know what a germ is and if they can describe what they look like. Ask them where germs are found and what we can do to protect ourselves from them.

▶ Lightly spray water on the hands of half of the children; sprinkle with baby powder or glitter. Ask children to shake hands with one another and then examine their hands.

▶ Coat children's hands with a thin layer of hand cream (make sure no one has any allergies). Sprinkle their hands lightly with glitter. Have them attempt to brush the "germs" off by

(continued)

CLASSROOM CORNER

Teacher Activities *(continued)*

Those Invisible Germs...

rubbing their hands together. Repeat this step using a paper towel. Finally, have children wash their hands with soap and warm water. After, ask the children which method was most effective for removing the "germs." Talk about why hand washing is important for keeping the germs away and staying healthy.

▶ Have children draw their own interpretations of what a germ looks like.

Evaluation

▶ Children can explain where germs are found and how they are spread.

▶ Children will demonstrate how to wash their hands correctly.

 Additional lesson plans for grades 3–5 are available on CourseMate.

Summary

▶ Communicable illnesses are common in group settings where there are young children. Reasons for this include children playing in close proximity, immature development of children's respiratory system, children's play and personal hygiene habits, adult carelessness, and poor hand washing practices.

▶ To be communicable, an illness requires a pathogen, a susceptible host, and a method for successful transmission.

  • Transmission occurs via airborne, fecal-oral, direct, or indirect methods.

▶ Communicable illnesses develop in four stages: incubation, prodromal, acute, and convalescence.

▶ Effective practices for controlling and managing communicable illness in group settings include conducting daily observations, implementing health policies and sanitation procedures, enforcing immunization requirements, modifying the environment, working collaboratively with families, and educating children.

Terms to Know

antibodies *p. 113*
communicable *p. 114*
pathogen *p. 114*
susceptible host *p. 114*
respiratory tract *p. 114*
immunized *p. 114*

airborne transmission *p. 115*
fecal-oral transmission *p. 115*
direct contact *p. 115*
indirect contact *p. 116*
incubation *p. 116*
contagious *p. 116*

prodromal *p. 116*
acute *p. 117*
convalescent *p. 117*
lymph glands *p. 117*
universal infection control
    precautions *p. 124*

Chapter Review

A. **By Yourself:**

1. Define each of the *Terms to Know* listed at the end of this chapter.

2. Describe two examples that illustrate how an illness can be spread via:

   a. airborne transmission

   b. indirect contact

3. What immunizations, and how many of each, are recommended for a 30-month-old child?

4. Where can families in your community obtain immunizations for their children?

5. During what stage(s) of communicable illnesses are children most contagious?

B. As a Group:

1. Identify and discuss three factors that are required for an infection to be communicable.

2. What early signs would you be likely to observe in a child who was coming down with a respiratory virus?

3. Discuss specific practices that teachers can use in their classrooms to limit the spread of illnesses transmitted via:

   a. the respiratory tract

   b. the fecal-oral route

   c. skin conditions

   d. contaminated objects such as toys, towels, or changing mats

4. Discuss when and how universal precautions should be implemented in the classroom.

5. What special accommodations would be necessary if a program wanted to allow mildly ill children to remain onsite?

◖ Case Study

Laura arrived at the child care center with a runny nose and cough. Her mother informed the teachers that it was probably "just allergies" and left before Laura could be checked in. When the head teacher finally completed a health check, she discovered that Laura had a fever, red throat, and swollen glands. Laura's mother is a single parent, a student at the local community college, and also works part time at an early childhood program in another part of town.

1. How should the teachers handle Laura's immediate situation? Should she be allowed to stay or should they try to contact Laura's mother?

2. If Laura is allowed to stay at the center, what measures can be taken to limit the risk of spreading illness to other children?

3. If this is a repeated occurrence, what steps can be taken to make sure Laura's mother complies with the center's exclusion policies?

4. How can the center help Laura's mother avoid similar situations in the future?

◖ Application Activities

1. Obtain several agar growth medium plates. With sterile cotton applicators, culture one toy and the top of one table. Observe the "growth" after 24 hours and again after 48 hours. Wash the same items with a mild chlorine bleach solution and repeat the experiment. Compare the results.

2. Contact the Office of Public Health in your state (province/territory). Obtain data on the percentage of children under 6 years of age who are currently immunized. How does this figure compare to national goals? What suggestions do you have for improving this rate in your community? What immunizations are children required to have before they can attend an early childhood or kindergarten program in your state.

3. Locate and read OSHA's regulations and guidelines for implementing a blood-borne pathogen workplace policy (document CFR 1910.1030) available on their website (http://www.osha .gov/SLTC/bloodbornepathogens/index.html). Develop a written compliance plan for an early childhood center or school building.

4. Discuss how you would handle the following situations:

   a. The father of a toddler in your center is upset because his child has frequent colds.

   b. You observe your teacher covering a cough with her hand and then continuing to prepare snacks for the children.

   c. Your toddler group has experienced frequent outbreaks of strep throat in the past six months.

   d. While reviewing immunization records, you discover that one child has received only one dose of DTaP, IPV, and Hib.

   e. Gabriel announces that he threw up all night. You notice that his eyes appear watery and his cheeks are flushed.

   f. You find that one of your aides has stored all of the children's toothbrushes together in a sealed, plastic container.

   g. You overhear one of your paraprofessionals offering to retrieve medication from her backpack for a child who is complaining of a headache.

5. Review and compare health care policies from an early childhood center, home-based program, Head Start program, and elementary school. How are they similar? How do they differ?

Helpful Web Resources

American Public Health Association	http://www.apha.org
Canadian Paediatric Society	http://www.cps.ca
Centers for Disease Control and Prevention (CDC)	http://www.cdc.gov
Maternal and Child Health Bureau	http://mchb.hrsa.gov
National Center for Emerging & Zoonotic Infectious Diseases (NCEZID)	http://www.cdc.gov/ncezid
National Foundation for Infectious Diseases	http://www.nfid.org
National Institutes of Health	http://www.nih.gov

Visit the Education CourseMate for this textbook to access the eBook, Did You Get It? quizzes, Digital Downloads, TeachSource Video Cases, flashcards, and more. Go to CengageBrain.com to log in, register, or purchase access.

References

Abrevaya, J., & Mulligan, K. (2011). Effectiveness of state-level mandates: Evidence from the varicella vaccine, *Journal of Health Economics*, 30(5), 966–976.

American Public Health Association (APHA) & American Academy of Pediatrics (AAP). (2011). *Caring for our children. National health and safety performance standards: Guidelines for out-of-home care.* (3rd. ed.). Washington, DC.

Armellino, D., Hussain, E., Schilling, M., Senicola, W., Eichorn, A., Dlugacz, Y., & Farber, B. (2012). Using high-technology to enforce low-technology safety measures: The use of third-party remote video auditing and real-time feedback in healthcare, *Clinical Infectious Diseases*, 54(1), 1–7.

Barile, J., Kuperminc, G., Weintraub, E., Mink, J., & Thompson, W. (2012). Thimerosal exposure in early life and neuropsychological outcomes 7–10 years later, *Journal of Pediatric Psychology*, 37(1), 106–118.

Cannon, M., Westbrook, K., Levis, D., Schleiss, M., Thackeray, R., & Pass, R. (2012). Awareness of and behaviors related to child-to-mother transmission of cytomegalovirus, *Preventive Medicine*, 54(5), 351–357.

Centers for Disease Control and Prevention (CDC). (2012). U.S. vaccination coverage reported via NIS. Accessed on May 10, 2012 from http://www.cdc.gov/vaccines/stats-surv/nis/default.htm#nis.

Egger, J., Konty, K., Wilson, E., Karpati, A., Matte, T., Weiss, D., & Barbot, O. (2012). The effect of school dismissal on rates of influenza-like illness in New York City schools during the spring 2009 novel H1N1 outbreak, *Journal of School Health*, 82(3), 123–130.

Fuller, C., Savage, J., Besser, S., Hayward, A., Cookson, B., Cooper, B., & Stone, S. (2011). "The dirty hand in the latex glove": A study of hand hygiene compliance when gloves are worn, *Infection Control & Hospital Epidemiology*, 32(12), 1194–1199.

Gaudino, J., & Robison, S. (2012). Risk factors associated with parents claiming personal-belief exemptions to school immunization requirements: Community and other influences on more skeptical parents in Oregon, 2006, *Vaccine*, 30(6), 1132–1142.

Gerald, L., Gerald, J., Zhang, B., McClure, L., Bailey, W., & Harrington, K. (2012). Can a school-based hand hygiene program reduce asthma exacerbations among elementary school children?, *Journal of Allergy & Clinical Immunology*, 130(6), 1317–1324.

Gidengil, C., Lieu, T., Payne, K., Rusinak, D., Messonnier, M., & Prosser, L. (2012). Parental and societal values for the risks and benefits of childhood combination vaccines, *Vaccine*, 30(23), 3445–3452.

Gleddie, D. (2012). A journey into school health promotion: District implementation of the health promoting schools approach, *Health Promotion International*, 27(1), 82–89.

Gonzalez-Mena, J. & Eyer, D. (2011). *Infants, toddlers, and caregivers: A curriculum of respectful, responsive, relationship-based care and education.* (5th ed.). NY: McGraw-Hill.

Johnson, T., Weed, D., & Touger-Decker, R. (2012). School-based interventions for overweight and obesity in minority school children, *Journal of School Nursing*, 28(2), 116–123.

Luthy, K., Beckstrand, R., Callister, L., & Cahoon, S. (2013). Reasons parents exempt children from receiving immunizations, *The Journal of School Nursing*, 28(2), 153–160.

Nandrup-Bus, I. (2011). Comparative studies of hand disinfection and handwashing procedures as tested by pupils in intervention programs, *American Journal of Infection Control*, 39(6), 450–455.

Nriagu, J., Martin, J., Smith, P., & Socier, D. (2012). Residential hazards, high asthma prevalence and multimorbidity among children in Saginaw, Michigan, *Science of the Total Environment*, 416(1), 53–61.

Occupational Safety and Health Administration (OSHA). (2011). OSHA Fact Sheet: Hepatitis B vaccination protection. Accessed on May 10, 2012 from http://www.osha.gov/OshDoc/data_BloodborneFacts/bbfact05.pdf.

OSHA. (2003). Model plans and programs for the OSHA bloodborne pathogens and hazard communication standards. Accessed on May 12, 2012 from http://www.osha.gov/Publications/osha3186.html.

Public Health Agency of Canada (2012). Canadian immunization guide. Accessed on April 23, 2013 from http://www.phac-aspc.gc.ca/publicat/cig-gci/index-eng.php.

Rowe, M., & Casillas, A. (2011). Parental goals and talk with toddlers, *Infant & Child Development*, 20(5), 475–494.

Schulte, J., Williams, L., Asghar, J., Dang, T., Bedwell, S., Guerrero, K., Hamaker, D., Stonecipher, S., Zoretic, J., & Chow, C. (2012). How we didn't clean up until we washed our hands: Shigellosis in an elementary and middle school in North Texas, *Southern Medical Journal*, 105(1), 1–4.

Stebbins, S., Downs, J., & Vukotich, C. (2011). The effect of grade on compliance with nonpharmaceutical interventions to reduce influenza in an urban elementary school setting, *Journal of Public Health Management*, 17(1), 65–71.

Tak, S., Groenewold, M., Alterman, T., Park, R., & Calvert, G. (2011). Excess risk of head and chest colds among teachers and other school workers, *Journal of School Health*, 81(9), 560–565.

U.S. Department of Health & Human Services (DHHS). (2012). Healthy People 2020–Improving the life of Americans. Accessed on May 10, 2012 from http://www.healthypeople.gov.

Vermeer, H., van IJzendorn, M., Groeneveld, M., & Granger, D. (2012). Downregulation of the immune system in low-quality child care: The case of the secretory immunoglobulin A (Slg A) in toddlers, *Physiology & Behavior*, 105(2), 161–167.

White, C., Statile, A., Conway, P., Schoettker, P., Solan, L., Unaka, N., Vidwan, N., Warrick, S., Yau, C., & Connelly, B. (2012). Utilizing improvement science methods to improve physician compliance with proper hand hygiene, *Pediatrics*, 129(4), e1042–e1050.

Wilson, S., Jacob, C., & Powell, D. (2011). Behavior-change interventions to improve hand-hygiene practice: A review of alternatives to education, *Critical Public Health*, 21(1), 119–127.

chapter **6** **Childhood Illnesses: Identification and Management**

▶ **#1 a, b, and c:** Promoting child development and learning
▶ **#2 a, b, and c:** Building family and community relationships
▶ **#3 a, c, and d:** Observing, documenting, and assessing to support young children and families

Learning Objectives

After studying this chapter, you should be able to:

LO 6-1 Explain how communicable childhood illnesses such as chickenpox, colds, pinkeye, and head lice are spread and identify the appropriate control measures to be taken.

LO 6-2 Describe the teachers' role in addressing common acute childhood illnesses, such as ear infections, Lyme disease, and Sudden Infant Death Syndrome (SIDS).

Because young children are especially vulnerable to a variety of communicable and acute illnesses, classroom teachers must be prepared to identify and implement policies and practices designed to limit their spread. Teachers can best prepare themselves for this role by becoming familiar with the signs and **symptoms** of common childhood illnesses and the precautionary control measures appropriate for each. This knowledge can be useful for establishing program guidelines, creating meaningful lessons for children, and communicating important health information with families.

6-1 Common Communicable Childhood Illnesses

Protecting children's health in group settings requires teachers to have a sound understanding of common communicable illnesses—what causes them, how they are transmitted, and how they can be controlled (Table 6–1). Their knowledge of childhood illnesses and ability to implement infection control procedures, including hand washing and disinfection, are essential to children's well-being.

Teachers should be familiar with local public health regulations that specify which communicable illnesses must be reported. Notifying health officials of existing cases enables them to monitor communities for potential outbreaks and to provide additional information that can be shared with families.

symptoms – *changes in the body or its functions that are experienced by the affected individual.*

TABLE 6–1   Common Communicable Childhood Illnesses

Communicable Illness	Signs and Symptoms	Methods of Transmission	Incubation Period	Length of Communicability	Control Measures
Airborne Transmitted Illnesses					
Chickenpox	Slight fever, irritability, cold-like symptoms. Red rash that develops blister-like head, scabs later. Most abundant on covered parts of body, e.g., chest, back, neck, forearms.	Airborne through contact with secretions from the respiratory tract. Transmission from contact with blisters less common.	2–3 weeks after exposure.	2–3 days prior to the onset of symptoms until 5–6 days after first eruptions. Scabs are not contagious.	Specific control measures: (1) Exclusion of sick children. (2) Practice good personal hygiene, especially careful hand washing. Children can return to group care when all blisters have formed a dry scab (approximately 1 week). Immunization is now available.
Common cold	Highly contagious infection of the upper respiratory tract accompanied by slight fever, chills, runny nose, fatigue, muscle ache, and headaches. Onset may be sudden.	Airborne through contact with secretions from the respiratory tract, e.g., coughs, sneezes, eating utensils, etc.	12–72 hours.	About 1 day before onset of symptoms to 2–3 days after acute illness.	Prevention through education and good personal hygiene. Avoid exposure. Exclude first day or two. Antibiotics not effective against viruses. Avoid aspirin products (possible link to Reye's syndrome). Observe for complications, e.g., earaches, bronchitis, croup, pneumonia.
Fifth disease	Appearance of bright red rash on face, especially cheeks.	Airborne contact with secretions from the nose/mouth cf infected person.	4–14 days.	Prior to appearance of rash; probably not contagious after rash develops.	Children don't need to be excluded once rash appears. Frequent hand washing; frequent washing/disinfecting of toys/surfaces. Use care when handling tissues/nasal secretions.
Haemophilus influenza Type b (Hib)	An acute respiratory infection; frequently causes meningitis. Other complications include pneumonia, epiglottitis, arthritis, infections of the bloodstream, and conjunctivitis.	Airborne via secretions of the respiratory tract (nose, throat). Some children are carriers and may/may not have symptoms.	2–4 days.	Throughout acute phase; as long as organism is present. Noncommunicable 36–48 hours after treatment with antibiotics.	Identify and exclude sick children. Treatment with antibiotics 3–4 days before returning to group care. Notify families of exposed children to contact their physician. Immunize children. Practice good hand washing techniques; sanitize contaminated objects.

(continued)

TABLE 6–1 Common Communicable Childhood Illnesses *(continued)*

Communicable Illness	Signs and Symptoms	Methods of Transmission	Incubation Period	Length of Communicability	Control Measures
Airborne Transmitted Illnesses *(continued)*					
Measles (Rubeola)	Fever, cough, runny nose, eyes sensitive to light. Dark red blotchy rash that often begins on the face and neck, then spreads over the entire body. Highly communicable.	Airborne through coughs, sneezes, and contact with contaminated articles.	8–13 days; rash develops approximately 14 days after exposure.	From beginning of symptoms until 4 days after rash appears.	Most effective control method is immunization. Good personal hygiene, especially hand washing and covering coughs. Exclude child for at least 4 days after rash appears.
Meningitis	Sudden onset of fever, stiff neck, headache, irritability, and vomiting; gradual loss of consciousness, seizures, and death.	Airborne through coughs, nasal secretions; direct contact with saliva/nasal discharges.	Varies with the infectious organism; 2–4 days average.	Throughout acute phase; noncommunicable after antibiotic treatment.	Encourage immunization. Exclude child from school until medical treatment is completed. Use universal precautions when handling saliva/nasal secretions, frequent hand washing, and disinfecting of toys/surfaces.
Mononucleosis	Characteristic symptoms include sore throat, intermittent fever, fatigue, and enlarged lymph glands in the neck. May also be accompanied by headache and enlarged liver or spleen.	Airborne; also direct contact with saliva of an infected person.	2–4 weeks for children; 4–6 weeks for adults.	Unknown. Organisms may be present in oral secretions for as long as 1 year following illness.	None known. Child should be kept home until over the acute phase (6–10 days). Use frequent hand washing and careful disposal of tissues after coughing or blowing nose.
Mumps	Sudden onset of fever with swelling of the salivary glands.	Airborne through coughs and sneezes; direct contact with oral secretions of infected persons.	12–26 days.	6–7 days prior to the onset of symptoms until swelling in the salivary glands is gone (7–9 days).	Immunization provides permanent protection. Peak incidence is in winter and spring. Exclude children from school or group settings until all symptoms have disappeared.
Roseola infantum (6–24 mos.)	Most common in the spring and fall. Fever rises abruptly (102–105°F) and lasts 3–4 days; loss of appetite, listlessness, runny nose, rash on trunk, arms, and neck lasting 1–2 days.	Person to person; method unknown.	10–15 days.	1–2 days before onset to several days following fading of the rash.	Exclude from school or group care until rash and fever are gone.

Disease	Symptoms	Incubation	Transmission	Period of Communicability	Management
Rubella (German Measles)	Mild fever; rash begins on face and neck and rarely lasts more than 3 days. May have arthritis-like discomfort and swelling in joints.	4–21 days.	Airborne through contact with respiratory secretions, e.g., coughs, sneezes.	From one week prior to 5 days following onset of the rash.	Immunization offers permanent protection. Children must be excluded from school for at least 7 days after appearance of rash.
Streptococcal infections (strep throat, scarlatina, rheumatic fever)	Sudden onset. High fever accompanied by sore, red throat; may also have nausea, vomiting, headache, white patches on tonsils, and enlarged glands. Development of a rash depends on the infectious organism.	1–4 days.	Airborne via droplets from coughs or sneezes. May also be transmitted by food and raw milk.	Throughout the illness and for approximately 10 days afterward, unless treated with antibiotics. Medical treatment eliminates communicability within 36 hours. Can develop rheumatic fever or become a carrier if not treated.	Exclude child with symptoms. Antibiotic treatment is essential. Avoid crowding in classrooms. Practice frequent hand washing, educating children, and careful supervision of food handlers.
Tuberculosis	Many people have no symptoms. Active disease causes productive cough, weight loss, fatigue, loss of appetite, chills, night sweats.	2–3 months.	Airborne via coughs or sneezes.	As long as disease is untreated; usually noncontagious after 2–3 weeks on medication.	TB skin testing, especially babies and young children if there has been contact with an infected person. Seek prompt diagnosis and treatment if experiencing symptoms; complete drug therapy. Cover coughs/sneezes. Practice good hand washing.
Acquired Immuno-deficiency Syndrome (AIDS)	Flu-like symptoms, including fatigue, weight loss, enlarged lymph glands, persistent cough, fever, and diarrhea.	6 weeks to 8 years.	Children acquire virus when born to infected mothers, from contaminated blood transfusions, and possibly from breast milk of infected mothers. Adults acquire the virus via sexual transmission, contaminated drug needles, and blood transfusions.	Lifetime	Exclude children 0–5 years if they have open lesions, uncontrollable nosebleeds, bloody diarrhea, or are at high risk for exposing others to blood-contaminated body fluids. Use universal precautions when handling body fluids, including good hand washing techniques. Seal contaminated items, e.g., diapers, paper towels in plastic bags. Disinfect surfaces with bleach/water solution (1:10) or other disinfectant.

(continued)

TABLE 6-1 Common Communicable Childhood Illnesses (continued)

Communicable Illness	Signs and Symptoms	Methods of Transmission	Incubation Period	Length of Communicability	Control Measures
Blood-Borne Transmitted Illnesses					
Hepatitis B	Slow onset; loss of appetite, nausea, vomiting, abdominal pain, and jaundice. May also be asymptomatic.	Through contact with blood/body fluids containing blood.	45–180 days; average 60–80 days.	Varies; some persons are lifetime carriers.	Immunization is preferable. Use universal precautions when handling any blood/body fluids; use frequent hand washing.
Contact (Direct and Indirect) Transmitted Illnesses					
Conjunctivitis (Pinkeye)	Redness of the white portion (conjunctiva) of the eye and inner eyelid, swelling of the lids, yellow discharge from eyes, and itching.	Direct contact with discharge from eyes or upper respiratory tract of an infected person; through contaminated fingers; indirect contact with surfaces and objects (tissues, towels).	1–3 days.	Throughout active infection; several days up to 2–3 weeks.	Antibiotic treatment. Exclude child for 24 hours after medication is started. Frequent hand washing and disinfection of toys/surfaces is necessary.
Cytomegalovirus (CMV)	Often no symptoms in children under 2 years; sore throat, fever, fatigue in older children. High risk of fetal damage if mother is infected during pregnancy.	Person-to-person contact with body fluids, e.g., saliva, blood, urine, breast milk, in utero.	Unknown; may be 4–8 weeks.	Virus present (in saliva, urine) for months following infection.	No need to exclude children. Always wash hands after changing diapers or contact with saliva. Avoid kissing children's mouths or sharing eating utensils. Practice careful hand washing with children; wash/disinfect toys and surfaces frequently.
Hand-foot-and-mouth disease	Affects children under 10 years. Onset of fever, followed by blistered sores in the mouth/cheeks; 1–2 days later raised rash appears on palms of hands and soles of feet.	Person-to-person through direct contact with saliva, nasal discharge, or feces.	3–6 days.	7–10 days.	Exclude sick children for several days. Practice frequent hand washing, especially after changing diapers. Clean/disinfect surfaces.

asymptomatic – *having no symptoms.*

Herpes simplex (cold sores)	Clear blisters develop on face, lips, and other body parts that crust and heal within a few days.	Direct contact with saliva, on hands, or sexual contact.	Up to 2 weeks.	Virus remains in saliva for as long as 7 weeks following recovery.	No specific control. Frequent hand washing. Child does not have to be excluded from school.
Impetigo	Infection of the skin forming crusty, moist lesions usually on the face, ears, and around the nose. Highly contagious. Common among children.	Direct contact with discharge from sores; indirect contact with contaminated articles of clothing, tissues, etc.	2–5 days; may be as long as 10 days.	Until treated with antibiotics and all lesions are healed.	Exclude from group settings until lesions have been treated with antibiotics for 24–48 hours. Cover areas with bandage until treated.
Lice (head)	Lice are seldom visible to the naked eye. White nits (eggs) are visible on hair shafts. The most obvious symptom is itching of the scalp, especially behind the ears and at the base of the neck.	Direct contact with infected persons or with their personal articles, e.g., hats, hair brushes, combs, or clothing. Lice can survive for 2–3 weeks on bedding, carpet, furniture, car seats, clothing, etc.	Nits hatch in 1 week and reach maturity within 8–10 days.	While lice remain alive on infested persons or clothing; until nits have been destroyed.	Exclude infected children until treated. Wash hair with a special medicated shampoo; follow with a vinegar/water rinse (any concentration will work) to make nit removal easier (use a fine-toothed comb). Heat from a hair dryer helps to destroy eggs. All friends and family should be carefully checked. Thoroughly clean child's environment: vacuum carpets, furniture, car seats; wash/dry clean bedding, clothing, hairbrushes. Seal nonwashable items (hair ribbons, clips) in plastic bag and freeze for 1 week.
Ringworm	A fungal infection of the scalp, skin, or nails. Causes flat, spreading, oval-shaped lesions that may become dry and scaly or moist and crusted. When it is present on the feet it is commonly called athlete's foot. Infected nails may become discolored, brittle, or chalky or they may disintegrate.	Direct or indirect contact with infected persons, their personal items, showers, swimming pools, theater seats, etc. Dogs and cats may also be infected and transmit it to children or adults.	4–10 days (unknown for athlete's foot).	As long as lesions are present.	Exclude children from gyms, pools, or activities where they are likely to expose others. May return to group care following treatment with a fungicidal ointment. All shared areas, such as pools and showers, should be thoroughly cleansed with a fungicide.

(continued)

TABLE 6-1 Common Communicable Childhood Illnesses *(continued)*

Communicable Illness	Signs and Symptoms	Methods of Transmission	Incubation Period	Length of Communicability	Control Measures
Contact (Direct and Indirect) Transmitted Illnesses *(continued)*					
Rocky Mountain spotted fever	Onset usually abrupt; fever (101–104°F); joint and muscle pain, severe nausea and vomiting, and white coating on tongue. Rash appears on 2nd to 5th day over forehead, wrist, and ankles; later covers entire body. Can be fatal if untreated.	Indirect transmission: tick bite.	2–14 days; average 7 days.	Not contagious from person to person.	Prompt removal of ticks; not all ticks cause illness. Administration of antibiotics. Use insect repellent on clothes when outdoors.
Scabies	Characteristic burrows or linear tunnels under the skin, especially between the fingers and around the wrists, elbows, waist, thighs, and buttocks. Causes intense itching.	Direct contact with an infected person. Indirect contact with towels, bedding, and personal items of infected person.	Several days to 2–4 weeks.	Until all mites and eggs are destroyed.	Children should be excluded from school or group care until treated. Affected persons should bathe with prescribed soap and carefully launder all bedding and clothing. All contacts of the infected person should be notified.
Tetanus	Muscle spasms and stiffness, especially in the muscles around the neck and mouth. Can lead to convulsions, inability to breathe, and death.	Indirect: organisms live in soil and dust; enter body through wounds, especially puncture-type injuries, burns, and unnoticed cuts.	4 days to 2 weeks.	Not contagious.	Immunization every 8–10 years affords complete protection.
Fecal/Oral Transmitted Illnesses					
Dysentery (shigellosis)	Sudden onset of vomiting; diarrhea, may be accompanied by high fever, headache, abdominal pain. Stools may contain blood, pus, or mucus. Can be fatal in young children.	Fecal-oral transmission via contaminated objects; indirectly through ingestion of contaminated food or water, and via flies.	1–7 days.	Variable; may last up to 4 weeks or longer in the carrier state.	Exclude child during acute illness. Careful hand washing after bowel movements. Proper disposal of human feces; control of flies. Strict adherence to sanitary procedures for food preparation.

E. coli	Diarrhea, often bloody.	Spread through contaminated food, dirty hands.	3–4 days; can be as long as 10 days.	For duration of diarrhea; usually several days.	Exclude infected children until no diarrhea; practice frequent hand washing, especially after toileting and before preparing food.
Encephalitis	Sudden onset of headache, high fever, convulsions, vomiting, confusion, neck and back stiffness, tremors, and coma.	Indirect spread by bites from disease-carrying mosquitoes; in some areas transmitted by tick bites.	5–15 days.	Not contagious.	Spraying of mosquito breeding areas and use of insect repellents; public education.
Giardiasis	Many persons are asymptomatic. Typical symptoms include chronic diarrhea, abdominal cramping, bloating, pale and foul-smelling stools, weight loss, and fatigue.	Fecal-oral transmission; through contact with infected stool (e.g., diaper changes, helping child with soiled underwear), poor hand washing; passed from hands to mouth (toys, food). Also transmitted through contaminated water sources.	7–10 days average; can be as long as 5–25 days.	As long as parasite is present in the stool.	Exclude children until diarrhea ends. Scrupulous hand washing before eating, preparing food, and after using the bathroom. Maintain sanitary conditions in bathroom areas.
Hepatitis (infectious; type A)	Fever, fatigue, loss of appetite, nausea, abdominal pain (in region of liver). Illness may be accompanied by yellowing of the skin and eyeballs (jaundice) in adults, but not always in children. Acute onset.	Fecal-oral route. Also spread via contaminated food, water, milk, and objects.	1C–50 days (average range 25–30 days).	7–10 days prior to onset of symptoms to not more than 7 days after onset of jaundice.	Exclude from group settings a minimum of 1 week following onset. Special attention to careful hand washing after going to the bathroom and before eating is critical following an outbreak. Report disease incidents to public health authorities. Immunoglobulin (IG) recommended for protection of close contacts.

(continued)

TABLE 6–1 Common Communicable Childhood Illnesses *(continued)*

Fecal/Oral Transmitted Illnesses *(continued)*

Communicable Illness	Signs and Symptoms	Methods of Transmission	Incubation Period	Length of Communicability	Control Measures
Pinworms	Irritability, and itching of the rectal area. Common among young children. Some children have no symptoms.	Infectious eggs are transferred from person to person by contaminated hands (oral-fecal route). Indirect spread through contaminated bedding, food, clothing, swimming pool.	Life cycle of the worm is 3–6 weeks; persons can also re-infect themselves.	2–8 weeks or as long as a source of infection remains present.	Infected children must be excluded from school until treated with medication; may return after initial dose. All infected and non-infected family members must be treated at one time. Frequent hand washing is essential; discourage nail biting or sucking of fingers. Daily baths and change of linen are necessary. Disinfect school toilet seats and sink handles at least once a day. Vacuum carpeted areas daily. Eggs are also destroyed when exposed to temperatures over 132°F. Education and good personal hygiene are vital to control.
Salmonellosis	Abdominal pain and cramping, sudden fever, severe diarrhea (may contain blood), nausea and vomiting that lasts 5–7 days.	Fecal-oral transmission via dirty hands. Also spread via contaminated food (especially improperly cooked poultry, milk, eggs), water, and infected animals.	12–36 hours.	Throughout acute illness; may remain a carrier for months.	Attempt to identify source. Exclude children/adults with diarrhea; may return when symptoms end. Carriers should not handle or prepare food until stool cultures are negative. Practice good hand washing and sanitizing procedures.

▼ **Identifying the early signs of childhood illnesses is an important control measure.**

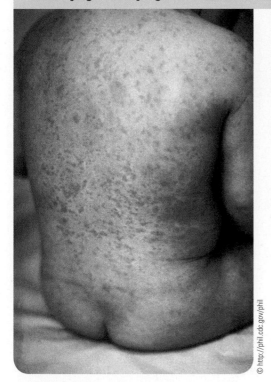

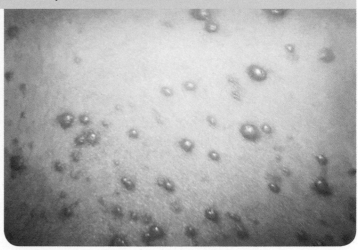

© http://phil.cdc.gov/phil

Did You Get It?

Chicken pox is a highly infectious disease caused by the varicella zoster virus. A child who has had chickenpox can return to the classroom when all blisters have:

a. disappeared completely
b. formed dry scabs
c. started oozing
d. started to decrease in number

Take the full quiz on CourseMate.

6-2 Common Acute Childhood Illnesses

Children experience many forms of acute illness; however, not all of these are contagious (Fiore et al., 2012; Sun & Sundell, 2011). Teachers must be able to distinguish conditions that are communicable from those that are limited to an individual child. *However, teachers must never attempt to diagnose children's health conditions.* Their primary responsibilities are to identify children who are ill, make them comfortable until parents arrive, and advise the family to contact their health care provider. The remainder of this chapter is devoted to descriptions of several common childhood illnesses and acute health conditions.

6-2a Colds

Children may experience as many as seven to eight colds during a typical year. This number tends to decrease as children mature and their respiratory passageways increase in size, their immune systems become more effective at warding off illness, and they begin to develop healthy personal habits. Cold symptoms can range from frequent sneezing and runny nose to fever, sore throat, cough, headache, and muscle aches.

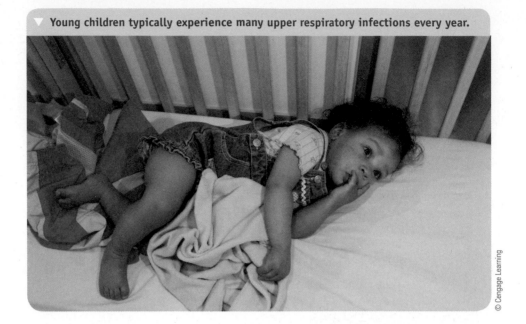

▼ **Young children typically experience many upper respiratory infections every year.**

Cause Most colds are caused by a viral **infection**, primarily rhinoviruses and coronaviruses. They spread rapidly and have a short incubation stage of 1 to 2 days.

Management Because colds are highly contagious during the first day or two, it is best to exclude children from group settings. Rest and increased fluid intake (water, fruit juices, soups) are recommended. Non-aspirin fever-reducing medication is usually adequate treatment for a cold and may help children rest more comfortably. (Note: Schools must obtain a physician's approval before administering any medication.)

Antibiotics are not effective against most viruses and are therefore of limited value for treating simple colds. However, a physician may prescribe antibiotics to treat complications or secondary infections, such as fever, red throat, white patches on tonsils (one indication of strep throat), or yellow nasal drainage. Toddlers and young children are more susceptible to these conditions and should be observed closely. Families should be advised to seek immediate medical attention for children who do not improve after 4 to 5 days or if they develop any secondary complications.

Some children who have developmental disabilities such as Down syndrome or special medical conditions such as leukemia, or allergies, may experience chronic cold-like symptoms including runny nose and a productive cough. It isn't necessary for these children to be excluded from school unless they also show signs of a secondary infection (e.g., fever, yellow nasal discharge, productive cough).

6-2b Diaper Rash (Diaper Dermatitis)

Diaper rash is an irritation of the skin in and around the buttocks and genital area. Infants who have sensitive skin or who are formula-fed versus breast-fed are more likely to experience periodic outbreaks of diaper rash (Hockenberry & Wilson, 2012).

Cause Prolonged contact with ammonia in urine and organic acids in stools can burn an infant's skin and cause patches of red, raised areas, or tiny pimples. In severe cases, areas that are open and weeping may become infected with yeast or bacteria. Reactions to fabric softeners, soaps, lotions, powders, antibiotics, foods, and certain brands of disposable diapers may also cause some infants and toddlers to develop diaper rash.

infection – *a condition that results when a pathogen invades and establishes itself within a susceptible host.*

CONNECTING TO EVERYDAY PRACTICE

Children's Cough and Cold Medications

Pharmacy shelves are lined with an abundance of non-prescription cold remedies that range from cough suppressants and expectorants to antihistamines and decongestants for relieving a stuffy nose. Warnings have been issued by the Food and Drug Administration (FDA) against giving these types of medications to children under 6 years of age (Isbister, Prior, & Kilham, 2012). Consumers are also being advised not to administer multiple medications (such as liquid acetaminophen and a decongestant) that may include the same ingredients because this can cause an overdose (Aschenbrenner, 2012). These directives have left many parents frustrated and wondering what they can do when children do get sick.

Think About This:

▶ Why are cold and cough remedies not recommended for use with children under 6 years?

▶ What would you tell parents to do with these medications if they still have them in their cabinets?

▶ How would you respond to a parent who brings in an over-the-counter cough medicine and asks you to give it to his 3-year-old daughter?

▶ What alternative measures could you suggest that a parent use to make a child with a cold feel better?

Management Prompt changing of wet or soiled diapers followed by a thorough cleansing of the skin is often sufficient to prevent and treat diaper rash. Baby products, such as powders and lotions, should be avoided because they can encourage bacterial growth when combined with urine and feces. In addition, infants are apt to inhale fine powder particles and some products contain phthalates, which may have harmful effects on children's development and reproductive systems (Lampel & Jacob, 2011). A thin layer of petroleum jelly or zinc oxide ointment applied to irritated areas will help to protect the skin. Allowing the infant to go without diapers (when at home) and exposing affected areas to the air can also speed the healing process. If the diaper rash does not improve in 2 or 3 days, parents should be encouraged to contact their health care provider.

6-2c Diarrhea

The term "diarrhea" refers to frequent watery or very soft bowel movements. At times they may be foul-smelling or contain blood or mucus, especially if a child is taking antibiotics or has an intestinal infection. It is not uncommon for young children to experience occasional episodes of diarrhea in response to dietary changes or food sensitivities. However, diarrhea that is frequent (more than seven or eight stools in 8 hours) or prolonged (lasting 6 or 7 days) and accompanied by fever, vomiting, and dehydration requires medical attention.

Cause Diarrhea can either be infectious or noninfectious. Infectious forms of diarrhea include:

▶ viral or bacterial infections, such as rotavirus, hepatitis A, or salmonellosis
▶ parasitic, such as giardia

Causes of noninfectious diarrhea can include:

▶ fruit juices containing fructose and sorbitol (Jones et al., 2013)
▶ antibiotic therapy
▶ recent dietary changes
▶ food allergies, such as lactose or gluten intolerance
▶ food poisoning
▶ illnesses, such as earaches, colds, strep throat, or cystic fibrosis

Until new vaccines became available in 2006, approximately 55,000–70,000 children were hospitalized each year for severe diarrhea caused by rotavirus (Dennehy, 2012). Because children under age 3 are the most frequent victims of this illness, infants are now being immunized against the disease at 2, 4, and 6 months of age. Consequently, the numbers of children who experience rotavirus infections and hospitalizations have declined significantly.

Frequent or prolonged diarrhea can result in **dehydration**, especially in infants and toddlers. Dehydration involves a loss of body water and can occur quickly in young children due to their poor fluid regulation and small body size. Because excessive dehydration can be fatal in infants and young children, they should be observed closely for:

- dryness of the mouth
- **listlessness**
- sunken eyes
- absence of tears
- decreased or no urinary output
- rapid, weak pulse
- skin that loses elasticity and becomes dough-like

Management It is important to monitor and record the frequency (number) and amount (small, large) of bowel movements. The color, consistency, and presence of any blood, mucus, or pus should also be noted. Be sure to check the child's temperature and observe for any signs of discomfort. Prompt medical advice should be sought if diarrhea is severe or prolonged, or the child becomes lethargic or drowsy. Adults and children should practice meticulous hand washing to avoid infecting themselves and others.

Most cases of diarrhea can be treated by temporarily replacing solid foods in the child's diet with a commercially prepared electrolyte solution. This solution supplies important fluids and salts lost through diarrhea and helps to restore normal function. Liquids and soft foods can gradually be added back into the child's diet once the diarrhea has ended. Any complaint of pain that is continuous or located in the lower right side of the **abdomen** should be reported promptly to the child's family and checked by a physician.

Children who have experienced diarrhea during the past 24 hours should be excluded from group settings. Exceptions to this policy would include children whose diarrhea resulted from noncontagious conditions such as food allergies, dietary changes, or recent antibiotic treatment. However, even these children may not feel well enough to attend school and to participate in the day's activities. The problem and inconvenience of frequent accidental soiling may also be too time-consuming for teachers to manage.

Diarrhea lasting longer than a week should be cause for concern, especially if it is accompanied by bloating, change of appetite, or weight loss. The child should remain at home until a cause is determined and conditions such as giardia, dysentery, or hepatitis A have been ruled out.

6-2d **Dizziness**

It is not unusual for children to complain of momentary dizziness or a spinning sensation after vigorous play. However, repeated complaints of dizziness should be noted and reported to the child's family. They should be advised to contact the child's physician to determine a possible underlying cause.

Cause Dizziness can be a symptom of other health conditions, including:

- ear infections
- fever

dehydration – *a state in which there is an excessive loss of body fluids or extremely limited fluid intake. Symptoms may include loss of skin tone, sunken eyes, and mental confusion.*

listlessness – *a state characterized by a lack of energy or interest in one's affairs.*

abdomen – *the portion of the body located between the diaphragm (located at the base of the lungs) and the pelvic or hip bones.*

- headaches
- head injuries
- anemia
- nasal congestion and sinus infections
- brain tumor (rare)

Management Temporary episodes of dizziness usually respond to simple first aid measures. Have the child lie down quietly or sit with head resting on or between the knees until the sensation has passed. Quiet play can be resumed when the child no longer feels dizzy. Inform the child's family of this experience so they can continue to monitor the condition at home.

If dizziness is accompanied by any loss of balance or coordination, parents should be encouraged to check with the child's physician at once. Dizziness that results from an underlying health problem will usually not respond to most first aid measures.

6-2e Earaches

Ear infections, also known as otitis media, are relatively common during the first three or so years of a child's life and affect boys more often than girls. More than half of all infants, especially those who are not breast-fed, experience an ear infection before their first birthday (Salone, Vann, & Dee, 2013). However, by age 5, children usually begin to have fewer ear infections as their resistance (antibody production) improves and structures in the ear, nose, and throat increase in size.

Certain groups of children appear to be more susceptible to ear infections. Children of Native American and Eskimo ethnicity are known to experience a higher rate of ear infections, possibly related to structural differences in the ear canal (Said et al., 2011). Children who are exposed to second-hand smoke are also at greater risk (Jones et al., 2012). Ear infections are also more common among children who have medical conditions such as cleft palate or developmental disabilities such as Williams syndrome, Turner's syndrome, Down syndrome, fragile X, or autism (Schieve et al., 2012). Infants who are fed in a reclining position experience more ear infections because milk can enter the Eustachian tube (passageway connecting the ear, nose, and throat) when the baby swallows. For this reason, it is important to always hold an infant in a semi-upright position (with head slightly elevated) during feedings. Additionally, studies have shown that children in group care are exposed to more upper respiratory infections and, thus, also experience more ear infections than those who remain at home (AAO-HNS, 2012).

Cause Ear infections are generally caused by a bacterial or viral infection that affects the middle ear (behind the ear drum). The resulting inflammation and fluid buildup (effusion) can result in considerable ear pain, fever, irritability, and temporary hearing loss. Ear pain in children can also be caused by several additional conditions, including:

- allergies
- nasal congestion
- dental cavities and eruption of new teeth
- excessive ear wax
- foreign objects, such as plastic beads, food, small toy pieces, or stones
- feeding infants in a reclining position

Young children, especially infants and toddlers who have limited language, should be closely monitored for signs of a potential ear infection, including:

- nausea, vomiting, and diarrhea
- tugging or rubbing of the affected ear
- refusal to eat or swallow
- redness of the outer ear
- fever
- dizziness or unsteady balance
- irritability

▸ discharge from the ear canal
▸ difficulty hearing
▸ crying when placed in a reclining position

Management   Ear infections are not contagious, but the bacteria or virus that caused the initial upper respiratory infection (such as a cold) is easily spread. For this reason, children who develop otitis media may not need to be excluded from group settings unless they are too ill to participate in daily activities or have other symptoms that are contagious. Teachers may be able to provide temporary relief from earache pain by having the child lie down with the affected ear on a soft blanket; the warmth helps to soothe discomfort. A small, dry cotton ball placed in the outer ear may also help reduce pain by keeping air out of the ear canal. If excess wax or a foreign object is causing the child's ear pain, it must be removed only by a health care provider.

Persistent complaints of ear pain or earache should not be ignored and need to be checked by the child's health care provider if symptoms last longer than 3 or 4 days. In most cases, the infection and fluid will resolve without treatment. However, some children may develop chronic otitis media and continue to have middle ear fluid even though the initial infection has cleared up. If left untreated, this condition can interfere with a child's speech and language development (Cunningham et al., 2012; Boudewyns et al., 2011; Danhauer, Johnson, & Caudle, 2011).

Physicians now use several approaches to treat acute bacterial ear infections. Current guidelines recommend taking a wait-and-see approach and limiting the use of antibiotics to reduce the potential of drug resistance. If children are placed on oral antibiotics, it is important that all medication be taken; failure to finish medication can result in a recurrence of the infection. Children's ears should be rechecked by a health care provider after the prescribed course of medication has been completed to be certain the infection and fluid are gone. In some cases, a second round of medication may be needed. Children who have recurrent infections and chronic fluid buildup may have small plastic tubes surgically inserted in the eardrum to drain the fluid and decrease the risk of permanent hearing loss (Robb & Williamson, 2012). Teachers should be alert to any children who have tubes in their ears. Special precautions must be taken to avoid getting water in the outer ear canal during activities that involve water play, such as swimming, bathing, or playing in pools or sprinklers. Ear plugs or a special plastic putty are commonly used for this purpose.

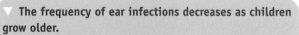

▾ **The frequency of ear infections decreases as children grow older.**

© Cengage Learning

6-2f   Fainting

Fainting, a momentary loss of consciousness, occurs when blood supply to the brain is temporarily reduced.

Cause   Possible causes for this condition in young children include:

▸ anemia
▸ breath-holding
▸ **hyperventilation**
▸ extreme stress, excitement, or hysteria
▸ drug reactions
▸ illness, infection, or extreme pain
▸ poisoning

---

hyperventilation – *rapid breathing often with forced inhalation; can lead to sensations of dizziness, lightheadedness, and weakness.*

Management Children may initially complain of feeling dizzy or weak. Their skin may appear pale, cool, and moist shortly before they collapse. If this occurs, lay the child down, elevate the legs 8 to 10 inches on a pillow or similar object, and observe breathing and pulse frequently. A light blanket can be placed over the child for extra warmth. Clothing should be loosened from around the neck and waist to make breathing easier. No attempt should be made to give the child anything to eat or drink until consciousness is regained. The child's family should be notified and encouraged to consult with their health care provider.

6-2g Fever

Fever is not an illness, but it is the body's way of indicating that a system is not functioning properly or is trying to fight infection. Activity, age, eating, sleeping, and the time of day can cause normal fluctuations in children's temperature. However, a persistent elevated **temperature** should be evaluated, especially if the child also complains of headache, coughing, nausea, or sore throat.

Cause Common causes of fever in children include:

- viral and bacterial illnesses, such as ear, skin, and upper respiratory infections
- urinary tract infections
- heat stroke and overheating

Changes in children's appearance and behavior may be an early indication of **fever**. Other signs may include:

- flushed or reddened face
- listlessness or desire to sleep
- "glassy" eyes
- loss of appetite
- complaints of not feeling well
- chills
- warm, dry skin; older children may have increased perspiration

Management Children's temperature should be checked if there is reason to believe that they may have a fever. Only digital and infrared **tympanic** thermometers are recommended for use in schools and group-care settings because of safety and liability concerns (Table 6–2). These thermometers are quick and efficient to use, especially with children who may be fussy or uncooperative, and they provide readings that are reasonably accurate (Table 6–3) (Padilla-Raygoza et al., 2011). Infrared forehead thermometers are currently being marketed, but studies have shown them to be unreliable. Glass mercury thermometers are considered unsafe to use with young children and also pose hazardous environmental concerns.

TABLE 6–2 Preferred Methods for Checking Children's Temperature in Group Settings (in Rank Order)

Age	Method
Infants and toddlers	axillary
2-5 year-olds	tympanic
	axillary
	oral
5 years and older	oral
	tympanic
	axillary

temperature – *a measurement of body heat; varies with the time of day, activity, and method of measurement.*
fever – *an elevation of body temperature above normal; a temperature over 99.4°F or 37.4°C orally is usually considered a fever.*
tympanic – *referring to the ear canal.*

TABLE 6–3   A Comparison of Thermometer Options

Type	Advantages	Disadvantages	Normal Range	How to Use	How to Clean
Digital thermometer	Can be used to check oral and axillary temperatures.	Takes 1–2 minutes to obtain a reading.	(Axillary) 94.5–99.0°F (34.7–37.2°C)	Turn switch on; wait for beep to signal ready.	Remove disposable cover.
	Safe, unbreakable.	Requires child to sit still.	(Oral) 94.5–99.5°F (34.7–37.5°C)	Apply disposable sanitary cover (optional).	Wipe with alcohol or clean with soap and cool water.
	Numbers are easy to read.	Axillary readings are less accurate than oral.		Place under tongue (oral) or in crease of armpit; hold in place; wait for beep to signal reading.	
	Beeps when ready.	Must purchase batteries and disposable covers.			
	Easy to clean.				
Tympanic thermometer	Yields a quick reading.	Thermometer is expensive to buy (approximately $40–60).	96.4–100.4°F (35.8–38°C)	Apply disposable earpiece.	Wipe instrument (probe) with alcohol.
	Easy to use.	Accuracy of reading depends on correct positioning in child's ear canal (differs from child to child).		Turn on start button.	
	Can check child's temperature while asleep.	Must purchase batteries and disposable ear piece coverings.		Insert probe carefully into ear canal opening; reading appears in seconds.	
	Requires limited child cooperation.				

Children with an axillary temperature over 99.1°F (37.2°C) or a tympanic reading over 100.4°F (38°C) should be observed carefully for other symptoms of illness. Unless a program's exclusion policies require children with fevers to be sent home, they can be moved to a separate room or quiet area in the classroom and monitored closely. If there are no immediate indications of acute illness, children should be encouraged to rest. Lowering the room temperature, removing warm clothing, and offering extra fluids can also help to make a child feel more comfortable. Fever-reducing medications should be administered only with a physician's approval. Families should also be notified so they can decide whether to take the child home or wait to see if any further symptoms develop.

6-2h Headaches

Headaches are not a common complaint of young children, but when they do occur they are usually a symptom of some other condition. Repeated complaints of headache should be brought to the family's attention.

Cause Children may experience headaches as the result of several conditions, including:

- bacterial or viral infections
- allergies
- head injuries
- emotional tension or stress
- reaction to medication
- lead poisoning
- hunger
- eye strain
- nasal congestion
- brain tumor (rare)
- constipation
- carbon monoxide poisoning

Management In the absence of any fever, rash, vomiting, or **disorientation**, children who experience headaches can remain in care but should continue to be observed for other indications of illness or injury. Frequently, their headaches will disappear with rest. However, patterns of repeated or intense headaches should be noted and families encouraged to discuss the problem with the child's physician.

6-2i Heat Rash

Heat rash is most commonly seen in infants and toddlers.

Cause Heat rash is caused by a blockage in the sweat glands. It occurs more commonly during the summer months, but can also develop when an infant or child is dressed too warmly. Some children have sensitive skin and may develop a heat rash from clothing made of synthetic fabrics.

Management Heat rash is not contagious. However, several measures can be taken to make a child more comfortable. Affected areas can be washed with cool water, dried thoroughly, and dusted sparingly with cornstarch.

6-2j Lyme Disease

Lyme disease is a tick-borne infection most prevalent along the East Coast, although it has been identified in nearly every U.S. state and many provinces of Canada (Eisen et al., 2012). The number of cases continues to increase. There were approximately 22,000 confirmed cases and 7,000 probable cases reported in 2010, with children ages birth to 15 years (especially boys 5 to 9 years) experiencing the highest incidence (CDC, 2012b).

---

disorientation – *lack of awareness or ability to recognize familiar persons or objects.*
Lyme disease – *bacterial illness caused by the bite of infected deer ticks found in grassy or wooded areas.*

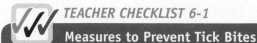

TEACHER CHECKLIST 6-1

Measures to Prevent Tick Bites

- Encourage children to wear long pants, a long-sleeved shirt, socks, shoes, and a hat; light-colored clothing makes it easier to spot small deer ticks.
- Apply insect/tick repellent containing DEET to clothing and exposed skin areas. Be sure to follow manufacturer's directions and avoid aerosol sprays that children might inhale.
- Discourage children from rolling in the grass or sitting on fallen logs.
- Remove clothing as soon as children come indoors and check all body areas (under arms, around waist, behind knees, in the groin, on neck) and hair.
- Bathe or shower to remove any ticks.
- Wash clothing in soapy water and dry in dryer. (Heat will destroy ticks.)
- Continue to check children for any sign of ticks that may have been overlooked on a previous inspection.
- Promptly remove any tick discovered on the skin and wash the area carefully. (See Chapter 9).

TeachSource Digital Download   Download from CourseMate.

Cause   This bacterial illness is caused by the bite of a tiny, infected deer tick; however, not all deer ticks are infected, nor will everyone who is bitten develop Lyme disease. Many species of the deer tick are commonly found in grassy and wooded areas during the summer and fall months.

Management   The most effective way to prevent Lyme disease is to take preventive measures whenever children will be spending time outdoors, especially in grassy or wooded areas (Teacher Checklist 6-1). It is important that these practices also be followed while children are attending school (Hamlen, 2012).

Because deer ticks are exceptionally small, they are easily overlooked. Development of any unusual symptoms following a tick bite should be reported immediately to a physician. However, Lyme disease can be difficult to diagnose in some cases because the early symptoms are easily mistaken for other less serious illnesses. In the early weeks following a bite, a small, red, and flat or raised area may develop at the site, followed by a localized rash that gradually disappears. Flu-like symptoms, including fever, chills, fatigue, headache, and joint pain, may also be experienced during this stage. If the bacterial infection is not diagnosed early and treated with antibiotics, complications, including arthritis, heart, or neurological problems can develop within 2 years of the initial bite. A simple blood test is available for early detection.

6-2k **Sore Throat**

Sore throats are a relatively common complaint among young children, especially during the fall and winter seasons. Teachers must rely on their observations to determine when infants and toddlers may be experiencing a sore throat because children of this age are unlikely to verbalize their discomfort. Fussiness, lack of interest in food or refusal to eat, difficulty swallowing, enlarged lymph glands, fever, and fatigue may be early indications that the child is not feeling well.

Cause   Most sore throats are caused by a viral or bacterial infection. However, some children may experience a scratchy throat as the result of sinus drainage, mouth breathing, or allergies.

Management   It is extremely important not to ignore a child's complaint of sore throat. A small percentage of sore throats are caused by a highly contagious streptococcal infection (Table 6–1). Although most children are quite ill with these infections, some may experience only mild symptoms, such as headache or stomachache and fever, or none at all. Unknowingly, they may also become carriers of the infection and capable of spreading it to others. A routine throat culture is necessary to determine if a strep infection is present and which antibiotic will provide the most effective treatment. If left untreated, strep throat can lead to serious health complications, including rheumatic fever, arthritis, heart valve damage, and kidney disease (Hockenberry & Wilson, 2012).

Sore throats resulting from viral infections are not usually harmful, but they may cause the child considerable discomfort. Cool beverages (and popsicles) can soothe an irritated throat. Antibiotics are not effective against viral infections and, therefore, seldom prescribed.

6-2l Stomachaches

Most children experience an occasional stomachache from time to time. However, children may use this term to describe a range of discomforts, from hunger or a full bladder to actual nausea, cramping, or emotional upset. Teachers can use their observation and questioning skills to determine a probable cause.

Cause   Children's stomachaches are often a symptom of some other condition. There are many possible causes, including:

- food allergies or intolerance
- appendicitis
- **intestinal** infections (e.g., giardiasis, salmonella, E. coli)
- urinary tract infections
- gas or constipation
- side effect to medication, especially antibiotics
- change in diet
- emotional stress or desire for attention
- hunger
- diarrhea and vomiting
- strep throat

Management   There are several ways to determine whether or not a child's stomach pain is serious. Is the discomfort continuous or a cramping-type pain that comes and goes? Does the child have a fever? Is the child able to continue playing? If no fever is present, the stomachache is probably not serious. Encourage the child to use the bathroom and note if **urination** or having a bowel movement relieves the pain. Have the child rest quietly to see if the discomfort goes away. Check with the child's family to determine if there has been a dietary change or new medication prescribed. Stomach pain or stomachaches should be considered serious if they:

- disrupt a child's activity, such as running, playing, eating, sleeping
- cause tenderness of the abdomen
- are accompanied by diarrhea, vomiting, or severe cramping
- last longer than 3 to 4 hours
- result in stools that are bloody or contain mucus

If any of these conditions occur while the child is attending school or group care, the family should be notified and advised to seek prompt medical attention.

6-2m Sudden Infant Death Syndrome (SIDS)

Sudden infant death syndrome (SIDS) refers to the unexplainable death of an infant under 12 months of age. It is a leading cause of infant mortality and typically peaks between the second and fourth months. Deaths are more likely to occur during sleep (nighttime and naps), and especially during the fall and winter months. Despite aggressive awareness campaigns, approximately 2,200 infants die each year (CDC, 2012d).

....

intestinal – *pertaining to the intestines and intestinal tract.*
urination – *the act of emptying the bladder of urine.*

Cause   It was previously thought that infants who died of SIDS were otherwise healthy. However, new evidence suggests that defects may exist in areas of the infant's brain (brainstem) that control breathing, temperature regulation, heart rate, and sleep patterns (Rand et al., 2013). These abnormalities appear to increase the infant's vulnerability to certain environmental conditions, such as second-hand smoke and respiratory infections, that would not pose the same risk for typically developing babies. Additional factors that increase an infant's risk of dying from SIDS include:

- prematurity
- weighing less than 3.5 pounds at birth
- being a male child
- being of African American or American Indian/Alaska Native ethnicity (CDC, 2012c)
- having a sibling who also died of SIDS
- family poverty
- prenatal exposure to alcohol or illicit drugs, such as cocaine, heroin, or methadone
- maternal smoking (during and after pregnancy) (Trachtenberg, et al, 2012)
- being born to a teenage mother

Children born into families with limited education and financial resources seem to experience the highest rate of SIDS deaths (Rowley & Hogan, 2012). Many of these mothers failed to obtain routine prenatal care or they engaged in unhealthy practices during and after their pregnancy. Infants who die of SIDS often experience repeated interruptions of breathing called **apnea**. Researchers continue to investigate possible connections between this breathing disturbance and other factors, including:

- toxic mattress fumes
- immunizations
- use of pacifiers
- air pollution
- bed sharing or co-sleeping with parents
- respiratory infections (such as colds and flu)
- swaddling

To date there has been no scientific evidence linking toxic mattress fumes or immunizations to SIDS. In fact, infants who are immunized are less likely to die from SIDS (AAP, 2011). Positive relationships between SIDS and air pollution have led to recommendations that families avoid exposing infants to second-hand smoke and other indoor pollutants. The practice of bed-sharing has also been linked to an increased risk of SIDS and is strongly discouraged (Schnitzer, Covington, & Dykstra, 2012).

Management   An infant's sleeping position has proven to be the most effective practice for preventing SIDS. This discovery led to a nationwide "Back to Sleep" campaign, which has been ongoing and credited with significantly reducing SIDS deaths (NICHD, 2012). Multiple child and maternal government and private agencies continue to educate parents about proper sleep positioning for infants—*that babies must always be placed on their backs for sleeping*—and have extended their efforts to include early childhood teachers and caregivers. Although fewer than 20 percent of SIDS fatalities occur while infants are being cared for outside of their home, it is essential that teachers take the same precautionary steps to avoid any preventable death (AAP, 2012a). Despite ongoing educational efforts, researchers have found that many non-parental caregivers continue to place infants in unsafe conditions and sleeping positions. As a result, many states now address infant sleep position in their child care licensing regulations so that programs will no longer be able to ignore this critical safety practice.

Initial fears that infants would be more likely to choke when placed on their back for sleeping have not proven true. It isn't clear whether back-sleeping improves infants' oxygen intake or reduces their breathing in of carbon dioxide. However, the SIDS death rate

apnea – *momentary absence of breathing.*

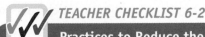

TEACHER CHECKLIST 6-2

Practices to Reduce the Risk of Sudden Infant Death Syndrome (SIDS)

- Always put infants to sleep on their back for naptimes and bedtimes unless a health condition prevents this.
- Use a firm mattress that fits snugly in a safety-approved crib; cover mattress with a tight-fitting sheet. Never place infants on a waterbed, sheepskin, comforter, sofa cushions, or other soft bedding material.
- Remove pillows, thick or fluffy blankets, bumper pads, positioning wedges, and soft toys from an infant's bed.
- Cover infants with a thin blanket, tucking the bottom half under the mattress (never cover their head) (Figure 6–1).
- Dress infants in light sleepwear and maintain room temperature between 68–72° F to avoid overheating.
- Remove all objects in the surrounding area that could cause entrapment, such as window blind cords, baby monitors, light or appliance cords, and mobiles.
- Offer a pacifier to infants who use them; breast-fed infants should be offered a pacifier only after feeding.
- Avoid exposing infants to second-hand smoke, car exhaust, wood smoke, and other air pollutants.
- Limit infants' exposure to persons who have colds or other respiratory infections.
- Provide brief periods of tummy time so infants build stronger neck muscles and don't develop flat spots on their heads.
- Encourage mothers to obtain professional prenatal care for themselves *and* recommended well-child checkups and immunizations for their infant.
- Encourage and support breastfeeding for as long as mothers are able; breast milk aids in protecting infants against SIDS.
- Know how to respond to medical emergencies.

TeachSource Digital Download | Download from CourseMate.

has decreased by nearly 50 percent since this practice was initially recommended (CDC, 2012d).

Infants should not share a crib with another infant nor sleep in a bed with adults; both of these practices have been found to increase the risk of SIDS. However, researchers have also discovered that the risk of SIDS is reduced when an infant's crib is placed in the same room with parents (Vennemann et al., 2012). The use of pacifiers has also been shown to reduce SIDS deaths although it is unclear why this practice is beneficial (Trachenberg et al., 2012). Additional guidelines for safe infant sleep are outlined in Teacher Checklist 6-2.

Because infants spend many hours sleeping, it is important to change their position often during times when they are awake. Weak neck muscles make it difficult for infants to turn their head from side to side. As a result, flat spots may develop if an infant is left in the same position for extended periods. These can be prevented by placing the infant on her tummy for brief periods or propping her on either side when she is awake. Alternating an infant's position in the crib is also beneficial—one day the head should be placed at the head of the crib, the following day the head should be placed at the foot of the bed. This prevents the infant from consistently laying on the same side of his or her head every day.

Because there is often no identifiable cause for SIDS, families tend to blame themselves for having been negligent or using poor judgment. They may believe that somehow this tragedy could have been prevented. Consequently, families who have experienced the unexpected death of an infant from SIDS require special emotional support and counseling. Siblings may also be affected by an infant's death and should be included in counseling therapy. Information and

Figure 6–1 Putting infants to sleep on their backs significantly reduces the risk of SIDS.

support groups are available to help families cope with their grief, including local chapters of several national SIDS organizations:

▶ First Candle/SIDS Alliance (http://www.sidsalliance.org)
▶ American SIDS Institute (http://www.sids.org)
▶ National SUID/SIDS Resource Center (http://www.sidscenter.org)
▶ Association of SIDS and Infant Mortality Programs (http://www.asip1.org)
▶ Canadian Foundation for the Study of Infant Deaths (http://www.sidscanada.org)

6-2n Teething

Teething is a natural process. Infants usually begin getting their first teeth around 4 to 7 months of age. Older children will begin the process of losing and replacing their baby teeth with a permanent set about the time they reach their fifth or sixth birthday.

Cause   New teeth erupting through gum tissue can cause some children mild discomfort. However, most children move through this stage with relatively few problems.

Management   Increased drooling and chewing activity may occur for several days or weeks before a tooth erupts and may be the only indication that an infant is teething. Some infants become a bit more fussy, run a low-grade fever (under 100°F), and may lose interest in eating. High fevers, diarrhea, and vomiting are usually not caused by teething, but may be an indication of illness. Chilled teething rings and firm objects for children to chew often provide comfort and relief to swollen gums.

6-2o Toothache

Young children do not typically experience toothaches. They may have temporary periods of discomfort during times when a tooth is being lost or new teeth are erupting. However, untreated oral health problems can cause significant pain and suffering, interfere with speech and language development, make eating difficult, affect school performance, and lead to early tooth loss. For this reason, it is important that children practice preventive measures such as brushing, eating a healthy diet, and seeing a dentist regularly. Limited finances should not prevent families from seeking necessary dental treatment for children. Low-cost insurance (CHIP), Medicaid, and community resources such as clinics and dental schools, are often available to help families obtain essential dental care (Kenney et al., 2011).

Cause   Although tooth decay is the most common cause of toothache, gum disease and injury can also be quite painful. Children may complain of a throbbing discomfort that sometimes radiates into the ear. Redness and swelling may also be observed around the gumline of the affected tooth. Foods that are hot or very sweet may intensify pain.

▶❚❚ **TeachSource Video Connections**

Video supplied by the BBC Motion Gallery

SIDS: Is There a Biological Cause?

The possibility that an infant may stop breathing is a frequent and genuine concern of parents and caregivers. Although many preventive measures can be taken to reduce the risk of SIDS, only recently have we learned that a biological defect may be involved. As you watch the learning video, *SIDS: Is There a Biological Cause?*, consider the following questions:

1. What is Sudden Infant Death Syndrome?

2. What is serotonin, and what biological functions does it regulate?

3. Note the crib bumper pads that appear in an early scene. Why should they never be used in an infant's crib?

4. How do you think that knowing SIDS is caused by a genetic abnormality will help parents who have lost an infant to the condition?

Watch on CourseMate.

▼ **Brushing teeth after eating helps to promote good oral health.**

© Cengage Learning

Management Complaints of toothache require prompt dental attention. In the meantime, an icepack applied to the cheek on the affected side may make the child feel more comfortable. Aspirin-free products can also be given for temporary pain relief. However, prevention, including proper brushing after eating and reduction of dietary sugars, is always the preferred approach for limiting tooth decay.

6-2p Vomiting

Vomiting can be a frightening and unpleasant experience for children. True vomiting is different from an infant who simply spits up after eating. Vomiting is a symptom often associated with an acute illness or other health problem (Hockenberry & Wilson 2012).

Cause A number of conditions can cause children to vomit, including:

- emotional upset
- viral or bacterial infection, such as stomach flu or strep throat
- drug reactions
- ear infections
- meningitis
- **salmonellosis**
- indigestion
- severe coughing
- head injury
- poisoning

Management The frequency, amount, and composition of vomited material is important to observe and record. Dehydration and disturbances of the body's chemical balance can occur with prolonged or excessive vomiting, especially in infants and toddlers. Children should be observed carefully for:

- high fever
- abdominal pain
- signs of dehydration
- headache
- excessive drowsiness
- difficulty breathing
- sore throat
- exhaustion

salmonellosis – *a bacterial infection that is spread through contaminated drinking water, food, or milk or contact with other infected persons. Symptoms include diarrhea, fever, nausea, and vomiting.*

Children who continue to vomit and show signs of a sore throat, fever, or stomach pains should be sent home as soon as possible until a cause can be determined. The teacher should also advise the child's family to contact their physician for further advice.

In the absence of any other symptoms, a single episode of vomiting may simply be due to an emotional upset, food dislike, excess mucus, or reaction to medication. Usually the child feels better immediately after vomiting and should be encouraged to rest quietly while remaining at school.

In addition to not feeling well, some children are upset by the act of vomiting itself. Extra reassurance and comforting can help make the experience less traumatic. Infants should be positioned on their stomachs, with their hips and legs slightly raised to allow any vomited material to flow out of the mouth and prevent choking. Older children should also be watched closely so they don't choke or inhale vomitus.

6-2q West Nile Virus

Did You Know...
there is no treatment to kill the West Nile virus? That is why prevention is so critical.

?

Humans have long considered mosquitoes to simply be annoying insects that buzz in the ear, feast on exposed skin, and leave an itchy raised welt as their calling card. However, they are also capable of transmitting disease. The Centers for Disease Control and Protection (CDC) reported 712 West Nile virus cases in the United States during 2011 (CDC, 2012a); a total of 110 cases were reported in Canada for 2011 (Public Health Agency of Canada, 2012).

A majority of persons infected with the West Nile virus will have no symptoms of the illness. Some people will experience mild flu-like symptoms; a small percent will develop more serious symptoms, such as high fever, muscle weakness, rash, stiff neck, tremors, disorientation, coma, and even death. Young children and the elderly are at the greatest risk for developing the West Nile virus.

Cause   West Nile virus is caused by the bite of an infected mosquito. The incidence is highest during the summer and fall seasons. However, there have also been limited reports of transmission via blood transfusion, organ donation, and the breast milk of an infected mother.

Management Prevention is the most important and effective strategy for avoiding this infectious illness (AAP, 2012b). Eliminating standing water in flower pots, water fountains, bird baths, buckets, tire swings, small pools, and similar sources removes mosquito breeding sites. A number of products containing natural chemicals and bacteria are available to spray or to use in ponds that cannot be drained. Additional precautionary measures include applying mosquito repellents containing DEET (maximum of 30 percent) whenever going outdoors, wearing protective clothing (long sleeves, long pants), staying indoors during early morning and evening hours when mosquitoes are at their peak activity, making sure that screen doors and windows are in good repair, and placing mosquito netting over infant strollers. In most cases, persons with mild symptoms will recover without medical treatment. However, prompt medical attention should be sought for prolonged illness or if any serious complications develop.

Finally, rely on your intuition. Don't hesitate to call the doctor if you are unsure about the symptoms your child may be experiencing. Most physicians would rather be notified of a child's condition than to be called only when there is a crisis.

Did You Get It?

A typically healthy and energetic kindergarten student is complaining of dizziness and seems unsteady. These symptoms might indicate:

a. dehydration

b. anemia

c. an ear infection

d. food poisoning

Take the full quiz on CourseMate.

PARTNERING with FAMILIES

When to Call the Doctor

Dear Families,

It is not uncommon for young children to experience frequent illness. With time, their bodies will mature, resistance (immunity) to many illnesses will develop, and their immunizations will have been completed. In the meantime, families may face the difficult task of deciding at what point a child is sick enough to warrant calling the doctor. Although each child's symptoms and needs are different, there are guidelines that may be helpful in making this decision. Call the physician if your child:

▶ Experiences serious injury, bleeding that cannot be stopped, or excessive or prolonged pain.

▶ Is less than one month old and develops a fever, or is between 1 and 3 months of age and has a rectal temperature over 100.4°F. Call if the child's fever lasts more than 3 days.

▶ Has difficult, rapid, or noisy breathing.

▶ Experiences any loss of consciousness, including a seizure.

▶ Complains of unusual pain in an arm or leg. X-rays may be necessary to rule out a fracture.

▶ Has repeated episodes of vomiting or diarrhea and is unable to keep down liquids. Symptoms of dehydration include urination fewer than three times per day, dry lips or tongue, headache, lack of tears, and excessive drowsiness. A sunken fontanel (soft spot) is an additional symptom in infants. Young children can become dehydrated quickly.

▶ Develops an unusual skin rash, especially one that spreads.

▶ Has blood in her vomit, urine, or stool.

▶ Suffers an eye injury or develops an eye discharge. Children who have sustained an eye injury should always be seen by a physician.

▶ Develops stomach pain that is prolonged or interferes with appetite or activity.

▶ Becomes excessively sleepy or difficult to arouse.

CLASSROOM CORNER

Teacher Activities

Gear Up for Health...

Concept: Physical activity is important for staying healthy. (Grades 3–5; National Health Education Standards 1.5.1 and 6.5.1)

Learning Objectives

▶ Children will learn the importance of moving to stay healthy.

▶ Children will improve their aerobic condition.

Supplies

▶ worksheet for recording activities

▶ kick balls

(continued)

CLASSROOM CORNER

Teacher Activities (*continued*)

Gear Up for Health...

▶ pedometers

▶ charts or graph paper

▶ Mylar balloons

▶ masking tape

Learning Activities

▶ Read and discuss any of the following books:

- *Anna Banana: 101 Jump-Rope Rhymes* by Joanna Cole

- *Norma Jean, Jumping Bean* by Joanna Cole

- *Song and Dance Man* by Karen Ackerman

- *Snow Dance* by Lezlie Evans

▶ As a group, discuss the benefits of physical activity in terms of improving the body's immune system to fight off germs and protect against illness. Encourage the children to brainstorm activities that will increase their respiratory and heart rates (jumping rope, running, riding bikes, going for a walk, playing soccer, etc.).

▶ Introduce the terms *aerobic* (activities that increase heart and breathing rates) and *anaerobic* (activities that improve muscle strength) and explain the differences. Prepare a worksheet with two columns: one headed "aerobic activities," the other "anaerobic activities." Have the children list as many activities as they can in each appropriate column. As a group, ask the children to share one activity listed on their sheet and compile a master class list. Challenge the children to engage in at least one of these activities each day.

▶ Set up a game of kickball and give each child a pedometer to wear during the activity. At the end of 15 minutes, have each child record the number of steps he has taken. As an alternative, set up two cones and have children run laps; each week, increase the distance or number of laps children must run. Older children can graph their data (number of steps) while younger children might simply keep a daily tally. Varying the distance between cones, the number of laps run, or the length of playing time is an effective way to help children grasp the relationship between activity and health benefits. Children can also set weekly goals for themselves and gradually increase the number of steps they want to accumulate on their pedometer.

▶ Play balloon volleyball (great indoor activity). Group children into small teams, place a tape line on the floor, and instruct children to keep the balloon in motion by batting it back and forth. Have the children compare and describe how they felt before (heart beating slowly, easy to breathe) and after (breathing hard, heart beating fast, sweaty) the activity.

Evaluation

▶ Children will describe how physical activity improves health.

▶ Children will improve aerobic capacity by setting goals and recording their progress.

Additional lesson plans for grades PreK–2 are available on this text's Education CourseMate website.

Summary

▶ Communicable illnesses are common among young children in group settings.

- Teachers can utilize multiple strategies to control the spread of communicable illnesses:
  - continuous observation and early identification of sick children
  - implementation of exclusion policies
  - thorough hand washing
  - environmental sanitation
  - ongoing health education

▶ Teachers should also be familiar with the signs and symptoms, method of transmission, and control measures of common acute childhood illnesses.

Terms to Know

symptoms *p. 136*
asymptomatic *p. 140*
infection *p. 146*
dehydration *p. 148*
listlessness *p. 148*
abdomen *p. 148*

hyperventilation *p. 150*
temperature *p. 151*
fever *p. 151*
tympanic *p. 151*
disorientation *p. 153*
Lyme disease *p. 153*

intestinal *p. 155*
urination *p. 155*
apnea *p. 156*
salmonellosis *p. 159*

Chapter Review

A. By Yourself:

1. Define each of the *Terms to Know*.

2. Match each of the following signs and symptoms in Column I with the correct communicable illness in Column II.

Column I	Column II
1. swelling and redness of white portion of the eye	a. chickenpox
2. frequent itching of the scalp	b. strep throat
3. flat, oval-shaped lesions on the scalp, skin; infected nails that become discolored, brittle, chalky, and may disintegrate	c. head lice
	d. shigellosis
4. high fever; red, sore throat	e. conjunctivitis
5. mild fever and rash that lasts approximately 3 days	f. ringworm
6. irritability and itching of the rectal area	g. German measles
7. red rash with blister-like heads; cold-like symptoms	h. scabies
8. sudden onset of fever; swelling of salivary glands	i. pinworms
9. burrows or linear tunnels under the skin; intense itching	j. mumps
10. vomiting, abdominal pain, diarrhea that may be bloody	k. Lyme disease

B. As a Group:

1. Discuss what a teacher should do in each of the following situations:

   a. You have just finished serving lunch to the children, when Kara begins to vomit.

   b. The class is involved in a game of keep-away. Theo suddenly complains of feeling dizzy.

   c. During check-in, a parent mentions that his son has been experiencing stomachaches every morning before coming to school.

d. Lucy wakes up from her afternoon nap crying and is holding her ear.

e. You have just changed a toddler's diaper for the third time in the last hour because of diarrhea.

f. Chris enters the classroom sneezing and blowing his nose.

g. While you are helping Jasmine put on her coat to go outdoors, you notice that her skin feels very warm.

h. Randy refuses to eat his lunch because it makes his teeth hurt.

i. While you are cleaning up the blocks, Sean tells you that his throat is sore and it hurts to swallow.

j. You have just taken Monique's temperature (orally) and it is 102°F.

k. Your assistant teacher mentions that his son has chickenpox and that he has never had it.

2. The concepts of illness and pain are often viewed differently by various cultural groups. Select two or three predominant cultures and research their beliefs about illness, pain, and traditional medicine. How might these differences in cultural values and beliefs influence your response in each of the situations described in Question #1?

◖◗ Case Study

The teacher noticed that Carrie seemed quite restless today and was having difficulty concentrating on any task that she started. She continuously squirmed, whether in her chair or sitting on the floor. On a number of occasions the teacher also observed Carrie tugging at her underwear and scratching her bottom. She recalled that Carrie's mother had mentioned something about getting her younger brother tested for pinworms and wondered if this might be what she was observing.

1. If you were the teacher, what actions would you take in this situation?

2. What control measures should be implemented? At school? At home?

3. When can Carrie return to school?

4. Is this a reportable illness in your state?

5. If Carrie does have pinworms, for what length of time should the other children be observed for similar problems?

6. What special personal health measures should be emphasized with the other children?

◖◗ Application Activities

1. With a partner, practice taking each other's axillary, oral, and tympanic temperatures. Follow steps for the correct cleaning of the thermometer between each use. Were there differences in the readings you obtained?

2. Divide the class into groups of five to six students. Discuss how each member feels about caring for children who are ill. Could they hold or cuddle a child with a high fever or diarrhea? What are their feelings about being exposed to children's contagious illnesses? How might they react if an infant just vomited on their new sweater? If they feel uncomfortable around sick children, what steps could they take to better cope with the situation?

3. Select another student as a partner and observe that person carefully for 20 seconds. Now look away. Write down everything you can remember about this person, such as eye color, hair color, scars or moles, approximate weight, height, color of skin, shape of teeth, clothing, and so on. What can you do to improve your observational skills?

4. Do you know if your immunizations are up-to-date with current recommendations? Take the quiz on the CDC's immunizations website: http://www.cdc.gov/vaccines/schedules/index.html. What boosters or newer immunizations do you need? Why is it especially important that teachers keep their immunizations current?

Helpful Web Resources

Center for Disease Control	http://www.cdc.gov
Health Canada	http://www.hc-sc.gc.ca
Keep Kids Healthy	http://www.keepkidshealthy.com
Morbidity & Mortality Weekly	http://www.cdc.gov/mmwr
National Initiative for Children's Healthcare Quality (special needs)	http://www.nichq.org/
National Institutes of Health	http://www.nih.gov
Office of Minority Health	http://minorityhealth.hhs.gov

Visit the Education CourseMate for this textbook to access the eBook, Did You Get It? quizzes, Digital Downloads, TeachSource Video Cases, flashcards, and more. Go to CengageBrain.com to log in, register, or purchase access.

References

American Academy of Otolaryngology—Head and Neck Surgery (AAO-HNS). (2012). *Fact sheet: Day care and ear, nose, and throat problems.* Accessed on May 29, 2012 from http://www.entnet.org/HealthInformation/dayCareENT.cfm.

American Academy of Pediatrics (AAP). (2012a). A child care provider's guide to safe sleep. Accessed on May 30, 2012 from, http://www.healthychildcare.org/pdf/SIDSchildcaresafesleep.pdf.

AAP. (2012b). Preventing West Nile virus. Accessed on May 30, 2012 from, http://www.healthychildren.org/English/health-issues/conditions/skin/Pages/Preventing-West-Nile-Virus.aspx.

AAP. (2011). Technical Report –SIDS and other sleep-related infant deaths: Expansion of recommendations for a safe infant sleeping environment, *Pediatrics*, 128(5), e1341–e1367.

Aschenbrenner, D. (2012). Safety warnings for new concentration of liquid acetaminophen, *American Journal of Nursing*, 1112(4), 28–29.

Boudewyns, A., Declau, F., Van den Ende, J., Kerschaver, E., Dirckx, S., Hofkens-Van den Brandt, A., & Van de Heyning, P. (2011). Otitis media with effusion: An underestimated cause of hearing loss in infants, *Otology & Neurotology*, 32(5), 799–804.

Centers for Disease Control & Prevention (CDC). (2012a). Final 2011 West Nile virus human infections in the United States. Accessed on May 30, 2012 from, http://www.cdc.gov/ncidod/dvbid/westnile/surv&controlCaseCount11_detailed.htm.

CDC. (2012b). Lyme disease data—2001 to 2010. Accessed on May 29, 2012, from http://www.cdc.gov/lyme/stats/index.html.

CDC. (2012c). Postneonatal mortality among Alaska native infants—Alaska, 1989–2009, *Morbidity & Mortality Weekly Report (MMWR)*, 61(1):1–5.

CDC. (2012d). Sudden Unexpected Infant Death (SUID). Accessed on May 30, 2012 from, http://www.cdc.gov/SIDS/index.htm.

Cunningham, M., Guardiani, E., Kim, H., & Brook, I. (2012). Otitis media, *Future Microbiology*, 7(6), 733–753.

Danhauer, J., Johnson, C., & Caudle, A. (2011). Survey of K–3rd grade teachers' knowledge of ear infections and willingness to participate in prevention programs, *Language, Speech, & Hearing Services in Schools*, 42(2), 207–222.

Dennehy, P. (2012). Effects of vaccine on rotavirus disease in the pediatric population, *Current Opinion in Pediatrics*, 24(1), 76–84.

Eisen R., Piesman, J., Zielinski-Gutierrez, E., & Eisen, L. (2012). What do we need to know about disease ecology to prevent Lyme disease in the Northeastern United States?, *Journal of Medical Entomology*, 49(1), 11–22.

Fiore, A., Epperson, S., Perrotta, D., Bernstein, H., & Neuzil, K. (2012). Expanding the recommendations for annual influenza vaccination to school-age children in the United States, *Pediatrics*, 129(2), S54–S62.

Hamlen, R. (2012). Tick-borne infections—A growing public health threat to school-age children: Prevention steps that school personnel can take, *NASN School Nurse*, 27(2), 94–100.

Hockenberry, M., & Wilson, D. (2012). *Wong's essentials of pediatric nursing*. (9th ed.). New York: Mosby.

Isbister, G., Prior, F., & Kilham, H. (2012). Restricting cough and cold medicines in children, *Journal of Paediatrics*, 48(2), 91–98.

Jones, H., Butler, R., Moore, D., & Brooks, D. (2013). Developmental changes and fructose absorption in children: Effect on malabsorption testing and dietary management, *Nutrition Reviews*, 71(5), 300–309.

Jones, L., Hassanien, A., Cook, D., Britton, J., & Leonardi-Bee, J. (2012). Parental smoking and the risk of middle ear disease in children, *Archives of Pediatrics & Adolescent Medicine*, 166(1), 18–27.

Kenney, G., Marton, J., Klein, A., Pelletier, J., & Talbert, J. (2011). The effects of Medicaid and CHIP policy changes on receipt of preventive care among children, *Health Services Research*, 46(1), 298–318.

Lampel, H., & Jacob, S. (2011). Phthalates in baby skin care products, *Dermatitis*, 22(5), 272–276.

National Institute of Child Health & Human Development (NICHD). (2012). Back to sleep public education campaign. Accessed on May 30, 2012 from http://www.nichd.nih.gov/sids/.

Padilla-Raygoza, N., Diaz-Guerrero, R., Garcia-Valenzuela, G., & Pantoja-Hernandez, P. (2011). Comparison of measurements of body temperature with four thermometers in a children health care setting, *The Internet Journal of Pediatrics & Neonatology*, 13(2). Accessed online from http://www.ispub.com/journal/the-internet-journal-of-pediatrics-and-neonatology/volume-13-number-2/comparison-of-measurements-of-body-temperature-with-four-thermometers-in-a-children-health-care-setting-comparison-of-thermometers.html.

Public Health Agency of Canada. (2012). West Nile virus monitor. Accessed on April 30, 2013 from http://www.phac-aspc.gc.ca/wnv-vwn/mon-hmnsurv-eng.php.

Rand, C., Patwari, P., Carroll, M., & Weese-Mayer, D. (2013). Congenital central hypoventilation syndrome and sudden infant death syndrome: Disorders of autonomic regulation, *Seminars in Pediatric Neurology*, 20(1), 44–55.

Robb, P., & Williamson, I. (2012). Otitis media with effusion in children: Current management, *Paediatrics & Child Health*, 22(1), 9–12.

Rowley, D., & Hogan, V. (2012). Disparities in infant mortality and effective, equitable care: Are infants suffering from benign neglect?, *Annual Review of Public Health*, 33, 75–87.

Said, M., O'Brien, K., Nuorti, J., Singleton, R., Whitney, C., & Hennessy, T. (2011). The epidemiologic evidence underlying recommendations for use of pneumococcal polysaccharide vaccine among American Indian and Alaska Native populations, *Vaccine*, 29(33), 5355–5362.

Salone, L., Vann, W., & Dee, D. (2013). Breastfeeding: An overview of oral and general health benefits, *The Journal of the American Dental Association,* 144(2), 143–151.

Schieve, L., Gonzalez, V., Boulet, S., Visser, S., Rice, C., Van Naarden Braun, K., & Boyle, C. (2012). Concurrent medical conditions and health care use and needs among children with learning and behavioral disabilities, National Health Interview Survey, 2006–2010, *Research in Developmental Disabilities,* 33(2), 467–476.

Schnitzer, P., Covington, T., & Dykstra, H. (2012). Sudden unexpected infant deaths: Sleep environment and circumstances, *American Journal of Public Health*, 102(6), 1204–1212.

Sun, Y., & Sundell, J. (2011). Early daycare attendance increase the risk for respiratory infections and asthma of children, *Journal of Asthma*, 48(8), 790–796.

Trachtenberg, F., Haas, E., Kinney, H., Stanley, C., & Krous, H. (2012). Risk factor changes for sudden infant death syndrome after initiation of back-to-sleep campaign, *Pediatrics*, 129(4), 630–638.

Vennemann, M., Hense, H., Bajanowski, T., Blair, P., Complojer, C., Moon, R., & Kiechl-Kohlendorfer, U. (2012). Bed sharing and the risk of Sudden Infant Death Syndrome: Can we resolve the debate?, *The Journal of Pediatrics*, 160(1), 44–48.

UNIT 2

Keeping Children Safe

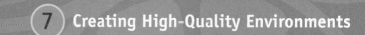

Creating High-Quality Environments

▶ **#1 a, b, and c:** Promoting child development and learning
▶ **#4 a, b, and d:** Using developmentally effective approaches to connect with children and families
▶ **#6 b, c, d, and e:** Becoming a professional
▶ Field experiences

Learning Objectives

After studying this chapter, you should be able to:

LO 7-1 Discuss how to identify high-quality programs.

LO 7-2 Explain how licensure and registration of early childhood programs differ.

LO 7-3 Identify the features of high-quality programs and discuss how teachers' educational preparation affects children's development.

LO 7-4 Describe at least ten ways to make children's indoor and outdoor environments safe.

Children's growth and development are continually being shaped and influenced by their **environment**. Growth is enhanced through nurturing and responsive care, a healthy diet, homes and schools that are clean and safe, access to dental and health care, and communities free of drugs, violence, excessive traffic, and air pollution. Children's intellectual and psychological development are fostered through environments that provide new challenges, opportunities for learning, and positive social interactions. For these reasons, careful attention must be given to creating physical, **cognitive**, and psychological settings that will have positive effects on children's growth and development.

7-1 Identifying High-Quality Programs

Families frequently rely on out-of-home arrangements for child care. Some families simply want their children to benefit from enrichment experiences and opportunities to socialize with their peers. Others may enroll children with special developmental needs in early intervention programs where they can receive individualized learning experiences and intervention services such as speech or physical therapy (Allen & Cowdery, 2012). Older children may require a safe, educational place to stay before and after regular school hours. Regardless of their reasons, families often find it challenging to identify and secure high-quality, affordable

▼ Environments should support and promote children's growth and development.

© Cengage Learning

---

environment – *the sum total of physical, emotional, cultural, and behavioral features that surround and affect an individual.*
cognitive – *the aspect of learning that refers to the development of skills and abilities based on knowledge and thought processes.*

programs for children. New programs are continuously being opened to meet increased demand, but quality is not always a priority.

Research continues to demonstrate that high-quality programs make a difference in children's development and family relationships (Tucker-Drob, 2012). Children enrolled in high-quality care show long-term gains in language and cognitive skills, improved readiness for school, and fewer problem behaviors (Sripada, 2012; Wen et al., 2012). Although most families would prefer to have their child in an excellent program, the urgency and, at times, desperation of simply finding an available opening may force them to overlook this important issue. Cost and location considerations may understandably overshadow a family's concern about quality.

It is also true that many families simply do not know how to determine the quality of a program or even what features to look for. Some parents feel uncomfortable questioning teachers. Others may not be able to find a convenient high-quality program in their area even when they are dissatisfied with poor conditions in a current arrangement.

7-1a Educating Families

Advocacy groups and professional organizations have launched initiatives to help educate families about the characteristics associated with excellence in early childhood programs. Families can also retrieve similar information from a number of professional websites.

Researchers have identified three characteristics common to high-quality early childhood programs (Ma et al., 2013; Hebbeler, Spiker, & Kanhn, 2012):

- small group size
- low teacher-child ratio (fewer children per teacher)
- teachers who have advanced educational training in early childhood education and child development

Families should always take time to observe any new program they are considering for their child and determine how the program measures up to these criteria. Additional areas that should also be noted include:

- physical facilities (clean, safe, spacious, licensed)
- program philosophy; developmentally appropriate goals and objectives
- nutritious meals and snacks
- opportunities for family involvement
- attention to diversity
- toys and educational activities (developmentally appropriate, variety, adequate in number, organized learning experiences)
- health services (trained personnel, established policies, and procedures)

Educating families about how to identify high-quality programs has obvious benefits for children. Programs that fail to improve their services may be forced out of business as demand for higher quality increases.

7-1b Resource and Referral Services

Many communities have resource and referral agencies devoted to helping families locate center- and home-based early childhood programs, as well as before- and after-school care. Families can request a list of available openings based on their specific child care needs, such as location, cost, preferred hours, philosophy, and child's age. Many independent agencies have been networked into state and national computerized databases; Child Care Aware (formerly the National Association of Child Care Resource and Referral Agencies) is one of the largest.

Child care resource and referral agencies do not necessarily restrict their listings to high-quality programs. Some agencies will include any program with available openings, while others screen programs carefully to ensure high standards. Consequently, families must spend time investigating individual programs to find one that best suits their needs and personal preferences.

Resource and referral agencies in many areas also play an active role in educating families about how to select an early childhood program. They are also vocal advocates for improved program quality and are committed to providing inservice training for early childhood teachers.

7-1c Professional Accreditation

A national system of voluntary **accreditation** for early childhood programs was established in 1985 by the National Association for the Education of Young Children (NAEYC). Its primary objective is aimed at promoting excellence and improving the quality of early education through a process of self-study (NAEYC, 2012). The accreditation process identifies and recognizes outstanding early-education programs and provides an added credential that acknowledges a commitment to quality. Programs are accredited for 3 years, at which time they must reapply. NAEYC continuously updates its accreditation standards to reflect the latest research findings and promote better quality in early childhood classrooms (http://www.naeyc.org/academy).

A number of organizations, including Head Start, the National Association for Family Child Care (NAFCC), and the National AfterSchool Association, have developed similar endorsement plans to recognize outstanding programs. Individual states have also begun to establish their own quality standards and voluntary accreditation systems.

Did You Get It?

Which environmental factor is not likely to foster healthy intellectual and psychological development for young children?

a. positive social interactions

b. new and continuously available challenges

c. opportunities for learning and "teachable moments"

d. rigid expectations and constant feedback

Take the full quiz on CourseMate.

7-2 Early Childhood Program Licensure

Licensing standards are established by individual states. They represent an attempt to ensure that environments are safe, appropriate, and healthful for young children. However, these regulations typically reflect only minimal health and safety requirements and also vary considerably from one state to another (Hillemeier et al., 2012). They in no way guarantee high-quality conditions, programs, or child care. This is an issue of great concern, as programs are increasing their numbers of infants and young children who have special behavior, developmental, and medical needs.

Licensing **regulations** serve a twofold purpose. First, they are aimed at protecting children's physical and psychological well-being by monitoring environmental and program safety. Second, they afford minimal protection to the program and its personnel. Programs that comply with licensing regulations are less likely to overlook situations that could result in negligence charges.

Early attempts to regulate child care programs dealt primarily with the sanitation and safety of physical settings. However, most current licensing regulations go beyond this narrow scope to also address teacher qualifications and the educational content of programs planned for children.

Each state has a designated agency that is authorized and responsible for conducting inspections and issuing or revoking licenses to operate. This agency also oversees the review and development of licensing standards and methods for enforcing **compliance**. Again, there are significant differences in licensing standards and levels of enforcement from one state to another. This fragmented approach also lacks a system for ensuring that individual states are actually performing their licensing responsibilities.

---

accreditation – *the process of certifying an individual or program as having met certain specified requirements.*
licensing – *the act of granting formal permission to conduct a business or profession.*
regulations – *standards or requirements that are set to ensure uniform and safe practices.*
compliance – *the act of obeying or cooperating with specific requests or requirements.*

▼ Licensing standards help to ensure that children's environments are safe and healthy.

© Cengage Learning

In many states, home-based child care programs are governed by a separate set of regulations that often include an option for becoming either licensed or registered. Those choosing to be licensed are inspected by a licensing agent and required to meet specific standards. In contrast, the requirements for **registration** are often minimal. Teachers may simply be asked to place their name on a list, complete a self-administered checklist attesting to safe conditions, and attend a brief preservice informational program. An on-site home inspection is seldom conducted unless a complaint is registered. Child care programs based in churches and public schools and relative care are exempt from licensing regulation in many states.

Controversy continues to surround the issue of early childhood program licensure. Establishing licensing requirements that adequately protect young children's health and safety—yet are realistic for teachers and programs to achieve—can be challenging. In addition, some people believe that too much control or standards that are set too high will reduce the number of available openings and programs. The licensing process is also costly to administer and often difficult to enforce, so that lowering the standards may be a tempting option. On the other hand, many families and teachers favor stricter regulations to ensure higher-quality programs and improved respect for the early childhood profession.

Despite the ongoing controversy, licensing of early childhood programs is necessary. Ideally, licensing standards should adequately safeguard children, yet not be so overly restrictive that qualified individuals and programs are eliminated.

7-2a Obtaining a License

A license permits an early childhood program to operate on a routine basis. As previously mentioned, the process for obtaining a license differs from state to state. However, the steps described here are generally representative of the procedure involved. In some cases, the process may require considerable time and effort, especially if major renovations must be made to the proposed facility. For others, approval may be obtained in a reasonably short time. Persons interested in operating an early childhood or after-school program should first contact their state or local licensing agency. Questions regarding the applicant's qualifications and specific program requirements can usually be answered at this time.

Child care facilities must comply with local laws and ordinances in addition to state licensing regulations. Zoning codes must be checked carefully to determine whether or not a program can be operated in a given location or neighborhood. Often this requires meeting with local planning authorities and reviewing proposed floor plans. Programs located in public school buildings may also be required to meet state building codes and regulations.

Buildings that house early childhood programs must also pass a variety of inspections to ensure they meet fire, safety, and sanitation codes. These inspections are usually conducted by personnel from the local fire and public health departments. Any renovations necessary to comply with licensing regulations will be determined during the inspections. In most cases, the changes are relatively simple; in other cases, the required changes may not be feasible or economical to make.

registration – *the act of placing the name of a child care program on a list of active providers; usually does not require on-site inspection.*

Application for a permanent license can be made once all these steps have been completed. Licensing authorities may also request copies of the program's plans for review. Final approval usually includes an on-site inspection of the facilities to ensure that all requirements and recommendations have been satisfied.

7-2b Federal Regulations

In addition to meeting state licensing requirements, early childhood programs that receive federal funds, such as Head Start, Early Head Start, and Even Start programs, must comply with an additional set of regulations. All schools and child care facilities, with the exception of religion-affiliated programs, built or remodeled after 1990 must also meet standards established by the Americans with Disabilities Act (ADA) (Child Care Law Center, 2009).

<aside>
Did You Get It?

Child care licensing regulations:

a. are uniform from state to state

b. ensure that programs are safe and of high quality

c. protect children from physical and emotional harm

d. reflect minimal standards

Take the full quiz on CourseMate.
</aside>

7-3 Features of High-Quality Programs

Researchers are continually studying children in schools, home-, and center-based programs to determine what conditions and experiences are best for promoting learning and healthy development. Through the years, they have identified several key components that distinguish high-quality programs from those considered to be of mediocre or poor value (Belsky & Pluess, 2012). NAEYC, the largest organization representing early care and education in the United States, and similar professional organizations have embraced these findings and incorporated them into their accreditation standards and recommended guidelines (APHA & AAP, 2011).

7-3a Teacher Qualifications

Perhaps one of the weakest areas in many state licensing regulations pertains to staff qualifications. Primary attention is often focused on the safety of the physical setting, while staff requirements, such as years of experience, educational preparation, and personal qualifications are often lacking or poorly defined. Even when these issues are addressed in the licensing regulations, there is little consistency from one state to another.

Research has documented a positive correlation between a teacher's educational preparation and the ability to provide high-quality early childhood education (Dennis & O'Connor, 2013; Whitebook & Ryan, 2011). Teachers who have a strong background in child development, value family involvement and communication, understand and respect diversity, and know how to create developmentally appropriate experiences are more effective in facilitating positive learning outcomes for children (Essa, 2014). As increasing numbers of children with behavior problems, developmental disabilities, and medical conditions are enrolled in early childhood programs, teachers must also be prepared to meet their special needs (Fults & Harryl, 2012). In addition, teachers must be able to work and communicate effectively with all children and families of diverse abilities, languages, and backgrounds.

Unfortunately, the licensing requirements in many states do not reflect what we currently know about the importance of employing teachers with formal training in early childhood education. Often, a person who is 18 years of age, has a high school diploma, and passes a background check is qualified to be hired as an early childhood teacher. As a result, many of these individuals are not prepared to effectively handle the daily challenges involved in working with young children (Nicholson & Reifel, 2011). The combination of low salaries, long working hours, and lack of preparation contribute to a high turnover rate which, in turn, has a negative effect on children's development (Tran & Winsler, 2011). Initiatives to improve teacher preparation and salaries are being studied, funded, and incorporated into licensing regulations in an effort to improve the quality of care and education that young children receive. However, teachers must also take steps to continue their education and prepare themselves to work with increasingly challenging child populations. Scholarship programs and professional opportunities are available to assist teachers in pursuing advanced education, including:

- on-the-job training/inservice training
- CDA (Child Development Associates credential)
- 1-year vocational training; child care or child development certificate
- 2-year associate degree (A.A.) (community college)
- 4-year bachelor degree (B.A.)
- advanced graduate training (M.A. and Ph.D.)

Although many of these degree programs are offered on traditional campuses, an increasing number are now available online.

At a minimum, all directors and head teachers should have a 2-year associate degree with specialized training in early childhood (Rhodes & Huston, 2012; Whitebook & Ryan, 2011). However, in many areas of the country, teachers and directors with advanced preparation are in short supply. Individual states are beginning to establish director credentialing programs in an effort to improve the quality of care and leadership provided in early childhood centers.

Early childhood programs often include paraprofessionals as part of their teaching team. These individuals may be aides who work for wages or are unpaid volunteers. Regardless of their position or previous experience, it is essential that paraprofessionals receive a thorough orientation to their job responsibilities and program procedures before they work in the classroom. This preparation enables paraprofessionals to provide safe and effective care when they assume their role and also improves employee retention.

Teachers who work in high-quality programs often bring many special personal qualities and skills to their position. They value communication and know how to develop meaningful relationships with children, families, and colleagues. They understand and respect diversity and make it a priority. They also possess qualities of warmth, patience, sensitivity to children's needs, respect for individual differences, and a positive attitude. They have the ability to plan, organize, make decisions, and resolve conflict. They also enjoy good personal health, which allows them to cope with the physical and emotional demands of long, action-packed days. Individuals with these qualities are not only better teachers, but also are more likely to have a positive effect on young children's lives.

7-3b Staffing Ratios

Staff/child ratios are determined by individual states and typically reflect only the minimal number of adults considered necessary to protect children's well-being. However, the ability to provide positive learning experiences, individualized care, and conditions that safeguard children's health and safety requires more teachers than are generally mandated.

Ideally, high-quality early childhood programs provide one full-time teacher for every seven to eight children 3 to 6 years of age. Programs serving children who have behavioral or developmental disabilities should be staffed with one teacher for every four to five children, depending on the age group and severity of their needs. If children younger than 2 years are included, there should be at least one full-time teacher for every three to four children. A list of substitutes should also be available in the event of teacher illness or other absence.

Research suggests that small group size and low teacher/child ratios improve the quality of educational experiences that children receive (Rhodes & Huston, 2012). However, low ratios do not always guarantee that children will be safer. Much depends on the knowledge and supervisory skills of individual teachers.

Teachers who are part of high-quality programs understand the importance of continuing their professional education by attending professional conferences, inservice programs, workshops, and college classes. Participation in these experiences exposes teachers to new concepts, ideas, and approaches and promotes continued professional growth and competence. They also provide forums where teachers can discuss common problems, share ideas, and discover unique solutions.

These opportunities are especially important for teachers who work in home-based programs and have limited interaction with other educators.

7-3c Group Size and Composition

When a license is issued to an early childhood program, specific conditions and restrictions under which it is allowed to operate are clearly defined. These conditions usually spell out:

- ages of children that can be enrolled
- group size per classroom
- maximum enrollment per program
- special populations of children to be served (e.g., children with behavior problems, children who have developmental disabilities, infants, school-age, etc.)
- teacher-child ratios

For example, a program might be licensed to provide three half-day sessions for children 3 to 5 years of age, with a maximum enrollment of eighteen children and two teachers per classroom. An in-home program might be licensed for a total of six children, ages birth to 4 years.

Group size is also recognized as an important indicator of high-quality programs (NAEYC, 2012). For this reason, restrictions are typically placed on the number of children a program is permitted to enroll. This figure is determined by the square footage of available space, children's ages, and any special needs children may have, as well as the number of teachers on site. However, it should be remembered that state regulations allow group sizes that are often much larger than is ideal for quality care.

A program's educational philosophy and range of services provided should be described in the admission policies. The age range, special needs, and total number of children that a program is licensed to serve must also be clearly stated to avoid parent misunderstandings.

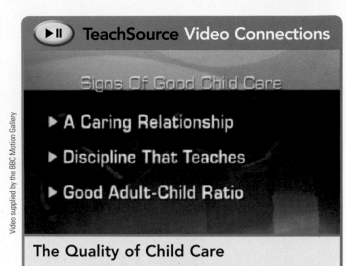

Video supplied by the BBC Motion Gallery

The Quality of Child Care

Numerous studies have demonstrated positive outcomes for children who are enrolled in high-quality early childhood and after-school programs. As you watch the learning video, *The Quality of Child Care,* consider the following questions:

1. What features are associated with high-quality programs?

2. What have the studies shown us about the effects that attending an early childhood program can have on children from disadvantaged families?

3. What is temporary distress syndrome? What should parents do if their child exhibits these behaviors?

Watch on CourseMate.

7-3d Program Curriculum

The benefits children derive from participating in high-quality early childhood programs have been consistently documented (Ma et al., 2013; Rhodes & Huston, 2012). Because many children spend the majority of their waking hours in out-of-home early childhood programs, it is essential that **developmentally appropriate practices (DAP)**—learning environments and enriching opportunities—be provided. High-quality early education programs plan learning experiences that address children's needs across all developmental areas, including:

- physical
- cognitive
- motor
- social-emotional
- language
- self-care

developmentally appropriate practices (DAP) – *learning experiences and environments that take into account children's individual abilities, interests, and diverse needs. DAP also reflects differences among families and values them as essential partners in children's education.*

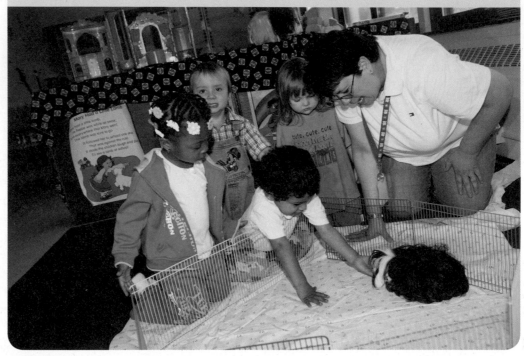

▼ Small group size provides children with more individualized attention and is a feature of high-quality programs.

© Cengage Learning

Curriculum delivery and content should be designed to address children's interests and to help them acquire new developmental skills. Learning experiences should be planned to take advantage of times when children are most likely to learn. Activities that alternate active and quiet play reduce the risk of children becoming overly fatigued and/or of losing interest. For example, a vigorous walk outdoors might be followed by a teacher-directed flannel board story or puppet show. It is also important that daily activity schedules and lesson plans be posted where families can learn what children will be doing throughout the day.

7-3e Health Services

Safeguarding children's health and well-being is a fundamental responsibility of teachers and school administrators (Green et al., 2012; APHA & AAP, 2011). Only when children are healthy can they fully benefit from everyday experiences and learning opportunities. High-quality programs take this role seriously and address children's health needs by:

- having written policies and procedures
- maintaining comprehensive health and safety records
- training personnel to administer first aid and emergency care
- providing clean, safe indoor and outdoor environments
- developing emergency response plans
- planning for health, safety, and nutrition education

State child care licensing regulations generally determine the types of policies and records that programs are required to maintain. Similar guidelines are issued by state departments of education for public schools. Although states' requirements differ, high-quality programs may find it prudent to take a more comprehensive approach to recordkeeping for improved understanding and legal protection. Basic records that are important for programs to maintain include:

- children's health assessments
- attendance
- emergency contact information

- ◗ developmental profiles
- ◗ staff health assessments
- ◗ fire and storm drills
- ◗ injuries
- ◗ daily health checks

Licensing authorities will review information in these records carefully during their renewal visits. Teachers in high-quality early childhood programs are trained to handle emergencies and to provide first aid and emergency care to ill or injured children. They also have completed training in cardiopulmonary resuscitation (CPR). Programs choosing to only meet minimal standards should have at least one staff member who is trained in these techniques and always available to respond to an emergency.

Notarized emergency contact forms, similar to the one shown in Figure 7–1, listing the name, address, and telephone number of the child's family and health care provider, should be completed at the time a child is enrolled. This step ensures that teachers can respond promptly, administer emergency care, and have a child transported to an emergency medical facility if necessary. Emergency numbers for fire, police, ambulance, and poison control should be posted next to the telephone for quick reference.

Programs that provide care for mildly ill children must establish policies that address their special health needs. A quiet area should be provided in either a separate corner of the classroom or a room designated specifically for this purpose so sick children can rest and not expose others to their illnesses. Medical supplies, equipment, and hand washing facilities should be located nearby so they are easy to access.

Early childhood programs must also have emergency plans and procedures in place so teachers are prepared to respond to unexpected events in a prompt and organized manner (Teacher Checklist 7-1). These plans should outline steps for protecting children's safety in emergencies, including fire, severe storms such as tornadoes, major disasters such as earthquakes, floods, or hurricanes, and unauthorized intruders. Representatives from local fire and law enforcement departments, the Red Cross, and emergency preparedness groups are available to assist programs in developing their emergency plans. Families should receive a copy of this information so they know what to expect in the event of an emergency and can also use it to develop similar procedures at home.

> ### Did You Get It?
> Staffing an institution properly is an ultimate and attainable goal. One of the weakest areas in many state licensing regulations is that of staff:
> **a.** motivation
> **b.** qualification
> **c.** education
> **d.** multiculturalism
> Take the full quiz on CourseMate.

TEACHER CHECKLIST 7-1

Principles of Emergency Preparedness

- Remain calm—do not panic.
- Be informed. Tune in to a local station on your battery-powered radio.
- Move to a safe place. Develop and practice an appropriate disaster plan.
- Keep a first aid kit, bottled water, and flashlight (along with extra batteries) handy.
- Take along children's health forms, emergency contact information, attendance records, and a cell phone.
- Learn basic emergency and first aid procedures.

TeachSource Digital Download Download from CourseMate.

notarized – *official acknowledgment of the authenticity of a signature or document by a notary public.*

FIGURE 7–1   **Sample emergency contact information form.**

EMERGENCY CONTACT INFORMATION

Child's Name _____ Date of Birth _____

Address _____ Home Phone _____

Mother's Name _____ Business Phone _____

Father's Name _____ Business Phone _____

Name of other person to be contacted in case of an emergency:

1. _____ Address _____

    Relationship (sitter, relative, friend, etc.) _____ Phone _____

2. _____ Address _____

    Relationship (sitter, relative, friend, etc.) _____ Phone _____

Authorization is hereby given for the Child Development Center Staff to release the above named child to the following persons, provided proper identification is first established (list all names of authorized persons, including immediate family):

1. _____ Relation: _____

2. _____ Relation: _____

3. _____ Relation: _____

Physician to be called in an emergency:

1. _____ Phone _____ or _____

2. _____ Phone _____ or _____

Dentist to be called in an emergency:

1. _____ Phone _____ or _____

I, the undersigned, authorize the staff of the Child Development Center to take what emergency medical measures are deemed necessary for the care and protection of my child enrolled in the Child Development Center program.

_____   _____
(Signature of Parent or Guardian/date)   Signature witnessed by:
                                                          (Notary)

_____   The above statement sworn
(Signature of Parent or Guardian/date)   before me on:

                                             _____

                                             _____

7-4 Guidelines for Safe Environments

Nowhere is health and safety more important than in group programs serving young children. When families enroll children in a program, they expect teachers to safeguard their child's well-being. They assume the facilities, toys, and equipment will be safe for children's use, that teachers will carefully supervise their children's activities, that the environment is clean, and the food is safe and nutritious.

Although no uniform child care licensing standards currently exist in this country, several organizations have developed recommendations for out-of-home programs based on years of research data. NAEYC has consistently defined and supported high standards for early-childhood programs. The American Public Health Association (APHA) and American Academy of Pediatrics (AAP) have released their newly revised document, *Caring for Our Children: National Health and Safety Performance Standards Guidelines for Out-of-Home Child Care Programs* (3rd ed.), in which they identify approximately 180 regulation standards and recommended safety practices. The remainder of this chapter addresses features in children's indoor and outdoor environments that require special attention. An indoor and outdoor safety checklist is provided in Teacher Checklist 7-4.

7-4a Indoor Safety

A great deal of thought and preparation is needed to create rooms that are safe for children. Everything from the traffic flow, furniture arrangement, and choice of floor coverings to the design of changing tables, sink placement, and proper storage requires careful study. Knowledge of children's abilities at each stage of development plays a key role in anticipating and eliminating potential safety hazards. (Refer to Table 8–2.) A safe environment encourages children to explore and learn through play, and is also less stressful for adults to work in (Vidoni & Ignico, 2011).

Building and Site Location In a time of shrinking budgets and increasing demand for child care, the selection of an appropriate building site often requires a creative approach. Although it would be ideal to plan and design a facility specifically for this purpose, few programs have sufficient funds for new construction. More often, existing buildings such as unused classrooms in public

© 2015 Cengage Learning

▶❚❚ **TeachSource** Video Connections

Creating a Safe Physical Environment for Toddlers

Toddlers are notorious for their boundless energy, curiosity, and questioning ways. However, these endearing qualities also place children at greater risk for unintentional injury. Teachers who work with toddlers must take extra care to safeguard children's well-being by creating safe environments and providing continuous supervision. As you watch the learning video, *Creating a Safe Physical Environment for Toddlers*, consider the following questions:

1. What safety features did you observe in this classroom?
2. What steps has the program taken to accommodate children who have special needs?
3. What qualities make toys safe for toddlers?
4. What security measures has the program implemented to protect the children's safety?

Watch on CourseMate.

schools, older houses, unoccupied stores, church basements, or places of business such as factories or hospitals are modified or remodeled to make them suitable for children. Although renovations can be expensive, it may be possible to reduce the cost by recruiting families and volunteers to assist with a portion of the work. In some cases, remodeling may simply not be a practical solution.

With the exception of church-affiliated programs, home- and center-based programs are considered public facilities under the 1990 Americans with Disabilities Act (ADA) even if they are privately owned (Child Care Law Center, 2009). Consequently, they too must comply with guidelines set forth in this historical piece of legislation, which requires the removal of physical barriers that would otherwise deny access to individuals who have disabilities. Early childhood programs cannot refuse to admit children on the basis of their disabilities. Program directors are expected to make reasonable adjustments in policies, practices, and facilities in order to accommodate all children. Admission can be denied only in special circumstances, such as if the required modifications are unreasonably difficult or costly to complete, or if there is no alternative solution for meeting a child's special needs (U.S. Department of Justice, 1997). Consequently, this law has important implications throughout the site selection, building, or remodeling stages as more children with disabilities are enrolling in early childhood programs.

CONNECTING TO EVERYDAY PRACTICE

Security in Early Childhood Programs

Media reports of school shootings, child mistreatment, unauthorized visitors, and workplace violence have heightened concerns about security. Although many public schools have installed additional security devices in buildings and enhanced their security procedures, early childhood programs have been somewhat slower to respond (Hong & Eamon, 2012). Employee background checks, photo identification cards for teachers and staff, and signed release forms authorizing child pickups are a few of the more common safety measures that programs utilize. Some centers have begun to install technology devices, such as touch keypads, Internet cameras that allow families to view children from work, and electronic surveillance cameras to improve security in their buildings (Bracy, 2011). However, the cost of these systems is simply more than many programs can afford.

Think About This:

▶ What resources are available to schools and community-based early childhood programs for addressing basic security issues and improvement measures?

▶ What workplace policies and procedures can programs implement to protect the safety of children and teachers?

▶ Are there any disadvantages to increasing security? What might they be?

▶ What message does the need for increased security in schools and early childhood programs say about contemporary society?.

Location is always important to consider when selecting an appropriate site. However, local zoning codes may make it difficult to locate programs in residential neighborhoods where they are often most needed. Ideally, buildings housing early childhood programs should be situated away from heavy traffic, excessive noise, air pollution, animals, ground contaminants (chemicals), bodies of water, large equipment, and other similar hazards to protect children's health and safety. Programs located in inner city and rural areas may find it difficult to avoid these conditions. It then becomes important to devote additional time and effort to safety awareness, policy development, and providing educational programs for children, teachers, and families. Buildings and building sites should be tested for radon, a colorless and odorless radioactive gas known to cause lung cancer (EPA, 2012). Inexpensive testing kits can be purchased locally or online or a certified radon professional can be hired to test the facilities. (The EPA also encourages individuals to test their personal homes for radon gas.)

Local fire codes will also affect building selection. Older buildings and those not originally designed for infants and young children may require extensive changes before they pass inspection. Rooms that children occupy must have a minimum of two exits, one leading directly outdoors. All doors should be hinged so they swing out of the room; this prevents doors from slowing the evacuation process in an emergency. Programs located on upper levels should have an enclosed stairwell for safe escape in the event of a fire.

How much space is needed depends to some extent on the type of program and services that will be offered. A minimum of 40 square feet of usable floor space per child is considered adequate for child care. However, teachers often find this amount of space crowded and difficult to work in. High-quality programs often provide 45 to 50 square feet of space per child for improved functionality and classroom safety. Additional space may be needed to accommodate large indoor play structures, special equipment for children with physical disabilities, or cribs for infants. However, it should also be kept in mind that large spaces are more difficult to supervise. Ground floor levels are always preferable for infants and preschool-aged children, although basement areas can be used for several hours at a time provided there are at least two exits.

▼ Rooms should be designed to accommodate different types of activities.

Space The arrangement of space, or basic floor plan, should be examined carefully to determine the ease of conducting specific activities. For example, the traffic flow should allow ample room for children to arrive and depart without disturbing others who are playing. It should also accommodate separate areas for active or noisy play and quiet activities. Small rooms that lack storage space, adequate lighting, accessible bathrooms, or suitable outdoor play areas are inconvenient and frustrating for the staff and children.

Play spaces for infants and toddlers should be separated from those of older children to avoid injuries, confrontations, and the spread of illness. Large, open space that is free of obstacles encourages young children to move about and to explore without hesitation.

Building Security Added precautions should be taken to protect children from unauthorized individuals while ensuring that families and legitimate visitors have safe access (Teacher Checklist 7-2). Buildings and outdoor play spaces should be evaluated carefully to determine if they are secure. Safety measures, such as locking outside doors and gates, issuing card keys (used in hotels), or installing keypads (with security codes) or buzzers on doors can be implemented to control unauthorized visitors. Teachers and staff members should always be alert to persons entering the building and acknowledge their presence by making a point to greet them. Surveillance cameras can also be installed to monitor entrances and exits. Programs should develop and review plans for handling unauthorized visitors and summoning assistance in the event of an emergency. They may also want to establish a safe area of the building where children can be moved for added protection.

Fire Safety Local fire officials can assist schools and in-home programs in the development and review of emergency procedures. They can be invited to tour the building layout and offer expert advice about planning efficient evacuation routes and notification procedures. Copies of the floor plans should be given to local fire authorities so they can familiarize themselves with the building layout and design. This will enable them to respond more efficiently if there is an actual emergency.

TEACHER CHECKLIST 7-2

Inventory Checklist: Planning for Program Security

Program administrators should work closely with local law enforcement, fire, and safety officials to assess a program's risk and to develop security plans that will protect children and staff members. Critical documents should be prepared and stored in a designated folder or box. All program staff should be familiar with its location and contents for quick retrieval in an emergency, such as fire, earthquake, hurricane, or unauthorized intruders. Items that should be addressed when planning for program security include:

- Obtaining a copy of the building floor plan or blueprint
- Preparing a list of employees by name and room, and attaching their photograph
- Preparing a roster of the children by room and attaching their photograph; note any children who have special needs
- Knowing where all shut-off valves are located and how to turn them off
- Preparing an evacuation plan with alternate exit routes
- Posting evacuation plans in each classroom and reviewing them periodically with teachers
- Conducting monthly evacuation drills with children
- Maintaining hallways and exits that are clear of obstructions
- Making copies of parent authorization forms and emergency contact information
- Compiling a list of emergency personnel and telephone numbers
- Assigning specific emergency responsibilities to individual personnel and outlining each role on a master plan
- Informing families about the program's security plans and including the information in parent handbooks
- Keeping an emergency food and water supply on hand

TeachSource Digital Download) Download from CourseMate.

Smoke and carbon monoxide detectors should be present in rooms occupied by children, especially those where infants and young children will be sleeping. Detectors should be tested monthly to be sure they are functioning properly and have the batteries replaced annually (unless the system is wired). All floor coverings and draperies should be flame-retardant and at least one multipurpose fire extinguisher should be available. Staff should be familiar with the location of building exits and emergency evacuation procedures. Monthly fire drills should be conducted with the children so they become familiar with the routine and are less likely to be frightened in an actual emergency (Teacher Checklist 7-3). Alternate evacuation routes should be planned and practiced so teachers will know where to exit the building if an area is blocked by fire. Plans for evacuating children with special needs should also be given careful attention.

Extension cords should not be used in classrooms. All electrical outlets should be covered with safety caps, which can be purchased in most grocery or hardware stores. However, remember that caps are only a temporary solution. They are frequently removed by teachers and cleaning personnel, not always replaced, and pose a choking hazard for young children if they are left lying around. An electrician can replace conventional outlets with childproof receptacles that do not require safety covers.

Bathroom Facilities Adequate bathroom facilities are essential for convenience and health concerns. They should be accessible to both indoor and outdoor play areas. Installation of child-sized fixtures, including sinks, toilets, soap dispensers, and towel racks, allow children to care for their own needs. If only adult-sized fixtures are available, foot stools, large wooden

Child-sized fixtures encourage independence.
© Cengage Learning

TEACHER CHECKLIST 7-3

How to Conduct a Fire Drill

Develop an Evacuation Plan

- Plan at least one alternate escape route from every room.
- Post a written copy of the plan by the door of each room.
- Review plans with new personnel.

Assign Specific Responsibilities

- Designate one person to call the fire department, preferably from a telephone outside of the building. Be sure to give the fire department complete information: name, address, approximate location of the fire in the building, and whether or not anyone remains inside. Do not hang up until the fire department does so first.
- Designate several adults to assemble children and lead them out of the building; assign extra adults, such as cooking or clerical staff, to assist with the evacuation of younger children or those needing extra help.
- Designate one adult to bring a flashlight and the notarized emergency cards or class list.
- Appoint one person to turn off the lights and close all classroom doors.

Establish a Meeting Place

- Once outside, meet at a designated location so everyone can be accounted for.
- DO NOT GO BACK INTO THE BUILDING!

Practice Fire Evacuation Drills

- Conduct drills at least once a month; plan some of these to be unannounced.
- Practice alternate routes of escape.
- Practice fire evacuation safety; for example, feel closed doors before opening them, select an alternate route if hallway or stairwells are filled with smoke, stay close to the floor (crawl) to avoid heat and poisonous gases, learn the stop-drop-roll technique.
- Use a stopwatch to time each drill and record the results; strive for improvement.

TeachSource Digital Download   Download from CourseMate.

---

blocks, or platforms securely anchored to the floor will facilitate children's independence. One toilet and sink should be available for every ten to twelve children. Programs serving children with disabilities should be designed to meet their special needs and comply with ADA standards (Child Care Law Center, 2009). A separate bathroom area should also be available for adults.

Hand-washing facilities located near toilets and sleeping areas encourage children and teachers to wash their hands when needed. Hot water temperatures should be maintained between 105°F (40.5°C) and 120°F (48.9°C) to protect children from accidental burns. Liquid or foam soap dispensers placed near sinks encourage hand washing, are easier for children to use, and less likely (than bar soap) to end up on the floor. The use of individual paper towels and cups improves sanitation and limits the spread of infectious illnesses. Smooth surfaces on walls and floors facilitate cleaning. Light-colored paint on walls makes dirty areas easy to notice and more likely to be cleaned.

Fixtures such as mirrors, light switches, and towel dispensers placed within children's reach, adequate lighting, and bright paint create a functional and pleasant atmosphere in which young children can manage self-care skills.

Surface and Furnishings Furniture and equipment should be selected to be comfortable, nontoxic, and safe. Children are less likely to be injured if chairs and tables are appropriately proportioned and safely constructed. Furniture should meet federal safety standards and be sturdy enough to withstand frequent use. (See Chapter 8.) Items with sharp corners or edges should be avoided; many manufacturers now construct children's furniture with rounded corners.

Did You Know...

that room colors are thought to affect human mood and behavior? Red, yellow, and orange are energizing; blue, pink, and brown are calming; green is restful; and purple fosters creativity.

Bookcases, lockers, pianos, televisions, and other heavy objects must be anchored securely to the wall or floor to prevent children from tipping them over. Tall bookshelves should be replaced or cut in half to scale them down to child-size. Children should also not have access to adult exercise equipment.

Materials such as tile, vinyl, and plastics (free of BPA, PVC, or phthalates) are ideal for wall and floor coverings because they are easy to clean. However, floors covered with any of these materials can become quite slippery when wet. Injuries can be avoided by taking extra precautions such as positioning non-skid rugs or newspapers where liquids are likely to be spilled and wiping up any spills immediately. Rooms that include a combination of carpeted and tiled areas address children's needs for soft, comfortable play spaces and areas for potentially messy activities.

Each child should have an individual storage space, cubby, or locker where personal belongings can be kept. A child's private space is particularly important in group settings where most other things must be shared. Individual cubbies also help to minimize the loss of prized possessions and aid in controlling infectious illnesses that can be transmitted through direct and indirect contact (such as head lice and pinkeye).

Additional features that make children's classrooms safer include having locked cabinets for storing medicines and other potentially poisonous substances, such as cleaning products and paint. A telephone should also be located conveniently in the building along with a list of emergency phone numbers (e.g., fire, police, hospital, ambulance, poison control center) posted directly nearby. A sample checklist for evaluating the safety of indoor and outdoor areas is provided in Teacher Checklist 7-4.

▼ **Space should be provided where children can store their personal items.**

© Cengage Learning

Lighting and Ventilation Low windows and glass doors should be constructed of safety glass to prevent serious injuries if they are broken. Colorful pictures or decals placed at children's eye level will help prevent children from accidently walking into the glass. Doors and windows should be covered with screens to keep out unwanted insects; screens that can be locked also prevent children from falling out. Drapery and blind cords should hang freely (not be knotted or looped together) to prevent strangulation and also be fastened up high and out of children's reach.

Adequate lighting is essential in classrooms and hallways. Natural light from windows and glass doors creates rooms that are bright, attractive, and inviting to teachers and children. Sunlight is also a cost-free, sustainable resource known to have a positive psychological effect on children's and adults' moods (Veitch & Galasiu, 2012).

Proper arrangement of artificial lighting is equally as important as the amount of brightness it produces. Additional lighting may be needed in areas such as reading and art centers. Compact fluorescent lights are ideal for this purpose because they give off more light, create less glare, cost less to operate, and are environmentally friendly.

Heating and cooling systems should be energy efficient and maintained annually. Room temperatures set between 68°F (20°C) and 85°F (29.4°C) year-round are ideal for children. Hot radiators, exposed pipes, furnaces, fireplaces, portable heaters, or fans should not be accessible

TEACHER CHECKLIST 7-4

Teachers' Safety Checklist: Indoor and Outdoor Spaces

Indoor Areas	Date Checked	Pass/Fail	Comments

1. A minimum of 35–40 square feet of usable space is available per child.
2. Room temperature is between 68°–85°F (20°–29.4°C).
3. Rooms have good ventilation:
   a. Windows and doors have screens.
   b. Mechanical ventilation systems are in working order.
4. There are two exits in all rooms occupied by children.
5. Carpets and draperies are fire-retardant.
6. Rooms are well lighted.
7. Glass doors and low windows are constructed of safety glass.
8. Walls and floors of classrooms, bathrooms, and kitchen appear clean; floors are swept daily, bathroom fixtures are scrubbed at least every other day.
9. Tables and chairs are child-sized and sturdy.
10. Electrical outlets are covered with safety caps.
11. Smoke detectors are located in appropriate places and in working order.
12. Furniture, activities, and equipment are set up so that doorways and pathways are kept clear.
13. Play equipment and materials are stored in designated areas; they are inspected frequently and safe for children's use.
14. Large pieces of equipment (e.g., lockers, piano, TV, bookshelves) are firmly anchored to the floor or wall.
15. Cleaners, chemicals, and other poisonous substances are locked up.
16. If stairways are used:
    a. Handrail is placed at children's height.
    b. Stairs are free of toys and clutter.
    c. Stairs are well-lighted.
    d. Stairs are covered with a nonslip surface.
17. Bathroom areas:
    a. Toilets and washbasins are in working order.
    b. One toilet and washbasin is available for every 10–12 children; potty chairs are provided for children in toilet training.
    c. Water temperature is no higher than 120°F (48.9°C).
    d. Powdered or liquid soap is used for hand-washing.
    e. Individual or paper towels are used for each child.
    f. Diapering tables or mats are cleaned after each use.
18. At least one fire extinguisher is available and located in a convenient place; extinguisher is checked annually by fire-testing specialists.
19. Premises are free from rodents and undesirable insects.
20. Food preparation areas are maintained according to strict sanitary standards.
21. At least one individual on the premises is trained in emergency first aid and CPR; first aid supplies are readily available.
22. All medications are stored in a locked cabinet or box.
23. Fire and storm/disaster drills are conducted monthly.

(continued)

TEACHER CHECKLIST 7-4

Teachers' Safety Checklist: Indoor and Outdoor Spaces (continued)

Indoor Areas	Date Checked	Pass/Fail	Comments
24. Security measures (plans, vigilant staff, keypads, locked doors, video cameras) are in place to protect children from unauthorized visitors.			

Outdoor Areas

1. Play areas are located away from heavy traffic, loud noises, and sources of chemical contamination.

2. Play areas are located adjacent to the premises or within safe walking distance.
3. Play areas are well drained; if rubber tires are used for play equipment, holes have been drilled to prevent standing water.
4. Bathroom facilities and a drinking fountain are easily accessible.
5. A variety of play surfaces (e.g., grass, concrete, and sand) is available; shade is provided.
6. Play equipment is in good condition (e.g., no broken or rusty parts, missing pieces, splinters, sharp edges, frayed rope, open "S" hooks, or protruding bolts).
7. Selection of play equipment is appropriate for children's ages and developmental skills.
8. Soft ground covers, approximately 12 inches in depth, are present under large climbing equipment; area is free of sharp debris (glass, sticks).
9. Large pieces of equipment are stable and anchored securely in the ground; finishes are non-toxic and intact.
10. Equipment is placed sufficiently far apart to allow a smooth flow of traffic and adequate supervision; an appropriate safety zone is provided around equipment.
11. Play areas are enclosed by a fence at least four feet high, with a gate and workable lock for children's security and safety.
12. There are no poisonous plants, shrubs, or trees in the area.
13. Chemicals, insecticides, paints, and gasoline products are stored in a locked cabinet.
14. Grounds are maintained on a regular basis and are free of debris; grass is mowed; broken equipment is removed.
15. Wading or swimming pools are always supervised; water is drained when not in use.

TeachSource Digital Download   Download from CourseMate.

to children; if they cannot be removed, protective insulation or wire screening must be placed around them to prevent injuries.

Indoor Air Quality Every day, children are exposed to a variety of indoor air pollutants, including formaldehyde (in carpet and building materials), carbon monoxide, radon, asbestos, cigarette smoke, paint fumes, lead, numerous household chemicals, and pesticides (EPA, 2013). Studies continue to demonstrate a close relationship between these pollutants and an increased rate of childhood respiratory illnesses, allergies, asthma, and cancer (Lin et al., 2012). Because children's bodies

TABLE 7-1   Common Air Pollutants and Their Health Effects

Sources

- organic particles (e.g., dust mites)
- molds
- pollen
- carbon monoxide
- formaldehyde and other VOCs
- insulation (e.g., asbestos, fiberglass)
- ozone

Common Health Effects

- chronic cough
- headache
- dizziness
- fatigue
- eye irritation
- sinus congestion
- skin irritation
- shortness of breath
- nausea

are still growing and maturing, they are especially vulnerable to the toxic chemicals found in these substances (Table 7-1).

Although it is not possible to avoid exposure to all toxic chemicals in an environment, steps can be taken to increase awareness and eliminate some sources. For example, labels on toys and art materials should always be checked to make certain they are nontoxic. Indoor air quality can be significantly improved by simply increasing ventilation (opening doors and windows daily, turning on the air conditioning), maintaining heating and cooling systems, and avoiding the use

▼ Children's toys should always be made of nontoxic materials.

© Cengage Learning

of aerosol sprays around children. Many new alternative building materials (low volatile organic compounds [VOC]) and cleaning products, often labeled as "green products" or "building green," are being manufactured without toxic chemicals. Information about green school initiatives, alternative cleaning products, and safer cleaning practices can be accessed on the Environmental Protection Agency's website (www.epa.gov/sc3), the Children's Environmental Health Network website (http://www.cehn.org), and from several other organizations dedicated to maintaining healthy environments.

7-4b Outdoor Safety

The outdoors provides an exciting environment for children's learning and imaginative play. It also offers important health benefits by encouraging children to be physically active. Studies continue to link time spent in outdoor play with reductions in childhood obesity, diabetes, mental health disorders, and behavior problems (Copeland et al., 2012; Milteer & Ginsburg, 2012). However, children's outdoor play areas are also a major source of unintentional injury and, therefore, require a heightened awareness of design, maintenance, and supervisory strategies. Schools that use public parks for outdoor recreation should be particularly alert to safety hazards, such as animal waste, needles, glass, and poorly maintained play equipment (CPSC, 2012b).

Space Safety must be a primary consideration in the design of outdoor play spaces. Separate play areas should be designated for infants and toddlers, preschoolers, and school-age children to accommodate their different developmental needs and abilities. A minimum of 75–100 square feet per child (using the area at the same time) is necessary to encourage active play and to reduce the potential for unintentional injury. The National Health and Safety Performance Standards recommend that play areas for infants include a minimum of 33 square feet per child; 50 square feet per child is suggested for toddlers (APHA & AAP, 2011). Ideally, play areas should be located adjacent to the building so that bathrooms are readily accessible and children are not required to walk long distances. Traveling even a short distance to playgrounds with young children requires considerable time and effort, and often discourages spontaneous outdoor play.

A fence at least 4 to 5 feet in height should surround the play area and include two exits with latched gates to prevent children from wandering away. Railings or slats should be spaced less than 3½ inches or more than 9 inches apart to prevent children's heads or bodies from becoming entrapped. Sharp wire and picket-type fences are inappropriate and should not be used around young children.

An important design element in children's play areas involves how the space will be used (Dotterweich, Greene, & Blosser, 2012; Woolley & Lowe, 2012). Play areas should be arranged so children are clearly visible from all directions. Large open areas encourage activities such as running and tossing balls. Hard, flat surfaces allow children to use riding toys and to play outdoors during inclement weather, especially if these areas are covered. Flower beds provide children with space for gardening, whereas sand and water promote imaginative play. Grassy areas and trees create a natural touch and offer protection from the sun. If trees are not available, large colorful canvas sails can be purchased from play equipment companies or home improvement stores to provide shade. Separate areas designed for quiet and active play also help to reduce potential injuries. Always check with a local nursery or county extension office to be sure that flowers, trees, and other plantings are not poisonous to children. (See Figure 7-2 and Table 7-2 for a partial list.) Photographs and a comprehensive listing of poisonous plants are also available from the Cornell University Department of Animal Science website (http://www.ansci.cornell.edu/plants; click on "Find - by common name.")

FIGURE 7–2 **Examples of common poisonous vegetation.**

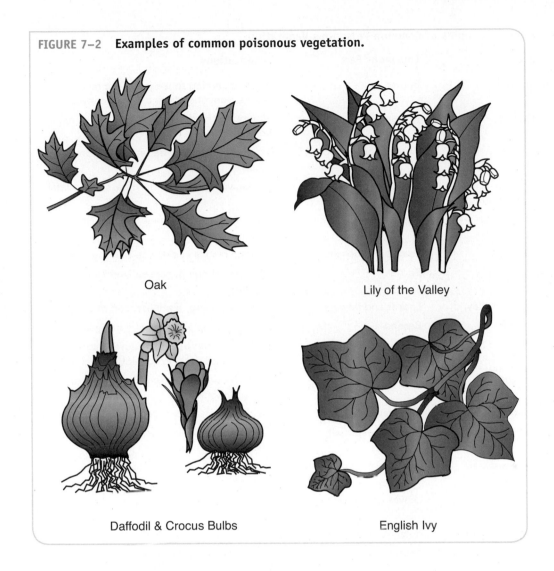

Oak

Lily of the Valley

Daffodil & Crocus Bulbs

English Ivy

Designing outdoor playgrounds so they can be enjoyed by children of all abilities presents another unique challenge. Solid, flat surfaces at least 3½ feet wide allow children to maneuver safely in wheelchairs. Bright colors, textures, ramps, and handrails can easily be incorporated into play environments to improve their visibility and accessibility. Most manufacturers now offer a selection of modified outdoor play equipment designed for children who have a range of abilities and special needs. ADA guidelines for planning accessible facilities and playgrounds are available on their website (http://www.ada.gov; click on "ADA design standards".)

Equipment Each year approximately 220,000 children under the age of 14 are treated in emergency rooms for playground-related injuries (Safe Kids USA, 2011). Because most injuries involve play equipment, careful attention must be given to its selection, placement, and maintenance (Teacher Checklist 7-5; also see Chapter 8). Equipment choices should be based on:

- amount of available play space
- age and developmental appropriateness
- variety of learning experiences provided
- quality and safety of construction
- accessibility to all children

Large pieces of equipment and portable climbing structures should be securely anchored in the ground; posts should be sunk 12 to 18 inches below the ground surface if anchored with

TABLE 7–2   Examples of Common Poisonous Vegetation

Vegetation	Poisonous Part	Complications
Bittersweet	Berries	Causes a burning sensation in the mouth. Nausea, vomiting, dizziness, and convulsions.
Buttercup	All parts	Irritating to the digestive tract. Causes nausea and vomiting.
Castor bean	Beanlike pod	Extremely toxic. May be fatal to children and adults.
Daffodil, hyacinth, narcissus, jonquil, iris	Bulbs Underground roots	Nausea, vomiting, and diarrhea. Can be fatal.
Dieffenbachia	Leaves	Causes immediate burning and swelling around mouth.
English ivy	Leaves and berries	Ingestion results in extreme burning sensation.
Holly	Berries	Results in cramping, nausea, vomiting, and diarrhea.
Lily of the valley	Leaves and flowers	Nausea, vomiting, dizziness, and mental confusion.
Mistletoe	Berries	Extremely toxic. Diarrhea and irregular pulse.
Oleander	Flowers and sap	Highly toxic; can be fatal. Causes nausea, vomiting, diarrhea, and heart irregularities.
Philodendron	Leaves	Ingestion causes intense irritation and swelling of the lips and mouth.
Rhubarb	Raw leaves	Can cause convulsions, coma, and rapid death.
Sweet pea	All parts, especially the seeds	Shallow respirations, possible convulsions, paralysis, and slow pulse.
Black locust tree	Bark, leaves, pods, and seeds	Causes nausea and weakness, especially in children.
Cherry tree	Leaves and twigs	Can be fatal. Causes shortness of breath, general weakness, and restlessness.
Golden chain tree	Beanlike seed pods	Can cause convulsions and coma.
Oak tree	Acorns and leaves	Eating large quantities may cause poisoning. Gradually causes kidney failure.
Rhododendron	All parts	Causes vomiting, convulsions, and paralysis.
Wisteria	Seed pods	Causes severe diarrhea and collapse.
Yews	Berries and foliage	Foliage is very poisonous and can be fatal. Causes nausea, diarrhea, and difficult breathing.

metal pins or at least 6 inches if set in concrete. The safe height of play equipment should be determined by the age of children who will be using it (Table 7–3). Stationary equipment should be located at least 6 to 8 feet from other equipment or hard surfaces such as concrete and asphalt to avoid injury in the event of a fall; this distance should be increased to 15 feet if the equipment has moving parts such as swings.

TABLE 7–3   Recommended Equipment Heights

Age Group	Maximum Equipment Height
Infants & toddlers	32 inches
Preschoolers	48 inches
School-age	6–6 1/2 feet

Many states no longer recommend or permit programs to include swings and teeter-totters on newly constructed playgrounds because they are a frequent source of injury. The Consumer Product Safety Commission (CPSC) also discourages swings in public parks unless they meet strict safety standards (CPSC, 2012b). Existing swing seats should be constructed of plastic or rubber to decrease the risk of impact injuries. Holes must be drilled in tire swings to prevent mosquitoes from breeding in water that may collect. The size of any opening on equipment should also be carefully checked (openings must be less than 3½ inches or greater than 9 inches) to prevent children's heads from becoming entrapped.

▼ A safe fall zone must be established around play equipment.

© Cengage Learning

Large trampolines have increased in popularity but are not appropriate in early childhood programs or school settings. The American Academy of Pediatrics discourages families from having trampolines in their backyards or schools from using them for physical education classes or athletic activities. Trampolines are also not recommended for use by children younger than 6 years due to the risk of serious injury (Lovejoy et al., 2012).

For many years, decks and children's climbing structures were constructed with chromated copper arsenic (CCA)-treated lumber, which gave it a green tint. CCA-treated lumber is no longer sold because there are health risks associated with these chemicals, which can rub off on children's hands. However, many play structures constructed with this material still exist on playgrounds and in children's backyards. Researchers have determined that an annual application of oil-based sealant significantly reduces children's exposure to the arsenic-based chemicals (CPSC, 2012a; Hayward, Lebow, & Brooks, 2011). Soil around the base of treated timbers should be

Did You Know...

that plastic, rubber, and other non-metal surfaces on outdoor play equipment can become hot enough on a sunny day to cause serious burns?

TEACHER CHECKLIST 7-5

General Guidelines for Purchasing Outdoor Play Equipment

Consider:

- Height of platforms and decks; no higher than 32 inches for infants and toddlers, 4 feet for preschoolers, and 6–6 1/2 feet for school-age children.
- Railings (height and design) present on all decks and platforms, especially those more than 30 inches above ground.
- The size of all openings (including those between rungs and guardrails) should be less than 3½ inches or greater than 9 inches apart to prevent entrapment.
- Hardware such as "S" hooks, protruding nuts and bolts, or moving pieces of rope that could injure fingers or catch on clothing; rope swings that could cause strangulation.
- Materials used in construction. (Wood/wood products require maintenance to avoid splintering and deterioration. Metal is strong, but becomes hot in sunlight and slippery when wet. Paints and chemicals used for wood treatment must be nontoxic.)
- The type of surface material that will be needed under equipment.
- The amount of area required for safe installation. (A clearance area of 9 feet is necessary for stationary equipment; 15 feet is needed for equipment with moving parts such as swings.)
- Ladders that are set straight up and down (vs. on an angle) encourage children to hold onto rungs more securely when climbing.

removed periodically or covered with fresh surface material because these chemicals also leach into the ground.

Sand boxes require special care to keep them safe for children (Teacher Checklist 7-6). Play sand made specifically for children's sandboxes can be purchased from local garden centers, building contractors, or cement suppliers. (**Note:** Sands used in construction may contain hazardous materials, such as asbestos, and should not be used for children.) Sandboxes should have good drainage and a tightly fitting cover to keep out animals and insects. If they cannot be covered, sand should be raked and inspected daily for animal feces, spiders, insects, sticks, stones, or other sharp debris before children begin to play. Locating sandboxes in wind-protected areas decreases the chances of having sand blown into children's eyes. Adjoining surfaces, especially sidewalks, should be swept frequently to reduce the potential for slipping and falling.

Wading or swimming pools can add interest to outdoor play areas. However, they require extra supervision, safety, and sanitation precautions. Every teacher should be familiar with water safety procedures and rescue breathing procedures, and at least one adult on site should be CPR certified. Limiting the number of children participating in water activities at any given time improves teachers' ability to monitor and improve safety. Safety rules should be carefully explained to the children before a water activity begins and then strictly enforced.

⚠ CAUTION

Children must never be left unattended around any source of water, including sprinklers, wading pools, water tables, puddles, ditches, fountains, buckets, or toilets.

It is essential that pool water be tested and disinfected (7.2–7.7 ph) prior to use by each group of children to prevent the spread of diseases such as giardia and **cryptosporidiosis**. (See Table 6–1). Inexpensive water-quality test kits are available from pool supply stores. Disinfecting chemicals must be guarded closely and removed from the area once they have been used to protect children from accidental poisoning. Permanent pools and natural bodies of water must be fenced (at least 5 feet in height; be sure to check local codes) and have self-closing gates. Gate alarms, pool safety covers, motion alarms, and the availability of proper flotation and rescue devices provide additional protection against accidental drownings.

Tricycles and other small riding toys are always children's favorites. However, they also are involved in many serious childhood injuries and are a common cause of head trauma. Children should always wear bike helmets when they are riding, but it is also important that the helmets fit properly, are worn correctly, and meet safety standards established by the Consumer Product Safety Commission (Figure 7–3). *Warning*: Children must not wear helmets while on play equipment to prevent entrapment and strangulation. A designated area located away from where other children are playing can make riding activities less hazardous. Safe

TEACHER CHECKLIST 7-6
Teacher Checklist: Sandbox Care and Maintenance

Purchase only special play sand for children's sandboxes.

- Make sure there is adequate drainage to prevent water from pooling.
- Rake and check sand daily for spiders, stones, and sharp objects.
- Cover sand if at all possible; if not, be sure to check for animal feces before children play.
- Sweep adjoining surfaces to prevent slipping and falling.

TeachSource Digital Download) Download from CourseMate.

cryptosporidiosis – *an infectious illness caused by an intestinal parasite. May be present in water (e.g., swimming pools, hot tubs, streams) contaminated with feces or from unwashed hands. Often causes severe diarrhea in children.*

riding rules should be determined and explained to the children. For example, only one child should be allowed on a bike or wheeled-toy and all bikes should be ridden in the same direction to avoid collisions and subsequent injury.

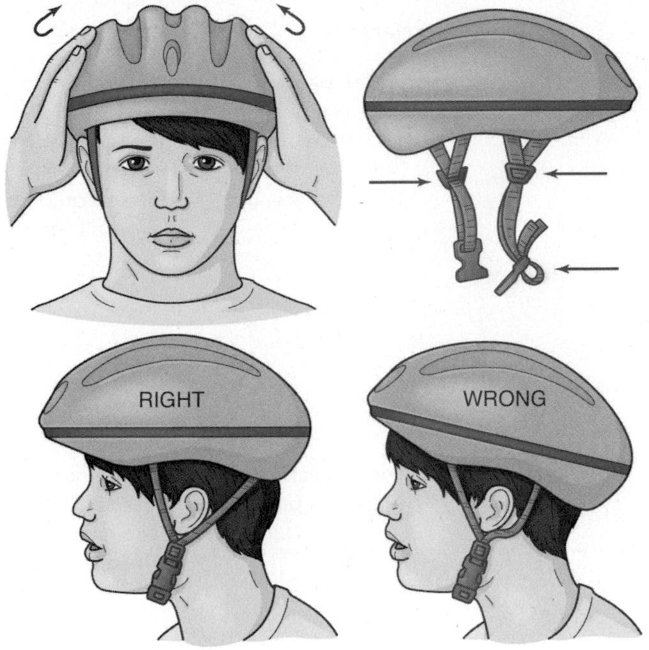

Impact Surface Materials Protective materials that are soft and resilient should be placed under all play equipment and extend approximately 4 to 6 feet out in all directions to create an adequate fall zone (Table 7–4) (CPSC, 2012b). These materials must be loosened frequently to prevent them from compacting and replaced periodically to maintain the recommended depths. Impact surface materials must also be checked daily for any sharp debris or animal waste. Special rubber matting has been developed as an alternative to natural fall zone materials and can be purchased through most outdoor equipment catalogues. Although the initial costs may be considerably greater, rubber matting tends to last longer under children's constant wear. Synthetic grasses, sprinkled with finely ground rubber tire particles for added cushioning, are being installed more often in city parks and school playgrounds. Questions have been raised about the safety of chemicals used in manufacturing these products and the potential for children inhaling or ingesting the fine, rubber particles (Kim et al., 2012).

FIGURE 7–3 **Helmets must fit and be worn properly to protect children from serious head injury.**

Maintenance Hazardous conditions can often be spotted if outdoor play areas are inspected carefully each day before children begin to play. Equipment with broken pieces, jagged or sharp edges, loose screws or bolts, or missing parts should be removed or made off-limits to children. Frequent inspections of play areas and removal of any poisonous vegetation, snakes, rodents or other small animals, sharp sticks, fallen branches, broken glass, or other harmful debris is essential for preventing unintentional injury. Play equipment with wooden surfaces should be sanded and repainted regularly.

Supervision Although adults may go to great lengths to design attractive playgrounds and safe equipment, there is no substitution for first-rate supervision. Children must never be left unattended, and the younger they are the more closely adults need to supervise their play. Teacher supervision and safety management will be addressed in greater detail in Chapter 8.

7-4c Transportation

Some early childhood programs transport children to and from other school settings or on occasional field trips. Large passenger vans are often used for this purpose, but they are not considered safe and, in the event of an accident, may actually place occupants at increased risk for serious injury. Vans have a tendency to roll over and offer passengers limited structural protection. As a result, federal transportation officials currently recommend that early childhood programs replace existing passenger vans with small-scale school buses. These buses are designed with improved structural safety features (roof and fuel tanks) and, thus, offer greater protection.

Any vehicle used to transport children should be fitted with an appropriate safety restraint system (based on height, weight, and age) for each child: an infant-only carrier for infants

TABLE 7-4 Comparison of Impact Surface Materials

Material	Advantages	Disadvantages	Protects to Fall Height (feet)
Gravel, pea (3/8-inch diameter) (9-inch depth)	• Relatively inexpensive • Readily available • Long-lasting; won't decompose • Drains quickly • Doesn't attract animals • Easy to install	• Requires a barrier for containment • Becomes compact if wet and freezes • Must be replenished periodically; may mix with soil below • Not recommended with children under 5 years; small pebbles may be thrown or stuffed into noses, ears, or mouths • Not wheelchair accessible; hazardous if gravel is scattered on hard surfaces nearby; can cause slipping and falls	5
Wood mulch (9-inch depth)	• Inexpensive • Easy to install • Drains quickly • Readily available	• Decomposes rapidly • Must be contained with barriers; can wash away with heavy rains • Absorbs moisture and freezes • Compacts easily • Difficult to find sharp objects (e.g., broken glass, sticks, nails, stones) in loose mulch • Prone to microbial infestations	7
Wood chips (9-inch depth)	• Air trapped between chips promotes cushioning effect • Low in cost • Accessible to wheelchairs	• Washes away with heavy rains • Decomposes and must be replenished to maintain cushioning effect • May be thrown about by children but not likely to cause injury	10
Sand (coarse or masonry sand) (9-inch depth)	• Easy to obtain • Inexpensive • Does not deteriorate over time • Easy to install • Not as prone to microbial or insect infestation • Accessible by wheelchairs	• Must be replenished periodically to maintain cushioning effect • May be thrown about or eaten by children • Gets into shoes and clothing • Hazardous when spilled onto nearby hard surfaces such as cement and tile floors; can cause slipping and falls • Attractive to animals (especially cats) if area is not covered • Must be raked and sifted frequently to check for undesirable objects (e.g., sticks, broken glass, stones) • Requires good drainage beneath	4
Shredded rubber (6-inch depth)	• Relatively low initial cost • Doesn't deteriorate over time • Not as likely to compact • Less conducive to microbial and insect infestation • Wheelchair accessible	• Is flammable • May stain clothing if not treated • May contain metal particles from steel belted tires • Easily thrown about by children but unlikely to cause injury • Requires good drainage system	10

(continued)

TABLE 7–4 **Comparison of Impact Surface Materials** (*continued*)

Material	Advantages	Disadvantages	Protects to Fall Height (feet)
Rubber tiles or mat systems (check manufacturer's recommendations)	• Uniform cushioning effect • Easy to clean and maintain • Material remains in place • Foreign objects are easily noticed • Wheelchair accessible	• Expensive to install • Requires a flat surface; difficult to use on hills or uneven area • Mat or tile edges may curl up and present a tripping hazard • Some materials affected by frost	Varies by manufacturer

Note: Suggested material depths (noncompacted).
Source: *Public Playground Safety Handbook,* U.S. Consumer Product Safety Commission (CPSC) (2012). (http://www.cpsc.gov/PageFiles/116134/325.pdf).

(birth–1 year) weighing up to 22 pounds (9.9 kg) (installed in the back seat, facing the rear of the car) with a three- or five-point harness. A convertible safety seat for heavier infants should be purchased for children under 1 year who weigh 20–35 pounds (9.1–15.9 kg).

  ▸ a child safety seat for children (1–4 years) weighing 20–40 pounds (9.1–18.1 kg) and who are able to sit up by themselves (installed in the back seat, facing forward)
  ▸ a booster seat, secured in the back seat, used in combination with a lap belt and shoulder harness for children (4–8 years) who have outgrown child safety seats and are under 4 feet 9 inches (57 inches; 144.8 cm) in height
  ▸ a vehicle lap belt and shoulder harness for children (age 8 years and older) who are at least 55–58 inches (139.7–147.3 cm) in height; children should always ride in the back seat.

It is also critical that safety seats and restraints be installed according to manufacturer's specifications and used correctly whenever children are in transit:

  ▸ They must be installed correctly (facing the front or back as is appropriate) and securely anchored in the vehicle.
  ▸ They must meet federal manufacturing standards. (See, http://www.nhtsa.gov/nhtsa_eou/info.jsp?type=all for car seat ratings.) Additional child car seat guidelines and comparison lists are posted at www.healthychildren.org. (Click on "Safety and Prevention," "On the Go.")
  ▸ Children must always be buckled into the seat.

Children and adults must be buckled in securely on every trip even though it may be a time-consuming process. Young children should always ride in the back seat of a vehicle to avoid injury from airbags.

Designated drivers must be responsible individuals who are in good health and possess a current license appropriate for the vehicle-type and number of passengers they will be transporting. They should present evidence of a safe driving history and have no criminal convictions. In addition, they must abstain from alcohol, drug, and tobacco use for several hours prior to and while driving. Families of children who are transported on a regular basis should get to know the driver so they feel comfortable with the arrangement. Written parental permission and special instructions should always be obtained from families before children are transported in any vehicle.

Transport vehicles must be inspected and maintained regularly to ensure their safe performance. Air conditioning and heating should be operational to protect children from temperature extremes. An ABC-type fire extinguisher should be secured in the front of the vehicle where it is accessible for emergencies. Liability insurance should be purchased to cover the vehicle, driver, and maximum number of intended passengers. Copies of children's health forms and emergency contact information should always be stored safely in the vehicle.

Special off-street areas should be designated for the sole purpose of loading and unloading children. If programs do not have space sufficient to accommodate this activity, they will need to dedicate additional effort to providing safety education for children and families. Children should always enter

▼ **Children should always enter and exit from the curb-side of a car.**

© Cengage Learning

and exit vehicles from the curb-side rather than the street-side. Adequate parking should be available around school buildings to reduce traffic congestion and protect children's safety. Families must also be reminded *never* to leave children alone in a vehicle, even for a few minutes, to prevent abduction or overheating. (**Note:** Temperatures inside of a vehicle can become dangerously high in a short time even on mild or cloudy days.)

Families are sometimes asked to provide transportation for off-site field trips. However, this practice is risky and has the potential for creating serious legal problems in the event of an accident. Programs have no guarantee that privately owned vehicles or individual drivers meet the standards and qualifications previously discussed. As a result, programs may be even more vulnerable to lawsuits and charges of negligence. To avoid this risk, programs may opt to use public transportation, such as a city bus, or contract with a private transportation company.

When private vehicles are used for transportation, several steps can be taken to protect children's safety. Travel routes should be planned in advance, reviewed with the director, and followed precisely by all drivers. Names of drivers, supervising adults, and children riding in each vehicle, as well as anticipated departure and arrival times, should be left with a program administrator. Rules for safe traveling should be reviewed with all drivers and children before each excursion. Plans for handling an unplanned emergency, such as an ill child, flat tire, carjacking, or unusual weather, should also be discussed and gone over carefully with drivers. At least one adult traveling with the group should have first aid and CPR training.

Did You Get It?

_____ is an important design feature to consider when planning a new indoor or outdoor space for children.

a. Cost
b. Ease of supervision
c. Visual appeal
d. Staffing

Take the full quiz on CourseMate.

PARTNERING with FAMILIES

How to Identify High-Quality Programs

Dear Families,

Choosing an early childhood or after-school program that is right for your child can be a challenging task. It is important to take time and to carefully research each program until you are satisfied with the arrangement. Note how well the program measures up to the three key indicators of a quality program: small group size; a low ratio of adults to children; and, teachers who have educational preparation in child development and early childhood education. Spend

(continued)

How to Identify High-Quality Programs *(continued)*

time visiting and observing each program and seek answers to the following questions before enrolling your child:

▶ Does the environment appear to be clean, safe, and appealing to children? For example, are electrical outlets covered, are poisonous and sharp items stored out of children's reach, is the carpet intact and free of snags or stains, and do children wash their hands before eating and at other appropriate times?

▶ Is the program accredited or licensed?

▶ Do the children seem happy and under control? Are children encouraged in their efforts and allowed to express their feelings? Are teachers playing and talking with the children? Do they involve children in solving their own problems?

▶ Are children treated with respect and as individuals? Is the teacher's tone of voice warm and friendly versus harsh, demanding, or demeaning?

▶ Is there adequate adult supervision? Are there sufficient numbers of adults present who can respond to an injured child or classroom emergency while ensuring the safety of other children?

▶ Are there a sufficient number and variety of toys and materials for all children to use, or must children wait for others to finish? Are items easily accessible to children? Do some of the toys reflect the diversity of children enrolled?

▶ Is the food served to children nutritious, age appropriate, and adequate in amount? Is food stored, prepared, and served in a safe manner? If your child has food allergies, would her special needs be accommodated? Are weekly menus posted?

▶ Have the teachers been trained to work with young children? Do they appear to enjoy interacting with the children and take pride in their efforts? Are they knowledgeable about how to facilitate children's development, identify problems, and support diversity? Be sure to ask about their educational preparation and years of experience.

▶ Do you feel welcomed and encouraged to ask questions? Are there opportunities for you to become involved in your child's classroom?

▶ Are learning experiences planned for children, or are they left to wander or to watch television?

▶ Is a schedule of the children's daily activities posted for you to read?

▶ Do you agree with the program's philosophy, and is it appropriate for your child's needs?

▶ Have the program's policies been explained clearly, and are they acceptable to you?

CLASSROOM CORNER

Teacher Activities

Recycle Everyday

(NHES PreK–2; National Health Education Standard 2.2.2)

Concept: You can recycle items instead of throwing them away in the trash.

Learning Objectives

▶ Children will learn that items can be recycled and then made into other products.

▶ Children will learn how to sort different items.

(continued)

CLASSROOM CORNER

Teacher Activities (continued)

Recycle Everyday

Supplies

▶ boxes (the size that reams of paper come in); newspapers, chipboard boxes, magazines/ catalogs; milk jugs and plastic bottles; cans (emptied out and clean; make sure cans don't have a sharp ring)

Learning Activities

▶ Read and discuss the books:
  - *Recycle Every Day* by Nancy Elizabeth Wallace
  - *Recycle* by Gail Gibbons
  - *The Adventures of a Plastic Bottle: A Story About Recycling* by Alison Inches

▶ Decorate each box so children will know which items need to go in it (picture of a milk jug, a water or soda bottle, newspaper, etc.). Children can help decorate the boxes ahead of time.

▶ Spread items out on the floor to show how much space discarded items take up. Talk about how items can be sorted and recycled and not thrown away.

▶ Demonstrate how items need to be sorted according to the pictures on the box.

▶ Have children come up and pick an item to place in the correct box. Sort all items. If possible, plan a field trip to a recycling center.

▶ Discuss what happens to items that are tossed in the garbage. Talk about where all of the garbage is taken. Ask children for their ideas about ways that families can reduce the amount of garbage they throw away.

Evaluation

▶ Children can sort items.

▶ Children will explain that items can be recycled and made into other items instead of thrown away as trash.

Additional lesson plans for grades 3-5 are available on CourseMate.

◖ Summary

▶ Identifying high-quality early care and education programs that are available, affordable, and convenient can be challenging for families.
  - The environment affects all aspects of children's growth and development.
▶ Licensing regulations and procedures reflect minimal standards and vary from state to state. However, they provide some assurance that children's health and safety will be protected. Not everyone agrees about how much regulation is necessary.
  - Adhering to licensing regulations can help protect teachers from potential claims of negligence.

▶ Key indicators of high-quality programs include: small group size, low teacher/child ratios, and teachers' educational preparation and experience.

▶ Care attention must be given to planning and monitoring environments so they are safe for young children.

- Location, security, fire safety, plumbing, surfaces and furnishings, and air quality should be considered when planning children's indoor environments.
- Space, play equipment, vegetation, impact surface materials, adult supervision, and transportation must be addressed when planning outdoor play areas.

◑ Terms to Know

environment *p. 169*
cognitive *p. 169*
accreditation *p. 171*
licensing *p. 171*

regulations *p. 171*
compliance *p. 171*
registration *p. 172*

developmentally appropriate
    practice (DAP) *p. 175*
notarized *p. 177*
cryptosporidiosis *p. 192*

◑ Chapter Review

A. By Yourself

1. Match the definition in **Column I** with the term in **Column II**.

Column I	Column II
1. local ordinance permitting specific types of facilities or businesses to operate in an area	a. regulation
	b. minimal
2. legal standard that outlines procedures	c. small group size
3. child development credential	d. staff qualifications
4. legally recognized signature	e. notarized
5. indicator of a quality program	f. CDA
6. skills possessed by an employee	g. zoning codes
7. least restrictive requirements	h. accreditation

2. Identify and describe eight features of a high-quality early childhood program.

3. Outline the steps involved in obtaining a license to operate an early childhood program?

4. What type of car seat or restraint is appropriate for a 3 years old? What about an 11-month-old infant who weighs 27 pounds?

B. As a Group

1. Locate and review the child care licensing regulations for your state posted online. Discuss the pros and cons of the following question: Should the quality of state child care licensing standards be raised?

2. In what ways does the environment influence a child's growth and development?

3. Describe several features that make an outdoor play yard safe for 2½- to 5-year-old children.

4. What steps can programs take to make their facilities secure from unwanted intrusions?

5. Discuss how a teacher's educational training affects the quality of a child's experiences in an early childhood program.

6. Brainstorm several ways that a school can "go green" and discuss what effect(s) this could potentially have on children's health.

◑ Case Study

Reya Gonzales has offered to help out her best friend Manuela by watching her three children several afternoons each week. Manuela has had difficulty finding child care because her new job requires her to work on different weekdays. Although she assured Reya this arrangement would only last a short time, two months have already passed. In the meantime, three of Manuela's coworkers have also asked Reya to watch their children on a regular basis. As a result, Reya now has seven children ranging in age from 15 months to 7 years who are in her care four days a week. Their parents are grateful and pleased with Reya's nurturing care. However, she fears the neighbors will report her to the local licensing agency or that the licensing authorities will soon discover her activities. Reya enjoys working with the children and has considered opening a child care business in her home. However, she is reluctant to contact the licensing agency because she has no formal training in early childhood and is unsure that her house and yard will pass the safety inspection. Reya also knows that her friends depend on her for child care and could lose their jobs if they are unable to locate an affordable program with openings.

1. What advice would you offer to Reya regarding her options?
2. What steps could Reya take to improve her success in becoming licensed?
3. Do you think family child care programs should be licensed or registered? Explain your position.
4. If Reya is unable to meet all of the state licensing standards during the initial inspection, should her child care activities be stopped? Why or why not?
5. How can the need to improve early childhood program quality be balanced with meeting increased demands for care?

◑ Application Activities

1. Develop a safety checklist that teachers and families can use when inspecting children's outdoor play areas for hazardous conditions. Use your list to conduct an inspection of two different play yards (for example, public vs. private), or the same play area on two separate occasions and summarize your findings. Repeat the process for indoor areas.

2. Contact your local child care licensing agency. Make arrangements to accompany licensing personnel on an on-site visit of a center-based program; be sure to review the state licensing regulations beforehand. Observe how the licensing inspection is conducted. Prepare a short paper in which you describe your reactions to this experience.

3. Licensing personnel are often viewed as unfriendly or threatening authority figures. However, their major role is to offer guidance and to help teachers create safer environments for children. Role-play how you would handle the following situations during a licensing visit. Keep in mind the positive role of licensing personnel (e.g., offering explanations, providing suggestions, and planning acceptable solutions and alternatives):
   - electrical outlets not covered
   - all children's toothbrushes found stored together in a large plastic bin
   - open boxes of dry cereals and crackers in kitchen cabinets
   - an adult-sized toilet and wash basin in the only bathroom
   - a swing set located next to a cement patio
   - incomplete information on children's immunization records
   - a teacher who prepares snacks without first washing his or her hands

4. Create a PowerPoint presentation to help families identify quality features to look for in an early childhood program. Include photographs of actual programs to illustrate your points. Prepare a modified version for families in your community who may not speak English as their predominant language. Make presentations to several parent groups and have them evaluate the effectiveness of your program.

5. Learn more about the CDA credential by searching online (http://www.cdacouncil.org) or contacting the Council for Professional Recognition (800-424-4310). After reading through the materials, prepare a brief summary describing the program and its requirements.

6. Locate and read through the *Public Playground Safety Handbook* (http://www.cpsc.gov /CPSCPUB/PUBS/325.pdf ; CPSC, 2010). Summarize the recommended safety standards for at least six different outdoor play equipment items. Prepare a safety checklist that families can use when they take children to public parks or playground areas. Test and revise your checklist before distributing it to families.

Helpful Web Resources

Canadian Child Care Federation	http://www.cccf-fcsge.ca
Child Care Aware	http://www.naccrra.org
Health Canada (Consumer Product Safety)	http://www.hc-sc.gc.ca
National Association for Family Child Care	http://www.nafcc.org
National Association for the Education of Young Children (NAEYC)	http://www.naeyc.org
National Network for Child Care	http://www.nncc.org
National Program for Playground Safety	http://playgroundsafety.org
U.S. Product Safety Commission	http://www.cpsc.gov
U.S. Product Safety Commission	http://www.cpsc.gov

Visit the Education CourseMate for this textbook to access the eBook, Did You Get It? quizzes, Digital Downloads, TeachSource Video Cases, flashcards, and more. Go to CengageBrain.com to log in, register, or purchase access.

References

Allen, K. E., & Cowdery, G. (2012). *The exceptional child: Inclusion in early childhood education.* (7th ed.). Belmont, CA: Wadsworth Cengage Learning.

American Public Health Association (APHA) and American Academy of Pediatrics (AAP). (2011). *Caring for our children: National health and safety performance standards for out-of-home care.* (3rd ed.). Washington, DC. Available online at http://nrckids.org/CFOC3/index.html.

Belsky, J., & Pluess, M. (2012). Differential susceptibility to long-term effects of quality of child care on externalizing behavior in adolescence?, *International Journal of Behavioral Development,* 36(1), 2–10.

Bracy, N. (2011). Student perceptions of high-security school environments, *Youth & Society,* 43(1), 365–395.

Child Care Law Center. (2009). Questions and answers about the Americans with Disabilities Act: A quick reference for child care providers. Accessed on June 4, 2012 from http://www.childcarelaw.org/docs/ADA%20Q%20and%20A%202009%20Final%203%2009.pdf.

Consumer Product Safety Commission (CPSC). (2012a). Chromated copper arsenate (CCA) – Treated wood use in playground equipment. Accessed on June 6, 2012 from, http://www.cpsc.gov/phth/ccafact.html.

Consumer Product Safety Commission (CPSC). (2012b). *Public playground safety handbook.* Accessed on May 2, 2013 from http://www.cpsc.gov/PageFiles/116134/325.pdf .

Copeland, K., Sherman, S., Kendeigh, C., Kalkwarf, H., & Saelens, B. (2012). Societal values and policies may curtail preschool children's physical activity in child care centers, *Pediatrics,* 129(2), 265–274.

Dennis, S., & O'Connor, E. (2013). Reexamining quality in early childhood education: Exploring the relationship between the organizational climate and the classroom, *Journal of Research in Childhood Education,* 27(1), 74–92.

Dotterweich, A., Greene, A., & Blosser, D. (2012). Using innovative playgrounds and cross-circular design to increase physical activity, *Journal of Physical Education, Recreation, & Dance*, 83(5), 1–60.

Environmental Protection Agency (EPA). (2013). *America's children and the environment*. (3rd ed.). Accessed on May 3, 2013 from http://www.epa.gov/ace .

Environmental Protection Agency (EPA). (2012). Managing radon in schools. Accessed on June 9, 2012 from http://www.epa.gov/iaq/schools/managing_radon.html.

Essa, E. (2014). *Introduction to early childhood education*. 7th ed. Belmont, CA: Wadsworth Cengage.

Fults, R., & Harryl, B. (2012). Combining family centeredness and diversity in early childhood teacher training programs, *Exceptional Children*, 35(1), 27–48.

Green, B., Malsch, A., Kothari, B., Busse, J., & Brennan, E. (2012). An intervention to increase early childhood staff capacity for promoting children's social-emotional development in preschool settings, *Early Childhood Education Journal*, 40(2), 123–132.

Hayward, D., Lebow, S., & Brooks, K. (2011). *Methods for mitigating the environmental risks associated with wood preservatives*. Accessed on June 6, 2012 from http://www.fpl.fs.fed.us/documnts/pdf2011/fpl_2011_hayward001.pdf.

Hebbeler, K., Spiker, D., & Kanhn, L. (2012). Individuals with Disabilities Act's early childhood programs powerful vision and pesky details, *Topics in Early Childhood Special Education*, 31(4), 199–207.

Hillemeier, M., Morgan, P., Farkas, G., & Maczuga, S. (2012). Quality disparities in child care for at-risk children: Comparing Head Start and non-Head Start settings, *Maternal & Child Journal*. Advanced online publication. DOI: 10.1007/s10995-012-0961-7.

Hong, J., & Eamon, M. (2012). Student's perceptions of unsafe schools: An ecological systems analysis, *Journal of Child & Family Studies*, 21(3), 428–438.

Kim, S., Yang, J., Kim, H., Yeo, I., Shin, D., & Lim, Y. (2012). Health risk assessment of lead ingestion exposure by particle sizes in crumb rubber on artificial turf considering bioavailability, *Environmental Health & Toxicology*, 27. DOI: 10.5620/eht.2012.27.e2012005.

Lin, S., Kielb, C., Reddy, A., Chapman, B., & Hwang, S. (2012). Comparison of indoor air quality management strategies between the school and district levels in New York State, *Journal of School Health*, 82(3), 139–146.

Lovejoy, S., Weiss, J., Epps, H., Zionts, L., & Gaffney, J. (2012). Preventable childhood injuries, *Journal of Pediatric Orthopedics*, 32(7), 741–747.

Ma, X., Shen, J., Lu, X., Brandi, K., Goodman, J., & Watson, G. (2013). Can quality improvement system improve childcare site performance in school readiness?, *The Journal of Educational Research*, 106(2), 146–156.

Milteer, R., & Ginsburg, K. (2012). The importance of play in promoting healthy child development and maintaining strong parent-child bond: Focus on children in poverty, *Pediatrics*, 129(1), e204–e213.

National Association for the Education of Young Children (NAEYC). (2012). Accreditation of programs for young children. Accessed on June 4, 2012 from http://www.naeyc.org/academy.

Nicholson, S., & Reifel, S. (2011). Sink or swim: Child care teachers' perceptions of entry training experiences, *Journal of Early Childhood Teacher Education*, 32(1), 5–25.

Rhodes, H., & Huston, A. (2012). *Building the workforce our youngest children deserve, Social Policy Report*, 26(1), 1–32. Available online at http://www.naccrra.org/sites/default/files/default_site_pages/2012/srcdworkforcerept2012.pdf.

Safe Kids USA. (2011). Playground safety fact sheet. Accessed on June 5, 2012 from http://www.safekids.org/our-work/research/fact-sheets/playground-safety-fact-sheet.html.

Sripada, K. (2012). Neoscience in the Capital: Linking brain research and Federal early childhood policies, *Early Education & Development*, 23(1), 120–130.

Tran, H., & Winsler, A. (2011). Teacher and center stability and school readiness among low-income ethnically diverse children in subsidized, center-based child care, *Child & Youth Services Review*, 33(11), 2241–2252.

Tucker-Drob, E. (2012). Preschools reduce early academic achievement gaps: A longitudinal twin approach, *Psychological Science*, 23(3), 310–319.

U.S. Department of Justice. (1997). Commonly asked questions about child care centers and the Americans with Disabilities Act. Accessed on June 10, 2012 from http://www.ada.gov/childq&a.htm.

Veitch, J., & Galasiu, A. (2012). The physiological and psychological effects of windows, daylight, and view at home: Review and research agenda. NRC-IRC Research Report RR-325. Accessed on June 4, 2012 from http://www.nrc-cnrc.gc.ca/obj/irc/doc/pubs/rr/rr325.pdf.

Vidoni, C. & Ignico, A. (2011). Promoting physical activity during early childhood, *Early Child Development & Care*, 181(9), 1261–1269

Wen, X., Bulotsky-Shearer, R., Hahs-Vaughn, D., & Korfmacher, J. (2012). Head Start program quality: Examination of classroom quality and parent involvement in predicting children's vocabulary, literacy, and mathematics achievement trajectories, *Early Childhood Research Quarterly*. Advanced online publication. http://dx.doi.org/10.1016/j.ecresq.2012.01.004.

Whitebook, M., & Ryan, S. (2011). *Degrees in context: Asking the right questions about preparing effective teachers of young children*, Preschool Policy Brief Vol. 22. New Brunswick, NJ: National Institute for Early Education Research.

Woolley, H., & Lowe, A. (2012). Exploring the relationship between design approach and play value of outdoor play spaces, *Landscape Research*. Advanced online publication. DOI:10.1080/01426397.2011.640432.

chapter **8** **Safety Management**

⏵ **#1 a and c:** Promoting child development and learning
⏵ **#2 a:** Building family and community relationships
⏵ **#3 d:** Observing, documenting, and assessing to support young children and families
⏵ **#4 b, and d:** Using developmentally effective approaches to connect with children and families
⏵ **#5 a, b, and c:** Using content knowledge to build a meaningful curriculum
⏵ **#6 b, c, d, and e:** Becoming a professional
⏵ Field experience

Learning Objectives

After studying this chapter, you should be able to:

LO 8-1 Define the term "unintentional injury," and explain why the victims are most often young children.

LO 8-2 Describe the four basic principles of risk management.

LO 8-3 Discuss safety practices that teachers should implement in the classroom and outdoors to safeguard children.

LO 8-4 Explain the process that programs should follow when developing emergency and disaster response plans.

Unintentional injuries are the leading cause of death and permanent disability among children under the age of 14 (CDC, 2012; Judy, 2011). They are also responsible for thousands of nonfatal injuries and are costly in terms of time, energy, suffering, and medical expense. Although children experience frequent mishaps, the most common causes of death (Table 8–1) due to unintentional injury include:

⏵ motor vehicles–as pedestrians; riding a tricycle, bicycle, or wheeled toy
⏵ drowning–in swimming pools, spas, bathtubs, ponds, toilets, buckets
⏵ burns–from fireplaces, appliances, grills, chemicals, electrical outlets, residential fires, fireworks
⏵ suffocation–from plastic bags, entrapment in chests or appliances, bedding, or aspiration of small objects
⏵ falls–from stairs, furniture, play equipment, windows
⏵ poisoning–from pain relievers, vitamins with iron, carbon monoxide, cleaning products, insecticides, cosmetics

Knowing that young children are especially vulnerable to unintentional injury makes it imperative that teachers and families understand how to organize environments, provide safe activities, and supervise children of all ages and developmental abilities.

TABLE 8–1   Leading Causes of Childhood Death Due to Unintentional Injury

Cause of Death	1- to 4-year-olds	5- to 9-year-olds
Motor vehicle/pedestrian	32.3 %	51.6 %
Drowning	30.7 %	15.4 %
Fire/burns	11.5 %	11.4 %
Suffocation	8.5 %	3.4 %
Falls	3.1 %	1.6 %
Poisoning	2.5 %	1.7 %
Total Deaths	1610	1044

Source: CDC. (2010). National Center for Injury Prevention & Control. WISQARS Leading causes of death reports, national and regional, 1999–2009.

8-1 What Is Unintentional Injury?

The term *unintentional injury* has replaced *accidents* when referring to injuries sustained by children. This is because in most instances, factors contributing to an injury are preventable. Childhood injuries are most often attributed to environmental hazards, lack of appropriate planning and adult supervision, or a child's immature development—conditions that are all manageable with improved knowledge and awareness.

Infants and toddlers are at highest risk for sustaining life-threatening injuries and medical emergencies. Their zealous interest and curiosity in learning about their surroundings, impulsive play, and immature development can unfortunately lead children into new and unexpected dangers. Likewise, older children continue to explore their environment with an even greater sense of enthusiasm, yet they still lack advanced motor skills, experience, and ability to anticipate the consequences of their behavior. Thus, adults must be continuously aware of children's developmental abilities and behavioral characteristics, as well as potential environmental hazards, in their efforts to protect children from injury (Table 8–2).

Teachers and administrators assume a major role and responsibility for protecting the safety of children in their care. This can be a particularly challenging task given the ages of children typically enrolled in early education programs, elementary schools, and before-and-after school programs. However, teachers' unique training and experience enables them to implement safety measures that can eliminate needless childhood injuries.

▼ Teachers have a professional and ethical responsibility to protect children's safety.

© Cengage Learning

Did You Know...

that no federal regulations govern the safety of rides in amusement facilities, fairs, water parks, shopping malls, restaurants, or public playgrounds? Or, that owners and operators are not required to report injuries and fatalities? Some states have passed minimal oversight laws, but they are not always enforced.

Did You Get It?

When referring to children, the term "accident" has been replaced by the phrase:

a. unintentional injury
b. random trauma
c. inadvertent harm
d. unforeseen bodily damage

Take the full quiz on CourseMate.

TABLE 8–2   Developmental Characteristics and Injury Prevention

Age	Developmental Characteristics	Hazards	Preventive Measures
Birth to 4 months	Eats, sleeps, cries; rolls off flat surfaces	Burns	Set hot water heater to a maximum of 120° F. Always keep one hand on baby.
	Wriggles	Falls	Never turn back or walk away from an infant who is on a table or bed.
		Toys	Select toys that are too large to swallow, too tough to break, have no sharp points or edges, and have nontoxic finishes.
		Sharp objects	Keep pins and other sharp objects out of an infant's reach.
		Suffocation	Filmy plastics, harnesses, zippered bags, and pillows can smother or strangle. Place infant on firm mattress; remove all blankets, pillows, and bumper pads.
4–12 months	Grasps and moves about	Play areas	Keep infants in sight at all times. The floor, adult bed, and yard are unsafe without close supervision.
	Puts objects in mouth	Bath	Check temperature of bath water with elbow. Keep baby out of reach of faucets. Never leave alone in bath.
		Toys	Large beads on strong cord, unbreakable, rounded toys made of smooth wood or plastic (phthalate-free) are safe.
		Small objects	Keep buttons, beads, coins, batteries and other small objects out of infants' reach.
		Poisoning	Store medicines, cleaners, and other toxic substances in locked cabinets.
		Falls	Don't turn your back or walk away when baby is on an elevated surface. Place gates in doorways and on stairways.
		Burns	Place guards around registers and floor furnaces. Keep hot liquids, hot foods, and electric cords (e.g., curling irons, toasters, coffee pots) out of infants' reach. Use sturdy and round-edged furniture. Avoid hot steam vaporizers.
1–2 years	Investigates, climbs, opens doors and drawers; takes things apart; likes to play	Gates, windows, doors	Securely fasten doors leading to stairways, driveways, and storage. Install gates on stairways and porches.
		Play areas	Keep screens locked or nailed. Fence the play yard. Provide sturdy toys with no small removable parts or unbreakable materials. Keep electric cords to coffee pots, toasters, irons, and computers out of reach.
		Water	Never leave child alone in tub, wading pool, or around open or frozen water. Fence and gate pools; keep locked at all times. Learn CPR.
		Poisons	Store all vitamins, medicines, and poisons in locked cabinets. Store cosmetics and household products, especially caustics and pesticides, out of child's reach. Store kerosene and gasoline in metal cans and locked cabinet.
		Burns	Provide guards for wall heaters, registers, and floor furnaces. Never leave children alone in the house. Supervise children closely to protect them from injuries.

(continued)

Age	Characteristics	Hazard	Safety measures
2–3 years	Fascinated by fire; moves about constantly; tries to do things alone	Traffic	Keep child away from street and driveway with strong fence and consistent discipline. Use appropriate car seat restraints.
	Imitates and explores; runs and is lightning fast; is impatient with restraint	Water	Eliminate water sources such as shallow wading pools, fountains, and garden ponds, unless carefully supervised.
		Toys	Provide large sturdy toys with rounded edges and no small parts.
		Burns	Lock up matches and cigarette lighters. Teach children about the danger of fire. Never leave them alone in the house. Keep hot liquids out of reach.
		Dangerous objects	Lock up medicine, household and garden poisons, dangerous tools, firearms, and garden equipment. Teach safe ways of handling appropriate tools and kitchen equipment.
		Playmates	Injuries occur more often when playmates are older; 2-year-olds may be easily hurt by bats, hard balls, bicycles, rough play.
3–6 years	Explores the neighborhood; climbs on objects; enjoys riding tricycles; plays and likes rough games	Tools and equipment	Store in a safe place, out of reach and locked. Teach safe use of tools and kitchen equipment.
	Frequently out of adult sight; likes to imitate adult actions	Poisons and burns	Keep medicines, household cleaning products, and matches locked up.
		Falls and injuries	Check play areas for attractive hazards such as old refrigerators, deep holes, trash heaps, wires, construction, and old buildings.
		Drowning	Teach the danger of water and begin swimming instruction.
		Traffic	Help children learn rules and dangers of traffic. Insist on obedience where traffic is concerned. Use appropriate car seat restraints; always buckle children in.
6–12 years	Enjoys spending time away from home; participates in active sports, is part of a group, and will "try anything once" in traffic, on foot, or on a bicycle; teaching must gradually replace supervision	Traffic	Set a good example: drive safely, wear seat belt, and avoid texting or using cell phone while driving. Teach pedestrian and bicycle safety rules. Don't allow play in streets or alleys.
		Personal	Teach self-protection skills: what to do if bullied; Internet and cell phone safety; resisting drugs and alcohol.
		Firearms	Store unloaded in a locked cabinet. Teach children to stay away from guns and tell an adult if they find a gun.
		Sports	Provide sound instruction, safe area, and equipment. Supervise any competition.
		Drowning	Teach swimming and boating safety.

8-2 Risk Management: Principles and Preventive Measures

Prevention of **unintentional injury** requires continuous awareness and implementation of **risk management** measures (Bowman et al., 2012; Pollack et al., 2012). Teachers and families must consider the element of safety in everything they do with young children (Table 8–2). This includes the rooms they organize, toys they purchase, and learning activities they plan. To new teachers or busy parents, this step may seem unnecessarily time-consuming. However, these are precisely the times when it is important to focus extra attention on children's safety. Any preventive effort is worth the time if it spares even one child from injury!

Knowledge of children's developmental skills is essential for protecting their safety (Marotz & Allen, 2013). Understanding the differences in their cognitive, motor, social, and emotional abilities at various stages helps adults anticipate children's actions and take steps to avoid unintentional injury. For example, knowing that infants put everything into their mouths should alert teachers to be extra vigilant of small items, such as a paper clip or pen cap, or coin that might have been dropped on the floor. Understanding that toddlers enjoy climbing should alert adults to the importance of fastening bookshelves, televisions, and large pieces of play equipment securely to the wall or floor so they won't tip over. Recognizing that 4-year-olds' limited understanding of cause and effect makes them more vulnerable to hazardous situations in their environment becomes useful when designing a classroom or play yard. Or, knowing that boys are more likely to be involved in accidents than are girls due to their preference for play that involves active, aggressive, and risk-taking behaviors can be used when planning large motor activities (Morrongiello et al., 2012; Little, Wyver, & Gibson, 2011). When adults are familiar with typical child development and also understand that children develop at different rates, they are able to use this information for:

- planning children's environments
- preparing learning activities
- selecting appropriate play equipment (indoor and outdoor)
- establishing safety guidelines
- supervising children's learning and play experiences
- developing safety education programs

It is important to recognize that circumstances, such as fatigue, illness, change, and distraction increase the risk of unintentional injury (Table 8–3). It is also known that children in group-care settings are more likely to be injured while playing outdoors, especially on swings, climbing apparatus, and

TABLE 8–3 Conditions That Contribute to Unintentional Injury

The risk of injury is greatest when:

- adults are not feeling well and suffering from symptoms of illness, discomfort, or fatigue.
- adults are angry, emotionally upset, or faced with a difficult situation, such as an uncooperative child, an unpleasant conversation with a parent, a strained relationship with a staff member, or a personal problem.
- new teachers, staff members, or visitors who are unfamiliar with the children and their routines are present.
- conditions are rushed or planned late in the day.
- there is a shortage of teachers or too few adults to provide adequate supervision.
- children are not able to play outdoors due to inclement weather.
- new children are included in a group and are unfamiliar with the environment, rules, and expectations.
- rules have not been formulated or explained carefully to children.

unintentional injury – *an unexpected or unplanned event that may result in physical harm or injury.*
risk management – *measures taken to avoid an event such as an injury or illness from occurring; implies the ability to anticipate circumstances and behaviors.*

slides (Loder & Abrams, 2011). For this reason, some states no longer permit swings, teeter-totters, or large slides on new playgrounds. When children are at home, they are more likely to sustain injuries indoors, particularly in the kitchen and bathroom areas (Smithson, Garside, & Pearson, 2011).

Environmental design and maintenance are also important considerations to address in the prevention of children's injuries. Local building codes, state child care licensing regulations, and the Americans with Disabilities Act (ADA) architectural requirements provide guidelines for the construction of facilities that are safe and accessible (U.S. Department of Justice, 2010). Consulting with licensing personnel during the planning phase of any new construction or remodeling project is also helpful for identifying important safety features and ensuring that facilities will comply with recommended standards.

Several organizations, including the National Association for the Education of Young Children (NAEYC) and Child Care Aware (formerly NACCRRA) have also developed safety recommendations for children's environments. The American Public Health Association and the American Academy of Pediatrics have also collaborated to produce the *National Health and Safety Performance Standards: Guidelines for Early Care and Education Programs* (http://nrckids.org). Recommendations outlined in these documents are based on what is currently known about best practices and, when followed, can help schools identify and eliminate potentially hazardous conditions in children's environments.

It is not always possible to prevent a child from being injured despite adults' best efforts. Some circumstances are simply beyond a teacher's or parent's ability to control regardless of the care taken to make areas safe. For example, no amount of careful planning or supervision can prevent a toddler from suddenly bumping into a table edge or an older child from unexpectedly losing his grip while climbing. However, the number and seriousness of injuries can be significantly reduced when basic risk management principles are followed:

- planning in advance
- establishing safety policies and guidelines
- maintaining high-quality supervision
- providing safety education

8-2a Advanced Planning

Considerable thought and planning should go into the selection of equipment and activities that are appropriate for young children (Copeland et al., 2012). Choices must take into account children's developmental abilities and also encourage the safe acquisition of new skills. Activities should be planned and equipment selected to stimulate children's curiosity, exploration, and sense of independence without endangering their safety (Wakes & Beukes, 2012; Frost, Wortham, & Reifel, 2011). When teachers invest time in planning, children are less likely to sustain injury because they will find the activities interesting, engaging, and appropriately suited to their abilities.

Organization is also fundamental to effective planning. Teachers must review each step of an activity and the materials that will be used before they are presented to children. Forgetting supplies or having any doubts about how to proceed greatly increases the risk of unintentional injury. Thinking a project through from start to finish allows the teacher to make adjustments and to substitute safer alternatives for those that may be potentially hazardous. Advanced planning also implies that a teacher is prepared for children's often unpredictable behaviors by developing appropriate safety guidelines. It also provides opportunities for teachers to check the safety of play equipment (indoor and outdoor) before children begin to play.

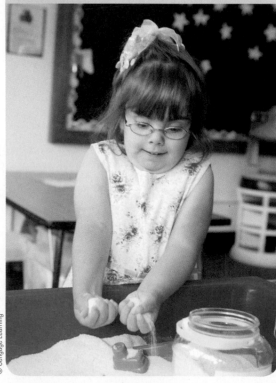

▼ Teachers must be able to anticipate children's unpredictable behaviors.

© Cengage Learning

An examination of injury records can also be useful during the planning stage. If it is noted that children are repeatedly being hurt on the same piece of outdoor play equipment or during a similar classroom activity, a cause must be investigated and addressed immediately. Modifying safety guidelines, the amount of supervision, or the equipment itself may be necessary to protect children from any additional occurrences.

8-2b Establishing Safety Policies and Guidelines

Safety guidelines are statements that describe acceptable behavior as it relates to the welfare of an individual child, concern for group safety, and respect for shared property (Teacher Checklist 8-1). Too often, guidelines let children know only what they should not be doing— for example, "Don't throw the truck" or "Don't jump off the ladder." This approach leaves children unsure about what behaviors are valued or considered appropriate.

 TEACHER CHECKLIST 8-1

Guidelines for the Safe Use of Play Equipment

Climbing Apparatus

Guidelines for Children

- Always hold on with both hands.
- Keep hands to self.
- Look carefully before jumping off equipment; be sure the area below is clear of objects and other children.
- Be extra careful if equipment or shoes are wet.

Guidelines for Adults

- Inspect equipment before children begin to play on it. Check for broken or worn parts and sharp edges; touch surfaces to make sure they are not too hot for children; be sure equipment is firmly anchored in the ground.
- Check the depth of impact surface material under equipment; be sure it is adequate and free of sharp stones, sticks, and toys.
- Limit the number of children on climber at any one time.
- Always have an adult in direct attendance when children are on the equipment.
- Supervise children carefully if they are wearing slippery-soled shoes, sandals, long dresses or skirts, mittens, bulky coats, long scarves, or hooded jackets with drawstrings.

Swings

Guidelines for Children

- Wait until the swing comes to a full stop before getting on or off.
- Always sit on the swing seat.
- Only one child per swing at any time.
- Only adults should push children.
- Stay away from moving swings.
- Hold on with both hands.

Guidelines for Adults

- Check equipment for safety, e.g., condition of chain/rope and seat, security of bolts or open-ended "S" rings (must be closed); also check ground beneath swings for sharp debris and adequate cushioning material.
- Designate a "safe" area where children can wait their turn.
- Plan for more than one adult to be in attendance at all times.

Fostering children's appropriate behavior begins by stating safety guidelines in positive terms such as, "Slide down the slide on your bottom, feet first, so you can see where you are going" or "Hold on with both hands when you climb the ladder." The only time the words "don't," "no," or "not" should be used is when a child's immediate safety is endangered. When children are given instructions that clearly describe how equipment is to be used correctly, they are more likely to comply and to remain safe.

There are no universal safety rules. Individual programs must develop their own policies and guidelines based on the:

- population of children being served
- type of program, equipment, and available space (indoor and outdoor)
- number of adults available for supervision
- nature of the activity involved

Programs serving very young children and children whose behavior is difficult to manage may need to establish limits that are more explicit and detailed. The type of equipment and whether it is being used in the classroom, outdoors, on large school playgrounds, or in home-based settings also influence how specific the guidelines must be to protect children from potential harm.

When safety guidelines are established, they must be enforced consistently or children quickly learn that they have no meaning. However, a teacher must never threaten children or cause them to be afraid in order to gain compliance. Rather, children should be acknowledged when they engage in appropriate safety behaviors. For example, a teacher might recognize a child's efforts by saying, "Carlos, I like the way you are riding your bike carefully around where the other children are playing," or "Tricia, you remembered to lay your scissors on the table before getting up to leave." Through repeated positive encouragement and adult modeling, children quickly learn to adopt appropriate safety behaviors.

Occasionally, a child will misuse play equipment or not follow directions. A gentle reminder is usually sufficient, but if this approach fails and the child continues to behave inappropriately, the teacher must remove the child from the activity or area. A simple statement such as, "I cannot allow you to hit the other children," lets the child know this is not acceptable behavior. Permitting the child to return later to the same activity conveys confidence in his ability to follow expectations.

Safety policies and guidelines never replace the need for careful adult **supervision**. Young children tend to forget quickly and often need frequent reminders, especially when they are busy playing or excited about what they are doing. Guidelines should be realistic and allow children sufficient freedom to play within the boundaries of safety. If they are overly restrictive, children may be discouraged from exploring and experimenting. The need for extensive policies and guidelines can gradually be reduced as children become more dependable, aware of dangerous situations, and able to practice safe behaviors without reminders.

8-2c Quality Supervision

Although families and teachers have many responsibilities, their supervisory role is, beyond question, one of the most important (Cavalari & Romanczyk, 2012; Guilfoyle et al., 2012). Children depend on responsible adult guidance for protection, as well as for learning appropriate safety behaviors. The younger children are, the more comprehensive and protective this supervision must be. As children gain

▼ **Rules never replace the need for adult supervision.**

© Cengage Learning

supervision – *monitoring the behaviors and actions of children and others.*

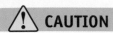

CAUTION

Never leave children unattended. If a teacher must leave an area, it should be supervised by another responsible adult.

additional motor coordination, cognitive skill, and experience in handling potentially dangerous situations, adult supervision can become less restrictive.

The nature of children's activities also influences the type of adult supervision required. For example, a cooking project that involves the use of a hot appliance must be supervised more directly than if children are painting at an easel or putting together a puzzle. Certain pieces of play equipment may also be more challenging for some children and, thus, require close teacher supervision at all times. The nature of an activity also affects the number of children a teacher can safely manage. One adult may be able to oversee several children building with hollow blocks or riding their bikes around a play yard, whereas a field trip to the fire station would require several adults to supervise.

Occasionally, there are children who are known to be physically aggressive or who engage in behaviors that could potentially bring harm to themselves or others (Little, Wyver, & Gibson, 2011). Teachers are legally and ethically obligated to supervise these children more closely and to protect the other children from harm. However, their responsibility goes beyond merely issuing a verbal warning for the child to stop—they must intervene and actually stop the child from continuing the dangerous activity even if it means physically removing the child from the area. Failure to intervene can result in legal action taken against the teacher (Marotz, 2000). However, there are a number of additional approaches that teachers can use to effectively manage children's disruptive behaviors (Teacher Checklist 8-2).

An appropriate number of adults must always be available to supervise children, especially in out-of-home programs. Minimal adult/child ratios for indoor and outdoor settings are generally established by individual state child care licensing regulations. NAEYC has recommended that there never be fewer than two adults present with any group of children. However, there are also considerable differences in adults' abilities to supervise and manage children's behavior. Some teachers are less effective at controlling unruly or disruptive children. In these situations, it may be necessary to have more than the required number of adults available to safely monitor children's play.

8-2d Safety Education

One of the primary methods for avoiding unintentional injury is through safety education (Pearson et al., 2012). Children can begin learning safe behaviors as soon as they understand the meanings of words. The earlier children learn about safety, the more naturally they will develop the attitudes and respect that lead to lifelong patterns of safe behavior.

A considerable amount of safety education occurs through **incidental learning** experiences and imitation of adult behaviors. Children who exhibit safe attitudes and practices can also serve

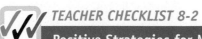

TEACHER CHECKLIST 8-2

Positive Strategies for Managing Children's Inappropriate Behavior

- Acknowledge and give attention for appropriate and desired behavior.
- Redirect the child's attention to some other activity.
- Provide the child with an opportunity for choices.
- Model the appropriate and desired behavior.
- Teach and encourage children to use problem-solving techniques.
- Ignore inappropriate behaviors, unless doing so is unsafe.
- Make changes in the environment to discourage inappropriate behavior.

TeachSource Digital Download Download from CourseMate.

incidental learning – *learning that occurs in addition to the primary intent or goals of instruction.*

as role models for other children. For example, several children may be jumping from the top of a platform instead of climbing down the ladder. Suddenly, one child yells, "You shouldn't be doing that. You could get hurt!" As a result, the children stop and begin using the ladder. Taking advantage of teachable moments can also prove to be an effective educational tool. For example, when children stand up on a swing or run with sharp objects in their hands, teachers can use these opportunities to explain why the behavior is not appropriate and help children to problem-solve safer alternatives. This form of learning is often most effective and meaningful for young children.

Safety education should also prepare children to cope with emergencies. Personal safety awareness and self-protection skills enable even young children to avoid potentially harmful situations, including being bullied on the playground. Children must know what to do in an emergency and how to get help. They should learn their home address and phone number as well as how to use the telephone. Older children can also begin to learn basic first aid skills.

Teachers must not overlook their own safety in their concern for children. It is easy for adults to be careless when they are under stress or have worked long, hard hours. Sometimes teachers take extraordinary risks in their zealous efforts to help children; however, it is at these times that even greater caution must be exercised. Planning scheduled breaks and practicing healthy eating and physical activity habits will improve a teacher's stamina, alertness, and ability to make sound decisions.

Did You Get It?

Measures taken to minimize instances of unintentional injury are commonly referred to as:

 a. injury mitigation
 b. trauma deterrence
 c. safety inoculation
 d. risk management

Take the full quiz on CourseMate.

8-3 Implementing Safety Practices

Much of the responsibility for maintaining a safe classroom environment belongs to teachers. Their knowledge of child development and daily contact with children gives them an advantageous position for identifying problem areas. However, safety must be a concern of all school personnel, including support staff such as classroom aides, cooks, receptionists, bus drivers, maintenance, and housekeeping personnel. Each person observes the environment differently, and may detect a safety hazard that had previously gone unnoticed.

Safety must also be a continuous concern. Every time teachers rearrange the classroom, take children on a field trip or walk, add new play equipment, or plan a new activity, they must first stop to determine if there are any potential risks involved for the children or themselves. Differences in children's personalities and in group dynamics also make it necessary for teachers to continuously reevalute the safety guidelines currently in place. Extra precautions may be needed when children who have special needs, medical conditions, or behavior problems are present (Haney, 2012; Morrongiello et al., 2012). In these cases, it may be necessary for teachers to modify activities or equipment so they are safe and allow all children to participate.

▼ Developmentally appropriate toys and learning materials are less likely to be a source of unintentional injury.

© Cengage Learning

FIGURE 8–1 Special devices can be purchased to determine the choking potential of small toys. Notice that the domino gets caught in the tube, but the die passes through the opening, which indicates a choking hazard.

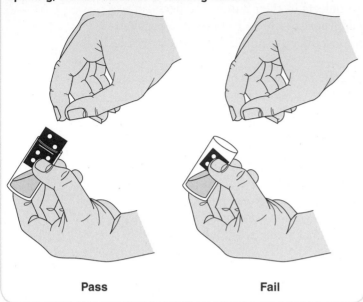

Pass   Fail

Did You Know...

that more than 181,000 children under age 15 suffered toy-related injuries last year? Balloons, small balls, and rubber balls were responsible for more than half of all fatalities.

8-3a Toys and Equipment

The majority of childhood deaths and injuries involving toys and play equipment are due to choking and improper use (Nichols et al., 2011). Many of these injuries can be prevented by carefully selecting equipment and toys that are developmentally appropriate (Marotz & Allen, 2013; NAEYC, 2012). Children's interests, behavioral characteristics, and developmental abilities should serve as key considerations when choosing these items (Teacher Checklists 8-3 and 8-4). Age warnings on product labels do not take into account children's individual differences and, therefore, are not always reliable. Some toys on the market meet only minimal U.S. safety standards and, thus, may pose a hazard for children whose skills are not as developmentally advanced. Injuries are also more likely to occur when children attempt to use educational materials and play equipment intended for older children, such as:

- toys that are too heavy for young children to lift
- rungs that are too large for small hands to grip securely
- steps that are spaced too far apart
- climbing equipment and platforms that are too high above the ground
- balloons and small objects that can cause choking or suffocation (Figure 8–1)
- equipment that is unstable or not securely anchored

The opposite may also occur. When play equipment has a singular purpose or is designed for younger children, older children may misuse it in their effort to create interest and challenge.

The amount of available classroom or play yard space will also influence choices. Equipment or toys that require a large area for their use will be a constant source of accidents if they are set up in spaces that are too small.

✓✓ *TEACHER CHECKLIST 8-3*

Guidelines for Selecting Safe Toys and Play Equipment

1. Consider children's age, interests, and developmental abilities (including problem-solving and reasoning skills); check manufacturers' labels carefully for recommendations and warnings.
2. Check postings for toys and equipment that may have been recalled (www.cpsc.gov).
3. Choose fabric items that are washable and labeled flame-retardant or nonflammable.
4. Look for high-quality construction; check durability, functional design, stability, absence of sharp corners or wires, and strings shorter than 12 inches (30.5 cm).
5. Select toys that are made from nontoxic paints and materials.
6. Avoid toys and play materials that have small pieces that a child could choke on.
7. Select toys and equipment that are appropriate for the amount of available play and storage space.
8. Avoid toys that make loud noises, have electrical parts, or are propelled through the air.
9. Choose play materials that children can use with minimal adult supervision.

TeachSource Digital Download Download from CourseMate.

TEACHER CHECKLIST 8-4

Examples of Appropriate Toy Choices for Infants, Toddlers, and Preschoolers

Infants	Toddlers	Preschoolers
nonbreakable mirrors	peg bench	puppets
cloth books	balls	dolls and doll houses
wooden cars	records	dress-up clothes
rattles	simple puzzles	simple art materials (e.g., crayons,
mobiles	large building blocks	markers, watercolors, play
music boxes	wooden cars and trucks	dough, blunt scissors)
plastic telephone	dress-up clothes	books, puzzles, lacing cards
balls	bristle blocks	simple musical instruments
toys that squeak	large wooden beads	cars, trucks, fire engines
blocks	to string	tricycle
nesting toys	cloth picture books	simple construction sets (e.g.,
teething ring	nesting cups	Lego® bricks, bristle blocks)
washable, stuffed animals	pull and riding toys	play dishes, empty food
	plastic dishes, pots and	containers
	pans,	
	chunky crayons and paper	

TeachSource Digital Download Download from CourseMate.

Quality must also be considered when purchasing toys and play equipment. The materials and construction should be examined carefully and not purchased if they have:

- sharp wires, pins, or staples
- small pieces that could come loose, such as buttons, "eyes," screws, or magnets
- moving parts that can pinch fingers
- pieces that are smaller than 1.5 inches (3.8 cm) or balls less than 1.75 inches (4.4 cm) in diameter (for children under 3 years) (Figure 8–1)
- objects too heavy or large to be handled easily
- unstable bases or frames
- toxic paints or materials, such as polyvinyl chloride (PVC) or phthalates
- sharp metal edges or rough surfaces
- defective parts or construction that will not hold up under hard use
- strings or cords (longer than 12 inches) that could cause strangulation
- electrical toys (for children under age 8)
- brittle plastic or glass parts that could easily break
- objects that become projectiles, such as darts, arrows, air guns, and rocket launchers
- toys with small magnets that may become dislodged and swallowed

The amount of noise a toy produces should also be evaluated. Children's hearing is more sensitive than that of an adult's and can easily be damaged through repeated exposure to loud noises. Many children's toys emit sounds that exceed the 85- to 90-decibel threshold recommendation for safe hearing levels (ASHA, 2012). Toys that produce loud music or sounds should be avoided to protect children from early hearing loss.

Not all new toys and children's products are manufactured according to U.S. safety standards, especially those that are imported. For this reason, extreme care should be taken when purchasing children's toys or equipment on the Internet. Hazard warnings and age recommendations may be absent, misrepresented, or not in compliance with statutory label requirements (U.S. Public Interest Research Groups, 2011). Occasionally, products that have been recalled because of hazardous features remain on store shelves, websites, and in garage sales. Families and teachers must take time to inspect items carefully and to make sure they meet all existing safety regulations.

▼ **An adult should always be positioned in direct attendance where children are playing.**

© Cengage Learning

Toys and play equipment should be inspected daily, especially if they are used frequently by groups of children or are located outdoors and exposed to variable weather conditions. These items must be in good repair and free of splinters, rough edges, protruding bolts or nails, and broken or missing parts. Ropes on swings or ladders should be examined routinely and replaced if they begin to fray. Large equipment should be checked often to make sure it remains firmly anchored in the ground and that impact surface materials are of adequate depth and free of debris (see Chapter 7) (CPSC, 2012c).

Regularly scheduled maintenance ensures that toys and play equipment remain safe for children's use. Equipment that is defective or otherwise unsafe for children to use should be removed promptly until it can be repaired. Items that cannot be repaired should be discarded.

Special precautions are necessary whenever large equipment or climbing structures are set up indoors. Positioning equipment in an open area away from furniture or other objects reduces children's risk for injury. Mats, foam pads, or large cushions placed around and under elevated structures will also help to protect children in the event of an unexpected fall. Guidelines for the safe use of indoor climbers should be demonstrated and explained carefully to children before they begin to play. The potential for injuries can be further reduced by positioning an adult next to the equipment so children's activities can be closely monitored.

Whenever new equipment, toys, or educational materials are introduced into a classroom or outdoor setting, safety is a prime concern. Policies and safety guidelines must be established and carefully explained to children. However, caution should be exercised not to establish too many restrictions that might otherwise dampen children's enthusiasm and interest. If several new items are being introduced into a classroom or outdoor environment, it is best to do this over a period of time so children are not overwhelmed by too many instructions.

Children's furnishings, such as beds, cribs, playpens, strollers, carriers, and toys for infants and toddlers, must be selected with great care. As a consumer, it is important to remember that product design is most often responsible for childhood deaths. Strict manufacturing standards for children's furniture are continuously being updated by the U.S. Consumer Safety Product Commission (CSPC) and Canadian Consumer Corporate Affairs (Table 8–4). However, toys and furniture purchased at second-hand shops, garage sales, or on the Internet do not always meet these criteria and should be examined carefully. Information concerning children's toy and product recalls is available from the CSPC at (http://www.cpsc.gov) or from Safe Kids USA (http://www.safekids.org).

8-3b Classroom Activities

Safety must always be a priority when teachers select, plan, and implement children's learning activities. The potential for injury is present in nearly every activity, whether it is planned for indoor or outdoor settings. Even small metal trucks or plastic golf clubs can cause harm when children use them incorrectly. Teachers should ask themselves the following questions when evaluating the safety of any activity:

- Is the activity age- and developmentally appropriate?
- What potential risks or hazards does this activity present?
- What special precautions do I need to take to make the activity safe?
- How should I respond if a child misuses the equipment or doesn't follow directions?
- What would I do in the event that a child is hurt while the activity is in progress?

After these questions have been given careful thought, teachers can begin to consider how to implement basic risk management principles—advanced planning, formulating safety guidelines, determining appropriate supervision, and providing safety education.

TABLE 8–4 **Infant Equipment Safety Checklist**

Back Carriers (not recommended for use before 4–5 months)	Yes	No

Carrier has restraining strap to secure child.
Leg openings are small enough to prevent child from slipping out.
Leg openings are large enough to prevent chafing.
Frames have no pinch points in the folding mechanism.
Carrier has padded covering over metal frame near baby's face.

Bassinets and Cradles

Bassinet/cradle has a sturdy bottom and a wide base for stability.
Bassinet/cradle has smooth surfaces-no protruding staples or other hardware that could
  injure the baby.
Legs have strong, effective locks to prevent folding while in use.
Mattress is firm and fits snuggly against sides of bed.
If cradle has slats, they must be spaced no more than 2 3/8 inches (6 cm) apart.

Carrier Seats

Carrier seat has a wide, sturdy base for stability.
Carrier has nonskid feet to prevent slipping.
Supporting devices lock securely.
Carrier seat has crotch and waist strap.
Buckle or strap is easy to use.

Changing Tables

Table has safety straps to prevent falls
Table has drawers or shelves that are easily accessible without leaving the baby unattended.

Cribs

Slats are spaced no more than 2 3/8 inches (6 cm) apart.
No slats are missing, loose, or cracked.
Mattress fits snugly—less than two fingers width between edge of mattress and crib
  side.
Mattress support is securely attached to the head and footboards.
Corner posts are no higher than 1/16 inch (1.5 mm) to prevent entanglement.
There are no cutouts in head and footboards to allow head entrapment.
All screws or bolts that secure components of crib together are present and tight.
**No drop-side cribs should be in use; they cannot be manufactured or sold after June
  2011. Child care programs *must* replace all drop-side cribs by December 2012.

Crib Toys

Components of toys are large enough not to be a choking hazard.
Crib gym or mobile has warning label to remove equipment when baby begins to push
  up on hands and knees or turns five months of age (whichever comes first).

Gates and Enclosures

Gate or enclosure has a straight top edge.
Openings in gate are too small to entrap a child's head.
Gate has a pressure bar or other fastener so it will resist forces exerted by a child.

High Chairs

High chair has restraining straps that are independent of the tray.
High chair has a crotch strap; it must be used whenever baby sits in the high chair.
Tray locks securely.
Buckle on waist strap is easy to fasten and unfasten.

(*continued*)

TABLE 8–4   Infant Equipment Safety Checklist   *(continued)*

	Yes	No
High Chairs *(continued)*		

High chair has a wide base for stability.
High chair has caps or plugs on tubing that are firmly attached and cannot be pulled off
  and choke a child.
If it is a folding high chair, it has an effective locking device.

Hook-on Chairs

Hook-on chair has a restraining strap to secure the child.
Hook-on chair has a clamp that locks onto the table for added security.
Hook-on chair has caps or plugs on tubing that are firmly attached and cannot be pulled
  off and become a choking hazard.
Hook-on chair has a warning never to place chair where child can push off with feet.

Pacifiers

Pacifier has no ribbons, string, cord, or yarn attached.
Shield is large enough and firm enough so it cannot fit in child's mouth.
Guard or shield has ventilation holes so baby can breathe if shield does get
  into mouth.
Pacifier nipple has no holes or tears that might cause it to break off in baby's mouth.

Playpens

Drop-side mesh playpen or mesh crib has warning label about never leaving a side in the
  down position.
Playpens or travel cribs have top rails that automatically lock when lifted into the normal
  use position.
There are no rotating hinges in the center of the top rail.
Playpen mesh has small weave (less than 1/4-inch openings).
Mesh has no tears or loose threads.
Mesh is securely attached to top rail and floor plate.
Wooden playpen has slats spaced no more than 2 3/8 inches (6 cm) apart.

Rattles/Squeeze Toys/Teethers

Rattles and teethers have handles too large to lodge in baby's throat.
Rattles have sturdy construction that will not cause them to break apart in use.
Squeeze toys do not contain a squeaker that could detach and choke a baby.
Rattles with large, ball-like ends should not be given to babies.

Strollers

Stroller has a wide base to prevent tipping.
Seat belt and crotch strap are securely attached to frame.
Seat belt buckle is easy to fasten and unfasten.
Brakes securely lock the wheel(s).
Shopping basket low on the back and located directly over or in front of rear wheels.
Leg holes can be closed when used in a carriage position.

Toy Chests

Toy chest has no latch to entrap child within the chest.
Toy chest has a spring-loaded lid support that will not require periodic adjustment and
  will support the lid in any position to prevent lid slam.
Chest has ventilation holes or spaces in front or sides, or under lid.

Source: Adapted from Consumer Product Safety Commission (CPSC). (2012b). *The Safe Nursery.* Accessed on May 2, 2013 from
http://www.cpsc.gov/PageFiles/115485/202.pdf.

Materials selected for classroom activities should always be evaluated for safety risks before they are presented to children. Added safety precautions and more precise planning may be necessary whenever the following high-risk items are used as part of an activity:

▼ **Only nontoxic art materials should be used with children.**

© Cengage Learning

- pointed or blunt objects such as scissors, knives, and woodworking tools (e.g., hammers, nails, saws)
- pipes, boards, blocks, or breakable objects
- electrical appliances (e.g., hot plates, radio, mixers, iron)
- hot liquids (e.g., wax, syrup, oil, water)
- cosmetics or cleaning supplies

For added safety, projects that include any of these items should be set up in an area separated from other activities. Boundaries created with portable room dividers or a row of chairs improve a teacher's ability to closely monitor children's actions.

Restricting the number of children who can participate in an activity at any one time is another effective way to ensure safe conditions. Some activities may need to be limited to only one or two children so that a teacher can closely monitor their participation. Several methods can be used to control the number of children in a given area at any one time, including the use of color-coded necklaces or badges, or limiting the number of chairs at a table. These systems also help children determine if there is room to join the activity.

When an activity involves the use of an electrical appliance, its condition must be carefully inspected and safety guidelines for its use be explained to the children (Teacher Checklist 8-5). Equipment with frayed cords or plugs should be discarded. Extension cords should not be used as they can be a tripping hazard. Electrical appliances should always be placed on a table nearest the outlet and against the wall for safety. Never use appliances near a water source, including sinks, wet floors, or large pans of water, to avoid electrical shock.

Safety must also be a concern in the selection of children's art media and activities (CPSC, 2012a; OEHHA, 2009). Only nontoxic art materials, such as paints, glue, markers, crayons, and clay, should be purchased. Liquids, such as paints and glue, should always be stored in plastic containers to prevent the danger of broken glass. Dried beans, peas, berries, or small beads should not be used because children may swallow or stuff them into their ears or nose. Toothpicks and similar sharp objects are also inappropriate. Fabric pieces, dried leaves or grasses, Styrofoam, packing materials, yarn, or ribbon provide safer alternatives for children's art creations. Additional safe substitutions for potentially hazardous art materials are provided in Teacher Checklist 8-6.

Special precautions should be taken in classrooms that have hard-surfaced or highly polished floors. Spilled water, paint, or other liquids and dry materials such as beans, rice, sawdust, flour,

---

✓✓ *TEACHER CHECKLIST 8-5*

Guidelines for the Safe Use of Electrical Appliances

Special precautions must be taken whenever an activity involves the use of an electrical appliance, including:

- placing the appliance on a low table or the floor so that children can easily reach.
- reminding children to stand back from appliances that have moving parts to prevent their hair, fingers, or clothing from getting caught or burned.
- turning handles of pots and pans toward the back of the stove or hot plate.
- always detaching cords from the electrical outlet, never the appliance.
- promptly replacing safety caps in all electrical outlets when the project is finished.

TEACHER CHECKLIST 8-6

Safe Substitutes for Hazardous Art Materials

Avoid	Safe Substitutes
Powders: dry tempera paints, silica, pastels, chalk, dry clay, and cement can be inhaled. Use plaster of Paris only in well-ventilated area.	Use liquid tempera paints, water colors, crayons, and nontoxic markers.
Aerosol sprays: adhesives, fixatives, paints.	Use brushes or spray bottles with water-based glues, paints, glue sticks, or paste.
Solvents and thinners: turpentine, rubber or epoxy cements, or those containing benzene, toluene, lacquers, or varnish. Avoid enamel-based paints that require solvents for cleanup.	Select water-based paints and glues, glue sticks, and inks.
Glitter (metal) can cause eye abrasion if rubbed.	Use salt crystals for a sparkling effect.
Permanent markers, dyes, and stains.	Prepare natural vegetable dyes (e.g., beets, walnuts, onions) or commercial cold-water dyes.
Minerals and fibers: instant papier-mâché. (may contain lead and asbestos fibers); glazes, printing inks (colored newsprint, magazines), paints (especially enamels, which may contain lead); builder's sand (may contain asbestos).	Use black-white newspaper and water-based glue to make papier-mâché; choose water-based paints and inks; purchase special sandbox sand that has been cleaned.
Photographic chemicals	Use blueprint or colored paper set in the sun.

Additional precautions:
- Read ingredient labels carefully. Choose only those materials that are labeled nontoxic. Older supplies may not comply with new federal labeling requirements and may contain harmful chemicals.
- Mix and prepare art materials (adults only) in a well-ventilated area away from children.
- Make sure children always wash their hands after working with art materials.
- Keep food and beverages away from areas where art activities are in progress.

TeachSource Digital Download) Download from CourseMate.

or cornmeal can cause floors to become extremely slippery and should be cleaned up promptly. Newspapers or rugs spread out on the floor help prevent children and adults from slipping and falling.

Environments and activities that are safe for young children are also less stressful for adults. When classrooms and play yards are free of potential hazards, teachers can concentrate their attention on selecting safe activities, encouraging active play, and providing better supervision. Also, being familiar with a program's safety policies and procedures and having proper emergency training, such as first aid and CPR, can increase teacher confidence and lessen stress levels.

8-3c Field Trips

Excursions away from a program's facilities can be an exciting part of children's educational experiences. However, field trips present added risks and liability concerns and require that schools and early childhood programs take special precautions.

Most importantly, programs should have written procedures to be followed when children are taken off of school premises. Scheduling these excursions for midweek gives teachers' adequate time to review procedures, finalize plans, and prepare the children. Families should be notified in advance and give their written permission for children to participate in each field trip. On the day of the outing, a notice should be posted on the classroom door reminding families and staff of the children's destination and when they will be leaving and returning to the building. At least one adult accompanying the group should have first aid and CPR training. A first aid kit that includes medications a child(ren) may need and a cell phone should also be taken along. Tags can be pinned on children with the center's name and phone number. However, *do not* include the children's names: This enables strangers to call children by their names and makes it easier to lure them away from the group. A complete list of the children's emergency contact information, including families' telephone numbers, child's health care provider, and emergency service (e.g., ambulance, fire) numbers, should also be taken along. Procedures and safety policies should be carefully reviewed with the staff and children prior to the outing.

Special consideration should be given to the legal issues involved in conducting field trips (Armenta, 2011; Child Care Law Center, 2011). Transporting children in the private vehicles of other families, staff, or volunteers, for example, can present serious liability risks (see Chapter 7) (Marotz, 2000). There is almost no way of ensuring that a car is safe or an adult is a competent driver. Also, most states have laws that require appropriate safety restraints for each passenger, and not all vans or cars are properly equipped to provide these for multiple children (Huang et al., 2011). Therefore, it may be in a program's best interest not to use private vehicles for transporting children on field trips. Vehicles owned and operated by a program are usually required to carry liability insurance and are therefore preferable. However, neighborhood walks and public bus rides are always safe alternatives.

8-3d Pets

Pets can be a special classroom addition, but care must be taken so the experience is safe for both the children and animals (CDC, 2011; Columbus Public Health, 2007). Children's allergies should be considered before arrangements are made for pets to visit or become permanent classroom residents. Precautions should also be taken to make sure animals are free of disease and have current immunizations (if appropriate). Some animals, such as turtles, fish, reptiles, and birds (including baby chicks), are known carriers of illnesses that are communicable to humans, such as salmonella and E. coli, and are therefore not appropriate to include in the classroom (AAP & APHA, 2011). Instructions for the animal's care should be posted to serve as both a guideline and reminder to staff. Precautions must also be taken to protect pets from curious and overly exuberant children who may unknowingly cause harm or injury to the animal. Children must be reminded to wash their hands carefully after handling or petting animals in the classroom, zoo, or petting farm because animals are often carriers of infectious illnesses.

CONNECTING TO EVERYDAY PRACTICE

Transporting Children

Evening news anchors described the tragic death of a toddler forgotten in a child care center van. The child had been picked up from his home early that morning, placed in a car safety seat, and transported to a local child care center. However, personnel did not realize the child was missing until the end of the day when it was time for the children to return home. The unconscious toddler was found still strapped in his car seat. Temperatures outside of the van had climbed into the 90s during the day. Despite emergency medical efforts, heat stroke had claimed the child's life.

Think About This:

▶ What steps should have been taken to prevent this tragedy?

▶ What policies and procedures would keep this unfortunate event from being repeated?

▶ What measures should be taken to ensure children's safety during transportation? In private vehicles? In center vans? In school buses?

TEACHER CHECKLIST 8-7

Personal Safety Practices for the Home Visitor

- Check with your organization to learn about policies and procedures that home visitors are expected to follow.
- Become familiar with the neighborhood; visit the area and address beforehand. Learn about the community and families living there.
- Talk with local police for information about the area and to determine if your concerns or fears are warranted.
- Let a supervisor know when you leave and where you are heading; provide your planned travel route and be sure to follow it.
- Take along a cell phone or pager; carry a whistle.
- Check in frequently with your supervisor; advise him of your location and share any immediate safety concerns.
- Schedule visits during the daytime. If evening visits are necessary, go in teams.
- Be alert and aware of your surroundings. Listen for unusual sounds, watch for suspicious people or activity, and leave if you feel uncomfortable.
- Know where to get help if something should happen.
- Complete a personal safety defense class and learn protective techniques to improve self-confidence.

TeachSource Digital Download) Download from CourseMate.

8-3e Personal Safety

Not all teachers work in classrooms. Some organizations, such as Head Start and Parents as Teachers, employ educators and other professionals to work with children and families in their homes. Opportunities to work independently and one-on-one with clients are attractive options for many teachers. However, working alone and in neighborhoods that may be unfamiliar or are noted for high crime rates may present additional risks and concerns. It is important that organizations establish policies and procedures in advance to protect the safety of personnel who work in these conditions. Individuals can also take a number of steps to ensure their own personal safety (Teacher Checklist 8-7).

8-3f Legal Considerations and Safety Management

Safety issues always generate a great deal of concern for teachers, school administrators, and program directors. Recent lawsuits, legal decisions, and increased public awareness have contributed to a greater sense of uneasiness, scrutiny, and need for stricter regulation. Families want and have a right to be assured that schools are safe and children will be closely supervised during the hours they spend away from home. For these reasons, it is imperative that teachers and administrators be familiar with the legal issues and responsibilities that accompany their positions.

One of the most important legal concerns for teachers is that of **liability** (Yudof et al., 2012; Essex, 2011; Rothstein & Johnson, 2010). The term "liability" refers to the legal obligations and professional responsibilities, especially those related to safety, that are accepted by administrators and teachers when they agree to work with children. Failure to perform these duties in a reasonable and acceptable manner is considered **negligence**.

Negligence involves a teacher's failure to prevent an avoidable injury. For legal purposes, negligent acts are generally divided into two categories based on the circumstances and resulting damages or injuries. The first category involves situations in which a teacher fails to take appropriate precautionary measures to protect children from harm, such as not providing adequate supervision or permitting children to play on equipment in need of repair. A second category of negligent acts addresses circumstances in which the teacher's actions or decisions actually place children at risk, such as allowing them to be transported by volunteers in uninsured vehicles or exposing them to toxic chemicals or dangerous animals.

liability – *legal responsibility or obligation for one's actions owed to another individual.*
negligence – *failure to practice or perform one's duties according to certain standards; carelessness.*

Prevention is always the best method for ensuring children's safety and avoiding unpleasant legal problems and lawsuits. However, there are additional protective steps that teachers, administrators, and programs can take (Marotz, 2000). It is advisable for teachers and administrators to obtain personal liability insurance unless they are already covered by their program's policy (Child Care Law Center, 2011). Liability insurance can be purchased from most private insurance companies and through NAEYC. Programs can also purchase accident insurance on children who are enrolled for added protection.

Administrators and teachers should not hesitate to seek legal counsel on issues related to their roles and professional responsibilities. Programs may want to seek legal counsel whenever developing policies to make certain they are consistent with the laws. Including a member of the legal profession on a program's board of directors or advisory council provides ready access to legal advice.

Teachers should always examine job descriptions carefully and be familiar with employer expectations before accepting a new position. This step helps to ensure that they have the appropriate qualifications and training to perform all required duties. For example, if a teacher will be responsible for administering first aid to injured children, she should have completed basic first aid and CPR training prior to beginning employment. It is also essential that administrators screen potential candidates for teaching positions through careful interviewing and follow up contacts with the individual's references. Background checks also help to identify persons with a history of criminal behavior or serious mental health problems. Although these initial steps may seem time-consuming, they will help to protect a program from hiring unqualified personnel.

Accurately maintained injury reports also provide added legal protection (Figure 8–2). Information included in these reports can be used as evidence in court if a teacher or program is ever charged with negligence. An individual report should be completed each time a child is hurt, regardless of how minor or unimportant the injury may seem at the time. This step is important because the outcome of some injuries may not be immediately apparent. Complications can develop months or years later, making it difficult for teachers to recall a particular incident or injury in detail sufficient to defend themselves. Injury reports should be completed by the teacher who witnessed the incident and administered first aid treatment. Information should be recorded in clear, precise, and descriptive language. It should describe the nature and location of the injury in detail, how it occurred, the names of witnesses, and any treatment administered. Injury records are considered legal documents and must be retained on file for a minimum of 5 years.

© 2015 Cengage Learning

▶II TeachSource Video Connections

Preschool: Safety and Emergency Preparedness

Emergency situations can be frightening for young children unless they know how to respond. It is important that teachers provide opportunities to help children learn how to handle emergencies so they are less likely to panic. As you watch the learning video, *Preschool: Safety and Emergency Preparedness*, consider the following questions:

1. Why is it important to practice fire drills and emergency evacuations frequently with children?

2. What skills are children and adults likely to develop by participating in repeated fire and other emergency drills?

3. What information is important for children to know and be able to provide when they call for emergency assistance?

4. What additional learning activities could be used to teach children about emergency preparedness?

Watch on CourseMate.

Did You Get It?

_____ learning occurs when a child learns as a result of passive experiences and/or imitation of adult behaviors.

  a. Incidental
  b. Ancillary
  c. Coincidental
  d. Contingent

Take the full quiz on CourseMate.

FIGURE 8–2 Sample individual injury report form.

INDIVIDUAL INJURY REPORT FORM

Child's Name _____ Date of Injury _____

Parent (or legal guardian) _____ Time _____ AM ____ PM ____

Address _____ Family notified _____ AM ____ PM ____

Description of injuries _____

_____

First aid or emergency treatment administered: _____

_____

Was a doctor consulted? _____ Doctor's name and address _____

Doctor's diagnosis_____

_____

Number of days child was absent as a result of injury _____

Adult in charge when injury occurred _____

Description of activity, location in facility, and circumstances immediately before and at the time of the injury

_____

_____

_____

_____

_____

_____

_____

Report prepared by (full name): _____ Date _____

8-4 Emergency and Disaster Preparedness

Schools and early childhood programs seldom expect to be involved in a disaster or emergency situation. However, it is essential that they be prepared to safeguard children's physical and mental well-being if such an event were to occur. Children depend on adults for support and protection, and have needs that are unique from those of an adult's. Their immature cognitive development and inexperience can lead to significant fear, misunderstanding, and immediate- and long-term psychological disturbances (Grasso, Ford, & Briggs-Gowan, 2013). Toddlers and preschoolers may exhibit signs of regression, clinginess, anger, irritability, repeated reenactments of the event, bed-wetting, sleep disturbances, and appetite loss. School-age children may develop similar behaviors in addition to excessive fear, apathy, withdrawal from friends and family, health complaints, nightmares, and poor school performance. These behaviors are symptomatic of post-traumatic stress disorder (PTSD) and require professional counseling if they persist.

Children are also more likely to experience physical disorders as a result of exposure to natural and man-made disasters. Their immature bodies are especially susceptible to the harmful effects of chemical, **thermal**, and biological agents. Young children are also relatively defenseless when it comes to fleeing danger or to understanding the consequences of their actions or inaction. Disrupted routines and unpredictable schedules can leave children feeling insecure and affect eating and sleeping patterns. Intense fear, anxiety, and uncertainty also weaken children's immune system and increase their likelihood of developing an acute illness.

8-4a Planning for Disasters and Emergencies: Where to Begin

An important first step in developing emergency readiness plans is to determine the types of local crises that are most likely to occur. The Federal Emergency Management Agency (FEMA) recognizes several major emergency categories and provides extensive planning information on their website specific to each (www.fema.gov):

- *natural disasters*, such as severe winter storms, earthquakes, wildfires, hurricanes, floods, tornadoes, and landslides (many events are seasonal)
- *technological and accidental hazards*, such as toxic chemical spills, electrical blackouts, radioactive leaks (nuclear power plants), biological threats, and building fires
- *pandemic illness*, such as H1N1 influenza, cholera, and severe acute respiratory syndrome (SARS)
- *threats against personal safety*, such as bomb threats, unauthorized intruders, neighborhood violence ("crack houses," meth labs), gunfire, a missing child

Local emergency response agencies are often able to provide information about specific high risk situations in a community that may not be common knowledge, such as railroad transport of nuclear or hazardous waste. They will also work with early childhood programs and schools to develop effective response plans and policies. Several major points that should be addressed during the initial planning stage include:

- identifying a safe location – within the building, outside, and at a nearby facility (approximately 1 mile away) where children can be transferred if necessary
- arranging for emergency transportation (in the event that children and personnel need to be evacuated – consider accommodations for children who are non-ambulatory or have special needs (Baker, Baker, & Flagg, 2012)
- planning evacuation and alternative escape routes – use building blueprints to sketch in exits and evacuation routes from each classroom
- determining how communications will be handled – who will establish contact with emergency personnel and children's families; having access to two-way radios and cell phones; and posting emergency numbers near a telephone
- locating and learning how to operate main utility shut-off valves (e.g., water, gas, electricity)
- considering how children will be informed, cared for, and comforted
- assembling important documents – class and staff rosters, children's emergency contact information and medical records, insurance papers, inventory lists, contact information for local disaster assistance resources
- establishing guidelines for when and what emergency measures will be implemented – developing signals to communicate different emergencies, deciding to evacuate or to remain, how children and staff will be transported

Protecting children's safety is a prime consideration in any disaster or emergency (Hull, 2011). For this reason, a program's emergency response plans should include guidelines for determining

thermal – *caused by heat.*

when it is safe to remain in the building or necessary to evacuate. In most cases, the appropriate option will depend on the nature of the emergency:

- *sheltering-in-place* – when occupants can safely remain in the building. Conditions, such as a storm or power outage, may necessitate moving to an interior safe room or lower level for added protection.
- *building lockdown* – when an external danger such as nearby robbery or potential intruder makes it unsafe for occupants to leave the building. All interior and exterior doors should be locked, children moved away from doors and windows, and lights turned off.
- *evacuation* – when conditions such as a fire, gas leak, or chemical spill make it unsafe to remain in the building. An outdoor location or alternative facility (including transportation measures) must be identified in a program's emergency response plans.

Time spent planning for emergency situations that are unlikely to ever happen may seem unproductive. However, when programs and staff are prepared to act in a crisis situation, they will be able to do so efficiently, effectively, and without panic.

8-4b   Preparing for Action

Once basic disaster and emergency preparedness plans have been developed, programs can begin to act on each recommendation. Plans should be shared with local emergency response agencies and arrangements confirmed with relocation shelter facilities. Important documents and records can be copied and stored in waterproof containers; they should be reviewed and updated every 6 months. Computerized records should be backed up on an external server or portable hard drive that can be removed from the facility. Daily attendance records should be located where teachers can quickly grab them if the classroom must be evacuated. These lists can be used to help teachers account for all children.

Emergency supplies, such as blankets, first aid kit, and battery-operated radio, need to be assembled and reevaluated every 6 months (Teacher Checklist 8-8). A selection of age-appropriate play materials (Table 8–5) and personal care items (e.g., diapers, wipes, formula, sippy cups, medications) should be also be included. Careful thought must also be given to equipment and supplies that children who have medical or other special conditions may need. Emergency provisions should also include a 3-day supply of water (1 gallon per person per day) and nonperishable, ready-to-eat food (Table 8–6); items should be replaced every 6 months.

Staff members should be assigned specific roles and responsibilities to perform in the event of an emergency. For example, who will contact 911, who will check to be certain everyone is out of the building, who will bring the emergency kits or food supplies, and who will lead the children out of each classroom? Teachers and administrators will be able to respond quickly, confidently, and efficiently when they each understand their role and how it fits into the program's

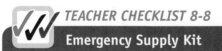

TEACHER CHECKLIST 8-8
Emergency Supply Kit

blankets	water (3 gallons per person)
extra clothing	non-perishable food
first aid kit	manual can opener
battery-operated radio (and extra batteries)	paper towel
flashlight (and batteries)	paper plates, cups, and plastic utensils
hand sanitizer & wipes	duct tape
toilet paper	plastic sheeting
plastic bags (small & garbage)	disposable gloves
soap & bleach (unscented)	infant supplies (e.g., diapers, formula,
whistle	bottles) (optional)
scissors	

TABLE 8–5   Evacuation Kits: Suggested Play Materials

paper and markers/crayons	play dough
music and stories on CDs or DVDs (and player)	puzzles
story books	inflatable beach balls
finger puppets	game ideas
manipulatives (e.g., building bricks, lacing cards)	jump ropes
coloring books	

TABLE 8–6   Emergency Food Supplies

Remember to check for food allergies	
breakfast bars	dried or dehydrated fruits
dry cereals	non-perishable or dry milk
crackers (include a variety)	canned or non-perishable meats
peanut butter	infant formula and jar foods (optional)
canned fruits, vegetables, & juices	

overall emergency response plan. Any oversights can be identified and corrected after staff members have had opportunities to participate in actual drills or mock scenarios.

8-4c Practice and Revise

It is important that programs have an emergency response plan in place and practice it often. Although a plan may seem functional on paper, it does not always work out the way it was intended. Rehearsing drills on a regular basis provides opportunities to correct oversights and misjudgments at a time when there is no imminent danger. Practice builds teacher confidence and skill in protecting children's safety during a time of crisis. It also helps children become more familiar and comfortable with evacuation routines so they are less likely to be frightened in a true emergency situation. Practice drills should be scheduled on different days of each month so that part-time teachers and volunteers are present and able to participate. Alternative evacuation routes and destinations (e.g., sheltering-in-place, lockdown, relocation) should also be practiced from time to time.

How often a particular emergency response plan should be rehearsed depends on the likelihood of an occurrence. For example, programs located in areas where tornadoes or wild fires are a seasonal event may want to practice monthly safety drills. In contrast, drills for earthquakes or ice storms may need to be conducted only every 6 months if the local risk is relatively low. Programs are also encouraged to participate in local, state, and national emergency exercises when they are planned.

8-4d Helping Children After A Disaster or Emergency

Children's concrete and egocentric thinking make it difficult for them to fully comprehend the significance of a disaster or an emergency event. They are generally aware that something unusual or disruptive has occurred, but may not understand what it means or how it will affect their lives. Their reactions typically reflect the behaviors of the adults and children around them, so it is important to maintain a calm, confident atmosphere. Although young children may have difficulty expressing what they are thinking and feeling, their behavioral changes may suggest considerable inner turmoil and anxiety. In most cases, this emotional tension is temporary and will pass with compassionate support and understanding (Table 8–7). However, it may be necessary to seek professional help if the child does not improve within 2–3 weeks following a traumatic event.

Encouraging children to ask questions can be helpful in determining what they know and understand (Hull, 2012). Answers should be factual, explained in simple terms, and appropriate for the child's developmental stage. Resuming routines and schedules as soon as is feasible can be reassuring and help children regain a sense of safety and normalcy. Limiting children's exposure to news media and visual reminders of an event can also speed the healing process.

TABLE 8–7   Strategies to Help Children Cope After a Disaster or an Emergency

- Listen to what children say and encourage their questions—much can be learned about what they understand and are feeling.
- Hold, hug, and touch children—personal contact is comforting.
- Model positive ways of dealing with adversity and explain why these are effective.
- Provide factual information in simple, understandable terms—don't offer more information than children are able to handle.
- Limit children's exposure to news media—graphic pictures can be frightening.
- Resume daily routines and schedules—children feel secure when things are predictable.
- Give children simple tasks where they can exert some control—this allows children to feel that they are helping.
- Spend extra time with children—read books together and engage in activities they enjoy.
- Let children know it is okay to cry—help them find ways to express their grief.

Source: Adapted from Federal Emergency Management Agency (FEMA). (2013). *Helping kids cope with disaster*. Retrieved from http://www.fema.gov/coping-disaster#4.

Did You Get It?

What is a teacher's failure to uphold legal and professional responsibilities associated with his or her position?

a. negligence
b. malpractice
c. culpability
d. accountability

Take the full quiz on CourseMate.

Teachers must not overlook their own recovery needs following an emergency event. It is important that they maintain a strong support system, follow a healthy diet, engage in daily physical activity, set aside time to relax, participate in pleasurable activities, and understand that full recovery takes time.

PARTNERING with FAMILIES

Sun Safety

Dear Families,

Exposure to too much sun over a lifetime can have harmful health consequences, including skin cancer, premature aging of the skin, eye damage, and difficulty fighting off infections. Children's skin—even that of dark-skinned children—is especially sensitive to the sun's ultraviolet (UV) rays and tends to burn quickly and easily. Therefore, it is important that you always take precautions to protect children's skin (and your own) and to minimize their sun exposure.

▶ Avoid going outdoors between 10 A.M. and 4 P.M. when the sun's rays are the strongest and most damaging.

▶ Encourage children to play in the shade whenever possible. Rule of thumb—you shouldn't be able to see their shadow!

▶ Dress in protective clothing that is cool and loose fitting. Keep as much skin surface covered as possible. Discourage children from wearing tank or halter tops. Wearing a hat with a brim will provide shade protection for the face and eyes.

▶ Apply sunscreen with a sun protection factor (SPF) of at least 15 or higher approximately 30 minutes before going outdoors. Reapply every 2 hours or more often if children are swimming, perspiring, or drying themselves with a towel. Sunburn occurs more quickly when the skin is wet.

▶ Wear sunglasses to protect eyes from UV radiation. Light-colored eyes (blue, gray) are particularly sensitive to sunlight and are more susceptible to damage.

▶ Encourage your child's school to become a "Sun Wise" school by registering at http://www.epa.gov/sunwise/becoming.html.

CLASSROOM CORNER

Teacher Activities

Fire Safety

(Grades 3–5, NHES 1.5.3 and 1.5.4)

Concept: It is important that children know how to evacuate a building in the event of a fire.

Learning Objectives

▶ Children will identify the three components of the fire triangle.

▶ Children will name potential fire safety hazards in their home.

▶ Children will conduct a home fire safety inspection.

Supplies

▶ A home fire safety checklist for each child. These can be downloaded from several online sites, including http://www.sparky.org/PDF/SparkyChecklist.pdf.

Learning Activities

▶ Have children read one of the following books and discuss it as a class.

- *The Case of the Blazing Sun* by John Erickson
- *Fire Safety* by Lucia Raatma (series)
- *Firefighting Behind the Scenes* by Maria Ruth

▶ Introduce the fire triangle concept (heat, fuel, oxygen). Ask the children to provide examples for each component (e.g., fuel/newspaper, heat/matches). Have children work together to create a bulletin board display illustrating the fire triangle; include the children's examples of common household sources.

▶ Provide each child with a copy of the home fire safety checklist. Instruct children to conduct a room-by-room inspection of their own home for potential fire hazards. Discuss the children's findings as a group.

▶ Have each child write a fire safety tip on a small piece of paper and place all suggestions in a container. Have the children take turns drawing a suggestion from the box and reading it aloud. Discuss each tip as a group. Alternatively, have the children take digital pictures of potential home fire hazards and upload them to a designated website. The teacher can then project individual photographs on a large screen, ask children to identify the potential hazards, and discuss a solution to correct each problem.

Evaluation

▶ Children will name the three fire triangle components and give an example of each.

▶ Children will conduct a home fire safety inspection.

▶ Children will identify at least three potential fire safety hazards in their homes.

Additional lesson plans for grades PreK–2 are available on CourseMate.

◑ Summary

❱ Unintentional injuries are the leading cause of death among young children.

- Limited motor, problem-solving, and anticipatory skills increase young children's risk of experiencing unintentional injury.

❱ The incidence of unintentional injury among children can be reduced when adults adhere to the principles of risk management, advanced planning, establishing safety policies and guidelines, providing appropriate supervision, and conducting safety education.

❱ Teachers must continuously be aware of safety in children's environments, from the toys and equipment presented to all planned activities including field trips.

- Teachers have a professional and moral obligation to implement precautionary measures that will protect children's well-being. Failure to uphold this responsibility may result in negligence charges.

❱ Programs must develop emergency response plans to address the types of potential disasters and emergencies that may occur locally.

- Emergency first aid, food and water, and supply kits should be assembled and located where they can be accessed quickly.
- Conducting frequent emergency drills helps children become familiar with the routine and enables adults to respond efficiently and effectively.

◑ Terms to Know

unintentional injury *p. 208*	incidental learning *p. 212*	negligence *p. 222*
risk management *p. 208*	liability *p. 222*	thermal *p. 225*
supervision *p. 211*		

◑ Chapter Review

A. By Yourself

1. Match the item in **Column I** with those in **Column II**.

Column I	**Column II**
1. remaining in a building during an emergency	a. foresight
2. legal responsibility for children's safety	b. supervision
3. the ability to anticipate	c. education
4. limits that define safe behavior	d. planning
5. failure to protect children's safety	e. safety guidelines
6. monitoring children's behavior	f. safe
7. environments free of hazards	g. negligence
8. the process of learning safe behavior	h. prevention
9. a key factor in injury prevention	i. liability
10. measures taken to ensure children's safety	j. shelter-in-place

2. Fill in the blanks with one of the words listed below:

removed	unintentional injury	anticipate
legal	responsible	risk management principles
safety education	safety	inspected

A.   The leading cause of death among young children is _____.

B.   Adults must be able to _____ children's actions as part of advanced planning.

C. Families expect teachers to be _____ for their child's safety.

D. Basic _____ _____ include(s) advanced planning, establishing safety policies and guidelines, appropriate supervision, and safety education.

E. Injury records are considered _____ documents.

F. Children's _____ must be a continuous teacher concern and responsibility.

G. Toys and play equipment should be _____ daily.

H. A prime method for reducing the incidence of unintentional injuries can be achieved through _____ _____.

3. What criteria would you use to determine if it is safe for the occupants to remain in a building or to be evacuated to another location in the event of an emergency?

B. As a Group

1. Discuss why safety policies and guidelines must not be considered a replacement for adult supervision.

2. What actions must teachers take if they notice that a piece of playground equipment is broken?

3. Discuss why infants and toddlers experience the highest rate of unintentional injury.

4. What preparations do teachers need to make before taking children on a field trip?

5. Divide into two groups and debate the advantages and disadvantages of taking children on field trips.

6. Discuss how teachers can best help children cope following a disaster or emergency event?

◖ Case Study

Teachers at the Sunrise Early Childhood Center, located in a downtown urban neighborhood, know that field trips can enrich children's learning. They have discussed organizing a trip to the local city zoo as part of a curriculum unit about animals. However, the teachers also realize the challenges involved in taking a group of twenty 3- and 4-year-olds on such an excursion, but believe the experience is especially valuable for these children. Since the zoo is located on the other side of town, the teachers have made arrangements to ride the city bus.

1. What criteria can teachers use to determine if a field trip is a worthwhile experience?

2. What types of planning are necessary to ensure a safe and successful field trip?

3. What are the advantages/disadvantages of using public transportation?

4. What safety precautions must teachers take before leaving the premises?

5. How might visiting a site ahead of time help teachers better plan for a field trip?

6. What problems should teachers anticipate when taking children on field trips?

7. What information should families be given?

8. Are off-premises field trips typically covered by school liability insurance policies?

◖ Application Activities

1. Role-play how a teacher might handle a child who is not riding a tricycle in a safe manner.

2. Visit an early childhood program play yard or a public playground. Select one piece of play equipment and observe children playing on it for at least 15 minutes. Make a list of observed

or anticipated dangers that could result from improper use. Prepare a set of developmentally appropriate guidelines for children's safe use of the equipment.

3. You have been asked to purchase outdoor play equipment for a new child development center. List the safety features you would look for when making your selections. Conduct an Internet search for companies that offer playground equipment and look over their options. Use this information to select basic outdoor equipment for the play yard of a small early childhood center that has three classes of twenty children each and a budget of $8,000. Be sure to include several pieces that are accessible to all children.

4. Prepare a room-by-room home safety checklist for families of (a) infants, (b) toddlers, and (c) preschool-age children.

5. Continue to research legal issues in early childhood programs. Prepare a 1-hour inservice training to increase teachers' awareness of high-risk situations and measures that can be taken to prevent legal action.

6. Visit with the local emergency preparedness agency in your community. Find out what types of disasters and/or emergencies they recommend that schools be prepared to address. Select one and draft a plan that includes personnel roles, evacuation routes, and emergency supplies.

Helpful Web Resources

American Society for Testing and Materials	http://www.astm.org
Canadian Institute of Child Health	http://www.cich.ca
Canadian Safety Council	http://canadasafetycouncil.org
Child Care Law Center	http://www.childcarelaw.org
Injury Control Resource Information Network	http://www.injurycontrol.com
CDC: National Center for Injury Prevention and Control	http://www.cdc.gov/injury/index.html
National Program for Playground Safety	http://playgroundsafety.org
Safety Link	http://www.safetylink.com
U.S. Consumer Product Safety Commission	http://www.cpsc.gov

 Visit the Education CourseMate for this textbook to access the eBook, Did You Get It? quizzes, Digital Downloads, TeachSource Video Cases, flashcards, and more. Go to CengageBrain.com to log in, register, or purchase access.

References

American Public Health Association (APHA) and American Academy of Pediatrics (AAP). (2011). *Caring for our children: National health and safety performance standards for out-of-home care.* (3rd ed.). Washington, DC. Accessed on May 2, 2013 from http://nrckids.org/CFOC3/index.html. Click on "Standard 3.4.2 Animals."

American Speech-Language-Hearing Association. (ASHA). (2012). *Noisy toys can damage your hearing.* Accessed on June 11, 2012 from http://www.asha.org/about/news/tipsheets/Watch-Out-for-Noisy-Toys.htm.

Armenta, T. (2011). Playing it smart: Safety in extracurricular activities, *Journal of Educational Strategies*, 84(4), 155–159.

Baker, M., Baker, R., & Flagg, L. (2012). Preparing families of children with special health care needs for disasters: An education intervention, *Social Work in Health Care*, 51(5), 417–429.

Bowman, S., Aitken, M., Robbins, J., & Baker, S. (2012). Trends in US pediatric drowning hospitalizations, 1993-2008, *Pediatrics*, 129(2), 275–281.

Cavalari, R., & Romanczyk, R. (2012). Supervision of children with an autism spectrum disorder in the context of unintentional injury, *Research in Autism Spectrum Disorders*, 6(2), 618–627.

Centers for Disease Control and Prevention (CDC). (2012). National action plan for child injury prevention. Accessed on June 11, 2012 from http://www.cdc.gov/safechild/nap/index.html.

CDC. (2011). Animals in schools and daycare settings. Accessed on June 12, 2012 from http://www.cdc.gov/Features/AnimalsInSchools.

CDC. (2010). National Center for Injury Prevention & Control. WISQARS Leading causes of death reports, national and regional, 1999 – 2009. Accessed on June 11, 2012 from http://webappa.cdc.gov/sasweb/ncipc/leadcaus10_us.html.

Child Care Law Center. (2011). Liability insurance for family child care providers. Accessed on June 12, 2012 from http://www.childcarelaw.org/docs/QA_Liability_Insurance_2011.pdf.

Columbus Public Health. (2007). School safe: Classroom pets. Accessed on June 12, 2012 from http://publichealth.columbus.gov/uploadedFiles/Public_Health/Content_Editors/Environmental_Health/Animal_Program/ClassPets.pdf.

Consumer Product Safety Commission (CPSC). (2012a). *Art and craft safety guide*. Accessed on May 2, 2013 from http://www.cpsc.gov/PageFiles/125203/5015.pdf.

CPSC. (2012b). *The safe nursery*. Accessed on May 2, 2013 from http://www.cpsc.gov/PageFiles/115485/202.pdf

CPSC. (2012c). *Public playground safety handbook*. Accessed on May 2, 2013 from http://www.cpsc.gov/PageFiles/116134/325.pdf.

Copeland, K., Kendeigh, C., Saelens, B., Kalkwarfl, H., & Sherman, S. (2012). Physical activity in child-care centers: Do teachers hold the key to the playground?, *Health Education Research*, 27(1), 81–100.

Essex, N. (2011). Bullying and school liability—Implications for school personnel, *Journal of Educational Strategies, Issues, & Ideas*, 84(5), 192–196.

Federal Emergency Management Agency (FEMA). (2013). Helping kids cope with disaster. Accessed May 2, 2013 from http://www.fema.gov/coping-disaster#4.

Frost, J., Wortham, S., & Reifel, S. (2011). *Play and child development*. (4th ed.). Upper Saddle River, NJ: Prentice Hall.

Grasso, D., Ford, J., & Briggs-Gowan, M. (2013). Early life trauma exposure and stress sensitivity in young children, *Journal of Pediatric Psychology*, 38(1), 94–103.

Guilfoyle, S., Karazsia, B., Langkamp, D., & Wildman, B. (2012). Supervision to prevent childhood unintentional injury: Developmental knowledge and self-efficacy count, *Journal of Child Health Care*. Advanced online publication. DOI: 10.1177/1367493511423855.

Haney, M. (2012). After school care for children with autism spectrum, *Journal of Child & Family Studies*, 21(3), 466–473.

Huang, P., Kallan, M., O'Neil, J., Bull, M., Blum, N., & Durbin, D. (2011). Children with special physical health care needs: Restraint use and injury risk in motor vehicle crashes, *Maternal & Child Health*, 15(7), 949–954.

Hull, R. (2012). Recovery and resiliency after a disaster in educational settings, *National Association of School Nurses*, 37(3), 144–149.

Hull, B. (2011). Changing realities in school safety and preparedness, *Journal of Business Continuity & Emergency Planning*, 5(1), 440–451.

Judy, K. (2011). Unintentional injuries in pediatrics, *Pediatrics in Review*, 32(10), 431–439.

Little, H., Wyver, S., & Gibson, F. (2011). The influence of play context and adult attitudes on young children's risk-taking during outdoor play, *European Early Childhood Education Research Journal*, 19(1), 113–131.

Loder, R., & Abrams, S. (2011). Temporal variation in childhood injury from common recreational activities, *Injury*, 42(9), 945–957.

Marotz, L. R. (2000). Childhood and classroom injuries. (2000). In, J. L. Frost (Ed.), *Children and injuries*. Tucson, AZ: Lawyers & Judges Publishing Co.

Marotz, L., & Allen, K. E. (2013). Developmental Profiles: Pre-birth through adolescence. Belmont, CA: Wadsworth Cengage Learning.

Morrongiello, B., Kane, A., McArthur, B., & Bell, M. (2012). Physical risk taking in elementary-school children: Measurement and emotion regulation issues, *Personality & Individual Differences*, 52(4), 492–496.

National Association for the Education of Young Children (NAEYC). (2012). *Good toys for young children*. Accessed on June 11, 2012 from http://www.naeyc.org/ecp/resources/goodtoys.

Nichols, B., Visotcky, A., Aberger, M., Braun, N., Tarima, S., & Brown, D. (2011). Pediatric exposure to choking hazards is associated with parental knowledge of choking hazards, *International Journal of Pediatric Otorhinolaryngology*, 76(2), 169–173.

Office of Environmental Health Hazard Assessment (OEHHA). (2009). *Guidelines for the safe use of art and craft materials* (updated October 2009). Accessed on June 12, 2012 from http://www.oehha.ca.gov/education/art/artguide.html.

Pearson, M., Hunt, H., Garside, R., Moxham, T., Peters, J., & Anderson, R. (2012). Preventing unintentional injuries to children under 15 years in the outdoors: A systematic review of the effectiveness of educational programs, *Injury Prevention*, 18(2), 113–123.

Pollack, K., Kercher, C., Frattaroli, S., Peek-Asa, C., Sleet, D., & Rivara, F. (2012). Toward environments and policies that promote injury-free active living—It wouldn't hurt, *Health Place*, 18(1), 106–114.

Rothstein, L., & Johnson, S. (2010). *Special education law (4th Ed.)*. Thousand Oaks, CA: Sage Publications.

Smithson, J., Garside, R., & Pearson, M. (2011). Barriers to, and facilitators of, the prevention of unintentional injury in children in the home: A systematic review and synthesis of qualitative research, *Injury Prevention,* 17(2), 119–126.

U.S. Department of Justice. (2010). 2010 ADA standards for accessible design. Accessed on June 11, 2012 from http://www.ada.gov/2010ADAstandards_index.htm.

U.S. Public Interest Research Groups. (2011). *Trouble in toyland: The 26th annual survey of toy safety.* Accessed on June 11, 2012 from http://uspirg.org/reports/usp/trouble-toyland.

Wakes, S., & Beukes, A. (2012). Height, fun, and safety in the design of children's playground equipment, *International Journal of Injury Control & Safety Promotion*, 19(2), 101–108.

Yudof, M., Levin, B., Moran, R., Ryan, J., & Bowman, K. (2012). *Educational policy and the law*, Belmont, CA: Wadsworth Cengage Learning.

chapter 9

Management of Injuries and Acute Illness

naeyc Standards Chapter Links

▸ **1 a and b:** Promoting child development and learning
▸ **#2 a and b:** Building family and community relationships
▸ **#3 a, c and d:** Observing, documenting, and assessing to support young children and families
▸ **#3 c:** Knowing about and using observation, documentation, and other assessment tools and approaches
▸ **#6 b:** Becoming a professional

Learning Objectives

After studying this chapter, you should be able to:

LO 9-1 Discuss the steps schools should take to prepare for medical emergencies.

LO 9-2 Describe how emergency care and first aid differ.

LO 9-3 Name six life-threatening conditions and demonstrate the emergency treatment for each.

LO 9-4 Identify six non-life-threatening conditions and describe the first aid treatment for each.

Prevention of unintentional childhood injuries is a major responsibility of families and teachers. This goal is best achieved by creating safe environments, providing health and safety education for children and first aid training for teachers, and establishing procedures for handling illness and injury emergencies (Copeland et al., 2012).

9-1 Responding to Medical Emergencies

High-quality programs have policies and procedures in place so they can respond to children's health emergencies quickly and efficiently. They have supplies available and provide advanced training to ensure that staff are ready to address emergencies in a prompt and knowledgeable manner (Figure 9–1). Points that should be addressed in a school's comprehensive emergency response plan include:

▸ training of personnel in infant and child CPR and basic first aid techniques
▸ designating staff who are responsible for administering emergency care
▸ obtaining contact information and notarized permission from each child's parent or guardian that authorizes emergency medical treatment (Note: Most medical facilities will not treat minor children without the notarized consent of their legal parent or guardian.)
▸ having an accessible telephone
▸ posting emergency telephone numbers (e.g., families and their designated emergency contacts, hospital emergency room, fire department, emergency medical technicians [EMTs], law enforcement, local poison control) next to the telephone
▸ making arrangements for emergency transportation
▸ providing a fully equipped first aid kit that is stored in a central location (Teacher Checklist 9-1); modified kits can be prepared for individual classrooms and for taking along on field trips (Teacher Checklist 9-2)

FIGURE 9–1 **Planning guidelines for serious injury and emergency illness.**

1. Remain with the child at all times. Keep calm and reassure the child that you are there to help. Your presence can be comforting to the child, especially when faced with unfamiliar surroundings or pain.
2. Do not move a child who has a serious injury unless there is immediate danger from additional harm, such as fire or electrical shock.
3. Begin appropriate emergency care procedures immediately. Meanwhile, send for help. Have another adult or child alert the person designated to handle such emergencies in your school or program.
4. Do not give food, fluids, or medications unless specifically ordered by the child's physician or Poison Control Center.
5. Call 911 for emergency medical assistance if in doubt about the child's condition. Don't attempt to handle difficult situations by yourself. A delay in contacting emergency authorities could make the difference in saving a child's life. If you are alone, have a child dial the emergency number in your community (911).
6. If the child is transported to a medical facility before parents arrive, a teacher should accompany, and remain with the child until a family member is present. You are able to provide medical personnel with valuable information about events preceding the injury or illness, symptoms the child exhibited, and any treatment administered.
7. Contact the child's family. Inform them of the illness or injury and the child's general condition. If the child's condition is not life-threatening, discuss plans for follow-up care (e.g., contacting the child's physician, observing for signs of infection). If the family cannot be reached, call the child's emergency contact person or physician.
8. Record all information concerning serious injury or illness on appropriate forms within 24 hours; place in the child's folder and provide the family with a copy. If required, notify local licensing authorities.

TeachSource Digital Download Download from CourseMate.

TEACHER CHECKLIST 9-1

Basic First Aid Supplies for Schools

adhesive tape, 1/2- and 1-inch widths	safety pins
antibacterial soap or cleanser	scissors, blunt tipped
bandages, assorted sizes	soap, preferably liquid
space blanket (Mylar)	spirits of ammonia
bulb syringe	SAM rolled splints (small)
thermometer	cotton balls
flashlight and extra batteries	plastic bags (sealable)
gauze pads, sterile, 2×2s, 4×4s	tongue blades
instant cold packs or plastic bags for ice cubes	towels, large and small
needle (sewing type)	triangular bandages for slings
roller gauze, 1- and 2-inch widths	tweezers
disposable gloves	first aid book or reference cards
pen and small notepad	emergency telephone numbers
saline eye wash solution	

TeachSource Digital Download Download from CourseMate.

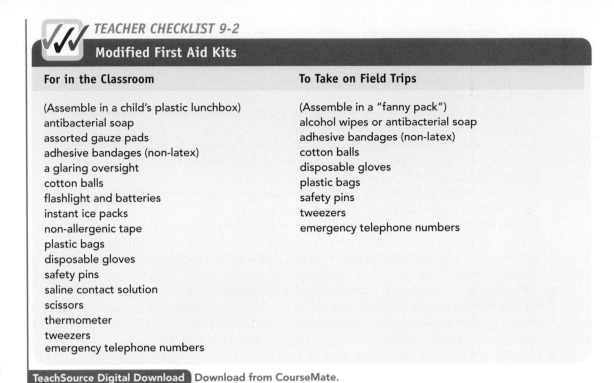

TEACHER CHECKLIST 9-2
Modified First Aid Kits

For in the Classroom	To Take on Field Trips
(Assemble in a child's plastic lunchbox)	(Assemble in a "fanny pack")
antibacterial soap	alcohol wipes or antibacterial soap
assorted gauze pads	adhesive bandages (non-latex)
adhesive bandages (non-latex)	cotton balls
a glaring oversight	disposable gloves
cotton balls	plastic bags
flashlight and batteries	safety pins
instant ice packs	tweezers
non-allergenic tape	emergency telephone numbers
plastic bags	
disposable gloves	
safety pins	
saline contact solution	
scissors	
thermometer	
tweezers	
emergency telephone numbers	

TeachSource Digital Download Download from CourseMate.

Copies of a program's emergency response plans should be made available to families and reviewed on a regular basis with staff members.

Information about universal precautions must be addressed in a program's emergency policies and procedures. Universal precautions are special infection-control guidelines that have been developed to prevent the spread of diseases transmitted via blood and other body fluids, such as hepatitis B and C, and AIDS/HIV. (See Chapter 5.) These guidelines include several areas of precaution—barrier protection (including the use of disposable gloves and hand washing), environmental disinfection, and proper disposal of contaminated materials—that must be strictly followed when caring for children's injuries.

Despite careful planning and supervision, childhood injuries and illnesses are inevitable. For this reason, it is important that teachers learn the fundamentals of emergency care and first aid (APHA & AAP, 2011). Appropriate training and continued participation in refresher courses enable personnel to handle emergencies with skill and confidence (Banghart & Kreader, 2012).

Teachers are responsible for administering initial and urgent care to children who are seriously injured or acutely ill. These measures are considered to be temporary and aimed at saving lives, reducing pain and discomfort, and preventing complications and additional injury. Once

TABLE 9-1 Initial Injury Assessment

Take a deep breath, survey the situation, and consider the following points before taking action:

- Safety – Determine if it is safe to proceed or if precautions must first be taken to protect you and or the child from additional risks (e.g., traffic, electricity, chemical fumes, glass).

- Location – Note whether the child may have fallen from play equipment, had access to toxic chemicals, been stung by an insect, or cut on a sharp object.

- Child's appearance – Observe the child for breathing, bleeding, choking, skin color (e.g., pallor, blue-grey, flushed), seizures, lying in an unusual position, and so on.

- Child's reaction – Note whether the child is crying and inconsolable, lethargic, confused, unresponsive, or able to respond appropriately.

the child has been stabilized, responsibility for obtaining further medical treatment can be transferred to the child's family (Marotz, 2000).

9-2 Emergency Care vs. First Aid

Emergency care refers to immediate treatment administered for life-threatening conditions. It includes a quick assessment of the child and conditions that may have contributed to the emergency (Table 9–1). First aid refers to treatment administered for injuries and illnesses that are not considered life-threatening. Emergency care and first aid treatments are based on principles that should be familiar to anyone who works with children:

1. Call 911 to summon emergency medical assistance for any injury or illness that requires more than simple first aid.
2. Stay calm and proceed cautiously.
3. Always remain with the child. If necessary, send another adult or child for help.
4. Don't move the child until the extent of injuries or illness can be determined. If in doubt, have the child remain in the same position and await emergency medical help.
5. Quickly evaluate the child's condition, paying special attention to signs of respiratory distress and significant bleeding.
6. Carefully plan and administer appropriate emergency care. Improper treatment can lead to other injuries.
7. Don't give any medications unless they are prescribed for certain lifesaving conditions.
8. Don't offer diagnoses or medical advice. Refer the child's family to seek professional health care.
9. Contact the child's family and inform them of the child's injury and any first aid care that has been administered.
10. Record all facts concerning the injury and treatments administered on the appropriate forms; file in the child's permanent folder.

All states grant legal protection to individuals who do not have medical training but volunteer to administer emergency treatment to an injured person. The **Good Samaritan Law** protects individuals from liability as long as they provide reasonable care to the best of their ability and without intentional harm. Teachers are also protected by this law and should not hesitate to give emergency care to an injured child.

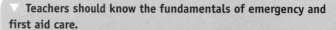
▼ **Teachers should know the fundamentals of emergency and first aid care.**

© Cengage Learning

....

Good Samaritan Law – *legal protection afforded to an individual who renders emergency or first aid care in a reasonable manner.*

9-3 Life-Threatening Conditions

Did You Know...

that after the heart stops, the human brain can live only 4 minutes without oxygen before irreversible brain damage occurs?

Situations that require emergency care to prevent death or serious disability are discussed in this section. The emergency techniques and suggestions included here are not intended as substitutes for certified first aid and cardiopulmonary resuscitation (CPR) training. Rather, they are provided as a review of basic instruction and to enhance the teacher's ability to respond to children's emergencies. A course involving hands-on practice is necessary to master these skills. It is also important to complete a refresher course every few years.

9-3a Absence of Breathing

Breathing emergencies accompany many life-threatening conditions, such as asthma, drowning, electrical shock, convulsions, poisoning, severe injuries, suffocation, choking, cardiac arrest, and Sudden Infant Death Syndrome (SIDS). For this reason, adults who work with children should complete certified training in basic first aid and CPR. This training is available from most chapters of the American Red Cross and the American Heart Association (AHA) or from a local ambulance service, rescue squad, fire department, high school, or community parks and recreation departments.

The current AHA guidelines for administering CPR recommend a single compression-to-ventilation rate of 30:2 for persons of all ages (with the exception of newborns) (Berg et al., 2010). A rescue breath is defined as being one second in length and sufficient to cause the chest to rise and fall. The CPR sequence of chest compressions and rescue breaths should be delivered as follows: Compressions first, open Airway, give Breaths (C-A-B) (Figure 9–2). The AHA continues to stress the slogan, "push hard and push fast," to convey the critical importance of administering high-quality chest compressions (approximately 100 per minute) sufficient to maintain adequate blood flow to vital organs. An adequate compression should depress the chest cavity by approximately one-third of its depth or 1.5 inches (3.8 cm) in infants and 2 inches (5.1 cm) in children.

It is important to remain calm while administering emergency lifesaving procedures and to perform them quickly and with confidence (Figure 9–3). Have someone call for an ambulance or emergency medical assistance while you begin chest compressions. If

FIGURE 9–2 Using C-A-B to perform CPR.

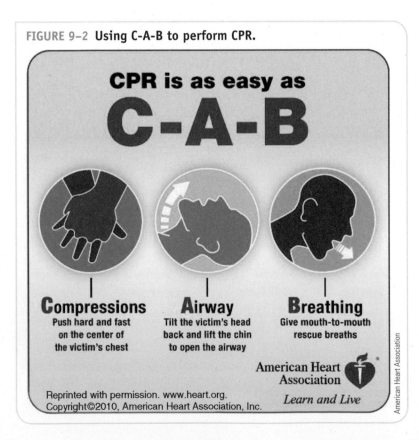

CPR is as easy as

C-A-B

Compressions
Push hard and fast on the center of the victim's chest

Airway
Tilt the victim's head back and lift the chin to open the airway

Breathing
Give mouth-to-mouth rescue breaths

American Heart Association
Learn and Live

Reprinted with permission. www.heart.org.
Copyright©2010, American Heart Association, Inc.

American Heart Association

you are alone, administer five cycles (30 chest compressions, 2 breaths) for approximately 2 minutes before leaving the victim to call 911 for emergency assistance.

To perform CPR:

1. **For an infant** (0–12 months):

    a. Have someone call 911 to summon emergency assistance.

    b. Check for a response. Shake the infant and shout, "(Child's name), are you sleeping?" or "Are you okay?" to determine if he is conscious. If the infant responds, check for injuries. If the infant isn't breathing and doesn't respond, begin CPR immediately.

FIGURE 9–3 Cardiopulmonary resuscitation (CPR) for infants and children.

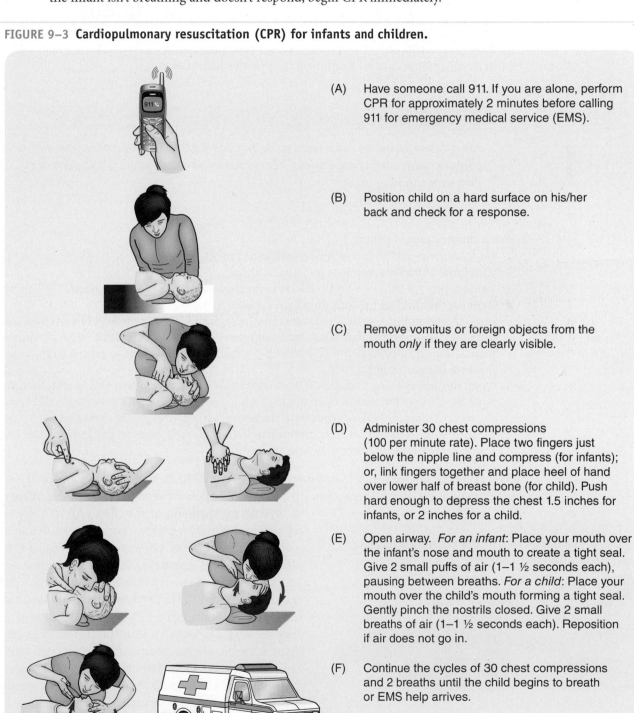

(A) Have someone call 911. If you are alone, perform CPR for approximately 2 minutes before calling 911 for emergency medical service (EMS).

(B) Position child on a hard surface on his/her back and check for a response.

(C) Remove vomitus or foreign objects from the mouth *only* if they are clearly visible.

(D) Administer 30 chest compressions (100 per minute rate). Place two fingers just below the nipple line and compress (for infants); or, link fingers together and place heel of hand over lower half of breast bone (for child). Push hard enough to depress the chest 1.5 inches for infants, or 2 inches for a child.

(E) Open airway. *For an infant*: Place your mouth over the infant's nose and mouth to create a tight seal. Give 2 small puffs of air (1–1 ½ seconds each), pausing between breaths. *For a child*: Place your mouth over the child's mouth forming a tight seal. Gently pinch the nostrils closed. Give 2 small breaths of air (1–1 ½ seconds each). Reposition if air does not go in.

(F) Continue the cycles of 30 chest compressions and 2 breaths until the child begins to breath or EMS help arrives.

c. Position the infant on her back on a hard surface. Remove vomitus or foreign object from the mouth only if it is clearly visible.

d. Immediately administer 30 quick chest compressions by placing two fingers just below the nipple line; each compression should depress the chest by one-third of its depth (1.5 inches [3.8 cm]). Let the chest return to its normal position between each compression by lifting your hand slightly.

e. Use the head tilt-chin lift to open the airway. Do not tip the head back too far to avoid obstructing the airway. Keep your fingers on the jawbone, not on the soft tissue under the chin.

f. Place your mouth over the infant's nose and mouth to create a tight seal. Give 2 small puffs of air (one second per breath with a short pause in between). Observe the chest (rise and fall) to be sure air is entering the lungs.

g. Continue cycles of 30 chest compressions (100 per minute) followed by 2 breaths (30:2) until the infant resumes breathing or emergency help arrives.

 CAUTION

*Too much air forced into an infant's lungs may also fill the stomach (causes vomiting and an increased the risk of **aspiration**). Always remember to use small, gentle puffs of air from your cheeks.*

2. ***For a child*** (1 year to puberty):

a. Have someone call 911 to summon emergency medical assistance.

b. Check the child for a response (i.e., shake, shout).

c. Remove any vomitus or foreign objects from the mouth only if clearly visible.

d. Position the child on his back on a hard surface.

e. Immediately administer 30 quick chest compressions by placing the heel of your hand over the lower half of the breast bone; each compression should depress the chest by approximately one-third of its depth (2 inches [5.1 cm]). Allow the chest to return to its normal position between compressions.

f. Open the airway using the head tilt-chin lift. Gently pinch the nostrils closed and place your open mouth over the victim's open mouth, forming a tight seal. Give 2 breaths of air (1 second per breath), pausing between breaths to make sure air is going into the child's lungs.

g. Continue cycles of 30 chest compressions followed by 2 breaths (30:2) until the child resumes breathing or emergency help arrives.

DO NOT STOP OR GIVE UP! Continue administering CPR (30 compressions, 2 breaths) until the infant or child is breathing or emergency medical service personnel arrive. If air does not appear to be entering the lungs or the chest does not rise and fall while administering CPR, check the mouth and airway for foreign objects. Only remove the object if it is clearly visible and easy to reach. (Refer to section 9.3b, Foreign Body Airway Obstruction.) If the child resumes breathing, keep her lying down and roll (as a unit) onto one side; this is called the **recovery position** (Figure 9–4). Placing a child in the recovery position helps keep the airway open and decreases the risk of aspiration and choking. Maintain body temperature by covering with a light blanket, and continue to monitor the child's breathing closely until medical help arrives.

FIGURE 9–4 Placing a child in the recovery position prevents aspiration and choking.

aspiration – *accidental inhalation of food, fluid, or an object into the respiratory tract.*
recovery position – *placing an individual in a side-lying position*

TEACHER CHECKLIST 9-3

Teacher Checklist: Foods Commonly Linked to Childhood Choking

raw carrots	seeds (sunflower), peanuts,
hot dogs	and other nuts
pieces of raw apple	chewy cookies
grapes (whole)	cough drops
fruit seeds and pits	chewing gum
gummy or hard candies	hard pretzels
peanut butter sandwich	popcorn

TeachSource Digital Download   Download from CourseMate.

Occasionally, families of children with special medical problems or life-threatening conditions make a decision not to have their child resuscitated and will obtain a Do Not Attempt to Resuscitate (DNAR) order from their physician. A copy of this document should be kept on file and honored in the event of a breathing emergency. School personnel should be made aware of the family's request.

9-3b Foreign Body Airway Obstruction

Children under 5 years of age account for nearly 90 percent of deaths due to airway obstruction (Kaushal et al., 2011). More than 66 percent of these deaths occur in infants. Certain foods (Teacher Checklist 9-3) and small objects (Teacher Checklist 9-4) are the most common causes of aspiration and should not be accessible to children under age 5 without supervision (Sih et al., 2012). However, developmental delays and disabilities may place some older children at higher risk for choking and the need for close supervision.

In most instances, children will be successful in coughing out an aspirated object without requiring emergency intervention. It is best not to interfere as long as the child continues to cough. However, emergency lifesaving measures must be started immediately if:

- Breathing is labored or absent.
- Lips and nail beds turn blue.
- Cough is weak or ineffective.
- The child is unable to speak.
- The child becomes unresponsive.
- A high-pitched sound can be heard when the child inhales.

Respiratory infections can sometimes cause swelling and obstruction of children's airway. If this occurs, call immediately for emergency medical assistance. Time should not be wasted on attempting

TEACHER CHECKLIST 9-4

Objects Commonly Linked to Childhood Choking

latex balloons (uninflated or pieces)
small batteries (calculator, hearing aid)
magnets
marker or pen caps
paper clips
small objects (less than 1.5 inches [3.8 cm]) in diameter
toys with small pieces
coins
marbles
small balls, blocks, beads, or vending machine toys
plastic film on toys and packages

TeachSource Digital Download   Download from CourseMate.

FIGURE 9-5 The infant's head should be positioned lower than the chest.

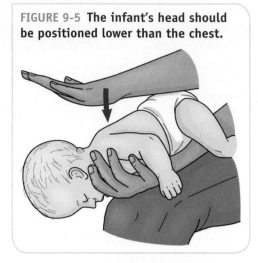

FIGURE 9-6 Location of fingers for chest compressions on an infant.

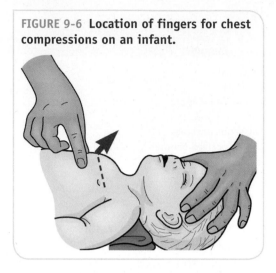

techniques for clearing an airway obstruction (foreign body). They are not effective and may actually cause the child more harm. Emergency techniques to relieve an airway obstruction should be attempted only if a child is known to be choking on an object or is unconscious and not breathing after attempts have been made to open the airway and to breathe for the child.

Different emergency techniques are used to treat infants, toddlers, and older children who are choking (AHA, 2010). Attempts to retrieve the object from the child's mouth should be made only if the object is clearly visible. Extreme care must be taken not to push the object further back into the airway.

For an infant: If the object cannot be removed easily and the infant is conscious, quickly:

▶ Have someone call 911 to summon emergency medical assistance.
▶ Position the infant face down over the length of your arm, with the child's head lower than her chest and the head and neck supported in your hand (Figure 9–5). The infant can also be placed (face down) in your lap with the head lower than the chest.
▶ Use the heel of your hand to give five quick back blows between the infant's shoulder blades.
▶ Support and turn the infant over, face up, with the head held lower than the chest.

⚠ **CAUTION**

Do not use excessive force as this could injure the infant.

▶ Give five chest thrusts. Place two fingers just below the nipple line (Figure 9–6). Rapidly compress the infant's chest approximately 1/2–1 inch (1.3–2.5 cm); release pressure completely between thrusts, allowing the chest to return to its normal position.
▶ Look inside the child's mouth for the foreign object. If clearly visible and reachable, remove it.
▶ Repeat the steps, alternating five back blows and five chest thrusts until the object is dislodged and the infant begins to cry or lose consciousness.

For the child: If the object cannot be removed easily and the child is conscious, quickly:

▶ Call 911 to summon emergency medical assistance.
▶ Administer the Heimlich maneuver. Stand or kneel behind the child with your arms around the child's waist (Figure 9–7).
▶ Make a fist with one hand, thumbs tucked in.
▶ Place the fisted hand (thumb-side) against the child's abdomen, midway between the base of the rib cage (xiphoid process) and the navel.
▶ Press your fisted hand into the child's abdomen with a quick, inward and upward thrust.
▶ Continue to repeat abdominal thrusts until the object is dislodged or the child regains consciousness.
▶ If the child loses consciousness and is still breathing, lower him to the floor and continue to administer abdominal thrusts until the object is dislodged (Figure 9–8).

If the infant or child LOSES CONSCIOUSNESS AND IS NOT BREATHING:

▶ Have someone call 911 for emergency medical assistance (if this has not already been done).
▶ Place the child on the floor or other hard surface on his back and begin CPR immediately (30 chest compressions, open the airway, and give 2 rescue breaths).

FIGURE 9-7 The Heimlich maneuver.

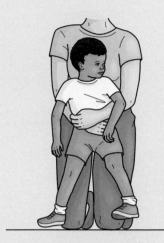

Stand or kneel behind the child with your arms around the child's waist.

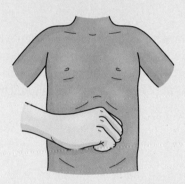

Make a fist with one hand. Place the fisted hand against the child's abdomen below the tip of the rib cage, slightly above the navel.

Grasp the fisted hand with your other hand. Press your fists into the child's abdomen with a quick upward thrust.

▶ Continue the cycle of chest compressions and rescue breaths until emergency help arrives.

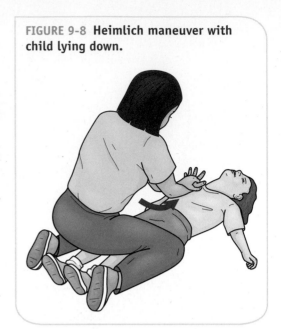

FIGURE 9-8 Heimlich maneuver with child lying down.

The AHA suggests that CPR chest compressions alone are sufficient to dislodge an object in the airway. Look inside of the child's mouth (for the foreign object) before each cycle of breaths is given and remove only if the object is visible.

If the infant or child begins to breathe on her own, stop CPR and continue to monitor the child closely until emergency medical personnel arrive. Roll the child (as a unit) onto his side (recovery position). Always be sure the child receives follow-up medical attention after the object has been dislodged and breathing is restored.

9-3c Anaphylaxis: Life-Threatening Allergic Reaction

A severe allergic reaction to an allergen such as food, medication, insect bite, or latex can cause some children (and adults) to experience a life-threatening condition known as anaphylaxis or anaphylactic shock. It is essential that teachers be aware of children who are predisposed to this condition and work closely with their families to establish emergency plans (Ercan et al., 2012). The symptoms of an anaphylactic reaction usually develop within minutes of exposure to the offending allergen and include:

▶ difficulty breathing, talking, and/or swallowing
▶ wheezing and/or cough
▶ hives
▶ swelling of the lips, tongue, eyes, and/or face
▶ abdominal pain, nausea, and/or vomiting
▶ dizziness, confusion
▶ slurred speech
▶ unusual restlessness or agitation

Anaphylaxis requires immediate treatment:

▶ Lay the child down and keep her as quiet as possible. If breathing is difficult, allow the child to sit up.
▶ Call 911 at once.
▶ If the child has injectable epinephrine (EpiPen), administer it immediately.
▶ Do not give the child any food or fluids to drink.
▶ Monitor breathing closely; begin CPR if breathing stops.

The family should be contacted as soon as the child is stable so they can seek medical attention. In some cases, the child may require a second dose of epinephrine because the medication's effects will begin to wear off.

9-3d Shock

Shock frequently accompanies injuries, especially those that are severe, and should therefore be anticipated. However, it can also result from extreme emotional upset and injuries, such as bleeding, pain, heat exhaustion, poisoning, burns, and fractures. Shock is considered a life-threatening condition that requires prompt emergency treatment. Early indicators of shock include:

▶ skin that is pale, cool, and clammy
▶ confusion, anxiety, restlessness
▶ increased perspiration
▶ weakness
▶ rapid, shallow breathing

Signs of more serious shock may develop, and include:

- rapid, weak pulse
- bluish discoloration around lips, nails, and ear lobes
- dilated pupils
- extreme thirst
- nausea and vomiting
- unconsciousness

To treat a child in shock:

1. Have someone call 911 for emergency medical assistance.
2. Quickly assess the child to identify what may have caused the shock (e.g., bleeding, poisoning, broken bone) and treat the cause first.
3. Keep the child lying down.
4. **Elevate** the child's feet 8 to 10 inches, if there is no indication of back injuries or fractures to the legs or head.
5. Maintain body heat by covering the child lightly with a blanket.
6. Moisten a clean cloth and use it for wetting the lips and mouth if the child complains of thirst; do not give food or fluids.
7. Stay calm and reassure the child until emergency medical help arrives.
8. Observe the child's breathing closely; begin CPR if the child is unresponsive and stops breathing.

9-3e Asthma

Asthma is a chronic disorder of the respiratory system characterized by periods of wheezing, gasping, and labored breathing. Numerous factors are known to trigger an acute asthma attack, including allergic reactions, respiratory infections, emotional stress, air pollutants, and physical exertion (Pawankar et al., 2012; Price et al., 2012). Asthma attacks make breathing intensely difficult and, therefore, must be treated as a life-threatening event (Allen et al., 2012). Schools should have an action plan in place for any child with a known history of asthma. (See Chapter 4).

Remaining calm and confident during a child's asthmatic attack is crucial. To treat a child who is having an asthma attack:

> **Did You Know...**
> that every day approximately 36,000 children are absent from school due to asthma? In a given school year, it is estimated that children miss more than 14 million days because of an asthma attack. This makes asthma a major cause of school absenteeism.

1. Call 911 to summon emergency medical help immediately if the child shows signs of anxiety, wheezing, restlessness, loss of consciousness, or blue discoloration of the nail beds or lips. Fatigue, inability to recognize teachers, or loss of consciousness are dangerous signs of impending respiratory failure or cardiac arrest.
2. Reassure the child.
3. Administer any medications (such as an inhaler) prescribed for the child's acute asthmatic symptoms immediately.
4. Encourage the child to relax and breathe slowly and deeply. (Anxiety makes breathing more difficult.)
5. Have the child assume a position that is most comfortable. (Breathing is usually easier when sitting or standing up.)
6. Notify the child's family.

9-3f Bleeding

Occasionally, children receive injuries, such as a deep gash or head laceration, that will bleed profusely. Severe bleeding requires prompt emergency treatment. Again, it is extremely important that the teacher act quickly, yet remain calm. To stop bleeding:

1. Summon emergency medical assistance immediately if bleeding comes in spurts or is profuse and cannot be stopped.
2. Follow universal infection control precautions (wear disposable gloves, wash hands, seal and dispose of contaminated items, clean and disinfect surfaces).

elevate – *to raise to a higher position.*

⚠ **CAUTION**

Tourniquets should be used only as a last resort and with the understanding that the extremity will probably need to be amputated.

3. Place a **sterile** gauze pad or clean material over the wound.
4. Apply firm pressure (5–10 minutes) directly over the site, using the flat parts of the fingers; do not let up, as bleeding may resume.
5. Place additional pads on top of the first bandage if blood soaks through. Do not remove the original gauze pad; bleeding may resume if the wound is disturbed.
6. Secure the gauze pad(s) in place with tape or an elastic bandage when bleeding has stopped.

Save all blood-soaked dressings. Doctors will use them to estimate the amount of blood loss. Contact the child's family when bleeding is under control and advise them to seek prompt medical attention.

9-3g Diabetes

Two potentially life-threatening emergencies associated with diabetes are hypoglycemia and hyperglycemia. Teachers must be able to quickly distinguish between these two conditions in order to determine appropriate emergency measures (American Diabetes Association, 2012). The causes and symptoms associated with these complications are often opposites of each other (Teacher Checklist 9-5).

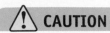 **TEACHER CHECKLIST 9-5**

Teacher Checklist: Signs and Symptoms of Hyperglycemia and Hypoglycemia

Hyperglycemia (diabetic coma)	**Hypoglycemia** (insulin reaction)
Causes	**Causes**
High blood sugar caused by too little available insulin, improper diet, illness, stress, or omitted dose of insulin	Low blood sugar caused by too much insulin, insufficient amounts of carbohydrates, increased activity, decreased food intake, and illness
Symptoms	**Symptoms**
• Slow, gradual onset • Slow, deep breathing • Increased thirst • Skin flushed and dry • Confusion • Staggering; appears as if drunk • Drowsiness • Sweet smelling, wine-like breath odor • Nausea, vomiting • Excessive urination	• Sudden onset • Skin cool, clammy, and pale • Dizziness • Shakiness • Nausea • Headache • Hunger • Rapid, shallow breathing • Confusion, abrupt moodiness • Seizures • Unconsciousness
Treatment	**Treatment**
Summon emergency medical assistance. Keep the child quiet and warm.	Summon emergency medical assistance if the child's state of consciousness is altered. If conscious and alert, quickly administer orange juice or a concentrated glucose source, such as glucose tablets or gel. If unconscious, maintain airway, summon emergency medical assistance, or rush the child to the nearest hospital.

TeachSource Digital Download) Download from CourseMate.

---

sterile – *free from living microorganisms.*

Hypoglycemia, or insulin reaction, is caused by low glucose (blood sugar) levels. It can occur whenever a diabetic child either receives an excessive dose of insulin or an insufficient amount of food. Other causes may include illness, delayed eating times, or increased activity. Similar symptoms are experienced by nondiabetic children when they become overly hungry. Hypoglycemia can often be quickly reversed by administering a sugar substance. Orange juice is ideal for this purpose because it is absorbed rapidly by the body. Regular soda (not diet) or 1–2 tablespoons of honey mixed into a small amount of water will also work. Concentrated glucose gel or tablets can also be purchased and used for emergency purposes. Hard candies, such as Life Savers® or lollipops, should not be used because a child could easily choke.

Hyperglycemia (which can lead to diabetic coma), results when too much sugar is circulating in the blood stream, and is a potential complication for children who have diabetes. Illness, infection, emotional stress, poor dietary control, fever, or a dose of insulin that is too small or forgotten can lead to hyperglycemia. Local emergency medical assistance should be contacted immediately if a child who has diabetes develops symptoms of hyperglycemia. Emergency treatment usually requires medical personnel to administer intravenous (IV) insulin. The child's family should be notified so they can consult with their health care provider.

9-3h Drowning

Drowning is a leading cause of unintentional death among young children (Laosse, Gilchrist, & Rudd, 2012). For this reason, every parent and teacher should complete basic CPR training. Even small amounts of water, such as toilet bowls, buckets, wading pools, bathtubs, outdoor water features, and fish ponds pose a serious danger. Poor muscle coordination and large upper body proportion make it difficult for young children to escape from water hazards. Older children who drown often have overestimated their swimming abilities or engaged in unsafe water activities.

CPR must be started as soon as the child is removed from the water. If the rescuer is alone, she should complete five cycles of chest compressions and rescue breaths (30:2) before calling 911. The child may vomit during **resuscitation** attempts because large amounts of water are often swallowed.

CONNECTING TO EVERYDAY PRACTICE

Water Safety

Several times each month, the Arizona 5 o'clock news and local newspapers carry heartbreaking stories of childhood drownings. More often than not, the victim is a toddler who momentarily escapes a parent's watchful eye, wanders through an unlocked gate, and falls into a residential swimming pool. Although current regulations require new houses and pool installations to meet strict building codes, many existing homes do not have these safety features in place. However, pools and spas are not the only water hazards that contribute to childhood drowning.

Think About This:

- What water sources are present in and around most homes that could contribute to a potential childhood drowning?

- What characteristics place the toddler at greater risk for drowning?

- What safety measures should be taken to protect children from drowning in residential pools or spas?

- How would you care for a toddler who has just been pulled from the water and is unconscious?

- What safety rules and regulations are pool owners in your community required to follow?

resuscitation – *to revive from unconsciousness or death; to restore breathing and heartbeat.*

To reduce the risk of choking, the child should be placed in a recovery position (side-lying) and observed closely for signs of shock. Even if a child appears to have fully recovered from a near drowning incident, medical care should be obtained immediately. Complications, such as pneumonia, can develop from water, chemicals, or debris remaining in the lungs.

9-3i Electrical Shock

Exposure to electrical shock can be a life-threatening condition in children. Although it is a natural reaction to immediately want to grab the child, this must never be attempted until the main electrical source has been turned off or disconnected. This can be accomplished by unplugging the cord, removing the appropriate fuse from the fuse box, or turning off the main breaker switch. Always stand on something dry such as a board or cardboard while attempting to rescue the child (after the electrical source has been turned off) if there is water in the area.

Severe electrical shock can cause breathing to cease, surface burns, deep tissue injury, symptoms of shock, and the heart to stop beating (cardiac arrest). To treat an infant or young child who has received an electrical shock:

1. Have someone call 911 while you attend to the child.
2. Check the child's breathing.
3. Begin CPR immediately if the child is not breathing.
4. Observe for, and treat, signs of shock and burns.
5. Have the child transported to a medical facility as quickly as possible.

9-3j Head Injuries

Head injury can occur from a bump, blow, or force that directly strikes the skull. Serious complications such as internal bleeding and swelling, can accompany any head injury, including those that may initially appear to be minor. These developments can occur within minutes, hours, or even several days following the initial injury (Bailey et al., 2012; Hockenberry & Wilson, 2012). Large-scale campaigns have recently been launched to increase public awareness and knowledge about the potential dangers of head injury and concussion. Early warning signs of mild to moderate head injury may include:

- repeated or forceful vomiting
- bleeding or clear fluid coming from nose or ears
- disorientation (e.g., confusion, aggressive behavior, apathy)
- loss of consciousness
- drowsiness
- severe headache

Symptoms associated with more severe head injury may appear immediately or several hours later, including:

- weakness or **paralysis**
- poor balance, coordination, or gait
- unequal size of the pupils of the eye (Figure 9–9)
- slurred speech
- blurred or double vision
- seizures
- an area of increasing swelling beneath the scalp
- unexplained restlessness or agitation

If any of these signs or symptoms are observed, call 911 to summon emergency medical services and contact the child's family immediately.

---

paralysis – *temporary or permanent loss of sensation, function, or voluntary movement of a body part.*

Children who receive even a minor blow or bump to the head should not be moved until it can be determined that there are no fractures or additional injuries. If the injury does not appear to be serious, the child should be encouraged to rest or play quietly for the next few hours. Always inform families of any blow or injury to a child's head regardless of how insignificant it may seem at the time. It is important to continue observing the child closely during the next 24 to 48 hours for any changes in behavior or appearance that may indicate the development of complications.

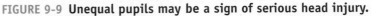
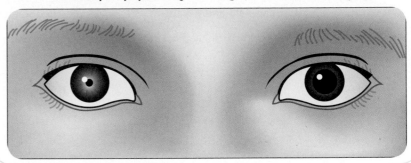

FIGURE 9-9 Unequal pupils may be a sign of serious head injury.

Scalp wounds have a tendency to bleed profusely, causing even minor injuries to appear more serious than they actually are. Therefore, when a child receives an injury to the scalp, it is important to avoid becoming overly alarmed at the sign of extensive bleeding. Pressure applied directly over the wound with a clean cloth or gauze dressing is usually sufficient to stop most bleeding. An ice pack can also be applied to the area to decrease swelling and pain. Families should be advised of the injury so they can continue to monitor the child's condition at home.

Did You Know...

that more than 1.7 million concussions are suffered in the United States each year? Children 0 to 14 years of age are at highest risk and account for nearly half a million annual emergency room visits for head injury.

9-3k Poisoning

Unintentional poisoning results when harmful substances have been inhaled, **ingested**, absorbed through the skin, or injected into the body. The majority of incidences occur in children under 6 and involve substances that have been swallowed (MMWR, 2012). Signs of poisoning may develop quickly or be delayed, and can include:

- nausea or vomiting
- abdominal cramps or diarrhea
- unusual odor to breath
- skin that feels cold and clammy
- burns or visible stains around the mouth, lips, or skin
- restlessness
- difficulty breathing
- convulsions
- confusion, disorientation, apathy, or listlessness
- loss of consciousness
- seizures

The emergency treatment for accidental poisoning is determined by the type of poison the child has ingested. For this reason, it is important to provide the name of the substance and time of exposure when contacting the Poison Control Center or emergency medical personnel. Poisons are divided into three basic categories: strong acids and **alkalis**, petroleum products, and all others. Examples are included in Table 9–2.

ingested – *the process of taking food or other substances into the body through the mouth.*
alkalis – *group of bases or caustic substances that are capable of neutralizing acids to form salts.*

TABLE 9–2 Poisonous Substances

Strong Acid and Alkalis	Petroleum Products	All Others
bathroom, drain, and oven cleaners	charcoal lighter	medicines
battery acid	cigarette lighter fluid	plants
dishwasher soaps	furniture polish and wax	berries
lye	gasoline	cosmetics
wart and corn remover	kerosene	nail polish remover
ammonia	naphtha	insecticides
bleach	turpentine	mothballs
	floor wax	weed killers
	lamp oil	

▶❚❚ **TeachSource** Video Connections

© 2015 Cengage Learning

Working with Children Who Have Physical Disabilities

Children's physical limitations may place them at higher risk for certain types of injuries and life-threatening conditions. For this reason, teachers who work in inclusive classrooms must be prepared to respond quickly in an emergency situation. As you watch the learning video, *Maddie: Positive Collaboration Between School Professionals and Parents to Serve a Student with Physical Disabilities* consider the following questions:

1. Which of the emergency conditions described in this chapter would you expect to encounter most often in an inclusive setting?

2. Why is a positive family-school partnership especially beneficially in these situations?

Watch on CourseMate.

If a child is suspected of swallowing a poisonous substance:

❭ Quickly check for redness or burns around the child's lips, mouth, and tongue. These are indications of a chemical burn, usually caused by strong acids or alkalis. Do not give the child anything to drink; do not make the child vomit.

❭ Smell the child's breath. If the poison is a petroleum product, the odor of gasoline or kerosene will be present. Do not give the child anything to drink; do not make the child vomit.

If the child is **conscious**:

❭ Quickly try to locate the container; it will provide clues about what the child has ingested. Also, try to estimate how much of the product the child may have swallowed and the approximate time when this incident may have occurred.

❭ If you cannot locate the container, do not delay in calling Poison Control.

❭ Call the nearest Poison Control Center (1-800-222-1222) or your city's emergency number (911) and follow their instructions.

❭ Observe the child closely for signs of shock and difficulty breathing.

❭ Do not give the child anything to eat or drink unless instructed to do so.

If the child is **unconscious**:

❭ Call 911 immediately to summon emergency medical assistance.

❭ Monitor the child's airway, breathing, and circulation; administer CPR if breathing stops or is absent.

❭ Do not give the child anything to eat or drink.

❭ Position the child in the recovery position (side-lying) to prevent choking on vomited material. Continue to observe the child for signs of breathing difficulty.

Always check with the Poison Control Center and follow their instructions before attempting to treat childhood poisoning. If the child begins to vomit, keep his head lowered to prevent aspiration and choking. Contact the child's family as soon as possible.

Did You Get It?

When you begin performing CPR on an infant who is not breathing, the first step should be to:

a. administer a series of quick chest compressions
b. remove any airway obstructions that can hinder breathing
c. shake the child to determine whether he or she is responsive
d. open the airway and breathe in

Take the full quiz on CourseMate.

9-4 Non–Life-Threatening Conditions

The majority of children's injuries and illnesses are not life-threatening but may require first aid. Teachers who have received proper training can administer this type of care, but they are not qualified or expected to provide comprehensive medical treatment. Initial first aid treatment of children's injuries is important for reducing complications and making children feel more comfortable until their family arrives. The remainder of this chapter addresses conditions typically encountered by young children that may require first aid care.

Did You Know...

that cleaning scrapes and abrasions from the center outward with an increasingly larger circular motion reduces the risk of infection?

9-4a Abrasions, Cuts, and Minor Skin Wounds

Minor cuts, scrapes, and abrasions are among the most common types of injury young children experience. First aid care is concerned primarily with the control of bleeding and the prevention of infection. To care for the child who has received a simple skin wound:

1. Follow universal infection control precautions, including the use of disposable gloves.
2. Apply direct pressure to the wound, using a clean cloth or sterile pad to stop any bleeding.
3. Wash the wound under running water for at least 5 minutes or until all foreign particles have been removed.
4. Cover the wound with a sterile bandage. A thin layer of antibiotic ointment can be applied to superficial abrasions if permitted.
5. Apply a cold pack, wrapped in a disposable paper towel or plastic bag, to the area; this can help slow bleeding and reduce pain and swelling.
6. Inform the child's family of the injury. Advise them to check on the child's tetanus immunization and to watch for signs of infection (e.g., warmth, redness, swelling, drainage).
7. Record the incident.

Puncture-type wounds and cuts that are deep or ragged require medical attention because of the increased risk of infection. Stitches may be needed to close a gash greater than 1/2 inch (1.3 cm), especially if it is located on the child's face, chest, or back.

9-4b Bites

Human and animal bites are painful and can lead to serious infection (Boat, 2012). The possibility of rabies should be considered with any animal bite that is unprovoked, unless the animal is known to be free of the virus. A suspected animal should be confined and observed by a veterinarian. In cases where the bite was provoked, the animal is not as likely to be rabid. First aid care for human and animal bites includes the following:

1. Follow universal infection control precautions, including the use of disposable gloves.
2. Allow the wound to bleed for a short while if the skin is broken (to remove any saliva) before applying direct pressure to stop bleeding.

▼ **Families must always be informed of children's injuries.**

© Cengage Learning

3. Cleanse the wound thoroughly with soap and water or hydrogen peroxide and cover with a clean dressing.
4. Notify the child's family and advise them to have the wound checked by the child's physician.
5. Notify local law enforcement authorities immediately if the injury is due to an animal bite; provide a description of the animal and its location (unless it is a classroom pet).
6. Record the incident.

Most insect bites cause little more than local skin irritations. However, some children are extremely sensitive to certain insects, especially bees, hornets, wasps, and spiders. Signs of severe allergic reaction (anaphylaxis) include:

- sudden difficulty breathing
- joint pain (delayed reaction)
- abdominal cramps
- vomiting
- fever
- red, swollen eyes
- hives or generalized itching
- shock
- weakness or unconsciousness
- swollen tongue

Allergic reactions to insect bites can be life-threatening and require immediate emergency treatment. (See the "9.3c Anaphylaxis: Life-Threatening Allergic Reaction" section in this chapter for emergency procedures.) First aid treatment for insect bites is aimed at relieving discomfort and preventing infection. If a stinger remains in the skin, an attempt should be made to remove it by scraping the area with the back of a flatware knife or clean credit card (removing with a tweezers may inject more venom into the skin). The area should then be washed and a cold pack applied to decrease swelling and pain. Calamine lotion or a paste of baking soda and water applied to the area will also provide temporary pain relief.

9-4c **Blisters**

A blister is a collection of infection-fighting fluid (white blood cells) that builds up beneath the skin's surface. Blisters most commonly develop from rubbing or friction, burns, or allergic reactions.

First aid care of blisters is aimed at protecting the affected area from infection. Efforts should be made to avoid breaking a blister. However, if it does break, wash the area with soap and water and cover with a bandage.

9-4d **Bruises**

Bruises result when small blood vessels rupture beneath the skin. They are often caused by falls, bumps, and blows. Fair-skinned children tend to bruise more easily. First aid care is designed to control subsurface bleeding and swelling. Apply a cold pack to the bruised area for 15 to 20 minutes and repeat three to four times during the next 24 hours. Later, warm moist packs can be applied several times daily to improve circulation and healing. Alert the child's family to watch for signs of infection or unusual bleeding if the bruising is extensive or severe.

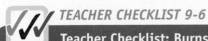

TEACHER CHECKLIST 9-6

Teacher Checklist: Burns—When to Call for Emergency Medical Assistance (911)

Always call for emergency medical assistance if:

- A child or elderly person is involved.
- The victim experiences any difficulty breathing.
- Burned areas are located on the face, head, neck, feet, hands, or genitalia.
- Multiple areas of the body have been burned.
- Burned area is larger than 2 to 3 inches (5.1 to 7.6 cm).
- Chemicals, electrical current, smoke, or an explosion has caused the burn.

TeachSource Digital Download Download from CourseMate.

9-4e Burns

Burns occur when body surfaces come in contact with heat, electrical current, or chemicals. Several factors affect the severity of an accidental burn and the need to call for emergency medical assistance, including the source, temperature of the source, affected body part or area, length of exposure, and victim's age and size (Teacher Checklist 9-6).

Burns are always considered more serious when they are sustained by children due to their smaller body surface area (De Young et al., 2012; Hockenberry & Wilson, 2012). Burns caused by heat are classified according to the degree (depth and extent) of tissue damage:

- first degree – Surface skin is red with some pain and swelling.
- second degree – Surface skin is red and blistered with swelling and severe pain.
- third degree – Burn is deep; skin and underlying tissues may be brown, white, or charred. Pain is often minimal, but these burns require emergency medical attention—call for help immediately.

First aid care of minor burns (first and second degree) that cover less than 3 inches (7.6 cm) of surface area includes the following:

1. Use caution to protect yourself from the heat source.
2. Quickly **submerge** the burned areas in cool water, hold under running water, or cover with a cool, wet towel for 5 to 10 minutes. Cool water temperatures reduce the depth of a burn as well as lessen swelling and pain.
3. Cover the burn with a sterile gauze dressing and tape in place. Do not use greasy ointments because dirt and bacteria can collect in these creams and increase the risk of infection.
4. Elevate the burned extremity to relieve discomfort.
5. Burns that involve feet, face, hands, or genitals, cover a large area (greater than 2 to 3 inches/5.1 to 7.6 cm) or cause moderate blistering are critical and require immediate medical attention. Families should be advised to contact the child's health care provider.

In the case of third degree burns, stop the burning process but do not attempt to cool the burn or to remove burnt clothing. Cover any open areas with a dry, sterile dressing and call immediately for emergency medical assistance.

Chemical burns should be rinsed for 10 to 15 minutes under cool, running water. Put on gloves and gently remove any clothing that may still have the chemical on it. Call for emergency medical assistance or the nearest Poison Control Center for further instructions. The child's family should also be advised to contact their health care provider.

Burns caused by smoke or electrical current require immediate medical attention and should not be cooled with water.

submerge – *to place in water*

9-4f Eye Injuries

Most eye injuries are not serious and can be treated by teachers. However, because eyes are delicate structures, it is important to know how to properly care for different types of injuries. Families should always be informed of any injury to a child's eye(s) so they can continue to observe and consult with a physician if they have concerns.

A sudden blow to the eye from a snowball, wooden block, or other hard object can be quite painful. First aid treatment includes the following:

1. Keep the child quiet.
2. Apply a cold pack to the eye for 15 minutes if there is no bleeding.
3. Use direct pressure to control any bleeding around the eye. Do not apply pressure to the eyeball itself. Cleanse and cover skin wounds with a sterile gauze pad.
4. Summon emergency medical assistance at once if the child complains of inability to see or is seeing spots or flashes of light.
5. Inform the child's family about any blow to the eye so they can continue to monitor the child's condition.
6. Record the incident.

Foreign particles such as sand, cornmeal, or specks of dust frequently find their way into children's eyes. Although children may want to rub their eyes, this must be discouraged to prevent the eyeball from becoming scratched. Spontaneous tearing is often sufficient to wash out the object. If the particle is visible, it can also be removed with the corner of a clean cloth or by flushing the eye with saline eye wash solution or lukewarm water. If the particle cannot be removed easily, the eye should be covered and medical attention sought.

An object that penetrates the eyeball must never be removed (Kelly & Reeves, 2012). Place a paper cup, funnel, or small cardboard box over both the object and the eye. Cover the uninjured eye with a gauze pad and secure both dressings (cup and gauze pad) in place by wrapping an elastic roller bandage around the head. Movement of the injured eyeball should be kept to a minimum and can be achieved by covering both eyes. Seek immediate medical treatment.

Did You Know...

that picking up or swinging children by their arms can easily cause joints to dislocate? This is a painful injury that requires prompt medical treatment.

A thin cut on the eye's surface can result from a piece of paper, toy, or child's fingernail. Injuries of this type cause severe pain and tearing. Both of the child's eyes should be covered with a gauze dressing and the child's family advised to seek immediate medical attention.

Chemical burns to a child's eye are very serious (Blackburn et al., 2012). Ask another staff member to call 911 immediately for emergency medical assistance so the child can be transported to the nearest medical facility. Begin immediately to flush the child's eye with lukewarm water or saline eye wash solution. Tip the child's head toward the affected eye and use a small bulb syringe or bottle to rinse the eye for at least 15 minutes. Meanwhile, contact the child's family.

9-4g Fractures

A fracture is a break or crack in a bone. It is always best to treat an injured extremity as if it were broken until the child can be examined by a health care provider. A child who sustains a mild break may be able to move the injured part and present few notable symptoms. The only way to confirm a fracture is by X-ray. Signs of a potential fracture may include:

- particular areas of extreme pain or tenderness
- an unusual shape or deformity of the bone
- a break in the skin with visible bone edges protruding
- swelling
- a change in skin color around the injury site
- numbness or a tingling sensation

A child who complains of pain after falling should not be moved, especially if a back or neck injury is suspected.

1. Have someone call 911 immediately for emergency medical assistance.
2. Keep the child warm and observe carefully for signs of shock.
3. Do not give the child anything to eat or drink in the event that surgery is necessary.
4. Stop any bleeding by applying direct pressure.
5. Contact the child's family and record the incident.

If no emergency medical help is available, only persons with prior first aid training should attempt to splint a fracture before the child is moved. Splints can be purchased from medical supply stores or improvised from items such as a rolled-up magazine, pillow or blanket, a ruler, or a piece of board. Never attempt to straighten a fractured bone. Call 911 at once if the injured extremity turns blue or pale. Cover open wounds with a sterile pad but do not attempt to clean the wound. Elevate the splinted part on a pillow and apply an ice pack to reduce swelling and pain. Observe the child closely for signs of shock and contact the child's family immediately so they can notify their physician.

> If a child shows any signs of a potential fracture, always treat the bone as if it were broken until ruled out by X-ray.

©the24studio/Shutterstock.com

9-4h Frostbite and Hypothermia

Frostbite results when body tissues freeze from exposure to extremely cold temperatures. Exposed areas such as ears, nose, fingers, and toes are especially prone to frostbite, particularly if clothing or shoes become wet. Frostbite can develop within minutes, causing the skin to take on a hard, waxy, gray-white appearance with or without blisters. For this reason, infants and young children should be monitored closely during cold weather so they don't remove hats, boots, or mittens. Initially, the child may experience considerable pain or have no discomfort. However, when tissues begin to warm, there is often a tingling and painful sensation. First aid treatment for minor frostbite consists of the following:

‣ Bring the child indoors and into a warm room.
‣ Remove wet clothing; replace with dry clothing or wrap the child in blankets for warmth.
‣ Do not rewarm the affected part(s) unless medical care is unavailable.
‣ Handle the frostbitten part(s) with care; avoid rubbing or massaging the area as this could further damage frozen tissue.
‣ Elevate the affected area(s) to ease pain and prevent swelling.
‣ Contact the child's family and encourage them to seek medical care for the child.
‣ Record the incident.

Exposure to cold temperatures can also cause **hypothermia**, a drop in body temperature that slows heart rate, respirations, and metabolism. This slowing of body functions reduces the amount of available oxygen and can lead to shivering, drowsiness, loss of consciousness, and cardiac arrest. Emergency medical personnel should be summoned at once.

hypothermia – *below-normal body temperature caused by overexposure to cold conditions.*

9-4i Heat Exhaustion and Heat Stroke

First aid treatment of a heat-related illness requires the teacher to distinguish between heat exhaustion and heat stroke. A child who has lost considerable fluid through sweating and is overheated may be suffering from **heat exhaustion**. The following symptoms would be observed:

- skin is pale, cool, and moist with perspiration
- weakness, dizziness, or fainting
- thirst
- nausea
- abdominal or muscle cramps
- headache
- normal or below-normal body temperature

Heat exhaustion is not considered life-threatening, but can become a serious condition if it is not treated quickly. It usually occurs when a child has been playing vigorously in extreme heat or humidity. First aid treatment for heat exhaustion is similar to that for shock:

1. Have the child lie down in a cool place.
2. Elevate the child's feet 8–10 inches (20–25 cm).
3. Loosen or remove the child's clothing.
4. Sponge the child's face and body with tepid (lukewarm) water or spray with cool water.
5. Offer frequent sips of cool water.

Heat stroke is a life-threatening condition that requires immediate treatment. The child's temperature begins to rise quickly and dangerously as perspiration stops and the body's temperature-regulating mechanism fails (Mattis & Yates, 2011). For example, children left in a parked car with the windows rolled up on a warm day (70°F and over) can quickly develop heat stroke and die (Figure 9–10). Symptoms of heat stroke include:

- high body temperature (102–106°F; 38.8–41.1°C)
- dry, flushed skin
- headache or confusion
- seizures
- diarrhea, abdominal cramps
- loss of consciousness
- shock

Emergency treatment for heat stroke is aimed at cooling the child as quickly as possible:

1. Call 911 to summon emergency medical assistance at once.
2. Move the child to a cool place and remove outer clothing.
3. Place the child in a shallow tub of cold water or gently spray her with a garden hose. Do not leave child unattended!
4. Elevate the child's legs to decrease the potential for shock.
5. Offer small sips of cool water only if the child is fully conscious; do not force.
6. Notify the child's family and record the incident.

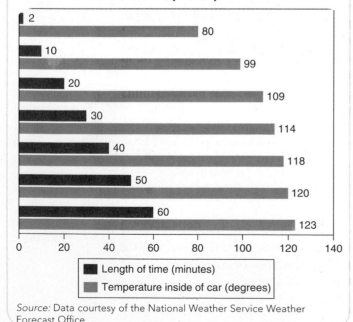

FIGURE 9–10 How quickly temperatures rise inside a closed car when it is 80°F (26.7°C) outside.

Length of time (minutes) / Temperature inside of car (degrees)

2	80
10	99
20	109
30	114
40	118
50	120
60	123

Source: Data courtesy of the National Weather Service Weather Forecast Office.

----

heat exhaustion – *overheating that occurs when a person is exposed to high outdoor temperatures. and humidity during vigorous activity*
heat stroke – *failure of the body's sweating reflex to function properly during exposure to high temperatures; causes body temperature to rise*

9-4j Nosebleeds

Accidental bumps, allergies, nose picking, or sinus congestion can all cause a child's nose to bleed. Most nosebleeds are not serious and can be stopped quickly. However, if a nosebleed continues for more than 30 minutes, get medical help. To stop a nosebleed, do the following:

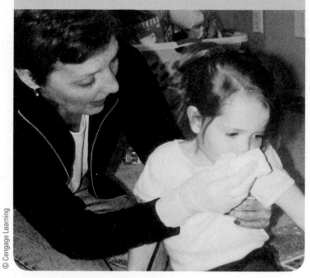

▼ **Firmly grasp and squeeze the child's nostrils to stop a nosebleed.**

© Cengage Learning

1. Place the child in a sitting position, with his head tilted slightly forward, to prevent any swallowing of blood. Ask the child to breathe through her mouth.
2. Follow universal infection control precautions, including the use of disposable gloves.
3. Firmly grasp the child's nostrils (lower half) and squeeze together for at least 5 minutes before releasing the pressure.
4. If bleeding continues, pinch the nostrils together for another 10 minutes.
5. Once the bleeding has stopped, avoid nose-blowing and encourage the child to play quietly for the next hour or so to prevent the bleeding from resuming.
6. Advise parents to discuss the problem with the child's health care provider if nosebleeds occur repeatedly.
7. Record the incident.

9-4k Seizures

Infants and young children experience seizures for a variety of reasons. Simple precautionary measures can be taken during and immediately after a seizure to protect a child from injury and should include the following:

1. Call 911 for emergency medical assistance if this is the first time a child has experienced a seizure. If the child has a known seizure disorder, call for emergency help if the seizure lasts longer than 3 to 4 minutes or the child experiences severe difficulty breathing or stops breathing.
2. Encourage the other children and adults to remain calm.
3. Carefully lower the child to the floor. Protect the child's head from striking the floor or nearby objects by placing a small pillow or item of soft clothing under the child's head.
4. Move furniture and other objects out of the way.
5. Do not hold the child down.
6. Do not attempt to force any protective device into the child's mouth.
7. Loosen tight clothing around the child's neck and waist to make breathing easier.
8. Observe closely to make sure the child is breathing.
9. Place the child in the recovery position (side-lying) with head slightly elevated when the seizure ends. This prevents choking by allowing oral secretions to drain out of the mouth.
10. Inform the child's family and record the incident.

When the seizure has ended, move the child to a quiet area and encouraged him to rest or sleep. An adult should continue to monitor the child closely.

9-4l Splinters

Most splinters under the skin's surface can be easily removed with a sterilized needle and tweezers. (Only bleach or alcohol should be used to clean the instruments.) Clean the skin with soap and water or alcohol before and after removing the splinter. Cover the area with a bandage. If the splinter is very deep, do not attempt to remove it; inform the child's family to seek medical attention and to make sure the child's tetanus immunization is current.

9-4m Sprains

A sprain is caused by injury to the ligaments and tissue surrounding a joint and often results in pain and considerable swelling. In most cases, only an X-ray can confirm whether an injury is a sprain or fracture. If there is any doubt, it is always best to splint the injury and treat it as if it were broken. Elevate the injured part and apply ice packs intermittently for 15 to 20 minutes at a time for several hours. Notify the child's family and encourage them to have the child examined by a physician.

9-4n Tick Bites

Ticks are small, oval-shaped insects that generally live in wooded areas and on wild animals and dogs. On humans, ticks frequently attach themselves to the scalp or base of the neck. However, the child is seldom aware of the tick's presence. Diseases, such as Rocky Mountain spotted fever and Lyme disease, are rare but serious complications of a tick bite (Hamlen, 2012). If a child develops chills, fever, or rash following a known tick bite, medical treatment should be sought at once.

Ticks must be removed carefully. Grasp the tick closely to the skin with tweezers, pulling steadily and straight out to remove all body parts; do not squeeze or twist. Wash the area thoroughly with soap and water and apply a disinfectant such as alcohol. The child's family should be advised to observe the site closely for several days and to contact their health care provider if any signs of infection or rash develop.

9-4o Tooth Emergencies

The most common injuries to children's teeth involve chipping or loosening of a tooth. Blood may be involved, so universal infection control precautions must be followed when caring for the child or handling the tooth. A tooth that has been knocked loose by a blow or fall will often retighten itself within several days. Care should be taken to keep the tooth and gum tissue clean, avoid chewing on hard foods, and watch for signs of infection (redness, swelling).

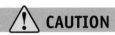 **CAUTION**

To avoid accidental choking, do not attempt to reinsert the tooth into the socket or have a child hold the tooth in place.

If a tooth has been completely dislodged, the child should be seen by a dentist and monitored for signs of infection. Although dentists will seldom attempt to replace a baby tooth, it is important to save the tooth and send it home with the child. Dentists are more apt to reimplant children's permanent teeth, but this process requires prompt emergency treatment to be successful.

- Rinse out the tooth socket (hole remaining in the gum); apply direct pressure to stop bleeding.
- Handle the tooth with care; do not to touch the root-end (part beneath the gum).
- Place the tooth in a small cup of milk or water; if this isn't available, wrap the tooth in a damp cloth.
- Get the child to a dentist or emergency room as quickly as possible (Turkistani & Hanno, 2011).

Did You Get It?

What is not a critical factor in determining whether or not to call for emergency assistance for burns?

a. the size of the burns
b. expressed pain associated with the burns (the amount of pain a child is experiencing)
c. specific location of the burns
d. degree of blistering associated with the burns

Take the full quiz on CourseMate.

PARTNERING with FAMILIES

Poison Prevention in the Home

Dear Families,

Children under the age of 6 are the most frequent victims of unintentional poisonings. Their curiosity and limited understanding often lead them unknowingly into risky situations. In many households, items such as cleaning products, garden chemicals, automobile waxes, charcoal lighter, lamp oil, and medications are commonly left in places accessible to young children. Often, simple precautions can be taken to make children's environments safe.

▶ Always place potentially dangerous substances in a locked cabinet. Don't rely on your child's ability to "know better."

▶ Supervise children closely whenever using harmful products. Take them with you if the doorbell rings or if you must leave the room.

▶ Teach children not to put anything into their mouths unless it is given to them by an adult.

▶ Test the paint on your house, walls, children's furniture, and toys to be sure it doesn't contain lead. Contact the National Lead Information Center for information (1-800-424-LEAD).

▶ Check before purchasing plants and flowers (indoor and outdoor) to make certain they are not poisonous.

▶ Insist that vitamins and medications, including those purchased over-the-counter, are in child-resistant containers. Store them in a locked cabinet.

▶ Post the number of the nearest Poison Control Center near the telephone.

▶ Caution visitors to keep purses, suitcases, and backpacks out of children's reach.

CLASSROOM CORNER

Teacher Activities

Preventing Burns

(**NHES** PreK–2; National Health Education Standards 5.2.1 and 5.2.2)

Concept: There are things that are safe to touch and play with and other things that can hurt you.

Learning Objectives

▶ Children will be able to identify items that are safe to touch and other items that are not safe.

▶ Children will explain what to do if they aren't sure that an item is safe to touch.

Supplies

▶ pictures of a stove, lighter, matches, campfire, candle, barbeque grill, ball, car, apple, crayons, a stuffed toy, and a block

▶ two pieces of string (long enough to make two big circles to sort the cards in)

▶ picture of a smiling face and a frowning face

Learning Activities

▶ Read and discuss one of the following books:

• *Fire Fighters* by Robert Maass

(continued)

CLASSROOM CORNER

Teacher Activities *(continued)*

- *Tonka Fire Truck to the Rescue* by Ann Martin
- *What If There Is a Fire?* by Anara Guard

▶ Tell the children you are going to talk about some items that are safe to touch and play with and others that aren't safe and can hurt them.

▶ Hold up the picture cards and talk about each item.

▶ Tell the children they are to sort the picture cards according to items that are safe to touch and those that are not. Put the smiling face in the middle of one circle and the frowning face in the middle of the other.

▶ Call a child to come up and pick a card and tell the other children if it is a safe item to touch and play with or an unsafe item. Continue until all cards have been sorted.

▶ Tell the children if they are not sure an item is safe or not to ask a grownup.

Evaluation

▶ Children will name at least two items safe to touch and two items they should not touch.

▶ Children will state what to do when they aren't sure if an object is safe to touch.

Additional lesson plans for grades 3–5 are available on CourseMate.

Summary

▶ Written emergency policies and procedures enable teachers to respond quickly and effectively to children's injuries and illnesses.
- Plans should include: personnel who are trained in first aid and CPR and are available at all times when children are in attendance; emergency telephone numbers; and first aid supplies

▶ Emergency care is administered for life-threatening conditions. First aid treatment is provided for conditions not considered to be life-threatening.
- Teachers never diagnosis or offer medical advice.
- Families are responsible for obtaining follow-up medical treatment after initial emergency or first aid care has been administered.

▶ Life-threatening conditions, such as severe bleeding, absence of breathing, shock, and head injuries require immediate emergency treatment.

▶ Treatment for life-threatening conditions, such as abrasions, fractures, burns, and frost bite is aimed at alleviating pain and further complications.

Terms to Know

Good Samaritan Law *p. 239*
aspiration *p. 242*
recovery position *p. 242*
elevate *p. 247*
sterile *p. 248*

resuscitation *p. 249*
paralysis *p. 250*
ingested *p. 251*
alkalis *p. 251*
submerge *p. 255*

hypothermia *p. 257*
heat exhaustion *p. 258*
heat stroke *p. 258*

Chapter Review

A. By Yourself

1. Complete each of the statements with a word selected from the following list. Take the first letter from each answer and place it in the appropriate space following question (j) to spell out one of the basic principles of first aid.

activate	evaluate	emergency
breathing	plans	rescue breaths
diagnose	pressure	anaphylaxis
elevate	responsible	

    a. Always check to be sure the child is _____.

    b. The immediate care given for life-threatening conditions is called _____ care.

    c. Schools and early childhood programs should develop _____ for handling emergencies.

    d. If an infant is found unconscious and not breathing, immediately give 30 chest compressions followed by 2 _____.

    e. The first step in providing emergency care is to quickly _____ the child's condition.

    f. Bleeding can be stopped by applying direct _____.

    g. If a child is seriously injured, you would immediately _____ emergency medical services (EMS) by calling 911.

    h. Families are _____ for arranging follow-up medical treatment for a child's injuries.

    i. To treat a child for shock, you would _____ the child's legs 8 to 10 inches.

    j. Teachers never _____ or give medical advice.

    A basic principle of first aid is _ _ _ _ _ _ _ _ _ _.

2. Explain the Good Samaritan Law and the purpose it serves.

3. What clues would help you determine if a child has swallowed a petroleum-based liquid or an acid/strong alkali?

4. Describe the classification of burns and how each level should be treated.

B. As a Group

1. Explain why a child who has fallen and bumped his head must be closely monitored for the next 48 hours despite the fact that he appears to be okay.

2. Assume that you are the teacher in the following scenarios. Role-play how you would respond:
    a. Child is having a nose bleed.
    b. Child appears to be experiencing a seizure.
    c. Toddler is choking on a bead that she found on the floor.
    d. Child is having an acute asthma attack.
    e. Child was pushed off of a piece of playground equipment and fell several feet to the ground; child appears disoriented, is pale, and has cool, clammy skin.

3. Discuss why you wouldn't begin the Heimlich maneuver immediately on a child who was choking but still able to cough. At what point would you initiate this emergency measure?

4. Describe how a teacher would determine if a child who has diabetes was experiencing hypoglycemia or hyperglycemia. How does the treatment of each differ?

Case Study

It was a beautiful spring morning and Myesha and Tyrell had taken their class of eager 4-year-olds outside to work in the school's newly established garden. The children had been reading books about flowers and vegetables for several weeks, purchased plants and seeds at a local market, and even helped to prepare the soil for planting. Today, they were going to weed and water the rows of lettuce, cucumbers, squash, and tomato plants that were beginning to grow. Myesha looked up from where she was working with the children and saw Jade running toward her with the watering can. Before Jade reached the garden gate, she suddenly dropped the can, fell to the sidewalk, and appeared to be having a seizure. Tyrell ran to check on Jade while Myesha tried to calm the other children.

1. What immediate measures should Tyrell take to care for Jade?

2. In what ways would his response differ if Jade had a known history of seizures or if she had never experienced a seizure prior to this one?

3. Should he notify Jade's family? At what point? Why?

4. If Jade's seizure continues longer than 3 to 4 minutes, what should the teachers do?

5. What information should Tyrell note during the seizure, observe afterwards, and record in Jade's file?

Application Activities

1. Complete basic CPR and first aid courses. Volunteer to assist with first aid trainings at local school or early childhood program.

2. Design a poster or bulletin board illustrating emergency first aid for a young child who is choking. Offer your project to a local school or early childhood program where it can be displayed for families to read.

3. Divide the students into small groups. Discuss and demonstrate the emergency care or first aid treatment for each of the following situations. A child who:
   - burned several fingers on a hot plate
   - ate de-icing pellets
   - splashed turpentine in her eyes
   - fell from a climbing gym
   - is choking on popcorn
   - slammed fingers in a door
   - is found chewing on an extension cord

4. Learn how to use an EpiPen and know what precautions need to be taken.

5. Observe two to three teachers at five different schools or early childhood programs during recess or outdoor time. Record the number of children who experience an injury during this period, the type of injury sustained, and the nature of teacher supervision (i.e., proximity, attentiveness, response). Summarize your findings. Provide recommendations for measures that can be taken to prevent similar injuries in the future and for teacher inservice training.

◗ Helpful Web Resources

Children's Safety Network (CSN)	http://www.childrenssafetynetwork.org
International Bicycle Fund (bicycle safety materials)	http://www.ibike.org/education
Learn CPR (children)	http://depts.washington.edu/learncpr/childrencpr.html
Learn CPR (infants)	http://depts.washington.edu/learncpr/infantcpr.html
Safe Kids Worldwide	http://www.safekids.org
National Safety Council	http://www.nsc.org
PoisonPrevention.org	http://www.poisonprevention.org

Visit the Education CourseMate for this textbook to access the eBook, Did You Get It? quizzes, Digital Downloads, TeachSource Video Cases, flashcards, and more. Go to CengageBrain.com to log in, register, or purchase access.

◗ References

Allen, K., Henselman, K., Laird, B., Quiñones, A., & Reutzel, T. (2012). Potential life-threatening events in schools involving rescue inhalers, epinephrine autoinjectors, and glucagon delivery devices. Reports from school nurses, *The Journal of School Nursing*, 28(1), 47–55.

American Public Health Association (APHA) and American Academy of Pediatrics (AAP). (2011). *Caring for our children: National health and safety performance standards for out-of-home care*, (3rd ed.). Washington, DC. Available online at http://nrckids.org/CFOC3/index.html.

American Diabetes Association. (2012). Safe at school. Accessed on June 21, 2012 from http://www.diabetes.org/living-with-diabetes/parents-and-kids/diabetes-care-at-school.

American Heart Association (AHA). (2010). 2010 American Heart Association guidelines for cardiopulmonary resuscitation and emergency cardiovascular care, *Circulation*, 122, S862–S875.

Bailey, B., Liesemer, K., Statler, K., Riva-Cambrin, J., & Bratton, S. (2012). Monitoring and prediction of intracranial hypertension in pediatric traumatic brain injury: Clinical factors and initial head computed tomography, *Journal of Trauma & Acute Care Surgery*, 72(1), 263–270.

Banghart, P. & Kreader, J. (2012). *What can CCDF learn from the research on children's health and safety in child care?* Urban Institute. Office of Planning, Research, and Evaluation. U.S. Department of Health & Human Services. Accessed June 21, 2012 from http://www.acf.hhs.gov/programs/opre/resource/what-can-ccdf-learn-from-the-research-on-childrens-health-and-safety-in-child.

Berg, M., Schexnayder, S., Chameides, L., Terry, M., Donoghue, A., Hickey, R., Berg, R., Sutton, R., & Hazinski, M. (2010). Pediatric basic life support: 2010 American Heart Association guidelines for cardiopulmonary resuscitation and emergency cardiovascular care, *Pediatrics*, 126(5), e1345–e1360.

Blackburn, J., Levitan, E., MacLennan, P., Owsley, C., & McGwin, G. (2012). The epidemiology of chemical eye injuries, *Current Eye Research*, 37(9), 787–793.

Boat, B., Dixon, C., Pearl, E., Thieken, L., & Bucher, S. (2012). Pediatric dog bite victims, *Clinical Pediatrics*, 51(5), 473–477.

Copeland, K., Sherman, S., Kendeigh, C., Kalkwarf, H., & Saelens, B. (2012). Societal values and policies may curtail preschool children's physical activity in child care centers, *Pediatrics*, 129(2), 265–274.

De Young, A., Kenardy, J., Cobham, V., & Kimble, R. (2012). Prevalence, comorbidity, and course of trauma in young burn-injured children, *Journal of Child Psychology & Psychiatry*, 53(1), 56–63.

Ercan, H., Ozen, A., Karatepe, H., Berber, M., & Cengizlier, R. (2012). Primary school teacher's knowledge about and attitudes toward anaphylaxis, *Pediatric Allergy & Immunology*. Advanced online publication. DOI:10.1111/j.1399-3038.2012.01307.x.

Hamlen, R. (2012). Tick-borne infections—A growing public health threat to school-age children. Prevention steps that school personnel can take, *NASN School Nurse*, 27(2), 94–100.

Hockenberry, M., & Wilson, D. (2012). *Wong's essentials of pediatric nursing*. (9th ed.). New York: Mosby.

Kaushal, P., Brown, D., Lander, L., Brietzke, S., & Shah, R. (2011). Aspirated foreign bodies in pediatric patients, 1968–2010: A comparison between the United States and other countries, *International Journal of Pediatric Otorhinolaryngology*, 75(10), 1322–1326.

Kelly, S., & Reeves, G. (2012). Penetrating eye injuries from writing instruments, *Clinical Ophthalmology*, 6, 41–44.

Laosse, O., Gilchrist, J., & Rudd, R. (2012). Drowning — United States, 2005–2009, *Morbidity & Mortality Weekly Report (MMWR)*, 61(19), 344–347.

Marotz, L. (2000). Childhood and classroom injuries. In J. L. Frost (ed.), *Children and injuries*. Tuscon, AZ: Lawyers & Judges Publishing Co.

Mattis, J., & Yates, A. (2011). Heat stroke: Helping patients keep their cool, *Nurse Practitioner*, 36(5), 48–52.

Morbidity & Mortality Weekly Report (MMWR). (2012). Vital signs: Unintentional injury deaths among persons aged 0–19 years — United States, 2000–2009. Accessed on June 21, 2012 from http://www.cdc.gov/mmwr/preview /mmwrhtml/mm61e0416a1.htm.

Pawankar, R., Canonica, G., Holgate, S., & Lockey, R. (2012). Allergic diseases and asthma: A major global health concern, *Current Opinion in Allergy & Clinical Immunology*, 12(1), 39–41.

Price, K., Plante, C., Goudreau, S., Boldo, E., Perron, S., & Snargiassi, A. (2012). Risk of childhood asthma prevalence attributable to residential proximity to major roads in Montreal, Canada, *Canadian Journal of Public Health*, 103(2), 113–118.

Sih, T., Bunnag, C., Ballali, S., Lauriello, M., & Bellussi, L. (2012). Nuts and seed: A natural yet dangerous foreign body, *International Journal of Pediatric Otorhinolaryngology*, 76(Suppl.1), S49–S52.

Turkistani, J., & Hanno, A. (2011). Recent trends in the management of dentoalveolar traumatic injuries to primary and young permanent teeth, *Dental Traumatology*, 27(1), 46–54.

chapter **10** # Maltreatment of Children: Abuse and Neglect

Juanmonino/Getty Images

267

▶ **#1 a, b, and c:** Promoting child development and learning
▶ **#2 a, b, and c:** Building family and community relationships
▶ **#3 a, c, and d:** Observing, documenting, and assessing to support young children and families
▶ **#4 a and c:** Using developmentally effective approaches to connect with children and families
▶ **#5 c:** Using content knowledge to build meaningful curriculum
▶ **#6 a, b, c, and e:** Becoming a professional

Learning Objectives

After studying this chapter, you should be able to:

LO 10-1 Explain the significance of Public Law 93-247.

LO 10-2 Describe how discipline and punishment differ.

LO 10-3 Provide an example of each form of abuse (physical, emotional/verbal, sexual) and neglect (physical and emotional/psychological).

LO 10-4 Describe factors that may perpetuate abusive or neglectful acts.

LO 10-5 Discuss the protective steps programs can take to avoid allegations of abuse.

LO 10-6 Identify individuals who are mandated by law to report abuse and neglect.

LO 10-7 Explain how teachers can help children who have been maltreated.

For many reasons, the true extent of **abuse** and **neglect** may never be known. Although an estimated three million cases are reported to investigative authorities in the United States each year, many more incidences are unreported. An average of four children die each day from maltreatment, but the actual number may be considerably higher than the data reveal (Child Welfare Information Gateway, 2013). Thousands of additional children are known to suffer serious and sometimes permanent physical and emotional injuries that are also never reported (Leventhal, Martin, & Gaither, 2012).

Did You Know...

that hospital emergency rooms in the United States treat more than 84 abused children with injuries (many uninsured) every hour?

Child maltreatment creates significant emotional and economic burdens for the individuals involved as well as for their communities and society at large. Researchers have estimated the lifetime costs, based on 1,740 confirmed cases for one year, to be approximately $124 million, or $210,012 per victim (significantly more than the costs associated with stroke or diabetes 2) (Fang et al., 2012). State and local agency resources are strained by the number of reported cases (more than six cases every minute) they must investigate. Community expenditures for prevention programs, interventions, and court costs continue to consume a significant portion of their annual budgets.

Although numbers are helpful for understanding the magnitude of child maltreatment, they overlook the enormous human toll and impact this problem creates. Witnessing or experiencing violence affects children's brain development and wires it for survival rather than for

abuse – *to mistreat, attack, or cause harm to another individual.*

neglect – *failure of a parent or legal guardian to properly care for and meet the basic needs of a child under 18 years of age.*

learning. These changes cause children who have been abused to have long-term difficulty with attention, recall, forming positive social relationships, and understanding emotions (Hart & Rubia, 2012). Researchers have also discovered that children who are abused develop permanent changes in their DNA that increase the risk for illness and chronic disease (Keeshin, Cronholm, & Strawn, 2012).

10-1 Historical Developments

Accounts of child abuse date from ancient times to the present. Throughout history, young children, especially those who have developmental disabilities, have suffered abusive and neglectful treatment. They have also been subjected to cultural practices that by today's standards would be considered inhumane. In many societies, children had no rights or privileges whatsoever, including the right to live.

One of the first child abuse cases in this country to attract widespread public attention involved a young girl named Mary Ellen. Friends and neighbors were concerned about the regular beatings Mary Ellen received from her adoptive parents. However, in 1874, there were no organizations responsible for dealing with the problems of child abuse and neglect. Consequently, Mary Ellen's friends contacted the New York Society for the Prevention of Cruelty to Animals on the basis that she was a human being and, therefore, also a member of the animal kingdom. Her parents were found guilty of cruelty to animals and eventually Mary Ellen was removed from their home. This incident brought gradual recognition to the need for establishing some form of protection for the many maltreated and abandoned children in this country.

It wasn't until 1961 that the subject of child abuse once again received national attention despite the fact that it continued to occur. For a period of years, Dr. C. Henry Kempe studied various aspects of child abuse and was concerned about children whose lives were endangered. He first introduced the phrase "battered child syndrome" in 1961 during a national conference that he organized to address problems related to the harsh treatment of children (Kempe & Helfer, 1982).

The passage of Public Law (PL) 93-247, the Child Abuse Prevention and Treatment Act (CAPTA), on January 31, 1974, signified a turning point in the history of child abuse and neglect. For the first time, national attention was drawn to the issue of childhood maltreatment. This law created the National Center on Child Abuse and Neglect, and required individual states to establish a central agency with legal authority to investigate and prosecute incidences of abuse and neglect. PL 93-247 also mandated states to develop policies, procedures, definitions, and laws that addressed maltreatment. In October 1996, CAPTA was reauthorized and amended to more clearly define circumstances related to the withholding of medical treatment in life-threatening situations. Changes in the 2003 reauthorization required states to expand their services to include adoption, foster care, abandoned infants, and family violence prevention. Additional funding was also appropriated for child protective worker training and efforts to strengthen collaboration among community agencies (Child Welfare Information Gateway, 2011). CAPTA was last reauthorized and amended in December 2010.

Although child abuse and neglect have occurred throughout history, it is only recently that public attention has acknowledged the magnitude of this problem. And, only now are professionals realizing the full impact and prolonged effects that maltreatment has on children's development.

Did You Get It?

The Child Abuse Prevention and Treatment Act (CAPTA) authorized and mandated that _____ establish centralized agencies tasked to investigate and prosecute instances of child maltreatment.

a. the federal government
b. individual states
c. local governments
d. counties

Take the full quiz on CourseMate.

10-2 Discipline vs. Punishment

The term **discipline** is derived from the word disciple and refers to the act of teaching or guiding. When used appropriately, discipline can be effective for helping children learn socially acceptable behavior. However, when it is used improperly or involves threats, fear, or harsh physical **punishment**, it teaches children only anger and violence.

For decades, the right to punish or discipline children as families saw fit was considered a parental privilege. Consequently, outsiders often overlooked or ignored incidences of cruelty to children so as not to interfere in a family's personal affairs. However, public attitudes regarding family privacy and the rights of families to discipline children as they wished began to change. Educators, health and law enforcement professionals, neighbors, and concerned friends grew intolerant of the abusive and neglectful treatment of young children. They began to speak out against such behavior and to serve as advocates for innocent children who were being victimized by adults.

One of the most difficult aspects of this problem is deciding at what point discipline or punishment becomes maltreatment. For example, when does a spanking or verbal **reprimand** constitute abuse? Is sending a child to his room without dinner neglect? In an attempt to establish clear guidelines, federal legislation forced states to define abuse and neglect and to establish policies and procedures for addressing individual cases.

Did You Get It?

One of the most difficult aspects involved in identifying and prosecuting child maltreatment cases is:

- **a.** why these acts occur
- **b.** at what point the line between reasonable discipline and abuse is crossed
- **c.** when, where, and how often these acts occur
- **d.** whether there is sufficient evidence to prosecute and convict the perpetrator

Take the full quiz on CourseMate.

10-3 Abuse and Neglect

Child maltreatment refers to any situation or environment in which a child is not safe due to inadequate protection, exposure to hazardous conditions, exploitation, or harm intentionally inflicted by adults. For legal purposes, a child is defined as an individual under 18 years of age. The most commonly recognized categories of maltreatment include:

▼ A child is legally defined as an individual under the age of 18 years.

© Cengage Learning

- physical abuse
- emotional or verbal abuse
- sexual abuse
- physical neglect
- emotional or psychological neglect

Physical abuse is the most common form of abuse and is characterized by a range of visible, non-accidental injuries, such as cuts, burns, welts, fractures, scratches, and missing hair (Figure 10–1). The explanations families provide for these injuries are often inconsistent or unreasonable based

discipline – *training or enforced obedience that corrects, shapes, or develops acceptable patterns of behavior.*
punishment – *a negative response to what the observer considers to be wrong or inappropriate behavior; may involve physical or harsh treatment.*
reprimand – *to scold or discipline for unacceptable behavior.*
physical abuse – *injuries, such as welts, burns, bruises, or broken bones, that are caused intentionally.*

on the child's age or developmental stage (Petska, Sheets, & Knox, 2013; Debelle, 2012). A combination of new and older or untreated injuries may suggest repeated abuse. In almost every instance, observable changes in the child's behavior, including shyness, fearfulness, passiveness, anger, aggression, or apprehension will accompany physical injuries (Teacher Checklist 10-1).

Abusive head trauma, formerly known as **shaken baby syndrome**, is a form of physical abuse most often observed in infants and young children. It is caused by vigorously shaking or tossing a child into the air, often because of persistent crying (Figure 10–2). The whiplash motion causes internal bleeding and trauma to the infant's brain that can result in blindness, deafness, fractures, learning disabilities, seizures, and death (Vitale et al., 2012). Prevention of this senseless tragedy requires adults to understand that shaking a child can have devastating effects and that crying is normal because it is an infant's primary mode of communication.

Physical abuse frequently begins as an innocent act of frustration or punishment. In other words, most adults do not set out to intentionally harm a child. However, in the process of disciplining the child, quick tempers and uncontrollable anger may lead to punishment that is severe and sufficiently violent to cause injuries and sometimes even death. In some cases, this outburst represents a one-time, regrettable incidence of poor judgment, while in others maltreatment may become a repetitive pattern. Regardless of the circumstances, the hurtful treatment of children is never considered acceptable.

Emotional or **verbal abuse** occurs when caregivers repeatedly and unpredictably criticize, verbally assault, ignore, or belittle a child's behavior or achievements. In many cases, adult demands and expectations are unrealistic given the child's age and developmental abilities. Chronic exposure to negative statements, such as "Why can't you ever do things right?" or "I knew you were too stupid" have lifelong effects on children's emotional and intellectual development (Rosenkranz, Muller, & Henderson, 2012). Verbal assaults frequently turn into physical abuse over time. Toddlers and preschoolers are the most frequent victims of emotional abuse because they trust adults, do not always fully understand adult expectations, and are relatively defenseless.

Notable changes in a child's behavior are often an early indicator of verbal abuse

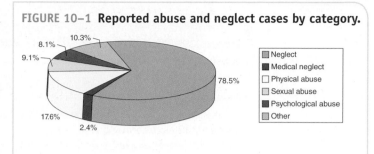

FIGURE 10–1 Reported abuse and neglect cases by category.

10.3%
8.1%
9.1%
78.5%
17.6%
2.4%

- Neglect
- Medical neglect
- Physical abuse
- Sexual abuse
- Psychological abuse
- Other

Source: U.S. Department of Health and Human Services, Administration for Children and Families, Administration on Children, Youth and Families, Children's Bureau. (2012). *Child Maltreatment 2011.* Retrieved from http://www.acf.hhs.gov/sites/default/files/cb/cm11.pdf.

Did You Know...

the rate of arrest for juvenile crime is nearly 60 percent higher among children who have experienced abuse or neglect?

FIGURE 10–2 Tossing or shaking young children can cause permanent brain injury.

---

shaken baby syndrome – *forceful shaking of a baby that causes head trauma, internal bleeding, and sometimes death.*
Emotional abuse – *repeated humiliation, ridicule, or threats directed toward another individual.*
verbal abuse – *to attack another individual with words.*

TEACHER CHECKLIST 10-1

Identifying Signs of Abuse and Neglect

Physical Abuse

- has frequent or unexplained injuries (e.g., burns, fractures, bruises, bites, eye, or head injuries)
- complains frequently of pain
- wears clothing to hide injuries; clothing may be inappropriate for weather conditions
- reports harsh treatment
- is often late or absent; arrives too early or stays after dismissal from school
- seems unusually fearful of adults, especially parents
- appears malnourished or dehydrated
- avoids logical explanations for injuries
- is withdrawn, anxious, or uncommunicative or may be outspoken, disruptive, and aggressive
- lacks affection, both giving and seeking
- receives inappropriate food, beverages, or drugs

Emotional/Verbal Abuse

- seems generally unhappy; seldom smiles or laughs
- is aggressive and disruptive or unusually shy and withdrawn
- reacts without emotion to unpleasant statements and actions
- displays behaviors that are unusually adult-like or child-like
- has delayed growth or emotional and intellectual development

Sexual Abuse

- wears underclothing that may be torn, stained, or bloody
- complains of pain or itching in the genital area
- has symptoms of venereal disease
- has difficulty getting along with other children, e.g., withdrawn, infant-like, anxious
- has rapid weight loss or gain
- experiences sudden decline in school performance
- engages in delinquent behaviors, including prostitution, running away, alcoholism, or drug abuse
- is fascinated with body parts, uses sexual terms and talks about sexual activities that are unfamiliar to children of this age

Physical Neglect

- has a bad odor from dirty clothing, body, or hair; repeatedly arrives unclean
- is in need of medical or dental care; may have untreated injuries or illness
- is often hungry; begs or steals food while at school
- dresses inappropriately for weather conditions; shoes and clothing often sized too small or too large
- is chronically tired; falls asleep at school, lacks the energy to play with other children
- has difficulty getting along with other children; spends much time alone

Emotional/Psychological Neglect

- performs poorly in school
- appears apathetic, withdrawn, and inattentive
- is frequently absent or late to school
- uses any means to gain teacher's attention and approval
- seldom participates in extracurricular activities
- engages in delinquent behaviors, e.g., stealing, vandalism, sexual misconduct, abuse of drugs or alcohol

TABLE 10-1   Tips for Determining If Children Are Ready to Be Left Home Alone

- Has your child expressed interest in staying home alone?
- Does your child typically understand and abide by family rules?
- Is your child reliable and able to handle responsibility in a mature manner?
- Does your child handle unexpected events in a positive way?
- Is your child able to entertain herself for long periods of time or does she require constant supervision?
- Have you rehearsed safety and emergency procedures so your child knows how to respond in the event of a fire, an unwanted telephone call, or someone knocking at the front door?
- Does your child know how to reach you if necessary? Is there another adult your child can contact if you are not available?
- Has your child experienced being left home alone for short periods?
- Does your child have any fears that would be problematic if he were left alone?

Teacher Checklist 10-1. Careful observation and documentation of adult-child interactions can be useful for identifying the potential signs of emotional maltreatment. Unlike the immediate harm caused by an act of physical abuse, the effects of verbal abuse may not appear until years later. This fact makes it difficult to identify and treat the problem before the abuse has left permanent scars on the child's personality and development. Sadly, many children who have endured emotional abuse will go on to engage in antisocial behaviors and to experience serious psychiatric disorders later in life (Gray & Montgomery, 2012; Jonson-Reid, Kohl, & Drake, 2012).

Sexual abuse involves any sexual involvement between an adult and a child, including fondling, exhibitionism, rape, incest, child pornography, and prostitution. Such acts are considered abusive regardless of whether or not the child agreed to participate. This belief is based on the assumption that children are incapable of making a rational decision or may not be able to refuse because of adult pressure. For this reason, the incidence of sexual abuse is probably much greater than reported and often not discovered until years later. Girls are sexually abused at a rate nearly twice that of boys (APA, 2012). More often, the perpetrator is male and not a stranger to the child, but rather someone the child knows and trusts, such as a babysitter, relative, caretaker, parent, stepparent, coach, teacher, or neighbor. Victims may be exposed to sexually transmitted diseases (STDs) and should be observed for characteristic symptoms (Teacher Checklist 10-2). Children who have been sexually abused also suffer a high rate of adult-onset mental health disorders (Nelson, Baldwin, & Taylor, 2012). Many sexually abused adolescents become runaways or prostitutes, or engage in a range of violent or dependency behaviors (Oshri, Tubman, & Burnette, 2012).

Did You Know...

that teen pregnancy is 25–30 percent higher among children who have been abused?

Physical neglect is defined as a family's abandonment of a child or their failure to provide for the child's basic physical needs and care. More than half of all substantiated maltreatment cases involve some form of neglect, including inadequate or inappropriate food, shelter, clothing, or cleanliness. Medical neglect is also considered a form of physical neglect that places a child at risk for disability or death (USLegal, Inc., 2012). Parents may be prosecuted if they fail to obtain appropriate medical treatment (e.g., immunizations, surgery, medications, dental care) necessary to address children's health needs. Charges are also being brought against families for educational neglect if they fail to enroll children in school, allow them to drop out prematurely, or permit children to be truant from school.

Failure to protect children's safety can also result in prosecution for criminal neglect and endangerment. For example, adults who supply drugs or alcohol to underage children or knowingly permit children to have access to, or use, illegal substances are considered guilty of exposing children to extreme risk. Parents who leave children alone and unsupervised are also being

---

sexual abuse – *any sexual involvement between an adult and child.*
physical neglect – *failure to meet children's fundamental needs for food, shelter, medical care, and education, including abandonment.*

✓✓ TEACHER CHECKLIST 10-2

Identifying Symptoms of Common Sexually Transmitted Diseases (STDs)

Gonorrhea	May cause painful or burning discomfort when urinating, increased vaginal discharge (yellow, green), or vaginal bleeding. Discharge, anal itching, soreness, bleeding, or painful bowel movements are characteristic of rectal infections. May cause sore throat (oral sex). Many victims have no symptoms, but are contagious; serious complications can develop if left untreated.
Chlamydia trachomatis	May cause abnormal vaginal discharge or burning discomfort when urinating 5 to 7 days following infection. Victims may not have any immediate symptoms; however, if left untreated infection can damage reproductive organs.
Syphilis	Symptoms appear in stages following infection. Initial stage: within 10 days to 3 months a chancre (painless sore) appears at the point of contact (vagina, rectum, mouth, penis) and heals. Second stage: 6 weeks to 6 months after sore heals a generalized rash appears along with fever and enlarged lymph glands. Curable with antibiotics.
Trichomoniasis	The most common and curable STD. Symptoms appear within 5 to 28 days and typically include a frothy, yellow-green, foul-smelling vaginal discharge, burning during urination, irritation, and itching around the genital area.
Genital herpes	Many victims have no symptoms. Others may develop painful blister-like sores (around vagina, rectum, penis, mouth), fever, flu-like symptoms, and swollen glands several days following infection; sores heal in 2 to 4 weeks. Reoccurrence of sores is common.
Condyloma (genital warts)	Caused by the human papilloma virus (HPV); single or clusters of warts may develop around the genital area within weeks or months following infection. Not everyone will develop symptoms. A vaccine is currently available.
HIV/AIDS	Infected persons usually have no initial symptoms. Blood tests can detect the HIV virus 6 weeks after exposure.

TeachSource Digital Download   Download from CourseMate.

charged with neglect and endangerment. The term **latch-key** has been used to describe children who are consistently left home alone during the hours before and after school. A shortage of programs, lack of trained personnel, and cost has made it difficult for many working families to secure adequate before- and after-school care for school-aged children. Questions remain unanswered about when it is appropriate for children of any age to be left home alone and if they are at greater risk for injury or emotional distress as a result (Table 10–1) (Ruiz-Casares et al., 2012).

Emotional or psychological neglect is perhaps the most difficult form of maltreatment to recognize and document. For this reason, not all states include this category in their reporting laws. Emotional neglect reflects a basic lack of parental interest or responsiveness to a child's psychological needs and development (Spratt et al., 2012) (Teacher Checklist 10-1). They fail to understand the need for affection, nurturing, and conversing with their child. The absence of any emotional connection, such as hugging, kissing, touching, conversation, or facial expressions, can result in developmental delays and stunted growth (Moxley, Squires, & Linstrom, 2012). The term **failure to thrive** describes this condition when it occurs in infants and young children. A lack of measurable gains in weight or height is often one of the first indications of psychological neglect.

---

latch-key – *a term that refers to school-age children who care for themselves without adult supervision before and after school hours.*
emotional or psychological neglect – *failure to meet a child's psychological needs for love and attention.*
failure to thrive – *a term used to describe an infant whose growth and mental development are severely slowed due to lack of nurturing or mental stimulation.*

CONNECTING TO EVERYDAY PRACTICE

Cultural Practices and Child Abuse

Members of a local Vietnamese community were irate following the arrest of a boy's 23-year-old parents for child abuse. Teachers had noted purple "bruises" on the little boy's back and chest when he arrived at school one day. The couple denied any wrongdoing, insisting they were merely performing "cao gio," a traditional Vietnamese practice used to cure fever. Following the application of medicated oil to the skin, a warm coin or spoon is scraped along the spine and chest until reddened patches appear. The boy's parents believed this would eliminate "bad winds" that had caused his fever.

Think About This:

▶ Is this practice a form of abuse?

▶ How do cultural differences affect parental practices and values?

▶ Should families be expected to give up traditional cultural practices related to healing and medicine when they immigrate to this country?

▶ Why is it important for teachers to acquire an understanding of cultural differences?

Did You Get It?

Which of the following forms of abuse and/or neglect is the most difficult to detect, document, report, and potentially prosecute?

  a. emotional/psychological abuse or neglect

  b. child exploitation

  c. physical abuse

  d. sexual abuse

Take the full quiz on CourseMate.

10-4 Understanding the Risk Factors for Maltreatment

Abusive adults come from all levels of social, economic, educational, ethnic, religious, and occupational backgrounds (Children's Bureau, 2011). They live in rural areas, as well as small towns and large cities. Some are well-educated professionals, whereas others dropped out of school early. Also, not all abusive adults are poor, alcoholics, or drug abusers, as is often believed. Although the incidence tends to be significantly higher among these groups, such generalizations are overly simplistic and do not address the complex social and economic issues that are involved.

One explanation for why the incidence of child abuse or neglect appears to be greater among disadvantaged families may relate to their increased reliance on public and social service programs. Frequent communication and visits with these families allow agency personnel to more closely monitor their actions. Furthermore, families living in poverty often face circumstances that make daily living more stressful and limit their options (Leventhal, Martin, & Gaither, 2012). Simply finding adequate food, clothing, housing, and transportation can prove to be overwhelming. In contrast, families with greater financial resources may have more choices available to them and can afford private medical care, move from doctor to doctor, and even seek treatment in neighboring cities. This flexibility limits their contact with a single health care provider and makes it easier for families to avoid immediate suspicion.

Researchers continue to study childhood maltreatment in an effort to better understand the complex nature of this problem. To date, they have identified three major risk factors:

▶ characteristics of adults who have a potential for committing maltreatment
▶ vulnerable children
▶ family and environmental stressors

It is believed that for abuse and neglect to take place, all three risk factors must occur at approximately the same time.

10-4a Characteristics of Abusive or Neglectful Adults

Certain adult behaviors and predispositions are commonly associated with abusive tendencies, including:

- a history of repeated fear, anger, and rejection
- low self-esteem
- difficulty in forming long-term relationships (e.g., friendships, marriage) that leads to social isolation and loneliness; depending on a child for love
- lack of trust
- early marriage and pregnancy
- maternal depression, post-traumatic stress disorder (PTSD), and other mental health conditions (Feldman, McConnell, & Aunos, 2012)
- belief in, and use of, harsh punishment to "discipline" children (Lansford et al., 2012)
- impulsive; poor anger control
- low stress tolerance
- drug and alcohol addictions
- poor problem-solving abilities

© 2015 Cengage Learning

▶❚❚ TeachSource Video Connections

0–2 Years: Observation Module for Infants and Toddlers

Caring for infants and toddlers is a demanding and, at times, stressful responsibility. Many adults are overwhelmed by the experience and may unintentionally harm a young child out of frustration. Linking families to informational and supportive resources is critical to reducing the risk of childhood maltreatment. As you watch the learning video, *0–2 Years: Observation Module for Infants and Toddlers,* consider the following questions:

1. Why do you think infants and toddlers experience a high rate of maltreatment?

2. What behaviors did you observe in this video that some parents might find frustrating or difficult to handle?

3. What resources would you recommend to help these parents cope and to enjoy their child's early years?

Watch on CourseMate.

Although not every adult who exhibits these characteristics is abusive or neglectful, likewise not every abusive or neglectful caregiver will necessarily display all of these behaviors. In many cases, adults simply lack the knowledge and skills needed to be successful parents. Their lack of understanding can lead to expectations that may be unrealistic and developmentally inappropriate based on the child's age and abilities. For example, a parent may become upset because a 15-month-old wets the bed, a toddler spills milk, or a 7-year-old loses a mitten despite the fact that these behaviors are typical and to be expected. Intolerance, frustration, and uncontrolled anger can, in turn, lead to a subsequent lashing out of abusive behavior. Drugs and alcohol addictions may further reduce an adult's ability to be nurturing or to respond appropriately to children's needs. Evidence also suggests that adults who grew up in abusive families are more likely to treat their own children in a similar manner.

10-4b Vulnerable Children

Victims of child maltreatment include an almost equal number of boys and girls. Children under age 4 years and those who have developmental delays or disabilities, especially autism, are at highest risk for physical abuse (Leeb et al., 2012; Stalker & McArthur, 2012). Infants under 12 months and children over the age of 6 years are more likely to suffer from neglect, whereas adolescents experience the highest rate of sexual abuse. Although age and disability increase children's risk for abuse and neglect, additional factors can include:

- difficult temperament (e.g., fussy, defiant, overly active)
- living in a single parent family (especially with father absent)
- poverty
- gender (sexual abuse)

▶ frequent or chronic illness

▶ gender nonconformity (Roberts et al., 2012)

Occasionally an abusive or neglectful caregiver will single out a child who does not live up to their expectations. This child may be perceived as being physically unattractive, disobedient, clumsy, weak, unintelligent, or similar to someone else whom the adult dislikes. These qualities may be real or imagined; in either case, the adult is convinced that they truly exist.

The risk of maltreatment is also greater for children who are born outside of marriage, from unwanted or unplanned pregnancies, stepchildren, or living in a foster home. Researchers have also established a strong connection between domestic violence and child abuse. Children living in households where domestic violence is also occurring are at significantly greater risk for abuse and neglect (Miller et al., 2012).

10-4c Family and Environmental Stresses

All individuals and families face conflict and crises from time to time. However, the economic recession, frequent military deployments, natural disasters, and incarcerations have caused extraordinary hardships for many families with children (Valentino et al., 2012; Waliski et al., 2012). Some are able to cope with these stressful events. Others are unable to handle the pressures or to maintain emotional control during difficult times. In many maltreatment cases, stress is identified as the **precipitating** factor. That is, the perceived conflict is sufficient to push an adult to action (abuse) or withdrawal (neglect) as a caretaker (Easterbrooks et al., 2011).

Adults who mistreat children often have difficulty discriminating between events that are significantly stressful and those that are not. Instead, they find all crises equally threatening, overwhelming, and difficult to manage (Schneiderman et al., 2012). The following examples illustrate the range of personal and environmental stressors that can potentially lead to a loss of control, especially when they occur in combination with other challenging events:

▶ flat tire, lost keys, clogged sink, or broken window

▶ unemployment or underemployment

▶ illness, injury, or death

▶ poverty, financial pressures, home foreclosure

▶ partner violence, divorce, or marital conflict

▶ moving

▶ birth of another child

▶ single parenting

▶ military deployment (James & Countryman, 2012)

Some events may seem trivial in comparison to others. Yet, any one may become the "straw that breaks the camel's back" and trigger abusive behavior. The level of an adult's anger may be inappropriate and out of proportion to the actual event and ultimately be directed toward a child.

▼ Children who have developmental disabilities are at greater risk for abusive and neglectful treatment.

© Cengage Learning

Did You Get It?

Poverty, disability, living in a household where domestic violence is occurring, and _____ increase a child's risk for maltreatment.

a. being the youngest child

b. having older parents

c. residing in a rural community

d. living in a single-parent household

Take the full quiz on CourseMate.

precipitating – *factors that trigger or initiate a reaction or response.*

10-5 Protective Measures for Programs and Teachers

It is essential that early childhood programs and school personnel take steps to protect themselves from potential accusations of child maltreatment. Special attention should be given to careful hiring practices, policy development, and ongoing personnel training, including:

- conducting background checks on potential employees for any prior record of child abuse or felony convictions (These are mandated in most states and performed by state law enforcement agencies.)
- hiring individuals who have formal training in early education and child development
- contacting an applicant's references (nonrelative) and requesting information about the applicant's prior work performance
- reviewing an employee's past employment record, including reasons for leaving previous jobs
- establishing a code of conduct regarding appropriate child-teacher behavior
- providing continued inservice training, especially on topics related to identification of abuse or neglect, effective behavior management strategies, and teaching children self-protection skills (Teacher Checklist 10-3)
- establishing a program policy of nontolerance regarding any form of abusive behavior, including harassment, bullying, or harsh discipline

Teachers can take additional measures to protect themselves against the possibility of false allegations. Conducting daily health checks upon a child's arrival and documenting all findings can protect teachers from being blamed for a bruise or scratch that may have occurred elsewhere. Teachers should also maintain thorough records of children's injuries so there is factual evidence that describes the circumstances and treatment administered. It is also preferable not to leave a teacher alone with children. A second teacher who serves as an eyewitness can eliminate any suspicions of wrongdoing. Teachers should also participate in inservice training opportunities to improve their understanding of child maltreatment and their role in successful identification and intervention. Finally, teachers may want to purchase their own professional liability insurance unless they are covered by their employer's policy.

TEACHER CHECKLIST 10-3

Strategies for Positive Behavior Management

- **Reinforce** desirable behaviors. Give lots of hugs and pats, adult attention, and verbal acknowledgment for things the child is doing appropriately; reinforcement should be given often and immediately following the appropriate behavior. For example: "I really like the way you are sharing your toys" or "That was nice of you to let Mat have a turn on the bike."
- **Redirect** the child's attention to another activity or area when he is behaving inappropriately; don't comment on the inappropriate behavior. "Juan, could you come and help me set the table?" or "Let's go to the block area and build a zoo together."
- **Consistent expectations** help children understand their limits and the way in which adults expect them to behave. Expectations should be realistic and state behavior that is considered appropriate. Keep explanations simple and brief. "Mika, you need to sit on the sofa; feet go on the floor" or "We need to walk in the hallways."
- **Consequences** can be used together with other management strategies. Most children understand consequences from an early age on. "When your hands are washed we can eat" or "I will have to take the ball away if you throw it at the window again."
- **Ignoring** undesirable behaviors, such as tantrums or throwing things can be effective for decreasing the attention-getting response children may be seeking. Don't look at the child or discuss the behavior with the child.
- **Practice** desirable behaviors when the child behaves inappropriately. For example, if the child scatters crayons across the floor, she needs to pick them up and then be acknowledged for doing what was asked. An adult may also model the desired behavior by helping the child to pick up the crayons.

10-5a Inservice Training

Teachers are morally, professionally, and legally responsible for reporting children whom they suspect are being maltreated (Feng et al., 2012; Goldman & Grimbeek, 2011). However, to be effective, they must know what signs to look for, to whom a report should be made, and what community resources are available to help families. These topics make ideal subjects for inservice training, in addition to:

- relevant state laws
- teachers' rights and responsibilities
- physical and behavioral signs of maltreatment
- development of school policies and procedures for handling suspected cases
- teacher and staff management of abuse and neglect
- community resources and services
- classroom strategies for helping children who have been maltreated
- stress reduction and time management skills.

Teachers also play a valuable role advocating for laws, policies, and programs that protect children's rights and well-being.

Did You Get It?

Teachers, administrators, and school counselors have the authority to assess children for signs of physical and/or sexual abuse without an eyewitness present.

a. Never

b. Yes, but doing so is not recommended

c. Yes, but only with prior written consent of authorities

d. Only if witnessed by the child's parent or legal guardian

Take the full quiz on CourseMate.

10-6 Reporting Laws

Reporting laws support the philosophy that parenthood carries with it certain obligations and responsibilities toward children. Therefore, punishment of abusive adults is not the primary objective. Rather, the purpose of these laws is to protect children from maltreatment and exploitation. Every attempt is made to preserve family unity by helping parents find solutions to problems that may be contributing to the abuse or neglect. Contrary to common belief, removing children from their homes is not always the best solution. Alternative placements and frequent moves may not improve the stability or quality of a child's life. Criminal action against parents is usually reserved for cases in which they are unwilling or unable to cooperate with prescribed educational and treatment programs.

Each case of maltreatment involves a unique and complex set of conditions such as home environments, economic obligations, individual temperaments, cultural differences, and parenting skills that must be taken into consideration. For this reason, states have intentionally written their child maltreatment laws to address the basic federal mandates established by CAPTA while remaining somewhat open-ended. This approach allows the legal system and social agencies flexibility in determining, on a case-by-case basis, whether or not an adult has acted irresponsibly.

Laws in every state identify specific groups and professionals who are required to report suspected incidences of maltreatment, including:

- teachers, assistants, paraprofessionals, and student teachers
- center directors and principals
- health care providers (e.g., doctors, nurses, dentists, pharmacists, psychologists, mental health counselors)
- law enforcement personnel
- social workers
- clergy

✓✓ **TEACHER CHECKLIST 10-4**

What to Include in a Written Child Abuse/Neglect Report

1. The child and parents' or caretakers' name(s) and address (if known).
2. The child's age.
3. The nature and extent of the child's injuries or description of neglect including any evidence of previous injuries or deprivation.
4. The identity of the offending adult (if known).
5. Any additional information the reporting person believes may be helpful in establishing the cause of injuries or neglect.
6. The name, address, telephone number, and professional title of the individual making the report.

TeachSource Digital Download Download from CourseMate.

10-6a Program Policy

Schools and early childhood programs should have a written action plan for addressing suspected incidences of abuse and neglect (Moxley, Squires, & Lindstrom, 2012). These policies and procedures should be reviewed frequently with staff to ensure their understanding and compliance. In larger programs, teachers may report directly to the director, principal, head administrator, or health consultant who, in turn, contacts appropriate local authorities and files a report. However, if at any time teachers are not satisfied that their concerns have been properly acted upon, they are obligated by law to personally report the incident. In home-based programs or smaller centers, an individual staff member may be responsible for filing a report. Failure to do so may prolong a potentially harmful situation for the child, and result in criminal prosecution and monetary fines for the teacher.

Initial reports are usually made by telephone and followed up with a written report that is completed several days later (Teacher Checklist 10-4). All information is kept strictly confidential, including the identity of the person making the report. State laws protect anyone who reports abuse or neglect from liability and criminal charges as long as the information provided is not intended to deliberately harm another individual.

It is not the teacher's role to prove suspicions of abuse and neglect before making a report. Local child protective services or the National Child Abuse Hotline (800-422-4453) should be contacted immediately if there is reason to believe that a child is being inadequately cared for or mistreated. As long as a report is made in good faith, the teacher is merely indicating that a family may be in need of help. The law does not require the family or adult in question to be notified when a report is filed. In some cases, doing so could place the child in additional danger, especially if sexual or harsh physical abuse is involved. Some families may actually experience relief when their problems are finally recognized. Therefore, the decision about whether or not to inform the family or adult in question may depend on the particular circumstances.

Reporting a family, colleague, or acquaintance can be difficult. However, as advocates for children's rights, teachers must always be concerned about children's safety and welfare. Unless the child is in immediate danger, trained personnel will generally meet with the family or caregiver within days to evaluate circumstances surrounding the incident. Legal action may be taken depending on the seriousness of the situation or arrangements may be made to provide family-centered support services.

▼ **Parenthood implies that an adult is willing to accept responsibility for a child's care and protection.**

© Cengage Learning

Did You Get It?

Teachers play a multifaceted role in dealing with potential instances of child abuse and/or neglect. What is not the teacher's responsibility?
a. detecting signs of maltreatment
b. documenting findings
c. reporting findings
d. proving allegations

Take the full quiz on CourseMate.

10-7 The Teacher's Role

A teacher may be one of the few adults children can turn to when they are being mistreated. Teachers serve as important child advocates by establishing effective communication, providing emotionally supportive and accepting environments, identifying and reporting suspicions of abuse or neglect, and helping children to learn socially appropriate behaviors.

10-7a Early Identification and Reporting

Teachers are in an ideal position to identify and help children who are being mistreated (Katz et al., 2012). Daily health checks and frequent interactions with children enable teachers to recognize early changes in children's behavior or appearance. (See Teacher Checklist 10-1 and Chapter 2). Patterns of non-accidental injury or neglect often become apparent when these observations are documented. This information may also be used by child protective services and the courts to determine if maltreatment is occurring. Therefore, it is important that teachers include the following information in their reports:

- a precise description of the nature, location, color, size, and severity of any suspected injury (Figure 10-3)

FIGURE 10-3 Form for reporting location, size, and nature of suspected abuse-related injuries.

Child's Name: _____
Date: _____
Comments: _____
Description of Injury: _____
Location and Size of Injury: _____
Color of Injury: _____
Description of Child's Behavior: _____
Additional Comments/Concerns: _____
Reported by: _____

- the child's explanation of how the injury occurred
- the family's or caretaker's explanation for the incident
- obvious signs of neglect (e.g., malnutrition, uncleanliness, inappropriate dress, excessive fatigue, lack of medical or dental care)
- recent or significant changes in the child's behavior
- nature of parent/child interactions

Comprehensive documentation provides child protective authorities with supporting evidence and also aids in determining the services and intervention programs most appropriate for the child and family.

Teachers must not ignore their professional and legal responsibilities to protect children's safety. In many cases, a teacher may be the only adult whom a child trusts enough to reveal maltreatment. Teachers must be able to identify the signs of abuse and neglect and know when and how to report suspected cases to the appropriate authorities. They must also be aware of cultural differences in parenting skills, expectations, and practices so as not to misinterpret what they may observe (Lilly & Kundu, 2012; Raman & Hodes, 2012).

10-7b Providing a Supportive Environment for Children

Teachers play an important role in helping children to understand and cope with the effects of abusive and neglectful treatment. They must be positive role models and accept children for who they are, listen to their concerns without judgment, encourage their efforts, and acknowledge their successes. For many children, teachers may be the only adult in their lives who accepts them unconditionally and shows a sincere interest in their well-being without making threatening demands or causing them harm.

Establishing a trusting relationship with children who have suffered maltreatment is a critical step in helping them begin to open up and to verbalize their feelings. This process takes time and cannot be forced or hurried. It often requires teachers to initially meet children on their own terms. For example, a teacher might start out by offering several books to the child who is reluctant to join a group story-time. Later, the teacher might sit alone with the child and read a story together. Finally, the child may be gently coaxed to participate with her peers in a group activity.

Play therapy can also be beneficial for drawing children out and allowing them safe opportunities for expressing anger, fears, and anxieties related to abusive treatment (Mishna et al., 2012; Thompson & Trice-Black, 2012). Activities such as housekeeping, puppets, and doll play are ideal for this purpose. For example, talking about how the puppet or doll (child) feels when it is mistreated may encourage children to talk about their true feelings. At the same time, teachers can model effective parenting skills for children, such as appropriate ways of talking to, treating, and caring for the puppets or dolls.

Artwork and story-telling can also be effective means for encouraging children to talk about their feelings, anxieties, and concerns related to traumatic events. For example, self-portraits may reveal an exaggeration of certain body parts or circumstances that children have experienced. Pictures may also depict unusual practices that children have been subjected to, such as being tied up, locked in a closet, or struck with an object. However, extreme caution must be exercised whenever attempting to interpret children's artwork. A child's immature drawing skills and lack of perspective can easily cause an inexperienced observer to misinterpret or reach false conclusions. Therefore, it is best to view unusual items in children's drawings as additional clues, rather than as absolute indicators of abusive or neglectful treatment. Small group discussions and story-telling (verbal, child-written, or dictated to a teacher) also provide valuable outlets for articulating feelings and helping children to explore effective solutions.

Teachers can be instrumental in helping children learn how to manage anger and to express emotions in ways that are positive and appropriate (Kim-Spoon et al., 2012). For example, a teacher might say, "Rosa, if you want another cracker, you need to say 'Please can I have another cracker.' We can't understand when you whine or cry." Or, "I can't let you hit Rodney. You need to ask him, 'May I please have a turn on the bike?'" Children can also be taught strategies that will help them to regain self-control when tension begins to escalate.

10-7c Building Children's Resilience

Teachers have many unique opportunities to help children develop and practice developmental skills that also promote **resilience** (see Chapter 1, Table 1–3) (Bruster & Foreman, 2012; Lee, Cheung, & Kwong, 2012). Victims of child abuse and neglect often have poor self-esteem and blame themselves for the way they have been treated. Letting children know they are safe, accepted, and loved is an important first step in helping them to overcome their fears and to regain trust. Teachers can facilitate this process by:

- responding to children in a consistent and supportive manner
- providing private space that children can call their own
- establishing gradual limits for acceptable behavior; following predictable routines and schedules to create order in children's lives
- letting children know you are available whenever they need someone, whether it be for companionship, extra attention, or reassurance
- taking time to prepare children for new experiences; informing children of expectations in advance enhances the "safeness" of their environment
- accepting children's initial fears and reluctance to participate; gradually involving them in activities
- encouraging children to talk about their feelings, fears, and concerns

Educational programs and materials are available to improve children's awareness and ability to respond to maltreatment (Table 10–2). Many excellent resources can be accessed on the Internet or through local public libraries, schools, and pediatric and mental health clinics. Materials should be selected and reviewed carefully so they are developmentally appropriate, instructive, and not frightening to young children. Social workers, nurses, doctors, mental health specialists,

TABLE 10–2   Children's Books about Maltreatment

Bentrim, W. (2009). *Mommy's black eye: Children dealing with domestic violence.* USA: CreateSpace.

Dietzel, M. (2000). *My very own book about me: A personal safety book.* Spokane, WA: ACT for Kids.

Federico, J. (2009). *Some parts are not for sharing.* Mustang, OK: Tate Publishing & Enterprises (also available in Spanish).

Foltz, L. (2003). *Kids helping kids break the silence of sexual abuse.* Lighthouse Point, FL: Lighthouse Point Press (for older children).

Girard, L. (1992). *My body is private.* Morton Grove, IL: Albert Whitman & Co.

Gross, P. (1996). *Stranger safety.* Southfield, MI: Roo Publishing.

Guard, A. (2011). *What if a stranger approaches you?* Mankato, MN: Picture Window Books.

Holmes, M. (2000). *A terrible thing happened: A story for children who have witnessed violence or trauma.* Washington, DC: Magination Books.

Kehoe, P. (1987). *Something happened and I'm scared to tell: A book for young victims of abuse.* Seattle, WA: Parenting Press.

King, K., & Rama, S. (2008). *I said no! A kid-to-kid guide to keeping your private parts private.* Weaverville, CA: Boulden Publishing.

Kleven, S., & Bergsma, J. (1998). *The right touch.* Bellevue, WA: Illumination Arts.

Kraizer, S. (1996). *The safe child book: A commonsense approach to protecting children and teaching children to protect themselves.* New York: Fireside Press.

Loftis, C. (1997). *The words hurt: Helping children cope with verbal abuse.* New York: Horizon Press.

Pendziwol, J. (2006). *Once upon a dragon: Stranger safety for kids (and dragons).* Tonawanda, NY: Kids Can Press.

Saltz, G. (2008). *Amazing you! Getting smart about your private parts.* New York: Puffin.

Schor, H. (2002). *A place for Starr: A story of hope for children experiencing family violence.* Charlotte, NC: Kidsrights Press.

Spelman, C., & Weidner, T. (1997). *Your body belongs to you.* Morton Grove, IL: Albert Whitman & Co.

Susewitt, L. (2011). *Is there love after abuse? The story of Kobe.* USA: CreateSpace.

Wachter, O. (2002). *No more secrets for me.* London: Little Brown & Co.

resilience – *the capacity to endure or overcome difficult conditions.*

Caring adults provide children with much needed companionship, reassurance, and individualized attention.

teachers, and public service groups can also be called upon to provide educational programs for children and families.

It is also important to help children develop effective communication, problem-solving, conflict resolution, and self-protection skills. Although children may not fully comprehend the complexity of abuse or neglect, these skills improve children's ability to recognize "uncomfortable" situations, how and when to tell a trusted adult, and how to assert themselves by saying no when someone attempts an inappropriate behavior. Informed children can be the first line of defense against abuse and neglect if they know that being beaten, forced to engage in sexual activity, or left alone for long periods is not normal or the type of treatment they deserve.

10-7d Reaching Out to Families

Raising young children is a challenging and demanding task. Many adults today have not had the same opportunities to learn parenting skills that past generations once had. They have often grown up in smaller families and had fewer opportunities to practice parenting firsthand until their own children arrive. Employment opportunities may require relocation to distant cities and result in the loss of extended family contact and support. And, more often than not, today's parents are holding down full-time jobs in addition to raising children. As a result, daily stress levels and economic worries may challenge some parents' ability to be patient, nurturing, and responsive to children's developmental needs. These circumstances in no way excuse the harsh or neglectful treatment of children. However, they signal the importance of early recognition and intervention.

There are many ways teachers can assist families who may be struggling (Haskett et al., 2012). Daily contacts provide opportunities for identifying families in crises and directing them to community services and programs, such as:

- child protective services
- day care and "crisis" centers
- family counseling
- help or "hot" lines
- temporary foster homes
- homemaker services
- transportation
- financial assistance
- parenting classes
- employment assistance
- home visitors
- self-help or support groups

Partnerships can be formed and strengthened when teachers also reach out to support families and encourage their involvement in children's education. Information can be shared about many topics that will enhance parents' confidence and child-rearing skills, including:

- child growth and development
- positive behavior management
- nutritious meals and snacks; how to manage feeding problems
- meeting children's social and emotional needs at different stages
- preventive health care
- activities that promote children's learning
- locating and utilizing community resources
- stress and tension relievers for parents
- creating safe environments; injury prevention
- financial planning

▶ time management

▶ organizing a family support group

Teachers must always be sensitive to cultural differences when providing families with information. Although most parents do their best to raise children, they may not share the same values and practices that teachers' consider to be important. Maintaining open communication with families promotes mutual understanding and lessens the risk of misinterpreting parenting ideas and behaviors as potentially abusive.

Legislation creating **safe havens** for unwanted infants has been passed in every state in an effort to eliminate maltreatment and abandonment. Although the laws vary somewhat from state to state, they basically allow a parent(s) to relinquish custody of an unharmed infant to authorities without fear of criminal prosecution. The laws typically declare a time/age limit and identify facilities such as hospitals, police precincts, or fire stations where infants can be safely left. The concept of safe havens is not without controversy, but has proven successful in saving the lives of many infants who might otherwise have been harmed or abandoned.

Did You Get It?

Laws creating "safe havens" have been passed in all 50 states and have paved the way for parents to more easily:

a. gain or regain lost custody of a child

b. relinquish custody of a child

c. find round-the-clock support services for themselves and their infant

d. locate community shelter for themselves and their child(ren)

Take the full quiz on CourseMate.

PARTNERING with FAMILIES

Anger Management

Dear Families,

Being a parent has many positive rewards, but it can also be a challenging and stressful role to fulfill. At times, children are likely to behave in ways that we find upsetting and cause us to react in anger. Although this behavior is understandable, it does not teach children how to handle their feelings of frustration or disappointment in a positive manner. Instead, our actions may teach children how to shout, say hurtful words, and respond in an emotional or physical manner, rather than in ways that are thoughtful and constructive. When adults practice effective anger management strategies, they become positive role models for children. The next time your child makes you angry, try several of the following techniques:

▶ Take a deep breath. Thoroughly assess the situation before you react.

▶ Leave the room. Take a brief "time out" and regain control of your emotions.

▶ Consider whether the situation or the child's behavior is actually worth your becoming upset. Could the outcome affect the long-term relationship you have with your child?

▶ Tell children what has upset you and why.

▶ Avoid lengthy explanations and arguments with your child. Children understand statements when they are brief and to the point.

▶ Learn to recognize your tolerance limits and what behaviors are most likely to make you upset.

▶ Always find something good to say about your child soon afterward. This helps children to understand that you still love them despite their unacceptable behavior.

safe haven – *a designated place, such as a hospital or fire station, where parents can leave their infant and give up parental rights without fear of criminal charges.*

CLASSROOM CORNER

Teacher Activities

We Have Many Kinds of Feelings

(NHES PreK–2; National Health Education Standards 4.2.1)

Concept: We all have feelings and it is important to talk about our feelings.

Learning Objectives

▶ Children will learn that there are many different types of feelings.

▶ Children will learn that it is important to talk about their feelings.

Supplies

▶ large piece of paper to write down comments from the children

▶ marking pen

▶ two puppets (any kind)

▶ small pile of blocks

▶ three small cars

▶ box of crayons

▶ two pieces of paper

Learning Activities

▶ Read and discuss the following books (see Appendix D for additional titles):
  - *The Way I Feel* by Janan Cain
  - *What to Do When You Worry Too Much* by Dawn Huebner
  - *How to Take the Grrrrr Out of Anger* by Elizabeth Verdick
  - *Big Feelings* by Talaris Institute

▶ Ask children if they have felt the same as the children in the story. Ask children to talk about what makes them feel scared, happy, angry, and so on.

▶ Next, role-play with the puppets. Have puppet 1 playing with three cars and have puppet 2 come over to play. Have puppet 1 ask puppet 2 if she would like to play with a car. Ask the children how they think puppet 2 feels when she got to play with a car.

▶ Next, have puppet 1 stacking and playing with blocks. Then have puppet 2 come over and knock down his blocks. Ask the children how they think puppet 1 is feeling after his block building was knocked down. Talk about what puppet 2 should have done differently (asked to play, asked a teacher for other blocks, and so on).

▶ Finally, have puppet 1 drawing with paper and crayons. Have puppet 2 come over and ask puppet 1 if she can play. Have puppet 1 say, "No, I am playing with these." Ask children how puppet 2 is feeling, and talk about what puppet 2 can do to get some crayons and paper (grab them—not appropriate; ask a teacher to get them some crayons and paper—appropriate).

Evaluation

▶ Children will name several different kinds of feelings.

▶ Children will describe behaviors that evoke specific feelings.

Additional lesson plans for grades 3–5 are available on the Education CourseMate website for this book.

Summary

▶ Public Law 93-247, the Child Abuse Prevention and Treatment Act (CAPTA):
  - was the first national law that addressed the problems of child abuse and neglect
  - provides legal protection to children who are maltreated
  - requires states to pass laws, designate an investigative and enforcement agency, and establish policies
  - has addressed contemporary maltreatment issues, including adoption, foster care, abandoned infants, family violence, and improved interagency collaboration in recent reauthorizations.
▶ Discipline involves guiding or teaching children how they should behave.
  - Punishment teaches children negative behaviors, including anger and violence.
▶ Children under 18 years are protected by law from harm, exploitation, and inadequate care.
  - Most states recognize four categories of abuse/neglect, including physical abuse, sexual abuse, emotional abuse, and physical neglect; emotional/psychological neglect is recognized in some states.
▶ The potential for abuse or neglect is thought to be greatest when three factors exist at approximately the same time: an adult who has abusive tendencies, a child who is vulnerable because of certain characteristics (e.g., age, disability, temperament), and family or environmental stressors.
▶ Programs and schools must take steps to protect themselves against potential abuse or neglect allegations by implementing thorough hiring practices and inservice training.
▶ Teachers are required to report suspected incidences of abuse or neglect and are protected by the law if reports are made in good faith.
  - Programs should have a procedure in place for handling incidences of abuse and neglect.
▶ Teachers play an important role in the prevention and treatment of child abuse/neglect through early identification and reporting, providing emotional support to children, reaching out to families, helping children develop skills to improve resilience (e.g., communication, social, problem-solving, conflict resolution), and advocating on behalf of children.

Terms to Know

abuse *p. 268*
neglect *p. 268*
discipline *p. 270*
punishment *p. 270*
reprimand *p. 270*
physical abuse *p. 270*

shaken baby syndrome *p. 271*
emotional *p. 271*
verbal abuse *p. 271*
sexual abuse *p. 273*
physical neglect *p. 274*
latch-key *p. 274*

emotional or/pychological
  neglect *p. 274*
failure to thrive *p. 274*
precipitating *p. 277*
resilience *p. 283*
safe havens *p. 285*

Chapter Review

A. **By Yourself:**

1. Define each of the *Terms to Know*.

2. Select a word from the list below to complete each of the following statements.

teachers   definition   childhood

trust   expectations   safe haven

physical   neglect   reported

psychological   identify

sexual   confidential

1. A child's excessive fascination with body parts and talk about sexual activities may be an indication of _____ abuse.

2. Public Law 93-247 requires states to write a legal _____ of child abuse and neglect.

3. Injury that is intentionally inflicted on a child is called _____ abuse.

4. Malnutrition, lack of proper clothing, or inadequate adult supervision are examples of physical _____.

5. Verbal abuse sometimes results because of unrealistic parent demands and _____.

6. Emotional or _____ neglect is one of the most difficult forms of neglect to identify.

7. Reporting laws usually require _____ to report suspected cases of child abuse and neglect.

8. Information contained in reports of child abuse or neglect is kept _____.

9. Many abusive adults were abused during their own _____.

10. Lack of _____ makes it difficult for many abusive and neglectful adults to form friendships.

11. Daily contact with children helps teachers to _____ children who are maltreated.

12. Suspected abuse or neglect does not have to be proven before it should be _____.

B. As a Group:

1. Describe five observable clues that might suggest a child is being physically maltreated.

2. Discuss what teachers should do if they suspect that a child is being abused or neglected.

3. Describe what information should be included in both an oral and written report.

4. Discuss four ways that teachers can help abused and neglected children in the classroom.

5. Why does the incidence of child abuse and neglect appear to be higher among disadvantaged families?

6. Discuss how you would respond to a parent or teacher who believes that families have a right to discipline children as they wish to in their own home.

◖ Case Study

When it was time to go outdoors, 3-year-old Casandra said she didn't want to play and headed for her locker. At the teacher's gentle insistence, Casandra reluctantly joined the other children on the playground. Tears rolled down her cheeks when the teacher boosted Casandra onto a swing seat and began to push her. The teacher stopped the swing and helped Casandra off. She held her closely for a few minutes and then asked why she was crying. Casandra initially denied that anything was wrong. However, when the teacher persisted, said she "had fallen the night before and hurt her bottom."

The teacher took Casandra inside and asked to see where she had been hurt. When Casandra pulled down her shorts, the teacher noted what appeared to be a large burn with blisters approximately 2 inches in length by 1 inch in width on her left buttock. Several small bruises were also evident along one side of the burn. Again, the teacher quietly asked Casandra how she had been hurt, and once again she replied that she "had fallen."

1. What actions should Casandra's teacher take?

2. Would you recommend that the teacher report the incident right away or wait until she gathered more evidence? Why?

3. Would your feelings and responses be different if this was a first-time versus a repeated occurrence?

4. How can the teacher begin to help Casandra cope with this experience?

5. What would you suggest the teacher do if this happens again?

Application Activities

1. Gather statistics on the incidence of child abuse and neglect for your city, county, and state. Compare your numbers to the national rates.

2. Write an incident report using the information presented in the Case Study.

3. Develop a pamphlet that illustrates self-protection skills for young children. Use it with a group of 3- to 4-year-olds. Evaluate their response.

4. Identify local agencies that assist abusive or neglectful families in your community. Collect materials from each. Prepare a resource list that includes contact information and a brief description of the services each agency provides. Offer your list to local schools and early childhood programs.

5. Conduct an Internet search to learn about the CASA (Court Appointed Special Advocates) program. What role do they play in helping abused and neglected children? Is there a CASA program in your area? What qualifications are required of volunteer participants?

Helpful Web Resources

American Professional Society on the Abuse of Children	http://www.apsac.org
Boys and Girls Clubs of America	http://www.bgca.org
Child Welfare Information Gateway	http://www.childwelfare.gov
Child Welfare League of America (CWLA)	http://www.cwla.org
Futures Without Violence	http://www.futureswithoutviolence.org/
Prevent Child Abuse America	http://www.preventchildabuse.org
Shaken Baby Alliance	http://www.shakenbaby.com

 Visit the Education CourseMate for this textbook to access the eBook, Did You Get It? quizzes, Digital Downloads, TeachSource Video Cases, flashcards, and more. Go to CengageBrain.com to log in, register, or purchase access.

References

American Psychological Association (APA). (2012). Child sexual abuse: What parents should know. Accessed on June 30, 2012 from http://www.apa.org/pi/families/resources/child-sexual-abuse.aspx.

Bruster, B., & Foreman, K. (2012). Mentoring children of prisoners: Program evaluation, *Social Work in Public Health*, 27(1–2), 3–11.

Child Welfare Information Gateway. (2013). *Child abuse and neglect fatalities 2011: Statistics and interventions.* Washington, DC: U.S. Department of Health & Human Services (HHS), Children's Bureau. Accessed on May 6, 2013 from https://www.childwelfare.gov/pubs/factsheets/fatality.cfm.

Child Welfare Information Gateway. (2011). *About CAPTA: A legislative history.* Washington, DC: U.S. Department of Health & Human Services, Children's Bureau.

Debelle, G. (2012). Interpreting physical signs of child maltreatment: 'grey cases' and what is 'reasonably possible', *Paediatrics & Child Health*, 22(11), 470–475.

Easterbrooks, M., Chaudhuri, J., Bartlett, J., & Copeman, A. (2011). Resilience in parenting among young mothers: Family and ecological risks and opportunities, *Children & Youth Services*, 33(1), 42–50.

Fang, X., Brown, D., Florence, C., & Mercy, J. (2012). The economic burden of child maltreatment in the United States and implications for prevention, *Child Abuse & Neglect,*36(2), 156–165.

Feldman, M., McConnell, D., & Aunos, M. (2012). Parental cognitive impairment, mental health, and child outcomes in a child protection population, *Journal of Mental Health Research in Intellectual Disabilities*, 5(1), 66–90.

Feng, J., Chen, Y., Fetzer, S., Feng, M., & Lin, C. (2012). Ethical and legal challenges of mandated child abuse reporters, *Children & Youth Services Review*, 34(1), 276–280.

Goldman, J., & Grimbeek, P. (2011). Sources of knowledge of departmental policy on child sexual abuse and mandatory reporting identified by primary school student-teachers, *Educational Review*, 63(1), 1–18.

Gray, C., & Montgomery, M. (2012). Links between alcohol and other drug problems and maltreatment among adolescent girls: Perceived discrimination, ethnic identity, and ethnic orientation as moderators, *Child Abuse & Neglect*, 36(5), 449–460.

Hart, H., & Rubia, K. (2012). Neuroimaging of child abuse: A critical review, *Frontiers in Human Neuroscience*, 6, 52. Retrieved from http://www.ncbi.nlm.nih.gov/pmc/articles/PMC3307045/.

Haskett, M., Stelter, R., Proffit, K., & Nice, R. (2012). Parent emotional expressiveness and children's self-regulation: Associations with abused children's school functioning, *Child Abuse & Neglect*, 36(4), 296–307.

James, T., & Countryman, J. (2012). Psychiatric effects of military deployment on children and families, *Innovations in Clinical Neuroscience*, 9(2), 16–20.

Jonson-Reid, M., Kohl, P., & Drake, B. (2012). Child and adult outcomes of chronic child maltreatment, *Pediatrics*, 129(5), 839–845.

Katz, C., Hershkowitz, I., Malloy, L., Lamb, M., Atabaki, A., & Spindler, S. (2012). Non-verbal behavior of children who disclose or do not disclose child abuse in investigative interviews, *Child Abuse & Neglect*, 36(1), 12–20.

Keeshin, B., Cronholm, P., & Strawn, J. (2012). Physiologic changes associated with violence and abuse exposure, *Trauma, Violence & Abuse*, 13(1), 41–56.

Kempe, C. H., & Helfer, R. (Eds.). (1982). *The battered child.* Chicago: University of Chicago Press.

Kim-Spoon, J., Haskett, M., Longo, G., & Nice, R. (2012). Longitudinal study of self-regulation, positive parenting, and adjustment problems among physically abused children, *Child Abuse & Neglect*, 36(2), 95–107.

Lansford, J., Wager, L., Bates, J., Dodge, K., & Pettit, G. (2012). Parental reasoning, denying privileges, yelling, and spanking: Ethnic differences and associations with child externalizing behavior, *Parenting: Science & Practice*, 12(1), 42–56.

Lee, T., Cheung, C., & Kwong, W. (2012). Resilience as a positive youth development construct: A conceptual review, *Scientific World Journal*. Retrieved from http://www.ncbi.nlm.nih.gov/pmc/articles/PMC3353472.

Leeb, R., Bitsko, R., Merrick, M., & Armour, B. (2012). Does childhood disability increase risk for child abuse and neglect?, *Journal of Mental Health Research in Intellectual Disabilities*, 5(1), 4–31.

Leventhal, J., Martin, K., & Gaither, J. (2012). Using US data to estimate the incidence of serious physical abuse in children, *Pediatrics*, 129(3), 458–464.

Lilly, E., & Kundu, R. (2012). Dermatoses secondary to Asian cultural practices, *International Journal of Dermatology*, 51(4), 372–382.

Miller, L., Grabell, A., Thomas, A., Bermann, E., & Graham-Bermann, S. (2012). The associations between community violence, television violence, intimate partner violence, parent–child aggression, and aggression in sibling relationships of a sample of preschoolers, *Psychology of Violence*, 2(2), 165–178.

Mishna, F., Morrison, J., Basarke, S., & Cook, C. (2012). Expanding the playroom: School-based treatment for maltreated children, *Psychoanalytic Social Work*, 19(1), 70–90.

Moxley, K., Squires, J., & Lindstrom, L. (2012). Early intervention and maltreated children: A current look at the Child Abuse Prevention and Treatment Act and Part C, *Infants & Young Children*, 25(1), 3–18.

Nelson, S., Baldwin, N., & Taylor, J. (2012). Mental health problems and medically unexplained physical symptoms in adult survivors of childhood sexual abuse: An integrative literature review, *Journal of Psychiatric & Mental Health Nursing*, 19(3), 211–220.

Oshri, A., Tubman, J., & Burnette, M. (2012). Childhood maltreatment histories, alcohol and other drug use symptoms, and sexual risk behavior in a treatment sample of adolescents, *American Journal of Public Health*, 102(S2), S250–S257.

Petska, H., Sheets, L., & Knox, B. (2013). Facial bruising as a precursor to abusive head trauma, *Clinical Pediatrics*, 52(1), 86–88.

Raman, S., & Hodes, D. (2012). Cultural issues in child maltreatment, *Journal of Paediatrics & Child Health*, 48(1), 30–37.

Roberts, A., Rosario, M., Corliss, H., Koenen, K., & Austin, S. (2012). Childhood gender nonconformity: A risk indicator for childhood abuse and posttraumatic stress in youth, *Pediatrics*, 129(3), 410–417.

Rosenkranz, S., Muller, R., & Henderson, J. (2012). Psychological maltreatment in relation to substance use problem severity among youth, *Child Abuse & Neglect*, 36(5), 438–448.

Ruiz-Casares, M., Rousseau, C., Currie, J., & Heymann, J. (2012). 'I hold on to my teddy bear really tight': Children's experiences when they are home alone, *American Journal of Orthopsychiatry*, 82(1), 97–103.

Schneiderman, J., Hurlburt, M., Leslie, L., Zhang, J., & Horwitz, S. (2012). Child, caregiver, and family characteristics associated with emergency department use by children who remain at home after a child protective services investigation, *Child Abuse & Neglect*, 36(1), 4–11.

Spratt, E., Friedenberg, S., LaRosa, A., De Bellis, M., Macias, M., Summer, A., Hulsey, T., Runyan, D., & Brady, K. (2012). The effects of early neglect on cognitive, language, and behavioral functioning in childhood, *Psychology*, 3(2), 175–182.

Stalker, K., & McArthur, K. (2012). Child abuse, child protection and disabled children: A review of recent research, *Child Abuse Review*, 21(1), 24–40.

Thompson, E., & Trice-Black, S. (2012). School-based group interventions for children exposed to domestic violence, *Journal of Family Violence*, 27(3), 233–241.

USLegal, Inc. (2012). Medical neglect law and legal definition. Accessed on June 30 2012 from http://definitions.uslegal.com/m/medical-neglect.

Valentino, K., Nuttall, A., Comas, M., Borkowski, J., & Akai, C. (2012). Intergenerational continuity of child abuse among adolescent mothers: Authoritarian parenting, community violence, and race, *Child Maltreatment*, 17(2), 172–181.

Vitale, A., Vicedomini, D., Vega, G., Greco, N., & Messi, G. (2012). Shaken baby syndrome: Pathogenetic mechanism, clinical features, and preventive aspects, *Minerva Pediatrica*, 64(6), 641–647.

Waliski, A., Bokony, P., Edlund, C., & Kirchner, J. (2012). Counselors called for service: Impact of parental deployment on preschool children, *The Family Journal*, 20(2), 157–163.

chapter 11

Planning for Children's Health and Safety Education

> **#1 a, b, and c:** Promoting child development and learning
> **#2 a, b, and c:** Building family and community relationships
> **#3 a, b, c, and d:** Observing, documenting, and assessing to support young children and families
> **#4 a, b, c, and d:** Using developmentally effective approaches to connect with children and families
> **#5 a, b, and c:** Using content knowledge to build meaningful curriculum
> **#6 c and d:** Becoming a professional
> Field experiences

Learning Objectives

After studying this chapter, you should be able to:

LO 11-1 Describe the benefits of including families in children's learning experiences.

LO 11-2 Discuss the role of teacher inservice training as it relates to children's health and safety education.

LO 11-3 Identify and describe the four basic elements of instructional design.

LO 11-4 Develop health and safety activity plans based on the format outlined in this chapter.

Many of today's health problems result from a combination of environmental and self-imposed factors (CDC, 2012). Unhealthy eating habits, inactivity, pollution, increased stress, inequitable access to medical or dental care, poverty, violence, and substance abuse (alcohol, drugs, and tobacco) continue to challenge the quality of children's health (Hadley, Tessema, & Muluneh, 2012; Yoshikawa, Aber, & Beardslee, 2012). They also pose a threat to children's academic success and to their potential to become healthy, productive adults (Pirrie & Lodewyk, 2012; Singh & Ghandour, 2012).

The early years are an important time when lifelong health behaviors, **attitudes**, and **values** are being formed. It is also a time when children are open and more receptive to new ideas, changes, and suggestions. For these reasons, it is important to design developmentally appropriate learning experiences that provide children and their families with sound information for promoting a healthy lifestyle.

11-1 Family Involvement in Health and Safety Education

Families are children's first and most important teachers. They shape children's early attitudes and health/safety practices through an ongoing combination of direct instruction, **incidental learning**,

....

attitudes – *beliefs or feelings one has toward certain facts or situations.*
values – *the beliefs, traditions, and customs an individual incorporates and utilizes to guide behavior and judgments.*
incidental learning – *learning that occurs in addition to the primary intent or goals of instruction.*

Successful health and safety education is built on family involvement.

© Cengage Learning

and modeling of adult behaviors. Daily activities often become important teachable moments. For example, a parent may discuss the benefits of eating fruits and vegetables while the child washes (and samples) the broccoli for tonight's dinner or helps plant tomatoes in a vegetable garden.

Successful health and safety education programs are built on a strong foundation of family involvement (Serpell & Mashburn, 2012; Allensworth, 2011). When teachers collaborate with children's families they are able to learn about their unique values, goals, and priorities. This information can then be used to design responsive instruction that addresses children's individual needs (Fan, Williams, & Wolters, 2012). There are many resourceful ways that teachers can involve families in children's health and safety education, such as inviting them to:

- prepare and contribute to newsletters
- accompany children on field trips
- share special talents, skills, or cultural traditions
- serve as a guest speaker
- help with class projects, demonstrations, films, discussions
- assist with health assessments and policy development

Family involvement also provides unique opportunities for sharing information and learning experiences that can be reinforced in the child's home. This helps reduce the potential frustration children may encounter when they receive information at school that is inconsistent with family values and practices. Family members also benefit indirectly by learning how to make positive changes in their own health practices. Additional advantages of family involvement include:

- better understanding of children's developmental needs
- improved parental esteem
- positive contributions to children's learning
- enhanced parenting skills
- improved communication between home and school

The combined resources and efforts of families, children, and teachers can bring about meaningful improvements in health and safety behaviors for everyone.

Did You Get It?

Parents and/or guardians are children's primary educators. Which of the following parental scenarios *is not* an example of "incidental learning"?

- **a.** Establishing a rule after the child has misbehaved
- **b.** Modeling an appropriate action for the child to follow
- **c.** Using an incident as a teachable moment.
- **d.** Providing a formal lesson or discussion.

Take the full quiz on CourseMate.

11-2 Teacher Inservice in Health and Safety Education

Learning experiences that address health and safety issues are essential in children's educational programs. Yet most teachers have had only limited preservice training in health education and may not be adequately prepared to assume this responsibility. Teachers can acquire valuable information about developmentally appropriate content and effective instructional techniques for teaching health and safety through continued **inservice** opportunities.

Inservice education that is ongoing and focused on enriching teacher's knowledge and skills is a characteristic feature of high-quality programs. It can be delivered in a number of ways, such as providing financial incentives so teachers can attend educational conferences or subscribing to professional journals. Guest speakers can also be invited to present training sessions on a variety of relevant topics, such as:

- schools, early childhood programs, and the law
- emergency preparedness
- identifying child abuse
- advances in health screening
- review of sanitation procedures
- stress and anger management
- working with diverse families
- infectious disease updates
- current information on specific health problems (e.g., epilepsy, autism, diabetes, HIV/AIDS, allergies)
- review of first aid techniques and CPR training
- health promotion practices, including children's mental health
- nutrition education
- cultural awareness and sensitivity
- violence and bullying prevention

It is important that all teaching and support staff be included in inservice training opportunities. Care must be taken to ensure that information and materials provided are meaningful to participants whose educational backgrounds and professional roles may differ.

Did You Get It?

The Health Education Curriculum Analysis Tool (HECAT), is a functional guide that can be used for:

a. developing a comprehensive health education plan
b. identifying learning experiences that children will like
c. evaluating the validity of testing materials
d. locating informational sources to share with families

Take the full quiz on CourseMate.

11-3 Effective Instructional Design

Opportunities to promote children's health awareness and to bring about desired behavioral changes present exciting challenges for teachers. To successfully achieve this goal, teachers must create learning experiences that systematically build children's knowledge base and skills. They must also address the four basic elements of effective instructional design: topic selection; behavioral objectives; content presentation; and, evaluation.

---

inservice – *educational training provided by an employer.*

TABLE 11–1 HECAT Instructional Modules

Lesson modules can be accessed from the CDC/HECAT website on the following topics:

- Alcohol and other drugs
- Healthy eating
- Mental and emotional health
- Personal health and wellness
- Physical activity
- Safety
- Sexual health
- Tobacco
- Violence prevention

Source: Centers for Disease Control & Prevention (CDC). *Health Education Curriculum Analysis Tool* (*HECAT*). Atlanta, GA: CDC.

11-3a Topic Selection

The ability to select and prepare meaningful learning activities requires an understanding of children's developmental needs. Too frequently, instruction is approached in a haphazard fashion with topics selected at random rather than according to any long-range plan. Several tools are now available to assist teachers and schools in planning a curriculum that advances children's knowledge of health and safety along an increasingly complex continuum. The *National Health Education Standards* for grades PreK–12 provides such a framework and ensures that comprehensive health education is also developmentally appropriate (Appendix A) (Basch, 2011). The Centers for Disease Control & Prevention (CDC) have also developed an evidence-based instrument, the Health Education Curriculum Analysis Tool (HECAT), that can be accessed from their website (http://www.cdc.gov/HealthyYouth/hecat) (Table 11-1). Here you will also find lesson plans, student materials, and teacher resources by topic and grade level, and in multiple languages. This content is consistently aligned with the National Health Education Standards.

Thoughtful planning helps ensure that topics and learning activities will be of interest and hold children's attention. Lessons that focus on isolated facts or address topics on a one-time only basis are quickly forgotten (Essa, 2014). Teachers must also consider the diversity of children's backgrounds and abilities and prepare learning experiences that are free of gender, cultural, ethnic, and personal bias.

When teachers plan health and safety learning experiences that are meaningful and integrated across the entire curriculum (e.g., dramatic play, language arts, science, math, outdoor play), children's understanding, retention, and motivation are significantly improved (Copple & Bradekamp, 2010). This approach also helps children establish important connections between what they learn in the classroom and their personal lives. A simple explanation can be effective in helping children to understand the value of making healthy decisions, such as "Washing your hands gets rid of germs that can make you sick. When you are well, you can take part in the fun things we do at school."

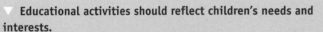

▼ **Educational activities should reflect children's needs and interests.**

© Cengage Learning

There are many developmentally appropriate health and safety **concepts** that can be introduced throughout the early curriculum. For example, toddlers enjoy learning about:

- body parts
- growth and development
- nutritious food
- social skills and positive interaction—getting along with others
- the five senses
- personal care skills—brushing teeth, hand washing, bathing, toilet routines, dressing
- friendship
- developing self-esteem and positive self-concepts
- cooperation
- physical activity and movement routines
- safe behaviors

Topics of interest to preschool children include:

- growth and development
- oral health
- safety and injury prevention—home, playground, water, firearms, traffic, poison, fire
- community helpers
- poison prevention
- emotional health—fostering positive self-image, feelings, responsibility, treating others with respect, dealing with stress, anger management
- personal cleanliness and grooming
- anger management and relaxation techniques
- healthful nutrition and where foods come from
- why sleep is important
- families
- how bodies benefit from physical activity
- disease prevention
- manners
- environmental health and safety
- personal protection skills

School-aged children are eager to explore topics in greater detail, including:

- personal appearance
- oral health
- dietary nutrients and food safety
- consumer health—taking medicines, understanding advertisements, reading labels, quackery, when to seek assistance
- factors affecting growth
- emotional health—personal feelings, making friends, family interactions, getting along with others, problem-solving, bullying, and harassment
- health professionals and their roles
- communicable illnesses and prevention measures
- personal safety and injury prevention—bicycle, pedestrian, water, playground, firearm, and home safety
- first aid techniques
- coping with stress—anger management, conflict resolution
- physical fitness
- Internet safety

concepts – *combinations of basic and related factual information that represent a broader statement or idea.*

11-3b Behavioral Objectives

The ultimate goal of health and safety education is the development and maintenance of positive knowledge, attitudes, and behaviors. Learning is demonstrated when children are able to make sound decisions and carry out health and safety practices that preserve or improve their current state of health. **Objectives** describe the desired changes in an individual's knowledge, behaviors, attitudes, or values that can be observed and measured upon completion of the learning experience (Orlich et al., 2013; Anderson, 2012).

Objectives serve several purposes:

- as a guide in the selection of content material
- as a means for identifying precise changes in learner knowledge or behavior
- as an aid in the selection of appropriate learning experiences
- as an evaluation or measurement tool

Functional objectives must be written in terms that are clear and meaningful; for example, "The child will select appropriate clothing to wear on a rainy day." The key word in this objective is "select." It is a specific behavioral change that can be observed and measured. In contrast, the statement, "The child will know how to dress for the weather," is vague, subjective, and cannot be accurately evaluated. Additional examples of precise and measurable terms include to:

- draw
- list
- discuss
- explain
- select
- write
- recognize
- describe
- identify
- answer
- demonstrate
- match
- compare

Measurable objectives are more difficult to develop for learning experiences that involve values, feelings, or attitudes. The behavioral changes resulting from this type of learning may not be immediately observable. Rather, it must be assumed that at some later point, children's behaviors will reflect what they have previously learned.

11-3c Content Presentation

Teachers serve as facilitators in the educational process, selecting instructional methods that are developmentally appropriate for children and support the stated objectives (Gordon & Browne, 2014). This is an important element in designing effective learning experiences for children and one that allows teachers to express their creativity. When deciding on a method, teachers should consider:

- presenting only a few, simple concepts during each session
- limiting presentations to a maximum of 5–10 minutes for toddlers, 10–15 minutes for pre-schoolers, and 15–25 minutes for school-aged children
- tailoring content presentation to address children's diverse needs, abilities, and interest levels
- taking into account class size, children's ages, the nature of content to be presented, and the available resources
- emphasizing the positive aspects of concepts; avoiding confusing combinations of do's and don'ts, good and bad comparisons
- creating learning experiences that involve children in hands-on activities with real-life materials
- explaining ideas in terms that are simple and familiar to children
- building in repetition to reinforce children's understanding and retention
- providing encouragement and positive reinforcement to acknowledge children's accomplishments

objectives – *clear, meaningful descriptions of specific behavioral outcomes; can be observed and measured.*

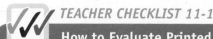

TEACHER CHECKLIST 11-1

How to Evaluate Printed Resource Material

Look for materials that:
- are prepared by reputable authorities in the field or by a reliable source
- contain unbiased information
- avoid promotion or advertisement of products
- present content that is current
- involve the learner
- are thought-provoking or raise questions and answers
- are attractive
- enhance the quality of the learning experience
- are worth the time and costs involved
- support your program's philosophy

TeachSource Digital Download   Download from CourseMate.

Several effective instructional methods can be used to present health and safety content, including:

- group discussion
- media (e.g., records, models, specimens, video)
- demonstrations, experiments, and role play
- teacher-made displays (e.g., posters, bulletin boards, booklets, flannel boards)
- art activities
- printed resource material (e.g., pamphlets, posters, charts) (See Teacher Checklist 11-1 for criteria to use for evaluating printed resource material.)
- puppet shows
- books and stories
- guest speakers
- personal example

Methods that actively involve young children in learning experiences are always the most desirable and effective. Learning activities in which children actually participate are more likely to hold their attention and also improve **retention**. Examples of instructional methods that actively engage children in learning include:

- dramatic play (e.g., family, animal groomer, dental office, restaurant, train station, airport, supermarket)
- field trips (e.g., visits to a hospital, pet store, exercise or dance class, supermarket, farm)
- art activities (e.g., posters, bulletin boards, displays, pictures, flannel boards created by children)
- hands-on experiences (e.g., hand washing, brushing teeth, grocery shopping, cooking projects, growing seeds, animal care, conducting simple science experiments)
- puppet shows (e.g., care when you are sick, protection from strangers, health checkups, good grooming practices)
- games and songs
- guest speakers (e.g., firefighter, dental hygienist, nurse, yoga instructor, dietitian, poison control staff, mental health professional)

▼ **Children learn best when they participate in the activity.**

© Cengage Learning

retention – *the ability to remember or recall previously learned material.*

When a topic or theme is presented over the course of several sessions, a variety of different instructional methods can be used to maintain children's interest, reinforce key concepts, and ensure an integrated approach. For example, a teacher might arrange an obstacle course one day, invite a yoga instructor to lead the class another day, and plan a math relay on a subsequent day to reinforce a lesson on physical activity.

Many governmental and commercial agencies offer excellent educational resource materials and lesson plans about health, safety, and nutrition topics that are appropriate for young children. A number of these websites are identified throughout the book.

11-3d Evaluation

Effective instructional design also requires that **evaluation** be conducted during all stages of lesson development and presentation. Evaluation yields feedback about the quality of instruction and whether or not students have learned what a teacher initially set out to teach. Evaluation procedures also help teachers to assess the strengths, weaknesses, and areas of instruction that require improvement (Sormunen et al., 2012).

Evaluation is accomplished by measuring positive changes in children's behavior. Goals and objectives established at the onset of instructional design are used to determine whether or not the desired behavioral changes have been achieved. Do children remember to wash their hands after using the bathroom without having to be reminded? Do children check for traffic before dashing out into the street after a runaway ball? Do children brush their teeth at least once daily? Are safety rules followed by the children when an adult is not there to remind them? In other words, evaluation is based on demonstrations of persistent change in children's observable behaviors.

Evaluation must not be looked upon as a final step. Rather, it should add a dimension of quality throughout the entire instructional program. Answers to the following evaluation questions will provide information that can be used for improvement:

- Do the objectives identify important areas where learning should occur?
- Are the objectives clearly stated, realistic, and measurable?
- Were children able to achieve the desired outcomes?
- Was the instructional method effective? Were children interested and engaged in the learning experiences?
- How can the lesson be improved?

Evaluation must also not be viewed as a self-critical process even if the findings suggest that the intended learner outcomes were not achieved. Rather, the evaluation process helps identify weaknesses in content, activity design, and presentation that may need to be addressed.

▶❚❚ **TeachSource** Video Connections

© 2015 Cengage Learning

Preschool: Health and Nutrition

Teaching young children about healthy lifestyle habits is an important adult responsibility. When children learn these skills as part of their daily activities, they are more likely to continue practicing them throughout their lifetime. As you watch the learning video, *Preschool: Health and Nutrition*, consider the following questions:

1. Why is it important to involve children in learning activities?

2. Do you think the teacher's approach to helping children learn about "good" and "bad" foods for healthy teeth was effective based on what you have learned in this chapter? Explain.

3. How would you change this activity to strengthen learning and improve retention?

4. What health and safety measures should the teacher in the video consider before presenting this lesson to children?

Watch on CourseMate.

---

evaluation – *a measurement of effectiveness for determining whether or not educational objectives have been achieved.*

CONNECTING TO EVERYDAY PRACTICE

Fire Safety

The headlines read, "Three young children found dead after fire guts basement apartment." Fire-fighters had worked frantically, but intense flames forced them out of the burning building before the children could be located. The children had been playing with matches in their mother's closet when flames quickly spread to nearby clothing. Smoke inhalation claimed the lives of all three children.

Think About This:

▶ What developmental characteristics may have contributed to this incident?

▶ What skills must young children learn to avoid a similar tragedy?

▶ What do families need to know?

▶ What classroom safety lessons can teachers introduce to help children learn the appropriate ways to respond in the event of a house fire?

▶ Describe how these learning experiences can be integrated across the curriculum.

Did You Get It?

Standardized measures meant to address targeted changes in behavior, thinking, actions, knowledge, and attitudes are formally referred to as:

a. goals
b. outcomes
c. objectives
d. targets

Take the full quiz on CourseMate.

11-4 Activity Plans

A teacher's day can be filled with many unexpected events. Activity plans encourage advanced planning and organization. Time spent on advanced planning enables a teacher to be better organized, prepared, and able to focus on presenting the learning activity.

Activity plans are often as individualized as the teachers who prepare them. However, health and safety instructional plans should include several basic features:

▶ subject title or concept to be presented
▶ specific learning objectives
▶ materials list
▶ step-by-step description of learning activities
▶ evaluation and suggestions for improvement

Activity plans should include sufficient detail so they can be implemented by a fellow colleague, a substitute teacher, classroom aide, or volunteer. Objectives should clearly indicate what children are expected to learn so that activities can be modified to meet the needs of a particular group. A description of materials, how they are to be used, and necessary safety precautions should also be addressed. Examples of several activity plans follow.

▼ Yoga helps children develop flexibility, strength, awareness, and self-control.

© waldru/Shutterstock.com

Activity Plan #1: Children's Yoga for Wellness

CONCEPT Children can begin to learn coordination, balance, and relaxation through simple yoga poses.

OBJECTIVES

- Children will identify and name body parts used in a pose.
- Children will follow simple directions.
- Children will demonstrate three yoga poses.

MATERIALS LIST

- Player and quiet music CDs
- Towels or mats

LEARNING ACTIVITIES

A. Read several of the following books and use with children:

Humphrey, M. (2008). *The kids' yoga book of feelings.* Tarrytown, NY: Marshall Cavendish Children's Books.

Lite, L. (2008). *Bubble riding: A relaxation story designed to help children increase creativity while lowering stress and anxiety levels.* Marietta, GA: Stress Free Kids.

Purperhart, H. (2008). *The yoga zoo adventure: Animal poses.* Alameda, CA: Hunter House.

Power, T. (2009). *The ABCs of yoga for kids.* Hixson, TN: Stafford House.

Whitford, R. (2005). *Little yoga: A toddler's first book of yoga.* New York: Henry Holt & Co.

B. Make yoga flash cards illustrating different poses (e.g., animals, shapes, easy). For each card, download and paste a picture of the pose on one side; write out step-by-step instructions on the other side. The cards will help children envision what the pose looks like. Teachers can vary poses for each session by selecting different cards. Continue adding cards to the collection.

C. Begin by completing several warm-up exercises with the children:

- Lie on back, raise arms overhead (palms up), and rest them on the floor. Breathe in slowly, hold, and blow out slowly like a whale. For variety, have children lie on their tummy and slide their hands underneath (placing palms over the bellybutton area) so they can feel their "breath" moving in and out.
- Stand and slowly rotate arms in large circles (like a windmill). Next, have children complete several jumping jacks.
- Stand and rise to tiptoes, stretch arms up and above the head; hold for 5 seconds. Stand with feet spread wide apart, arms extended to the sides. Lean slightly to the right, shift body weight to the right foot while lifting the left foot off of the floor. Then, lean left, shift body weight to the left foot while lifting the right foot off of the floor. Repeat the sequence, rocking back and forth from right to left foot while singing "Twinkle, Twinkle Little Star."

D. Continue to talk with the children about how to be healthy – eating nutritious foods, being physically active each day, sleeping and resting, learning how to relax, and so on.

E. Invite a children's yoga instructor to demonstrate several child-friendly poses.

EVALUATION

- Children correctly name the body parts involved in a pose.
- Children listen and follow directions.
- Children are able to demonstrate three yoga poses.

Activity Plan #2: Understanding Feelings (Emotional Health)

CONCEPT Feelings affect the state of one's mental as well as physical well-being.

OBJECTIVES

- Children will be able to name at least four feelings or emotions.
- Children will begin to express their feelings in words.

MATERIALS LIST

- Old magazines, glue, paper
- Large, unbreakable mirror
- Shoe boxes

LEARNING ACTIVITIES

A. Read and discuss with the children several of the following books:

Appelt, K. (2003). *Incredible me!* New York: Harper Collins.

Beaumont, K. (2004). *I like myself.* New York: Harcourt Children's Books.

Cain, J. (2000). *The way I feel.* Seattle, WA: Parenting Press.

Carle, E. (2000). *The grouchy ladybug.* New York: Scholastic.

Carle, E. (2000). *The very lonely firefly.* New York: Scholastic.

Dewdney, A. (2009). *Llama llama misses mama.* New York: Viking Juvenile.

Elliott, D. (2011). *Finn throws a fit!* Somerville, MA: Candlewick.

Lewis, P. (2002). *I'll always love you.* Wilton, CT: Tiger Tales.

Katz, K. (2002). *The color of us.* New York: Owlet Paperbacks.

Mciners, C. (2010). *Cool down and work through anger.* Minneapolis, MN: Free Spirit.

Milord, S. (2008). *Happy school year!* New York: Scholastic.

Nolan, A. (2009). *What I like about me.* New York: Reader's Digest.

Parr, T. (2009). *It's okay to be different.* New York: Little Brown.

Sakai, K. (2010). *Mad at mommy.* New York: Arthur A. Levine Books.

Shuman, C. (2003). *Jenny is scared! When sad things happen in the world.* Washington, DC: Magination Press.

Snow, T. & Snow, P. (2007). *Feelings to share from A to Z.* Oak Park Heights, MN: Maren Green Publishing.

Spelman, C. M. (2000). *When I feel angry.* Morton Grove, IL: Albert Whitman & Co.

Thomas, P. (2000). *Stop picking on me.* Hauppauge, NY: Barron's Juveniles.

B. During group time, encourage children to talk about the different feelings people experience. Stress that many of these feelings are normal and that it is important to learn acceptable and healthy ways of expressing them. Ask children, one at a time, to name a feeling (e.g., happy, sad, tired, bored, special, excitement, surprise, fear, lonely, embarrassed, proud, or angry). Have children act out the feeling and encourage them to observe the expressions of one another. Help children learn to recognize these feelings. "Have you ever seen someone look like this?" "Have you ever felt like this?" "What made you feel like this?" Discuss and role-play healthy ways to cope with these feelings.

C. Place an unbreakable mirror where children can see themselves. Encourage them to imitate some of the feelings they have identified and observe their own facial expressions.

D. Make a collage of feelings using pictures of people from old magazines. Help children identify the feelings portrayed in each picture.

E. Construct "I Am Special" boxes. Have the children decorate old shoe boxes with pictures that reflect their individuality, such as favorite foods, activities, toys, and so on. Ask children to fill their boxes with items that tell something special about themselves; for example, a hobby, favorite toy, photograph, souvenir from a trip, a pet, or pictures of their

▼ **Children can role-play different emotions.**

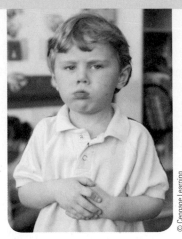

family. Children can share their boxes and tell something special about themselves during "Show and Tell" or large group time.

F. Older children can be involved in role play. Ask them to write out problem situations on small cards; for example, "You and another child want the same toy," "Someone knocks down the block structure you just finished building," "Another child pushes you," or "A friend says he doesn't like you anymore." Have pairs of children select a card and act out acceptable ways of handling their feelings in each situation. Discuss their solutions.

EVALUATION

▶ Children name at least four different feelings or emotions.
▶ Children use words rather than physical aggression to handle emotional situations.

Activity Plan #3: Germs and Illness Prevention

CONCEPT Sneezing and coughing release germs that can cause illness.

OBJECTIVES

▶ Children will be able to discuss why it is important to cover coughs and sneezes.
▶ Children will be able to identify the mouth and nose as major sources of germs.
▶ Children will cover their coughs and sneezes without being reminded.

MATERIALS LIST

▶ Two large balloons and a small amount of confetti
▶ Dolls or stuffed animals
▶ Doctor kit
▶ Stethoscopes
▶ Old lab coats or men's shirt to wear as uniforms

(Note: Check before conducting this activity to be sure no one has a latex allergy.)

LEARNING ACTIVITIES

A. Fill both balloons with a small amount of confetti. When the activity is ready to be presented to children, carefully inflate one of the balloons.

⚠ **CAUTION**

Remove your mouth from the balloon each time before inhaling.

When the balloon is inflated, quickly release pressure on the neck of the balloon, but do not let go of the balloon itself. Confetti will escape as air leaves the balloon, imitating germs as they leave the nose and mouth during coughs and sneezes. Repeat the procedure. This time, place your hand over the mouth of the balloon as the air escapes (as if to cover a cough or sneeze). Your hand will prevent most of the confetti from escaping into the air.

B. Discuss the differences between the two demonstrations with the children: "What happens when someone doesn't cover their mouth when they cough?" "How does covering your mouth help when you cough or sneeze?"

C. Include a discussion of why it is important to stay home when you are sick or have a cold.

D. Help children set up a pretend hospital where they can care for "sick" dolls or animals. Encourage children to talk about how it feels to be sick or when they must take medicine. Reinforce the importance of covering coughs and washing hands to prevent illness.

E. Have several books available for children to look at and discuss:

Capeci, A., & Cole, J. (2001). *The giant germ (Magic School Bus Chapter Book 6)*. New York: Scholastic.

Frantz, J. (2010). *Sid the science kid: The trouble with germs*. New York: HarperCollins.

Oetting, J. (2011). *Germs*. New York: Children's Press.

Rice, J. (1997). *Those mean, nasty, dirty, downright disgusting but invisible germs*. St. Paul, MN: Redleaf Press.

Romanek, T. (2003). *Achoo: The most interesting book you'll read about germs*. Toronto, ON: Kids Can Press.

Verdick, E., & Heinlen, M., (2006). *Germs are not for sharing*. Minneapolis, MN: Free Spirit Press.

Wilson, K., & Chapman, J. (2007). *Bear feels sick*. New York: Margaret K. McElderry Books.

> ### Did You Know...
> soap is a surfactant that loosens oils, dirt, and germs from the skin's surface and permits them to be washed away easily with running water?

EVALUATION

- Children can describe the relationship between germs and illness.
- Children identify coughs and sneezes as a major source of germs.
- Children voluntarily cover their own coughs and sneezes.

Activity Plan #4: Hand Washing

CONCEPT Germs on our hands can make us sick and spread illness to others.

OBJECTIVES

- Children can describe when it is important to wash their hands.
- Children can demonstrate the hand washing procedure without assistance.
- Children will value the concept of cleanliness as demonstrated by voluntarily washing their hands at appropriate times.

MATERIALS LIST

- Liquid or bar soap
- Paper towel
- Sink with running water

▼ **Correct hand washing is an important skill for children to learn.**

© Cengage Learning

LEARNING ACTIVITIES

A. Present the finger play "Bobby Bear and Leo Lion." Have children gather around a sink to observe a demonstration of the hand washing procedures as the story is read.

One bright, sunny morning, Bobby Bear and Leo Lion (make a fist with each hand, thumbs up straight), who were very good friends, decided to go for a long walk in the woods (move fists in walking motion). They walked and walked, over hills (imitate walking motion raising fists) and under trees (imitate walking motion lowering fists) until they came to a stream where they decided to cool off.

Bobby Bear sat down on a log (press palm of hand on faucet with adequate pressure to release water or turn on the faucet) and poured water on Leo Lion. Leo Lion danced and danced under the water (move hand and fingers all around underneath the water) until he was all wet. Then it was Bobby Bear's turn to get wet, so Leo Lion (hold up other fist with thumb up) sat down on a log (press palm of hand on faucet with adequate pressure to release water), and Bobby Bear danced and danced under the water until he was all wet (move other hand under water).

This was so much fun that they decided to take a bath together. They found some soap, picked it up (pick up bar of soap), put a little on their hands (rub a little soap on hands), then laid it back down on the bank (place soap in dish on side of sink). Then they rubbed the soap on their fronts and backs (rub hands together for 30 seconds) until they were all soapy.

After that, Bobby Bear jumped back on his log (press faucet) and poured water on Leo Lion until all his soap was gone (move hand under water). Then Leo Lion jumped back on his log (press other faucet), poured water on Bobby Bear, and rinsed him until all his soap was gone (move other hand under water).

Soon the wind began to blow and Bobby Bear and Leo Lion were getting very cold. They reached up and picked a leaf from the tree above (reach up and take a paper towel from the dispenser) and used it to dry themselves off (use paper towel to dry both hands). When they were all dry, Bobby Bear and Leo Lion carefully dropped their leaves into the trash can (drop paper towel into wastebasket). They joined hands (use fists, thumbs up and joined; walking motion, rapidly) and ran merrily back through the woods.[1]

B. Discuss the proper hand washing procedure with small groups of children. Ask simple questions and encourage all the children to contribute to the discussion.

   ▶ "When is it important to wash our hands?"
   ▶ "What do we do first? Let's list the steps together."
   ▶ "Why do we use soap?"
   ▶ "Why is it important to dry our hands carefully after washing them?"

C. Talk with children about the importance of washing hands after blowing their nose, coughing into their hands, playing outdoors, using the bathroom, and before eating. Model these behaviors and set a good example for children.

D. Set up a messy art activity, such as finger paint, clay, glue, or gardening. Practice hand washing. Have children look at their hands before and after washing them. Point out the value of washing hands carefully.

E. Have children practice washing their hands for as long as it takes them to sing the complete "ABC" or "Twinkle Twinkle Little Star" songs.

F. Read and discuss several of the following books with the children:

Boynton, S. (2007). *Bath time!* New York: Workman Publishing Company.
Brown, R. (2005). *All dirty! All clean!* Brentwood, TN: Sterling Publications.
Edwards, F. B. (2000). *Mortimer Mooner stopped taking a bath.* Kingston, ON: Pokeweed Press.

[1]The author would like to acknowledge Rhonda McMullen, a former student and graduate of the Early Childhood Program, University of Kansas, for sharing her delightful story and creative ways with young children.

Gerver, J. (2005). *Bath time.* New York: Children's Press.

Hammond, V. (2009). *Wash those hands!* Victoria, Ca: Trafford Publishing.

Katz, A. (2001). *Take me out of the bathtub, and other silly dilly songs.* New York: Scholastic.

Ross, T. (2006). *Wash your hands!* LaJolla, CA: Kane/Miller Book Publishers.

Woodruff, E. (1990). *Tubtime.* New York: Holiday House, Inc.

G. Observe children washing their hands to make sure they continue to follow good procedures.

H. Observe children at different times throughout the day to determine if they are using correct technique and washing hands at appropriate times.

EVALUATION

▶ Was the finger play effective for demonstrating the hand washing technique?

▶ Do the children wash their hands correctly without assistance?

▶ Do the children wash their hands at the appropriate times without being reminded?

Activity Plan #5: Dress Right for the Weather

CONCEPT Clothing helps to keep us healthy.

OBJECTIVES

▶ When given a choice, children will match appropriate items of clothing with different types of weather (e.g., rainy, sunny, snowy, hot, cold).

▶ Children will perform two of the following dressing skills: button a button, snap a snap, or zip up a zipper.

▶ Children will demonstrate proper care and storage of clothing by hanging up their coats, sweaters, hats, and so on, at least two out of three days.

MATERIALS LIST

▶ Items for a clothing store, such as clothing, cash register, play money, mirror

▶ Old magazines and catalogues containing pictures of children's clothing

▶ Paste

▶ Paper or newspaper

▶ Buttons, snaps, and zippers sewn onto pieces of cloth

▶ Dolls and doll clothes

▶ Books and pictures

LEARNING ACTIVITIES

A. Read and discuss with the children several of the following books:

Andersen, H. C. (2002). *The emperor's new clothes.* New York: North South Winds Press.

Kondrchek, J. & de la Vega, E. (2009). *What should I wear today?* Hockessin, DE: Mitchell Lane Publishers.

London, J. (2007). *Froggy gets dressed.* New York: Puffin

Scarry, H. (2002). *Richard Scarry's what will I wear?* New York: Random House.

Ziefert, H. (2004). *Bear gets dressed.* New York: Sterling Publishing Co.

B. Help children set up a clothing store. Provide clothing appropriate for boys and girls. Include items that could be worn for different types of weather conditions. Talk about the purpose of clothing and how it helps to protect our bodies. Help children identify qualities in clothing that differ with weather conditions (e.g., short sleeves vs. long sleeves, light colors vs. dark colors, lightweight fabrics vs. heavyweight fabrics, etc.).

C. Have children select two different seasons or weather conditions. Give children old magazines or catalogues from which they can choose pictures of appropriate clothing. Display completed pictures where families will see them. Younger children can point to and name various items of clothing.

D. Provide children with pieces of cloth on which a button, zipper, and snap have been sewn. Working with a few children at a time, help each child master these skills. Have several actual clothing items available for children to practice putting on and taking off.

EVALUATION

▶ Children select at least two appropriate items of clothing for three different types of weather.
▶ Children are able to complete two of the following skills—buttoning a button, snapping a snap, zipping a zipper.
▶ Children hang up their personal clothing (e.g., hats, coats, sweaters, raincoats) at least two out of three days.

Activity Plan #6: Tooth-brushing

CONCEPT Teeth should be brushed after meals and snacks to stay white and healthy.

OBJECTIVES

▶ Children can state appropriate times when teeth should be brushed.
▶ Children can demonstrate proper tooth-brushing technique.
▶ Children can describe one alternate method for cleaning teeth after eating.

MATERIALS LIST

▶ One white egg carton per child
▶ Cardboard
▶ Pink construction paper
▶ Several old toothbrushes
▶ Cloth
▶ Grease pencil
▶ Toothpaste and toothbrushes (donated)

LEARNING ACTIVITIES

A. Invite a dentist or dental hygienist to demonstrate proper tooth brushing to the children. Ask the speaker to discuss how often to brush, when to brush, how to brush, alternate ways of cleaning teeth after eating, what type of toothpaste to use, and the correct care of toothbrushes. This may also be an ideal opportunity to invite families to visit so they can learn about correct tooth-brushing skills to reinforce at home.

B. Help children construct a set of model teeth from egg cartons (Figure 11–1). Cut an oval approximately 14 inches in length from lightweight cardboard; crease oval gently along the center. Cut the bottom portion of an egg carton lengthwise into two strips. Staple egg carton "teeth" along the small ends of the oval. Glue pink construction paper along the edges where "teeth" are fastened to form "gums." Also cover the backside of the oval with pink construction paper. Use a grease pencil to mark areas of plaque on the teeth. Cover the head of an old toothbrush with cloth and fasten. With the toothbrush, have children demonstrate correct tooth-brushing technique to remove areas of plaque (grease pencil markings).

C. Obtain pamphlets about children's dental health from your local dental health association or download information from reliable dental websites. Prepare a newsletter and include information about the dental hygiene concepts children have been learning; distribute it to families or post online.

D. Send a note home to families and request that children bring a clean toothbrush to school. (Local dentists and dental associations may be willing to donate brushes.) Practice step-by-step tooth brushing with small groups of children.

E. Older children will enjoy designing posters or bulletin board displays that reinforce proper dental hygiene.

F. Read and discuss with children several of the following books:

Beeler, S. (2001). *Throw your tooth on the roof: Tooth traditions from around the world*, Queensland, AU: Sandpiper Publishing.

Civardi, A. (2010). *Going to the dentist.* London: Usborne Books.

Keller, L. (2000). *Open wide: Tooth school inside.* New York: Henry Holt & Co.

Miller, E. (2009). *The tooth book: A guide to healthy teeth and gums.* New York: Holiday House.

Ricci, C. (2005). *Show me your smile!* New York: Simon Spotlight/Nickelodeon.

Simms, L. (2002). *Rotten teeth.* Queensland, AU: Sandpiper Publishing.

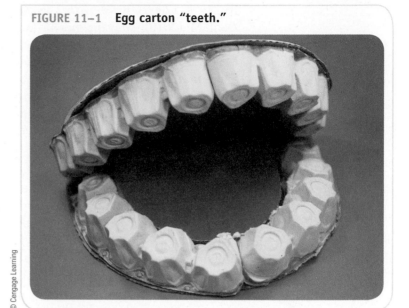

FIGURE 11–1   Egg carton "teeth."

© Cengage Learning

Evaluation

- Children identify times when teeth should be brushed.
- Children demonstrate correct tooth-brushing technique.
- Children correctly describe at least one alternate method for cleaning their teeth after eating.

Activity Plan #7: Dental Health

CONCEPT Proper dental hygiene helps keep teeth healthy.

OBJECTIVES

- Children will be able to identify at least two purposes that teeth serve.
- Children can name at least three foods that are good for healthy teeth.
- Children can describe three ways to promote dental health.

MATERIALS LIST

- Men's old shirts (preferably white) to use as dental uniforms
- Stuffed animals
- Tongue blades
- Children's books on dental health
- Old magazines
- Plastic fruits and vegetables
- Gardening tools

LEARNING ACTIVITIES

A. Information and resource materials about children's dental care can be located on the following websites:

American Dental Association (http://www.ada.org)

American Academy of Pediatric Dentistry (http://www.aapd.org)

National Maternal & Child Oral Health Resource Center/Head Start (http://www.mchoralhealth.org/Topics/hs.html)

CDC: Children's Oral Health (http://www.cdc.gov/oralhealth/topics/child.htm)

B. Read one or more of the following books during group time. Talk with the children about the role teeth play (e.g., for chewing, speech, smiling, a place for permanent teeth) and why it is important to take good care of them.

Bagley, K. (2000). *Brush well: A look at dental care.* Mankato, MN: Capstone Press.

Dahl, M. (2010). *Pony brushes his teeth.* Bloomington, MN: Picture Window Books.

Frost, H. (2006). *Food for healthy teeth.* Bloomington, MN: Capstone Press.

Mayer, M. (2001). *Just going to the dentist.* New York: Golden Books.

Palatini, M. (2004). *Sweet tooth.* New York: Simon & Schuster Children's Publishing.

Schoberle, C. (2000). *Open wide! A visit to the dentist.* New York: Simon Spotlight.

Schuh, M. (2008). *Brushing teeth.* Mankato, MN: Capstone Press.

Vrombaut, A. (2003). *Clarabella's teeth.* New York: Clarion Books.

C. Set up a "dentist" office for dramatic play. Have old white shirts available for children to wear as uniforms. Place stuffed animals in chairs so children can practice their "dentistry" skills using wooden tongue blades and cotton balls.

D. Spread out plastic fruits, vegetables, child-sized gardening tools, and baskets on the floor. Have children plant a garden with foods that are healthy for their teeth.

E. Discuss ways children can help to keep their teeth healthy (e.g., daily brushing with a fluoride toothpaste; regular dental checkups; eating nutritious foods, especially raw fruits, vegetables; avoiding chewing on nonfood items such as pencils, spoons, and keys; limiting sweets).

F. Help children construct "healthy food" mobiles. Use old magazines to cut out pictures of foods that promote healthy teeth. Paste pictures on paper, attach with string or yarn, and tie to a piece of cardboard cut in the shape of a smile.

G. Have children help plan snacks for several days; include foods that are nutritious and important for healthy teeth.

EVALUATION

▶ Children name at least two functions that teeth serve.

▶ Children identify at least three foods that are important for healthy teeth.

▶ Children describe three oral health practices that help keep teeth healthy.

Activity Plan #8: Safety in Cars

CONCEPT Safety rules are important to follow in and around vehicles.

OBJECTIVES

▶ Children will understand the purpose and importance of wearing seat belts or sitting in an appropriate safety car seat.

▶ Children can name at least one important safety rule to follow in and around cars.

MATERIALS LIST

▶ Educational materials about child passenger safety can be downloaded from many websites, including the Children's Safety Network (http://www.childrenssafetynetwork.org) and the National Highway Traffic Safety Administration (http://www.nhtsa.dot.gov).

▶ Photographs taken of children demonstrating the following safety rules:

a. Always hold an adult's hand when going to and from the car; never dash ahead.

b. Always get in and out of a car on the curbside.

c. Open and close car doors properly. Place both hands on the door handle to reduce the possibility of getting fingers caught in the door.

d. Sit in the car seat; never ride standing.

e. Put on seat belt or use safety car seat.

f. Lock all car doors before starting out.

g. Ride with arms, legs, head, and other body parts inside the car.

h. Only adults touch the controls inside of a car.

i. Ride quietly so as not to disturb the driver.

▼ **Children can begin to recognize traffic safety signs.**

© Cengage Learning

LEARNING ACTIVITIES

A. Download car safety information pamphlets from one of the websites listed above and discuss with the children. Stress the importance of wearing seat belts or riding in an appropriate car seat restraint. Print copies of car safety pamphlets for children to take home and to share with their family.

B. Mount photographs of children demonstrating safety rules on poster board or display them on a table. Encourage children to identify the safe behavior demonstrated in each picture.

C. Use large group time to discuss with the children the importance of the safety rule illustrated in each of the photographs.

D. For dramatic play, use large wooden blocks, cardboard boxes or chairs, and a "steering wheel" to build a pretend car. Have children demonstrate the car safety rules as they play.

E. Prepare a chart with all of the children's names. Each day, have children place a checkmark next to their name if they rode in a car seat and wore their seat belt on the way to school.

F. Establish a parent committee to plan a "Safe Riding" campaign. On randomly selected days, observe families and children as they arrive and depart from the center; record whether or not they were wearing seat belt restraints. Enlist children's artistic abilities to design and make awards to be given to families who ride safely. Repeat the campaign again in several months.

EVALUATION

▸ Children are observed wearing seat belts or sitting in a proper safety car seat.

▸ Children name one safety rule to observe when riding in a car.

Activity Plan #9: Pedestrian Safety

CONCEPT Children can begin to learn safe behaviors to follow in and around traffic and develop a respect for moving vehicles.

OBJECTIVES

▸ Children will be able to identify the stop, go, and walk signals.

▸ Children will describe two rules for safely crossing streets.

▸ Children will begin to develop respect for moving vehicles.

MATERIALS LIST

▸ Flannel board and characters

▸ Cardboard pieces, poster paint, wooden stakes

▸ Masking tape, yarn or string

▸ 6-inch paper plates

▸ Red, green, and yellow poster paint

▸ Black marker

LEARNING ACTIVITIES

A. Read and discuss with the children several of the following books:

Baraclough, S. (2007). *Road safety.* Mankato, MN: Heineman-Raintree.

Berenstain, S., & Berenstain, J. (1999). *My trusty car seat: Buckling up for safety.* New York: Random House.

Committee, C. B. (2000). *Buckles buckles everywhere.* Columbia, SC: Palmetto Bookworks.

Llewellyn, C. (2006). *Watch out! On the road.* Hauppauge, NY: Barron Education Series.

Mattern, J. (2007). *Staying safe in the car.* New York: Weekly Reader Early Learning.

Rathmann, P. (1995). *Officer Buckle and Gloria.* New York: Putnam Publishing Group.

Thomas, P. (2003). *I can be safe.* Hauppauge, NY: Barron Education Series.

B. Discuss rules for safely crossing streets:

1. Always have an adult cross the street with you. (This is a must for preschool children.)
2. Cross streets only at intersections.
3. Always look both ways before stepping out into the street.
4. Use your ears to listen for oncoming cars.
5. Don't walk out into the street from between parked cars or in the middle of a block.
6. Ask an adult to retrieve balls and toys from streets.
7. Always obey traffic signs.

C. Introduce basic traffic signs (only those that have meaning to young pedestrians) such as stop, go, walk, pedestrian crossing, one-way traffic, bike path, and railroad crossing. Help children learn to recognize each sign by identifying distinguishing features such as color, shape, and location.

D. Help children to construct the basic traffic signs using cardboard and poster paint. Attach signs to wooden stakes. Set up a series of "streets" in the outdoor play yard by using string, yarn, or pieces of cardboard to mark paths; place traffic signs in appropriate places. Select children to ride tricycles along designated "streets" while other children practice pedestrian safety.

E. Prepare a flannel board story and characters to help children visualize pedestrian safety rules.

F. Help children construct a set of stop-go-walk signs. Have each child paint three paper plates—one red, one green, one yellow. On a plain white plate, write the word WALK. Fasten all four plates together with tape or glue to form a traffic signal.

EVALUATION

▸ Children respond correctly to traffic signals: stop, go, walk.

▸ Children state two rules for safely crossing streets. (Puppets can be used to ask children questions.)

▸ Children demonstrate caution in the play yard as pedestrians and when riding tricycles and other wheeled toys.

Did You Know...

that approximately 400 children under the age of 10 die in house fires each year? Children younger than 5 years are at highest risk.

Activity Plan #10: Fire Safety

CONCEPT Fire safety rules are important to know in the event of a fire.

OBJECTIVES

▸ Children can describe what they would do if there was a fire at their house or school.

▸ Children can demonstrate stop, drop, and roll.

▸ Children can state what firefighters do and how they put out fires.

MATERIALS LIST

- Large cardboard boxes
- Poster board
- Photograph of each child
- Chalk and paint in fire colors (red, orange, and yellow)
- Small spray bottles
- Paper and plastic wrap
- Rolling pin
- Tape

▼ **Learning about fire safety is important for young children.**

© Cengage Learning

LEARNING ACTIVITIES

A. Read and discuss with the children several of the following books:

Brown, M. (2000). *Arthur's fire drill*. New York: Random House.

Cuyler, M. (2001). *Stop, drop & roll*. New York: Simon & Schuster Children's Publishing.

Demarest, C. (2003). *Firefighters A to Z*. New York: Margaret K. McElderry Books.

MacLean, C. (2004). *Even firefighters hug their moms*. New York: Puffin.

Pendziwol, J. (1999). *No dragons for tea: Fire safety for kids (and dragons)*. Tonawanda, NY: Kids Can Press.

Rau, D. (2009). *Fire safety*. New York: Benchmark Books.

B. Invite a firefighter to speak about important safety skills, such as stop, drop, and roll; crawling low on the floor to stay away from smoke and heat; and, planning alternative evacuation routes.

C. Construct a fire obstacle course. Build a tunnel out of cardboard boxes. Establish a "designated meeting place" at the end of the tunnel by displaying a poster with children's photographs. Have children begin the obstacle course by demonstrating the correct stop, drop, and roll technique. Next, have children crawl through the tunnel on their hands and knees; this shows children the appropriate way for navigating through a smoke-filled room before arriving at the designated safe area. Be sure to encourage and reinforce children's efforts.

D. Take cardboard boxes outside and have the children decorate them to look like buildings. Have children draw fire on the buildings using red, yellow, and orange chalk. Children can then use small spray bottles filled with water to put out the fire.

E. Add firefighter figures, ladders, fire trucks, and other fire-related materials to the block area.

F. Create a fire painting. Have the children paint a picture with thick red and yellow tempera paint. While the paint is still wet, cover with plastic wrap and secure to the back of the painting with tape. Have the child use a rolling pin to roll back and forth over their painting (colors will merge)

EVALUATION

- Children describe how they would get out of their house or school safely during a fire and where they would go once outside the building.

▶ Children demonstrate how to stop, drop, and roll.
▶ Children explain what firefighters do and how they put out fires.[2]

Activity Plan #11: Poisonous Substances—Poison Prevention

CONCEPT Identification and avoidance of known and potentially poisonous substances.

OBJECTIVES

▶ Children will name at least three poisonous substances.
▶ Children can identify at least one safety rule that will help prevent accidental poisoning.

MATERIALS LIST

▶ Old magazines
▶ Large sheet of paper
▶ Glue
▶ Small squares of paper or self-adhesive labels
▶ Marking pens

LEARNING ACTIVITIES

A. Invite a guest speaker from your local hospital emergency room or public health department to talk with the children about poison prevention.
B. Show children pictures or actual labels of poisonous substances. Include samples of cleaning items, personal grooming supplies, auto maintenance products, medicines, perfumes, plants, and berries.
C. Discuss rules of poison prevention:

1. Only food should be put into the mouth.
2. Medicine is not candy and should be given only by an adult.
3. An adult should always inform children that they are taking medicine, not candy.
4. Never eat berries, flowers, leaves, or mushrooms before checking with an adult.

D. Make a wall mural for the classroom displaying pictures of poisonous substances. Be sure to include a sampling of cleaning products, personal grooming supplies, medicines, plants; products commonly found in garages, such as insecticides, fertilizers, gasoline, and automotive fluids. Glue pictures of these products on a large sheet of paper. Display the mural where parents and children can look at it.

EVALUATION

▶ Children point to or name at least three poisonous substances.
▶ Children state and role-play at least one safety rule that can help prevent accidental poisoning.

TEACHER RESOURCES

Nelson, L., Shih, R., & Balick, M. (2007). *Handbook of Poisonous and Injurious Plants*, Warren, MI: Springer.
U.S. Environmental Protection Agency. (2002). *Learn about chemicals around your house.* (A virtual room-by-room tour available online at http://www.epa.gov/kidshometour).
American Association of Poison Control Centers. Prevention materials. (Available online at http://www.aapcc.org/prevention)
National Capital Poison Center. *Quills up – Stay away!* (Teacher guide and resource materials available online at http://www.poison.org/prevent/preschool.asp).

[2]The author would like to thank Allison Moore, a former student and graduate of the Early Childhood program, Department of Human Development and Family Life, University of Kansas, for her innovative lesson plan.

Did You Get It?

For the next two days you are presenting your sixth grade class with a series of lessons on "listening versus hearing." Lesson plans should be documented in enough detail to allow a colleague, substitute teacher, classroom aide, or volunteer to _____ the learning experience.

a. enjoy

b. conduct

c. critique

d. modify

Take the full quiz on CourseMate.

PARTNERING with FAMILIES

Evaluating Health and Safety Information on the Internet

Dear Families,

The Internet has improved access to a vast amount of health and safety information. Consumers are able to learn about new developments, the pros and cons of various treatments, product recalls, and background information for making informed decisions. However, it is important to view websites with caution because many include considerable misinformation due to the lack of any regulatory control. There are several questions that can be asked to help you determine the reliability of health and safety information posted online:

◗ What individual or group is sponsoring and responsible for this site? Check the URL (web address): information on sites maintained by the government (.gov) and educational institutions (.edu) is generally considered trustworthy.

◗ Are the individuals who prepared and maintain the site qualified? (Often the credentials of advisory board members, an individual who has reviewed the content, or webmaster will be included.)

◗ Who is the intended audience? Is the purpose to entertain, inform, or educate?

◗ Is the site current? How recently was the information updated? It may be difficult to know if the date posted on a web page refers to when the information was originally written, last revised, or actually posted.

◗ Does the information appear to be objective and free of bias? Sites run by private individuals or commercial groups may reflect personal opinion or an attempt to sell a product. Facts and figures should include a reference to the original information source.

◗ What links are included? Anyone can establish a link to another web page, so this may not prove to be a valid strategy for evaluating a site's credibility.

◗ Does the site include a way to contact the owner if you have questions or wish to obtain additional information?

Summary

◗ Including families in children's health and safety education encourages consistency between school and home.

- Unhealthy lifestyle practices and attitudes are responsible for many contemporary health problems. They also interfere with children's ability to learn.

- When families know what children are learning at school, it is easier for them to reinforce the same information, practices, and values at home.
- When teachers are aware of differences (e.g., cultural, linguistic, ethnic) in families' values regarding health, they are better able to create learning experiences that are more responsive to children's needs.

▶ Ongoing inservice opportunities help teachers stay current, especially in the areas of health and safety, where new developments and information are always emerging.

- Education is a key element in reducing health problems.
- Educating children about health and safety raises their awareness and ability to make informed decisions. It also strengthens children's early efforts to assume some responsibility for their personal well-being.

▶ Effective health and safety instruction is based on four key design elements:

- Health and safety topics selected to appeal to children's interests, address their developmental needs, and be free of bias.
- Learning objectives that describe expected changes in children's behavior.
- Instructional methods that are varied, inspire creativity, capture children's attention, and convey information in ways that children can understand.
- Evaluation that is continuous and assesses all aspects of the instructional process.

▶ Lesson plans that are prepared in advance improve the teacher's ability to be organized, safe, creative, and focused on the learning activity.

◐ Terms to Know

attitudes *p. 293*	inservice *p. 295*	retention *p. 299*
values *p. 293*	concepts *p. 297*	evaluation *p. 300*
incidental learning *p. 293*	objectives *p. 298*	

◐ Chapter Review

A. **By Yourself:**

1. Match each of the following definitions in **Column I** with the correct term in **Column II**.

Column I	Column II
1. to assess the effectiveness of instruction	a. education
2. favorable changes in attitudes, knowledge, or practices	b. outcome
3. a sharing of knowledge or skills	c. positive behavior changes
4. ideas and values meaningful to a child	d. attitude
5. subject or theme	e. relevance
6. feeling or strong belief	f. topic
7. occurs in conjunction with daily activities and routines	g. incidental learning
8. the product of learning	h. evaluation
	i. retention

2. The following is a list of suggested health and safety topics. Place an A (appropriate) or NA (not appropriate) next to each statement. Base your decision on whether the topic is or is not suitable for preschool-aged children.

_____ dental health

_____ feelings and how to get along with others

_____ primary causes of suicide

_____ consumer health (e.g., understanding advertisements, choosing a doctor, medical quackery)

_____ eye safety

_____ the hazards of smoking

_____ how to safely light matches

_____ physical fitness for health

_____ cardiopulmonary resuscitation (CPR)

_____ the importance of rest and sleep

_____ safety at home

_____ animal families

B. **As a Group:**

1. Discuss why it is essential to provide health and safety learning experiences during a child's early years.

2. Explain why learning experiences must be evaluated continuously and not only after the lesson has ended. How can this information be used to improve future lessons?

3. Debate the pros and cons of including families in children's health and safety education.

4. Explain how programs and schools benefit from investing in inservice training for teachers.

5. Discuss how teachers can determine if health and safety resource materials are reliable.

Case Study

Eduardo, a new assistant, was asked by his head teacher to develop a "Healthy Eating Helps Us Grow" lesson. Although eager to be given this assignment, Eduardo was apprehensive about planning activities that 4-year-olds would enjoy. He arrived early that morning and set up a grocery store for dramatic play, books about food for the children to read, and magazine pictures of foods for the children to sort into the MyPlate food categories. The children played "grocery shopping" for a while, looked at several of the books, but weren't interested in the sorting activity.

1. Were the activities Eduardo planned appropriate for 4-year-olds?

2. How effective was this lesson for teaching children about healthy eating habits?

3. What are some realistic learning objectives that Eduardo might have established in preparation for this lesson?

4. How would Eduardo evaluate what the children actually learned from these activities?

5. What changes would you make in Eduardo's instructional strategies?

Application Activities

1. Interview a toddler, preschool, and a first- or second-grade teacher. Ask each to describe the basic health and safety concepts they emphasize in their classrooms.

2. Arrange to observe one of the teachers while she is conducting a health and safety learning activity with children. What were the teacher's objectives? Was the instructional method effective? Did the teacher involve children in the learning activities? Were the children attentive? Were the learning objectives met?

3. Visit several websites that provide information about appropriate child seat-belt restraints and car safety seats. Read and compare the information. Do all statements agree? If not, in what ways does the information differ? For what audience is the material written (e.g., families, children, teachers, and other professionals)?

4. Develop a lesson plan for a unit on "What makes us grow?" Include objectives, length of time, materials, learning activities, measures for evaluation, and teacher resource information. Exchange lesson plans with another student; critique each other's plan for clarity of ideas, thoroughness, organization, and creativity.

5. Make arrangements to present your "What makes us grow?" lesson plan to a class of the same-age children at two different schools. Compare the experience in each setting. Did the children respond similarly to the lesson? Were you able to achieve the learning objectives? What factors may have contributed to differences in children's learning styles? What would you have changed?

Helpful Web Resources

American Dental Association	http://www.ada.org
American Heart Association	http://www.americanheart.org
Awesome Library	http://www.awesomelibrary.org
Canadian Childcare Resource & Research Unit	http://www.childcarecanada.org
Children, Stress, & Natural Disasters (University of Illinois)	http://web.extension.uiuc.edu/disaster/teacher/teacher.html
Children's Safety Network	http://www.childrenssafetynetwork.org/
Environmental Protection Agency	http://www.epa.gov
National Dairy Council	http://www.nationaldairycouncil.org
National Fire Protection Association	http://www.nfpa.org
National Highway Traffic Safety Administration	http://www.nhtsa.dot.gov
PE (physical education) Central	http://www.pecentral.org
The Weather Channel Kids!	http://www.weatherchannelkids.com

Visit the Education CourseMate for this textbook to access the eBook, Did You Get It? quizzes, Digital Downloads, TeachSource Video Cases, flashcards, and more. Go to CengageBrain.com to log in, register, or purchase access.

References

Allensworth, D. (2011). Addressing the social determinants of health of children and youth, *Health Education & Behavior*, 38(4), 331–338.

Anderson, L. (2012). What every teacher should know: Reflections on "Educating the developing mind", *Educational Psychology Review*, 24(1), 13–18.

Basch, C. (2011). Healthier students are better learners: A missing link in school reforms to close the achievement gap, *Journal of School Health*, 81(10), 593–598.

Centers for Disease Control & Prevention (CDC). (2012). Chronic disease prevention and health promotion. Accessed on July 3, 2012 from http://www.cdc.gov/chronicdisease/.

CDC. (2007). *Health education curriculum analysis tool (HECAT)*. Accessed on July 3, 2012 from http://www.cdc.gov/HealthyYouth/hecat/.

Copple, C., & Bradekamp, S. (Eds.). (2010). *Developmentally appropriate practice (in early childhood programs, serving children birth through age 8)*. Washington, DC: National Association for the Education of Young Children (NAEYC).

Essa, E. (2014). *Introduction to early childhood education* (7th ed.). Belmont, CA: Wadsworth Cengage Learning.

Fan, W., Williams, C., & Wolters, C. (2012). Parental involvement in predicting school motivation: Similar and differential effects across ethnic groups, *Journal of Educational Research*, 1015(1), 21–35.

Gordon, A., & Browne, K. (2014). *Beginnings and beyond.* (9th ed.). Belmont, CA: Wadsworth Cengage Learning.

Hadley, C., Tessema, F., & Muluneh, A. (2012). Household food insecurity and caregiver distress: Equal threats to child nutritional status?, *American Journal of Human Biology*, 24(2), 149–157.

Orlich, D., Harder, R., Callahan, R., Trevisan, M., & Brown, A. (2013). *Teaching strategies.* (10th ed.). Belmont, CA: Wadsworth Cengage Learning.

Pirrie, A., & Lodewyk, K. (2012). Investigating links between moderate-to-vigorous physical activity and cognitive performance in elementary school students, *Mental Health & Physical Activity*, 5(1), 93–98.

Serpell, Z., & Mashburn, A. (2012). Family-school connectedness and children's early social development, *Social Development*, 21(1), 21–46.

Singh, G., & Ghandour, R. (2012). Impact of neighborhood social conditions and household socioeconomic status on behavioral problems among US children, *Maternal & Child Health Journal*, 16(1 Supp.), 158–169.

Sormunen, M., Saaranen, T., Tossavainen, K., & Turunen, H. (2012) Process evaluation of an elementary school health learning intervention in Finland, *Health Education*, 112(3), 272–291.

Yoshikawa, H., Aber, J., & Beardslee, W. (2012). The effects of poverty on the mental, emotional, and behavioral health of children and youth: Implications for prevention, *American Psychologist*, 67(4), 272–284.

Foods and Nutrients: Basic Concepts

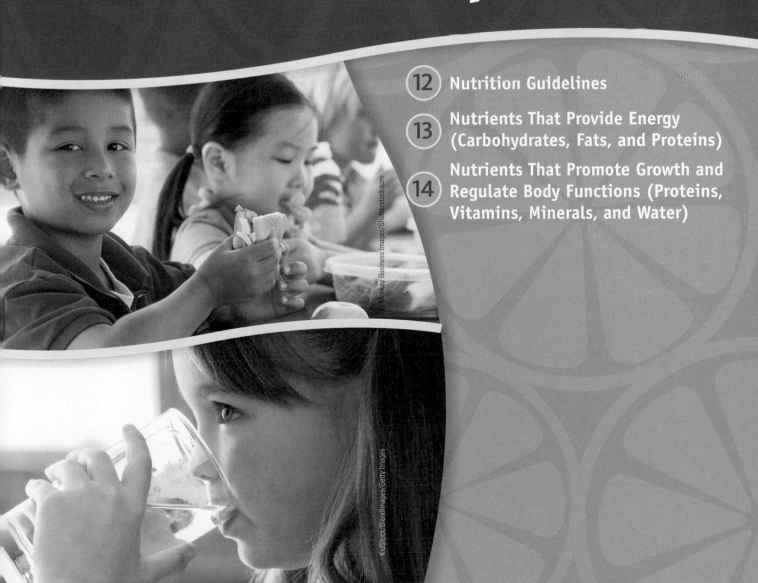

Nutrition Guidelines

▶ **#1 a, b, and c:** Promoting child development and learning
▶ **#2 a and c:** Building family and community relationships
▶ **#3 a, b, c, and d:** Observing, documenting, and assessing to support young children and families
▶ **#6 b, c, and e:** Becoming a professional

Learning Objectives

After studying this chapter, you should be able to:

LO 12-1 Calculate the nutrient content of a meal.
LO 12-2 Use the *Dietary Guidelines for Americans* to achieve your personal nutritional goals.
LO 12-3 Identify the five MyPlate food groups and the major nutrient contributions of each.
LO 12-4 Evaluate the nutritional quality of a food item from its package label.

Diet has a direct effect on the quality of a person's health and well-being. Foods contain **nutrients** that play important roles in supporting and maintaining normal body functions. They:

▶ supply energy
▶ provide materials for growth and maintenance of body tissue
▶ regulate body processes

It is important to note that all persons require the same nutrients throughout their lifetime, but in different amounts. Factors such as age, activity, gender, health status, and lifestyle determine how much of a particular nutrient is needed. For example, young children have a significant need for nutrients that support growth and provide energy; older children and adults require nutrients to maintain and repair body tissue and to provide energy.

Approximately 50 nutrients are known to be essential for humans. **Essential nutrients** can be obtained only from food because they are not produced in the body in adequate amounts. An inadequate intake or poor utilization of nutrients can lead to **malnutrition** or **undernutrition** and disrupt normal body functions that support good health. Malnutrition can also develop from an excessive intake (supplementation) of one or more nutrients to the exclusion of others. This, too, can interfere with normal body functions and cause health problems. Information about the nutrient contributions of specific foods can be accessed online (http://ndb.nal.usda.gov) and in many books.

Nutrition is the study of food and how nutrients are used in the body—from the time food is ingested, digested, nutrients are absorbed and distributed throughout the body, and waste is eliminated. Table 12–1 shows the relationship between nutrients and their primary functions. Note that most nutrients serve one or two main purposes, whereas protein plays a critical role in all three.

....

nutrients – *the chemical substances in food that the body requires to function properly.*
essential nutrient – *nutrient that must be provided in food because it cannot be synthesized by the body at a rate sufficient to meet its needs.*
malnutrition – *prolonged inadequate or excessive intake of nutrients and/or calories required by the body.*
undernutrition – *an inadequate intake of one or more required or essential nutrients.*
nutrition – *the study of food and how it is used by the body.*

TABLE 12–1 Nutrients and Their Roles

	Calories per Gram	Energy	Build/Maintain Body Tissues	Regulators
Carbohydrates	4	×		
Fats	9	×		
Proteins (needed for every function)	4	×	×	×
Minerals			×	×
Water			×	×
Vitamins				×*

*required in a regulatory role only.

▼ A healthful diet includes a variety of nutrient-dense foods.

© Cengage Learning

A healthful diet is based on a daily intake of nutritious foods and meals. Consuming a wide variety of foods ensures that all essential nutrients will be obtained. Some foods contain many nutrients; others yield few. No single food supplies all of the nutrients in amounts adequate to support life. What should we eat? What should we not eat? How much should we eat? The answers to these important questions have led to the development of several nutrition tools and guidelines. Each provides information that promotes healthy eating habits. However, it is up to the individual to make the right choices.

12-1 Dietary Reference Intakes

The "master guideline" for nutrition planning in the United States and Canada is the **Dietary Reference Intakes (DRIs)**. The current DRI guidelines reflect major philosophical and format changes from the original 1941 plan previously known as the Recommended Daily Dietary Allowances (RDAs). DRI recommendations now emphasize the critical relationship that exists between dietary intake, health, and the reduced risk of chronic disease. Table 12–2 illustrates the first two sections of the DRI document, which consists of four basic components:

- Recommended Daily Allowance (RDA) – the ideal nutrient intake goals for individuals.
- Adequate Intake (AI) – goals for nutrient intake when an RDA has not been determined.
- Estimated Average Requirement (EAR) – the amount of a nutrient that is estimated to meet the requirements of 50 percent of the individuals in a given life-stage or gender group; this number is used to establish the RDAs.
- Tolerable Upper Intake Level (UL) – the highest intake level that is likely to pose no health risk; exceeding this limit could cause potential toxicity and health risks.

The DRIs are used to set national nutritional policy as well as for planning diets and assessing the nutrient intakes of individuals or groups. They are also used for determining

Dietary Reference Intake (DRI) – *a plan that presents the recommended goals of nutrient intakes for various age and gender groups.*

TABLE 12-2 Dietary Reference Intakes: RDA and AI for Vitamins and Elements
Food and Nutrition Board, Institute of Medicine, National Academies

Life Stage Group	Vitamin A (µg/d)[a]	Vitamin C (mg/d)	Vitamin D (µg/d)[bc]	Vitamin E (mg/d)[d]	Vitamin K (µg/d)	Thiamin (mg/d)	Riboflavin (mg/d)	Niacin (mg/d)[e]	Vitamin B6 (mg/d)	Folate (µg/d)[f]	Vitamin B12 (µg/d)	Pantothenic Acid (mg/d)	Biotin (µg/d)	Choline (mg/d)[g]
Infants														
0 to 6 mo	400*	40*	10	4*	2.0*	0.2*	0.3*	2*	0.1*	65*	0.4*	1.7*	5*	125*
6 to 12 mo	500*	50*	10	5*	2.5*	0.3*	0.4*	4*	0.3*	80*	0.5*	1.8*	6*	150*
Children														
1–3 y	300	15	15	6	30*	0.5	0.5	6	0.5	150	0.9	2*	8*	200*
4–8 y	400	25	15	7	55*	0.6	0.6	8	0.6	200	1.2	3*	12*	250*
Males														
9–13 y	600	45	15	11	60*	0.9	0.9	12	1.0	300	1.8	4*	20*	375*
14–18 y	900	75	15	15	75*	1.2	1.3	16	1.3	400	2.4	5*	25*	550*
19–30 y	900	90	15	15	120*	1.2	1.3	16	1.3	400	2.4	5*	30*	550*
31–50 y	900	90	15	15	120*	1.2	1.3	16	1.3	400	2.4	5*	30*	550*
51–70 y	900	90	15	15	120*	1.2	1.3	16	1.7	400	2.4[h]	5*	30*	550*
>70 y	900	90	20	15	120*	1.2	1.3	16	1.7	400	2.4[h]	5*	30*	550*
Females														
9–13 y	600	45	15	11	60*	0.9	0.9	12	1.0	300	1.8	4*	20*	375*
14–18 y	700	65	15	15	75*	1.0	1.0	14	1.2	400[i]	2.4	5*	25*	400*
19–30 y	700	75	15	15	90*	1.1	1.1	14	1.3	400[i]	2.4	5*	30*	425*
31–50 y	700	75	15	15	90*	1.1	1.1	14	1.3	400[i]	2.4	5*	30*	425*
51–70 y	700	75	15	15	90*	1.1	1.1	14	1.5	400	2.4[h]	5*	30*	425*
>70 y	700	75	20	15	90*	1.1	1.1	14	1.5	400	2.4[h]	5*	30*	425*
Pregnancy														
14–18 y	750	80	15	15	75*	1.4	1.4	18	1.9	600[j]	2.6	6*	30*	450*
19–30 y	770	85	15	15	90*	1.4	1.4	18	1.9	600[j]	2.6	6*	30*	450*
31–50 y	770	85	15	15	90*	1.4	1.4	18	1.9	600[j]	2.6	6*	30*	450*
Lactation														
14–18 y	1,200	115	15	19	75*	1.4	1.6	17	2.0	500	2.8	7*	35*	550*
19–30 y	1,300	120	15	19	90*	1.4	1.6	17	2.0	500	2.8	7*	35*	550*
31–50y	1,300	120	15	19	90*	1.4	1.6	17	2.0	500	2.8	7*	35*	550*

Note: This table (taken from the DRI reports, see www.nap.edu) presents Recommended Dietary Allowances (RDAs) in **bold type** and Adequate Intakes (AIs) in ordinary type followed by an asterisk (*). An RDA is the average daily dietary intake level; sufficient to meet the nutrient requirements of nearly all (97–98 percent) healthy individuals in a group. It is calculated from an Estimated Average Requirement (EAR). If sufficient scientific evidence is not available to establish an EAR, and thus calculate an RDA, an AI is usually developed. For healthy breastfed infants, an AI is the mean intake. The AI for other life stage and gender groups is believed to cover the needs of all healthy individuals in the groups, but lack of data or uncertainty in the data prevent being able to specify with confidence the percentage of individuals covered by this intake.

[a] As retinol activity equivalents (RAEs). 1 RAE = 1 µg retinol, 12 µg β-carotene, 24 µg α-carotene, or 24 µg β-cryptoxanthin. The RAE for dietary provitamin A carotenoids is two-fold greater than retinol equivalents (RE), whereas the RAE for preformed vitamin A is the same as RE.

[b] As cholecalciferol. 1 µg cholecalciferol = 40 IU vitamin D.

[c] Under the assumption of minimal sunlight.

[d] As α-tocopherol. α-Tocopherol includes RRR-α-tocopherol, the only form of α-tocopherol that occurs naturally in foods, and the 2R-stereoisomeric forms of α-tocopherol (RRR-, RSR-, RRS-, and RSS-α-tocopherol) that occur in fortified foods and supplements. It does not include the 2S-stereoisomeric forms of α-tocopherol (SRR-, SSR-, SRS-, and SSS-α-tocopherol), also found in fortified foods and supplements.

[e] As niacin equivalents (NE). 1 mg of niacin = 60 mg of tryptophan; 0–6 months = preformed niacin (not NE).

[f] As dietary folate equivalents (DFE). 1 DFE = 1 µg food folate = 0.6 µg of folic acid from fortified food or as a supplement consumed with food = 0.5 µg of a supplement taken on an empty stomach.

[g] Although AIs have been set for choline, there are few data to assess whether a dietary supply of choline is needed at all stages of the life cycle, and it may be that the choline requirement can be met by endogenous synthesis at some of these stages.

[h] Because 10 to 30 percent of older people may malabsorb food-bound B12, it is advisable for those older than 50 years to meet their RDA mainly by consuming foods fortified with B12, or a supplement containing B12.

[i] In view of evidence linking folate intake with neural tube defects in the fetus, it is recommended that all women capable of becoming pregnant consume 400 µg from supplements or fortified foods in addition to intake of food folate from a varied diet. It is assumed that women will continue consuming 400 µg from supplements or fortified food until their pregnancy is confirmed and they enter prenatal care, which ordinarily occurs after the end of the periconceptional period—the critical time for formation of the neural tube.

Sources: Dietary Reference Intakes for Calcium, Phosphorous, Magnesium, Vitamin D, and Fluoride (1997); Dietary Reference Intakes for Thiamin, Riboflavin, Niacin, Vitamin B6, Folate, Vitamin B12, Pantothenic Acid, Biotin, and Choline (1998); Dietary Reference Intakes for Vitamin C, Vitamin E, Selenium, and Carotenoids (2000); Dietary Reference Intakes for Vitamin A, Vitamin K, Arsenic, Boron, Chromium, Copper, Iodine, Iron, Manganese, Molybdenum, Nickel, Silicon, Vanadium, and Zinc (2001); Dietary Reference Intakes for Water, Potassium, Sodium, Chloride, and Sulfate (2005); and Dietary Reference Intakes for Calcium and Vitamin D (2011). These reports may be accessed via www.edu.

the nutrient information provided on food labels (Batada et al., 2012). It is suggested that RDAs, AIs, and ULs be used in planning diets for individuals, whereas the EAR is more effectively used for planning and assessing the nutrient intake of individuals and groups (Bucholz, Desai, & Rosenthal, 2011).

The DRI can be used to evaluate the nutrient contributions of an individual's 24-hour food intake. This can be determined by:

1. Listing the amounts of all foods and beverages consumed during one 24-hour period.
2. Looking up the nutrients in each food item and beverage consumed.
3. Totaling the values for each nutrient (e.g., calcium, sodium, protein).
4. Comparing each nutrient total with the DRIs (for the correct age and gender) (Table 12–2) to determine if it is deficient or adequately meets recommendations.

12-2 Dietary Guidelines for Americans

The National Nutrition Monitoring and Related Research Act of 1990 requires the Secretaries of Health and Human Services (HHS) and the U.S. Department of Agriculture (USDA) to issue a joint report, called the *Dietary Guidelines for Americans*, at least every 5 years. This document reflects the Advisory Committee's efforts to establish recommendations based on latest scientific evidence regarding nutrition's role in health maintenance and disease prevention. The current edition is available online (http://www.cnpp.usda.gov/DGAs2010-PolicyDocument.htm). A new document, *Dietary Guidelines for Americans, 2015*, is scheduled to be released in the fall of 2015.

The *Dietary Guidelines* have come to serve as the basis for nearly all nutrition information in the United States (USDA, 2010). Whereas the DRIs focus on specific nutrients and age groups, the *Dietary Guidelines* assume a broader approach and provide advice about healthy eating, weight management, and increasing physical activity for persons 2 years of age and older. The document includes 23 health-promoting recommendations, which are summarized in Table 12–3.

Canada has developed similar guidelines in a document entitled, *Canada's Food Guide*. Citizens are encouraged to achieve good health by choosing nutritious foods and limiting foods that are

Did You Know...

that salt occurs naturally in many foods, but added salt in restaurant, fast food, and processed foods accounts for nearly 80 percent of a person's total daily intake?

FIGURE 12–1   Physical activity recommendations for children.

The American Academy of Pediatrics (AAP), National Association for Sport & Physical Education (NASPE), and Canadian Academy of Sport Medicine (CASM) encourage daily physical activity for children of all ages:

– *infants* should have ample opportunities to explore their environment and should not be confined to a stroller or carrier for longer than 60 minutes/day.

– *toddlers* should accumulate at least 30 minutes of structured, vigorous physical activity and at least 60 minutes or more of free play.

– *preschoolers and school-age children* should participate in at least 60 minutes of structured physical activity during the day. They should also be given opportunities to engage in several hours of unstructured physical activity.

Dietary Guidelines for Americans – *a report that provides recommendations for daily food choices, to be balanced with physical activity, to promote good health and reduce certain disease risks.*

TABLE 12–3   Dietary Guidelines for Americans 2010: Key Recommendations

Balancing calories to manage weight:

- Prevent or reduce overweight and obesity through improved eating and physical activity behaviors during each stage of life.
- Control total calorie intake to manage body weight; consume fewer calories from foods and beverages if currently overweight.
- Increase physical activity and reduce time spent in sedentary behaviors.

Foods and food components to increase:

Recommendations for healthy eating should be made while staying within calorie needs.

- Increase vegetable and fruit intake. Eat a variety of vegetables, especially dark green, red, and orange vegetables, beans, and peas.
- Consume at least half of all grains as whole grains.
- Increase intake of fat-free or low-fat milk and dairy products (e.g., yogurt, cheese, or fortified soy beverages).
- Choose a variety of lean protein foods (e.g., seafood, meat and poultry, eggs, beans, peas, soy products, and unsalted nuts and seeds).
- Replace solid fats with oils where possible.
- Choose foods that provide potassium, dietary fiber, calcium, and vitamin D (often low in American diets): vegetables, fruits, whole grains, milk, and milk products.

Foods and food components to reduce:

- Reduce sodium to 2,300 milligrams (mg); African Americans, persons 51 and older, or anyone who has high blood pressure, diabetes, or chronic kidney disease should further reduce this level to 1,500 mg (Figure 12–2).
- Consume less than 10 percent of calories from saturated fatty acids; replace them with monounsaturated and polyunsaturated fats.
- Consume less than 300 mg per day of dietary cholesterol.
- Keep trans-fatty acid consumption as low as possible.
- Reduce intake of calories from solid fats, added sugars, and refined grains.
- If alcohol is consumed, it should be done in moderation (1 drink per day for women, 2 for men).

Building healthy eating patterns:

- Select an eating pattern that meets nutrient needs over time and within an appropriate calorie level.
- Follow food safety recommendations when preparing and eating foods to reduce the risk of foodborne illnesses.

Source: Adapted from, *Dietary Guidelines for Americans 2010: Executive Summary*. Accessed online from http://www.cnpp. usda.gov/Publications/DietaryGuidelines/2010/PolicyDoc/ExecSumm.pdf.

high in sodium, sugar, fats, and calories. A companion document, *Canada's Physical Activity Guide to Healthy Active Living*, stresses the importance of maintaining an active lifestyle.

Early childhood programs have an obligation to promote healthy eating and physical activity behaviors given the significant increase in childhood obesity. Excessive weight and sedentary lifestyles have been linked to the development of many chronic diseases and, thus, pose a serious public health concern. Schools must take an active role in addressing this problem by adhering to Dietary Guideline recommendations when serving food to children and by incorporating more physical activity throughout the day (AHA, 2012; NASPE, 2012).

12-2a Additional Nutrition Guidelines

The U.S. Public Health Service continues to update the original *Healthy People* guidelines. Several statements in the *Healthy People 2020* document that specifically address children's nutritional needs are:

- eliminating very low food insecurity among children in U.S. households
- reducing the proportion of children who are overweight or obese

TeachSource Video Connections

Young Children's Stages of Play: An Illustrated Guide

Children are inherently active individuals and express this behavior through their lively play. Nutrition guidelines urge all of us to maintain a healthy weight by balancing calorie intake with physical activity. As you watch the learning video, *Young Children's Stages of Play: An Illustrated Guide,* consider the following questions:

1. Why do you think children become more sedentary as they get older?

2. How can teachers and parents use play to help children maintain a physically active lifestyle?

3. What activities could you plan to keep children physically active during each stage of play described in this video?

Watch on CourseMate.

increasing the contribution of fruits, vegetables, whole grains, and calcium to the diets of children 2 years and older

reducing the consumption of calories from solid fats and added sugars in the population aged 2 years and older

increasing the number of states and school districts that require regularly scheduled elementary school recess

increasing the proportion of consumers who follow key food safety practices

Several non-profit organizations, including the American Heart Association and the National Cancer Institute, also advise similar healthy eating and physical activity behaviors. Their guidelines call for reducing dietary fat, cholesterol, sodium, and alcohol and increasing vegetable, fruit, low-fat dairy, and whole grain consumption.

© 2015 Cengage Learning

Did You Get It?

The Dietary Guidelines for Americans report recommends that all individuals reduce their sodium intake, especially those of which race or ethnicity?

a. Hispanic-American

b. Asian-American

c. Native-American

d. African-American

Take the full quiz on CourseMate.

12-3 MyPlate

The new MyPlate model replaces the Food Guide Pyramid and provides a graphic representation of the Dietary Guidelines for Americans (Figure 12–2). The Food Pyramid proved to be confusing for many consumers and presented information in a way that had limited appeal and functionality. The simplified MyPlate format presents critical dietary recommendations in a concise manner that is easier for the public to understand and to implement. It also conveys a strong preventive message and emphasizes the importance of balancing caloric intake with physical activity, consuming a greater variety of foods from each food group, and limiting foods high in sugar, fats, and calories. MyPlate also encourages consumers to incorporate more low-fat dairy products into their diet, and to fill half of their plate with fruits and vegetables, one-fourth with whole grains, and the remaining fourth with a lean protein food.

Did You Know...

studies have shown that eating a diet rich in a variety of fruits and vegetables can reduce a person's risk of developing some cancers?

The ChooseMyPlate website (http://www.choosemyplate.gov) has also been improved and now offers comprehensive food charts, portion sizes (based on age), nutrient contributions and health benefits, and preparation suggestions for each food category. Separate sections address the specific health and nutrition needs of young children, children over 5 years, pregnant and breastfeeding women (locate by clicking on "Site Map"). The site also gives consumers access to extensive resource information about calories, weight management, physical activities, healthy eating suggestions (e.g., vegetarian, food safety, recipes, sample menus), and tips for eating out. The SuperTracker feature provides an opportunity for individuals to plan and monitor their food calorie intake and expenditures, as well as offering menu plans and information about portion sizes and reading food labels. The ChooseMyPlate website is easy to navigate and provides consumers with sound nutritional information for making healthy choices. It also offers extensive resources that teachers can use and incorporate into health and nutrition lessons.

12-3a Vegetables

The Vegetable group is composed of food items in an array of colors and flavors. Vegetables contribute notable amounts of minerals, vitamins, and fiber to a person's diet and are low in fat and calories (Table 12–4). The vegetable group is organized into five subgroups according to their nutrient strengths: dark green; starchy; red and orange; beans and peas; and other. Daily food selections should include dark green vegetables such as broccoli and leafy greens, which are rich in vitamins A and C, as well as orange-red foods such as sweet potatoes, squash, tomatoes, and carrots, which are rich in vitamin A (Table 12–4). Adults should consume 2½–3 cups of vegetables daily (based on a 2,000-calorie intake); children 2 to 3 years old require 1 cup and 4- to 8-year-olds should have 1½ cups.

Dietary fiber continues to receive attention for its health-promoting benefits, yet many children's (and adults') intake is deficient because their diet lacks fruits and vegetables (Osborne & Forestell, 2012; Pabayo et al., 2012). Efforts to increase children's acceptance of different vegetables is an important issue to address (see Chapter 17). However, too much fiber in a child's diet can interfere with the absorption of essential vitamins and minerals. A practical recommendation for fiber intake for children over 2 years of age is the "age plus 5" rule. For example, Tasha, age 3 years, would require 8 grams of fiber per day. A sampling of food sources and their fiber contribution is presented in Table 12–5.

12-3b Fruits

The Fruit group is a major contributor of vitamins, especially vitamins A, C, potassium, folate (folic acid), and dietary fiber. Choosing a variety of fruits that are of different colors improves nutrient intake. Children are usually more receptive to eating fruit because it is sweet. Fruit can be prepared and served in many ways to increase its appeal to children (e.g., frozen, in smoothies, in muffins, with a nutritious yogurt dip). Adults are encouraged to consume the equivalent of 2 cups of fruit daily, whereas children 2 to 3 years old need 1 cup and 4- to 8-year-olds require 1 to 1 1/2 cups. At least one vitamin C–rich and one vitamin A–rich selection should be included in a child's diet every day (Table 12–4 and Table 12–6).

FIGURE 12–2 The MyPlate model presents extensive nutrition and physical activity information in a clear and easy-to-use manner.

TABLE 12–4   Good to Excellent Vitamin A Sources

cantaloupe	winter squash
carrots	greens
pumpkin	apricots
sweet potatoes	watermelon*
spinach	broccoli

*May cause allergic reactions.

TABLE 12–5   Dietary Fiber in Common Foods

Food	Amount	Fiber (gram)
Cheerios®	1/2 cup	1.5
Raisin bran	1/2 cup	2.5
oatmeal	1/4 cup	1.9
macaroni, enriched	1/2 cup	1.3
bread, whole wheat	1/2 slice	0.9
bread, white	1/2 slice	0.6
graham crackers	1 square	0.5
orange sections	1/2 cup	2.2
banana, sliced	1/2 cup	1.9
apple with skin	1/2 cup	1.3
acorn squash	1/4 cup	2.3
green peas	1/4 cup	2.2
corn, frozen	1/4 cup	1.0
pinto beans	1/2 cup	5.5
black beans	1/2 cup	7.5

12-3c   Grains

Foods such as breads, breakfast cereals, pastas, and a variety of whole grains make up the Grains group. Items from this group provide complex carbohydrates, B vitamins, minerals, and dietary fiber and are known to decrease the risk of chronic diseases, such as diabetes, heart disease, and hypertension. The Grains group is divided into two subcategories: whole grains and refined grains. Recommendations suggest that at least half of the grains an individual consumes each day should be whole grain. Whole grain products retain all of their original nutrients and are an ideal source of dietary fiber. Some grains are refined to improve their texture and shelf-life but the process removes important vitamins and minerals. Manufacturers are required to restore these nutrients so they are equivalent to the original whole grain. Breads and cereals are examples of foods that must be fortified or enriched with iron, calcium, thiamin, riboflavin, and niacin. Most grain products today are also fortified with folacin (folic acid), which reduces the incidence of spina bifida, cleft lip, and cleft palate birth defects (Colapinto et al., 2012).

A typical serving from the Grain group consists of one slice of bread, 1 cup of dry, ready-to-eat cereal, or 1/2 cup (1 ounce) of cooked rice, cereal, or pasta. A child's serving size is approximately one-half that of an adult's. Adults should consume the equivalent of 6 ounces of grains daily; children 2 to 3 years require 3 ounces, and 4- to 8-year-olds should have 5 ounces.

TABLE 12–6   Good to Excellent Vitamin C Sources

orange*	tomatoes*
orange juice*	grapefruit*
strawberries*	mustard greens
cauliflower	spinach
broccoli	cabbage
sweet peppers, red or green	tangerine*

*May cause allergic reactions.

12-3d Protein Foods

The Protein Foods group consists of meats (e.g., beef, veal, pork, lamb, wild game), seafood, poultry, eggs, beans and peas, nuts and seeds (nut butters), and soy products. Food items in this group play an important role in promoting children's growth. They provide critical nutrients, including **protein**, B vitamins, iron, zinc, and magnesium. Foods from this group should be selected carefully to avoid those high in calories, fat, and cholesterol. Consumers are encouraged to include more non-meat protein sources (e.g., beans, peas, nuts and seeds, soy products) in their diet to lower fat and cholesterol intake (Akbaraly et al., 2011). Information to help individuals make healthier choices is offered on the ChooseMyPlate website.

The recommended daily intake from the Protein Foods group, as with the other groups, varies according to age, gender, and level of physical activity. Children 2 to 3 years old require approximately 2 ounces of protein equivalents daily; children 4 to 8 should receive 4 ounces; adults should consume between 5 and 6 1/2 ounces. The following foods contain protein that is approximately equivalent to 1 ounce of meat, poultry, or fish:

1 egg
1/4 cup cooked dried peas or beans
2 tablespoons peanut butter
1/2 ounce nuts or seeds
1/4 cup tofu
2 tablespoons hummus

12-3e Dairy

This group includes milk and milk-based products that retain their **calcium** content, such as home-made pudding, frozen yogurt, ice cream; hard cheeses such as Swiss and cheddar; soft cheeses such as ricotta and cottage cheese; yogurt; and calcium-fortified soy milk. This group is a major supplier of the mineral calcium, which is essential for healthy bone development and tooth formation. Dairy products that provide little or no calcium include butter, cream cheese, and cream and are not considered part of the Dairy group. Food examples that provide the amount of calcium equivalent to one cup of milk include:

1 1/2 ounces cheddar, mozzarella,	2 cups cottage cheese or Swiss cheese
1 cup pudding or frozen yogurt	1 cup plain yogurt
1 1/2 cups ice cream	1 cup calcium-enriched soy milk

The Dairy group is a primary source of dietary calcium, potassium, and vitamin D, but also a poor source of iron and vitamins A and C. Children 2 to 3 years old should consume 2 cups of milk daily or the equivalent from this group; 4- to 8-year-olds require 2 1/2 cups; adults should have 3 cups. Servings may be divided into 1/2-cup portions in consideration of children's smaller appetites and stomach capacity. The number of servings reflects new recommendations that have been increased for calcium and vitamin D intake. Whenever possible, low-fat or fat-free items should be selected because foods in the Dairy group tend to be high in fat and cholesterol. However, children should not be given low-fat milk and dairy products prior to the age of 2. Infants and toddlers require the critical fats and fat-calories contained in whole milk and milk products to meet their high energy needs and to support healthy nervous system development (Parletta, Milte, & Meyer, 2013).

12-3f Oils

Oils are not considered a food group but they are present in many food items. The Oils group consists of two subgroups: oils and solid fats. Oils, such as canola, corn, cottonseed, olive, and

protein – *class of nutrients used primarily for structural and regulatory functions.*
calcium – *mineral nutrient; a major component of bones and teeth.*

▼ Children's nutrient needs are influenced by age, gender, and activity level.

© Cengage Learning

sunflower, are liquid at room temperature and are often used in cooking. Some oils, such as walnut oil and sesame oil, are used primarily for flavoring. Plant oils contain no cholesterol and are considered beneficial. Foods such as nuts, olives, avocados, and fish have a high oil content that also offers health benefits. Mayonnaise, certain salad dressings, and soft (tub or squeeze) margarines that do not contain trans-fats are considered oils.

Solid fats are food products, such as butter, that have been prepared from animal sources. Stick and soft margarines are also classified as solid fats because they are made by converting liquid oil to a solid form through a process called hydrogenation. In general, the nutrient contribution of this group is low and the calorie content is high. Adults should limit their daily oil intake to a maximum equivalent of 5 to 7 teaspoons; young children should have no more than 3 to 4 teaspoons.

12-3g Empty Calories

Foods from each of the MyPlate groups yield calories for energy. How many calories an individual requires varies according to age, gender, and level of physical activity. The new interactive SuperTracker feature on the ChooseMyPlate website allows individuals to monitor their food intake, record calories burned, and use the information to make healthier decisions.

Many foods also include empty calories, primarily sugars and fats. They are called "empty" because they contribute only calories to a person's diet and few other nutrients. Empty calories add up quickly and can lead to weight gain. They also dilute the quality of a person's healthy diet when too many food items with empty calories are included (Isoldi et al., 2012). For example, the potassium and vitamin C contribution of a banana are significantly altered when sugars, fats, and flour are added (Table 12–7).

Did You Get It?

Citrus fruits, strawberries, and tomatoes are all excellent sources of vitamin C and share what other trait that should be considered when preparing a classroom snack?

a. They all promote healthy teeth and bones
b. They can all cause allergic reactions
c. They improve memory
d. They can help prevent osteoporosis

Take the full quiz on CourseMate.

TABLE 12–7   **How Added Sugar and Fats Alter a Food's Calories and Nutrient Contribution**

	Calories	Potassium	Vitamin C
Banana, 1/2 cup sliced	67	211 mg	5.0 mg
Banana chips, 1 ounce	147	152 mg	1.8 mg
Banana pudding, 1/2 cup	72	62 mg	0.3 mg
Banana bread, 1 slice	196	80 mg	1.0 mg
Banana cream pie, 1/8 pie	387	238 mg	2.3 mg
Banana waffle, 1 small round	212	140 mg	1.1 mg

CONNECTING TO EVERYDAY PRACTICE

Eat Locally Campaign

Consumers are increasingly being encouraged to purchase and eat more locally grown foods. Concerns about sustainability practices, energy costs, and food safety have contributed significantly to this recent movement. Produce grown within a 100 mile radius retains more of its nutrients and is often more affordable. Eating locally also supports the farmers and has economic benefits for communities.

Think About This:

▶ In what ways does the MyPlate nutrition guide support this trend?

▶ What key recommendations in the *Dietary Guidelines for Healthy Americans* would be reinforced by eating locally?

▶ How might this trend contribute to lower obesity rates and improve children's intake of vitamins A and C?

12-4 Food Labels

The Nutritional Labeling and Education Act of 1990 led to significant changes in food product labeling. The food label, regulated by the U.S. Food and Drug Administration (FDA) and the U.S. Department of Agriculture (USDA), underwent further revision in 1994 (Figure 12–3) and resulted in the current label format that appears on all packaged food products. The redesign makes it easier for consumers to locate, understand, and use nutrient information when purchasing foods (Miller & Cassady, 2012). Labels provide:

▶ Manufacturer's name and contact information (e.g., address, telephone number) and country of origin.
▶ Product net weight.
▶ Standardized serving sizes that are consistent for similar foods (e.g., cereals, crackers, canned/frozen vegetables) and in amounts that are typically consumed. This prevents manufacturers from basing nutrient information on a smaller serving size in order to make their food product appear healthier than that of competing brands.
▶ A list of all ingredients– in descending order according to weight.
▶ **Percent Daily Values (%DV)** that show how a serving of food fits into a person's daily diet.
▶ **Nutrition and health claims** that are regulated and based on proven scientific findings (Figure 12–4).
▶ Warnings about any potentially allergenic substances that might be included.

Food allergens (milk, eggs, tree nuts [such as almonds, walnuts], peanuts, shellfish [such as shrimp, crab, lobster], fish, wheat, and soy) that could potentially cause life-threatening reactions for some individuals must be clearly identified (U.S. FDA, 2013a). Manufacturers may include health claims, such as "reduces the risk of heart disease," as long as there is scientific evidence to support the statement.

Laws have been proposed by the FDA that would require nutrient labels on foods sold in vending machines and in chain restaurants (with more than twenty locations) (U.S. FDA, 2013b). The FDA is also working with food manufacturers to design a uniform format for front-of-package labels that would include key nutrient information. They believe this addition will help to address obesity and diet-related diseases in this country by encouraging consumers to compare brands and make healthier food choices. Some manufacturers have already begun to adopt new front-of-package labeling despite the lack of regulatory guidelines.

Percent Daily Values (%DV) – *measures of the nutritional values of food; used in nutrition labeling.*
nutrition claims – *statements of reduced calories, fat, or salt on the food labels.*

FIGURE 12–3   A typical food label.

Nutrition Facts

Serving Size 3/4 cup (30g)
Servings Per Container about 15

Amount Per Serving	Cereal	Cereal with 1/2 cup Skim Milk
Calories	100	140
Calories from Fat	5	5

	% Daily Value**	
Total Fat 0.5g*	**1%**	**1%**
Saturated Fat 0g	**0%**	**0%**
Polyunsaturated Fat 0g		
Monounsaturated Fat 0g		
Cholesterol 0mg	**0%**	**0%**
Sodium 220mg	**9%**	**12%**
Potassium 190mg	**5%**	**11%**
Total Carbohydrate 24g	**8%**	**10%**
Dietary Fiber 5g	**21%**	**21%**
Soluble Fiber 1g		
Insoluble Fiber 4g		
Sugars 6g		
Other Carbohydrate 13g		
Protein 3g		
Vitamin A	15%	20%
Vitamin C	0%	2%
Calcium	0%	15%
Iron	45%	45%
Vitamin D	10%	25%
Thiamin	25%	30%
Riboflavin	25%	35%
Niacin	25%	25%
Vitamin B$_6$	25%	25%
Folate	25%	25%
Vitamin B$_{12}$	25%	35%
Phosphorus	15%	25%
Magnesium	15%	20%
Zinc	10%	15%
Copper	10%	10%

*Amount in Cereal. One half cup skim milk contributes an additional 40 calories, 65mg sodium, 200mg potassium, 6g total carbohydrate (6g sugars), and 4g protein.

**Percent Daily Values are based on a 2,000 calorie diet. Your daily values may be higher or lower depending on your calorie needs:

	Calories:	2,000	2,500
Total Fat	Less than	65g	80g
Saturated Fat	Less than	20g	25g
Cholesterol	Less than	300mg	300mg
Sodium	Less than	2,400mg	2,400mg
Potassium		3,500mg	3,500mg
Total Carbohydrate		300g	375g
Dietary Fiber		25g	30g

FIGURE 12–4   Commonly used labeling terms defined.

WHAT SOME CLAIMS MEAN

high-protein: at least 10 grams (g) high-quality protein per serving

good source of calcium: at least 100 milligrams (mg) calcium per serving

more iron: at least 1.8 mg more iron per serving than reference food. (Label will say 10 percent more of the Daily Value for iron.)

fat-free: less than 0.5 g fat per serving

low-fat: 3 g or less fat per serving. (If the serving size is 30 g or less or 2 tablespoons or less, 3 g or less fat per 50 g of the food.)

reduced or fewer calories: at least 25 percent fewer calories per serving than the reference food

sugar-free: less than 0.5 g sugar per serving

reduced sugar: reduced sugar: at least 25% less sugar per serving when compared with a similar food

sodium-free: less than 5 mg of sodium per serving

light or lite (two meanings):

■ one-third fewer calories or 50% less fat per serving than the reference food. (If more than half of the food's calories are from fat, the fat must be reduced by 50 percent)

■ a "low-calorie" or "low-fat" food whose sodium content has been reduced by 50 percent of the reference food

low cholesterol: 20 mg or less of cholesterol and 2 g or less of saturated fat per serving

12-4a Calories from Fat

Food labels must disclose the amount of fat, saturated fat, trans-fats, and number of calories derived from fat in a product. Consumers can use this information to determine the percentage of total calories that are derived from fat:

$$\text{Percent of calories from fat} = \frac{\text{Calories from fat/serving}}{\text{Calories/serving}} \times 100$$

If a food is not labeled or does not include the number of calories from fat, you can determine this figure by multiplying the total fat grams by 9 (number of calories in 1 fat gram):

$$\text{calories from fat} = \text{grams (g) of fat/serving} \times 9 \text{ (cal/g)}.$$

Knowing the percentage of calories from fat can help the consumer make an educated decision about a food's nutrient quality and avoid being misled by claims that a product is low-fat, fat-free, nutritious, or healthy. The following examples illustrate this point:

Cheddar cheese 1 ounce = 115 calories and 9 g of fat:

Calories from fat = 9 × 9 = 81
Percent calories from fat = 81/115 × 100 = 70%

Eggs one egg = 75 calories and 6 g of fat:

Calories from fat = 6 × 9 = 54
Percent calories from fat = 54/75 × 100 = 72%

90% fat-free ground beef 3 ounces = 185 calories and 10 g of fat:

Calories from fat = 10 × 9 = 90
Percent calories from fat = 90/185 × 100 = 49%

Low-fat cream cheese 1 tablespoon = 30 calories and 2.3 g of fat:

Calories from fat = 2.3 × 9 = 20.7
Percent calories from fat = 20.7/30 × 100 = 69%

In each example, the grams of fat (9, 6, 10, and 2.3) appear to be relatively low, yet they represent more than 50 percent of the total calories. This may surprise many consumers and illustrates why this information is important to know. Should these foods be eliminated from our diets? No, but they should be consumed in moderation (portion size) and perhaps less often. For example, if you order a lean hamburger with 49 percent fat-calories, it might be better to skip the French fries at 47 percent fat-calories and substitute an apple, banana, or lettuce salad, which contain less than 10 percent of their calories from fat.

Did You Get It?

Food manufacturers are mandated to list all ingredients in descending order according to _____:
a. nutritional content
b. weight
c. volume
d. calories

Take the full quiz on CourseMate.

PARTNERING with FAMILIES

Children's Sugar Consumption

Dear Families,

Several meal-planning tools are available to help you meet children's nutrient needs for growth and well-being and limit those that are not beneficial. The *Dietary Guidelines for Americans*, for example, encourage individuals to reduce added sugars in their diet for better health.

▶ Follow a diet that is moderate in sugar. Many foods, such as milk/dairy products and fruit, supply naturally occurring sugars as well as important vitamins and minerals. Foods that have sugars added during processing or preparation contribute extra calories and are often low in essential dietary nutrients. Although sugar is not harmful when consumed in limited amounts, it also has no particular benefits.

(continued)

PARTNERING with FAMILIES

Children's Sugar Consumption (*continued*)

▶ Know your food labels: A *reduced sugar* food item contains at least 25 percent less sugar than the reference food. *No added sugar* or *without added sugar* foods indicate that no sugars were added during processing or packaging. *Sugar-free* foods contain less than 0.5 grams sugar per serving.

▶ The following terms, if listed as the first or second ingredient on a food label, indicate the food is likely high in sugar: brown sugar, corn sweetener or corn syrup, fructose, fruit juice concentrate, glucose, dextrose, high-fructose corn syrup, honey, lactose, maltose, molasses, raw sugar, table sugar (sucrose), agave syrup.

▶ Major food sources of sugar in the United States include sodas, cakes, candy, cookies, pies, fruit drinks and punches, and dairy desserts such as ice cream. Healthier foods that contain added sugar should also be limited in children's diet: chocolate milk, presweetened cereals, prepared puddings, and fruits packed in syrup. If these foods are served, do so in moderation and choose smaller serving sizes. (A serving of soda in the 1950s was 6.5 ounces compared to a 20-ounce serving today!)

You can find many suggestions and recipes for healthy snacks and meals that are low in sugars (and economical) on the ChooseMyPlate website (http://www.choosemyplate.gov).

CLASSROOM CORNER

Teacher Activities

Tasting a Rainbow . . .

(PreK–2; **NHES** National Health Education Standards 1.2.1 and 8.2.1)

Concept: Fruits and vegetables are healthy foods to eat and we should eat a variety of them.

Learning Objectives

▶ Children will learn that fruits and vegetables are healthy foods to eat.

▶ Children will experience tasting a variety of fruits and vegetables.

Supplies

▶ one red fruit and vegetable (apple, strawberry, tomato, watermelon, red pepper)

▶ one orange fruit and vegetable (orange, acorn squash, orange pepper, cantaloupe, yam, carrot)

▶ one green fruit and vegetable (grape, lime, spinach, kale, honeydew, green pepper, apple, pear, broccoli, bean, pea, kiwi)

▶ one yellow fruit and vegetable (banana, mango, pineapple, lemon, yellow squash, corn)

▶ one purple fruit and vegetable (purple grape, purple cabbage, purple potato)

▶ one blue fruit (blueberry)

▶ hand wipes, plates, forks

(*continued*)

CLASSROOM CORNER

Teacher Activities   *(continued)*

Learning Activities

◗ Read and discuss one of the following books:

- *Apples Grow on a Tree* (How fruits and vegetables grow) by Mari Schul
- *The ABCs of Fruits & Vegetables* by Steve Charney & David Goldbeck
- *The Vegetables We Eat* by Gail Gibbons

◗ Talk with the children about how bodies need nutritious foods, such as fruits and vegetables, to stay healthy and help us grow. Show children a picture of a rainbow; explain that fruits and vegetables come in many colors, like a rainbow.

◗ Have children wash their hands with wipes. Hand each child a plate with fruit, a plate with vegetables, and a fork. Make sure all the fruits and vegetables are cut into bite-sized pieces to prevent choking. Talk about how the colors of the food on their plates are the same as those in a rainbow.

◗ Give children an opportunity to sample each item and talk about how each tastes. Focus the activity on the importance of tasting a variety of fruits and vegetables instead of on children's likes and dislikes.

◗ Make a chart or flannel board with the following color labels across the top: red, yellow-orange, green, purple, white. One day, ask the children to name fruits that represent each of the colors. Another day, have the children identify vegetables that are these colors. Talk about why it is important to eat fruits and vegetables that are different colors.

◗ Older children can begin to identify and chart the primary nutrient strength of various fruits and vegetables. (For example, oranges, green peppers, strawberries, and watermelon are high in vitamin C. Carrots, sweet potatoes, and broccoli are rich in vitamin A.)

Evaluation

◗ Children will name several kinds of fruits and vegetables.

◗ Children will taste a variety of fruits and vegetables.

Additional lesson plans for grades 3–5 are available on CourseMate.

◗ Summary

◗ The Dietary Reference Intakes (DRIs) are nutrient goals based on gender and age that are considered essential for maintaining health. They are used for policy development, dietary assessment, meal planning, and determining the nutrient contribution on food labels.

◗ The *Dietary Guidelines for Americans* are a set of recommendations that encourage consumers to: make healthy food choices to meet nutrient needs and reduce the overconsumption of nutrient groups known to have health risks, increase their physical activity, and implement food safety practices.

◗ MyPlate is the newest nutrition tool. It offers practical advice for making healthier food choices and engaging in physical activity every day. Information provided on the ChooseMyPlate website (http://www.choosemyplate.gov) is attractive, comprehensive, and easy for consumers to use and understand.

▶ Food labels must include a list of all ingredients in a product; nutrient values, fat, and calories present in the item based on serving size. Warnings must identify ingredients that are known allergens. The manufacturer's contact information must also be provided.

- Determining the percentage of calories from fat in a given food serving is useful for comparing and choosing nutrient-rich foods and limiting excessive dietary fat intake.

◖ Terms to Know

nutrients *p. 321*
essential nutrient *p. 321*
malnutrition *p. 321*
undernutrition *p. 321*
nutrition *p. 321*

Dietary Reference Intake
  (DRI) *p. 322*
Dietary Guidelines for
  Americans *p. 324*
protein *p. 329*

calcium *p. 329*
Percent Daily Values (%DV)
  p. 331
nutrition and health claims
  p. 331

◖ Chapter Review

A. By Yourself:

1. Match the foods in **Column I** to the appropriate food group in **Column II**. Some foods may include more than one food group.

Column I	Column II
1. Black beans	a. Dairy group
2. Rice	b. Protein foods
3. Spaghetti with tomato sauce	c. Grain group
4. Fish taco	d. Vegetable group
5. Macaroni and cheese	e. Fruit group
6. Peanut butter sandwich	f. Oils
7. French fries	g. Empty calories
8. Frozen yogurt	
9. Popcorn	
10. Bacon	
11. Carbonated beverages	
12. Watermelon	

2. Practice calculating the percentage of calories from fat by using the labels on ten different food products. What did you learn that was surprising? How will you use this information in your diet?

B. As a Group:

1. Describe the energy sources in food. What nutrients yield energy and how much does each provide?

2. Discuss how an individual might use the Dietary Guidelines for Americans to improve their personal well-being.

3. Explain what Dietary Reference Intakes (DRIs) are and how they can be used for planning a child's daily diet.

4. Explore the ChooseMyPlate website (http://www.choosemyplate.gov). Have each student identify and discuss the features that were most informative and useful. Are there any limitations to the site and, if so, what are they?

5. Explain how foods labeled *low-fat, fat-free,* and *reduced calories* differ.

Case Study

Ruby runs a small child care program in her home. The preschool-age children begin arriving at 7 A.M. each morning and leave by 5:30 P.M. Ruby prepares and serves them breakfast, lunch, and two snacks throughout the day. This year, she has encountered several children who have challenging food allergies and food preferences. What suggestions would you offer to help Ruby in each of the following situations?

1. Layla, age 4, breaks out in hives whenever she has eaten too many strawberries or oranges. She will occasionally accept a small serving of applesauce or a few bites of banana but few other fruits. What two nutrients are probably deficient in Layla's diet? What other fruits or vegetables can Ruby serve to supply these essential vitamins?

2. Ailani, age 3, is lactose intolerant and unable to drink milk or to eat dairy products. What nutrient is most likely deficient in Ailani's diet? What other foods can Ruby serve to meet Ailani's nutrient needs?

3. Carlos, age 5, doesn't like milk and demands fruit juice or lemonade instead. What two nutrients are most likely deficient? What adjustments can Ruby make in his diet to meet these needs?

4. Mariko, age 2, prefers a daily diet of rice or noodles that have been drenched in soy sauce. She will take a few bites of tofu when her mother insists, but refuses meats, fish, and most vegetables. What nutrients is she missing? What health concerns would you have about Mariko's current dietary pattern? What can Ruby do to improve Mariko's dietary intake?

5. Sophia's favorite breakfast foods include bacon, sausages, doughnuts, and biscuits with gravy. What nutrients is she consuming in excess? What food groups and nutrients is she lacking? Should Ruby be concerned, and what can she do to encourage healthier eating habits?

Application Activities

1. Record your personal food intake for the past 24 hours. Go to http://www.choosemyplate.gov; locate the SuperTracker and use the Food-A-Pedia feature to analyze your 24-hour food intake. Compare your results to the RDAs for your age and gender. How did you measure up? Explore the other features on this site (e.g., Food Tracker, Physical Activity Tracker) and create a plan to help identify and reach your goals.

2. Plan a day's menu for a 4-year-old girl who does an extra 45 minutes of vigorous activity each day. Include the recommended servings from each food group and total calories she should consume each day.

3. What fruit and vegetable choices would supply vitamin C to a child who has a citrus allergy?

4. A 50 pound child burns approximately 300 calories per hour (or 5 calories per minute) during moderately vigorous play (e.g., walking, running, climbing). How many minutes would this child have to play to burn off the calories in each of the following foods?

Cheese pizza (1 slice)	= 380 calories
Beef tacos (2)	= 340 calories
Seafood sushi	= 260 calories
Chicken vegetable soup (1 cup)	= 130 calories
Apple pie (1 piece)	= 335 calories

Fruit smoothie, no dairy (1 cup)   = 130 calories

French fries (medium order)   = 410 calories

Strawberries (1 cup fresh)   = 46 calories

Helpful Web Resources

Academy of Nutrition & Dietetics	http://www.eatright.org
Canada's Food Guide	http://www.hc-sc.gc.ca/fn-an/food-guide-aliment/index-eng.php
Food and Drug Administration (FDA) (Food labels)	http://www.fda.gov/Food/default.htm
ChooseMyPlate for Preschoolers	http://www.choosemyplate.gov/preschoolers.html
Nutrition Action Health Newsletter	http://www.cspinet.org/nah/index.htm

 Visit the Education CourseMate for this textbook to access the eBook, Did You Get It? quizzes, Digital Downloads, TeachSource Video Cases, flashcards, and more. Go to CengageBrain.com to log in, register, or purchase access.

References

Akbaraly, T., Ferrie, J., Berr, C., Brunner, E., Head, J., Marmot, M., Singh-Manoux, A., Ritchie, K., Shipley, M., & Kivimaki, M. (2011). Alternative Healthy Eating Index and mortality over 18 years of follow-up: Results from the Whitehall II cohort, *American Journal of Clinical Nutrition*, 94(1), 247–253.

American Heart Association (AHA). (2012). Physical activity and children. Accessed on July 13, 2012 from http://www.heart.org/HEARTORG/GettingHealthy/Physical-Activity-and-Children_UCM_304053_Article.jsp.

Batada, A., Bruening, M., Marchlewicz, E., Story, M., & Wootan, M. (2012). Poor nutrition on the menu: Children's meals at America's top chain restaurants, *Childhood Obesity*, 8(3), 251–254.

Bucholz, E., Desai, M., & Rosenthal, M. (2011). Dietary intake in Head Start vs. non-Head Start preschool-aged children: Results from the 1999–2004 National Health and Nutrition Examination survey, *Journal of the American Dietetic Association*, 111(7), 1021–1030.

Colapinto, C., O'Connor, D., Dubois, L., & Tremblay, M. (2012). Folic acid supplement use is the most significant predictor of folate concentrations in Canadian women of childbearing age, *Applied Physiology, Nutrition, & Metabolism*, 37(2), 284–292.

Isoldi, K., Dalton, S., Rodriguez, D., & Nestle, M. (2012). Classroom "cupcake" celebrations: Observations of foods offered and consumed, *Journal of Nutrition Education & Behavior*, 44(1), 71–75.

Miller, L., & Cassady, D. (2012). Making healthy choices using nutrition facts panels: The roles of knowledge, motivation, modification goals, and age, *Appetite*, 59(1), 129–139.

National Association for Sport & Physical Education (NASPE). (2012). National guidelines for physical activity. Accessed on July 13, 2012 from http://www.aahperd.org/naspe/standards/nationalGuidelines/PAguidelines.cfm.

Osborne, C., & Forestell, C. (2012). Increasing children's consumption of fruit and vegetables: Does the type of exposure matter?, *Physiology & Behavior*, 106(3), 362–368.

Pabayo, R., Spence, J., Casey, L., & Storey, K. (2012). Food consumption patterns in preschool children, *Canadian Journal of Dietetic Practice & Research*, 73(2), 66–71.

Parletta, N., Milte, C., & Meyer, B. (2013). Nutritional modulation of cognitive function and mental health, *The Journal of Nutritional Biochemistry*, 24(5), 725–743.

U.S. Department of Agriculture (USDA). (2010). *Dietary Guidelines for Americans.* Accessed on July 13, 2012 from http://www.cnpp.usda.gov/dietaryguidelines.htm.

U.S. Food & Drug Administration (U. S. FDA). (2013a). Food Allergen Labeling and Consumer Protection Act of 2004. Accessed on May 7, 2013 from http://www.fda.gov/Food/GuidanceRegulation/GuidanceDocumentsRegulatoryInformation/Allergens/ucm106187.htm.

U.S. FDA. (2013b). Overview of FDA proposed labeling requirements for restaurants, similar retail food establishments and vending machines. Accessed on May 7, 2013 from http://www.fda.gov/Food/IngredientsPackagingLabeling/LabelingNutrition/ucm248732.htm.

chapter 13

Nutrients That Provide Energy (Carbohydrates, Fats, and Proteins)

- **#1 a, b, and c:** Promoting child development and learning
- **#2 a and c:** Building family and community relationships
- **#3 b, c, and d:** Observing, documenting, and assessing to support young children and families
- **#4 a:** Using developmentally effective approaches to connect with children and families
- **#6 c:** Becoming a professional

Learning Objectives

After studying this chapter, you should be able to:

LO 13-1 Identify the three nutrient groups that supply energy and the amount each contributes.

LO 13-2 Explain why children and adults are encouraged to consume more complex carbohydrates and fewer refined sugars.

LO 13-3 Plan a day's diet that meets the 30 percent of calories from fat recommendation and is low in saturated fatty acids and cholesterol.

LO 13-4 Discuss why proteins are not an ideal energy source.

Energy is defined as the ability to do work. Examples of work performed by the body are (1) locomotion and movement, (2) building new tissues, (3) maintaining body temperature, and (4) digesting, absorbing, and metabolizing food. In other words, energy is required for the performance of all body functions. In terms of survival, the need for energy is second only to the need for oxygen and water.

13-1 Food as an Energy Source

The body obtains its energy from three basic nutrient groups: carbohydrates, fats, and proteins. These are the only nutrients that have **calories** or supply energy. The amount of potential energy in a food is expressed in calories. For example, a 1-cup serving of ice cream supplies 185 calories, a medium apple provides 86 calories, and a serving of French toast has 356 calories. The caloric value of any given food is determined by its carbohydrate, fat, and protein content:

- Carbohydrates – 4 calories per gram
- Fat – 9 calories per gram
- Proteins – 4 calories per gram

The energy cost of a given activity is also measured and expressed in terms of calories. For example, over a 30 minute period a 125-pound female would burn approximately 94 calories while walking (at a moderate pace), 184 calories while engaged in aerobic dance (moderate), or 28 calories while sitting quietly.

energy – *power to perform work.*
calories – *units used to measure the energy value of foods.*

A **gram** is a metric unit of measurement for weight. The symbol for gram is "g." There are 28 grams in 1 ounce, and 454 grams in 1 pound. A metal paper clip weighs about 1 gram. A **milligram** is a metric unit of weight that is equal to one-thousandth of a gram: There are 1,000 milligrams in a gram. The symbol for milligram is "mg."

Vitamins, minerals, and water do not yield calories but they enable **enzymes**, **coenzymes**, and **hormones** to function. Enzymes and coenzymes are vitamin-containing substances that initiate and participate in the many metabolic reactions involved in releasing energy from carbohydrates, fats, and proteins. Hormones, such as thyroxin and insulin, although not directly involved in energy-releasing reactions, regulate many of these functions. For example, several hormones are required to maintain a steady blood sugar level so the body has sufficient energy to meet its needs.

Every individual has different energy requirements. These requirements vary slightly from day to day and are determined by a combination of:

- basal metabolic rate (BMR)
- physical activity
- calories used in the process of releasing energy in foods that have been consumed (thermic energy of food)

> **Did You Know...**
>
> that a 50-pound child will burn approximately 22 calories per hour while sleeping? A 110-pound adult burns about 45 calories per hour during sleep.

13-1a Energy Utilization

The term **basal metabolic rate (BMR)** describes the energy needed to carry on vital involuntary body processes, such as blood circulation, breathing, cell activity, body temperature maintenance, and heartbeat. A person's BMR varies only slightly from day to day. A child's BMR will be higher than an adult's due to a faster heartbeat, respiratory rate, and the additional energy required for growth. BMR does not reflect voluntary activity, although physical activity taken to the aerobic level will increase heartbeat and breathing rates, which temporarily increases BMR. For most children and adults, the energy required to meet basal metabolic needs is greater than energy expended for voluntary physical activity.

Physical activity is the aspect of an individual's energy need that is subject to the greatest conscious control (Niederer et al., 2012). For instance, participation in tennis or swimming as a recreational activity requires far more energy than reading or watching television. Although children seem to always be on-the-go, it is also important that they engage in daily periods of vigorous physical activity. The benefits of physical activity include improved cognitive function and motor development, opportunities for socialization, a sense of personal accomplishment, improved physical and mental health, and increased fitness. The calories burned during vigorous physical activity provide an opportunity to increase children's food intake and, thus, make it easier to meet their nutrient requirements.

▼ **The energy needs of active, growing children are considerably greater than those of an adult.**

© Cengage Learning

---

gram – *a metric unit of weight (g); approximately 1/28 of an ounce.*
milligram – *a metric unit of weight (mg); approximately 1/1,000 of a gram.*
enzymes – *proteins that catalyze body functions.*
coenzymes – *a vitamin-containing substance required by certain enzymes before they can perform their prescribed function.*
hormones – *special chemical substances produced by endocrine glands that influence and regulate specific body functions.*
basal metabolic rate (BMR) – *minimum amount of energy needed to carry on the body processes vital to life.*

Thermic energy of food refers to the energy required to **digest**, **absorb**, transport, and **metabolize** nutrients in food. This factor accounts for approximately 10 percent of an individual's total energy requirement.

Children require more energy per unit of body weight than do adults due to their rapid growth. In turn, the rate of growth (cell division and/or enlargement of existing cells) is determined by the availability of an adequate energy supply (Denny-Brown et al., 2012). Physical activity and body mass also affect the amount of energy an individual child requires. In general, a child's daily caloric requirement is calculated solely on the basis of normal body weight. For example, a 4-year-old child needs approximately 40 calories per pound of body weight. (The energy needs of infants are detailed in Chapter 15.) For comparison, a moderately active adult female requires approximately 18 calories per body pound; a moderately active adult male needs approximately 21 calories per body pound. (Moderately active is described as equal time "on the feet and on the seat.") Males have a higher BMR than do females due to their greater muscle-to-fat ratio; muscle tissue is more aerobically active than fat and requires additional BMR energy, whereas fat needs zero energy for storage or retrieval.

A stable body weight is maintained by balancing the number of calories eaten with the number of calories expended. (See *Dietary Guidelines for Americans* in Chapter 12.) Consuming fewer calories than are needed leads to weight loss. A calorie deficit in children can also slow their growth rate because body tissue must be utilized to meet energy demands. When children's

▼ **Quiet activities burn fewer calories than active play.**

© Cengage Learning

thermic energy of food – *energy required to digest, absorb, transport, and metabolize nutrients in food.*
digestion – *the process by which complex nutrients in foods are changed into smaller units that can be absorbed and used by the body.*
absorption – *the process by which the products of digestion are transferred from the intestinal tract into the blood or lymph or by which substances are taken up by the cells.*
metabolism – *all chemical changes that occur from the time nutrients are absorbed until they are built into body tissue or are excreted.*

diets provide adequate calories from carbohydrates and fat, proteins are spared and can be used to support growth. Carbohydrates should supply at least half of children's and adult's daily calories, with starches being the preferred carbohydrate because they contribute important vitamins, minerals, and fiber as well as energy.

13-1b Excess Energy and Obesity

Consuming an excess of calories over a period of time can lead to obesity. (Refer also to Chapter 3.) Children who are overweight are often less active than their slimmer playmates and may require fewer calories because fewer are burned. Their bulkier body mass can interfere with coordination and increase the risk of accidental injury (Adams et al., 2012). This may also contribute to the obese child's reluctance to engage in active play, which can lead to additional weight gain. Thus, it is important to interrupt this cycle during the child's early years because there is strong evidence that child obesity increases the risk for adult obesity (Halfon, Verhoef, & Kuo, 2012). There are also many known health problems associated with childhood obesity, including breathing disturbances during sleep, asthma, muscle and joint problems, diabetes, high blood pressure, and heart disease (Barton, 2012; Magnusson et al., 2012). Children who are significantly overweight may be subjected to teasing from their peers and excluded from play activities. This can foster additional problems for the child, including negative self-image, decreased fitness level, and fewer opportunities for socialization (Mustillo, Hendrix, & Schafer, 2012).

Effective weight management strategies for children include increasing their participation in physical activity and providing a healthful diet based on nutrient-dense foods (Teacher Checklist 13-1) (Collings et al., 2013).

TeachSource Video Connections

Video supplied by the BBC Motion Gallery

Child Obesity and School Nutrition

Many schools recognize that childhood obesity is a shared problem and have begun to assume some responsibility by making small changes in their meal programs and incorporating more physical activity into daily class schedules. It is clear that simple changes can have positive outcomes for children. As you watch the learning video, *Child Obesity and School Nutrition*, consider the following questions:

1. What strategies did the Cambridge school implement to increase children's acceptance of healthier food choices?
2. How does gardening foster children's interest in healthy eating?
3. What healthy food choices did you note during this video?
4. What evidence did the school have to show that the changes they made were having a positive effect?

Watch on CourseMate.

TEACHER CHECKLIST 13-1

Health Improvement Tips for Children Who Are Overweight

- Increase the amount of physical activity in which a child participates. This is often the most effective approach to healthy weight control.
- Make slight changes in a child's meals and snacks to help a child control his or her weight. Serve more low-fat cheese and dairy products, whole grains, fruits and vegetables, and fewer prepared and processed foods.
- Serve foods in the proper portion sizes to avoid overeating.
- Encourage water consumption and reduce a child's intake of sweetened beverages.
- Avoid clean plate requirements.
- Substitute fresh fruit or low-fat, low-sugar, dairy-based desserts for high-calorie desserts. For example, offer fat-free animal crackers, frozen yogurt, or fresh fruit in place of a chocolate cookie, brownie, doughnut, or ice cream. Do not exclude desserts because this can increase their importance for children.
- Be a positive role model for children and personally follow healthy eating and physical activity habits.

TeachSource Digital Download Download from CourseMate.

Children's calories should never be drastically reduced, as this can cause a deficiency of essential energy and nutrients and potentially contribute to eating disorders (Goncalves et al., 2012). A safer approach is to adjust calorie intake to maintain the child's current weight while he or she continues to grow taller. Over time, this will bring the weight–height ratio (also known as body mass index, or BMI) back into a normal range. Any time children are placed on a weight-reduction program, they must be closely monitored by a physician to ensure that all nutritional needs are being adequately met.

13-2 Carbohydrates as Energy Sources

The carbohydrate nutrient group is composed of sugars (simple carbohydrates) and starches (complex carbohydrates). Carbohydrates are an important energy source, especially for children, and supply 4 calories per gram (Figure 13–1). At least half of a child's caloric requirement should be derived from carbohydrates, particularly complex (starch) sources; refined sugars should supply no more than 10 percent of daily calories. For example, a child who requires 1,600 calories should get at least 800 calories from carbohydrates; 800 calories are supplied by 200 grams of carbohydrates. Many experts recommend that adults consume a minimum of 125 grams (500 calories) of carbohydrates daily.

Foods that contain complex and unprocessed carbohydrates are ideal choices for children's snacks. Fresh fruits and vegetables, fruit and vegetable juices, and whole grain products such as breads, cereals, and crackers are nutritious and usually readily accepted. The consumption of complex carbohydrates has steadily declined since the 1980s, whereas refined sugar intake continues to increase. Current dietary recommendations suggest that more complex carbohydrates be included in our diet and refined sugars be significantly decreased. This simply means that a person should consume less sugar and more starch and fiber from the grain, vegetable, and fruit groups.

FIGURE 13-1   Carbohydrates provide 4 calories per gram.

13-2a Sugars (Simple Carbohydrates)

The chemical structure of a sugar molecule determines whether it is a simple or compound sugar. Differences in their chemical makeup account for variations in flavor and the way each is broken down in the body.

Simple sugars Simple sugars consist of a single unit or molecule that requires no digestion prior to absorption. This means that the energy is immediately available. Examples of simple sugars are:

- glucose
- fructose
- galactose

Glucose is the only sugar form that body cells are able to utilize. However, most glucose that circulates in the blood stream results from the digestion of complex carbohydrates (starches). Fructose occurs naturally in honey and fresh fruits, but is also processed into high-fructose corn syrup and used to sweeten many commercial food

CONNECTING TO EVERYDAY PRACTICE

Are We Having an Obesity Epidemic?

The media tell us almost daily that we are fat and getting fatter. Depending on the source, the story will report that "30–50 percent of all Americans are obese," or 20 percent above their normal body weight. The message then proceeds to tell us that obesity increases our risk for several diseases.

Think About This:

▶ Why are Americans not taking these warnings seriously and trying to achieve a healthy weight?

▶ What role should early childhood programs and schools play in preventing childhood obesity?

▶ What changes can be made in the lunches served to children at your school to make them healthier?

▶ Studies show that families with young children are eating away from home and at fast-food restaurants more often.

   ▶ What foods are most commonly featured on children's restaurant menus?

   ▶ What healthier food options would you suggest?

   ▶ Should fast food chain restaurants be allowed to locate near schools? How might their proximity to schools contribute to obesity?

products. Fructose is the sweetest of all other sugars. Galactose results from the digestion of the sugars in milk but is not found freely in other foods.

Compound Sugars   Compound sugars consist of two simple sugar units joined together. Consequently, compound sugars must be digested and broken down into their simple sugar units before they can be absorbed and utilized by body cells. Two important compound sugars are:

▶ sucrose
▶ lactose

> **Did You Know...**
> that additional sugars are often added to low-fat products to improve their flavor? Read food labels carefully and be aware of hidden sugars (and empty calories)

In its refined form, sucrose is commonly known as table sugar and is found in sugar beets, sugar cane, fruits, vegetables, and honey. When sucrose occurs naturally in fruits and vegetables, it is accompanied by other essential nutrients including vitamins, minerals, and water. However, refined table sugar contributes no nutrients—only calories. For this reason, calories from table sugar are frequently called "empty calories." Consuming too many empty calories can lead to obesity accompanied by a deficiency of several essential nutrients. Children who are allowed to eat too many foods containing refined sugar may not be hungry for more healthful foods that contain the essential nutrients required for normal growth and development.

Refined sucrose, or table sugar, has also been linked to a number of health concerns, including tooth decay in children. Additional factors that increase the risk of tooth decay include the stickiness of the food containing sugar, the frequency and timing of eating, the frequency of tooth brushing, whether the sugar is part of a meal served along with other foods or in a stand-alone snack, and whether the sugar-containing food is accompanied by a beverage.

Lactose, commonly referred to as "milk sugar," is found in milk and dairy products including many processed foods. It is the only carbohydrate derived from an animal-source food. Lactose is present in the milk of mammals, including human breast milk. It is the least sweet of all common sugars, which explains why 1 cup of 2-percent milk with the equivalent of 1 tablespoon of sugar in the form of lactose does not taste sweet. It has advantages over other sugars in that

▼ **At least half of a child's daily calories should come from carbohydrates.**

© Monkey Business Images/Shutterstock.com

lactose aids in establishing and maintaining beneficial intestinal bacteria. Calcium is also used more efficiently by the body if lactose is present. Fortunately, calcium and lactose occur in the same food—milk.

Although lactose is usually a beneficial sugar, it can be problematic for some individuals. People who do not produce the enzyme lactase are unable to break lactose down to its simple sugar units so it can be absorbed. This condition is commonly referred to as lactose intolerance, and may cause considerable intestinal discomfort, cramping, gas, and diarrhea. Some individuals are able to tolerate dairy products if they are consumed in small amounts (1 to 2 cups a day) throughout the day. Dairy products such as yogurt and buttermilk are often better tolerated than milk. Lactose intolerance is more common among certain racial and ethnic populations, including persons of Native American, Asian American, Mexican American, African American, and Jewish descent (Brown-Esters, McNamara, & Savaiano, 2011). Adults are more likely to develop this condition and to experience its troublesome symptoms.

Artificial Sweeteners Questions continue to be raised about the use and safety of artificial sweeteners to reduce caloric intake. The FDA has approved a number of artificial sweeteners for human consumption, including saccharin, aspartame (NutraSweet®), acesulfame potassium (Sunett®), sucralose (Splenda®), neotame, and Stevia (National Cancer Institute, 2012). Used in moderation, these sweeteners are considered to be safe. However, their use in children's diets remains questionable because foods that typically include them are usually also poor sources of essential nutrients. Also, most children have from birth a strong natural preference for a sweet taste that does not need to be enhanced by "fake" sweeteners.

Children who are born with a condition known as phenylketonuria (PKU), a genetic disease characterized by an inability to properly metabolize the essential amino acid phenylalanine, must not use aspartame because it contains this compound. Accumulation of this toxic substance may cause severe and irreversible brain damage.

13-2b **Starches and Dietary Fiber (Complex Carbohydrates)**

Complex carbohydrates are composed of multiple simple sugar units that are joined together. Complex carbohydrates must be broken down into their simple sugar units before the body is able to absorb, use, and store them. The digestion of only one complex carbohydrate often results in thousands of simple sugars units. Complex carbohydrates that are important to human nutrition are:

- starch
- cellulose
- glycogen

Starch Starch is the only digestible form of complex carbohydrate found in foods. It is available in large amounts in grains, legumes (peas, peanuts), dried beans, and root vegetables such as potatoes, corn, winter squash, and carrots. Starches have the unfortunate reputation of being fattening, which can be true when they are consumed in excess. However, starches provide an efficient and steady fuel (energy) source while they are being digested. In addition, they are usually accompanied by a host of essential vitamins and minerals and, therefore, considered to be desirable components of a healthful diet.

Fiber Cellulose (fiber) is an indigestible complex carbohydrate found in whole grains, nuts, fruits, and vegetables. Because humans are unable to digest cellulose, it cannot be absorbed and used by body cells and, therefore, does not contribute any calories. Although it cannot be absorbed, cellulose plays a critical role in the human body. It is a primary source of insoluble fiber, which increases the rate of food transit through the intestinal tract by decreasing time for digestion, the absorption of food components, and cholesterol uptake. Studies have found that the risk for some cancerous formations is reduced when waste elimination is accelerated (Romaniero & Niyati, 2012). Soluble fiber helps to decrease the body's production of cholesterol. Cellulose is also thought to promote dental health by providing a detergent-like effect on the teeth.

Glycogen Another form of complex carbohydrate that has physiological importance is glycogen. It is often referred to as an animal starch and is the only form in which carbohydrates can be stored in the body for future conversion into sugar and subsequent energy.

Did You Get It?

Many foods now contain artificial sweeteners as substitutes for sugar. Foods containing artificial sweeteners are generally not recommended for inclusion in children's diets because they:

a. can exacerbate symptoms of ADHD
b. contain excess calories
c. are typically nutrient-poor foods
d. can be addictive for children

Take the full quiz on CourseMate.

13-3 Fats as Energy Sources

Fats make up the second group of energy-supplying nutrients. For decades, fat has been the target of much negative press and, as a result, the food industry has responded with a deluge of low-fat and fat-free foods. However, fat is an essential nutrient for young children and is required for normal growth, development, and the production of body function regulators. It also provides the most concentrated source of dietary energy, which is an important consideration when feeding young children who have a smaller stomach capacity than adults (Figure 13–2).

Each gram of fat consumed supplies approximately 9 calories. Foods in which fats are readily identified include butter, margarine, cheese, shortening, oils, and salad dressings. Less obvious fat sources are found in meats, whole milk, egg yolks, nuts, and nut butters. Fruits and vegetables contain little fat, with the exception of the avocado, which is quite rich in healthy fats. Most bread and cereal products are naturally low in fat. However, baked products such as cakes, pies, doughnuts, and cookies are usually high in added fats. Although some dietary fat is required for good health, recommendations encourage individuals to reduce fat intake to no more than 30 percent of their total daily calories. However, the American Academy of Pediatrics and the American Heart Association recommend that there should be no dietary fat restriction for children under 2 years of age unless they have a family history of obesity, heart disease, or diabetes (AAP, 2012; AHA, 2012a). The 2010 *Dietary Guidelines for Americans* advises that total fat intake be maintained "between 30 to 35 percent of calories for children 2 to 3 years of age and between 25 to 30 percent of calories for children and adolescents 4 to 18 years of age," with most fats coming from fish,

FIGURE 13–2 Fats provide 9 calories per gram.

nuts, and vegetable oils. Thus, if a child requires 1,600 calories, her diet should include a maximum of 50-55 fat grams or approximately 480 calories from fat. This amount is equivalent to approximately 4 tablespoons of butter, margarine, or vegetable oil.

Although fats provide more than twice the energy per gram as do carbohydrates, they are a less desirable energy source for children. Fat is more difficult for children to digest and is usually accompanied by fewer essential nutrients. However, fats are essential for children and should not be reduced below 30 percent of a child's daily calories because they:

❱ support normal growth and development of brain and nerve tissues
❱ contribute the essential fatty acids (**linoleic** and **linolenic**)
❱ serve as carriers for important fat-soluble vitamins
❱ provide a concentrated energy source that meets children's high caloric needs

Young children should not be served fat-free or skim milk to lower their fat intake. Most authorities believe this practice may lead to insufficient calorie intake and essential fatty acid (EFA) deficiency. In addition, infants and young children (under 2 years of age) who consume the same amount or more of skim milk as they previously consumed of breast milk or formula will receive excess protein and minerals. Young children's kidneys are still immature and may not be able to handle and excrete the added waste and minerals (Whitney & Rolfes, 2013). Low-fat (2 percent) milk may be given to children older than 2 years and may be advised if there is a strong family history of cardiovascular disease.

Fats must undergo digestion and absorption into the body to have their energy released. Digestion of dietary fats produces:

❱ fatty acids
❱ glycerol

The resulting fatty acids and glycerol are in forms that the body can readily absorb and utilize. Fatty acids in foods are either saturated or unsaturated.

13-3a Saturated Fats

The fats in animal-source foods such as meat, milk, cheese, and eggs yield fatty acids that are primarily saturated (Tables 13–1 and 13–2). Fats containing predominantly saturated fatty acids

TABLE 13–1 **Comparison of cooking oils (values for 1 tablespoon).**

	Saturated (grams)	Monounsaturated (grams)	Polyunsaturated (grams)
Safflower oil	0.8	2.0	10.0
Canola oil	1.0	8.9	3.9
Margarine (tub)	1.0	2.6	1.8
Flaxseed oil	1.2	2.5	9.2
Sunflower oil	1.4	7.8	3.9
Corn oil	1.7	3.8	7.4
Olive oil	1.9	9.8	1.4
Soybean oil	2.1	3.1	7.9
Margarine (stick)	2.3	5.5	3.0
Peanut oil	2.3	6.2	4.3
Palm oil	6.7	5.0	1.3
Butter	7.3	1.1	0.2
Coconut oil	11.8	0.8	0.3

Source: USDA National Nutrient Database for Standard Reference.

linoleic acid – *a polyunsaturated fatty acid that is essential (must be provided in food) for humans; also known as omega-6 fatty acid.*
linolenic acid – *one of the two polyunsaturated fatty acids that are recognized as essential for humans; also known as omega-3 fatty acid.*

TABLE 13-2 **Comparison of Saturated Fat Values in Foods**

Food Category	Portion	Saturated Fat Content (grams)	Calories
Cheese			
• Regular cheddar cheese	1 oz.	6.0	114
• Low-fat cheddar cheese	1 oz.	1.2	49
Ground beef			
• Regular ground beef (25% fat)	3 oz. (cooked)	6.1	236
• Extra lean ground beef (5% fat)	3 oz. (cooked)	2.6	148
Milk			
• Whole milk (3.25%)	1 cup	4.6	146
• Low-fat (1%) milk	1 cup	1.5	102
Breads			
• Croissant (med.) 1 medium	1 medium	6.6	231
• Bagel, oat bran (4")	1 medium	0.2	227
Frozen desserts			
• Regular ice cream	1/2 cup	4.9	145
• Frozen yogurt, low-fat	1/2 cup	2.0	110
Table spreads			
• Butter 1 tsp.	1 tsp.	2.4	34
• Soft margarine with zero *trans-fats*	1 tsp.	0.7	25
Chicken			
• Fried chicken (leg with skin)	3 oz. (cooked)	3.3	212
• Roasted chicken (breast no skin)	3 oz. (cooked)	0.9	140
Fish			
• Fried fish	3 oz.	2.8	195
• Baked fish	3 oz.	1.5	129

are usually solid at room temperature and are often accompanied by cholesterol. Cholesterol and saturated fats have been extensively investigated as undesirable dietary components that should be limited. However, after years of study, few definitive conclusions have been reached regarding dietary cholesterol's role in cardiovascular disease or the advisability of lowering children's intake of saturated fatty acids and cholesterol. The American Heart Association (AHA) does recommend that dietary intake of saturated and **trans-fats** be limited (AHA, 2012b; Cascio, Schiera, & Di Liego, 2012). It is important to remember that cholesterol is found only in animal-source foods. However, do not equate high fat with high cholesterol. For example, coconut derives 83 percent of its calories from fat, and 89 percent of its fatty acids are saturated, but it has no cholesterol.

13-3b Unsaturated Fats

Unsaturated fats are usually soft at room temperature or are in oil form. Monounsaturated fatty acids (**MUFAs**), which have only one point of unsaturation, are currently reported to be most effective in controlling the type and amount of fat and cholesterol circulating in the bloodstream. Thus, olive oil and canola oil, both high in MUFAs, are recommended for use, especially by persons who are prone to cardiovascular disease.

The fats in plant-source foods such as corn oil or sunflower oil are primarily unsaturated. Many plant oils are high in polyunsaturated fatty acids which are also known as **PUFAs**. Linoleic

trans-fats – *unsaturated fats that have been converted to a solid by a process called hydrogenation.*
MUFAs – *monounsaturated fatty acids; fatty acids that have one double hydrogen bond; nuts, avocados, and olive oil are high in this form of fat.*
PUFAs – *polyunsaturated fatty acids; fatty acids that contain more than one bond that is not fully saturated with hydrogen.*

and linolenic acids are polyunsaturated fatty acids that are essential for all humans, especially infants and children, who require them in larger amounts. These fats play a critical role in visual and neural system development, and can be obtained only from food sources. Plant-based foods are ideal choices as they do not contain cholesterol. Protein molecules link with fat to produce lipoproteins, which help to transport fat and cholesterol in the blood. A high blood level of high density lipoproteins (HDLs), which have a greater ratio of protein to fat, is currently thought to reduce the risk of cardiovascular disease. Physical activity has been identified as the most effective way to increase HDL (good cholesterol) levels in blood.

Did You Get It?

The American Academy of Pediatrics and the American Heart Association, with a few exceptions, take the stance that children aged two and under should have:

a. no fat restrictions in their diets
b. diets that contain approximately 30% of calories from fats
c. diets that contain at least 50% of calories from saturated fats
d. diets that include no more than 20% of calories from fats

Take the full quiz on CourseMate.

13-4 Proteins as Energy Sources

Proteins are the third nutrient group that provides energy. Each gram yields 4 calories, which is the same amount of energy provided by a gram of carbohydrate (Figure 13–3). Although they both yield the same number of calories per gram, proteins such as meats, seafood, and cheeses are generally more costly to purchase than are carbohydrates. Thus, relying on protein to supply energy is like filling your car's gas tank with premium fuel when a less expensive grade would work as well.

Proteins must be digested into their component amino acids prior to absorption and utilization by the body. Each protein is unique in the number, arrangement, and specific amino acids from which it is built. Because proteins (amino acids) function primarily as raw materials for building body tissues and regulating body functions, they will be discussed in greater detail in the next chapter.

FIGURE 13–3 **Proteins provide 4 calories per gram.**

Did You Get It?

Protein is an essential nutrient for ensuring healthy growth, development, and human body function. Each gram of protein supplies the body with how many calories?

a. two
b. four
c. seven
d. nine

Take the full quiz on CourseMate.

PARTNERING with FAMILIES

Healthy Families

Dear Families,

Children's early years are an important time to begin instilling healthy eating and physical activity habits. Encouraging children to be active and to eat a well-balanced diet also has important benefits for maintaining a healthy weight. You can use the BMI calculator provided on the Centers for Disease Control & Prevention (CDC) website (http://www.cdc.gov) to determine your child's current weight status: underweight, healthy weight, overweight, or obese. An adult BMI calculator is also available on this site. The higher a child's BMI, the greater the risk is for certain health-related diseases. Adopting healthy lifestyle changes is important for all family members, regardless of where your child's BMI appears on the chart.

▶ Plan to eat meals together as a family. Sit down and turn off all distractions including televisions, video games, cell phones, and computers. It is important that family members share mealtimes together and to engage in positive, non-stressful conversation.

▶ Use the MyPlate plan to guide your food choices. Incorporate a wide variety of foods and colors into your family's diet. Choose the majority of foods from the fruits, vegetables, and whole grains groups, serve low-fat dairy products, limit processed and highly sweetened foods, and practice portion control.

▶ Encourage healthy snacking at planned times. Use suggestions posted on the http://www.ChooseMyPlate.gov website to identify nutrient-dense snack foods that children will enjoy. Avoid snacks that have empty calories and don't let children eat throughout the day; this will cause them to eat poorly at meals.

▶ Join children in active games, neighborhood walks, field trips, and sports they enjoy. Doing these things together with children builds strong family bonds and a healthy lifestyle.

CLASSROOM CORNER

Teacher Activities

Roll the Cube and Move...

(PreK-2, NHES National Health Education Standard 1.2.1, 7.2.1)

Concept: Food gives us energy and energy is what helps us move.

Learning Objectives

▶ Children will learn that eating food provides the body with energy to move.

▶ Children will practice different movement activities: clapping, jumping, stomping, running, touching their toes, and tossing a bean bag.

Supplies

▶ Cube or small box with pictures representing each of the above actions

▶ Bean bags (one per child)

(continued)

CLASSROOM CORNER

Teacher Activities   *(continued)*

Learning Activities

▶ Talk about the importance of eating healthy foods such as fruits, vegetables, whole grains, meats, dairy, and proteins to give our body energy. Explain that energy is what enables the body to move.

▶ Explain the movement cube. Demonstrate the actions represented by each picture on the cube (hands together - clapping; toes - touch your toes, and so on).

▶ Have children take turns rolling the cube and performing the appropriate action.

Evaluation

▶ Children will name several foods that give them energy.

▶ Children will perform a variety of movement activities.

Additional lesson plans for grades 3–5 are available on CourseMate.

Summary

▶ The nutrient classes that yield energy are carbohydrates (4 calories/gram), fats (9 calories/gram), and proteins (4 calories/gram).

  • A person's total energy requirement is a composite of (a) basal metabolic need, (b) voluntary physical activity, and (c) metabolism to release energy for both of these activities (a) and (b).

▶ Carbohydrates yield 4 calories/gram and consist of sugars and starches.

  • Simple sugars are a one-unit molecule and include glucose, fructose, and galactose.
  • Compound sugars are two-unit molecules that require digestion and include sucrose and lactose.
  • Starch and dietary fiber are complex carbohydrates that are made up of many simple sugar units.

▶ Fat yields 9 calories per gram and is the richest energy source. The fatty acids in fats are either saturated or unsaturated. Two unsaturated fatty acids (linoleic and linolenic) are essential for children's growth.

▶ Proteins are an inefficient source of energy. They are not usually burned for energy unless too few carbohydrates and fats are available to meet energy needs.

Terms to Know

energy *p. 340*
calories *p. 340*
gram *p. 341*
milligram *p. 341*
enzymes *p. 341*
coenzymes *p. 341*

hormones *p. 341*
basal metabolic rate
    (BMR) *p. 341*
thermic energy of food *p. 342*
digest (digestion) *p. 342*
absorb (absorption) *p. 342*

metabolize (metabolism) *p. 342*
linoleic acid *p. 348*
linolenic acid *p. 348*
trans-fats *p. 349*
MUFAs *p. 349*
PUFAs *p. 349*

Chapter Review

A. By Yourself:

1. Match the terms in **Column II** to the correct phrase in **Column I.**

Column I	Column II
1. a simple sugar	a. amino acids
2. digestible complex carbohydrate	b. cellulose
3. found in meats, dairy products, legumes, and eggs	c. protein
4. building blocks in proteins	d. carbohydrate
5. found in grains, fruits, vegetables, and milk products	e. glucose
6. richest source of energy	f. fats
7. indigestible complex carbohydrate	g. starch
8. table sugar (complex sugar)	h. sucrose
	i. trans-fats

2. Explain why fat intake must not be restricted for children younger than 2 years of age.

3. Provide two examples of saturated and unsaturated fats.

4. Explain how the number of calories an individual requires is determined.

B. As a Group:

1. Conduct an online search of scholarly articles on childhood obesity. Why are more children overweight or obese today? In what ways can teachers begin to address this problem in their classrooms?

2. Discuss the cause of lactose intolerance, which groups of children are more likely to experience this condition, and what dietary modifications need to be made.

3. Prepare a convincing argument to counter the statement, "Carbohydrates are bad for you."

4. Discuss whether or not all fats are unhealthy and should thus be eliminated from one's diet.

5. Take the interactive portion distortion quiz posted on the National Institutes of Health website (http://hp2010.nhlbihin.net/portion). Create your own set of slides illustrating additional food examples along with their correct portion sizes and activity equivalents.

Case Study

The dietitian at the Women, Infant, and Child (WIC) office met with Olivia's mother during their last clinic visit to discuss the importance of limiting Olivia's sugar and sugary drink intake. Although Olivia is only 5, she has already had extensive dental work because of tooth decay. The dentist has also counseled Olivia's mother about supervising her daughter's tooth brushing practices and eliminating refined sucrose from her diet.

- Plan a day's menu (including snacks) for Olivia that contains at least 150 grams of carbohydrates without any refined sucrose (table sugar). Use the following average amounts of carbohydrates:

bread, cereals, pastas	15 grams/slice or ounce
fruits and juices	10 grams/ ½ adult serving
starchy vegetables	10 grams/ ½ adult serving
milk	6 grams/ ½ cup

- What nutrient-dense snack items would you suggest that Olivia's mother serve in place of those with refined sugars?

Application Activities

1. Use the cereal label in Figure 13-4 to determine: (a) the number of calories derived from carbohydrates; (b) the percentage of calories derived from sugar.

2. Which of the cereal's nutrient contributions are increased by adding milk?

3. Explain why cereal with milk has a higher carbohydrate value than cereal alone.

   a. Is this cereal predominantly starch or sucrose?

   b. Do starches and complex carbohydrates increase with the addition of milk?

4. Calculate the caloric requirement of a 4-year-old child who weighs 42 pounds.

5. Determine the number of calories in a serving of food that contributes the following: carbohydrate-12 grams; protein-8 grams; fat-10 grams.

FIGURE 13-4   A typical cereal label..

Nutrition Facts

Serving Size 3/4 cup (30g)
Servings Per Container about 15

Amount Per Serving	Cereal	Cereal with 1/2 cup Skim Milk
Calories	100	140
Calories from Fat	5	5

		% Daily Value**
Total Fat 0.5g*	**1%**	**1%**
Saturated Fat 0g	0%	0%
Polyunsaturated Fat 0g		
Monounsaturated Fat 0g		
Cholesterol 0mg	**0%**	**0%**
Sodium 220mg	**9%**	**12%**
Potassium 190mg	**5%**	**11%**
Total Carbohydrate 24g	**8%**	**10%**
Dietary Fiber 5g	**21%**	**21%**
Soluble Fiber 1g		
Insoluble Fiber 4g		
Sugars 6g		
Other Carbohydrate 13g		
Protein 3g		

Vitamin A	15%	20%
Vitamin C	0%	2%
Calcium	0%	15%
Iron	45%	45%
Vitamin D	10%	25%
Thiamin	25%	30%
Riboflavin	25%	35%
Niacin	25%	25%
Vitamin B6	25%	25%
Folate	25%	25%
Vitamin B12	25%	35%
Phosphorus	15%	25%
Magnesium	15%	20%
Zinc	10%	15%
Copper	10%	10%

*Amount in Cereal. One half cup skim milk contributes an additional 40 calories, 65mg sodium, 200mg potassium, 6g total carbohydrate (6g sugars), and 4g protein.

**Percent Daily Values are based on a 2,000 calorie diet. Your daily values may be higher or lower depending on your calorie needs:

		Calories:	2,000	2,500
Total Fat	Less than		65g	80g
Saturated Fat	Less than		20g	25g
Cholesterol	Less than		300mg	300mg
Sodium	Less than		2,400mg	2,400mg
Potassium			3,500mg	3,500mg
Total Carbohydrate			300g	375g
Dietary Fiber			25g	30g

Helpful Web Resources

American Dietetic Association	http://www.eatright.org
Center for Science in Public Interest (CSPI)	http://www.cspinet.org
Healthy Children	http://www.healthychildren.org
Women, Infants, and Children (WIC)	http://www.fns.usda.gov/wic
United States Department of Agriculture, Food & Nutrition	http://www.usda.gov

Visit the Education CourseMate for this textbook to access the eBook, Did You Get It? quizzes, Digital Downloads, TeachSource Video Cases, flashcards, and more. Go to CengageBrain.com to log in, register, or purchase access.

References

Adams, A., Kessler, J., Deramerian, K., Smith, N., Black, M., Porter, A., Jacobsen, S., & Koebnick, S. (2012). Associations between childhood obesity and upper and lower extremity injuries, *Injury Prevention*. DOI:10.1136/injuryprev-2012-040341.

American Academy of Pediatrics (AAP). (2012). Low fat diets for babies. Accessed on July 20, 2012 from http://www.healthychildren.org/English/ages-stages/baby/feeding-nutrition/pages/Low-Fat-Diets-For-Babies.aspx.

American Heart Association (AHA). (2012a) Dietary recommendations for healthy children. Accessed on July 20, 2012 from http://www.heart.org/HEARTORG/GettingHealthy/Dietary-Recommendations-for-Healthy-Children_UCM_303886_Article.jsp.

AHA. (2012b). Know your fats. Accessed on July 20, 2012 from http://www.heart.org/HEARTORG/Conditions/Cholesterol/PreventionTreatmentofHighCholesterol/Know-Your-Fats_UCM_305628_Article.jsp.

Barton, M. (2012). Childhood obesity: A life-long health risk, *Acta Pharmacologica Sinica*, 33, 189–193.

Brown-Esters, O., McNamara, P., & Savaiano, D. (2011). Dietary and biological factors influencing lactose intolerance, *International Dairy Journal*, 22(2), 98–103.

Cascio, G., Schiera, G., & Di Liegro, I. (2012). Dietary fatty acids in metabolic syndrome, diabetes, and cardiovascular diseases, *Current Diabetes Review*, 8(1), 2–17.

Collings, P., Brage, S., Ridgway, C., Harvey, N., Godfrey, K., Inskip, H., Cooper, C., Wareham, N., & Ekelund, U. (2013). Physical activity intensity, sedentary time, and body composition in preschoolers, *The American Journal of Clinical Nutrition*, 97(5), 1020–1028.

Denny-Brown, S., Stanley, T., Grinspoon, S., & Makimura, H. (2012). The association of macro- and micronutrient intake with growth hormone secretion, *Growth Hormone & IGF Research*, 22(3), 102–107.

Goncalves, S., Silva, M., Gomes, A., & Machado, P. (2012). Disordered eating among preadolescent boys and girls: The relationship with child and maternal variables, *Nutrients*, 4(4), 273–285.

Halfon, N., Verhoef, P., & Kuo, A. (2012). Childhood antecedents to adult cardiovascular disease, *Pediatrics in Review*, 33(2), 51–61.

Magnusson, J., Kull, I., Mai, X., Wickman, M., & Bergström, A. (2012). Early childhood overweight and asthma and allergic sensitization at 8 years of age, *Pediatrics*, 129(1), 70–76.

Mustillo, S., Hendrix, K., & Schafer, M. (2012). Trajectories of body mass and self-concept in Black and White girls: The lingering effects of stigma, *Behavior*, 53(1), 2–16.

National Cancer Institute. (2012). Artificial sweeteners and cancer. Accessed on July 20, 2012 from http://www.cancer.gov/cancertopics/factsheet/Risk/artificial-sweeteners.

Niederer, I., Kriemler, S., Zahner, L., Bürgi, F., Ebenegger, V., Marques-Vidal, P., & Puder, J. (2012). BMI group-related differences in physical fitness and physical activity in preschool-age children: A cross-sectional analysis, *Research Quarterly for Exercise and Sport*, 83(1), 12–19(8).

Romaneiro, S., & Niyati, P. (2012). Dietary fiber intake and colorectal cancer risk: Weighing the evidence from epidemiologic studies, *Topics in Clinical Nutrition*, 27(1), 41–47.

Whitney, E., & Rolfes, S. (2013). *Understanding nutrition*. (12th ed.). Belmont, CA: Wadsworth.

chapter 14 Nutrients That Promote Growth and Regulate Body Functions

▶ **#1 a, b, and c:** Promoting child development and learning
▶ **#2 a and c:** Building family and community relationships
▶ **#3 b, c, and d:** Observing, documenting, and assessing to support young children and families
▶ **#4 a:** Using developmentally effective approaches to connect with children and families
▶ **#6 c:** Becoming a professional

Learning Objectives

After studying this chapter, you should be able to:

LO 14-1 Identify four nutrients that are often inadequate in children's diet and explain why this occurs.

LO 14-2 Describe how complete and incomplete proteins differ and give several examples of each.

LO 14-3 Discuss the primary functions that vitamins serve in the body.

LO 14-4 Describe the major roles that minerals play in maintaining normal body functions.

LO 14-5 Explain why children have a greater need for water than adults do.

No nutrient is able to function independently. Each plays a specific role or roles and always teams up with other nutrients to perform complex processes in the human body. Some nutrients are precursors, which means they must complete their required step before additional nutrients can take over. For example, thiamin, niacin, and riboflavin must be available to trigger the sequential steps involved in the release of energy from carbohydrates, proteins, and fats. Nerve impulses will not travel from one nerve cell to another, nor will muscles contract, unless several B and C vitamins and minerals are present in adequate amounts when they are needed. Some nutrients are known for their ability to enhance another nutrients' performance. For example, the body's capacity for absorbing the iron in foods is significantly improved when vitamin C is present. The importance of consuming a rich variety of foods thus becomes clearer once it is understood how nutrients function and depend on one another.

Some nutrients are required in large amounts, whereas others, especially vitamins and minerals, are needed in extremely small quantities. Their RDAs are typically measured in **milligrams (mg)**, one-thousandth of a gram, and in **micrograms (mcg or μg)**, one-millionth of a gram (Table 12–2). Recall that a standard size metal paper clip weighs approximately 1 gram. Imagine that you smash that paper clip into one thousand pieces or one million pieces and try to envision 1 milligram or 1 microgram. Would you expect to see a particle that was 1 microgram in size?

....

milligram (mg) – *a metric unit of weight (mg); approximately 1/1,000 of a gram.*
microgram (mcg or μg) – *a metric unit of measurement; one microgram equals one-millionth of a gram.*

Proteins, vitamins, minerals, and water are vital to the growth, performance, and maintenance of the human body. These nutrients are especially critical for young children because they establish the cellular foundation that will continue to serve for a lifetime.

14-1 Children and At-Risk Nutrients

It is relatively easy to satisfy children's dietary needs for protein, carbohydrates, and fat despite the small amounts of food they are often willing and able to eat. However, meeting their dietary requirements for calcium, iron, and vitamins A and C can present significantly greater challenges. Foods that supply these nutrients are often not among children's favorites. It is for this reason the two minerals and two vitamins are frequently referred to as at-risk nutrients (Pabayo et al., 2012; Zhou et al., 2012).

There are many reasons why these particular nutrients are often deficient in children's diets. Food acceptance and preferences are strongly influenced by children's current developmental stage. For example, young children often dislike red meat because it requires considerable chewing—small teeth and weak jaw muscles make chewing difficult and less effective. Fruits and vegetables, especially those that are sour or have a strong flavor (e.g., broccoli, cabbage, beets) are more likely to be refused because children also have an acute sense of taste and sensitivity to texture during the early years. Foods that are unfamiliar, or to which children have had limited experience, are frequently rejected. However, children's diets may also be deficient because adults lack knowledge about foods that supply the at-risk nutrients. In addition, an increasing number of children are growing up in families for which economic hardship and food insecurity limit the foods (and nutrients) they are able to provide. As a result, milk (calcium), meat (iron), and fresh fruits and vegetables (vitamins A and C), are frequently missing from children's diets (Goldman, Radnitz, & McGrath, 2012; Kirkpatrick et al., 2012).

Studies have repeatedly found children's diets to be deficient in calcium and iron (Maxwell et al., 2012; Black et al., 2011). These minerals are not widely distributed in foods and often poorly absorbed. Simply because calcium or iron is present in a food does not guarantee that it will all be absorbed and utilized in the body. Factors that *increase* calcium and iron absorption (Table 14–1):

 ▶ Vitamin C makes calcium and iron more soluble so they are easier for the body to absorb.
 ▶ Vitamin C maximizes the absorption of calcium and iron in foods when it is consumed in the same meal.
 ▶ Calcium and iron absorption increases at times when the body requires more of these minerals, such as when intake is inadequate or during periods of rapid growth.

Factors that *decrease* calcium and iron absorption:

 ▶ Large single doses are not absorbed as efficiently as several smaller doses, especially when consumed in supplement form.
 ▶ A high fiber diet can speed up intestinal movement and decrease the time calcium and iron have contact with intestinal wall linings where they are absorbed.

TABLE 14–1 Factors That Affect Calcium and Iron Absorption

Calcium	Factor	Iron
↑	Adequate vitamin C	↑
↑	Increased need	↑
↓	Large dose	↓
↓	High fiber diet	↓
↓	High protein level	↑
↑	Physical activity	

14-2 Proteins

Proteins are the only class of nutrients that can perform all three general functions: they build and repair body tissue; regulate body functions; and, provide energy. However, the role they play in growth is the most important of these functions. Proteins supply the fundamental materials from which all body cells (tissues and fluids, such as hormones and antibodies) are built. They are concentrated in muscles, glands, organs, bones, blood, and skin and account for approximately 15 percent of person's body weight (Figure 14–1).

14-2a Proteins for Growth

Growth represents an increase in (1) the number of cells, and/or (2) the size of individual cells. It results in changes that may affect certain body parts or the entire body and is a distinguishing feature of childhood. For example, infants typically double their birth weight in the first 6 months and triple it by the end of the first year. Their length increases by 50 percent during the same period. Preschool- and school-age children grow more slowly but continue to add several inches and pounds each year. In contrast, adolescents once again experience dramatic growth spurts that gradually contribute to their adult-like appearance.

▼ **Protein is essential during the early years when rapid growth is occurring.**

© Cengage Learning

Although young children are continually growing, the rate is often irregular. Periods of linear growth (height) are followed by a brief plateau and then by a period of weight gain. Children's appetite and nutrient needs are greatest during the linear growth phase. Optimum growth during each of these stages is possible only when children have access to a nutrient-rich diet. Failure to meet nutrient needs for growth may result in a small-for-age child who develops fewer brain cells and has lowered resistance to disease, poor utilization of food eaten, lack of energy, and delayed development (Marotz, 2011; Watford & Wu, 2011).

Protein as Building Blocks Proteins are composed of hundreds of individual units called **amino acids**. The human body is able to manufacture some of the amino acids needed to build new proteins; these amino acids

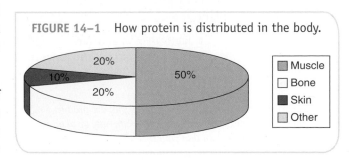

FIGURE 14–1   How protein is distributed in the body.

20%
10%
20%
50%

☐ Muscle
☐ Bone
☐ Skin
☐ Other

amino acids – *the organic building blocks from which proteins are made.*

are called **non-essential amino acids**. Amino acids that the body cannot produce in the required amounts must be supplied by proteins in food; these amino acids are called **essential amino acids**.

When all essential amino acids are present in adequate amounts in a given food item, the protein is said to be a **complete protein**. Complete proteins are typically found in animal-source foods such as meats, seafood, eggs, and milk and dairy products.

Incomplete proteins lack adequate amounts of one or more essential amino acids. They are found primarily in plant-based foods such as grains, legumes (peas, peanuts), dried beans, and vegetables (such as corn). One exception is the soybean (from which soy milk and tofu is made), which supplies amino acids that are adequate to support children's growth. However, soybeans and soybean products can interfere with iron absorption when consumed in large amounts.

Complete proteins are formed by combining two or more incomplete proteins that are complementary. A food is said to be complementary when it supplies amino acids that are insufficient or missing in another food item. For example, wheat is deficient in the amino acid lysine. When it is combined with peanuts, which contain adequate amounts of lysine but lack other essential amino acids that are available in wheat, a complete protein is formed. The wheat and peanut combination contains all the essential amino acids and is equivalent to a complete protein. This wheat-peanut combination could be served as a peanut butter sandwich or a peanut sauce on pasta. Plant proteins tend to be low in fat and less expensive to purchase than animal-source proteins. However, they must be consumed in some what larger amounts to achieve the equivalent of a complete protein. For instance, 1 cup of beans will complement 2⅔ cups of rice to form a complete protein. The amino acids in incomplete proteins are stored in the body for approximately 24 hours. If their complementary amino acids do not become available during this time, they will be eliminated.

Many favorite dishes are prime examples of incomplete protein combinations that result in a complete protein equivalent:

- ▶ **complementary proteins** – combining one or more incomplete proteins to form the equivalent of a complete protein.
  Examples: peanut butter sandwich, beans and rice, rice or macaroni salad with peas, lentil or bean soup with crackers, baked beans and cornbread, black bean tacos.
- ▶ **supplementary proteins** – combining a small amount of complete protein with an incomplete protein to yield a complete protein.
  Examples: macaroni and cheese, rice pudding, egg salad sandwich, cheese pizza, cereal and milk, grilled cheese sandwich.

Building a meal around complementary or supplementary proteins can be an effective way to obtain high-quality protein while controlling food costs.

Vegetarian Diets Many populations worldwide follow a plant-based diet. Their reasons for choosing a vegetarian diet vary widely and include religion, economics, health, personal choice, animal rights protection, and environmental concerns. Vegetarian diets are based primarily on plant-source foods but may also include some animal products:

- ▶ lacto-ovo-vegetarian—includes milk, dairy products, and eggs
- ▶ lacto-vegetarian—includes milk and dairy products, but not eggs

---

non-essential amino acids – *amino acids that are produced in the body.*
essential amino acids – *amino acids that can only be obtained from protein food sources.*
complete protein – *protein that contains all essential amino acids in amounts relative to the amounts needed to support growth.*
incomplete proteins – *proteins that lack required amounts of one or more essential amino acids.*
complementary proteins – *proteins with offsetting missing amino acids; complementary proteins can be combined to provide complete protein.*
supplementary proteins – *a complete protein mix resulting from combining a small amount of a complete protein with an incomplete protein to provide all essential amino acids.*

> ✓✓ *TEACHER CHECKLIST 14-1*
>
> ### Non-animal Food Sources of Essential Nutrients
>
> Vegetarians who consume no animal products may lack several critical nutrients unless careful attention is given to identifying alternative dietary sources. Nutrients that are most likely to be deficient and their non-animal food sources are:
>
> - **vitamin B$_{12}$**—fortified soy beverages and cereals
> - **vitamin D**—fortified soy beverages and sunshine
> - **calcium**—tofu processed with calcium, broccoli, seeds, nuts (almonds), kale, bok choy, legumes (peas and beans), and calcium-fortified orange juice
> - **iron**—legumes (dried beans, peas, lentils), tofu, green leafy vegetables, dried fruit, whole grains, and iron-fortified cereals and breads, especially whole-wheat (Absorption is improved when vitamin C is present in foods, such as citrus fruits and juices, tomatoes, strawberries, broccoli, peppers, spinach tortillas, leafy green vegetables, and potatoes with skins.)
> - **zinc**—whole wheat bread, whole grains (especially the germ and bran), legumes (dried beans, peas, lentils), nuts and nut butters, tofu
> - **protein**—tofu and other soy-based products, legumes, seeds, nuts, tempeh, grains, and vegetables

TeachSource Digital Download) Download from CourseMate.

- ovo-vegetarian—includes eggs, but no milk or dairy products
- vegan—no animal source foods are consumed, including items such as honey and gelatin

Plant-based diets must be planned carefully to include all essential amino acids while meeting a child's caloric needs. This can be somewhat challenging given children's smaller stomach capacity and the larger quantities of incomplete proteins required. Teacher Checklist 14-1 identifies nutrients that are most likely to be deficient in the vegetarian diet and includes examples of alternative (non-animal) food sources. Food manufacturers have responded to increasing interest in vegetarian diets by expanding their lines of plant-based items and fortifying many soy products with calcium and vitamin D.

It was formerly thought that a vegan diet would not adequately meet children's nutrient needs. However, the Academy of Nutrition and Dietetics (formerly the American Dietetic Association) has stated that, "Appropriately planned vegan, lacto-vegetarian, and lacto-ovo-vegetarian diets satisfy the nutrient needs of infants, children, and adolescents and promote normal growth" (Academy of Nutrition and Dietetics, 2009). This statement emphasizes the importance of a well-planned diet based on sound information about children's nutrient requirements for growth, development, and health (Mangels & Driggers, 2012).

14-2b Proteins as Regulators

Proteins (amino acids) are important components of the enzymes responsible for regulating energy metabolism and other chemical reactions in the body. They help to control fluid distribution, including fluid retention and loss. Proteins are also critical components of hormones, such as insulin and thyroxin that are secreted by glands. Hormones play critical roles in regulating many body functions, including energy metabolism. For example, thyroxin is secreted by the thyroid gland and regulates the rate at which energy is used for involuntary activities. Insulin is secreted by the pancreas and aids cells in absorbing glucose so that it can be used as an energy source for cellular activity.

14-2c Protein Requirements

Daily protein requirements are determined by an individual's body weight and life stage. Infants' rapid growth during the first year demands significantly more protein relative to their body size

Vitamins play important supporting roles in growth, energy release, and motor function.

© Cengage Learning

than an older child or adult would require. For example, an 8-month-old infant requires approximately 13.5 grams of protein daily, a 2-year-old requires 13 grams, and a 4-year-old needs 19 grams. Although school-age children are growing at a slower rate, they continue to need approximately 35 grams of high-quality protein each day. The following food selections illustrate how easy it is for children to obtain adequate protein.

Food	Protein
2 cups of milk	16.0 grams
1 slice whole wheat bread	2.7 grams
1 ounce meat	7.0 grams
1 slice provolone cheese	7.0 grams
1 egg	5.5 grams
1 ounce tofu (firm)	2.5 grams
3 wheat crackers	0.5 grams
2 ounces cooked pasta	7.0 grams

Table 14–2 illustrates a one-day menu that would more than adequately meet the daily recommended protein requirement for a 4- to 6-year-old child.

TABLE 14–2   Menu Supplying Recommended Daily Allowances of Protein for 4- to 6-Year-Olds

Breakfast	Grams of Protein
1/2 c. 100 percent fruit juice or 1/2 medium banana	trace
1/2 c. dry oat cereal	1.0
1/2 c. milk*	4.0
Midmorning Snack	
1/2 c milk*	4.0
1/2 slice buttered toast	1.0
Lunch	
1/2 fish taco ($^1/_2$ tortilla, $1^1/_2$ ounces tilapia)*	15.0
4 cherry tomatoes	0.5
1/2 medium apple	trace
1/2 c. milk*	4.0
Mid-afternoon Snack	
1/2 c. 100 percent fruit juice	trace
2 rye crackers	1.0
Dinner	
1 chicken leg (1 oz.)*	6.0
1/4 c. rice	1.0
1/4 c. broccoli	trace
1/4 c. strawberries	trace
1/2 c. milk*	4.0
	TOTAL: 41.5 gm protein

*Complete protein.

14-3 Vitamins

Vitamins are organic compounds that are naturally occurring in food. They play essential roles in maintaining and performing critical body functions, including growth, energy release and production, and neurological health and function.

Thirteen vitamins are considered to be essential for the human body and are classified as being either **fat soluble** (dissolved in and carried by fat molecules) or **water soluble** (dissolved in water) (Table 14–3). Fat-soluble vitamins (A, D, E, and K) are present in high-fat foods such as meats, milk and dairy products, eggs, nuts, avocados, and vegetable oils and offer important health benefits. However, toxicities can develop when fat-soluble vitamins are taken as large-dose supplements because they are absorbed and stored in the body. Water-soluble vitamins (B and C) are absorbed directly into the blood stream and cells and any excess or unused amounts are excreted in urine. Toxicities are unlikely to develop when these vitamins are acquired from food because the body does not store them. Consequently, deficiencies of water-soluble vitamins can develop within days if they are not consumed on a regular basis. Water-soluble vitamins are readily available in fruits, vegetables, whole grain products, milk and dairy products, and many meats. Table 14–4 summarizes the characteristics of both vitamin classes.

> **Did You Know...**
>
> that Americans spend approximately $28 billion annually on vitamin and herbal supplements? This is an unregulated industry and there are no guarantees that products are safe, effective, or contain the nutrient in the amount stated.

14-3a Vitamins that Support Growth

Folacin (also known as folate or folic acid) and vitamin B_{12} are essential for cell division and growth. Although they do not become structural parts of new tissue, they are involved in the production of **DNA** and **RNA**, which provide the genetic code or pattern for individual cell formation. For example, bones would not form properly or be maintained without the influence of vitamins A, D, and C; blood components could not be produced without vitamins C, B_6, B_{12}, and folic acid. So crucial are these vitamins that deficiencies quickly become noticeable, especially in tissues that are frequently replaced such as red blood cells and intestinal wall lining.

Young children are at greater risk for folacin and B_{12} deficiencies due to their rapid growth. Meals, especially vegetarian meals, must be carefully planned to include adequate vitamin B_{12} because it is found only in animal-source and some fortified foods. Vitamin B_{12} supplementation may be recommended when no animal products are included in children's diet. Several

---

fat-soluble vitamins – *vitamins that are dissolved, transported, and stored in fat.*
water-soluble vitamins – *vitamins that are dissolved and transported in water/fluids; cannot be stored.*
DNA – *deoxyribonucleic acid; the substance in the cell nucleus that codes for genetically transmitted traits.*
RNA – *ribonucleic acid; the nucleic acid that serves as messenger between the nucleus and the ribosomes where proteins are synthesized.*

TABLE 14–3   Vitamin Summary

Vitamin	Functions	Sources	Deficiency Symptoms	Toxicity Symptoms
Fat-Soluble Vitamins				
Vitamin A	Maintenance of: • remodeling of bones • all cell membranes • epithelial cells; skin • mucous membranes, glands Regulation of vision in dim light	Liver, whole milk, butter, fortified margarine, orange and dark green vegetables, orange fruits (apricots, nectarines, peaches)	Depressed bone and tooth formation, lack of visual acuity, dry epithelial tissue, increased frequency of infections related to epithelial cell vulnerability	Headaches, nausea, vomiting, fragile bones, loss of hair, dry skin Infant: hydrocephalus, hyperirritability
Vitamin D	Regulates calcium/phosphorus absorption; mineralization of bone	Vitamin D fortified milk, exposure of skin to sunlight	Rickets (soft, easily bent bones), bone deformities	Elevated blood calcium; deposition of calcium in soft tissues resulting in cerebral, renal, and cardiovascular damage
Vitamin E	Antioxidant	Vegetable oils, wheat germ, egg yolk, leafy vegetables, legumes, margarine	Red blood cell destruction; creatinuria	Fatigue, skin rash, abdominal discomfort
Vitamin K	Normal blood coagulation	Leafy vegetables, vegetable oils, liver, pork; synthesis by intestinal bacteria	Hemorrhage	None reported for naturally occurring vitamin K
Water-Soluble Vitamins Vitamin C (ascorbic acid)	Formation of collagen for: • bones/teeth • intercellular cement • wound healing Aid to calcium/iron absorption Conversion of folacin to active form Neurotransmitter synthesis	Citrus fruits, strawberries, melons, cabbage, peppers, greens, tomatoes	Poor wound healing, bleeding gums, pin-point hemorrhages, sore joints, scurvy	Nausea, abdominal cramps, diarrhea, precipitation of kidney stones in susceptible person; "conditioned scurvy"
Thiamin	Carbohydrate metabolism Energy metabolism Neurotransmitter synthesis	Whole or enriched grain products, organ meats, pork	Loss of appetite, depression, poor neuromuscular control, beriberi	None reported
Riboflavin	Metabolism of carbohydrates, fats, and proteins; energy metabolism	Dairy foods, meat products, enriched or whole grains, green vegetables	Sore tongue, cracks at the corners of the mouth (cheilosis)	None reported
Niacin	Carbohydrate, protein, and fat metabolism; energy metabolism; conversion of folacin to its active form	Meat products, whole or enriched grain products, legumes	Dermatitis, diarrhea, depression, and paranoia	Flushing, itching, nausea, vomiting, diarrhea, low blood pressure, rapid heartbeat, low blood sugar, liver damage
Pantothenic acid	Energy metabolism; fatty acid metabolism; neurotransmitter synthesis	Nearly all foods	Uncommon in humans	None reported

(continued)

Nutrient	Functions	Food Sources	Deficiency	Toxicity
Vitamin B_6 (pyridoxine)	Protein and fatty acid synthesis; neurotransmitter synthesis; hemoglobin synthesis	Meats, organ meats, whole grains, legumes, bananas	Can cause nervous system irritability, tremors, insomnia, convulsions (in infants)	Unstable gait, numbness, lack of coordination
Folacin	Synthesis of DNA and RNA: cell replication-protein synthesis	Liver, other meats, green vegetables	Macrocytic anemia characterized by unusually large red blood cells; sore tongue, diarrhea	None reported (large intake may hide B_{12} deficiency)
Vitamin B_{12} (cobalamin)	Synthesis of DNA and RNA: conversion of folacin to active form; synthesis of myelin (fatty covering of nerve cells); metabolism of carbohydrates for energy	Animal foods, liver, other meats, dairy products, eggs	Macrocytic anemia, nervous system damage, sore mouth and tongue, loss of appetite, nausea, vomiting (pernicious anemia results from faulty absorption of B_{12})	None reported
Biotin	Carbohydrate and fat metabolism; amino acid metabolism	Organ meats, milk, egg yolk, yeast; synthesis by intestinal bacteria	Nervous disorders, skin disorders, anorexia, muscle pain	None reported

macrocytic anemia – *a failure in the oxygen transport system characterized by abnormally large immature red blood cells.*

TABLE 14–4   Characteristics of Vitamins

	Fat-Soluble Vitamins	Water-Soluble Vitamins
Examples	A, D, E, K	Vitamin C (ascorbic acid), thiamin, niacin, riboflavin, pantothenic acid, B_6 (pyridoxine), biotin, folacin, B_{12} (cobalamin)
Stored in body	Yes	No (B_{12} is an exception)
Excreted in urine	No	Yes
Needed daily	No	Yes
Deficiency	Develops slowly (months, years)	Develops rapidly (days, weeks)

additional measures can be taken to ensure that children obtain the vitamins needed to support optimal growth, including:

- minimizing children's intake of less nutritious foods such as sweets and high-fat items.
- choosing whole or unrefined grain products in place of highly processed or refined foods.
- serving a variety of nuts, seeds, legumes, fruits, and vegetables, including foods rich in vitamin C to improve iron absorption.
- choosing a variety of low-fat dairy products.
- including foods fortified with B_{12}, such as soy beverages and cereals.

14-3b Vitamins and Blood Formation

Several vitamins (folacin, pantothenic acid, vitamins B_6, B_{12}, and E) play essential roles in the formation of blood cells and hemoglobin. Hemoglobin, the red pigment in red blood cells, carries oxygen to all living cells throughout the body and transports the waste product, carbon dioxide, back to the lungs. These vitamins are plentiful in many foods, including fruits, vegetables, meats, and enriched grain products.

14-3c Vitamins that Regulate Bone Growth

Although bones and teeth consist primarily of calcium and phosphorus, they depend on several vitamins, including vitamins A, C, and D, to regulate the growth and maintenance processes. For example, vitamin A helps to control the destruction and replacement of old bone cells through a process known as "remodeling." Vitamin C makes calcium soluble so it is easier to absorb and also promotes **collagen** formation (the flexible protein foundation upon which phosphorus and calcium crystals are deposited). Vitamin D ensures that calcium and phosphorus are available for absorption into bones and teeth. Fruits and vegetables are rich sources of vitamins A and C; milk and brief exposures to sunshine supply abundant vitamin D.

14-3d Vitamins that Regulate Energy Metabolism

Several B vitamins (thiamin, niacin, riboflavin, pantothenic acid) work together to efficiently metabolize and release energy from carbohydrates and fats. They ensure that energy is supplied in a slow, steady manner to sustain body needs and to prevent heat loss. This function is especially important in young children because they require greater amounts of energy per pound and lose it more quickly than do adults. Animal-source foods and enriched grain products are primary sources of the B vitamins.

collagen – *a protein that forms the major constituent of connective tissue, cartilage, bone, and skin.*

14-3e Vitamins that Regulate Neuromuscular Function

Vitamins play a supporting role in healthy **neuromuscular** functioning. For example, vitamin C and several B vitamins work closely together to produce neurotransmitters (chemical messengers) that regulate nerve-muscle activities and carry electrical messages to all organs. Vitamins B_6 and B_{12} are essential for the healthy formation of nerve cells and the myelin sheath that surrounds and protects nerve fibers. Mylenization is especially critical in young children and can result in numbness, tremors, or loss of coordination if it fails to develop properly.

Researchers have linked several birth defects, including cleft lip, cleft palate, and **spina bifida** to a folacin deficiency during the early months of a mother's pregnancy (Crider, Bailey, & Berry, 2011). Folacin is readily available in fruits (oranges, strawberries), vegetables (spinach, asparagus), dried beans and legumes, and fortified whole grain products. Prenatal vitamins also contain folacin; however, neural tube defects often occur before a mother even realizes she is pregnant. Consequently, many foods and grain products today are fortified with folacin as a preventive measure.

TeachSource Video Connections

School Age Children: Teaching about Nutrition

Grocery stores and markets are filled with an attractive array of fruits and vegetables in various shapes, colors, textures, and flavors. As adults, we have an important responsibility to encourage children to consume more fruits and vegetables and to try new food items they may not have previously tasted. As you watch the learning video, *School Age: Teaching about Nutrition*, consider the following questions:

1. Why do you think the teacher chose to use the rainbow colors as a framework for teaching children about the importance of eating a variety of fruits and vegetables each day?

2. Identify one fruit and one vegetable that represent each of the five rainbow colors described in the video.

3. Why might games be an effective way to teach school age children about fruit and vegetable consumption?

4. What other instructional strategies did the teacher use to reinforce the children's learning about fruits and vegetables?

Watch on CourseMate.

14-3f Vitamin Requirements

Vitamins are required in extremely small but specific amounts and are essential for normal body functions. Infants and young children require vitamins in proportionally larger amounts than do adults due to their rapid growth. Unless a vitamin deficiency has been identified, taking large doses in supplement form can have limited usefulness and may actually be harmful in some instances. For example, toxic effects have long been noted with large supplement doses of vitamins A and D (Duerbeck & Dowling, 2012; Rutkowski & Grzegorczyk, 2012). Researchers have also identified neurological damage from too much vitamin B_6, and kidney stone formation from vitamin C (ascorbic acid) **megadoses**. At present, toxic levels for most vitamins have not been established in children; however, the amount required to produce **toxicity** is certainly smaller for children than adults. Extreme caution should be used if children are given vitamin supplements without a physician's advice, especially

---

neuromuscular – *pertaining to control of muscular function by the nervous system.*
spina bifida – *a neural tube defect that occurs during early fetal development; a malformation (gap or opening) in the spinal column that affects the nerves and spinal cord.*
megadose – *an amount of a vitamin or mineral at least ten times that of the RDA.*

▼ **Calcium and phosphorus are essential for healthy teeth and bones.**

© Cengage Learning

those containing iron, because an excess can cause serious illness or death. "If a little bit is good, a lot is better" is a dangerous practice to follow with regard to vitamins.

Vitamins are a frequent subject of media attention and often promoted as "cures" for numerous conditions including cancer, common colds, fatigue, depression, and mental illness (Snyder & Brown, 2012). Many people take vitamins and give them to their children as an "insurance policy" (Bailey et al., 2012). Although vitamins can supplement "hit-or-miss" eating, they should not be considered a substitute for a nutritious diet. Vitamin and mineral supplements, by themselves, do not supply all of the essential nutrients that humans require. They also lack calories and protein, which are essential for growing children. Concerns have also been raised about other unknown substances that may be present in vitamin and mineral preparations. Consuming a well-balanced diet is always the preferred method for obtaining all essential nutrients.

Did You Get It?

Is there a problem with a parent of a child in your class asking you to give her child three capsules of a potassium (K) supplement (one in the morning, one at lunch, and one in the afternoon) when the directions on the bottle recommend taking one capsule per day?

  a. No, potassium is only a mineral.

  b. No, the dose is excessive but the unused nutrient will be excreted from the child's system.

  c. No, you should administer the supplement according to the mother's request even though it might be incorrect.

  d. Yes, the dose should be questioned because an excess of this mineral could lead to toxicity.

Take the full quiz on CourseMate.

14-4 Minerals

Minerals are inorganic elements that do not undergo any change in composition once they enter the human body. They are involved in the processes that help regulate body functions and build body tissue, but they yield no energy (Table 14–5). Some are required and present in the body in large quantities, whereas others are needed in exceedingly small or even trace amounts. For example, the RDA for calcium is 1,000 mg for children 4 to 8 years, which is equivalent to approximately 3 cups of milk. In contrast, the RDA for iron is 10 mg and 5 mg for zinc for children of the same age.

14-4a Minerals that Support Growth

Phosphorus, magnesium, and zinc are essential for cell reproduction and growth. Children who consume a well-rounded diet are likely to obtain sufficient amounts of these minerals because they are present in most foods. Some health conditions and medications may affect absorption and contribute to deficiencies, but this is a relatively uncommon occurrence. For example, large-dose supplementation with calcium and/or iron can seriously reduce the availability of zinc. Stunted growth, delayed sexual maturity, and a decreased sense of taste and smell can result from a zinc deficiency.

minerals – *inorganic chemical elements that are required in the diet to support growth, repair tissue, and regulate body functions.*

TABLE 14–5 Mineral Summary

Mineral	Functions	Sources	Deficiency Symptoms	Toxicity Symptoms
Calcium	Major component of bones and teeth; collagen formation; muscle contraction; secretion/release of insulin; neurotransmitters; blood	Dairy products, turnip or collard greens, canned salmon or sardines, soybeans or soybean curd (tofu)	Poor growth, small adult size, fragile and deformed bones, some form of rickets	Unlikely: absorption is controlled; symptoms usually result from excess vitamin D or hormonal imbalance
Phosphorus	Major component of bones and teeth; energy metabolism; component of DNA and RNA	Dairy products, meats, legumes, grains; additive in soft drinks	Rare with normal diet	Large amounts may depress calcium absorption
Magnesium	Major component of bones and teeth; activator of enzymes for ATP use; required for synthesis of DNA and RNA and for synthesis of proteins by RNA	Nuts, seeds, green vegetables, legumes, whole grains	Poor neuromuscular coordination, tremors, convulsions	Unlikely
Sodium	Nerve impulse transmission; fluid balance; acid-base balance	Meats, fish, poultry, eggs, milk (naturally occurring sodium): high levels (sodium, salt, MSG) are present in many processed and cured foods	Rare (losses from sweat may cause dizziness, nausea, muscle cramps)	Linked to high blood pressure in some persons; confusion; coma
Potassium	Nerve impulse transmission; fluid balance; acid-base balance	Fruits (bananas, orange juice), vegetables, whole grains, fresh meats, fish	Weakness, irregular heartbeat	Unlikely from food sources
Iron	Component of hemoglobin; enzymes involved in oxygen utilization	Liver, oysters, meats, enriched and whole grains, leafy green vegetables	Microcytic anemia (characterized by small, pale red blood cells), fatigue, pallor, shortness of breath	Unlikely (may be due to genetic defect)
Zinc	Component of many enzymes involved in: protein metabolism; DNA/RNA synthesis; collagen formation; wound healing	Liver, oysters, meats, eggs, whole grains, legumes	Retarded growth, loss of senses of taste and smell, delayed wound healing	Excess supplementation may interfere with iron/copper metabolism and cause nausea, vomiting, diarrhea, gastric ulcers
Iodine	Component of thyroxin, which regulates basal metabolic rate; regulates physical and mental growth	Iodized salt, seafood, many processed foods	Goiter, hypothyroidism, infertility, stillbirth; inhibits fetal growth and brain development (cretinism)	Hyperthyroidism, abdominal pain, diarrhea, metallic taste (in mouth), seizures, thirst

microcytic anemia – *a failure in the oxygen transport system characterized by abnormally small red blood cells.*

14-4b Minerals that Build Bones and Teeth

Calcium and phosphorus are the major mineral components of bones and teeth. Bone is formed as phosphorus and calcium crystals are deposited on a flexible collagen base. Young children's bones are relatively soft, small, and pliable because they are not yet fully calcified. As children age, their bones gradually become larger, denser, and stronger as they are infused with minerals. Although mature bone appears to be solid and unchanging, calcium and phosphorus crystals are continually moving in and out and being replaced. Consequently, children require more calcium for bone growth and replacement of existing bone cells; adults require calcium only for replacement.

Fluoride also plays an important role in bone and tooth formation and dental health (Palmer & Gilbert, 2012). It is incorporated into growing tooth structures and increases resistance to decay by strengthening the enamel. Many communities add fluoride to their municipal water supply. Dental application of fluoride varnish appears to be less effective in hardening tooth enamel, but it is thought to significantly reduce dental caries (decay) (Douglass, 2011). Children who drink fluoridated water should be taught not to swallow toothpaste because excess fluoride consumption can cause mottling and brown discoloration of the teeth.

> **Did You Know...**
>
> that the calcium in your bones replaces itself every five years? This is why calcium-rich foods need to be included in a person's diet throughout a lifetime.

Milk and dairy products, such as cheese and yogurt, are the major food sources of dietary calcium and phosphorus. Custards, pudding, and ice cream also supply both minerals, but the added sugars and fat reduce their nutrient contribution. Small amounts of calcium are present in some vegetables (e.g., broccoli, collard greens, kale, Chinese cabbage), oranges, and almonds but few other rich sources exist. All flours and many food products, such as breads, pastas, cereals, crackers, and soy milks are currently fortified with additional calcium. Some orange juice brands are also adding calcium to their product. This is an ideal combination because vitamin C in the orange juice improves calcium absorption.

14-4c Minerals and Blood Formation

Blood is the liquid of life and affects the health of every living cell and organ in the body. **Hemoglobin**, the iron-containing protein in red blood cells, transports oxygen to the cells and removes waste (carbon dioxide) from the cells. Inadequate intake or poor absorption of dietary iron can lead to **iron-deficiency anemia**. This condition is characterized by low levels of hemoglobin in red blood cells, which reduces the cells' ability to carry oxygen to tissues. Iron-deficiency anemia is more common in children 1 to 3 years of age and can cause slow growth, fatigue, lack of energy, learning deficits, and lowered resistance to infections (Algarin et al., 2013; Black et al., 2011).

Heme iron (the type of iron in meats) is especially high in red meats such as beef and liver, and is more readily absorbed than the iron in grains and other plant-source foods. Although liver is especially rich in iron, it is also exceptionally high in cholesterol (and not a food that is well-accepted by most adults or children). Many red meats are refused by children because they can be difficult to chew and swallow. Milk, which is often a major component of children's diets, contains very little iron. Consequently, a child who drinks large amounts of milk to the exclusion of iron-containing foods may develop iron-deficiency anemia.

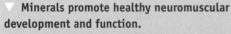

▼ **Minerals promote healthy neuromuscular development and function.**

© Cengage Learning

---

hemoglobin – *the iron-containing, oxygen-carrying pigment in red blood cells.*
iron-deficiency anemia – *a failure in the oxygen transport system caused by too little iron.*

CONNECTING TO EVERYDAY PRACTICE

The Necessity of Water

The aftermath of a Gulf coast hurricane left streets flooded and houses filled with stagnant water for days. Electrical outages and the potential for contamination forced several water treatment plants to temporarily shut down. This left residents scrambling for alternative sources of drinking water despite being surrounded by miles of floodwaters. Heat, humidity, and strenuous clean-up efforts increased the urgency for access to safe drinking water simply to stay alive. Although humans are able to go without food for long periods (weeks), they cannot survive more than a few days without water.

Think About This:

1. How much water does a child require per day? What about an adult?

2. What steps should your program or school take to prepare for a potential shortage of drinkable water?

3. What measures will you take in your own home?

4. What methods can be used to disinfect contaminated water and make it safe to drink?

14-4d Minerals that Regulate Energy

Several minerals are indirectly involved in the production, storage, and steady release of energy. Phosphorus, magnesium, iodine, and iron are important components of the enzymes, coenzymes, and hormones that control energy metabolism. They are also responsible for regulating the rate at which the body uses energy for involuntary activities (basal metabolic rate).

14-4e Minerals that Regulate Neuromuscular Function

Sodium, potassium, calcium, and magnesium are all necessary for the successful transmission of nerve impulses from nerve cell to nerve cell or from nerve cell to muscle. They make it possible for an individual to perform voluntary activities such as walking, running, writing, and talking. They are also involved in the processes that maintain a host of involuntary functions, including heartbeat, breathing, and circulation.

Did You Get It?

Three glasses of milk would meet the Recommended Daily Allowance of _____ milligrams of calcium for 4- to 8-year-olds.
   a. 2,500
   b. 1,500
   c. 1,000
   d. 500

Take the full quiz on CourseMate.

14-5 Water and Growth

Water is an important constituent of all body tissue and is essential for survival. It acts as a solvent in which nutrients (e.g., vitamins, minerals, glucose, proteins) are dissolved and distributed throughout the body. It rids the body of soluble wastes and transports them out in urine (which is 95 percent water). Water is a major component of body fluids and secretions such as salivary juice, gastric juice, bile, and perspiration and aids cells in maintaining their distinctive shapes. Joints and eyes also benefit from water's shock-absorbing and lubricating properties.

▼ **Water is essential for the regulation of many body functions.**

© Cengage Learning

Water accounts for approximately 70 to 75 percent of an infant's and 60 percent of an adults' total body weight. This percentage continues to decrease as a person ages. Each day the body replaces approximately 15 percent of its water. Several factors determine how much replacement water an individual requires, including total body surface area, environmental conditions (temperature and humidity), and physical activity. Vomiting and diarrhea also cause significant water loss and can quickly lead to serious dehydration in infants, toddlers, and young children.

Water is supplied to the body through drinking water and other beverages, the digestion of solid foods, and as a by-product of energy metabolism. Thirsty children should be offered water instead of fruit juices. Sugars in fruit juices and sweetened beverages slow water absorption and are less likely to quench a child's thirst. They can also dull a child's appetite and contribute to several health problems:

> Diarrhea. Some fruit juices, notably apple juice, contain sorbitol, a naturally occurring sugar that can be difficult for children to digest. This can cause loose stools or diarrhea if children drink several glasses during the day (Zella & Israel, 2012).

> Tooth decay. Toddlers who are given a bottle containing fruit juice are at risk for developing baby bottle tooth decay (BBTD). Prolonged exposure to the sugars in fruit juices can gradually cause extensive tooth decay (Knowlden et al., 2012).

> Excess weight gain. Fruit juices contain natural sugars that can contribute to weight gain when they are consumed in excess (Wojcicki & Heyman, 2012).

14-5a Water as a Regulator

Water plays a critical role in regulating internal body temperature during changes in environmental conditions and activity-related heat production. Keeping children hydrated is especially important during periods of vigorous physical activity and when weather conditions are hot or humid (AAP, 2011). Water is lost quickly through perspiration and must be replaced to prevent dehydration. Children should always have ready access to drinking water and be reminded frequently to stop playing and drink.

Did You Get It?

Which statement about water, an essential nutrient for all age groups, is incorrect?

a. Water serves as a medium in which nutrients are dissolved and transported throughout the body.

b. Water functions in the human joints the way shock absorbers do in a car.

c. Water binds with excess protein molecules to form a reliable energy source.

d. Water regulates human body temperature.

Take the full quiz on CourseMate.

14-6 Nutrient Functions: A Recap

Approximately 40 nutrients are recognized as essential for providing energy, allowing normal growth for the child and maintenance for the adult. Each nutrient has its special function(s). Some nutrients share functions and in many cases the function of any given nutrient depends on the presence of one or more other nutrients. Table 14–6 provides a summary of these functional relationships and highlights what nutrients really do in the body.

TABLE 14–6   Summary of Nutrients and Their Biological Functions

Functional Unit	Nutrients Involved	Specific Function
Blood formation and maintenance	Calcium Vitamin K Protein Iron Copper	Blood clotting
	Vitamin B_6 Folacin Vitamin B_{12}	Red blood cell and hemoglobin production
Bone and teeth development	Calcium Phosphorus Magnesium	Components of bones and teeth
	Vitamin C Vitamin A Vitamin D	Promote building and remodeling of bones
Nerve-muscle development and activity	Vitamin C Thiamin Niacin Vitamin B_6 Pantothenic acid Calcium Potassium	Required for transmission of nerve impulses
	Calcium Magnesium Potassium Sodium Thiamin Pantothenic acid	Regulates muscle contraction and relaxation
Growth and maintenance of cells and body organs	Protein Phosphorus Zinc Selenium Vitamin B_6 Folacin	Regulates cell division and synthesis of needed cell proteins
	Iodine	Regulates physical and mental growth
Availability of energy for cellular activity	Carbohydrates Fats Proteins	May be "burned" to release energy
	Phosphorus Magnesium Thiamin Riboflavin Niacin Pantothenic acid Biotin	Roles in enzyme and coenzyme production to release energy
	Iodine	Regulates basal metabolic energy needs

Did You Get It?

A _____ deficiency can interfere with blood clotting.
a. vitamin C
b. vitamin K
c. magnesium
d. phosphorous

Take the full quiz on CourseMate.

PARTNERING with FAMILIES

Sugary Drinks vs. Water: A Weighty Problem

Water is essential for growth and the regulation of many body functions. Although it is abundantly available, getting children to drink water can sometimes be a challenge. Water has many glorified competitors including sodas, fruit drinks and juices, designer waters, and sport drinks that children often find more appealing. These beverages come in a rainbow of colors and flavors and are heavily marketed to susceptible audiences. However, they are costly and provide little nutritional value while adding significant calories and sugar. These are important considerations given the increasing rates of childhood obesity and tooth decay. Set a good example and encourage children to ask for water when they are thirsty!

▶ Limit or avoid purchasing sweetened beverages. If these items are not readily available in the home or at school, your child is more likely to drink water and other nutritious beverages such as milk and 100 percent fruit juices.

▶ Keep a pitcher of water in the refrigerator and small cups where children can reach. Smaller cups are less intimidating and more manageable for children. Lemon or lime slices can be added for flavor interest and variation. Freeze ice cubes in fun-shaped trays.

▶ When traveling from home or participating in physical activities, provide your child with a reusable water bottle (and water) to quench her thirst. Bringing your own water is more economical than purchasing beverages from a vending machine or convenience store; offers more health benefits than sodas, fruit drinks, and fruit beverages; and, is eco-friendly.

CLASSROOM CORNER

Teacher Activities

Calcium Helps to Make Strong Bones and Teeth . . .

(Grades 3–5; NHES National Health Standards 6.5.1; 7.5.1)

Concept: Some foods supply calcium, which is important for strong bones and teeth.

Learning Objectives

▶ Children will learn how calcium helps to make strong bones and teeth.

▶ Children will learn about foods that are good sources of calcium.

▶ Children will monitor their calcium intake and take steps to achieve the Dietary Referenced Intake (DRI) for calcium.

Supplies

▶ Two chicken drumstick bones (cooked; with meat removed)

▶ Two glass jars with lids

(continued)

CLASSROOM CORNER

Teacher Activities   (continued)

▶ Vinegar

▶ Internet connection and PowerPoint software

▶ A five-day chart/worksheet for each child

Learning Activities

▶ Have children place one chicken bone in each glass jar. Fill one jar with vinegar, the other with water and screw on the lids. Each day, have children observe the bones and note any changes (calcium crystals will gradually form on the bone immersed in vinegar). At the end of three weeks, remove both bones from their respective containers and let them air dry for at least 10 to 12 days. Have children break the bones and describe how they differ (in terms of strength and appearance). Discuss how calcium aids in building strong bones.

▶ Have children work in teams to conduct an Internet search for foods that are good calcium sources. Each team should prepare a PowerPoint presentation highlighting their findings to share with the class.

▶ Provide each child with a five-day chart. Have them record the primary calcium sources they consume each day, total the number of daily servings, and compare this figure with MyPlate recommendations. Ask older children to calculate the amount of daily calcium they have consumed (provide a worksheet with approximate values for serving equivalents: for example, 1 cup milk = 300 mg, 1 piece string cheese = 214 mg; ½ cup macaroni and cheese = 180 mg, and so on). Ask children to identify foods they can include each day to continue meeting or to increase their calcium intake; have them chart their progress toward achieving the recommended goals.

Evaluation

▶ Children will explain how calcium helps to make bones strong.

▶ Children will identify foods that provide calcium.

▶ Children will implement steps to achieve the Dietary Referenced Intake (DRI) for calcium.

 Additional lesson plans for PreK-2 are available on CourseMate.

◖ Summary

▶ Children's intake of vitamins A and C, iron, and calcium are often inadequate and thus referred to as at-risk nutrients.

▶ Proteins provide amino acids, which are the basic building materials for new cell and tissue formation. They are also an important component of the enzymes that help to regulate energy metabolism.

• Meat, fish, poultry, and dairy products supply complete proteins; grains, legumes, nuts, and dry beans contain incomplete proteins.

• Protein requirements are determined by a person's weight and life stage.

▶ Vitamins are involved in cell division (growth); blood and bone formation; energy metabolism; and, as an ingredient in the chemicals that regulate brain and nerve activities.

- Vitamins are required in small amounts; taking supplements in large doses can be harmful and offers few benefits unless there is a significant nutrient deficiency.

▶ Minerals are necessary for building tissue, teeth, and bones; regulating energy metabolism; and, are a part of chemical solutions that enable voluntary and involuntary neuromuscular activity.

- Calcium and phosphorus are major components of bones and teeth; they cause structures to harden as crystals are deposited on a protein collagen base.
- Calcium is found primarily in dairy products; phosphorus is available in milk and in meats, grains, beans, nuts, and cereal products.
- Iron is a critical component of hemoglobin that carries oxygen to all body cells. Best food sources are red meats and iron-fortified breads and cereals.

▶ Water is a major constituent of all living body cells; it makes up approximately 60 to 75 percent of total body weight.

- Water is critical for cell survival, especially during periods of active growth and physical activity.
- Water serves as a medium by which most nutrient functions take place. It also transports nutrients throughout the body and is a prime regulator of body temperature.

◗ Terms to Know

milligram (mg) *p. 357*	supplementary proteins *p. 360*	neuromuscular *p. 367*
microgram (mcg or µg) *p. 357*	fat-soluble vitamins *p. 363*	spina bifida *p. 367*
amino acids *p. 359*	water-soluble vitamins *p. 363*	megadose *p. 367*
non-essential amino acids *p. 360*	DNA *p. 363*	minerals *p. 368*
essential amino acids *p. 360*	RNA *p. 363*	microcytic anemia *p. 369*
complete protein *p. 360*	macrocytic anemia *p. 365*	hemoglobin *p. 370*
incomplete proteins *p. 360*	collagen *p. 366*	iron-deficiency anemia *p. 370*
complementary proteins *p. 360*		

◗ Chapter Review

A. By Yourself:

1. What role(s) does water play in the body?
2. Which vitamins are classified as fat soluble? Why are they more likely to cause toxicity?
3. What foods supply folacin (folate, folic acid)? What birth defect(s) is associated with a deficiency of this vitamin?
4. Identify six non-meat protein sources.
5. Match the terms in **Column II** with the definition in **Column I**. Use each term in **Column II** only once.

Column I	Column II
1. result when two incomplete proteins are paired	a. calcium
2. structure upon which calcium and phosphorus crystals are deposited	b. dairy
3. mineral component in hemoglobin	c. megadose
4. major mineral component of bones and teeth	d. fruits and vegetables
5. major source of calcium	e. complete protein
6. food group rich in vitamins A and C	f. iron
7. comprises approximately 70 percent of an infant's body weight	g. water
	h. collagen

B. **As a Group:**

1. Discuss why children are at risk for developing iron deficiency anemia.
2. How could you provide calcium to a child who is allergic to milk and dairy products?
3. Read and discuss the Academy of Nutrition & Dietetics' "Vegetarian Diets" position statement. What are the benefits and limitations of a vegetarian diet for young children?
4. React to the statement, "I take vitamins just to be sure I get everything I need."
5. Research and read about vitamin D deficiencies. Why has the concern increased in recent years?

Case Study

Mealtimes were frustrating for Akecheta's mother. Her four-year-old son often refused to drink his milk and begged for juice instead. He complained "that his stomach hurt" and would cry until his mother gave in to his requests. She was becoming extremely frustrated and finally decided to take him to the local health clinic for advice. After several visits and tests, the physician assistant determined that Akecheta was lactose intolerant and allergic to citrus fruits. Even small amounts of milk or cheese seemed to upset his stomach and orange juice caused him to break out in hives.

1. What nutrients will Akecheta lack if these food groups are eliminated from his diet?
2. Would you expect symptoms of a deficiency to appear immediately or long term? Explain.
3. Suggest several foods that have the same nutrient-strength and could be served in place of citrus fruits and dairy products?
4. Should Akecheta be given nutrient supplements to offset potential deficiencies? Why or why not?

Application Activities

1. Compare the nutrition information labels from several commercially prepared cereals. Which cereal(s) would give you the most nutrient value for your money? What food(s) could be served along with the cereal to improve iron absorption?
2. Explain why early childhood is a high-risk period for iron-deficiency anemia. Consider factors such as food groups in which iron occurs, typical food preferences, and relative ease of eating foods. Develop a list of snacks that would provide children with additional iron.
3. Determine the recommended amount of protein for a child who weighs 42 pounds.
4. Using the vitamin and mineral summaries in Tables 14–3 and 14–5:
   a. List two specific foods that are rich sources of each of the following nutrients:
      - magnesium   – thiamin
      - calcium   – riboflavin
   b. What foods are good sources of more than one of these nutrients?
   c. Which nutrients occur in the same types of foods?
   d. Which nutrients do not occur in the same types of foods?
   e. Which nutrients are found mostly in animal-source foods?
   f. Which nutrients are found mostly in plant-based foods?

Helpful Web Resources

American Academy of Pediatrics	http://www.aap.org
Academy of Nutrition and Dietetics	http://www.eatright.org
Dietitians of Canada	http://www.dietitians.ca
Fuel Up to Play 60 (National Dairy Council)	http://school.fueluptoplay60.com/home.php
Vegetarian Resource Group	http://www.vrg.org

Visit the Education CourseMate for this textbook to access the eBook, Did You Get It? quizzes, Digital Downloads, TeachSource Video Cases, flashcards, and more. Go to CengageBrain.com to log in, register, or purchase access.

References

Academy of Nutrition and Dietetics. (2009). Position of the American Dietetic Association: Vegetarian diets. Accessed on September 5, 2012 from, http://www.eatright.org/About/Content.aspx?id=8357.

Algarin, C., Nelson, C., Peirano, P., Westerlund, A., Reyes, S., & Luzoff, B. (2013). Iron-deficiency anemia in infancy and poorer cognitive inhibitory control at age 10 years, *Developmental Medicine & Child Neurology*, 55(5), 453–458.

American Academy of Pediatrics (AAP). (2011). Climatic heat stress and exercising children and adolescents, *Pediatrics*, 128(3), e741–e747.

Bailey, R., Fulgoni, V., Keast, D., Lentino, C., & Dwyer, J. (2012). Do dietary supplements improve micronutrient sufficiency in children and adolescents, *Journal of Pediatrics,*161(5), 837–842.

Black, M., Quigg, A., Hurley, K., & Pepper, M. (2011). Iron deficiency and iron-deficiency anemia in the first two years of life: Strategies to prevent loss of developmental potential, *Nutrition Reviews*, 69(Suppl. 1), S64–S70.

Crider, K., Bailey, L., & Berry, R. (2011). Folic acid food fortification—Its history, effect, concerns, and future directions, *Nutrients*, 3(3), 370–384.

Douglass, J. (2011). Fluoride varnish when added to caregiver counseling reduces early childhood caries incidence, *Journal of Evidence Based Dental Practice*, 11(1), 46–48.

Duerbeck, N., & Dowling, D. (2012). Vitamin A: Too much of a good thing? *Obstetrical & Gynecological Survey*, 67(2), 122–128.

Goldman, R., Radnitz, C., & McGrath, R. (2012). The role of family variables in fruit and vegetable consumption in preschool children, *Journal of Public Health Research*, 1(2). DOI: 10.4081/jphr.2012.e22. Available online at http://jphres.org/index.php/jphres/article/view/jphr.2012.e22.

Kirkpatrick, S., Dodd, K., Reedy, J., & Krebs-Smith, S. (2012). Income and race/ethnicity are associated with adherence to food-based dietary guidance among US adults and children, *Journal of the Academy of Nutrition & Dietetics*, 112(5), 624–635.

Knowlden, A., Hill, L., Alles-White, M., & Cottrell, R. (2012). Addressing tooth decay in Head Start children, *NHSA Dialog*, 15(2), 201–205.

Mangels, R., & Driggers, J. (2012). The youngest vegetarians, *ICAN: Infant, Child, & Adolescent Nutrition*, 4(1), 8–20.

Marotz, L. (2011). Children's dietary needs: Nutrients, interactions, and their role in health. In, D. Kilcast & F. Angus (Eds.), *Developing children's food products*. Cambridge, UK: Woodhead Publishing Ltd.

Maxwell, M., Lemacks, J., Coccia, C., Ralston, P., & Ilich, J. (2012). A student-led pilot project to improve calcium intake and a healthy lifestyle in African American communities, *Topics in Clinical Nutrition*, 27(1), 54–66.

Pabayo, R., Spence, J., Casey, L., & Storey, K. (2012). Food consumption patterns in preschool, *Canadian Journal of Dietetic Practice & Research*, 73(2), 66–71.

Palmer, C., & Gilbert, J. (2012). Position of the Academy of Nutrition and Dietetics: The impact of fluoride on health, *Journal of the Academy of Nutrition & Dietetics*, 112(9), 1443–1453.

Rutkowski, M., & Grzegorczyk, K. (2012). Adverse effects of antioxidative vitamins, *International Journal of Occupational Medicine & Environmental Health*, 25(2), 105–121.

Snyder, J., & Brown, P. (2012). Complementary and alternative medicine in children: An analysis of the recent literature, *Current Opinion in Pediatrics*, 24(4), 539–546.

Watford, M., & Wu, G. (2011). Protein, *Advances in Nutrition*, 2(1), 62–63.

Wojcicki, J., & Heyman, M. (2012). Reducing childhood obesity by eliminating 100% fruit juice, *American Journal of Public Health*, 102(9), 1630–1633.

Zella, G., & Israel, E. (2012). Chronic diarrhea in children, *Pediatrics in Review*, 33(5), 207–218.

Zhou, S., Gibson, R., Gibson, R., & Makrides, M. (2012). Nutrient intakes and status of preschool children in Adelaide, South Australia, *Medical Journal of Australia*, 196(11), 696–700.

Nutrition and the Young Child

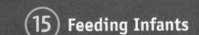

Feeding Infants

▶ **#1 a, b, and c:** Promoting child development and learning

▶ **#2 a, b, and c:** Building family and community relationships

▶ **#3 a, b and d:** Observing, documenting, and assessing to support young children and families

▶ **#4 a, b, and d:** Using developmentally effective approaches to connect with children and families

▶ **#5 a and c:** Using content knowledge to build a meaningful curriculum

▶ **#6 c:** Becoming a professional

Learning Objectives

After studying this chapter, you should be able to:

LO 15-1 Explain how the feeding relationship helps to satisfy the infant's needs in other developmental areas.

LO 15-2 Discuss the advantages and disadvantages of breast and formula feeding.

LO 15-3 Demonstrate how to feed an infant correctly (e.g., food preparation, positioning, burping).

LO 15-4 Describe how to determine when an infant is developmentally ready for semi-solid foods.

LO 15-5 Identify and discuss several health concerns associated with infant feeding.

15-1 Profile of an Infant

An infant's growth and development occurs at a rate that is significantly more rapid than at any other period in the life cycle (Marotz & Allen, 2013). Infants will double their birth weight during the first 5 to 6 months and nearly triple it by the end of the first year. Birth length typically increases by 50 percent as the child approaches his first birthday.

Food and the feeding relationship play important roles in meeting the infant's early biological, learning, and developmental needs. Feedings accompanied by close physical contact, emotional connections, verbal and non-verbal interchanges, and tender loving care (TLC) begin to foster a sense of self-awareness and trust. Failure to meet infants' physical and emotional needs can lead to serious delays in growth and development even though they are receiving all of the essential nutrients (Bigelow & Power, 2012). Infants also gradually begin to learn about the different flavors, colors, temperatures, textures, and variety of foods from adults who understand how to help them transition from a diet that consists solely of breast milk or formula to one that includes semi-solid foods and later involves them in family meals (Teacher Checklist 15-1).

Did You Know...

that an infant gains between 1 1/2 and 2 pounds per month during the first 6 to 7 months? Can you imagine what would happen if we continued to grow at this rate?

Did You Get It?

A baby born at 6 pounds should weigh approximately _____ pounds by his or her first birthday?

a. 12

b. 18

c. 24

d. 15

Take the full quiz on CourseMate.

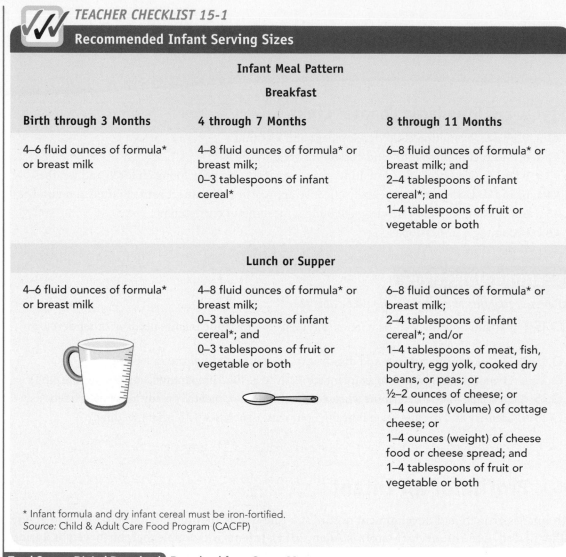

✓✓ *TEACHER CHECKLIST 15-1*

Recommended Infant Serving Sizes

Infant Meal Pattern

Breakfast

Birth through 3 Months	4 through 7 Months	8 through 11 Months
4–6 fluid ounces of formula* or breast milk	4–8 fluid ounces of formula* or breast milk; 0–3 tablespoons of infant cereal*	6–8 fluid ounces of formula* or breast milk; and 2–4 tablespoons of infant cereal*; and 1–4 tablespoons of fruit or vegetable or both

Lunch or Supper

Birth through 3 Months	4 through 7 Months	8 through 11 Months
4–6 fluid ounces of formula* or breast milk	4–8 fluid ounces of formula* or breast milk; 0–3 tablespoons of infant cereal*; and 0–3 tablespoons of fruit or vegetable or both	6–8 fluid ounces of formula* or breast milk; 2–4 tablespoons of infant cereal*; and/or 1–4 tablespoons of meat, fish, poultry, egg yolk, cooked dry beans, or peas; or ½–2 ounces of cheese; or 1–4 ounces (volume) of cottage cheese; or 1–4 ounces (weight) of cheese food or cheese spread; and 1–4 tablespoons of fruit or vegetable or both

* Infant formula and dry infant cereal must be iron-fortified.
Source: Child & Adult Care Food Program (CACFP)

TeachSource Digital Download) Download from CourseMate.

15-2 Meeting the Infant's Nutritional Needs for Growth and Brain Development

Infancy is characterized by a rapid rate of growth and development that must be supported by an adequate intake of protein, carbohydrates, and fat. Infants' nutrient and caloric needs remain high, relative to their body size, throughout the first year, but are greatest during the first 4 months when growth is most rapid. For example, a newborn requires approximately 50 calories per pound of body weight daily until 5 to 6 months of age. One-fourth to one-third of these calories is used for growth. As the infant progresses through the first year and becomes more mobile, fewer calories are needed for growth and more are required for physical activity. By 6 months of age, the infant requires only 40–45 calories per pound.

Meeting the infant's critical energy and nutrient needs presents a significant feeding challenge. Small stomach capacity limits the quantity of food they are able to consume at a given meal. As a result, infants need to be offered frequent, small feedings of nutrient-dense foods—sometimes as many as six to eight feedings in a 24-hour period during the first few months.

15-2a Prenatal Influence on Infants' Nutritional Needs and Brain Development

A well-balanced maternal diet that includes all essential nutrients supports healthy fetal development, including brain and central nervous system formation. A mother's nutritional status during pregnancy has immediate and long-term effects on the infant's early nutrient needs and well-being (Voss et al., 2012). Mothers who gain excessive weight during pregnancy give birth to infants who are more likely to become overweight as they mature (Poston, 2012). Mothers who do not obtain critical dietary nutrients (especially protein) and calories during pregnancy are more likely to have a **low-birthweight (LBW)** infant. These infants experience a high rate of serious illness and premature death during their first year. Low-birth weight infants are also at significant risk for additional problems such as:

▶ poor regulation of body temperature
▶ respiratory distress, including SIDS
▶ increased susceptibility to infection
▶ difficulty in metabolizing carbohydrates, fats, and proteins
▶ delayed development of kidneys and digestive organs
▶ poorly calcified bones—reduced bone density
▶ poor iron stores resulting in neonatal anemia
▶ vitamin deficiencies (especially vitamin E, folacin, and vitamin B_6) during neonatal period (birth to 28 days)
▶ attention disorders, cognitive delays, and behavior problems

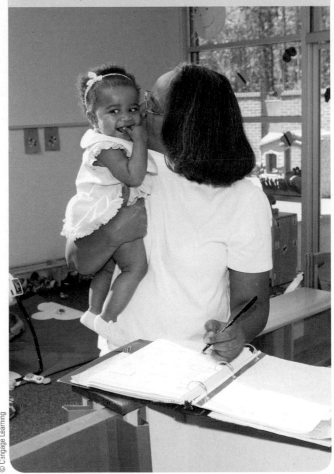

▼ A mother's nutrition during pregnancy influences her infant's early nutritional needs.

© Cengage Learning

Infants at highest risk for these problems are often born to teenage mothers, who must meet their own nutritional needs for growth in addition to providing nutrients for the developing fetus. Women who smoke, are pregnant with multiple babies, or who fail to consume adequate calories and nutrients during pregnancy are also more likely to give birth to LBW infants.

Common prenatal nutritional deficiencies that produce LBW infants include:

▶ protein
▶ energy
▶ folacin
▶ vitamin D
▶ vitamin B_6

Prenatal nutrient deficiencies may be partially corrected by supplementing the infant immediately after birth, but the effects of malnutrition are seldom completely reversed. The WIC (Special Supplemental Nutrition Program for Women, Infants, and Children) program, which provides supplemental food for income-eligible pregnant, breastfeeding and non-breastfeeding women and their infants and children up to the age of 5 who are at nutritional risk, has been effective in reducing the incidence of child malnutrition (Black et al., 2012). WIC currently provides nutrition, health care, and child care information in multiple languages for approximately 9 million clients in the United States, including 5 million children and 2 million infants (Figure 15–1) (USDA, 2012).

....

low-birthweight (LBW) – *weighing less than 5.5 pounds (2,500 grams) at birth.*

FIGURE 15–1   Breastfeeding information is available in multiple languages from WIC.

MiPirámide en Acción:
Consejos para Mamás en Período de Lactancia

¿Cómo Puedo Adelgazar Después de que Nazca Mi Bebé?

Amamantar es lo mejor para las mamás y para sus bebés por muchas razones. Una de las razones es que la lactancia facilita la pérdida del peso que gano durante el embarazo, al quemar las calorías extras. Además, la leche materna ayuda a combatir infecciones y reduce las alergias, de modo que los bebés alimentados con leche materna se enferman con menor frecuencia.

Siga su **Plan MiPirámide para Mamás** (ver reverso) para elegir la cantidad adecuada de cada grupo de alimentos. Además, visite a su médico. Mientras está amamantando, su médico puede monitorear su peso y decirle si está perdiendo peso como debería. Si está perdiendo peso muy lentamente, disminuya la cantidad de calorías que está consumiendo. La mejor manera de ingerir menos calorías es reduciendo la cantidad de "calorías extras."

¿Qué son las "calorías extras"?

Las calorías extras son los azúcares agregados o grasas sólidas en los alimentos. Los siguientes son algunos ejemplos de alimentos con "calorías extras":

- Refrescos o gaseosas
- Golosinas
- Postres
- Galletas
- Cereales azucarados
- Alimentos fritos
- Queso
- Leche entera
- Yogur endulzado
- Salchichas
- Carnes grasas

Busque opciones que sean de bajo contenido graso, sin grasa, sin azúcar ni edulcorantes o sin azúcares agregados.

United States Department of Agriculture

15-2b The First 6 Months

The months following an infant's birth are marked by rapid growth and critical neurological developments. Access to high-quality nutrition is especially important during this time to support the numerous changes that are occurring. Infants who are malnourished or who do not receive proper nutrition tend to be smaller in size, grow at a slow rate, and have fewer brain cells and poorer intellectual capacity (Galler et al., 2012). Providing a malnourished infant with proper nutrition will not completely reverse the negative effects it has had on brain development and other body systems.

During the first 6 months, the infant's nutritional needs can be met solely with formula or breast milk (and vitamin D supplementation). Breast milk and formula are both rich in fat and provide approximately 650 calories per quart to meet the infant's high energy needs (Kim & Friel, 2012). The full-term infant is born with a temporary store of iron and vitamin A that lasts for approximately the first 5 to 6 months. However, premature infants may require additional supplementation with these nutrients during this period because they have had less time to acquire adequate reserves. No semi-solid foods are needed or advised until the infant is at least 5 months of age. Younger infants are not developmentally or physiologically ready to ingest or digest solid foods. (This is discussed later in the chapter.)

The benefits of breastfeeding continue to gain increased attention and support. The American Academy of Pediatrics (AAP) and the American Academy of Family Physicians (AAFP) urge mothers to breastfeed infants exclusively for at least the first 6 months and, if possible, to continue until the infant turns 1 year of age (AAP, 2012). Scientific evidence has shown a positive relationship between breastfeeding and a reduced risk of some childhood health conditions, including SIDS, ear infection (otitis media), allergies and asthma, diabetes, and bacterial meningitis (Salone, Vann, & Dee, 2013; Gale et al., 2012). In addition, researchers have found that some children show small advantages in developmental and intellectual function (Andres et al., 2012; Isaacs et al., 2011). The nutrient advantages of breast milk are summarized in Table 15–1.

TABLE 15–1 Advantages of Breast Milk

Breast Milk:

- has all of the nutrients needed by the infant for the first 6 months (with the exception of adequate vitamin D)
- contains proteins that are more digestible than cow's milk protein
- contains lactose, the main carbohydrate component, which aids in calcium absorption and in establishing beneficial intestinal flora
- provides antibodies (immunoglobulin) that protect the infant from some infectious illnesses
- has a higher content of the essential fatty acids (omega 3 and 6)
- provides taurine* and dietary nucleotides**
- is associated with lower obesity rates
- is less likely to cause food allergies
- reduces the risk of bacteria entering the infant's body from unsanitary formula preparation
- is inexpensive, convenient, and always available at the correct temperature
- contains less sodium (salt) than formulas
- fosters emotional bonding between mother and infant
- is a biologically active substance that adjusts its nutrient composition to meet the infant's changing needs

*Taurine is a free amino acid (not found in proteins) that is particularly important for the normal growth and development of the central nervous system. It is now added to many formulas, especially those for premature infants.
**Dietary nucleotides play a role in infant cell growth and improved antibody production. The AAP recommends these nutrients be added to all commercial formulas.

Breastfeeding requires that mothers increase their intake of certain nutrients in order to maintain their own health and the quality of breast milk (Table 15–2).

Some mothers may elect formula feeding as the best approach after giving careful consideration to their health and lifestyle factors. Conditions that might cause a mother to choose formula feeding are:

- maternal illness or surgery
- medications the mother may need to take
- demands that require the mother to be away from the child for long periods of time
- personal preference
- use of addictive drugs, including alcohol and tobacco

Regardless of the feeding method that is chosen, teachers must be accepting and willing to assist families in meeting their infants' nutritional needs. Mothers should never be made to feel guilty or that they have made the wrong decision.

15-2c The Teacher and the Breastfeeding Mother

Many mothers continue to breastfeed their infants while employed outside of the home. They may use a breast pump or hand express milk and refrigerate or freeze it so the infant can be fed breast milk while her mother is at work. Breast milk can be refrigerated (40°F) in a sterile container and used

TABLE 15–2 Breastfeeding and a Mother's Dietary Needs

Mothers who are breastfeeding need to increase their daily intake of calories and nutrients, including:

- approximately 500 additional calories
- 15–20 additional grams of protein
- vitamins A, C, and folacin
- calcium (equivalent of one extra serving)
- an additional 4 cups of fluids
- vitamin B_{12} and D supplementation (if no animal products are consumed)

antibodies – *special substances produced by the body that help protect against disease.*

TEACHER CHECKLIST 15-2

Supporting the Nursing Mother

Early childhood programs can provide an environment that will support mothers who wish to nurse their infants at the facility by:

- creating a private area that is quiet and comfortable
- having a place where mothers can wash their hands before and after nursing
- providing a comfortable chair (a rocking chair if possible) and a foot rest to relieve back strain
- making water or other fluids available for mothers to drink
- having the infant ready (e.g., awake, diapers changed, infant's hands cleaned) when mother arrives

TeachSource Digital Download   Download from CourseMate.

within 48 hours; it can also be frozen (0°F), preferably in hard plastic containers (to avoid breakage or tears) and used within 3 months from the time it was expressed. Frozen breast milk must never be refrozen once it has thawed. Containers should be clearly labeled with the date and infant's name.

Some nursing mothers have flexible work schedules that allow them to take time off to feed their infants. Teachers should accommodate and assist mothers whenever they are able to make these arrangements during the day (Teacher Checklist 15-2).

Safe Handling of Breast Milk   Human milk varies in color, consistency, and odor, depending on the mother's diet and the container in which it is stored. Because breast milk is not homogenized, the cream may rise to the top of the container. Shaking it briefly before feeding helps blend the layers. For safe handling, the teacher should always follow these steps:

- Wash hands thoroughly before touching any milk containers. Avoid touching the inside of bottles or caps.
- Request that mothers label containers with the date when milk was collected; use the oldest milk first.
- If breast milk is to be stored for more than 48 hours, it should be frozen. (See Teacher Checklist 15-3 for safe thawing instructions.)
- Frozen breast milk may be safely stored in a freezer (0°F) for up to 3 months.

15-2d The Teacher and the Formula-Fed Infant

Although breastfeeding offers important health benefits, some infants in early childhood programs will be formula fed. The infant's family and health care provider will determine which formula is best for the infant. Commercial infant formulas are prepared to closely resemble breast milk in composition relative to the amount of protein, carbohydrate, and fat. Most infant formulas are made from

TEACHER CHECKLIST 15-3

Thawing Frozen Breast Milk Safely

1. Wash your hands with soap and water before touching the breast milk container.
2. Place the sealed container of breast milk in a bowl of warm water for about 30 minutes, or hold the container of 4 ounces of human milk under warm running water for approximately four minutes. **NEVER MICROWAVE BREAST MILK!** Microwaving can alter the nutritional composition of breast milk and also cause burns to the infant due to uneven heating.
3. Swirl the container to blend any fat that may have separated and risen during thawing.
4. Feed thawed milk immediately or store in the refrigerator for a maximum of 24 hours.

NEVER REFREEZE BREAST MILK.

TeachSource Digital Download   Download from CourseMate.

modified cow's milk or soy products and are available in powder, liquid concentrates, or as ready-to-feed solutions. Infants who have difficulty tolerating milk-based formulas may be switched to one that is soy-based. Although soy-based formulas are considered to be safe for infants, there has been some concern expressed about the plant-based estrogens they contain and their effect on infant growth. Soy can also cause allergic reactions in some infants (De Greef et al., 2012). Unmodified cow's milk should not be given to infants prior to 1 year of age because it often causes digestive disorders including intestinal bleeding. Goat's milk is also not recommended as it does not contain adequate nutrients.

15-2e **Preparation of Formula**

Two safety factors that are especially important to follow when preparing infant formula are:

1. *Sanitation*—Sanitary formula preparation using **aseptic procedures** prevents serious illness that can result when bacteria are introduced into the formula. Hands should be washed carefully and all utensils sanitized prior to mixing the formula. Sterilized (boiled) or bottled water should be used when preparing formula from a powdered concentrate. Honey should never be added to any formula for an infant younger than 1 year of age.

> **CAUTION**
>
> *Honey contains* Clostridium botulinum *spores, which, in an infant's intestine, can produce a dangerous, life-threatening toxin.*

Each formula type (ready-to-feed, concentrated liquid, powdered) requires different preparation techniques that must be followed precisely according to the manufacturers' directions on the label.

2. *Accuracy*—Accurate measuring and mixing of formula (according to directions) ensures that the infant will receive needed calories and nutrients in the amounts required for optimal growth and development. Adding too much water dilutes the formula and nutrients the infant receives and can lead to malnutrition. Adding too little water results in an "over-rich" formula that may cause digestive problems, excessive caloric intake, and obesity over time. Skim or low-fat milks should not be used in formula preparation because their low fat content is inadequate to satisfy daily caloric needs in the amount (volume) that infants are able to consume. It is recommended that 40 to 50 percent of the infant's calories come from fat. Adequate fat intake also plays a critical role in normal brain and central nervous system development and is needed to form the myelin sheath, or the insulation, around new nerve fibers. Essential fatty acids (linolenic and linoleic) in breast milk and formulas are also required for healthy cell growth and visual system development. The equivalent of 1 tablespoon of a polyunsaturated fat, such as corn oil or safflower oil, will meet the infant's need for these essential fatty acids. Table 15–3 provides a summary of common infant formulas.

TeachSource Video Connections

© 2015 Cengage Learning

Infants and Toddlers: Health and Nutrition

Successful feeding requires patience and an understanding of the infant's physical requirements and developmental abilities. With time, caregivers become sensitive to changes in the infant's behavior that signal different needs. As you watch the learning video, *Infants and Toddlers: Health and Nutrition*, consider the following questions:

1. Why did the teacher make a point of telling Ethan that she was putting him in the infant seat?
2. Why did the teacher wash the infant's hands as well as her own before the feeding?
3. Why is it important to feed an infant in an upright position?
4. Why did the caregiver gently stroke the infant's check before offering the bottle?

Watch on CourseMate.

aseptic procedure – *treatment to produce a product that is free of disease-producing bacteria.*

TABLE 15-3   Examples of Common Infant Formulas

Standard Formulas		
Enfamil®, Enfamil A+® Enfamil® Lower Iron; Similac® & Similac® with Iron; SMA & SMA Lo Iron; Gerber® Good Start®	20 cal./oz.	Modified cow's milk
Soy Formulas		
Similac® Soy Isomil®; Nursoy; Enfamil® ProSobee®; Gerber® Good Start® Soy Formula	20 cal./oz.	Hypoallergenic formula
Therapeutic Formulas		
Nutramigen®; Pregestimil®; Similac Expert Care® Alimentum	20 cal./oz.	Hypoallergenic formula
Phenyl-Free® 1	22 cal./oz.	For phenylketonurics (PKU)
Pedialyte®	3 cal./oz.	Electrolyte/fluid replacement
Pregestimil®; Similac Sensitive®	20–24 cal./oz.	Lactose-free milk
Enfamil® Premature; Enfamil® EnfaCare®; Similac® Special Care®; Similac Expert Care® NeoSure	20–24 cal./oz.	Premature infant formula

Did You Get It?

Which health risk or manifestation has not been directly linked to low-birth-weight infants?
 a. neonatal anemia
 b. high susceptibility to pathogens and infections
 c. ineffective regulation of body temperature
 d. increased hardening of the arteries

Take the full quiz on CourseMate.

15-3 Feeding Time for the Infant

How often an infant needs to be fed is determined by the family, infant, and health care provider. On-demand feeding is usually recommended for young infants. This approach allows caregivers to adjust the amount and frequency of feedings to meet the infant's unique needs. An infant will signal when he is hungry and is, therefore, the best source of information about when to feed or not to feed (Table 15–4). It is important that parents and teachers learn to read an infant's cues because not all crying indicates a desire for additional food (Thompson, 2012). Noting the infant's body language as well as the tone, intensity, and length of crying can be helpful in determining if she is indeed hungry, distressed about a wet diaper, or simply wants to be picked up and held. Although the frequency and amount of feeding varies from infant to infant, a typical pattern is:

0–1 months	6 feedings of 2–4 oz./feeding
1–2 months	6 feedings of 3–5 oz./feeding
2–3 months	5 feedings of 4–6 oz./feeding
4–5 months	5 feedings of 5–7 oz./feeding
6–7 months*	5 feedings of 6–8 oz./feeding
8–12 months*	3 feedings of 8 oz./feeding

*Also taking solid foods

TABLE 15–4   Behavioral Signs of Hunger and Fullness (Satiety)

Hunger Indicators
begins to suck on fingers or fist
makes lip smacking sounds
sticks tongue out
searches for breast or bottle (rooting)
squirms or appears restless
begins crying (a late sign)

Fullness Indicators
falls asleep
turns head away
releases nipple
clamps mouth/lips tightly
becomes distracted while feeding

An infant who is consuming adequate breast milk or formula will usually have at least six or more wet diapers and several bowel movements a day.

Feeding an infant involves much more than simply getting the nipple into the mouth. Cleanliness at feeding time is of prime importance. The caregiver's hands must be soap-washed prior to every feeding. Formula should be tested against the inside of the wrist to make sure it is the right temperature for the infant to drink.

 CAUTION

Infant formula in a bottle should not be heated in a microwave. The fluid formula may become dangerously hot while the outside of the bottle feels cool. This method of heating has severely burned some infants.

Feeding time should be relaxed and preceded by a few minutes of talking and playing with the infant. When adults cuddle, maintain eye contact, and verbally interact with the infant they are satisfying critical social, emotional, and communication needs. The feeding experience also meets the infant's need for close human contact (bonding).

The infant should be held in a sitting position with her head resting against the caregiver's upper arm. Tilting the bottle slightly upward will keep the nipple filled and prevent the infant from swallowing excess air, which can cause gas and **distention**. (See Figure 15–2 illustrates different nipples that can be used for bottle feeding.) Allow at least 20 minutes per feeding to avoid hurrying the infant. Infants will signal by turning their head away, releasing or playing with the nipple, or pushing away from the adult when they have had enough to eat. It is important to recognize these cues and not force the infant to continue feeding.

15-3a Burping

Because infants naturally swallow air when sucking, they should be burped two or three times during the feeding and again when they have finished eating. The infant can be placed

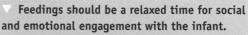

▼ **Feedings should be a relaxed time for social and emotional engagement with the infant.**

© Cengage Learning

distention – *the state of being stretched or enlarged.*

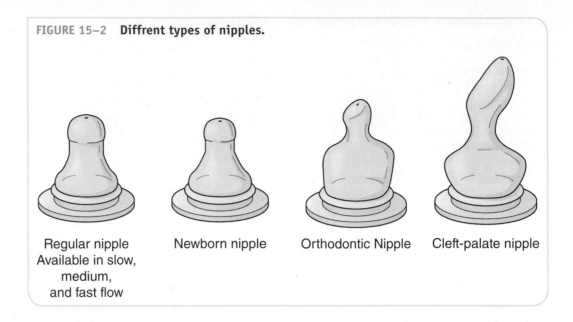

FIGURE 15–2   **Diffrent types of nipples.**

Regular nipple
Available in slow,
medium,
and fast flow

Newborn nipple

Orthodontic Nipple

Cleft-palate nipple

in either an upright position over the adult's shoulder or face-down across the adult's lap. In either position, the adult should gently pat or rub the infant's back. It is normal for infants, especially those who are formula-fed, to experience **regurgitation** and to spit up small amounts of their feeding. However, the frequency and amount spit up generally decreases with age.

⚠ **CAUTION**

An infant's bottle should never be propped up, nor should the baby ever be left unattended while feeding. Infants do not have sufficient motor control to remove the bottle from their mouth and may aspirate the milk after they fall asleep. This practice (bottle propping) also increases the risk of baby bottle tooth decay (BBTD) and ear infections.

15-3b Water

Breast milk or formula is usually sufficient to meet infants' water requirement until the time semi- or solid foods are added to their diet. However, there may be reasons, such as warm days, vomiting, or diarrhea, when an infant may need supplemental water to prevent dehydration. A thirsty infant often acts like a hungry baby. If the infant appears to be hungry shortly after feeding, a small amount of unflavored water can be offered. This amount should be limited to no more than 4 ounces daily to ensure that water does not replace the infant's milk consumption. *Water sweetened with sugar or flavored drinks should not be fed to infants.* Fluids with added **electrolytes** (salts and minerals) should be given only with a doctor's recommendation.

15-3c Supplements

Vitamin or mineral supplements are sometimes recommended for infants. In general, breast milk or formula is adequate to meet most of the infant's nutritional needs with the exception of vitamin D and the mineral fluoride. Breastfed infants are usually given a vitamin D supplement; however, the formula-fed infant receives adequate amounts of this vitamin and should

regurgitation – *the return of partially digested food from stomach to mouth.*
electrolytes – *substances that, when in solution, become capable of conducting electricity; examples include sodium and potassium.*

not be supplemented. Fluoride is present in breast milk in scant amounts and only added in low levels to concentrated and powdered formulas. However, the American Dental Association (ADA) and American Academy of Pediatric Dentistry (AAPD) do not recommend supplementation before 12 months of age because excess fluoride can have toxic effects and cause tooth discoloration (ADA, 2011). Infants who are breastfed longer than 6 months may require supplementation with iron because milk is a poor source of this mineral. Introducing iron-fortified foods around this time is also beneficial.

 CAUTION

Fluoride supplements combined with vitamin D are not safe to use with the formula-fed infant. Formulas are already fortified with vitamin D and excessive intake of this vitamin may have serious consequences for the infant.

▼ **Infants should be burped during and after feedings to decrease the risk of choking.**

© Cengage Learning

Did You Get It?

If you sense that an infant with a moderate case of diarrhea is thirsty after finishing her formula on a warm, dry day, you should:

a. provide additional water that has been sweetened with sugar to replace lost calories

b. provide a large amount of additional water to compensate for the water lost from diarrhea

c. provide a small addition of unsweetened water

d. not provide additional water

Take the full quiz on CourseMate.

15-4 Introducing Semi-Solid (Pureed) Foods

The teacher, family, and health care professional must cooperate closely when infants are being introduced to semi-solid foods. Finely cut, pureed foods high in fluid content, such as cereals, fruits, and vegetables can be introduced when the infant is about 5 or 6 months of age. It is around this time that infants have the **physiological** and **developmental readiness** to eat and digest semi-solid foods.

15-4a Developmental Readiness

At approximately 5 months of age, infants are able to move food to the back of their mouth and to swallow without an initial sucking action. They have also developed the ability to open their mouth and chew, to hold their head erect, to sit for short periods, and to lean forward toward the spoon. At about 4 to 5 months, infants begin showing interest in touching, holding, and tasting objects—food and otherwise. It is important to note that at this age infants are able to signal when they have had enough to eat by turning their head away from food. This behavior should be respected and the offering of food discontinued. Ignoring these signals can gradually lead to overeating and obesity.

developmental or physiological readiness – *growth (both physical and cognitive) and chemical processes that lead to the ability to perform a function.*

✓✓ *TEACHER CHECKLIST 15-4*

Age-Related Infant Eating Behaviors

Age	Common Infant Behaviors
1–3 months	• becomes fussy when hungry • turns face toward nipple • sucks vigorously but may choke on occasion
4–6 months	• assumes more symmetrical sitting position • grasps for objects • puts objects in mouth • closes hands around bottle • turns head away from food when no longer hungry • leans toward food-containing spoon
6–7 months	• teeth erupt • shows up-and-down chewing motions • grasps finger foods by using entire hand (**palmar grasp**) and gets them to mouth • drinks small amounts of liquid from a cup • holds bottle with both hands
7–8 months	• sits alone with little support • uses finger and thumb (**pincer grip**) to pick up small food pieces • is better able to manipulate food in the mouth • is more successful when drinking from a cup • begins self-feeding with help
9–12 months	• grasps and releases objects with greater precision • reaches for the spoon • feeds self with some help • drinks successfully from a cup • is more aware of surrounding environment • mimics motions and activities that are observed

TeachSource Digital Download Download from CourseMate.

15-4b Physiological Readiness

By 5 to 6 months of age, the infant's digestive system has matured and is now able to metabolize complex carbohydrates and proteins other than milk protein. This is also about the time that the iron stores present at birth are nearly depleted. Semi-solid foods such as iron-enriched cereals and pureed vegetables and fruits can gradually be introduced into the infant's diet to supplement dwindling iron reserves. High protein meat products should not be added until infants are approximately 6 to 8 months of age because the nitrogen-containing wastes from their digestion are difficult for immature kidneys to handle.

Teacher Checklist 15-4 presents age-related, developmental factors that influence infant feeding behavior. However, it is important to remember that infants are unique individuals and their rate of development can vary (Marotz & Allen, 2013). Infants who have developmental delays or special needs may require additional time to acquire some of these skills. Differences in cultural practices also influence when children are encouraged to attempt self-feeding (Holub & Dolan, 2012; Kuo et al., 2011). Foods should be introduced according to the individual infant's abilities, interests, and nutritional needs.

New foods should be introduced slowly with only a few baby spoonsful offered one or two times daily. (See Teacher Checklist 15-1 for appropriate serving sizes.) Iron-fortified infant cereals such as rice or barley are usually the first addition because they are less likely to cause allergic reactions.

palmar grasp – *using the entire hand to pick up objects.*
pincer grip – *using the thumb and finger to pick up an object.*

Cereals can be thinned with formula, breast milk, or water to make them more acceptable to the infant. Semi-solid foods should always be fed with a spoon and not from a bottle.

A suggested sequence for introducing semi-solid and solid foods is:

5–6 months	iron-enriched cereals
6–8 months	vegetables, followed by fruits
8–9 months	meat and meat substitutes

Initially, it is better to offer individual foods rather than mixtures. If an infant does experience an allergic or sensitivity reaction, the offending food can more easily be identified. Sugar, salt, and butter should not be added to an infant's food. Parents may choose to prepare pureed foods at home or to purchase commercially prepared food. Either is acceptable as long as the foods are nutritionally adequate. Table foods (removed before they have been seasoned) can be pureed in a blender. For example, if a family's meal consists of baked chicken, peas, and rice, an appropriate infant serving would be 2 tablespoons chicken, 2 tablespoons peas, and ¼ cup rice (all pureed). Preparing food in this manner begins to expose infants to a variety of flavors and allows families to control the ingredients. Initially, it may be wise to limit too many high-fiber foods. Home-prepared pureed food can also be frozen in ice cube trays, removed after frozen, stored in a tightly sealed container, and thawed for use as needed.

If commercially prepared infant foods are used, plain fruits, vegetables, and meats should be chosen rather than "dinners" or "desserts," which are typically extended with starches and other additives. Information on the labels of commercially prepared infant and toddler foods should be read carefully in order to make nutritious selections (Figure 15–3). Remember that ingredients on food labels are listed in descending order according to the amount present. The first ingredient in an acceptable infant food should always be fruit, vegetable, or meat—not water, cereal,

▼ **Older infants begin to show interest in feeding themselves.**

© Cengage Learning

FIGURE 15–3 Special labeling rules.

Nutrition Facts
Serving Size 1 jar (140g)

Amount Per Serving	
Calories 110	

Total Fat	0g
Sodium	10mg
Total Carbohydrate	27g
Dietary Fiber	4g
Sugars	18g
Protein	0g

%Daily Value

Protein 0%	•	Vitamin A 6%
Vitamin C 45%	•	Calcium 2%
Iron 2%		

Nutrition Label for
Foods for Children
Under Four Years Old.

Nutrition Facts
Serving Size 1 jar (140g)

Amount Per Serving	
Calories 110	Calories from Fat 0

Total Fat	0g
Saturated Fat	0g
Cholesterol	0mg
Sodium	10mg
Total Carbohydrate	27g
Dietary Fiber	4g
Sugars	18g
Protein	0g

%Daily Value

Protein 0%	•	Vitamin A 6%
Vitamin C 45%	•	Calcium 2%
Iron 2%		

Nutrition Label for
Foods for Children Two
to Four Years Old.

or other starch. When feeding a child prepared infant foods, a small portion should be removed from the jar, placed in a bowl, and the contents returned to the refrigerator. If infants are fed directly from the jar, bacteria and enzymes in saliva can cause the remaining contents to break down and become watery.

Infants may begin to drink small amounts of liquid from a cup at about 6 to 7 months of age. They like to help hold the cup and bring it to their mouth, although many spills should be expected. By 6 to 7 months, infants are also able to pick up and chew on finger foods. An infant's teeth are beginning to erupt at this age, and the provision of "chew foods" such as dry toast, dry cereal, or baby biscuits can aid the teething process. (Refer to Teacher Checklist 15-1.)

15-4c Infants with Special Needs

Although eating appears to be a natural process, infants who are born prematurely or who have a range of health problems, including genetic disorders and congenital malformations, may present special feeding challenges and nutritional needs. For example, infants born with Down syndrome typically have weak facial muscles, which make sucking difficult and less efficient. Later, these children have a tendency to overeat and to gain excessive weight. Some infants may have conditions that require surgery, which can increase their need for certain nutrients at a time when they may not be receptive to food. It is especially important that infants with special needs obtain all of the nutrients necessary for healthy growth and brain development during the months following birth.

An infant's eating behaviors may be further challenged by infection, medication side effects, unpleasant medical treatments, swallowing difficulties, dental problems, inactivity, special diets, and fatigue. These factors may make it difficult for the infant with special needs to eat and to maintain an interest in food. Families may be referred to a feeding clinic where the infant's physical and nutritional needs can be evaluated and where they can receive assistance. Nutritional services are also available through Early Head Start, IDEA (Individuals with Disabilities Education Act, Part C), WIC (Special Supplemental Nutrition Program for Women, Infants, and Children), hospital clinics, and other community-based programs.

CONNECTING TO EVERYDAY PRACTICE

Salty Beginnings

Adults worldwide are being encouraged to lower their salt intake. The *Dietary Guidelines for Healthy Americans* urge adults to limit their sodium intake to 2,300 mg (the equivalent of 1 teaspoon) daily. Recognized organizations, such as the World Health Organization (WHO), the American Medical Association (AMA), and the American Heart Association (AHA) continue to issue public warnings about the links between sodium intake, hypertension (high blood pressure), and heart disease (Frisoli et al., 2012). Certain populations, especially minorities, older adults, and the obese, are known to be at greater risk for these conditions. However, we are also learning that excessive salt intake can contribute to the early development of these same diseases in children. Although infants appear to initially dislike the taste of salt, they quickly learn to like it and even to acquire a preference for it as they transition to finger foods (Stein, Cowart, & Beauchamp, 2012). Adults who are aware of this connection can play an influential role in shaping children's early eating habits.

Think About This:

▶ What high-salt (sodium) finger foods are frequently offered to infants?

▶ How much salt (sodium) do the infants in your program receive in a typical day?

▶ What healthy, low-salt finger food options can you suggest for snacks?

▶ What can you do to encourage families to lower their salt intake and to substitute low-salt food items for infants?

Increasing numbers of infants with special needs are being enrolled in early childhood programs. Teachers must work closely with their families to learn as much about the child's condition, medical treatments, nutritional needs, and ways they can collaborate to ensure the infant's healthy development.

Did You Get It?

Should you introduce protein-rich meat products to a 4½-month-old infant who has progressed, slightly early, from formula to semisolid foods?
- **a.** Yes, the iron present in the body at birth is nearly depleted.
- **b.** Yes, the child needs this type of protein now more than ever.
- **c.** Yes, the child needs both iron and protein from meat.
- **d.** No, the child is still too young to digest and metabolize meat products.

Take the full quiz on CourseMate.

15-5 Common Feeding Concerns

15-5a Food Allergies

Allergic responses to food are common and may cause a variety of symptoms, including runny nose, wheezing, diarrhea, constipation, bloating, vomiting, hives, and eczema (Lack, 2012). An infant who experiences these symptoms should be seen by the child's health care provider. If there is a family history of allergies, introduction of semi-solid foods may be delayed until the infant reaches at least 6 months of age (Przyrembel, 2012). Allergic reactions are more commonly associated with certain foods such as citrus juice(s), eggs, cereal products (other than rice), chocolate, nuts and nut butters, and fish/shellfish. Parents may delay including these particular foods in the infant's diet and then introducing them only one at a time later on.

If an infant experiences an allergic reaction to a specific food, that food should be eliminated from the diet and reintroduced at a later time. If a milk-based formula seems to be the offending food, it may be necessary to replace it with one formulated from modified proteins or soybeans.

15-5b Colic

Some seemingly healthy infants develop colic-like symptoms between 3 and 16 weeks of age. They experience considerable distress, including abdominal discomfort, cramping, and prolonged periods of intense crying that often occur in late afternoon or evening and at approximately the same time each day (Kvitvaer, Miller, & Newell, 2012; Salisbury et al., 2012). Consoling an infant who has colic is difficult and typically ineffective. Although the exact cause of this condition is unknown there is some evidence to suggest that reflux may be a contributing factor and that changing the type of formula being fed will sometimes relieve the symptoms (Hasan & Ng, 2012). Mothers who are breastfeeding should continue to do so, but may want to monitor their diet closely for highly spiced or strongly flavored foods that may trigger or contribute to the infant's discomfort. Fortunately, most infants outgrow colic at about 3 to 4 months of age.

▼ **Children should be observed carefully for potential allergic reactions when new foods are being introduced into their diet.**

© Cengage Learning

15-5c Vomiting and Diarrhea

Common causes of vomiting and diarrhea in infants include:

- food allergies or food sensitivities
- overfeeding
- infections: systemic or food-borne
- introducing solid foods before an infant is able to digest them
- incorrect formula preparation
- use of fruit juice
- swallowed air
- reflux

It is normal for young infants to spit up or to vomit. The muscle (sphincter), positioned at the stomach opening, is responsible for keeping stomach contents in place. This sphincter requires time to fully develop before it is able to function properly; this process may take longer in some young infants and, until then, may cause them to spit up after almost every feeding. However, when vomiting is accompanied by back arching, difficulty feeding, and pulling away from the nipple, this condition is known as gastroesophageal reflux (GER). It is often resolved by feeding the infant in an upright position (and remaining upright for a short time afterward), changing formula type, and maturation (the condition usually disappears around 18 months-of-age). When the condition consistently interferes with feeding and growth or causes the infant to wheeze, cough, or have difficulty breathing, it is recognized as a disease (GERD) (Sullivan & Sundaram, 2012). Medication may be prescribed if the condition persists despite changes in feeding practices.

Fluid and electrolyte replacement are primary considerations when an infant has been ill and experienced repeated vomiting and diarrhea. These infants require approximately 3 ounces of replacement fluids per pound of body weight. There are also numerous commercial ready-to-feed (RTF) rehydrating formulas available (Pedialyte®, Equalyte®, Infalyte®, and Rehydralyte®); however, parents should check with their health care provider before giving any of these solutions to an infant. Fruit juices, carbonated beverages, tea, or adult electrolyte formulas are not recommended because of their high sugar and low electrolyte content. The ultimate goal is a gradual progression and eventual return to the infant's normal diet.

Acute diarrhea due to an infection, and characterized by accompanying fever, must be attended to immediately. The infant's physician should be contacted for advice and appropriate treatment.

15-5d Anemia

Inadequate iron intake can result in low-hemoglobin-type anemia that may delay the growth process and cause the infant to be lethargic (Gibbs et al., 2012). Iron stores present at birth are usually exhausted by 6 months of age unless the infant is receiving an iron-fortified formula. Adding iron-enriched cereals to an infant's diet at about 5 to 6 months of age is usually sufficient to prevent anemia from developing. Some infants may initially experience constipation or diarrhea when placed on an iron-fortified formula but this usually corrects itself with time.

15-5e Baby Bottle Tooth Decay

Infants who are allowed to recline or to sleep with a bottle or breast in their mouth may develop baby bottle tooth decay (BBTD). This condition, also referred to as early childhood caries, is caused by the prolonged presence of sugars in formula, breast milk, or juices in the child's mouth. Tooth decay can also develop when cavity-causing bacteria are transferred from an adult to the infant via saliva through practices such as cleaning the infant's pacifier in person's mouth or tasting food from the infant's spoon. Bacteria in saliva feed on the sugars in milk and juices and create acids that cause decay. When infants have finished a feeding, their gums should be wiped with a damp cloth. Weaning infants to a cup at about 8 months of age also reduces the risk of BBTD. Pacifiers should never be dipped in sugar or other sugary substances.

15-5f Ear Infection

Feeding an infant in a reclining position or propping the bottle while an infant is lying down (and not being held) increases the risk of ear infection (Abrahams & Labbok, 2011). An infant should always be held in a semi-upright position during feedings, and for a short while after a feeding is completed, to prevent milk from traveling back into the eustachian tubes and ear canals.

15-5g Obesity

Obesity results when energy intake exceeds an infant's needs for growth, maintenance, and activity. Infant feeding practices thought to play a role in obesity include overeating during bottle feedings, prolonged breastfeedings, early introduction of semi-solid foods, and feeding cereal (or other foods) from a bottle (Li et al., 2012).

It is important that caregivers be alert to signs that an infant is satisfied and has consumed enough during feedings. Stopping periodically gives the infant a chance to assess her own hunger and to respond appropriately when the bottle is again offered. It is important to respect the infant's judgment about the amount of food desired at a given time. Urging an infant to finish milk remaining in a bottle or to continue breastfeeding may ignore his or her signs of fullness (satiety), which include:

- closing the mouth or turning away from the bottle
- falling asleep
- crying or fussing at repeated attempts to continue feeding
- biting or playing with the nipple
- pushing the bottle or breast away

Some authorities believe that continuously ignoring these signs may cause the infant to stop recognizing and communicating signs of fullness and, thus, end an important means of regulating food intake. This can have serious, long-term consequences for children and adults who no longer know when to stop eating. To establish the point at which the infant is satisfied, the teacher should stop after a few minutes of solid-food feeding and play with the child before offering more food. This practice aids in determining whether the infant is eating because of hunger or simply to gain the caregiver's attention.

Introducing semi-solid foods before infants are old enough or serving foods high in sugar or fat may contribute to a calorie intake that is greater than needed and can lead to obesity (Schell & Gallo, 2012; Thompson, 2012). Continuing to offer solid food after the infant seems satisfied also contributes to obesity and may set the stage for overeating later in life.

Physical activity is also important for encouraging a healthy appetite and balanced weight. Infants should have multiple opportunities throughout the day to move about and should not remain in one position for longer than an hour at any time (unless sleeping). Repositioning an infant every 30 to 40 minutes also promotes the use of different muscle groups. For example, an infant might first be placed on his tummy to play, then rolled onto his back under an activity gym, and later moved to an infant seat. Older infants can be enticed to move about by placing toys out of their reach or by engaging them in rolling a ball back and forth. These are also important steps for helping children to continue developing an active lifestyle.

15-5h Choking

Occasional episodes of choking are not uncommon in young infants. The frequency of these events tends to diminish as the muscles used for swallowing continue to mature. The danger of choking is increased when infants are allowed to eat too quickly or to drink from a propped bottle while lying down. Choking can be minimized during breast or bottle feedings by holding the child in a semi-reclining position with the head elevated. Stopping for brief periods and burping the infant periodically are also effective strategies to prevent choking.

When 6- to 7-month-old infants begin to eat finger foods such as dry bread, crackers, or dry cereal, they must be monitored closely because these items may increase the risk of choking. Again, this danger can be minimized by placing the infant in a sitting position and breaking or cutting foods into small pieces that are easy to chew and swallow. Semi-solid foods can be ground or mashed with a small amount of liquid to prevent choking. Because the majority of choking episodes occur in infants, it is essential that parents and teachers be prepared by completing CPR training.

15-5i Teething

An infant's teeth begin to erupt at around 6 months of age. This can be a stressful period for some infants and may temporarily disrupt their feeding pattern. As a result, some infants may begin to wean themselves from breast or bottle feedings and prefer foods that can be chewed such as dry cereal pieces, toast, or teething biscuits. Cold or frozen teethers also help to relieve gum discomfort. Appropriate chewing toys and food items should be made available to discourage infants from picking up and chewing on inappropriate or unsafe objects. Diarrhea accompanying teething is usually due to infectious organisms and is not caused by the teething process. In an early childhood program, it is important to ensure that toys are frequently sanitized to reduce the risk of spreading illness from one infant to another.

15-5j Constipation

Breast-fed infants are generally not troubled by constipation. Because breast milk is so easily digested, only a small amount of waste product remains to be excreted. Infants who are formula-fed, especially with soy-based or iron-enriched products, are more likely to experience constipation. Giving them additional water is often sufficient to address the problem. However, if the formula-fed infant fails to have a bowel movement for more than three or four days, the family should contact their health care provider for advice.

Did You Get It?

You should administer approximately _____ oz of fluid per pound of bodyweight to an infant experiencing repeated diarrhea whose pediatrician recommended giving the infant an electrolyte replacement solution.

a. 3

b. 5

c. 8

d. 0 (You should never give this solution to a baby with diarrhea; it is for vomiting only.)

Take the full quiz on CourseMate.

PARTNERING with FAMILIES

Feeding Your Infant

Dear Families,

Birth (and even before) is an ideal time to begin addressing your child's nutritional well-being. What you eat during pregnancy influences your infant's health and food preferences. Following your infant's birth, you can encourage his or her development of healthy eating habits by serving nutritious foods and creating positive mealtime experiences.

▶ Breast milk and/or infant formula is recommended as the infant's primary source of nutrition for the first year. Cow's milk does not meet the infant's nutritional requirements for rapid growth rate and should not be offered until after the infant's first birthday.

▶ Always hold, cuddle, and talk with your infant during feedings. This practice fosters important emotional connections between you and your infant. It also reduces the potential for choking, ear infections, and baby bottle tooth decay.

▶ Wait until your infant is about 5 to 6 months old before introducing solid foods. Choose a single-grain (usually rice) iron-fortified cereal as the first food to feed to your infant. Only introduce one food at a time and serve it for several days to determine if your infant has any allergies or intolerances.

(continued)

PARTNERING with FAMILIES

Feeding Your Infant (continued)

▶ Be wary of food additives, especially in commercially produced infant foods. "Desserts" and "dinners" often contain additives and offer less nutritional value than plain cereal, vegetables, fruits, and meats. Experiment with making your own pureed infant foods.

▶ Introduce 100 percent fruit juices when your infant is about 6 to 7 months of age.

▶ Don't serve infants fruit drinks, sodas, or other beverages that are high in sugar and offer few nutrients.

▶ Always cut food in small pieces and avoid foods that cause choking (especially grapes, peanuts, hotdogs, popcorn, raw vegetables).

▶ Learn CPR!

CLASSROOM CORNER

Teacher Activities

Planning Healthy Snacks

(PreK–2; NHES grades 3–5; National Health Education Standards 1.2.1, 2.2.3, 6.2.1; 1.5.1, 2.5.5, 6.5.1)

Concept: Healthy food choices provide important energy.

Learning Objectives

▶ Children will learn to plan healthy snacks.

▶ Children will identify foods that help bodies stay healthy.

Supplies

▶ Paper

▶ Crayons or markers

▶ Computer and Internet access (for older children)

▶ MyPlate placemats (can be printed from http://www.choosemyplate.gov)

▶ Magazine pictures of healthy snack items

▶ Glue sticks

Learning Activities

▶ Discuss the importance of choosing healthy snacks (e.g., growth, energy, staying healthy/not sick). Use the MyPlate food guide to talk about and to illustrate foods that are considered healthy and why it is important to select a variety of foods (and colors) from each group, including some that are new.

▶ Draw a grid on a large sheet of paper (for each day of the week). Have younger children plan a week's worth of afternoon snacks by selecting items from two different food groups; teachers can fill in the grid with foods that children name or children can glue food pictures from magazines onto the grid. Older children can explore the ChooseMyPlate.gov website online and learn about healthy food options before developing their menu. Arrange to have the cook prepare snacks from the children's menu; older children may be able to prepare their own snacks each day.

Evaluation

▶ Children will make healthy food choices and state why this is important.

▶ Children will use the menu to create a healthy snack plan.

◑ Summary

▮ The first year of an infant's life is one of very rapid growth and developmental change.

- By 12 months of age, most infants will triple their birth weight and increase their length by 50 percent.
- Satisfying an infant's needs for all essential nutrients supports healthy growth and development.

▮ All nutrients that an infant requires for growth and development during the first 6 months can be supplied by either breast milk or formula. Formula is similar in nutrient composition but does not provide the infant with disease-protecting antibodies.

▮ It is important for caregivers to recognize and acknowledge an infant's behavioral signals that indicate hunger or satiety.

▮ Infants are developmentally and physiologically ready to eat semi-solid foods at around 5 to 6 months of age.

- Single-grain, iron-fortified cereals (usually rice) are the first semi-solid foods introduced at around 5 to 6 months of age.
- Vegetables, fruits, and meats are added over the next three months.

▮ Caregivers must anticipate common food-related problems such as allergies, colic, vomiting and diarrhea, anemia, ear infection, obesity, and choking.

◑ Terms to Know

low-birthweight (LBW) infant *p. 383*
antibodies *p. 385*
aseptic procedure *p. 387*
distention *p. 389*

regurgitation *p. 390*
electrolyte(s) *p. 390*
developmental or physiological readiness *p. 391*

palmar grasp *p. 392*
pincer grip *p. 392*

◑ Chapter Review

A. By Yourself:

1. Provide a rationale for why an infant's bottle should not be propped up during feedings.
2. In what order should the following foods be introduced?

   pureed peas   pureed meat products

   crisp toast   pureed peaches

   iron-fortified barley cereal

3. At approximately what age should an infant be introduced to each of these foods?
4. Describe three social factors that make feeding time more enjoyable for an infant.
5. Explain why unmodified cow's or goat's milk should not be given to an infant before 1 year of age.
6. What steps can teachers take to support a mother who wants to continue breastfeeding her infant?

B. As a Group:

1. Discuss why it is important not to feed infants semi-solid foods before 5 to 6 months of age.
2. Debate the advantages and disadvantages of breastfeeding versus formula feeding.
3. Describe several feeding practices that are thought to contribute to infant obesity.
4. Discuss baby bottle tooth decay (BBTD) and feeding practices that will prevent this condition.
5. Evaluate the nutrient contributions of several commercial infant foods by using the http://ndb.nal .usda.gov website. Make recommendations for healthy choices based on your findings.

6. Observe several mothers while they are feeding their infant. In what ways did the mothers and infants communicate verbally and nonverbally with each other? Discuss how you could use this information to help first-time mothers.

◖ Case Study

Donica M's first child, Leandra recently celebrated her 2-month birthday. Although she is thoroughly in love with her infant, Donica finds that being a new mother can be a demanding and frustrating experience at times. Since giving birth, she has been exceptionally tired because Leandra awakens several times during the night and seems to be hungry. Donica's mother lives nearby and occasionally helps out with Leandra's care. She has suggested that putting cereal in Leandra's nighttime bottle might help to "fill her up so she will sleep through the night." She has also advised Donica to cut larger holes in the nipple "so Leandra will get more food during each feeding and won't have to work as hard."

▶ Should Donica follow her mother's advice?

▶ What are the dangers, if any, of feeding an 8-week-old infant cereal from the bottle?

▶ How might feeding practices have changed since Donica was an infant?

▶ What are the potential short- and long-term consequences of feeding semi-solid food from a bottle?

▶ How would you respond if you were the teacher and Donica asked you to feed Leandra in this manner?

◖ Application Activities

1. Mrs. Jones, mother of 2-month-old Kelly, has been on maternity leave from her job. She is preparing to return to work and has made arrangements for Kelly to stay in a nearby family child care home. Mrs. Jones wants to continue breastfeeding, but is concerned that she will have to switch Kelly over to formula. In what ways can the care provider support Mrs. Jones' interests in continuing to breastfeed?

2. Visit the infant food section of your local grocery store and read the ingredient list on several food items. Select ten foods that you consider to be nutritious choices for a young infant based on the label ingredients. Discuss the criteria you used to make this determination.

3. Plan an instructional manual for new employees in an infant care facility. What social aspects of infant feeding would be important to address? What information should also be included regarding nutrition and sanitation?

4. If applicable, review state regulations relating to infant feeding guidelines in early childhood programs. Comment on the adequacy of information provided.

5. Identify and discuss the health and feeding problems that low-birthweight infants are more likely to experience. What prenatal nutrient deficiencies are more common among infants with low-birthweight?

◖ Helpful Web Resources

Administration for Children & Families   http://www.acf.hhs.gov

Healthy Children.org (AAP)   http://www.healthychildren.org

Keep Kids Healthy   http://www.keepkidshealthy.com

La Leche League   http://www.lalecheleague.org
National Network for Child Care   http://www.nncc.org
Office on Women's Health   http://www.womenshealth.gov
Public Health Agency of Canada   http://www.phac-aspc.gc.ca

 Visit the Education CourseMate for this textbook to access the eBook, Did You Get It? quizzes, Digital Downloads, TeachSource Video Cases, flashcards, and more. Go to CengageBrain.com to log in, register, or purchase access.

References

American Academy of Pediatrics (AAP). (2012). Breastfeeding and the use of human milk, *Pediatrics*, 129(3), e827–e841.

American Dental Association. (ADA). (2011). Fluoride and infant formula: Frequently asked questions. Accessed on July 26, 2012 from http://www.ada.org/4052.aspx.

Andres, A., Cleves, M., Bellando, J., Pivik, R., Casey, P., & Badger, T. (2012). Developmental status of 1-year-old infants fed breast milk, cow's milk formula, or soy formula, *Pediatrics*, 129(6), 1134–1140.

Bigelow, A., & Power, M. (2012). The effect of mother–infant skin-to-skin contact on infants' response to the Still Face Task from newborn to three months of age, *Infant Behavior & Development*, 35(2), 240–251.

Black, M., Quigg, A., Cook, J., Casey, P., Cutts, D., Chilton, M., Meyers, A., Ettinger de Cuba, S., Heeren, T., Coleman, S., Rose-Jacobs, R., & Frank, D. (2012). WIC participation and attenuation of stress-related child health risks of household food insecurity and caregiver depressive symptoms, *Archives of Pediatrics & Adolescent Medicine*, 166(5), 444–451.

De Greef, E., Hauser, B., Devreker, T., Veereman-Wauters, G., & Vandenplas, Y. (2012). Diagnosis and management of cow's milk protein allergy in infants, *World Journal of Pediatrics*, 8(1), 19–24.

Frisoli, T., Schmieder, R., Grodzicki, T., & Messerli, F. (2012). Salt and hypertension: Is salt dietary reduction worth the effort?, *The American Journal of Medicine*, 125(5), 433–439.

Gale, C., Logan, K., Santhakumaran, S., Parkinson, J., Hyde, M., & Modi, N. (2012). Effect of breastfeeding compared with formula feeding on infant body composition: A systematic review and meta-analysis, *American Journal of Clinical Nutrition*, 95(3), 656–669.

Galler, J., Bryce, C., Waber, D., Hock, R., Harrison, R., Eaglesfield, G., & Fitzmaurice, G. (2012). Infant malnutrition predicts conduct problems in adolescents, *Nutritional Neuro-science*, 15(4), 186–192(7).

Gibbs, C., Wendt, A., Peters, S., & Hogue, C. (2012). The impact of early age at first childbirth on maternal and infant health, *Paediatric & Perinatal Epidemiology*, 26(Suppl. 1), 259–284.

Hasan, N., & Ng, P. (2012). The management of reflux in infants, *InnovAiT*, 5(2), 69–75.

Holub, S., & Dolan, E. (2012). Mothers' beliefs about infant size: Associations with attitudes and infant feeding practices, *Journal of Applied Developmental Psychology*, 33(3), 158–164.

Isaacs, E., Ross, S., Kennedy, K., Weaver, L., Lucas, A., & Fewtrell, M. (2011). 10-year cognition in preterms after random assignment to fatty acid supplementation in infancy, *Pediatrics*, 128(4), e890–898.

Kim, J., & Friel, J. (2012). Lipids and human milk, *Lipid Technology*, 24(5), 103–105.

Kuo, A., Inkelas, M., Slusser, W., Maidenberg, M., & Halfon, N. (2011). Introduction of solid food to young infants, *Maternal & Child Health Journal*, 15(8), 1185–1194.

Kvitvaer, B., Miller, J., & Newell, D. (2012). Improving our understanding of the colicky infant: A prospective observational study, *Journal of Clinical Nursing*, 21(1-2), 63–69.

Lack, G. (2012). Update on risk factors for food allergy, *Journal of Allergy & Clinical Immunology*, 129(5), 1187–1197.

Li, R., Magadia, J., Fein, S., & Grummer-Strawn, L. (2012). Risk of bottle-feeding for rapid weight gain during the first year of life, *Archives of Pediatrics & Adolescent Medicine*, 166(5), 431–436.

Marotz, L., & Allen, K. (2013). *Developmental profiles: Pre-birth through adolescence* (7th ed.). Belmont, CA: Wadsworth Cengage.

Poston, L. (2012). Gestational weight gain: Influences on the long-term health of the child, *Current Opinion in Clinical Nutrition & Metabolic Care*, 15(4), 252–257.

Przyrembel, H. (2012). Timing of introduction of complementary food: Short- and long-term consequences, *Annals of Nutrition & Metabolism*, 60(2), 8–20.

Salisbury, A., High, P., Twomey, J., Dickstein, S., Chapman, H., Liu, J., & Lester, B. (2012). A randomized control trial of integrated care for families managing infant colic, *Infant Mental Health Journal*, 33(2), 110–122.

Salone, L., Vann, W., & Dee, D. (2013). Breastfeeding: An overview of oral and general health benefits, *The Journal of the American Dental Association*, 144(2), 143–151.

Schell, L., & Gallo, M. (2012). Overweight and obesity among North American Indian infants, children, and youth, *American Journal of Human Biology*, 24(3), 302–313.

Stein, L., Cowart, B., & Beauchamp, G. (2012). The development of salty taste acceptance is related to dietary experience in human infants: A prospective study, *American Journal of Clinical Nutrition*, 95(1), 123–129.

Sullivan, J., & Sundaram, S. (2012). Gastroesophageal reflux, *Pediatrics in Review*, 33(6), 243–254.

Thompson, A. (2012). Developmental origins of obesity: Early feeding environments, infant growth, and the intestinal microbiome, *American Journal of Human Biology*, 24(3), 350–360.

U.S. Department of Agriculture (USDA). (2012). "WIC Program data: National level annual summary." Accessed on July 26, 2012 from http://www.fns.usda.gov/pd/37WIC_Monthly.htm.

Voss, W., Jungmann, T., Wachtendorf, M., & Neubauer, A. (2012). Long-term cognitive outcomes of extremely low-birth-weight infants: The influence of the maternal educational background, *Acta Paediatrica*, 101(6), 569–573.

Feeding Toddlers and Young Children

⏵ **#1 a, b, and c:** Promoting child development and learning
⏵ **#2 a, b, and c:** Building family and community relationships
⏵ **#3 a, b, and d:** Observing, documenting, and assessing to support young children and families
⏵ **#4 a, b, and d:** Using developmentally effective approaches to connect with children and families
⏵ **#5 a, and c:** Using content knowledge to build meaningful curriculum
⏵ **#6 c:** Becoming a professional.

Learning Objectives

After studying this chapter, you should be able to:

LO 16-1 Discuss the developmental characteristics typical of toddlers, preschoolers, and school-age children.

LO 16-2 Explain the challenges involved in getting toddlers to eat and how these challenges can be addressed.

LO 16-3 Describe the unique nutrient requirements of preschoolers and school-age children and ways to meet their needs.

LO 16-4 Discuss how adults can foster children's healthy eating behaviors.

LO 16-5 Identify and discuss the common health problems associated with children's poor eating patterns.

16-1 Developmental Profiles: Toddlers, Preschoolers, and School-Aged Children

Toddlers (1- to 2½-year-olds) are delightful individuals, but they can be challenging at times. They are beginning to assert their independence, yet need and want limits. They have an insatiable curiosity, yet prefer most things to be predictable and always conducted in the same way. They are becoming increasingly mobile and active, but still need to be monitored closely and protected from unsafe conditions in their environment.

Many toddlers spend considerable time each day in early education programs while their parents work or attend school. These opportunities expose children to social and eating experiences that often differ from those they are accustomed to at home. Children begin to learn that other people may do things differently, but this doesn't necessarily translate into a willingness to join in.

Although toddlers are growing at a much slower rate than they did as infants, they continue to need adequate calories and essential nutrients to maintain growth and activity levels. However, the amount of food they are willing and able to eat often seems insufficient to adults. Children's small stomach capacity and short attention span limit what they are able to consume at any one time. One way to address mealtime challenges is to serve small amounts of food more often and on a consistent schedule. Yet toddlers may resist eating on a schedule and reject foods they are served as they struggle to become independent. They have learned the power of the word "no" and use it repeatedly. They quickly learn to shape adults' behavior by refusing to eat or, at other times, by eating to gain adult favor.

▼ Preschool-age children prefer to do things by themselves, but may still need adult assistance.

© Cengage Learning

The toddler is often described as being **neophobic**, especially when it comes to eating—that is, they become distressed and are often reluctant to try new or unfamiliar foods (Tan & Holub, 2012). This behavior may limit the toddler's willingness to eat an increasing variety of foods. When adults understand that this behavior is characteristic of most toddlers, they can begin to exercise more patience and ingenuity as they introduce new foods into children's diet (Musher-Eizenman et al., 2011).

Many toddlers also become avid television watchers. What they observe is likely to affect their behavior and food preferences. Researchers have noted that foods advertised on popular children's television programs are often of poor nutrient quality. They have also found that commercials create a desire for foods high in calories, refined sugars, and fat (Harris et al., 2012). Furthermore, hours spent sitting in front of the television reduce valuable time that toddlers should be spending in active play. Inactivity limits the calories that are burned and can ultimately contribute to childhood obesity.

Preschool-aged children (2½- to 6-year-olds) are generally more easygoing and cooperative than toddlers. They are willing to listen and to follow adult directions in an effort to please, but are not always compliant. Although they prefer to do things for themselves, they may still need some adult assistance to be successful. Structure continues to be important for preschoolers, who are also more likely to respect it than toddlers do. They are learning more appropriate ways of expressing themselves, yet may still be somewhat hesitant at times to accept change. Families and teachers can anticipate that many of these developmental characteristics will be reflected in the preschooler's eating behaviors and responses to food.

School-aged children are becoming increasingly aware of a much bigger world. They are energetic, curious, eager to learn, and able to understand increasingly complex situations. Friends and friendships gradually replace time spent with family, although school-aged children still need and find comfort in knowing they can rely on their parents. Watching television, playing electronic games, and participating in organized activities now consume more of their time.

Family meal practices, including cultural eating habits and food preferences, remain an important factor in determining the school-aged child's mealtime behaviors (Anderson et al., 2012). However, the favorite foods of friends and peers also begin to influence their food choices. School-aged children enjoy helping with meal planning, grocery shopping, and food preparation. Their appetite is generally good, but it also tends to fluctuate with growth spurts and activity levels.

Did You Get It?

Toddlers displaying _____ behavior frequently refuse new food options and experiences with which they are not familiar.
   a. ombrophobic
   b. nouveauphobic
   c. neophobic
   d. ailurophobic

Take the full quiz on CourseMate.

neophobic – *fear of things that are new and unfamiliar.*

16-2 The Challenges of Feeding Toddlers

Toddlers are driven to assert their independence and to let their preferences be known. This includes their firm announcement of the foods they will or will not eat. Fortunately, their "will" and "will not" foods change almost daily. However, great care must be taken so that families and teachers do not become involved in a battle of wills over what the toddler will eat and when it will be eaten. Mealtime friction can be minimized by respecting adult and child responsibilities in the feeding relationship (Satter, 2000). Adults are responsible for:

- serving a variety of nutritious foods
- deciding when food is offered
- setting a positive example by eating a variety of foods

The child is responsible for:

- choosing what foods will be eaten from those that have been offered
- deciding how much of the offered food to eat

16-2a What Foods Should Be Served and How Much

Families and teachers have a responsibility to provide children with a variety of nutritious foods each day. As discussed in Chapter 12, the MyPlate guidelines are easy to follow and ensure that children's daily nutrient needs will be met (Figure 16–1, or visit www.ChooseMyPlate.gov). Teacher Checklist 16-1 presents a summary of the basic food groups and recommended amounts that children should consume each day.

When feeding toddlers, it is preferable to serve slightly less than they are expected to eat. In this way toddlers are not overwhelmed by the amount of food on their plates and are able to assert their independence by requesting more. An appropriate serving size for a toddler is

FIGURE 16–1   ChooseMyPlate.

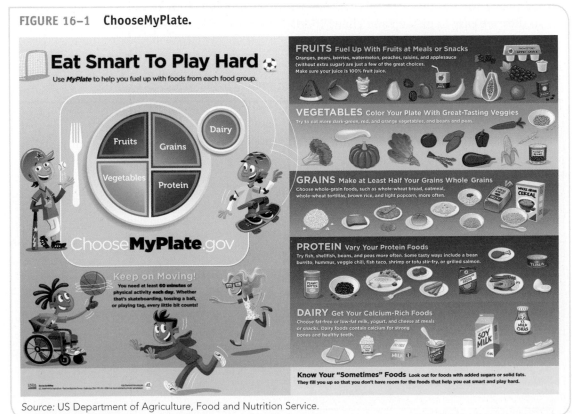

Source: US Department of Agriculture, Food and Nutrition Service.

United States Department of Agriculture

✓✓ TEACHER CHECKLIST 16-1
Recommended Daily Food Group Intakes

Food Group	Toddlers	Preschoolers	School-Aged
Grains	3 ounces	4-ounces	5–6 ounces
Vegetables	1 cup	1½ cups	2–2½ cups
Fruits	1 cup	1–1½ cups	1½ cups
Dairy	2 cups	2 cups	3 cups
Meat & meat alternates	2 ounces	3–4 ounces	5 ounces
Oils	Use sparingly		

TeachSource Digital Download   Download from CourseMate.

approximately one-fourth of an adult serving for each food group with the exception of the dairy group (see Figure 16–2):

Milk - 1/2 cup
Meat/meat alternate - 1 ounce
Fruits and Vegetables - 2 tablespoons
Breads and Cereals - 2 tablespoons rice, cereal, or pasta; 1/2 slice bread

The toddler's acceptance of foods is highly influenced by their sensory qualities, especially taste, texture, and temperature. Young children's mouths are sensitive to temperature extremes; foods that are too cold or too hot will often be refused. Hot foods that are comfortable for adults may burn the toddler's mouth. Toddlers also have an abundance of taste buds that intensify the flavors of some foods. This may explain, in part, why toddlers often refuse vegetables such as broccoli, spinach, brussels sprouts, and beets. Food textures may also be challenging, especially as toddlers are transitioning from soft, pureed foods to table foods. They still have an active gag reflex and are also prone to choking. For this reason, foods must be cut into small pieces (1/4 inch or less) so they are easy to pick up and chew. Toddlers also prefer foods that are served individually

FIGURE 16–2   Sample menu with serving sizes for toddlers.

BREAKFAST	LUNCH	DINNER
Whole milk (1/2 cup)	Whole milk (1/2 cup)	Whole milk (1/2 cup)
Pancake (small)	Beef patty (1 oz)	Finely diced chicken (1 oz)
or	Broccoli (2 tbsp)	Cooked carrots (2 tbsp)
Whole wheat toast (1/2 slice)	Diced watermelon (2 tbsp)	Diced plums (2 tbsp)
Fruit preserves (1 tsp)	Whole wheat bread (1/2 slice)	Brown rice (1/4 cup)
Diced peaches (1/4 cup)	Margarine (1 tsp)	Margarine (1 tsp)
MIDMORNING SNACK	**MIDAFTERNOON SNACK**	**EVENING SNACK**
Vanilla wafers (3)	Cheese cube (1/2 oz)	Applesauce (1/2 cup)
Orange juice (1/2 cup)	Whole wheat crackers (2)	Graham crackers (2)
	Water	Water

(and not touching) rather than combined in mixtures. For example, instead of serving spaghetti and meatballs, green beans, and a mixed fruit salad, the same basic foods could be presented as:

- Ground beef patty
- Green beans
- Whole grain bread or pasta
- Diced peaches
- Milk

Remember that toddlers' appetite typically decrease as their growth rate slows. Adults should not become overly concerned if children are suddenly eating less. It is also important to avoid pressuring, nagging, or forcing children to eat more food than they may want or need. Doing so can cause food to take on an emotional association and potentially lead to eating disorders.

Table 16–1 presents an overview of age-related eating behaviors that may be helpful in understanding children's changing responses to food. Adults can use this knowledge to establish realistic expectations and to create positive feeding experiences for children of all ages.

TABLE 16–1 Age-Related Eating Behaviors

Age	Behavior
12–24 months	Has a decreased appetite Is sometimes described as a finicky or fussy eater; may go on food jags Uses spoon with some degree of skill Helps feed self
2-year-old	Has fair appetite Expresses strong likes and dislikes; may go on food jags Prefers simple food, dislikes mixtures, wants food served in familiar ways Learns table manners by imitating adults and older children
3-year-old	Has fairly good appetite; prefers small servings; likes only a few cooked vegetables Feeds self independently, if hungry Uses spoon in semi-adult fashion; may spear with fork and spread with a blunt knife Dawdles over food when not hungry
4- to 5-year-old	Eats well, but not at every meal May develop dislikes of certain foods and refuse them to the point of tears if pushed; often adapts to preferences of family and teachers Enjoys helping with meal preparation Uses all eating utensils; becomes skilled at spreading jelly or peanut butter, pouring milk on cereal, or cutting soft foods such as bread
6- to 7-year-old	Has good appetite; eats most foods Is willing to try new foods, but is unpredictable Able to use eating utensils, but not always correctly Easily distracted; has difficulty sitting through a meal
8- to 9-year-old	Usually has a good appetite; boys eat more than girls Prefers to eat when hungry rather than at specified times Is open to trying new foods, but prefers certain "favorites" Enjoys cooking Eats quickly so they can resume previous activity
10- to 12-year-old	Always hungry; seems to eat non-stop and large amounts at one time Needs a big snack after school Dislikes few foods; interested in trying foods from other cultures and those seen on television Seems to forget manners that were previously learned

Source: Adapted from Marotz, L. R., & Allen, K. E. (2013). *Developmental profiles: Pre-birth through adolescence.* (7th ed.). Belmont, CA: Wadsworth Cengage.

16-2b When to Serve Food

The timing of meals and snacks is an important consideration when feeding toddlers. Too much time between feedings will result in an overly hungry, cranky child who may lose interest in food when it is finally presented. Meals and snacks spaced too closely together will not allow ample time for a child to become hungry again, resulting in a poor eating response. Most young children also eat better at meals if they are not tired and if they have been given an advanced warning so they can "wrap up" their play activities. Allowing time for a quiet story before mealtime can set the stage for a pleasant, relaxed, and more satisfying mealtime experience for everyone.

Because toddlers have a critical need for nutrients and a small stomach capacity, they must eat more often than the three-meal family pattern. An ideal eating pattern includes:

- breakfast
- midmorning snack
- lunch
- midafternoon snack
- dinner
- bedtime snack, if needed

Snacks chosen from each of the food groups can be planned to meet a portion of the child's daily nutrient needs. Foods commonly promoted on television as "snacks," such as chips, snack cakes, frosted cookies, candy bars, fruit "drinks," and sodas have no place in the toddler's daily meal pattern. These foods consist primarily of empty calories and provide little if any nutritional value. Healthy snack choices include:

- cheese cubes and pita wedges
- crackers with peanut butter or hummus
- 100 percent fruit juices – orange or other juices fortified with vitamin C
- diced, raw vegetables – cucumber slices, cherry tomatoes, mushrooms, zucchini, red and orange peppers, jicama
- lightly cooked (steamed) vegetables– broccoli florets, green beans, carrots, edamame, sweet potato strips
- fruits – apple and orange wedges, bananas, applesauce, diced peaches, pears, plums, nectarines, kiwi, pineapple
- whole grain crackers and breads
- dry, nonsweetened cereals
- yogurt with fresh fruit or granola

16-2c Making Mealtime Comfortable, Pleasant, and Safe

Children are more likely to eat in comfortable surroundings. Furniture should be of an appropriate size; table height should be comfortable for children to reach and chairs should permit their feet to rest flat on the floor. If a highchair or youth chair is used, it must have a stable base, washable eating tray, crotch safety strap, and support for the child's feet. Eating utensils should be child-sized and nonbreakable. Children's forks should have short, blunt tines and broad, short, easy-to-grasp handles. Spoons should also have short, blunt handles and shallow bowls for easy use. An upturned rim around plates provides a means for "trapping" elusive bits of food. Plates divided into two or three compartments can also reduce frustration for toddlers as they develop self-feeding skills. Small (4 to 6 ounces) plastic cups with a broad base are easy for children to hold and also reduce potential spills.

Toddlers are developing hand/eye coordination and improved fine motor skills that enable them to better handle utensils and to feed themselves. They should be encouraged to practice these skills but should not be given too many difficult-to-manage foods. Peas that roll off of a spoon or soups that spill before they reach the child's mouth can quickly discourage even the most determined toddler. Finger foods served along with foods that require a fork or spoon encourage self-feeding and reduce mealtime frustration. Meats and cheeses cut into small cubes and vegetables and fruits sliced into small pieces are easier (and safer) for toddlers to pick up and chew. Although adults may not think that peas, mashed potatoes, and rice are finger foods, toddlers often do. A little flexibility in the choice of feeding methods can pay off in terms of the toddler's increased willingness to eat.

Sanitation is also an important consideration in feeding the toddler. The aseptic environment required when they were infants is no longer necessary or possible to maintain. However, cleanliness is of prime importance when preparing, serving, and eating food. Hand washing before and after meals is mandatory for toddlers as they often eat with their hands. Teachers must also wash their hands carefully before handling or eating food and again after cleaning up from a meal.

> ### Did You Know...
> that french fries account for 25 percent of the vegetables consumed by children? Fewer than 20 percent of children eat five or more daily servings of fruits and vegetables.

Did You Get It?

To present toddlers with a variety of foods at each meal and minimize mealtime friction, adults should:

a. insist that the toddler eat a little bit of everything

b. tell the toddler to choose one or two options

c. take a bite from each option, model the behavior, and present the toddler with a small serving

d. allow the toddler to choose from the options according to his or her desire

Take the full quiz on CourseMate.

16-3 The Challenges of Feeding Preschoolers and School-Age Children

As children mature, they also become more willing to eat. However, some preschoolers will have even firmer ideas of the foods they do or do not like. During active growth periods, the child's appetite and food acceptance are usually quite good. However, as growth slows, so does the child's appetite. It is during this latter stage that parents and teachers may become unduly concerned. (This concern may have the consequence of establishing a food-emotion link that can lead to feeding problems and eating disorders.) In most cases, there is no real cause for concern; growing, energetic children will usually eat when they are hungry. Remember that during this age, food should be offered frequently. If the child does not finish lunch, a nutrient dense midafternoon snack can make up for nutrients that may be lacking.

Children's attitudes about food and eating patterns are formed during the preschool years and often carried over into adulthood. For this reason, it is important that teachers and families work together to help children develop healthful eating practices and positive feelings about food. Rules regarding acceptable eating behaviors should provide constructive guidance and be enforced consistently. However, they should also allow some flexibility for both the adult and child in order to avoid a power struggle during mealtimes.

▼ Creating a comfortable eating environment encourages children's independence and ability to feed themselves.

© Cengage Learning

16-3a Guidelines for Feeding the Preschooler

As with toddlers, the MyPlate model provides a simple guide for feeding preschoolers. Foods are needed from all of the food groups, but the amounts required are somewhat larger (Figure 16–3). Appropriate serving sizes for preschoolers are:

> 1/2 to 3/4 cup milk
> 1/2 to 1 slice of bread
> 1 tablespoon for each year of age for:
> > fruits (approximately 1/4 cup)
> > vegetables (approximately 1/4 cup)
> > meat or meat alternative (approximately 1 1/2 ounces)

The appearance and other sensory qualities of foods still influence the 3- to 5-year-olds' willingness to eat. Foods presented in colorful combinations, shapes, and textures are attractive and inviting. Preschool-age children also prefer their foods served lukewarm, and are likely to reject or play with items that are too hot or too cold until they reach an acceptable temperature. Serving slightly smaller food portions prevents children from feeling visually overwhelmed and provides them with an opportunity to ask for more. Involving children in meal preparation is also an effective strategy for improving their interest in trying a new food or meal they have helped to make.

Creating a comfortable mealtime environment continues to be important for preschool-age children. Appropriately sized furniture, dishes, and silverware encourage independence. Although many 3- to 5-year-olds still have difficulty managing eating utensils skillfully, they are becoming increasingly adept with continued practice. For example, younger children may find it easier to handle a plastic knife when initially learning how to spread and cut their bread. Including a few finger foods in meals and ignoring unintentional messes also promotes a positive eating experience.

16-3b Nutrient Needs of School-Aged Children

Although energy expenditures and growth rates are highly variable from child to child, the need for a well-balanced diet continues to be critical for school-aged children. For the most part, they

FIGURE 16–3   Sample menu with serving sizes for preschool-age children.

BREAKFAST	LUNCH	DINNER
Low-fat milk (3/4 cup)	Low-fat milk (3/4 cup)	Low-fat milk (3/4 cup)
Pancake (1)	Beef patty (1 1/2 oz)	Diced chicken (1 1/2 oz)
or	Broccoli (1/4 cup)	Cooked carrots (1/4 cup)
Whole wheat toast (1/2 slice)	Diced watermelon (1/4 cup)	Diced plums (1/4 cup)
Fruit preserves (1 tsp)	Whole-wheat bread (1/2 slice)	Brown rice (1/4 cup)
Diced peaches (1/2 cup)	Margarine (1 tsp)	Margarine (1 tsp)
MIDMORNING SNACK	**MIDAFTERNOON SNACK**	**EVENING SNACK**
Vanilla wafers (3)	Cheese cube (1 1/2 oz)	Applesauce (1/2 cup)
Orange juice (1/2 cup)	Whole wheat crackers (2)	Graham crackers (2)
	Water	Water

are eager eaters and open to trying new foods. Peers and social groups outside of the child's family, including school and television, begin to compete with long-standing family eating patterns and food preferences. However, families still play an important role in terms of their expectations, the foods they provide at home, and the importance they place on eating meals together.

School-aged children are able to consume considerably more food at a sitting and, thus, require fewer in-between-meal snacks than when they were younger. Although many children receive a portion of their daily nutrients from meals eaten at school, they are usually eager for, and need, a substantial after-school snack. Having access to a supply of healthy fruits, vegetables, low-fat dairy products, and whole grain foods allows children to independently select and prepare nutritious snacks that also reinforce healthy eating habits. Appropriate serving sizes for school-aged children are:

1 cup milk (2 percent)
1 slice bread or 3/4 cup dry cereal
1/2 to 3/4 cup fruits/vegetables
1 ounce meat or meat alternative (snack); 2 ounces (meals)

The MyPlate guide serves as an effective tool for ensuring that children's meals and snacks include all essential nutrients.

16-3c Feeding Children with Special Needs

Children who have developmental disabilities or special health conditions may present a range of unique nutritional needs and feeding challenges. Impaired motor abilities may make self-feeding and/or swallowing difficult. Medications, such as antibiotics and those taken for seizure disorders can increase a child's need for certain nutrients or interfere with a child's appetite. Some genetic conditions, such as **Down syndrome** and **Prader-Willi syndrome**, increase the tendency for obesity and, thus, make it necessary to carefully monitor children's food intake. Other children may have difficulty recognizing and communicating when they are hungry or have had enough to eat. Children who experience autism spectrum disorders often restrict their food intake to a select few items and may require considerable coaxing before they will even take a few bites (Rogers, Magill-Evans, & Rempel, 2012). Food intolerances and allergies to foods containing wheat, dairy, or gluten, for example, can make it challenging to meet children's essential nutrient requirements.

Because nutrition is essential to healthy development and well-being, teachers must pay careful attention to identifying and addressing each child's unique nutrient needs. Maintaining close communication ties with families can help teachers learn more specifically about a child's condition and how it may affect eating ability and nutrient requirements. Families should also be encouraged to keep teachers informed of changes in children's medical condition and treatments that might affect eating behavior. Teachers can be instrumental in monitoring children's growth and overall health by checking their height and weight periodically. They can also consult with hospital dietitians and public health nurses for advice or assistance with children's feeding problems.

▼ **Children must always wash their hands before and after eating.**

© Cengage Learning

- -

Down syndrome – *a genetic disorder that is characterized by unique facial features, intellectual disabilities, and motor delays.*
Prader-Willi syndrome – *a chromosomal disorder that causes learning and behavior problems, poor muscle tone, short height, and overeating that can lead to obesity.*

Did You Get It?

Because the temperature of food is an important factor in enticing young children to eat, you should consider serving food _____, as most children appear to prefer food at that temperature.

a. extremely hot
b. lukewarm
c. hot
d. cold

Take the full quiz on CourseMate.

16-4 Healthy Eating Habits

Children between the ages of 1 and 5 years are in the process of establishing lifelong eating patterns. This makes the feeding of toddlers and young children an especially important responsibility. Steps that families and teachers can take to promote children's healthy eating habits include:

▶ serving a variety of nutritious foods
▶ eating with the children and modeling an enjoyment of a variety of nutritious foods

One of the most important goals in helping children develop healthy eating habits is to expose them to an increasing number and variety of foods from each food group. It is especially important to cultivate their interest in the fruit and vegetable groups because these foods are the primary source of many vitamins and minerals. Children should also experience familiar foods prepared in a variety of different ways in order to broaden their eating experiences.

Toddlers and preschoolers have a strong preference for sweet foods and a dislike for most vegetables. Knowing this, parents and teachers can downplay sweets in children's diets while increasing their exposure to fruits and vegetables. One way to approach this challenge might be to involve children in planting vegetables in containers or a small classroom garden, harvesting the mature produce, and then helping to prepare the vegetables for a meal. Teachers can also set an example by eating a variety of vegetables in front of the children, commenting on how delicious they are, and indicating pleasure (such as smiling). This power of suggestion can have a contagious effect on children's willingness to at least try a few bites. Teacher Checklist 16-2 provides additional suggestions for introducing children to new or unfamiliar foods.

> ✓✓ **TEACHER CHECKLIST 16-2**
>
> **Introducing New or Unfamiliar Foods**
>
> 1. Introduce only one new food at a time.
> 2. Serve the new food along with other familiar foods.
> 3. Serve only small portions of the new food—begin with one bite or teaspoonful.
> 4. Introduce new foods when the child is hungry.
> 5. Allow the child time to examine an unfamiliar food in her own curious way.
> 6. Talk about the new food: its taste, color, texture, where it comes from.
> 7. Involve the child in grocery shopping and preparing the new food item.
> 8. Encourage the child to taste the new food. If rejected, accept the refusal and try again on another occasion. As foods become more familiar, they are also more readily accepted.
> 9. Determine what is not liked about a rejected food. Perhaps preparing it in a different manner will improve its appeal.
> 10. Let the child observe you eating and enjoying the new food!

TeachSource Digital Download   Download from CourseMate.

Children in group settings often begin to imitate the eating behaviors of their teachers and peers. For this reason, it is particularly important that adults sit and eat with the children at mealtime, engage in pleasant social conversation, taste a variety of foods, and avoid displaying a dislike for any food. Children are quick to pick up and copy negative reactions to foods.

Older children enjoy being involved in meal planning and preparation. For example, children in an after-school program might develop the weekly snack menu from a teacher-provided list of healthy foods rich in vitamins, minerals, and fiber. School-age children can also be assigned specific food preparation roles and trusted to perform them with skill and confidence. Not only does this acknowledgement appeal to the child's sense of responsibility, but it also fosters positive self-esteem. Involving school-aged children in food-related activities provides multiple opportunities to learn about foods and to reinforce healthy eating and physical activity habits. This is important because school-aged children are especially vulnerable to conflicting messages about body image and weight control. Their involvement with food contributes to a better understanding of the important connections between eating behaviors and well-being.

Rewards should not be offered to children for trying a new food, nor should food be used to reinforce any other form of desired behavior. Adults are often tempted to use food (especially dessert or popular sweet snacks) as an incentive to get children to eat the nutritious portion of a meal. This practice causes desserts to assume undue importance for the child and is unlikely to result in any long-term acceptance of unfamiliar or disliked foods. Appropriate desserts, such as fresh fruits or fruit-based dishes, should be nutritious (nutrient dense) and planned as a basic part of the meal. For example, a zucchini or carrot bar or slice of pumpkin bread may disguise vegetables that a child might otherwise refuse. Also, a child should never be asked to present a "clean plate" before receiving their dessert. This is one sure way to start the child on a road to obesity or eating disorders (Zhang & McIntosh, 2011).

Gardening helps children to learn about where food originates and improves their interest in trying vegetables they have grown.

© Cengage Learning

Did You Get It?

What is not one of the recommended practices to encourage children to try and even begin to like healthy fruits and vegetables?

a. modeling the eating and enjoyment of these foods
b. planting and cultivating a garden with these foods
c. explaining why fruits and vegetables are so vitally important
d. involving children in the preparation and cooking of these foods

Take the full quiz on CourseMate.

16-5 Health Problems Related to Eating Patterns

Teaching children healthful eating practices can have lifelong positive outcomes. A number of health conditions are now thought to be directly or indirectly related to dietary patterns, including:

- **dental caries** (tooth decay)
- obesity (excess body fat)
- **hypertension** (high blood pressure)
- cardiovascular disease (CVD)
- diabetes mellitus

16-5a Dental Caries

Dietary sugars are known to increase the occurrence of dental caries. However, several factors determine sugar's decay-causing potential, including the form (solid, in solution, sticky), frequency of consumption, and when it is eaten (meals versus snacks) more than does total sugar intake. Sugar obtained from fresh fruits and vegetables may actually offer some protection from tooth decay while also supplying essential nutrients for the actively growing child (Hess et al., 2012).

16-5b Obesity

The prevention of obesity begins with infant feeding. The infant's signals of **satiety** should be noted and feeding stopped when they occur. (See Table 15–4.) Toddlers and preschoolers will usually signal or stop eating when they have had enough food, unless eating or not eating is their best way to gain attention. Forcing children to continue eating interferes with their ability to recognize when they are full and can contribute to excessive weight gain and obesity. However, many children are also consuming more calories than are needed. Increased portion sizes have made it difficult for them to recognize what is actually an appropriate serving (Friedman et al., 2012) (Figure 16–4).

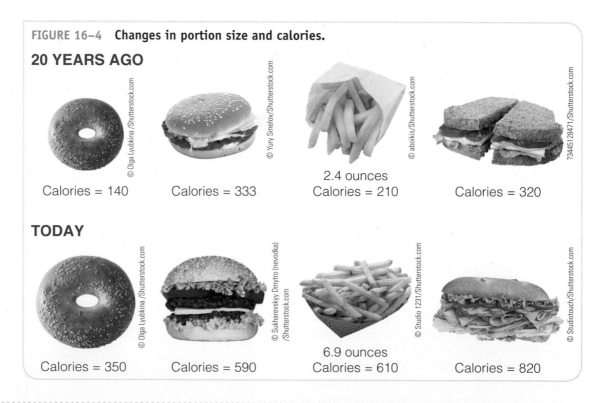

FIGURE 16–4   Changes in portion size and calories.

20 YEARS AGO

Calories = 140   Calories = 333   2.4 ounces
Calories = 210   Calories = 320

TODAY

Calories = 350   Calories = 590   6.9 ounces
Calories = 610   Calories = 820

---

dental caries – *tooth decay.*
hypertension – *elevation of blood pressure above the normally accepted values.*
satiety – *a feeling of satisfaction or fullness*

Approximately 33 percent of U.S. children are overweight or obese, an incidence that has nearly tripled over the past 20 years (AHA, 2012). Although a slight genetic potential for obesity exists in some families, this does not mean that all family members will become obese. Thus, serving children nutritious foods, teaching them to make wise choices, involving them in physical activity, and limiting their sedentary activities, such as television viewing and computer or video games, is critical for maintaining normal body weight and reducing the risk of childhood obesity (Lent et al., 2012; Skouteris et al., 2012) (Figure 16–5).

16-5c Hypertension

For many years hypertension (high blood pressure) has been correlated with a high intake of dietary sodium (salt). Children who have a family history of hypertension are at greater risk for developing the condition and may benefit from reducing their salt intake (Frisoli et al., 2012). Although sodium is an essential nutrient for infants and young children, their needs can easily be met without the use of a salt shaker. Many convenience, processed, and fast foods are high in sodium and should be avoided by individuals who may be genetically predisposed to hypertension. The amount of salt added to foods prepared at home or school can easily be controlled and often reduced without affecting the flavor outcome.

Did You Know...
the average child consumes the equivalent of 3,387 mg of salt per day? This is approximately 1,300 mg more than recommended.

FIGURE 16–5   **Physical activity for children.**

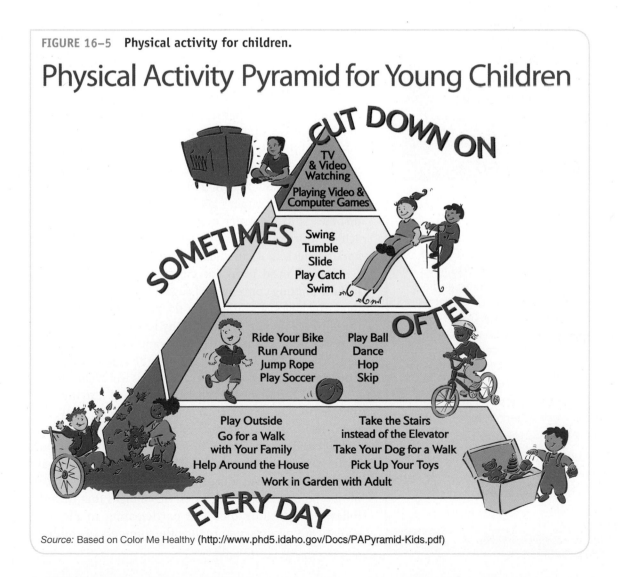

Physical Activity Pyramid for Young Children

CUT DOWN ON

TV & Video Watching
Playing Video & Computer Games

SOMETIMES

Swing
Tumble
Slide
Play Catch
Swim

OFTEN

Ride Your Bike
Run Around
Jump Rope
Play Soccer

Play Ball
Dance
Hop
Skip

Play Outside
Go for a Walk with Your Family
Help Around the House

Take the Stairs instead of the Elevator
Take Your Dog for a Walk
Pick Up Your Toys

Work in Garden with Adult

EVERY DAY

Source: Based on Color Me Healthy (http://www.phd5.idaho.gov/Docs/PAPyramid-Kids.pdf)

16-5d Cardiovascular Disease

Cardiovascular disease (CVD) is most often associated with high levels of certain fatty substances in the blood. Although cholesterol is frequently cited as the culprit, the true causative agents of CVD are high intakes of dietary fat and saturated fatty acids. Over 60 percent of overweight children ages 5 to 10 already have at least one risk factor for heart disease that can be attributed to a high fat diet (Halfon, Verhoef, & Kuo, 2012).

The testing and monitoring of young children's blood cholesterol levels remain controversial. The American Academy of Pediatrics has endorsed new recommendations issued by the National Heart, Lung, & Blood Institutes that all children be tested between 9 and 11 years of age and again when they reach 17 to 21 years (AAP, 2011). Some health professionals argue that this results in over-testing and contributes to increased health care costs. What all experts do agree upon is to lower dietary fat (e.g., cholesterol, saturated, trans-fats) and sodium intakes while increasing children's physical activity.

A child who has high blood cholesterol levels should have his diet monitored closely to include no more than 30 percent of calories from fat and 10 percent or less calories from saturated fat. However, dietary fats, including cholesterol, should not be restricted before the age of 2 (unless medically prescribed) because they provide essential fatty acids necessary for normal neurological development. Any adjustments made in a child's diet must ensure that all nutrient requirements for normal growth and development are being met. In many cases, increasing the child's physical activity level is sufficient to lower blood cholesterol.

▶❚❚ **TeachSource** Video Connections

Video supplied by the BBC Motion Gallery

Technology and Media Use by Children and Adolescents

Today's children are growing up surrounded by an array of advanced electronic and media devices. These items provide children with opportunities for socialization, entertainment, and learning and are considered commonplace and essential. However, experts are concerned that excessive use of these devices is having negative effects on children's health. As you watch the learning video, *Technology and Media Use by Children and Adolescents,* consider the following questions:

1. What negative outcomes are often attributed to children's extensive use of technology?

2. Why do you think these outcomes occur?

3. What types of foods are children most likely to consume while watching television or a video?

4. How can parents help children use their time and technology wisely?

Watch on CourseMate.

16-5e Diabetes

Although type 1 diabetes is most commonly diagnosed in children and adolescents, it is not caused by the quality of a child's diet. However, the disease does have a profound effect on a child's eating pattern and growth (Hockenberry & Wilson, 2012). There is no one "diabetic diet." The primary goal in feeding a child who has diabetes is to meet her essential nutrient needs and to achieve normal blood sugar levels by maintaining a balance between food, medication (insulin), and activity.

Typical meal plans for children who have diabetes include limiting concentrated sugars, planning meals with food exchanges, and matching the amount of medication (insulin) administered with activity levels and the amount of carbohydrates consumed in meals and snacks. It is important that children who have diabetes be able to eat foods similar to their peers so they don't always feel excluded.

Type 2 diabetes typically develops during the middle- to later years and in overweight adults. However, there has been a dramatic increase in the number of young children with type 2 diabetes in recent years due to the epidemic of childhood obesity. Approximately half of all children newly diagnosed with diabetes each year have type 2 (CDC, 2012). Lifestyle changes that include following a healthy diet and participating in physical activity are necessary to reduce the numbers of children at risk for this chronic disease.

16-5f Common Feeding Behaviors and Concerns

Consuming Excessive Milk Children who drink milk to the exclusion of other foods may be at risk for iron-deficiency anemia and vitamin C (ascorbic acid) deficiency because it is a poor source of both nutrients. Children who consume more than 16 to 24 ounces of milk daily may have difficulty eating enough food from other food groups to adequately meet their nutrient needs. Water offered between meals and when additional milk is requested can help to satisfy children's thirst and discourage excess dairy consumption. Special attention should also be paid to including iron-rich foods in daily meals to protect children from developing iron-deficiency anemia. Examples of foods high in iron are presented in Chapter 17 (Table 17–1).

Refusal to Eat and Selective Eating Toddlers and preschoolers occasionally refuse food either because they are overly tired, asserting their newly found independence, or simply not hungry. If health problems do not explain a child's short-term disinterest in food, it may be best to ignore the behavior. Remember that most active, growing children will soon become hungry and decide to eat. If nutritious food is provided for meals and snacks and if adults do not give in to children's requests for unhealthy food substitutions, hunger will eventually win over the challenge of refusal. However, it is also important that adults do not "try too hard" or attempt to coax or pressure children to eat because this can lead to unpleasant power struggles. In most cases, children will gradually grow out of this stage when adults refrain from nagging or pressuring them to eat.

Children who have autism spectrum disorders often exhibit a significant aversion to foods and are especially sensitive to their textures. Prolonged food refusal or selectivity may require professional behavioral intervention, close monitoring of children's nutrient intake, and nutrient supplementation (Sira & Fryling, 2012).

Dawdling and Messiness These are the trademarks of young children and cannot be avoided, although they can be controlled. Children dawdle for various reasons—they have eaten enough, they'd rather eat something else, or they have learned that it gets attention. Establishing and consistently enforcing mealtime rules will usually end dawdling behaviors. The teacher should decide upon an appropriate length of time for eating (approximately 20–25 minutes), warn the child when there is not much time remaining, and then remove the child from the table when time is up. This may result in some temporary unhappiness, but children quickly learn to eat when given the opportunity. However, it is important to avoid hurrying them at mealtimes and to allow children sufficient time to finish their food.

Although children need to learn to feed themselves and to manage eating utensils, they may find some foods especially challenging. This learning process can result in understandable and forgivable messiness that should be overlooked. However, some children intentionally create messes to gain adult attention. In these cases, the child's behavior should be ignored to avoid reinforcing or encouraging it from being repeated. Removing the child from the table can also be an effective way to extinguish undesirable behavior.

Food Jags Food jags are temporary phases during which children are willing to eat only a limited number of their favorite foods. These periods are not an uncommon occurrence among preschool-aged children and may simply reflect transitions in their tastes and interest in food. However, prolonged refusal of foods from all food groups can eventually result in nutrient deficiencies and the development of unhealthy eating habits. In most instances, adult patience and a few preventive measures offer the best approach.

Meals and snacks served to young children should always include a variety of choices from all food groups. Serving the same few favorite foods over and over strengthens children's preference for these items and narrows the range of foods they are willing to eat. Involving children in food preparation can also be an effective strategy for helping children to overcome food jags. Fortunately, most children soon tire of a limited food selection and will resume their normal eating pattern.

Inconsistent Adult Approaches to Feeding Problems This concern relates to several behavioral challenges that have previously been discussed. It is important that families and teachers

CONNECTING TO EVERYDAY PRACTICE

"Surfing the Web" for Information

The Internet has become a primary source of health and nutrition information for many consumers. Many of us have "surfed the Web" at one time or another to learn more about a particular condition, dietary recommendation, or research finding that was recently reported in the news. Public awareness and interest in wellness topics has significantly increased as a result of having online access to health and nutrition websites. However, limited regulation and oversight of information posted on many websites has concerned health care professionals (Boyer, 2013; Mager, 2012).

Think About This:

▶ How can you determine if the information provided is accurate and trustworthy?

▶ What are your thoughts about allowing commercial advertising on these websites?

▶ What nutrition and medical information websites would you recommend to friends, children's families, or visit for your own personal use?

communicate and agree on a consistent approach to handling children's food-related problems. It doesn't matter if the problem is weaning from excessive milk intake, decreasing dawdling behaviors, confronting eating refusals, or dealing with food jags. What is essential is that any interventions designed to address the child's problematic behaviors must be enforced consistently by teachers and the family. Children cannot be expected to learn acceptable behavior if the rules vary from setting to setting.

Did You Know...

that fast food restaurants serve more than 50 million Americans every day? Children who consume fast food meals several times a week drink less milk, eat fewer fruits and vegetables, take in more calories, and have a higher BMI.

Food Additives and Hyperactivity The Feingold diet, initially published in 1973, proclaimed a link between sugar, food additives, and children's hyperactivity (ADHD). However, several subsequent double-blind studies have failed to demonstrate any relationship. Recent studies have suggested that a small number of children may experience allergic-type responses to some additives, which could explain their behavior (Turner & Kemp, 2012). For these children, eliminating the offending agent from their diet did result in improvement. Sugar has also been thought to cause hyperactivity, but this association remains unfounded. Restricting a child's sugar intake has not been shown to improve behavior or learning. Actually, a biochemical case can be made for sugar as a calming and sleep-inducing agent. There is no harm in eliminating sugar and food additives, including artificial dyes, from children's diet as long as nutritious foods from all food groups are provided.

Fast-Food Consumption The current cultural pattern of two-working-parents and single-parent families has led to significant changes in eating practices. More meals are eaten outside of the home today, especially in fast-food restaurants, than in previous decades. Families have also become more reliant on convenience and processed foods from local grocery stores for meals. These collective changes have raised serious public health concerns about children's food intake, especially of fast foods, and their long-term effects on health (Saelens et al., 2012). Most fast foods are high in calories, cholesterol, fat, and salt, which over time can contribute to serious health problems such as cardiovascular disease, hypertension, diabetes, and obesity. Fast foods also tend to be low in fiber, vitamins A and C, and calcium (unless milk is the selected beverage). A too-frequent scenario is a mother and young child at a fast-food restaurant. The mother shares a few bites of her hamburger with the child, whose meal is rounded out with French fries and a small cola. An occasional fast-food meal for children is not problematic if care is taken to make up for any nutrient deficiencies by selecting healthy options and serving nutritious foods at other times in the day.

Commercial Advertising Television commercials and other media advertising formats exert a strong influence on children's ideas about food. It is estimated that a child is exposed to approximately 3 hours of commercial advertising per week and 20,000 to 30,000 commercials each year (Harrison & Liechty, 2012). More than half of these involve food, particularly sweetened cereals, cookies, candy, sugary beverages, and fast-food offerings (Andreyeva, Kelly, & Harris, 2011). Most advertised foods are high in sugar and/or fat and are too calorie-dense to be healthful choices for young children. An additional concern is the extent to which children's food preferences are being shaped by television food commercials and, in turn, influence adult food purchases.

Young children consider television to be reality and do not understand the persuasive nature of commercial advertising (Graff, Kunkel, & Mermin, 2012). For these reasons, it is important that adults talk with children about the purpose of commercial messaging, limit their television viewing time, and encourage more active play to address childhood obesity.

Did You Get It?

The genetic potential for obesity in families is:
- **a.** about equal to that of environmental factors
- **b.** great
- **c.** the single biggest cause of obesity
- **d.** slight

Take the full quiz on CourseMate.

PARTNERING with FAMILIES

Feeding Toddlers and Young Children

Dear Families,

Mealtimes should be pleasant, social opportunities when family members can spend time together and build positive connections. Having a child who is a "picky" or selective eater can be disruptive and cause considerable turmoil during an otherwise enjoyable mealtime experience. It is important never to force or bribe children to eat. This will only cause them to be even more resistant. Instead, show patience, encourage children to participate in food preparations, and mealtimes will gradually become pleasant eating experiences again.

- Let children help with menu planning. Take them along to the grocery store and give them a list with several items to find or have them help you pick out fresh fruits and vegetables. Challenge them to find a new (nutritious) food item for the family to try.

- Get children involved in preparing foods. Have them assist with mixing, washing and peeling vegetables, and setting the table.

- Serve foods that a child dislikes along with a favorite or familiar food.

- Prepare foods in different ways to add fun and interest to meals. For example, try freezing fresh fruits and serving them frozen, incorporate a new vegetable into muffins or cookie bars, or make a tropical fruit salsa to top off grilled fish or a veggie burger.

- Do not give up on a food item if your child does not accept it the first time. It may take ten to fifteen exposures to an unfamiliar food before the child is willing to eat it.

- Serve meals and snacks at scheduled times. Children are more likely to eat if there is adequate time planned between their meals and snacks.

- Avoid sharing and passing your own food dislikes on to your children.

- Engage children in family conversations during mealtimes. You are letting children know they are valued family members when you listen and show interest in what they have to say.

- Finally, most children will get the nutrients they need, even if only small amounts of food are consumed. Continue to offer a wide variety of colorful foods and make mealtime a positive, pleasant family experience.

CLASSROOM CORNER
Teacher Activities

Tasting Pears . . .

(PreK–2; NHES National Health Education Standards, 1.2.1, 1.2.2)

Concept: The same food can have different tastes and textures.

Learning Objectives

▶ Children will learn that pears come in a variety of tastes.

▶ Children will experience tasting three kinds of pears.

Supplies

▶ Two Anjou pears, two Bosc pears, two Bartlett pears, hand wipes, small plates, napkins

Learning Activities

▶ Read and discuss the following book:
  • *Too Many Pears!* by Jackie French
  • *Orange Pear Apple Bear* by Emily Gravett

▶ Tell children there are different varieties of pears. Talk about the importance of eating fruit each day (fiber, vitamins).

▶ Have children wash their hands with wipes and then pass around each pear for children to feel and look at the differences and similarities. Have children describe each pear's color, texture, and shape and talk about differences.

▶ Next, hand a napkin and a plate to each child. Place a small bite of each pear on a plate for children to taste; this can be done one at a time or the plate can have a sample of each pear on it.

▶ Give children an opportunity to taste each pear and talk about how each one tastes. Talk about the different tastes and textures.

▶ Repeat the activity using variations of other foods, such as vegetables, eggs, or grains.

Evaluation

▶ Children will state why pears are a healthy food choice.

▶ Children will taste a sample of each type of pear.

Additional lesson plans for grades 3–5 are available on CourseMate.

◖ Summary

▶ Children's growth rate begins to slow soon after their first birthday and contributes to a decreased interest in food. Children also begin to experience many behavioral changes as they transition from toddlers to preschoolers and on to the school-age years that directly influence their nutrient needs and eating patterns.

◗ Mealtimes with toddlers can be challenging. To minimize potential friction, adults are responsible for: (a) serving a variety of nutritious foods, (b) deciding when to offer food, and (c) setting a positive example by eating a variety of nutritious foods.

◗ Children are responsible for deciding: (a) what to eat and (b) how much to eat.

◗ It is important that children's meals include a range of nutritious foods from all food groups because lifetime food patterns are being formed during the toddler, preschool, and school-age years.

◗ Adults play an important role in shaping children's eating behaviors by planning and providing meals that include a variety of foods and serving as positive role models.

◗ Consuming a nutritious diet can minimize children's risk of developing food-related health problems, including dental caries, obesity, hypertension, heart disease, and diabetes.

◗ Terms to Know

neophobic *p. 406*   Prader-Willi syndrome *p. 413*   hypertension *p. 416*
Down syndrome *p. 413*   dental caries *p. 416*   satiety *p. 416*

◗ Chapter Review

A. By Yourself:

1. Name three ways to make mealtimes comfortable and pleasant for children.

2. Explain the teacher's major responsibilities in toddler feeding situations.

3. Suggest approximate serving sizes for a 2-year-old and a 4-year-old for each of the following foods: bread, peas, applesauce, orange juice, banana, cooked chicken, noodles, baked beans.

B. As a Group:

1. Watch 1 hour of Saturday morning cartoons on television and discuss the following:

   a. What foods were presented in the majority of commercials?

   b. What adjectives did the announcer use to describe the foods being advertised?

   c. What other media effects were used to capture and maintain children's interest?

   d. Imagine that you are a 4-year-old. On your next trip to the grocery store with your mother, what products would you want her to buy? Why?

2. Visit a fast-food restaurant that features hamburgers and observe the following:

   a. How many toddlers and preschoolers are present?

   b. What foods are the children eating and drinking?

   c. What foods might have been ordered from the menu to provide a more nutritious or healthier meal?

   d. Ask the restaurant for nutritional information or visit its website. Are you surprised by any of the calorie and nutrient values?

3. Visit a local supermarket and observe the advertising techniques used to draw children's attention to certain foods and products.

   a. What cereals are shelved at a child's eye level? Describe features on the boxes that are used to capture children's attention.

   b. What types of foods are displayed at the end of aisles?

   c. What food items are typically displayed at the checkout counter?

   d. What types of free food samples are being offered that would appeal to young children? What is the intended purpose of these promotions?

Case Study

Maria, age 7 years, is new to the community and has recently enrolled in your after-school program. She and her parents speak Portuguese, but very little English. The other children are intrigued with Maria and her "different" language. They eagerly attempt to teach her some English words by pointing to and repeating the names of foods and objects with exaggerated clarity. Although Maria seems to enjoy their attention and is responding to their efforts, you (teacher) are concerned that she still eats very little during snack time.

1. Why should you be concerned that Maria is not eating?

2. What steps can you take to learn more about her family's food preferences?

3. Where might you access information about foods and food preferences native to Maria's culture?

4. Where might you access materials to aid in Maria's care and your ability to communicate with her family?

5. Where might you locate an interpreter for assistance?

Application Activities

1. Jason, 18 months old, has recently been enrolled in an all-day early childhood program. His health assessment reveals that he is anemic. Observations of his eating habits suggest that he dislikes meat and vegetables but eats large quantities of fruits and drinks at least two cups of milk at every meal and snack. What changes in eating habits should the teacher try to foster to improve Jason's iron status?

2. Formulate plans for the dining area of an early childhood program that will promote children's self-feeding skills. Include a discussion of appropriate furniture and eating utensils. Plan a 1-day menu (one meal and two snacks) that will further enhance children's self-feeding efforts.

3. Flore, 4 years old, arrives at her family child-care provider's home every morning with a bag of doughnuts. Her mother informs the provider that it is okay for Flore to eat the doughnuts because she doesn't like what is being served for breakfast. The other children have also begun to ask for doughnuts. How should the provider handle this situation? What factors must be considered?

4. Prepare a 5-day snack menu for toddlers, preschoolers, and school-age children that features nutrient-dense foods.

Helpful Web Resources

American Diabetes Association	http://www.diabetes.org
American Heart Association (childhood obesity)	http://www.americanheart.org
Council for Exceptional Children	http://www.cec.sped.org
Food Allergy & Anaphylaxis Network	http://www.foodallergy.org

 Visit the Education CourseMate for this textbook to access the eBook, Did You Get It? quizzes, Digital Downloads, TeachSource Video Cases, flashcards, and more. Go to CengageBrain.com to log in, register, or purchase access.

References

American Academy of Pediatrics (AAP). (2011). Physicians recommend all children, ages 9–11, be screened for cholesterol. Accessed on August 27, 2012 from http://www.aap.org/en-us/about-the-aap/aap-press-room/pages/Physicians-Recommend-all-Children,-Ages-9-11,-Be-Screened-for-Cholesterol.aspx.

American Heart Association (AHA). (2013). Overweight in children. Accessed on May 8, 2013 from http://www.heart.org/HEARTORG/GettingHealthy/Overweight-in-Children_UCM_304054_Article.jsp.

Anderson, S., Must, A., Curtin, C., & Bandini, L. (2012). Meals in our household: Reliability and initial validation of a questionnaire to assess child mealtime behaviors and family mealtime environments, *Journal of the Academy of Nutrition & Dietetics*, 112(2), 276–284.

Andreyeva, T., Kelly, I., & Harris, J. (2011). Exposure to food advertising on television: Associations with children's fast food and soft drink consumption and obesity, *Economics & Human Biology*, 9(3), 221–233.

Boyer, C. (2013). The Internet and health: International approaches to evaluating the quality of web-based health information. In, G. Carlisle, P. Duquenoy, & D. Whitehouse (Eds.), *eHealth: Legal, Ethical and Governance Challenges*, Part 3, 245–274.

CDC. (2012). Children and diabetes. Accessed on August 26, 2012 from http://www.cdc.gov/diabetes/projects/cda2.htm.

Friedman, A., Bennett, T., Barbarich, B., Keaschuk, R., & Ball, G. (2012). Food portion estimation by children with obesity: The effects of estimation method and food type, *Journal of the Academy of Nutrition & Dietetics*, 112(2), 302–307.

Frisoli, T., Schmieder, R., Grodzicki, T., & Messerli, F. (2012). Salt and hypertension: Is salt dietary reduction worth the effort?, *Acta Pharmacologica Sinica*, 33, 189–193.

Graff, S., Kunkel, D., & Mermin, S. (2012). Government can regulate food advertising to children because cognitive research shows that it is inherently misleading, *Health Affairs*, 31(2), 392–398.

Halfon, N., Verhoef, P., & Kuo, A. (2012). Childhood antecedents to adult cardiovascular disease, *Pediatrics in Review*, 33(2), 51–51.

Harris, J., Speers, S., Schwartz, M., & Brownell, K. (2012). US food company branded advergames on the Internet: Children's exposure and effects on snack consumption, *Journal of Children & Media*, 6(1), 51–68.

Harrison, K., & Liechty, J. (2012). US preschoolers' media exposure and dietary habits: The primacy of television and the limits of parental mediation, *Journal of Children & Media*, 6(1), 18–36.

Hess, J., Latulippe, M., Ayoob, K., & Slavin, J. (2012). The confusing world of dietary sugars: Definitions, intakes, food sources and international dietary recommendations, *Food & Function*, 3, 477–486.

Hockenberry, M., & Wilson, D. (2012). *Wong's essentials of pediatric nursing*. (9th ed.). St Louis: Mosby.

Lent, M., Hill, T., Dollahite, J., Wolfe, W., & Dickin, K. (2012). Healthy children, healthy families: Parents making a difference! A curriculum integrating key nutrition, physical activity, and parenting practices to help prevent childhood obesity, *Journal of Nutrition Education & Behavior*, 44(1), 90–92.

Marotz, L. R., & Allen, K. E. (2013). *Developmental profiles: Pre-birth through adolescence*. (7th ed.). Belmont, CA: Wadsworth Cengage.

Mager, A. (2012). Search engines matter: From educating users towards engaging with online health information practices, *Policy & Internet*, 4(2), 1–21.

Musher-Eizenman, D., Oehlhof, M., Hauser, J., Galliger, C., & Sommer, A. (2011). Emerald dragon bites vs. veggie beans: Fun food names increase children's consumption of novel healthy foods, *Journal of Early Childhood Research*, 9(3), 191–195.

Rogers, L., Magill-Evans, & Rempel, G. (2012). Mother's challenges in feeding their children with autism spectrum disorder—Managing more than just picky eating, *Journal of Developmental & Physical Disabilities*, 24(1), 19–33.

Saelens, B., Sallis, J., Frank, L., Couch, S., Zhou, C., Colburn, T., Cain, K., Chapman, J., & Glanz, K. (2012). Obesogenic neighborhood environments, child and parent obesity: The Neighborhood Impact on Kids study, *American Journal of Preventive Medicine*, 42(5), e57–e64.

Satter, E. (2000). *How to get your child to eat . . . But not too much*. Palo Alto, CA: Bull Publishing Co.

Sira, B., & Fryling, M. (2012). Using peer modeling and differential reinforcement in the treatment of food selectivity, *Education & Treatment of Children*, 35(1), 91–100.

Skouteris, H., McCabe, M., Ricciardelli, L., Milgrom, J., Baur, L., Aksan, N., & Aquila, D. (2012). Parent–child interactions and obesity prevention: A systematic review of the literature, *Early Child Development & Care*, 182(2), 153–174.

Tan, C., & Holub, S. (2012). Maternal feeding practices associated with food neophobia, *Appetite*, 59(2), 483–487.

Turner, P., & Kemp, A. (2012). Intolerance to food additives—Does it exist?, *Journal of Paediatrics & Child Health*, 48(2), E10–E14.

Zhang, L., & McIntosh, W. (2011). Children's weight status and maternal and paternal feeding practices, *Journal of Child Health Care*, 15(4), 389–400.

chapter 17

Planning and Serving Nutritious and Economical Meals

naeyc Standards Chapter Links

▸ **#1 a, b, and c:** Promoting child development and learning

▸ **#2 b and c:** Building family and community relationships

▸ **#3 c and d:** Observing, documenting, and assessing to support young children and families

▸ **#4 a, b, c, and d:** Using developmentally effective approaches to connect with children and families

▸ **#5 b, and c:** Using content knowledge to build meaningful curriculum

▸ **#6 b, c, and d:** Becoming a professional

▸ Field Experience

Learning Objectives

After studying this chapter, you should be able to:

LO 17-1 Describe four criteria that must be addressed when developing children's menus.

LO 17-2 Explain how weekly and cycle menus differ.

LO 17-3 Plan snacks for toddlers, preschoolers, and school-aged children that meet their nutritional requirements.

LO 17-4 Create mealtime environments that are inviting for children.

LO 17-5 Outline a simple cost control plan to keep the menu within budget.

Eating is a sensory, emotional, and social experience that provides nourishment essential for human life. It should be an enjoyable time when children begin to establish positive attitudes toward food and healthy dietary habits. Teachers have many opportunities to encourage and support children in this process by planning nutritious meals and snacks and serving them in a pleasant atmosphere.

Did You Know...
your taste buds are able to detect the fat in foods, although scientists have discovered individual sensitivity variations in this genetic trait.

17-1 Developing the Menu

A menu is a list of foods to be served and is fundamental to any food service. Menu planning requires time and a careful evaluation of the physical, developmental, and social needs of those for whom it is being developed. Thoughtful planning is necessary whether the menu is designed to feed a family of three or an institution serving one-hundred meals a day. The difference between the two situations is largely one of scale. Creating menus for children requires that detailed attention be given to:

▸ meeting children's nutritional needs
▸ addressing any existing funding or licensing requirements
▸ providing sensory appeal (taste, texture, and visual interest)
▸ making children comfortable by including familiar foods
▸ encouraging healthy food habits by introducing new foods
▸ providing safe food and serving it in clean surroundings
▸ serving nutrient-dense foods while staying within budgetary limits
▸ providing alternatives for children who have food allergies, eating problems, or special nutritional needs

▼ Menus must be planned to provide nutrients essential for children's growth and development.

© Cengage Learning

17-1a A Well-Designed Menu Meets Children's Nutritional Needs

Children's nutrient and energy needs must be given priority during the initial steps of menu planning. For schools, this means determining what portion of children's daily nutrient requirements will be provided. Early childhood programs participating in federally funded food programs for children are required to meet at least one-third of the recommended daily requirements for calcium, iron, vitamin A, and vitamin C (these are considered at-risk nutrients for children; see Tables 17–1 through 17–4); supplying one-half of children's daily nutrient requirements is preferable. Schools serving older children should also aim to meet these recommendations. The MyPlate food guide and the Child and Adult Care Food Program (CACFP) guidelines, discussed later in this chapter, are excellent tools for determining what nutrients children require, what foods supply these nutrients, and in what amounts (serving sizes) they are needed (Ritchie et al., 2012).

TABLE 17–1   Sources of Iron and Suggested Preparations

Best Sources

Beef – ground beef patty, meat loaf, roast beef, meat balls with spaghetti, stews, beef burrito
Dried Peas, Beans, and Lentils – with rice, with vegetables, in soup or salads, in a tortilla, on pitas (hummus), as soy curd (tofu)
Pumpkin and Sunflower Seeds – roasted, in salads or baked goods
Spinach – raw, in salad with bacon, cooked and tossed with parmesan cheese or hard boiled eggs
Whole or Enriched Grain Products – as tortillas, fortified ready-to-eat cereals, breads, crackers, pastas, bran or cornmeal muffins

Good Sources

Chicken – with rice, with noodles, baked, as chicken salad
Ham – baked and sliced, ham salad, ham and scalloped sweet potatoes, sandwich
Peanut Butter – on flat bread sandwiches, blended in smoothies, in cookies
Potatoes – baked, boiled in their skins
Cooked Tomatoes and Tomato Products – in soups and sauces, as juice
Raisins – in bread or rice pudding, plain, added to cereals or baked products

TABLE 17–2   Sources of Calcium and Suggested Preparations

Best Sources

Milk – plain, in custards or puddings
Cheddar Cheese – sliced in sandwiches, cubed, in cream sauce, shredded in salads
Enriched Orange Juice – as a beverage, frozen in popsicles or fruit slush
Salmon (canned) or Sardines – as patties or loaf, in salad, or plain with crackers
Soy Products (enriched) – soy milk; tofu in stir fry, smoothies, or pudding
Yogurt – plain, with fruit, as dips for fruit or vegetables, frozen, in smoothies

Good Sources

Almonds – plain, in baked products
Bok Choy (Chinese cabbage) – in stir fry, diced raw in salads, braised
Broccoli – raw as florets with yogurt dip, cooked plain or served with a light cheese sauce, in stir fry
Enriched Grain Products – as tortillas, fortified ready-to-eat cereals, breads, crackers, pastas
Oranges – raw, sections, juice

TABLE 17–3   Sources of Vitamin C and Suggested Preparations

Best Sources

Broccoli – raw as florets with yogurt dip, cooked plain or served with a light cheese sauce
Cantaloupe – sliced, cubed in mixed fruit salad
Cauliflower – raw as florets with yogurt dip or in a tossed salad, cooked plain or served with a light cheese sauce
Green, Red, or Yellow Peppers – strips, rings, or included in sauces and mixed dishes
Kiwi – sliced, in mixed fruit salads
Oranges and Grapefruit – slices or wedges, juice (added to gelatin, as a beverage, or frozen in popsicles)
Strawberries – plain, with milk, sliced in a fruit cup, in smoothies
Tomatoes – cherry tomatoes, juice, stewed, broiled, cooked and added to mixed dishes; fresh and served as slices, wedges, or in tossed salads
Watermelon – slices or chunks, added to mixed fruit salads

Good Sources

Brussels Sprouts – sliced in salads, cooked and lightly buttered
Cabbage – raw in coleslaw or tossed salads, cooked and lightly buttered

TABLE 17–4   Sources of Vitamin A and Suggested Preparations

Best Sources

Beef Liver – baked or broiled
Sweet Potatoes – baked, mashed, in breads
Carrots – cooked, raw in salad with raisins, raw in sticks, curls, or "coins"
Pumpkin – cooked and mashed, in breads or muffins, custard
Cantaloupe – balls or cubes, in mixed fruit salad

Good Sources

Apricots – sliced fresh, canned in fruit juice
Broccoli – raw as florets with yogurt dip, cooked plain or served with a light cheese sauce, in stir-fry
Mango – cubed, blended in smoothies, tossed in a salad

17-1b A Well-Designed Menu Meets Funding and/or Licensing Requirements

Several federally sponsored food assistance programs are available to schools and early childhood programs for the purpose of improving children's nutrition. Perhaps the best known of these are the Child and Adult Care Food Program (CACFP) and the National School Lunch Program (NSLP).

Child and Adult Care Food Program   The CACFP program reimburses participating early childhood centers and family child care homes for meals served to children. The three-tier meal/ snack reimbursement rate is based on family-income eligibility and compensates programs, in part, for their food, labor, and administrative expenses (Table 17–5). CACFP is administered by the Department of Education in most states with funding provided by the U.S. Department of Agriculture. Participating programs must plan and serve meals according to specific CACFP guidelines to qualify for reimbursement (Table 17–6):

1. Minimum Breakfast Requirement
   ▷ whole grain or enriched bread or grain alternate
   ▷ fruit, vegetable, or full-strength fruit or vegetable juice
   ▷ milk, fluid

TABLE 17–5 CACFP Reimbursement Rates for Centers (2012–2013)

Contiguous States	Breakfast	Lunch/dinner	Snack
Paid	0.27	0.27	0.07
Reduced price	1.25	2.46	0.39
Free	1.55	2.86	0.78
Alaska			
Paid	0.41	0.44	0.11
Reduced price	2.18	4.23	0.63
Free	2.48	4.63	1.27
Hawaii			
Paid	0.31	0.32	0.08
Reduced price	1.51	2.95	0.46
Free	1.81	3.35	0.92

Source: Child & Adult Care Food Program (CACFP).

TABLE 17–6 CACFP Meal Requirements for Children Ages 1 Through 12

Child Meal Pattern - Breakfast

Select All Three Components for a Reimbursable Meal

Food Components	Ages 1–2	Ages 3–5	Ages 6–12[1]
1 milk[2]			
fluid milk	1/2 cup	3/4 cup	1 cup
1 fruit/vegetable			
juice,[3] fruit and/or vegetable	1/4 cup	1/2 cup	1/2 cup
1 grains/bread[4]			
bread or	1/2 slice	1/2 slice	1 slice
cornbread, biscuit, roll, muffin or	1/2 serving	1/2 serving	1 serving
cold dry cereal or	1/4 cup	1/3 cup	3/4 cup
hot cooked cereal or	1/4 cup	1/4 cup	1/2 cup
pasta, noodles, or grains	1/4 cup	1/4 cup	1/2 cup

Child Meal Pattern - Lunch or Supper

Include Foods from All Four Components for a Reimbursable Meal

Food Components	Ages 1–2	Ages 3–5	Ages 6–12[1]
1 milk[2]			
fluid milk	1/2 cup	3/4 cup	1 cup
2 fruits/vegetables			
juice,[3] fruit and/or vegetable	1/4 cup	1/2 cup	3/4 cup
1 grains/bread[4]			
bread or	1/2 slice	1/2 slice	1 slice
cornbread, biscuit, roll, muffin, or	1/2 serving	1/2 serving	1 serving
cold dry cereal or	1/4 cup	1/3 cup	3/4 cup
hot cooked cereal or	1/4 cup	1/4 cup	1/2 cup
pasta, noodles, or grains	1/4 cup	1/4 cup	1/2 cup

(continued)

TABLE 17–6 CACFP Meal Requirements for Children Ages 1 Through 12 (*continued*)

1 meat/meat alternate

meat, poultry, fish, or	1 ounce	1 1/2 ounces	2 ounces
alternate protein product or	1 ounce	1 1/2 ounces	2 ounces
cheese or	1 ounce	1 1/2 ounces	2 ounces
egg or	1/2 egg	3/4 egg	1 egg
cooked dry beans, or peas, or	1/4 cup	3/8 cup	1/2 cup
peanut or other nut or seed butters or	2 Tbsp.	3 Tbsp.	4 Tbsp.
nuts and/or seeds[5] or	1/2 ounce	3/4 ounces	1 ounces
yogurt[6]	4 ounces	6 ounces	8 ounces

[1] Children age 12 and older may be served larger portions based on their greater food needs. They may not be served less than the minimum quantities listed in this column.
[2] Milk served must be low-fat (1 percent) or non-fat (skim).
[3] Fruit or vegetable juice must be full strength.
[4] Breads and grains must be made from whole-grain or enriched meal or flour. Cereal must be whole-grain or enriched or fortified.
[5] Nuts and seeds may meet only one-half of the total meat/meat alternative serving and must be combined with another meat/meat alternate to fulfill the lunch or supper requirement.
[6] Yogurt may be plain or flavored, unsweetened or sweetened.

Child Meal Pattern - Snack

Select Two of the Four Components for a Reimbursable Snack

Food Components	Ages 1–2	Ages 3–5	Ages 6–12[1]
1 milk[2]			
fluid milk	1/2 cup	1/2 cup	1 cup
1 fruit/vegetable			
juice,[3] fruit and/or vegetable	1/2 cup	1/2 cup	3/4 cup
1 grains/bread[4]			
bread or	1/2 slice	1/2 slice	1 slice
cornbread, biscuit, roll, muffin, or	1/2 serving	1/2 serving	1 serving
cold dry cereal or	1/4 cup	1/3 cup	3/4 cup
hot cooked cereal or	1/4 cup	1/4 cup	1/2 cup
pasta, noodles, or grains	1/4 cup	1/4 cup	1/2 cup
1 meat/meat alternate	1/2 ounce	1/2 ounce	1 ounce
meat, poultry, fish[5], or	1/2 ounce	1/2 ounce	1 ounce
alternate protein product or	1/2 ounce	1/2 ounce	1 ounce
cheese or	1/2 ounce	1/2 ounce	1 ounce
egg[6] or	1/2 egg	1/2 egg	1/2 egg
cooked dry beans, peas, or	1/8 cup	1/8 cup	1/4 cup
peanut or other nut or seed butters or	1 Tbsp.	1 Tbsp.	2 Tbsp.
nuts and/or seeds or	1/2 ounce	1/2 ounce	1 ounce
yogurt[7]	2 ounces	2 ounces	4 ounces

[1] Children age 12 and older may be served larger portions based on their greater food needs. They may not be served less than the minimum quantities listed in this column.
[2] Milk served must be low fat (1%) or non-fat (skim).
[3] Fruit or vegetable juice must be full strength. Juice cannot be served when milk is the only other snack component.
[4] Breads and grains must be made from whole-grain or enriched meal or flour. Cereal must be whole-grain or enriched or fortified.
[5] A serving consists of the edible portion of cooked lean meat, poultry or fish.
[6] One-half egg meets the required minimum amount (1 ounce or less) of meat alternative.
[7] Yogurt may be plain or flavored, unsweetened or sweetened.

Source: Food and Nutrition Service, United States Department of Agriculture, 2013.

2. Minimum Snack Requirement (choose two different components).
   ◗ whole grain or enriched bread, or grain product
   ◗ milk, fluid
   ◗ fruit, vegetable, or full-strength fruit or vegetable juice
   ◗ meat, meat alternate, or yogurt

3. Minimum Lunch or Supper Requirement
   ◗ meat or meat alternate
   ◗ fruits and/or vegetables (two or more different kinds)
   ◗ whole grain or enriched bread, or grain product
   ◗ milk, fluid

CACFP meal planning guidelines follow a food-based menu approach, using Nutrient Standard or Assisted Nutrient Standard Menu Planning, or adopting an alternate menu planning approach developed by a state agency or by the school food authority with state agency approval. The guidelines specify the minimum amount of each food required to qualify as a full serving. Lists of alternative foods that are creditable for reimbursement within each food group can be accessed online. An example for the Grain group is illustrated in Table 17–7. The menu planner must work within these guidelines and take great care to keep up with current information as this program undergoes frequent and sometimes sweeping changes. For example, passage of the Healthy Hunger-Free Kids Act (2010) expanded program eligibility, simplified administrative responses, and included recommendations for improved meal requirements (e.g., more fruits, vegetables and whole grain foods; lowering salt, fat, and sugar intake; making drinking water available at all times; serving low-fat milk to children over 2 years).

Early childhood programs must be licensed by their state to participate in the CACFP program. Each state establishes its own regulations that govern nutrition and food service in these programs and typically address:

1. Administration and record keeping
   ◗ sample menus and appropriate menu substitutions
   ◗ production records
   ◗ number of meals served daily

2. Food service
   ◗ specifications for kitchens and equipment
   ◗ sanitation of dishes, utensils, and equipment
   ◗ requirements for transporting food when kitchen facilities are not available
   ◗ feeding equipment required for specific age groups

3. Staffing
   ◗ requirements of person in charge of food service

4. Nutrition policies
   ◗ number of meals and snacks to be served within the current week
   ◗ posting of menus and making them available to families
   ◗ seating of adults at the table with children
   ◗ posting of food allergies in the kitchen and eating area

National School Lunch Program   The National School Lunch Act (1946) established the National School Lunch Program (NSLP) and provided permanent funding so schools could offer meals that met children's minimum nutrient requirements. The program has continued to expand over the years and currently serves approximately 32 million U.S. children every school day. Although NSLP complied with the *Dietary Guidelines for Americans,* many authorities called for major reforms in the quality of school meals to address childhood obesity and cardiovascular heart

TABLE 17–7   Acceptable Bread and Bread Alternates (serving sizes for children under 6 years)

Important Notes:

- All products must be made of whole grain or enriched flour or meal.
- Serving sizes listed below are specified for children younger than 6 years of age.
- A "*full*" serving (defined below) is required for children 6 years of age and older.
- USDA recommends that cookies, granola bars, and similar foods be served in a snack no more than twice a week. They may be used for a snack only when:
  - whole grain or enriched meal or flour is the predominant ingredient as specified on the label or according to the recipe; and
  - the total weight of a serving for children younger than 6 years of age is a minimum of 18 grams (0.6 ounces) and for children over 6 years, a minimum of 35 grams (1.2 ounces).
- To determine serving sizes for products in Group A that are made at child care centers, refer to "Cereal Products" in FNS–86, "Quantity Recipes for Child Care Centers."
- Doughnuts and sweet rolls are allowed as a bread item in breakfasts and snacks only.
- French, Vienna, Italian, and Syrian breads are commercially prepared products that often are made with unenriched flour. Check the label or manufacturer to be sure the product is made with *enriched* flour.
- The amount of bread in a serving of stuffing should weigh at least 13 grams (0.5 ounces).
- Whole grain, enriched, or fortified breakfast cereals (cold, dry, or cooked) may be served for breakfast or snack only.

Group A

When you obtain these items commercially, a *full* serving should have a minimum weight of 20 grams (0.7 ounces). The serving sizes specified below should have a minimum weight of 10 grams (0.5 ounces).

Item	Serving Size
bread sticks (hard)	2 sticks
chow mein noodles	1/4 cup
crackers (saltines and snack)	4 squares
lavosh	1/2 serving
melba toast	3 pieces
pretzels (hard)	1/2 serving
stuffing (bread)	1/2 serving

Group B

When you obtain these items commercially, a *full* serving should have a minimum weight of 25 grams (0.9 ounces). The serving sizes specified below should have a minimum weight of 13 grams (0.5 ounces).

Item	Serving Size
bagels	1/2 bagel
biscuits	1 biscuit
breads (white, rye, whole-wheat, raisin, French)	1/2 slice
buns (hamburger, hot dog)	1/2 bun
cookie-crackers (graham, animal)	2 2¼ × 2¼ squares; 10 animal crackers
egg roll/wonton wrappers	1 serving
English muffins	1/2 muffin
pita bread	1/2 round
muffins	1/2 muffin
pizza crust	1 serving
pretzels (soft)	1 pretzel
rolls and sweet rolls (unfrosted)	1/2 roll

(continued)

TABLE 17–7 Acceptable Bread and Bread Alternates *(continued)*

| taco shells (whole, pieces) | 1 shell |
| tortillas | 1/2 tortilla |

Group C

When you obtain these items commercially, a *full* serving should have a minimum weight of 31 grams (1.1 ounces). The serving sizes specified below should have a minimum weight of 16 grams (0.6 ounces).

Item	Serving Size
cookies	1/2 serving
cornbread	1 piece
croissants	1/2 croissant
pie crust (meat or meat alternative pies)	1/2 serving
popovers	1/2 popover
waffles	1/2 serving

Group D

When you obtain these items commercially, a *full* serving should have a minimum weight of 50 grams (1.8 ounces). The serving sizes specified below should have a minimum weight of 25 grams (0.9 ounces).

Item	Serving Size
doughnuts (all types)	1/2 doughnut
granola bars (plain)	1/2 serving
hush puppies	1/2 serving
muffins/quick breads (all except corn bread)	1/2 serving
sopapillas	1/2 serving
sweet roll (unfrosted)	1/2 serving
toaster pastry (unfrosted)	1/2 serving

Group E

When you obtain these items commercially, a *full* serving should have a minimum weight of 63 grams (2.2 ounces). The serving sizes specified below should have a minimum weight of 31 grams (1.1 ounces).

Item	Serving Size
cookies (with nuts, raisins, chocolate pieces, fruit purees)	1/2 serving
doughnuts (all kinds)	1/2 serving
French toast	1/2 serving
fruit grain bars/granola bars (with fruit, nuts, chocolate pieces)	1/2 serving
sweet rolls	1/2 serving
toaster pastry (frosted)	1/2 serving

Group F

When you obtain these items commercially, a *full* serving should have a minimum weight of 75 grams (2.7 ounces). The serving sizes specified below should have a minimum weight of 38 grams (1.3 ounces).

Item	Serving Size
coffee cake	1/2 serving

(continued)

TABLE 17–7   **Acceptable Bread and Bread Alternates**   *(continued)*

Group G

When you obtain these items commercially, a *full* serving should have a minimum weight of 115 grams (4 ounces). The serving sizes specified below should have a minimum weight of 58 grams (2 ounces).

Item	Serving Size
brownies	1/2 serving

Group H

When you serve these items, a *full* serving should have a minimum of 1/2 cup cooked product. The serving sizes specified below are the minimum half servings of a cooked product.

Item	Serving Size
barley	1/4 cup
breakfast cereals (cooked)	1/4 cup
bulgur or cracked wheat	1/4 cup
couscous	1/4 cup
macaroni (all shapes)	1/4 cup
masa	1/4 cup
noodles (all varieties)	1/4 cup
pasta (all shapes)	1/4 cup
ravioli (noodle only)	1/4 cup
rice (enriched white or brown)	1/4 cup

Source: Courtesy of USDA, 2012.

disease. This effort resulted in passage of the Healthy Hunger-Free Kids Act (2010), which established significant changes to be phased in over a three-year period. The law set new standards for healthier meals and increased school food program funding. In addition, it permits schools to charge meal fees more aligned with actual costs, provides training to assist schools in complying with new recommendations, and requires nutrition standards to be applied to all foods and beverages sold in schools (Table 17–8).

CONNECTING TO EVERYDAY PRACTICE

CACFP and Positive Outcomes for Children

Recent studies conclude that meals planned according to CACFP guidelines have the potential to improve children's diets and health (Neelon et al., 2012; Ritchie et al., 2012). Children attending programs that participate in the CACFP are more likely to be served meals aligned with recommendations outlined in the *Dietary Guidelines for Americans*. Programs also tend to be better informed about the importance of providing physical activity opportunities to discourage childhood obesity and promote healthy lifestyle habits.

Think About This:

▶ How can teachers translate these findings into learning experiences for children?

▶ Of what importance are the results of these studies to menu planners?

▶ What are the "take home lessons" from these studies for families and teachers?

TABLE 17–8   New National School Lunch Program Meal Standards
Nutrition Standards in the National School Lunch and School Breakfast Programs.

Meal Pattern	Breakfast Meal Pattern			Lunch Meal Pattern		
	Grades K-5[a]	Grades 6–8[a]	Grades 9–12[a]	Grades K-5	Grades 6–8	Grades 9–12
	Amount of Food[b] Per Week (Minimum Per Day)					
Fruits (cups)[c,d]	5 (1)[e]	5 (1)[e]	5 (1)[e]	2½ (½)	2½ (½)	5 (1)
Vegetables (cups)[c,d]	0	0	0	3¾ (¾)	3¾ (¾)	5 (1)
Dark green[f]	0	0	0	½	½	½
Red/Orange[f]	0	0	0	¾	¾	1¼
Beans/Peas (Legumes)[f]	0	0	0	½	½	½
Starchy[f]	0	0	0	½	½	½
Other[f,g]	0	0	0	½	½	¾
Additional Veg to Reach Total[h]	0	0	0	1	1	1½
Grains (oz eq)[i]	7–10 (1)[j]	8–10 (1)[j]	9–10 (1)[j]	8–9 (1)	8–10 (1)	10–12 (2)
Meats/Meat Alternates (oz eq)	0[k]	0[k]	0[k]	8–10 (1)	9–10 (1)	10–12 (2)
Fluid milk (cups)[l]	5 (1)	5 (1)	5 (1)	5 (1)	5 (1)	5 (1)
Other Specifications: Daily Amount Based on the Average for a 5-Day Week						
Min-max calories (kcal)[m,n,o]	350–500	400–550	450–600	550–650	600–700	750–850
Saturated fat (% of total calories[n,o]	< 10	< 10	< 10	< 10	< 10	< 10
Sodium (mg)[n,p]	≤ 430	≤ 470	≤ 500	≤ 640	≤ 710	≤ 740
Trans fat[n,o]	Nutrition label or manufacturer specifications must indicate zero grams of <u>trans</u> fat per serving.					

Source: Food and Nutrition Service, U.S. Department of Agriculture. (2013).

[a]In the SBP, the above age-grade groups are required beginning July 1, 2013 (SY 2013-14). In SY 2012–2013 only, schools may continue to use the meal pattern for grades K-12 (see § 220.23).

[b]Food items included in each food group and subgroup and amount equivalents. Minimum creditable serving is ⅛ cup.

[c]One quarter-cup of dried fruit counts as ½ cup of fruit; 1 cup of leafy greens counts as ½ cup of vegetables. No more than half of the fruit or vegetable offerings may be in the form of juice. All juice must be 100% full-strength.

[d]For breakfast, vegetables may be substituted for fruits, but the first two cups per week of any such substitution must be from the dark green, red/orange, beans and peas (legumes) or "Other vegetables" subgroups as defined in §210.10(c)(2)(iii).

[e]The fruit quantity requirement for the SBP (5 cups/week and a minimum of 1 cup/day) is effective July 1, 2014 (SY 2014–2015).

[f]Larger amounts of these vegetables may be served.

[g]This category consists of "Other vegetables" as defined in §210.10(c)(2)(iii)(E). For the purposes of the NSLP, "Other vegetables" requirement may be met with any additional amounts from the dark green, red/orange, and beans/peas (legumes) vegetable subgroups as defined in §210.10(c)(2)(iii).

[h]Any vegetable subgroup may be offered to meet the total weekly vegetable requirement.

[i]At least half of the grains offered must be whole grain-rich in the NSLP beginning July 1, 2012 (SY 2012–2013), and in the SBP beginning July 1, 2013 (SY 2013–2014). All grains must be whole grain-rich in both the NSLP and the SBP beginning July 1, 2014 (SY 2014–15).

[j]In the SBP, the grain ranges must be offered beginning July 1, 2013 (SY 2013–2014).

[k]There is no separate meat/meat alternate component in the SBP. Beginning July 1, 2013 (SY 2013–2014), schools may substitute 1 oz. eq. of meat/meat alternate for 1 oz. eq. of grains after the minimum daily grains requirement is met.

[l]Fluid milk must be low-fat (1 percent milk fat or less, unflavored) or fat-free (unflavored or flavored).

[m]The average daily amount of calories for a 5-day school week must be within the range (at least the minimum and no more than the maximum values).

[n]Discretionary sources of calories (solid fats and added sugars) may be added to the meal pattern if within the specifications for calories, saturated fat, trans fat, and sodium. Foods of minimal nutritional value and fluid milk with fat content greater than 1 percent milk fat are not allowed.

[o]In the SBP, calories and trans fat specifications take effect beginning July 1, 2013 (SY 2013–2014).

[p]Final sodium specifications are to be reached by SY 2022-2023 or July 1, 2022. Intermediate sodium specifications are established for SY 2014–2015 and 2017–2018. See required intermediate specifications in § 210.10(f)(3) for lunches and § 220.8(f)(3) for breakfast

17-1c A Well-Designed Menu Is Appealing

The French say, "We eat with our eyes." Menu planners are able to create meals that will appeal to children when they take time to visualize how food will look on a plate. Figure 17–1 illustrates this principle: For example, apples can be sliced an alternative way to surprise and capture children's interest in eating. Consider the following **sensory qualities** when planning children's menus:

- color
- flavor (strong or mild; sweet or sour)
- texture (crisp, crunchy, or soft)
- shape (round, cubed, strings)
- temperature (cold or hot)

FIGURE 17–1 Slice apples horizontally for a novel and magical surprise!

Children's food acceptance and choices are highly influenced by the various sensory qualities of food items (Poelman & Delahunty, 2011). Toddlers and young children are unlikely to consider the nutrient content of food, but they will think of foods in terms of their color, flavor, temperature, texture, and shape. Creating menus that incorporate a variety of sensory qualities will improve their appeal and reinforce children's ability to interpret the environment through their physical senses.

The menus in Figure 17–2 illustrate how color improves a meal's visual appeal. Menu #1 is essentially a combination of yellow and brown tones. The color and vitamins A and C are significantly improved in Menu #2 by substituting broccoli for the cauliflower and watermelon for the banana. These simple changes enhance the meal's visual appeal and also add more flavor, texture, and fiber.

A meal's sensory qualities also provide opportunities for expanding children's language development. Children can be encouraged to identify and describe various food characteristics, such as being round or rectangular, red or yellow, hot or cold, smooth or rough, soft or crisp, sweet or salty. Songs and stories about foods also provide a fun way to reinforce language skills. For some children, simply talking about a food's qualities may improve their willingness to try it.

Although color is an important element in food appeal, other sensory aspects also contribute to its acceptability (Zampollo et al., 2012). Young children often prefer simple foods that are mild in flavor. Softer textured foods such as chicken or ground meats are more likely to be eaten because they are easier for children to chew and swallow. Plain foods are often preferred over those served in combination dishes. Young children also have a strong preference for sweet foods. Because the basis for this may be biological, care should be taken to limit their availability and to offer fresh fruits and nutritious whole grain baked products instead.

Did You Know...

that children have about 10,000 taste buds located across their tongue, lips, and cheeks? Half of these will disappear as the child ages.

17-1d A Well-Designed Menu Includes Familiar and New Foods

Although it is important to introduce children to new foods, a meal should also include items that are familiar. Much of this familiarity is learned from

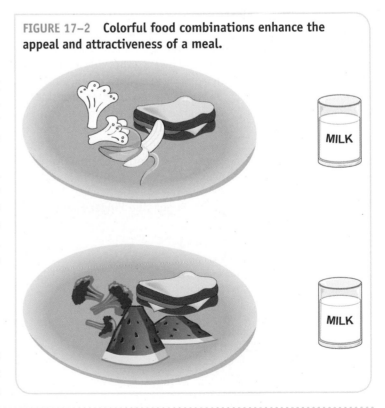

FIGURE 17–2 Colorful food combinations enhance the appeal and attractiveness of a meal.

MILK

MILK

sensory qualities – *aspects that appeal to sight, sound, taste, feel, and smell.*

▼ **Young children continue to enjoy finger foods while they are learning how to use eating utensils.**

© Cengage Learning

family eating practices, which help shape children's lifelong food preferences (Hamlin & Wynn, 2012; Lukasewycz & Mennella, 2012). Sharing information, menu plans, and recipes with families may encourage them to expand children's choices and also to serve new food items at home.

When introducing new foods, it is preferable to include only one at a time and to serve it along with other familiar foods. This ensures that children will not leave the table hungry if the new food is refused. (See Teacher Checklist 16-2 for suggestions about ways to introduce new foods to young children.) The menu planner might also consider serving unfamiliar foods for children to try at snack time, which avoids the new food being labeled as a "breakfast food" or "lunch food." New foods should be introduced with little fanfare and in small amounts to entice children's interest. Involving children in the preparation of an unfamiliar food is also an effective strategy for improving their willingness to try it (Anzman-Frasca et al., 2012; Williams, 2011).

It is always advisable to include finger foods when new foods are introduced in a meal or snack (Table 17–9). Young children who may still have difficulty managing eating utensils will find comfort in having small pieces of foods they can pick up. Finger foods also promote children's independence and decrease the risk of choking.

Children from a variety of cultural and ethnic backgrounds are represented in many classrooms today. A sensitive menu planner draws on this diversity and incorporates foods that are familiar to a variety of cultures. Incorporating **ethnic** foods into the menu serves several purposes:

⯈ Children from the featured culture are likely to be familiar with these foods. Their acceptance and enjoyment may encourage classmates to try foods that are unfamiliar.

⯈ Foods that are representative of different cultural groups add variety and interest to children's meals. They also provide a valuable forum for helping children to learn about other cultures.

⯈ Serving ethnic foods can be an effective way to reduce cultural barriers and to encourage rapport among the children. Families may be willing to contribute recipes that can be prepared and served to the children at school.

⯈ Educating children about various cultures fosters greater respect and appreciation for children who are from a culture that may differ from their own (Husband, 2012; Zakin, 2012). The sharing of food is often an effective way of helping children from all cultures and ethnicities gain acceptance and comfort in an unfamiliar group.

TABLE 17–9 Suggested Finger Foods

apricot pieces	grapefruit sections (seeded)
banana chunks	green grapes (halved)
blueberries	melon cubes
cauliflower buds	nectarines
cheese cubes	orange sections
cherry tomatoes	red and green pepper sticks
crackers	pineapple chunks
cucumbers	sliced mushrooms
diced fresh peaches	string cheese
diced fresh pears	strawberries, diced
kiwi slices	zucchini sticks

ethnic – *pertaining to races or groups of people who share common traits or customs.*

17-1e Steps in Menu Planning

A few simple steps are involved in planning nutritious meals. The entire process will proceed efficiently and effectively when the planner first takes time to assemble and organize the necessary supplies:

- menu forms
- a list of foods on hand that need to be used
- a list of children's allergies, food restrictions, or special food needs
- recipe file
- former menus with notes and suggestions
- calendar with special events and holidays noted
- grocery ads for short-term planning
- USDA list of available commodity foods

The menu form shown in Figure 17–3 can be used by a large center, small group, or home-based program and modified to include only the meals that will be served.

Step 1 List the main dishes to be served for lunch for the entire week. These should include a protein or protein alternative. Be sure to note children's food allergies or other special food requirements and plan for appropriate substitutes. Combinations of plant-based proteins (e.g., whole grains, beans, legumes, nuts, seeds) (see Chapter 13), are acceptable protein-source substitutes for meat, poultry, cheese, eggs, or fish. However, care must be taken to include other iron-rich foods because non-animal source proteins do not provide the same quality or quantity of iron found in meat and meat products.

Bean burrito with cheese	BBQ beef	Scrambled eggs	Vegetarian chili	Macaroni and cheese	Protein

Step 2 List vegetables and fruits, including salads, for the main meal. Be sure to use fruits and vegetables in season. Fresh produce in season is often less expensive, more nutritious, higher in fiber, and lower in sodium than canned or frozen varieties. Fresh fruits and vegetables also serve as excellent material for learning activities. If menus are planned in advance, local County Extension Offices can provide information regarding the availability of local and seasonal produce.

Zucchini Orange wedges	Broccoli Mango slices	Cherry tomatoes Banana	Carrots and celery Plum slices	Green beans Apple wedges	Fruits and Vegetables

Step 3 Add enriched or whole grain breads and cereal products.

Whole wheat tortilla	Enriched whole grain bun	Whole wheat toast	Corn muffin	Enriched macaroni (in casserole)	Bread

Step 4 Add a beverage. Be sure to include the required amount of milk.

Milk	Milk	Milk	Milk	Milk	Milk

Step 5 Plan snacks to balance the main meal. Pay special attention to including adequate amounts of vitamin C, vitamin A, iron, and calcium.

A.M. Snack	Prepared oat cereal Milk	Bran muffin Cantaloupe Water	Pumpkin bread Milk	Raisin toast Orange juice	Rye crackers Milk
P.M. Snack	Watermelon Wheat crackers Water	Cheese crackers Peanut butter Milk	Pizza biscuits Pineapple juice	Oatmeal cookies Milk	Egg salad sandwich Cranberry juice

FIGURE 17–3 A sample menu-planning form.

		Monday	Tuesday	Wednesday	Thursday	Friday
Breakfast	Fruit/Vegetable Bread Milk					
Snack (supplement)	Bread Fruit/Vegetable or Milk					
Lunch	Protein Fruit/Vegetable Fruit/Vegetable Bread Milk					
Snack (supplement)	Bread Fruit/Vegetable or Milk					
	# Served					
Notes						

TeachSource Digital Download Download from CourseMate.

Step 6 Review your menu.
- Does it meet funding and/or licensing regulations?
- Does it satisfy all nutrient and serving requirements?
- Does it include a variety of contrasting foods?
- Does it offer some foods that are familiar to children?
- Are several new foods included?

Step 7 Note changes on the menu and post where it can be viewed by teachers and families (Figure 17–4). The menu serves as an important form of communication between the school and families and helps ensure that children's daily and weekly nutrient needs are more likely to be met.

Step 8 Evaluate the menu. Did the children appear to eat and enjoy the foods that were served? Was there much plate waste? Do not eliminate a food from the menu because it was rejected. Repeated exposures to disliked foods, sometimes as often as ten to twelve times, have been shown to improve children's acceptance over time (Anzman-Frasca et al., 2012; Lynch & Batal, 2012). Children's likes and dislikes are continually changing and a rejected food this week may become a favorite in another week or two. However, be sure to note children's preferences and dislikes on your copy and use for future reference.

FIGURE 17–4 **Menus should be made available to families.**

WEEKLY MENUS

Week of _____

Lunch and Snacks

	Monday	Tuesday	Wednesday	Thursday	Friday
Snack	Bagel with cream cheese Orange juice	Blueberry muffin Milk	Mixed fresh veggies & dip Corn muffin Water	Waffles Applesauce Milk	Graham crackers Cranberry juice
Lunch	Turkey with gravy Mashed sweet potatoes Peas Apple slices Bread & butter Milk	Macaroni & cheese Broccoli Watermelon Milk	Scrambled eggs Green beans Plums Biscuits Milk	Beef barbecue Cooked carrots Whole wheat bread Pears Milk	Spaghetti with meat sauce Tossed salad Bread sticks Honeydew melon Milk
Snack	Peanut butter Bananas Milk	Yogurt-pineapple smoothies Water	Cheese cubes Whole wheat crackers Grape juice	Oatmeal cookies Milk	Mini pitas Hummus Tomato juice

Did You Get It?

What is not generally regarded as a function and need-meeting factor of a children's menu?

- **a.** cognitive
- **b.** developmental
- **c.** physical
- **d.** social

Take the full quiz on CourseMate.

17-2 Writing Menus

There are several approaches to menu-writing that the planner may wish to consider: weekly menus, cycle menus, and odd-day cycle menus. The program's scheduled hours of operation, personnel available to prepare the food, and method of purchasing food and supplies will determine which menu planning style is most efficient and functional. **Weekly menus** include a list of foods that are to be prepared and served for the entire week. This approach requires a greater time commitment than the others because the planner must repeat the process each week. Preparing two or three weeks' of menus simultaneously is often a more efficient use of the menu planner's time and allows utilization of larger, more economical amounts of food. It also enables the planner to better evaluate the nutrient contributions of menus over an extended period and to avoid repeating the same food items.

Cycle menus incorporate a series of weekly menus that are reused or recycled over a two- or three-month period. Cycle menus are usually written to parallel the seasons and incorporate fruits and vegetables that are most available and affordable. Although a well-planned cycle menu requires a greater initial time investment, it also saves time in the long run. Food ordering is more efficient and less time-consuming. However, the planner should not hesitate to change any part of the cycle that proves difficult to prepare or is not well accepted by the children. Seasonal cycle menus offer another distinct advantage in that they can be reused year after year with timely revisions.

Odd-day cycle menus involve planning menus for any number of days other than a week (e.g., four days, six days, nine days). This type of cycling avoids the association of specific food items with certain weekdays. However, it also requires careful planning to avoid serving dishes or foods on Mondays or Fridays that require advanced or lengthy preparation.

Did You Know...

that annually, Americans spend more than $30 billion on snack foods such as corn and potato chips, pretzels, popcorn, and their variations? This number does not include crackers, cookies, nuts, or cereal bars.

Did You Get It?

What perceived strength and unique advantage does the odd-day cycle menu offer?
a. Leftovers can be recycled and served in a creative manner.
b. Nutrients and calories can be easily counted.
c. It is a budget-friendly approach that reduces food costs.
d. It does not associate specific meals with specific days of the week.

Take the full quiz on CourseMate.

17-3 Nutritious Snacks

Offering nutrient-dense snacks can be an effective way to meet a portion of children's daily nutrient needs (Snelling & Yezek, 2012). Food choices should contribute vitamins, minerals, and other nutrients essential for children's health, growth, and development (Table 17–10). Empty-calorie snacks, those high in sugars and fat, are not appropriate choices for young children because they do not compensate for any nutrients that may be missing or not adequately consumed in previous meals.

Foods that are new or unfamiliar to children are best introduced at snack time. Tasting parties and learning experiences designed around new foods can increase children's interest and willingness to try something different.

Snacks can also be planned to meet children's high energy needs. Small stomach capacity and short attention spans often limit what children are able to consume at a given time or to sustain

weekly menus – *menus that are written to be served on a weekly basis.*
cycle menus – *menus that are written to repeat after a set interval, such as every three to four weeks.*
odd-day cycle menus – *menus planned for a period of days other than a week that repeat after the planned period; cycles of any number of days may be used. These menus are a means of avoiding repetition of the same foods on the same day of the week.*

TABLE 17–10 Snack suggestions for school-aged children

Active days and growing bodies make after-school snacks a must. Plan snacks that children can help to make.

- Water – encourage children to drink water often; thirst may be interpreted as hunger.
- Banana chunks dipped in yogurt and crispy rice cereal; freeze
- Yogurt "sundaes"—layer flavored yogurt with fruit pieces and granola
- Bagel melts—low-fat cheese slice on bagel half; microwave
- Baked pita chips (make your own) with salsa
- Tortilla rollups—roll a low-fat cheese and ham slice up in a tortilla; serve with fat-free ranch dip
- Fruit smoothies—blend yogurt with favorite fruits
- Trail mix—combine various cereals, dried fruit, and mini marshmallows
- Whole wheat tortilla spread with peanut butter, cinnamon sugar, and sliced fruit
- Raw veggies with homemade hummus
- Oatmeal raisin cookies or pumpkin bread (a great cooking activity)
- Egg salad on wheat crackers
- Apple wedges with peanut butter dip
- Chocolate tofu pudding

them until the next meal. A nutrient-dense snack served about two hours between meals is usually the best spacing for most children. This amount of time prevents children from becoming overly hungry or spoiling their appetite for the next meal.

17-3a Suitable Snack Foods

Fresh fruits, vegetables, low-fat dairy, and whole-grain products make ideal choices for snack foods because they contribute vitamins A and C, calcium, and fiber (which aids elimination) (Ohri-Vachaspati, Turner, & Chaloupka, 2012). The crispness of fresh fruits and vegetables also aids in removing food particles that may cling to teeth and stimulates the gums so they remain healthy. Fresh fruits and vegetables should be sectioned, sliced, or diced into small pieces so they are easy for children to pick up and chew and less likely to cause choking.

Low-fat dairy products (for children over 2 years) provide children with high-quality protein and additional calcium. Cheese, low-fat yogurt, unsweetened milk, and pudding are versatile to serve and easy for children to eat.

Whole grains or enriched breads and grain products are also ideal high-fiber snack choices. Foods from this group contribute a variety of flavors, textures, and interest to children's diets. **Enriched** breads and cereals are refined products to which iron, thiamin, niacin, riboflavin, and folic acid are added in amounts equal to the original whole grain product.

▼ **Children learn important self-regulation and motor skills when they are encouraged to serve themselves.**

© Cengage Learning

---

whole grains – *grain products that have not been refined; they contain all parts of the kernel of grain.*

enriched – *adding nutrients to grain products to replace those lost during refinement; thiamin, niacin, riboflavin, and iron are nutrients most commonly added.*

Unsweetened beverages such as **full-strength** fruit and vegetable juices offer another healthy snack food option. Orange, grapefruit, tangerine, and tomato juices are rich in vitamin C. Many manufacturers add vitamin C to their apple, grape, cranberry and pineapple juices; however, always check juice labels to determine if they are indeed fortified with vitamin C. Carbonated beverages, fruit punches, **fruit drinks**, fruit-ades, and sport drinks are unacceptable options and contribute to obesity (Lopez et al., 2012). These beverages consist primarily of sugar, water, and few other nutrients unless small amounts of vitamins have been added.

Water plays an important role in maintaining a healthy body. It should be made available to children at all times and can be served with meals and snacks. Allowing children to pour water from a pitcher, on demand, may encourage them to drink it more often. Special attention should be given to water intake following a period of physical activity and when environmental temperatures and humidity are high. A quick stop at the drinking fountain is an ideal way to replenish water lost during active outdoor play.

> ### Did You Get It?
>
> What is not one of the specific nutrients added to enrich bread products and return them to their original whole-grain level?
>
> **a.** iron
> **b.** riboflavin
> **c.** potassium
> **d.** folic acid
>
> Take the full quiz on CourseMate.

17-4 Meal Service

A nutritious meal is of no value to a child if it is not eaten. The mealtime atmosphere in which foods are presented can forestall, encourage, or further contribute to eating problems. Meals should be served in a peaceful, pleasant, and social atmosphere (van der Horst, 2012). Straightening up the classroom prior to mealtimes eliminates the distraction of scattered toys or an unfinished game. Quiet music playing in the background also helps children (and adults) to relax and focus on the meal.

Care should be taken to make the table and settings attractive. Child-made placemats add interest and give children an opportunity to contribute to the meal. Children can also make centerpieces from objects gathered on field trips or nature hikes. Plates, cups, utensils, and napkins should be laid out neatly and appropriately at each place. Involving children in setting the table provides a positive learning experience, promotes self-esteem, and improves interest in the meal.

Food served in an attractive manner also contributes to its appeal for children. Foods cooked at the correct temperature retain their color, shape, and texture. Arranging them neatly in serving dishes or on plates also creates visual interest. (White or warm-hued plates enhance food's natural colors; cool-hued dishes such as blues and greens detract from most food colors.) Fresh, edible garnishes may be used if time and budget permit. Contrived or "cute" foods are time-consuming to prepare and may actually result in the children saving them as "souvenirs" rather than in eating them.

Food may be served in a variety of styles:

▶ plate service
▶ family-style service
▶ combination of the above

Plate service involves placing food on individual plates in the kitchen before serving. This style offers the best option for **cost control** as it permits the food server to manage portion size and results in fewer leftovers and waste.

In family-style service, food is placed on the table in serving dishes. Children are encouraged to help themselves and pass the dish to the next child. Beverages are placed in small, easily managed pitchers, and each child pours the amount desired before passing it to the next child. Although this method does not permit the same degree of portion control as plate service, it does promote children's independence. Because children determine how much food to take and

---

full-strength – *undiluted (as in 100 percent fruit or vegetable juice).*
fruit drinks – *products that contain 0–10 percent real fruit juice, added water, and sugar.*
cost control – *reduction of expenses through portion control inventory and reduction of waste.*

to eat, they are learning important problem-solving, decision-making, and self-regulation skills. They are also practicing motor skills used to dip, serve, pass, and pour, as well as social skills such as cooperating and sharing. Many teachers believe the positive aspects of family-style service outweigh the benefits of portion and cost control associated with plate service.

Because both service styles offer distinct advantages, teachers may decide to use a combination of the two. For example, the teacher may place entrée servings on the plates (the amount determined by each child's request) while children pass and help themselves to the bread, fruit, and vegetables. Thus, cost savings are maintained by controlling the more expensive protein component. This approach also protects children from sustaining an accidental burn caused by a hot entrée food or serving dish. If the vegetables are hot, it may be prudent for the teacher to also serve them.

It is important that teachers sit at the table and eat meals together with the children. They serve as role models for appropriate behavior and attitudes concerning foods. Teachers are also able to engage children in pleasant table conversation and to assist those who may require extra help (Erinosho et al., 2012). Minimal attention should be focused on proper table manners to avoid creating a negative mealtime atmosphere. It is often best to ignore children's inappropriate behaviors (to a point) while acknowledging their desirable behaviors. Additional suggestions for making mealtime a relaxed, happy time are offered in Teacher Checklist 17-1.

▼ **Adults should sit and eat meals together with children.**

© Cengage Learning

Did You Get It?

When serving a meal to and eating with young children, whether at home or in an institutional/educational setting, talk of table manners should be:
- **a.** a primary and ongoing topic
- **b.** avoided as much as possible, but not taboo
- **c.** addressed, but not dwelled upon
- **d.** discussed in firm, open-ended terms

Take the full quiz
on CourseMate.

TEACHER CHECKLIST 17-1
Making Mealtime a Pleasant Experience

Creating a positive eating environment makes mealtime an enjoyable experience for children and adults if you:

- Provide meals that are nutritious, attractive, and tasty.
- Provide a transition or quiet time shortly before meals so children are relaxed.
- Avoid delays so children do not have to wait.
- Enlist children to help set the table, put serving dishes on the table, and assist with clean up after the meal.
- Create a room environment that is attractive, clean, and well lit; limit distractions.
- Get to know each child's personality and reaction to foods.
- Provide tables, chairs, dishes, glassware, eating, and serving utensils that are an appropriate size for children.
- Support and encourage children's efforts to feed themselves.
- Avoid rushing or pressuring children to hurry. Allow sufficient time for children to eat and enjoy their meal.
- Never force children to eat or to finish everything on their plate. There will be times when children are picky eaters.
- Offer a variety of foods prepared in different ways.
- Encourage social interaction.

17-5 Planning the Menu within Budget

While the menu identifies the foods to be served, the budget defines the resources allotted for implementing the plan. Food, personnel, and equipment costs are items that must be addressed in the budget. These expenses can be managed and controlled by paying careful attention to:

- menu planning
- food purchasing
- food preparation
- food service
- recordkeeping

Cost control is essential if a food service is to stay within the budget. The goal is to feed children appetizing, nutritious meals at a reasonably low cost. However, cost control should never be the defining factor at the expense of providing nutritious food.

17-5a Menu Planning

Cost control begins at the menu-planning stage. To plan menus that stay within a budget, it is important to begin by including inexpensive foods. To do so, the planner must be aware of current prices and seasonal supplies.

The menu planner can reduce food costs by utilizing supplies on hand and any remaining leftovers. (Note: *Leftovers must be refrigerated promptly and cannot be reclaimed for reimbursement.*) To ensure that high-quality foods are selected from supplies on hand, the **First-In-First-Out (FIFO) inventory method** should be used. Supplies are dated as they are brought into the storage area. Newly purchased foods are placed at the back of shelves and older items are moved forward so they are used first.

17-5b Food Purchasing

Food purchasing, or **procurement**, is a crucial step in cost control. Lowering food costs during the purchasing phase can be accomplished by obtaining food from local suppliers, using USDA commodities, and keeping abreast of price trends and market availability. Purchasing too much food or inappropriate foods can turn a menu that is planned around inexpensive foods into one that becomes expensive. The key step is to determine as accurately as possible the amount of food necessary to adequately feed everyone. The use of standardized recipes can make this process easier by determining how much and what kinds of food are needed. The U.S. Department of Agriculture has developed a series of healthy recipes, including ingredient lists and large group quantities, for use in school lunches and early childhood programs. (See "Helpful Web Resources" at the end of this chapter.)

Before purchasing food, a written food order should be prepared with the following specifications:

- name of product
- federal grade
- packaging procedures and type of package
- test or inspection procedures
- market units: ounces, pounds, can size, cases, and so on
- quantity (number) of units needed
- style of food desired: frozen, fresh, canned, slices, halves, chunks

If foods are purchased from local retail stores, a simple form that follows the store's floor plan will make shopping easier and more efficient. When preparing the market order, list items that must be purchased for the entire menu period (e.g., one week, four weeks) in the following order:

- meats or alternative proteins
- grains (breads, cereals, crackers, pastas)

First-In-First-Out (FIFO) inventory method – *a method of storage in which the items stored for the longest time will be retrieved first.*
procurement – *the process of obtaining services, supplies, and equipment in conformance with applicable laws and regulations.*

▶ fruits and vegetables
▶ dairy products

Frozen foods should be purchased last to minimize thawing between the store freezer and food service freezer.

17-5c Food Preparation

The nutrients in food are best retained when appropriate food preparation methods are utilized. Fruits and vegetables should be washed under running water; the use of soap or detergents is not recommended. If produce must be peeled for infants and young toddlers, only a thin outer layer should be removed as many important nutrients are present in the skin.

Utilizing correct heat and cooking times maintains critical nutrients and is also important for cost control. Foods cooked too long or at excessively high heat may burn or undergo significant shrinkage. In either case, this can increase costs because burned food is not usable and shrinkage results in fewer portions than originally planned. Equally important is the fact that some nutrients, such as thiamin and vitamin C, are readily destroyed when exposed to heat.

Standardized recipes, as previously described, help ensure that correct amounts of ingredients are purchased and leftovers are minimized. Leftover foods that have not been placed on the table may be promptly frozen and used when serving the same dish at a later date. Leftovers should be reheated in a separate pan and not combined with freshly prepared portions, nor should they ever be reheated more than once to prevent foodborne illness.

© 2015 Cengage Learning

▶❙❙ **TeachSource** Video Connections

School Age: Cooking Activities

Cooking activities provide an effective instructional opportunity for reinforcing children's learning across curricular areas. Children's involvement in cooking also increases their interest in food and willingness to taste new and unfamiliar items. As you watch the learning video, *School Age: Cooking Activities*, consider the following questions:

1. What safety precautions must the teacher take before and during a classroom cooking activity?

2. How can the teacher use this particular cooking activity to promote children's literacy development?

3. What social-emotional skills are the children learning?

4. What additional math and/or science concepts could be taught during this cooking activity?

Watch on CourseMate.

17-5d Food Service

If a recipe specifies a serving size, for example, 1/2 cup or 1 1/2 × 1 1/2 inch square, that amount is what must be served. When a family-style method is used, teachers may serve children standard portions as a means of portion control. In programs where children are encouraged to serve themselves, each child should be asked to initially take only as much as can be eaten and then request more.

Special serving utensils designed to measure out preselected amounts can be used to control food portions and costs. Examples of such utensils are soup ladles and ice cream scoops, which are available in a number of standardized sizes (e.g., 1/4 cup, 1/2 cup); these tools can be purchased online or from restaurant supply stores.

17-5e Recordkeeping

Records documenting actual food expenses are vital for determining whether the menu planner has stayed within the projected budget. The cost of feeding each child and adult (cost/person ratio) is also important information for the meal planner to determine:

▶ Calculate the total number of individuals served.
▶ Calculate the total food bills.
▶ Divide the total dollars spent on food by the total number of persons served to determine the weekly or monthly food costs per person.

The results of weekly or month-by-month expense records can be used to revise the following month's menu and stay within budget. An inventory of all foods remaining on hand should also be updated monthly (unless there is little variation from month to month).

Did You Get It?

First-in-first-out (FIFO) is a practice for dealing with:

a. meal service

b. grocery shopping

c. menu planning

d. food handling and storage

Take the full quiz on CourseMate.

PARTNERING with FAMILIES

Planning Healthy Meals

Dear Families,

The MyPlate model provides an easy-to-use tool for planning healthy, nutritious family meals. Extensive food lists, menu suggestions, nutrition information, and ideas for increasing physical activity (as a family) can be accessed on the http://www.ChooseMyPlate.gov website. Planning and writing out weekly menus and grocery lists may seem unnecessary at first, but the process offers significant benefits, including:

1. Making sure that family members are receiving all required nutrients.

2. Planning nutritious meals within a budget by taking advantage of seasonal produce and store sales.

3. Making fewer trips to the grocery store and purchasing fewer items on impulse.

4. Being more aware of calories, appropriate portion sizes, and the variety of available food items.

The process of planning weekly menus becomes easier with time and practice:

▶ Choose low fat proteins, such as fish, chicken, turkey, lean pork or beef, beans, legumes, egg whites, and tofu or other soy-based products.

▶ Build the main part of a meal around complex carbohydrates (pastas, rice, whole grains).

▶ Plan half of a meal to consist of vegetables and fruits (to replace sweets).

▶ Use appropriate serving sizes to determine the amount of each food item to purchase.

▶ Rely on fewer prepared or processed foods to control calories, fat, and sodium intake; foods prepared at home are also generally less expensive.

▶ Plan meals that include a variety of colors, flavors, and new items to try.

▶ Experiment with different ethnic cuisines and meatless meals that include beans, legumes, soy, or eggs.

▶ Use leftovers to save time and money. For example, serve half of a beef roast for one meal, use the other half for BBQ sandwiches, soup, or stew. Prepare a double batch of your family's favorite dish and freeze half for another meal.

▶ Avoid foods high in fat (and trans-fats) and empty calories, such as doughnuts, croissants, pastries, snack cakes, high-fat cookies, high-fat crackers, and snack chips; substitute water for sugar-laden beverages.

▶ Enlist your creativity when planning healthy snacks. This is an ideal time to experiment with new foods and preparation methods: serve frozen fruit or vegetables (slightly thawed), low-fat yogurt with granola or fresh fruit, hummus with fresh vegetables, low-fat cheese and fruit kebobs, tofu and fruit smoothies, or whole wheat tortilla with a blended cottage cheese spread and dried cranberries (or diced fresh fruit).

CLASSROOM CORNER

Teacher Activities

Amazing Pumpkins

(PreK–2; [NHES] National Health Education Standards, 1.2.1, 1.2.2)

Concept: Pumpkins are a type of food that is abundant in the fall. You can eat their seeds or use them to make many other food items.

Learning Objectives

▶ Children will learn about and explore pumpkins.

▶ Children will be given an opportunity to help make and taste two pumpkin products.

Supplies

▶ large pumpkin

▶ knife (teacher use only)

▶ newspaper

▶ medium-sized bowl for seeds

▶ baking pan

▶ oil

▶ pumpkin muffin recipe and ingredients

▶ muffin tins

▶ hand wipes

Learning Activities

▶ Read and discuss one of the following books:

   Pumpkin Day, Pumpkin Night by Anne Rockwell
   Miss Fiona's Stupendous Pumpkin Pies by Mark Moulton
   From Seed to Pumpkin by Wendy Pfeffer
   Duck and Goose Find a Pumpkin by Tad Hills
   The Very Best Pumpkin by Mark Moulton

▶ Examine a pumpkin together with the children and ask them to help describe its appearance. Ask children questions about the pumpkin (color, size, shape, what can be done with a pumpkin, if it is a vegetable, where does it grow, and if it can be eaten).

▶ Tell the children you are going to cut open the pumpkin and look inside. While the teacher cuts open the pumpkin, have children clean their hands with wipes. Call children up one at a time to put their hands in the pumpkin and remove some of the seeds. After everyone has had a turn, put the seeds aside; let children know that you will wash the seeds and bake them in the oven later.

▶ Next, have the children help make pumpkin muffins. They can add ingredients, stir, spoon batter into muffin cups, and so on.

▶ Serve the pumpkin seeds and muffins for snack with a glass of milk.

Evaluation

▶ Children will describe several characteristics and uses for pumpkins.

▶ Children will name at least two foods that can be made from a pumpkin.

Additional lesson plans for grades 3–5 are available on CourseMate.

Summary

▶ The menu is the basic tool of food service. It should be designed to meet the nutritional needs of the intended audience, introduce new foods, include some items that are familiar or well-liked, address food safety, and stay within budgetary limits.

▶ Menus can be planned for a week (weekly menu), multiple weeks (cycle menu), or an odd-number of days (odd-day menu).

▶ Snacks should be nutrient-dense and planned to address deficiencies in children's diet.

▶ Meals should be served in a comfortable environment with foods prepared and served in an attractive manner to enhance their appeal to children.

▶ Strategies for planning meals that stay within budget include: purchasing high-quality foods in season, storing foods promptly and at the correct temperature, cooking foods at correct temperatures, using standardized recipes and appropriate serving sizes, and accurate recordkeeping.

Terms to Know

sensory qualities *p. 437*
ethnic *p. 438*
weekly menus *p. 442*
cycle menus *p. 442*
odd-day cycle menus *p. 442*

whole grains *p. 443*
enriched *p. 443*
full-strength *p. 444*
fruit drinks *p. 444*

cost control *p. 444*
First-In-First-Out (FIFO)
    inventory method *p. 446*
procurement *p. 446*

Chapter Review

A. By Yourself:

1. State the appropriate serving size for a child 3 to 5 years old for each of the following foods:
   a. milk
   b. dry cereal
   c. fruit
   d. vegetable
   e. bread

2. Where can a program director locate information about state licensing requirements that address nutrition and food services for young children?

3. Name four sensory qualities that contribute to food's appeal.

4. What are two advantages of using fresh fruits and vegetables in season?

5. List two strategies the menu planner can use to control food costs.

B. As a Group:

1. Outline three ways to control food costs when preparing food.

2. Discuss how environment affects children's mealtime behaviors. Identify steps that adults can take to create a positive eating atmosphere for children.

3. Discuss how you might handle the following mealtime behaviors:
   • child refuses to eat any vegetables
   • child eats only the macaroni and cheese on his plate and then asks for more
   • child belches loudly to make the other children laugh
   • child is too busy talking to finish eating by the time others are done

4. Evaluate and comment on the nutrient quality of the following snacks:
   - strawberry jam and whole wheat bagel
   - cheese pizza and water
   - apple juice and plum slices
   - fruit punch and graham crackers
   - oatmeal/raisin cookie and milk

Case Study

Mark plans and prepares the meals for a local Head Start program that serves approximately seventy-five 3- and 4-year-olds. He has explored and likes the new MyPlate guidelines and wants to use several features when he develops his weekly menus for the coming school year. He is especially interested in including a greater variety of fruits and vegetables for the children to try and incorporating more plant-based proteins and ethnic foods into his meals. Mark and the teachers have fenced off a corner of the play yard where the children will be able to plant a garden when they return in the fall. They also worked together over the summer to design weekly lesson plans around featured foods and have decided to concentrate on colors during the first month.

1. Help Mark prepare a list of at least ten different fruits and/or vegetables for each of the following colors: purple, white, red, yellow/orange, green.

2. Suggest several ways that Mark might prepare the vegetables you identified (question #1) so they will appeal to children.

3. How should the menu planner respond to children's refusal to eat a new food(s)? Should these items be eliminated from future menus? Why or why not?

4. How are children likely to benefit from lessons that are designed around the menus?

5. Why is it important to include ethnic foods in children's menus?

Application Activities

1. Plan a five-day menu, including morning snack, lunch, and an afternoon snack, that would be appropriate for 4-year-old children. The menu should supply one-half of their daily required nutrients. Provide one strong source of vitamin C, calcium, and iron each day. Include at least three rich vitamin A sources over the five-day period.

2. Lilly's second grade teacher suspects that she doesn't eat breakfast most mornings before arriving at school. Lilly's parents leave for work before she wakes up and has to get herself ready for school. By mid-morning, Lilly seems inattentive, lethargic, and "off in her own world." She rarely plays with the other children and spends most of her recess just standing around. The lunchroom monitors have noted that Lilly eats only carbohydrates (e.g., breads, pasta, rice), milk, and an occasional bite of fruit. They have rarely seen her eat any vegetable or meat.

   a. In what ways might Lilly's diet be contributing to her behavior?

   b. How would you characterize Lilly's nutritional status?

   c. What nutrients are likely to be deficient in Lilly's diet?

   d. What steps would you take to improve Lilly's participation in recess activities, as well as her dietary habits and overall health?

3. Review the menu criteria discussed in this chapter. Rank the criteria as you perceive their degree of importance. Are there other factors that you believe should be considered in planning nutritious menus? Consider the needs of individual early childhood programs, family child care programs, and after-school programs. Are the important factors the same or different in each setting?

4. Eiswari, 3 years old, is allergic to eggs. Explain how this affects menu planning.

5. Plan a daily menu that meets all of the nutrient needs of a child who follows a vegan vegetarian diet. Then modify the menu for a child who is a lacto-ovo-vegetarian. Include appropriate serving sizes.

6. The following weekly menu is planned for an early childhood program during the month of January:

Meat loaf	Whole wheat roll with margarine
Fresh asparagus	Watermelon-blueberry fresh fruit cup
Milk	

   a. Evaluate this menu and suggest changes that would make it less expensive to serve yet still be equally or even more nutritious.

   b. How would the cost of this menu served in January compare to the cost of the same menu served in June or July?

Helpful Web Resources

Academy of Nutrition and Dietetics	http://www.eatright.org
FoodSafety.gov	http://www.foodsafety.gov
ChooseMyPlate.gov	http://www.choosemyplate.gov/
National Food Service Management Institute (See newsletters for menus.)	http://www.nfsmi.org
Nutrition.gov (Ethnic Cooking)	http://www.nutrition.gov/shopping-cooking-meal-planning/ethnic-cooking
USDA Center for Nutrition Policy and Promotion	http://www.cnpp.usda.gov/
USDA Healthy Meals Resource System (See "Recipes" and "Menu Planning.")	http://healthymeals.nal.usda.gov/
USDA Nutrition Assistance Programs	http://www.fns.usda.gov/fns

Visit the Education CourseMate for this textbook to access the eBook, Did You Get It? quizzes, Digital Downloads, TeachSource Video Cases, flashcards, and more. Go to CengageBrain.com to log in, register, or purchase access.

References

Anzman-Frasca, S., Savage, J., Marini, M., Fisher, J., & Birch, L. (2012). Repeated exposure and associative conditioning promote preschool children's liking of vegetables, *Appetite*, 58(2), 543–553.

Erinosho, T., Hales, D., McWilliams, C., Emunah, J., & Ward, D. (2012). Nutrition policies at child-care centers and impact on role modeling of healthy eating behaviors of caregivers, *Journal of the Academy of Nutrition & Dietetics*, 112(1), 119–124.

Hamlin, J., & Wynn, K. (2012). Who knows what's good to eat? Infants fail to match the food preferences of antisocial others, *Cognitive Development*, 27(3), 227–239.

Husband, T. (2012). "I don't see color": Challenging assumptions about discussing race with young children, *Early Childhood Education Journal*, 39(6), 365–371.

Lopez, N., Ayala, G., Corder, K., Eisenberg, C., Zive, M., Wood, C., & Elder, J. (2012). Parent support and parent-medicated behaviors are associated with children's sugary beverage consumption, *Journal of the Academy of Nutrition and Dietetics*, 112(4), 541–547.

Lukasewycz, L., & Mennella, J. (2012). Lingual tactile acuity and food texture preferences among children and their mothers, *Food Quality & Preference*, 26(1), 58–66.

Lynch, M., & Batal, M. (2012). Child care providers' strategies for supporting healthy eating: A quantitative approach, *Journal of Research in Childhood Education*, 26(1), 107–121.

Neelon, S., Vaughn, A., Ball, S., McWilliams, C., & Ward, D. (2012). Nutrition practices and mealtime environments of North Carolina child care centers, *Childhood Obesity*, 8(3), 216–223.

Ohri-Vachaspati, P., Turner, L., & Chaloupka, F. (2012). Fresh fruit and vegetable program participation in elementary schools in the United States and availability of fruits and vegetables in school lunch meals, *Journal of the Academy of Nutrition & Dietetics*, 112(6), 921–926.

Poelman, A., & Delahunty, C. (2011). The effect of preparation method and typicality of colour on children's acceptance for vegetables, *Food Quality & Preference*, 22(4), 355–364.

Ritchie, L., Boyle, M., Chandran, K., Spector, P., Whaley, S., James, P., Samuels, S., Hecht, K., & Crawford, P. (2012). Participation in the Child and Adult Care Food Program is associated with more nutritious foods and beverages in child care, *Childhood Obesity*, 8(3), 224–229.

Snelling, A., & Yezek, J. (2012). The effect of nutrient-based standards on competitive foods in 3 schools: Potential savings in kilocalories and grams of fat, *Journal of School Health*, 82(2), 91–96.

van der Horst, K. (2012). Overcoming picky eating: Eating enjoyment as a central aspect of children's eating behaviors, *Appetite*, 58(2), 567–574.

Williams, K. (2011). Increasing children's food choices: Strategies based upon research and practice. In D. Kilcast & F. Angus (Eds.), *Developing children's food products* (pp. 125–139), Cambridge, UK: Woodhead Publishing.

Zakin, A. (2012). Hand to hand: Teaching tolerance and social justice one child at a time, *Childhood Education*, 88(1), 3–13.

Zampollo, F., Kniffin, K., Wansink, B., & Shimizu, M. (2012). Food plating preferences of children: The importance of presentation on desire for diversity, *Acta Paediatrica*, 101(1), 61–66.

- **#1 c:** Promoting child development and learning
- **#2 c:** Building family and community relationships
- **#3 a, c, d:** Observing, documenting, and assessing to support young children and families
- **#4 c:** Using developmentally effective approaches to connect with children and families
- **#5 b:** Using content knowledge to build meaningful curriculum
- **#6 b, c, d and e:** Becoming a professional
- Field experience

Learning Objectives

After studying this chapter, you should be able to:

LO 18-1 Discuss why the incidence of food-borne illness is increasing and what audiences are at greatest risk.

LO 18-2 Outline basic safety and sanitation practices critical to preventing food-related illness.

LO 18-3 Explain how an HACCP plan is conducted to improve food safety.

LO 18-4 Identify common food-borne illnesses, including their food sources, symptoms, and prevention methods.

LO 18-5 Describe several large-scale efforts that are designed to make food safer for human consumption.

This unit introduces factors other than the menu that contribute to effective food service in schools and early childhood settings. The success of a carefully planned menu depends on the food being safe to eat.

18-1 Food-Related Illness

Food-borne illnesses are a major public health concern and pose an especially serious risk, including death and long-term disability, for young children (Hoffman, Batz, & Morris, 2012) (Figure 18–1).

A **food-borne illness outbreak** occurs when two or more people become ill after ingesting the same food and a laboratory analysis confirms that food was the source of the illness. The United States Centers for Disease Control and Prevention (CDC) estimates that 48 million people become ill each year as a result of food-borne illnesses (CDC, 2011). This accounts for 128,000 hospitalizations and 3,000 deaths annually. Those groups at greatest risk are:

- infants and children under 4 years
- pregnant women
- individuals 50 years of age and older
- persons who have chronic diseases or weakened immune systems

---

food-borne illness – *a disease or illness transmitted by the ingestion of food contaminated with bacteria, viruses, some molds, or parasites.*
food-borne illness outbreak – *two or more persons become ill after ingesting the same food and laboratory analysis confirms that food is the source of the illness.*

FIGURE 18–1   **Common causes of food-borne illness.**

Pathogen	Estimated Cases	Percent
Norovirus	5,461,731	58%
Salmonella	1,027,561	11%
Clostridium perfringens	965,958	10%
Campylobacter	845,024	9%
Staphylococcus aureus	241,148	3%

Source: CDC. (2011)

An increased reliance on mass food production, global imports, and restaurant meals exposes large numbers of people to food-borne illnesses each day. However, although outbreaks of food-related illnesses associated with fast-food chains and food processing plants receive extensive media coverage, many more cases are caused by home-cooked meals. (Remember the Thanksgiving when the whole family had "the flu" after the holiday dinner?) The connection between food and illness is often overlooked because the symptoms are similar to those experienced with other conditions affecting the digestive system. As a result, the true extent of food-borne illness in this and other countries is unknown.

18-1a Food-Borne Contaminants

Food can become unsafe in several ways. Hazards to food are present in the air, in water, in other foods, on work surfaces, and on a food preparer's hands and body. These hazards can be divided into three categories (Figure 18–2):

- biological
- chemical
- physical

Bacteria present in the environment pose the greatest threat to food safety. Some bacteria can cause serious and life-threatening complications, whereas others such as blue cheese and yogurt are beneficial. The risk of environmental contamination of foods can be reduced through two basic approaches:

- following strict personal health and cleanliness habits
- maintaining a sanitary food service operation

FIGURE 18–2   **Food-borne contaminants.**

Hazard	Examples
Biological	Bacteria
	Parasites
	Viruses
	Molds, yeasts
Chemical	Pesticides
	Metals
	Cleaning chemicals
Physical	Dirt
	Hair
	Broken glass
	Metal shavings
	Plastic
	Bones
	Rodent droppings

18-1b Conditions that Promote Bacterial Growth

Special precautions must be taken around food and food supplies because there are numerous bacteria present in the environment. In some respects, it is surprising that food-related illnesses don't occur more often. The following conditions are conducive to the development of a food-borne illness:

- *Potentially hazardous foods* – Bacteria generally prefer foods that are high in protein, such as meat, poultry, seafood, eggs, milk, and dairy products.

- *Oxygen* – Some bacteria require oxygen. Others thrive best in its absence. A few bacteria can grow in environments with or without oxygen.
- *Temperature* – Temperature is probably the most critical factor for bacterial growth. The hazard zone of 41–140°F is the ideal range in which bacteria grow most rapidly.
- *Time* – A single bacterial cell can multiply into one million cells in less than five hours under ideal conditions.
- *Water* – Bacteria grow in foods that have a higher moisture content.
- *Acidity* – Bacteria prefer conditions that are near neutral (pH 7.0).

Food infections result when food containing large amounts of viable (live), disease-producing bacteria is ingested. Salmonella, E. coli, and campylobacter are examples of bacteria that commonly cause this type of food-borne illness. Symptoms typically develop within 12 to 24 hours after contaminated food has been ingested and bacteria have had sufficient time to multiply. **Food intoxications** occur when food containing the bacterial toxins is consumed. Symptoms usually develop within a shorter time period (1–6 hours), with the exception of botulin toxins, which take longer to cause illness (8–36 hours).

Did You Get It?

What population group is not typically at high risk for food-borne illness?
a. infants and children
b. obese individuals (specifically those with diabetes)
c. the elderly
d. pregnant women

Take the full quiz on CourseMate.

18-2 Measures to Keep Food Safe

Efforts to educate consumers about the prevention of food-borne illness have intensified in recent years. Perhaps the most widely publicized initiative is the Fight BAC! movement created by the U.S. Department of Agriculture (USDA) and the Partnership for Food Safety Education (Figure 18–3). This organization unites scientists and representatives from trade and restaurant associations, food processors and manufacturers, and government agencies to work collaboratively toward reducing food-related illness. An additional campaign, *Fight BAC! Goes to Child Care*, offers a series of fact sheets and training materials designed specifically for early childhood programs.

The way food is handled, stored, transported, and prepared ultimately affects the health of those who consume it. Safe handling instructions appear on many food packages and must be followed carefully (Figure 18–4). The incidence of food-borne illness can be reduced significantly when basic safety measures are implemented:

- examine foods carefully
- maintain clean conditions
- separate foods
- store foods properly
- cook and serve foods correctly
- discard spoiled food

Because young children are more likely to be sickened by food-related illnesses, it is especially important that early childhood and school personnel understand and follow these practices precisely (Stinson et al., 2011).

----

food infections – *illnesses resulting from the ingestion of live bacteria in food.*
food intoxications – *illnesses resulting from the ingestion of food containing residual bacterial toxins in the absence of viable (live) bacteria.*

FIGURE 18–3   Keeping food safe from bacteria.

FIGURE 18–4   Safe handling instructions are present on every package of meat and poultry.

Safe Handling Instructions

This product was prepared from inspected and passed meat and/or poultry. Some food products may contain bacteria that could cause illness if the product is mishandled or cooked improperly. For your protection, follow these safe handling instructions.

 Keep refrigerated or frozen.
Thaw in refrigerator or microwave.

 Keep raw meat and poultry separate from other foods. Wash working surfaces (including cutting boards), utensils, and hands after touching raw meat or poultry.

 Cook thoroughly.

 Keep hot foods hot. Refrigerate leftovers immediately or discard.

18-2a Examine Food Carefully

All foods should be examined closely before they are purchased. The integrity of food wrappers should be intact (e.g., no broken film on meat, poultry, fish, or cheese packages, no dented cans) to protect the product from potential contamination. Eggs should be inspected and avoided if they are cracked. Fresh fruits and vegetables should be checked for bruises or signs of spoilage. Salads, fresh fruits such as melons and berries, and vegetables that have been cut should be securely packaged and refrigerated. Always note the "sell by" or "use by" dates printed on perishable foods; expired items may not be a bargain.

18-2b Maintain Clean Conditions

Special effort and attention are necessary to maintain a sanitary food preparation environment. Food handlers must practice good hand washing and personal hygiene, surfaces and equipment must be sanitized, and food items must be washed to protect children from food-borne illnesses.

Personal Health and Hygiene   Food preparation and service personnel must take great care to maintain a high level of personal health and hygiene. They must also adhere to health department and state child care licensing food service standards. These usually include providing evidence of a periodic physical examination, negative tuberculin test, and absence of infectious diseases such as hepatitis.

Teachers, cooks, paraprofessionals, and volunteers who assist with food preparation or serving meals to children must also be free of common communicable illnesses such as colds, respiratory or intestinal influenza, gastrointestinal upsets, sore throat, or sinus infections. These conditions can easily be transmitted to others even though an employee may be feeling well enough to work. A person who is ill should refrain from handling food until he is symptom free for at least 24 hours (Figure 18–5). Programs should be prepared for the

FIGURE 18–5   Food handlers and transmission of food-borne illness.

Condition	Guidelines
Abscess or skin infections	Avoid food preparation if lesions are open or draining. Disposable gloves should be worn if sores are present on hands.
Cough, cold, or respiratory infection (without fever)	Avoid handling or working with food if coughing is uncontrollable or nose-blowing is frequent. Wash hands often and step out of food preparation areas when coughing or sneezing.
Cuts or burns (not infected)	Keep affected area(s) bandaged. Wear disposable gloves if injuries are on hands or lower arms.
Diarrhea	Avoid contact with food, children and other personnel until 24 hours after diarrhea ends. Medical evaluation should be obtained for diarrhea lasting longer than 48 hours to rule out infectious diseases such as *E. coli*, giardia, salmonella, hepatitis A, and *campylobacter*. Contact local health department authorities if tested positive for any of these.
HIV/AIDS	No restrictions are necessary. Food handlers should practice good handwashing and personal hygiene.
Respiratory infections (with fever)	No contact should be had with food or food preparations until 24 hours after the fever ends. A throat culture may be needed to rule out strep infections.
Vomiting	Avoid contact with food, children, and other personnel until 24 hours after the vomiting ends.

possibility of a cook's absence by maintaining an emergency menu that includes easy-to-prepare foods, such as:

- canned soups (low salt)
- peanut butter
- canned or frozen vegetables, fruits, and fruit juices
- canned tuna or cooked chicken that has been frozen
- cheese (can be frozen)
- rice and pastas
- dried or canned beans
- eggs

Meals that require a minimum of time and cooking skill are easy for substitute cooks to prepare when supplies are readily available.

Food handlers should always wear clean, washable clothing and change aprons frequently if they become soiled. Hair should be covered with a net, cap, or scarf and shoulders checked for loose hair prior to entering the kitchen. Fingernails should be kept short, clean, and without polish or artificial nails. Jewelry should not be worn with the exception of a plain wedding band to prevent the transfer of trapped food particles and bacteria. Food handlers should also refrain from chewing gum or smoking around food to prevent contamination from saliva.

Hand Washing Hand washing is of utmost importance to food safety (Teacher Checklist 18-1). Hands should be washed thoroughly:

- upon entering the food preparation area
- before putting on gloves to work with food

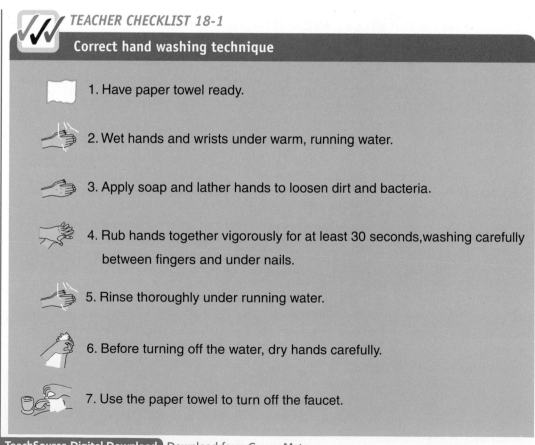

TEACHER CHECKLIST 18-1

Correct hand washing technique

1. Have paper towel ready.

2. Wet hands and wrists under warm, running water.

3. Apply soap and lather hands to loosen dirt and bacteria.

4. Rub hands together vigorously for at least 30 seconds, washing carefully between fingers and under nails.

5. Rinse thoroughly under running water.

6. Before turning off the water, dry hands carefully.

7. Use the paper towel to turn off the faucet.

- before touching food
- after handling nonfood items such as dirty dishes, cleaning or laundry supplies, garbage, or animals
- after handling raw meat, poultry, seafood, or eggs
- after using the bathroom
- after coughing, sneezing, or blowing the nose
- after using tobacco, eating, or drinking
- after touching hair or bare skin surfaces (e.g., face, ears, nose, arms)

▼ **Frequent and correct hand washing is essential for reducing the spread of food-borne illnesses.**

© Cengage Learning

Careful hand washing is mandatory after handling raw foods such as fish, shellfish, meat, poultry, and eggs to prevent cross-contamination with other foods. Disposable gloves offer an additional measure of protection but hands must still be washed carefully following their removal. Current recommendations suggest that soap and water remain the accepted method for cleaning hands in non–health–care settings (Soon, Baines, & Seaman, 2012). Although waterless, alcohol-based gels are increasingly being used in health care settings, they are never considered a substitute for hand washing. Any cuts or abrasions on the food handler's forearms, arms, or hands must be bandaged and covered with gloves (hands only). Gloves should always be changed between preparations that involve handling raw and cooked foods and if they become torn.

Did You Know...

that can openers are often the dirtiest utensil in peoples' kitchen? Do you wash yours after every use?

?

Food Preparation Areas and Equipment Traffic through kitchen areas should be minimized to reduce the potential for contaminating food with dirt and bacteria. Kitchen areas and equipment must be maintained according to strict sanitary procedures. A schedule, such as that shown in Figure 18–6, can be used to ensure that all areas of the kitchen, including floors, walls, ranges, ovens, and refrigerators, are cleaned regularly. Special care and attention must be given to equipment that comes in direct contact with food. Countertops and other surfaces on which food is being prepared should be disinfected with a chlorine bleach solution between every preparation of different food types (meat, salads, fruit). A fresh bleach solution must be mixed daily to retain its disinfecting strength.

⚠ **CAUTION**

Never mix bleach with anything other than water—a poisonous gas can result!

▼ **Use separate cutting boards for meats and fresh foods to prevent cross-contamination.**

© USDA

Cutting boards should be nonporous (preferably plastic) and in good condition. They should be washed with hot, soapy water and sanitized with a bleach solution after each use. Separate cutting boards should be designated for different food preparations (e.g., meat, raw poultry, salad, fresh fruits or vegetables) to reduce the potential for cross contamination (Soares et al., 2012). Cutting boards can be labeled or color coded to indicate their specific purpose.

The sink, faucet handles, and drain should be disinfected after any contact with raw meat, fish, shellfish, eggs, or poultry. Food particles trapped in a moist drain and the garbage disposal provide an excellent environment for bacterial growth. A disinfecting or chlorine bleach solution can be mixed and poured down the drain.

FIGURE 18–6   **Frequent, systematic cleaning is essential for maintaining a safe and sanitary kitchen.**

CLEANING SCHEDULE

Daily
▼ Cutting boards are sanitized after each use.
▼ Counter tops are washed and sanitized before food preparation is begun and between preparation of different foods.
▼ Tables are washed with sanitizing solution.
▼ Can openers are washed and sanitized.
▼ Range tops are cleaned and functional.
▼ Floors are damp mopped.
▼ Sink is scrubbed and disinfected.

Weekly
▼ Ovens are cleaned.
▼ Refrigerator is cleaned with soap and rinsed with vinegar water.

As Needed
▼ Refrigerator/freezer are defrosted.
▼ Walls are around countertops are washed.
▼ Floors are scrubbed and sanitized.

Dishwashing   Dishes should either be washed by hand or in a mechanical dishwasher. If washing by hand:

▶ Wash dishes with hot water and detergent.
▶ Rinse dishes in hot, clear water.
▶ Sanitize dishes with chlorine bleach solution or scald with boiling water.
▶ Air dry (not dried with a towel) all dishes, utensils, and surfaces.

If a mechanical dishwasher is used for dishwashing, the machine must meet local health department standards. Some state licensing regulations provide guidelines as to which dishwashing method is permitted based on the number of persons being served.

Food Service Areas   The eating area also requires special attention. Tables used for classroom activities must be washed and sanitized with a disinfecting solution:

▶ before and after each meal
▶ before and after each snack

Children and adults must always wash their hands carefully before eating and especially before they begin to set the table or to prepare and serve food. Children should also be taught that serving spoons are used to serve food and then replaced in the serving dishes. They must never be allowed to eat food directly from the serving dishes or serving utensils.

Continuous assessment of sanitation practices in the food preparation and service areas is essential for preventing food-related illness. A functional tool for monitoring the food environment and food handling practices is illustrated in Teacher Checklist 18-2.

18-2c Separate Foods

Steps must be taken to prevent the cross-contamination of minimally prepared foods with raw meat, poultry, or seafood juices or household chemicals. Bacteria present in meat juices will not be destroyed unless the food items are heated to the appropriate temperature prior to their

TEACHER CHECKLIST 18-2

Checklist for evaluating sanitary conditions in food service areas.

SANITATION EVALUATION

	EX	GOOD	FAIR	POOR
FOOD				
1. Supplies of food and beverages must meet local, state, and federal codes.				
2. Meats and poultry must be inspected and passed for wholesomeness by federal or state inspectors.				
3. Milk and milk products must be pasteurized.				
4. Home-canned foods must not be used.				
FOOD STORAGE				
1. Perishable foods are stored at temperatures that will prevent spoilage:				
a. Refrigerator temperature: 40°F (4.4°C) or below				
b. Freezer temperature: 0°F (−18°C) or below				
2. Thermometers are located in the warmest part of each refrigerator and freezer and are checked daily.				
3. Refrigerator has enough shelves to allow space between foods for air circulation to maintain proper temperatures.				
4. Frozen foods are thawed in refrigerator or quick-thawed under cold water for immediate preparation, or thawed as part of the cooking process (never thawed at room temperature).				
5. Food is examined for spoilage, dirt, and insect infestation when brought into the school or center.				
6. Foods are stored in rodent-proof and insect-proof covered metal, glass, or hard plastic containers.				
7. Food containers are stored above the floor (6 inches) on racks that permit moving for easy cleaning.				
8. Storerooms are dry and free from leaky plumbing or drainage problems. All holes and cracks in storeroom are repaired.				
9. Storerooms are kept cool: 50°F to 70°F (10°C to 21°C)				

(Continued)

TEACHER CHECKLIST 18-2

Checklist for evaluating sanitary conditions in food service areas. *(continued)*

SANITATION EVALUATION

	EX	GOOD	FAIR	POOR
10. All food items are stored separately from nonfood items.				
11. Inventory system is used to be sure that stored food is rotated.				
FOOD PREPARATION AND HANDLING				
1. All raw fruits and vegetables are washed before use. Tops of cans are washed before opening.				
2. Thermometers are used to check internal temperatures of: a. Poultry—minimum 165°F (73.9°C)				
b. Pork and pork products—minimum 160°F (71.1°C)				
3. Meat salads, poultry salads, potato salads, egg salad, cream-filled pastries, and other potentially hazardous prepared foods are prepared from chilled products as quickly as possible and refrigerated in shallow containers or served immediately.				
4. All potentially hazardous foods are maintained below 40°F (4.4°C) or above 140°F (60°C) during transportation and holding until service.				
5. Foods are covered or completely wrapped during transportation.				
6. Two spoons are used for tasting foods.				
7. Each serving bowl has a serving spoon.				
8. Leftover food from serving bowls on the tables is not saved. An exception would be raw fruits and vegetables that could be washed.				
9. Food is held in kitchen at safe temperatures and is used for refilling serving bowls.				
10. Foods stored for reuse are placed in shallow pans and refrigerated or frozen immediately.				
11. Leftovers or prepared dishes are held in refrigerator or frozen immediately.				

(Continued)

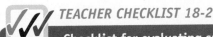

TEACHER CHECKLIST 18-2

Checklist for evaluating sanitary conditions in food service areas. *(continued)*

SANITATION EVALUATION

	EX	GOOD	FAIR	POOR

STORAGE OF NONFOOD SUPPLIES

1. All cleaning supplies (including dish sanitizers) and other poisonous materials are stored in locked compartments or in compartments well above children's reach and in areas separate from food, dishes, and utensils.

2. Poisonous and toxic materials other than those needed for kitchen sanitation are stored in locked compartments outside the kitchen area.

3. Insect and rodent poisons are stored in locked compartments in an area apart from other cleaning compounds to avoid contamination or mistaken usage.

CLEANING AND CARE OF EQUIPMENT

1. A cleaning schedule is followed:
   a. Floors are wet mopped daily and scrubbed as needed.

   b. Food preparation surfaces are washed and sanitized between preparation of different food items (as between meat and salad preparation).

   c. Cutting boards are made of hard nontoxic material, and are smooth and free from cracks, crevices, and open seams.

   d. Cutting boards are thoroughly washed and sanitized after use with any single meat, fish, or poultry item.

   e. Can openers are washed and sanitized daily.

   f. Utensils are cleaned and sanitized between uses on different food items.

2. Dishwashing is performed according to an approved method:
   a. *Hand washed*—three-step operation including sanitizing rinse.

(Continued)

SANITATION EVALUATION

	EX	GOOD	FAIR	POOR
b. *Mechanical*—dishwasher that meets local health department standards.				
3. Range tops are washed daily and as needed to keep them clean during preparation.				
1. Ovens are cleaned weekly or as needed.				
2. Refrigerator is washed once a week with vinegar.				
3. Freezer is defrosted when there is about 1/4-inch thickness of frost.				
4. Tables and other eating surfaces are washed with a mild disinfectant solution before and after each meal.				
5. All food contact surfaces are air-dried after cleaning and sanitizing.				
6. Cracked or chipped utensils or dishes are removed from use and discarded.				
7. Garbage cans are leak-proof and have tight-fitting lids.				
8. Garbage cans are lined with plastic liners, emptied and disinfected regularly.				
9. There is a sufficient number of garbage containers available.				
INSECT AND RODENT CONTROL				
1. Only an approved pyrethrin-base insecticide or fly swatter is used in the food preparation area.				
2. Insecticides do not come in contact with raw or cooked food, utensils, or equipment used in food preparation and serving, or with any other food contact surface.				
3. Doors and windows have screens in proper repair and are closed at all times. All openings to the outside are closed or properly screened to prevent entrance of rodents or insects.				

(Continued)

TEACHER CHECKLIST 18-2

Checklist for evaluating sanitary conditions in food service areas. *(continued)*

SANITATION EVALUATION

	EX	GOOD	FAIR	POOR
PERSONAL SANITATION				
1. Health of food service personnel meets standards: a. TB test is current.				
b. Physical examination is up to date.				
2. Personnel who work with or near food are free from communicable disease.				
3. Clean, washable clothing is worn.				
4. Hairnets or hair caps are worn in the kitchen.				
5. There is no use of tobacco or chewing gum in the kitchen.				
6. Hands are washed thoroughly before touching food, before work, after handling nonfood items, between handling of different food items, and after using bathroom, after coughing, sneezing, and blowing nose.				

TeachSource Digital Download Download from CourseMate.

consumption. Meats should always be separated from fresh fruits and vegetables, sealed in plastic bags, packed separately at the checkout counter, and refrigerated away from foods that will not be cooked.

18-2d Food Storage

Perishable foods must be stored at appropriate temperatures and used within a few days to prevent food-related illness. A thermometer should be placed in the warmest area of the refrigerator and freezer (i.e., nearest the front of shelves or drawers) to determine if appropriate temperatures are being maintained. Refrigerator temperatures should be set

▼ Refrigerator temperatures should be maintained and checked regularly to keep perishable foods safe.

© USDA

at or below 40°F (4.4°C) and freezers at or below 0°F (−18°C) . Foods must remain frozen until they are ready to be used, and then thawed:

- in the refrigerator
- in cold water (place food in watertight plastic bag; change water every 30 minutes)
- in a microwave oven
- during the cooking process

CAUTION

Frozen food should never be thawed at room temperature! Once thawed, food should be used and never refrozen.

Non-perishable foods, such as cereals, grains, dried beans, spices, and canned items should be stored in a cool, dry area away from sunlight. Although most non-perishable foods will keep for 12 to 24 months, it is always important to check and to use by their expiration date.

18-2e Cook and Serve Foods Correctly

Did You Know...

that many fruits, vegetables, and herbs contain naturally occurring pesticides to protect them from insects and animals? However, they are not harmful to humans.

The way food is prepared plays an important role in making sure it is safe to eat. Fresh fruits and vegetables can carry bacteria and pesticide residues that need to be washed off before they are used (Li et al., 2012; Winter, 2012) (Figure 18–7). Produce that will not be peeled, such as strawberries, potatoes, and green onions, can be cleaned under running water with a soft brush to remove surface dirt. Lettuce leaves should also be washed individually. Even produce that will be peeled, such as melons, bananas, oranges, and carrots should be rinsed. This prevents bacteria from being introduced into the edible portions when the fruit or vegetable is cut or touched with hands that have handled contaminated peel or rind. The tops of canned foods should always be washed before they are opened; this prevents contaminants from being introduced into the food or from contaminating other cans or work surfaces via a dirty can opener. (Can openers must be washed between every use to prevent cross-contamination.)

Cooking and holding foods at a proper temperature is critical for preventing the growth of infectious pathogens (Figure 18–8). It is NEVER safe for young children to eat raw or undercooked eggs, meat products, fish, or seafood because their immature immune systems leave them vulnerable to food-borne illness. Soups, salads, and dishes that include meat, poultry, seafood,

---

FIGURE 18–7   **Pesticide residues detected in fresh fruits and vegetables.**

"Dirty dozen": Produce with the highest residue levels	"Clean fifteen": Produce with the lowest residue levels
Apples	Onions
Celery	Sweet corn
Bell peppers	Pineapples
Peaches	Avocado
Strawberries	Cabbage
Nectarines (imported)	Sweet peas
Grapes	Asparagus
Spinach	Mangoes
Lettuce	Eggplant
Cucumbers	Kiwi
Blueberries (domestic)	Cantaloupe (domestic)
Potatoes	Sweet potatoes
	Grapefruit
	Watermelon
	Mushrooms

Source: U.S. Department of Agriculture (2012).

FIGURE 18–8   **Safe cooking temperatures for meats.**

"Is it *done* yet?"

You can't tell by *looking*. Use a **food thermometer** to be sure.

USDA Recommended Safe Minimum Internal Temperatures

Beef, Pork, Veal, Lamb Steaks, Roasts & Chops	Fish	Beef, Pork, Veal, Lamb Ground	Egg Dishes	Turkey, Chicken & Duck Whole, Pieces & Ground
145 °F with a 3-minute rest time	145 °F	160 °F	160 °F	165 °F

www.IsItDoneYet.gov

USDA Meat & Poultry Hotline: 1-888-MPHotline (1-888-674-6854)

USDA United States Department of Agriculture
Food Safety and Inspection Service

USDA is an equal opportunity provider and employer.
July 2005 • Slightly Revised August 2011

© USDA

dairy, or eggs are especially prone to spoilage. They should be prepared from ingredients that have been cooked and thoroughly chilled or held at temperatures below 40°F (4.4°C) until they are used. Protein based dishes should be assembled quickly (from chilled ingredients) and served or immediately refrigerated in shallow containers. Remember that cold temperatures **STOP** most (not all) bacterial growth, while heat **KILLS** most (not all) bacteria.

When food is being transported, it must be covered or wrapped to maintain appropriate temperatures and to lower the potential for **microbial** contamination. Each serving bowl, dish, or pan should have its own spoon; spoons should not be used to serve more than one food. Care must also be taken so that serving spoons do not touch children's plates to prevent contamination from saliva.

In group settings and schools, foods that have previously been served should not be saved. An exception to this rule are fresh fruits and vegetables that can be washed after removal from the table and served later or incorporated into baked

▼ **Children's hands should be washed after handling raw eggs to prevent food-borne illness.**

© Cengage Learning

microbial – *refers to living organisms, such as bacteria, viruses, parasites, or fungi that can cause disease.*

▶❚❚ TeachSource Video Connections

Promoting Children's Health: A Focus on Nutrition in an Early Childhood Setting

Learning about personal hygiene and other healthy habits is important for safeguarding children against illness. These practices can also help protect children from experiencing a food-related illness because many microorganisms are transmitted by dirty hands. As you watch the learning video, *Promoting Children's Health: A Focus on Nutrition in an Early Childhood Setting*, consider the following questions:

1. What learning objective was the teacher attempting to achieve with this lesson?

2. How did the teacher incorporate learning about sanitation and its relationship to wellness into this lesson?

3. Do you think this was an effective strategy for reinforcing children's hand washing skills? Explain.

4. What step of the hand washing procedure did the boy *not* perform correctly and, thus, may have unknowingly re-contaminated his hands?

Watch on CourseMate.

products such as quick breads and muffins. Foods held in the kitchen at proper temperatures (160°F [71.1°C] for hot food or 40°F [4.4°C] or below for cold foods) for no longer than two hours are safe to eat. Foods that are to be saved should be placed in shallow pans (3 inches or less in depth so they cool quickly) and immediately refrigerated or frozen.

18-2f Discard Spoiled Food

Foods that are visibly moldy, soured, discolored, have an unusual odor, or are beginning to liquefy should not be used. Likewise, food in bulging cans, cans in which the liquid is foamy or smells strange, or that "spew" when opened should be discarded immediately. A good motto to remember is: When in doubt, throw it out!

Did You Get It?

Fruits and vegetables such as melons, berries, and salad vegetables must be examined carefully to ensure they are properly packaged and refrigerated, especially if they:

a. have been cut
b. are fresh
c. are seasonal
d. have been processed

Take the full quiz on CourseMate.

18-3 Hazard Analysis and Critical Control Point

Great care must be taken when food is being purchased, prepared, and served to large groups and at-risk populations, including young children. Schools, hospitals, food banks, restaurants, and food processing plants have adapted the **Hazard Analysis and Critical Control Point (HACCP)** system for keeping foods safe. HACCP is a seven-step food safety and self-conducted inspection system that highlights potentially hazardous foods and how they are handled in the food service environment. The U.S. Food and Drug Administration (FDA) recommends the implementation of HACCP because it is one of the most effective and efficient ways to ensure that food products are safe (U.S. FDA, 2013). A sound HACCP plan is based on the following principles:

1. **Conducting a hazard analysis**. In this phase, an HACCP team is assembled. The team lists all food items used in the establishment with the product code, preparation techniques, and storage requirements for each one. A flowchart is then designed to follow food from the time it is received until it is served to identify potential hazards during each step of this process (Figure 18–9).

Hazard Analysis Critical Control Point (HACCP) – *a food safety and self-inspection system that highlights potentially hazardous foods and how they are handled in the food service department.*

© 2015 Cengage Learning

FIGURE 18–9 Recipe flowcharts are useful for identifying potential hazards in a food service program.

BASIC BEEF CHILI

INGREDIENTS	AMOUNT	25	50	100
Lean ground beef	Lbs	7	14	28
Canned tomatoes	Qts	1 1/2	3	6
Canned kidney beans	Qts	1 3/4	3 1/2	7
Tomato paste	Cups	1 3/4	3 1/2	7
Water	Gals	1/2	1	2
Dehydrated onions	Ozs	1	2	4
Chili Powder	Tbsp	3	6	12
Sugar	Tbsp	1 1/4	2 1/2	5
Cumin	Tbsp	2	4	8
Garlic powder	Tbsp	1	2	4
Onion powder	Tbsp	1	2	4
Paprika	Tbsp	1	2	4
Black pepper	Tbsp	1/2	1	2

PREPARATION

1. **CCP** Thaw ground beef under refrigeration (41°F).

2. Place ground beef in steam kettle or in large skillet on stove top. Cook meat using medium-high heat until lightly browned. While cooking, break meat into crumbs of about 1/2" to 1/4" pieces.

3. Drain meat well, stirring while draining to remove as much fat as possible. If desired, pour hot water over beef and drain to remove additional fat.

4. Mash or grind canned tomatoes with juice. Add to kettle or stock pot with cooked ground beef. Add remaining ingredients to mixture and stir well.

5. **CCP** Simmer chili mixture for 1 hour, stirring occasionally. Temperature of cooked mixture must register 160°F or higher.

Flowchart:

Ground beef → RECEIVING → STORAGE Freezer → PRE-PREPARATION CCP Thaw in refrigerator → PREPARATION (as directed) CCP Cook to minimum 160°F → HOLDING CCP Cover and maintain minimum 140°F

Tomatoes, Dehydrated onions, Kidney beans, Seasonings, Tomato paste, Sugar → RECEIVING → STORAGE Dry → PREPARATION (as directed) CCP Cook to minimum 160°F

(continued)

FIGURE 18–9 Recipe flowcharts are useful for identifying potential hazards in a food service program. *(continued)*

BASIC BEEF CHILI (cont'd)

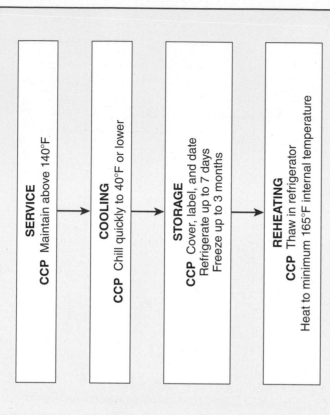

SERVICE
CCP Maintain above 140°F

↓

COOLING
CCP Chill quickly to 40°F or lower

↓

STORAGE
CCP Cover, label, and date
Refrigerate up to 7 days
Freeze up to 3 months

↓

REHEATING
CCP Thaw in refrigerator
Heat to minimum 165°F internal temperature

PREPARATION (cont'd)

6. **CCP** Remove from heat and portion into service pans. Cover and hold for service (140°F).

7. Portion: 1 cup (8 ounces) per serving

SERVICE

1. **CCP** Maintain temperature of finished product above 140°F during entire service period. Keep covered whenever possible. Take and record temperature of unserved product every 30 minutes. Maximum holding time, 4 hours.

STORAGE

1. **CCP** Transfer unserved product into clean, 2-inch deep pans. Quick-chill. Cooling temperature of product must be as follows: from 140°F to 70°F within 2 hours and then from 70°F to 40°F or below, within an additional 4-hour period. Take and record temperature every hour during chill-down.

2. **CCP** Cover, label, and date. Refrigerate at 40°F or lower for up to 7 days (based on quality maintained) or freeze at 0°F for up to 3 months.

REHEATING:

1. **CCP** Thaw product under refrigeration, if frozen (41°F).

2. **CCP** Remove from refrigeration, transfer into shallow, 2-inch deep pans and immediately place in preheated 350°F oven, covered. Heat for 30 minutes or until internal temperature reaches 165°F or above.

Discard unused product.

2. **Determining the critical control point (CCP).** These are critical points during food preparation at which potential and preventable hazards are identified (i.e., cooking foods to appropriate temperatures, using proper thawing techniques, maintaining proper refrigerator/freezer temperatures).

3. **Establishing critical limits.** Procedures and operating guidelines are developed during this step to prevent or reduce hazards in the food service area. Requirements are established and must be monitored continuously to ensure they are being met.

4. **Establishing monitoring procedures.** This principle is accomplished through consistent documentation in temperature logs, observation and measurement of requirements, frequent feedback, and monitoring by the food service manager.

5. **Establishing corrective actions.** Specific actions need to be developed and implemented if a critical control point procedure is not being met. Each event must be accurately documented so that future occurrences are prevented.

6. **Establishing record-keeping and documentation procedures.** Record-keeping is a key component of the HAACP process. Important records that must be maintained include recipes, time/temperature logs, employee training documentation, cleaning schedules, and job descriptions.

7. **Establish verification procedures.** Management must be diligent in observing staff members' routine behaviors and provide continued training to address any deficiencies.

Continuous monitoring and improvement efforts are necessary for the HAACP procedure to function successfully in any food service establishment.

Did You Get It?

In carrying out a HACCP plan, corrective action must be implemented immediately if a _____ is not being met or adhered to.
  a. hazard analysis
  b. critical control point procedure
  c. critical limit
  d. verification procedure

Take the full quiz on CourseMate.

18-4 Food-Borne Illnesses

The term food poisoning is often used to describe a variety of food-borne illnesses that are caused by the presence of bacteria, viruses, parasites, funguses, and several molds. Common food-borne illnesses, including their potential source of contamination, symptoms, and prevention methods, are presented in Table 18–1. Many foods infected with disease-producing organisms provide the consumer with few notable clues. These foods may smell and appear safe, yet be capable of causing severe illness and disability. For this reason, it is critical that food handlers always adhere to basic food safety measures when preparing meals.

Did You Get It?

Which food item is most likely to cause listeria, a food-borne illness whose symptoms range from fever and diarrhea to convulsions and even possible miscarriages?
  a. improperly canned foods
  b. unwashed lettuce and melons
  c. unpasteurized dairy products
  d. cooked shellfish

Take the full quiz on CourseMate.

---

critical control point (CCP) – *a point or procedure in a specific food system where loss of control may result in an unacceptable health risk.*

TABLE 18–1   Food-Borne Illnesses

Disease and Organism That Causes It	Source of Illness	Symptoms	Prevention Methods
salmonellosis *Salmonella* (bacteria; more than 2,000 varieties)	Especially common in raw meats, poultry, eggs, fish, milk, sprouts, and foods that include these items. Organism multiplies rapidly at room temperature.	Onset: 1–3 days after eating; symptoms may last 7 days; can be fatal. Nausea, fever, headache, abdominal cramps, diarrhea, and sometimes vomiting.	• Adhere to safe food handling practices. • Cook foods thoroughly. • Refrigerate foods promptly and properly.
E. coli *E. coli 0157:H7* (bacteria)	May occur in undercooked beef (primarily ground beef), unpasteurized apple cider, raw milk, raw fruits and vegetables, and person-to-person contact. Organism is naturally present in animals raised for food.	Onset: 1–7 days; symptoms can last 7–10 days. Watery, profuse diarrhea, fever. Diarrhea may be bloody.	• Cook ground meats to 165°F, the temperature high enough to inactivate *E. coli.* • Pasteurization.
Staphylococcal food poisoning staphylococcal enterotoxin (produced by *Staphylococcus aureus* bacteria)	Toxins are produced when food contaminated with the bacteria remains too long at room temperature. Meats, poultry, egg products; tuna, potato and macaroni salads; and cream-filled pastries are ideal environments for these bacteria to produce toxin.	Onset: 1–8 hours after eating; symptoms may last 24–48 hours; rarely fatal. Diarrhea, vomiting, nausea, abdominal cramps, and prostration. Mimics stomach flu.	• Use sanitary food handling practices. • Cook foods to proper temperatures. • Refrigerate foods promptly and properly.
botulism *Clostridium botulinum* (bacteria)	Bacteria are widespread in the environment. However, bacteria produce toxin only in an anaerobic (oxygen-less) environment of little acidity. Types A, B, and F may result from inadequate processing of low-acid canned foods, such as green beans, mushrooms, spinach, olives, beef, and lunch meats. Type E normally occurs in fish.	Onset: 6–36 hours after eating, but can develop up to 10 days after ingestion. Recovery is slow, some symptoms may remain forever. Symptoms include muscle weakness, double vision, slurred speech, difficulty swallowing and breathing, and progressive paralysis. OBTAIN MEDICAL HELP IMMEDIATELY. BOTULISM IS OFTEN FATAL.	• Use proper methods for canning low-acid foods. • Avoid commercially canned low-acid foods with leaky seals or cans that are dented or bulging. • Dispose of foods carefully to prevent animals from exposure.
Listeriosis *Listeria monocytogenes* (bacteria)	Raw animal and dairy products; fresh, soft cheeses; contaminated water.	Onset: 7–21 days or longer; recovery time varies. Muscle aches, mild fever, diarrhea, and miscarriage; can spread to the nervous system, causing headache, stiff neck, loss of balance, and convulsions.	• Pasteurization. • Adhere to proper cooking and refrigeration recommendations. • Wash hands to prevent cross-contamination.

Disease / Organism	Description	Symptoms	Prevention
parahaemolyticus food poisoning *Vibrio parahaemolyticus* (bacteria)	Organism thrives in warm waters and can contaminate fish and shellfish. Avoid eating raw fish and shellfish (e.g., mussels, oysters).	Onset: 12–24 hours after eating; lasts 1–7 days. Causes abdominal pain, nausea, vomiting, and diarrhea; can also bring on fever, headache, chills, and mucus and blood in the stools. Rarely fatal.	• Use sanitary food handling, including hand washing. • Cook seafood thoroughly.
gastrointestinal disease *norovirus, rotavirus* (virus)	Viruses are present in the human intestinal tract and expelled in feces; spread person-to-person and indirectly. Food can become contaminated: (1) when sewage is used to enrich garden/farm soil, (2) by direct hand-to-food contact during meal preparation, and (3) when shellfish grow in sewage-contaminated water.	Onset: 1–2 days; usually lasts 4–5 days but may last for weeks. Causes severe diarrhea, nausea, and vomiting.	• Maintain sanitary food handling procedures. • Wash hands and any contaminated clothing. • Disinfect all surfaces. • Use purified drinking water. • Ensure proper sewage disposal. • Cook foods adequately.
hepatitis *hepatitis A virus* (virus)	Chief food sources: shellfish harvested from contaminated areas, and foods that are handled a lot during preparation and then eaten raw (such as vegetables).	Onset: 5–50 days (average 28 days); recovery takes several weeks. Causes jaundice, fatigue, headache, diarrhea, and dark urine. May cause liver damage and death.	• Maintain sanitary food handling and cooking of foods. • Wash hands thoroughly. • Ensure proper sewage disposal.
mycotoxicosis *mycotoxins* (molds)	Produced in foods relatively high in moisture. Chief food sources: beans, grains, and peanuts that have been stored in warm, moist places.	May cause liver and/or kidney disease.	• Discard foods with visible mold. • Store susceptible foods properly.
giardiasis *Giardia lamblia* (parasite)	Parasites can reside in the intestinal tract of humans and animals and are expelled in feces. Parasites may be ingested from foods contaminated with sewage, from swallowing contaminated water (lake, pool, spring, river, spa), from dirty hands, and infected persons.	Onset: 1–2 weeks; lasts 2–6 weeks with treatment. Diarrhea, abdominal pain, flatulence, and nausea.	• Maintain sanitary food handling. • Wash hands carefully. • Drink only from approved water sources.
Perfringens food poisoning *Clostridium perfringens* (bacteria)	Bacteria are widespread in environment. Generally found in meat and poultry and dishes containing them. Bacteria multiply rapidly when food remains at room temperature too long. Destroyed by cooking.	Onset: 8–22 hours after eating (usually 12); symptoms last 1–2 days and are usually mild. Causes abdominal pain, diarrhea, nausea, and vomiting. Can be more serious in older or debilitated people.	• Maintain sanitary handling of foods, especially meat, meat dishes, and gravies. • Cook foods at appropriate temperatures. • Refrigerate foods promptly and properly.

(continued)

TABLE 18–1 Food-Borne Illnesses *(continued)*

Disease and Organism That Causes It	Source of Illness	Symptoms	Prevention Methods
shigellosis (bacillary dysentery) *Shigella* (bacteria)	Food becomes contaminated when a human carrier with poor sanitary habits handles liquid or moist food that is then not cooked thoroughly. Organisms multiply in food stored above room temperature. Found in milk and dairy products, poultry, potato salad, and contaminated water.	Onset: 1–7 days after eating; lasts 4–7 days. Causes abdominal pain, cramps, bloody diarrhea, fever, sometimes vomiting. Can be serious in infants, the elderly, or debilitated people.	• Maintain sanitary handling of food. • Cook food to proper temperatures. • Dispose of sewage and diapers properly. • Wash hands frequently and carefully.
campylobacterosis *Campylobacter jejuni* (bacteria)	Chief food sources: raw and undercooked poultry and meat, unpasteurized milk, and contaminated water.	Onset: 2–5 days after eating; lasts 6–7 days. Causes diarrhea (may be bloody), cramping, nausea, and fever.	• Cook foods thoroughly. • Wash hands frequently and carefully. • Avoid unpasteurized milk.
gastroenteritis *Yersinia enterocolitica* (bacteria)	Bacteria multiply rapidly at room temperature, and at refrigerator temperatures of 39.2° to 48.2°F (4° to 9°C). Generally found in raw vegetables, undercooked meats (especially pork), water, and unpasteurized milk. Also transmitted person-to-person via dirty hands.	Onset: 4–7 days after exposure; lasts 1–3 weeks or longer. Flu-like symptoms, including fever, headache, nausea, diarrhea, abdominal pain, and fatigue. An important cause of gastroenteritis in children, but affects those of all ages. If not treated, can lead to more serious diseases (such as lymphadenitis, arthritis, and Reiter's syndrome).	• Cook foods thoroughly. • Sanitize cutting instruments and cutting boards before preparing foods that are eaten raw. • Avoid unpasteurized milk and unchlorinated water. • Wash hands carefully.
cereus food poisoning *Bacillus cereus* (bacteria and possibly their toxin)	Illness may be caused by the bacteria, which are widespread in the environment, or by an enterotoxin created by the bacteria. Found in raw meat, fish, milk, and vegetables. Bacteria multiply rapidly in foods stored at room temperature.	Can cause two types of illness: a) onset of nausea and vomiting 1–6 hours after eating; b) abdominal cramps and diarrhea 8–16 hours after eating.	• Maintain sanitary handling of foods. • Cook foods thoroughly. • Refrigerate foods promptly and properly.
cholera *Vibrio cholera* (bacteria)	Present in raw milk, fruits, and vegetables; contaminated water; fish and shellfish harvested from waters contaminated by human sewage. (Bacteria may also occur naturally in Gulf Coast waters.) Chief food sources: seafood, especially types eaten raw (such as oysters).	Onset: 1–3 days. Can range from "subclinical" (a mild uncomplicated bout with diarrhea) to fatal (intense diarrhea with dehydration). Severe cases require hospitalization and antibiotics.	• Maintain sanitary handling of foods. • Cook foods thoroughly, especially seafood. • Avoid drinking untreated water.

18-5 National and International Food Supply Safeguards

The globalization of food production and distribution has made it necessary for countries to focus more attention on ways to protect the safety of food supplies. The World Health Organization (WHO) has played a key role in raising international awareness and developing food safety guidelines. Individual countries have also responded by establishing stricter regulations and laws and enhancing their surveillance of imported foods.

Several government regulatory agencies, including the FDA, USDA, and National Oceanic and Atmospheric Administration (NOAA), are responsible for overseeing food safety in the United States. The FDA Food Safety Modernization Act (FSMA), signed into law in 2011, significantly expanded the agencies' authority and established new mandates, including a more rigorous inspection system, tougher compliance standards, and improved access to records. This legislation represents the first major change to U.S. food safety laws in decades and shifts agency responsibilities from a food-borne illness outbreak response mode to one of disease prevention.

18-5a Commercial Food Production

One of the most familiar, large-scale efforts practiced throughout the world to make food safer for human consumption is **pasteurization**. This process involves heating a food product briefly (approximately 16 seconds) to destroy harmful bacteria and other disease-causing microorganisms. Foods that are commonly pasteurized include milk and dairy products, egg products, fruit juices, vinegars, and canned foods. All milk and dairy products served in schools and early childhood programs must be pasteurized.

Steam pasteurization is a technique being used to produce safer meat products. This technology exposes processed meats and animal carcasses to pressurized steam for approximately 6 to 8 seconds to destroy harmful bacteria (Chen et al., 2012). Researchers are also studying a variety of additional preventive measures to improve meat safety, including spraying baby chicks with antibiotic mist to reduce salmonella infections in poultry, and changing cattle feeding practices immediately before slaughter to control *E. coli* in beef.

The introduction of **irradiation** as a food preservation technique has also played an important role in reducing the incidence of some food-borne diseases (Moosekian et al., 2012). The FDA has approved this technology as a "processing aid" for destroying illness-producing microorganisms, such as salmonella and *E. coli* in beef and poultry products, lunch meats, fresh fruits and vegetables, and processed foods containing eggs. Irradiation is also used to eliminate parasites and insects in spices and teas, slow the sprouting process (as in potatoes), delay ripening, and decrease spoilage. This procedure involves briefly exposing foods to low levels of radiant energy from gamma rays or an electron beam; the amount of exposure and the types of foods that can be irradiated are closely regulated by the FDA. The USDA has approved the use of irradiated ground beef for the School Lunch Program since 2004.

▼ New technologies are being developed to make food safer for consumption.

© chalabala/Shutterstock.com

---

pasteurization – *the process of heating a food to a prescribed temperature for a specific amount of time necessary to destroy disease-producing bacteria.*

irradiation – *food preservation by short-term exposure of the food to gamma rays.*

FIGURE 18–10　Irradiated foods are required to display the radura symbol.

© U.S. Environmental Protection Agency

Irradiated foods must carry the international symbol and message shown in Figure 18–10. Irradiation is currently being practiced in more than 40 countries and is endorsed by the World Health Organization, the American Medical Association, and the CDC, among other groups (Griffin, Hallman, & Griffin, 2012). Although some consumer groups remain skeptical about food irradiation, the practice is considered to be a safe and effective method for improving food safety. Irradiated foods are not radioactive, nor do they retain radioactivity. Nutrient loss during irradiation, particularly of vitamins A, E, and C, and thiamin, is minimal and significantly less than losses that occur during most conventional food preservation methods.

Irradiation serves an important role in improving food safety, but it is not the only solution to preventing food-borne illness. Various advocacy groups have raised concerns that irradiation covers up unsanitary food processing procedures and that consumers will become careless and dependent on commercial industries to prevent food-related illnesses.

Pressure continues to be placed on the food industry to develop new strategies for controlling and preventing food contamination. One newly emerging method being tested on fresh produce, such as spinach and lettuce, involves electrostatic spraying with natural acid and oil extracts to reduce bacterial contamination (Ganesh et al., 2012). Improved animal-raising (e.g., feed, water, sanitation) and slaughtering practices are also being explored (Doyle & Erickson, 2012). New food packaging films that are capable of destroying existing microorganisms are currently being developed as well as rapid chilling and freezing techniques (Abreu, Cruz, & Losada, 2012; Davidson & Critzer, 2012).

Undoubtedly, many more innovative strategies will emerge as the food industry continues its efforts to eliminate diseases transmitted via food. However, advanced technologies will never replace the critical role that consumers' play in handling foods safely. Early childhood is an ideal time to begin teaching children and their families important practices, including personal hygiene and kitchen safety, to reduce their chances of experiencing a food-related illness.

CONNECTING TO EVERYDAY PRACTICE

Recreational Waters, Beaches, and *E. coli*

E. coli 0157:H7 is a deadly bacterium that is frequently in the news. It is commonly associated with outbreaks of contaminated and undercooked meats—especially ground beef. However, foods are not the only source of this infectious agent. A recent *E. coli* outbreak occurred at a popular water park when one of the children in attendance accidentally defecated in the wading pool. Six children were hospitalized and many more sickened with an *E. coli* 0157:H7 illness. It was later determined that chlorine levels had not been maintained at a level sufficient to destroy the bacteria. Additional *E. coli* outbreaks have been associated with hot tubs, swimming in lakes or rivers, and children's petting zoos. *E. coli* 0157:H7 infections have also been traced to beach sand (Heaney et al., 2012; Yamahara et al., 2012).

Think About This:

▶ Are your program's sanitation procedures adequate to prevent illnesses such as *E. coli* from spreading through water play?

▶ Are your food preparation and service methods safe?

▶ What sanitation precautions should you observe when taking children on an outing to prevent this illness?

Did You Get It?

Foods labeled with the international radura sign:

a. are organic
b. have been irradiated
c. have undergone pasteurization
d. contain genetically altered ingredients

Take the full quiz on CourseMate.

PARTNERING with FAMILIES

Wash Those Hands!

Dear Families,

Food safety is everyone's responsibility, and it is never too early to introduce children to practices that will help protect their well-being. Hand washing is the single-most effective tool for reducing infectious diseases, including food-borne illnesses, that are commonly transferred by food, people, and objects in the environment. For this reason, it is important that children be taught how to wash their hands correctly and times when hand washing is necessary. Parents and teachers serve as visible role models and must consistently practice the same handwashing techniques being taught to children.

▶ Be sure children wash their hands with warm, soapy water before and after eating, after using the toilet, after playing with a pet, after playing in sand, and after covering a cough or blowing their nose.

▶ Keep a step stool nearby so it is easy for children to reach the sink.

▶ Post a chart near the sink and have children make a mark for every time she has washed her hands. Acknowledge your child for a job well done.

▶ Make hand washing fun. Purchase colorful soaps and soap dispensers; design special towels (use fabric paints to add the child's name).

▶ Be creative! Make up your own words to favorite childhood songs or nursery rhymes, such as "Row, Row, Row Your Boat" or "Old McDonald Had a Farm." Have children wash their hands for the entire length of the song. They will have fun while ensuring that an appropriate amount of time is spent washing hands.

CLASSROOM CORNER

Teacher Activities

Cleaning and Setting the Table...

(NHES PreK–2; National Health Education Standards 1.2.1; 7.2.1;7.2.2)

Concept: Cleaning the table before eating and touching the correct parts of cups, plates, and silverware when placing them on the table can prevent the spread of germs.

Learning Objectives

▶ Children will learn how to clean classroom tables before meals.

▶ Children will learn how to properly place cups, plates, and silverware on the table.

(continued)

CLASSROOM CORNER

Teacher Activities   *(continued)*

Supplies

▶ Soapy water and disinfectant water in spray bottles

▶ One dishcloth per table

▶ One paper towel per table

▶ Silverware, cups, plates, and napkins for meal time

Learning Activities

▶ Choose one helper per table and demonstrate how a table is to be washed and set for meal time.

▶ Have each child wash his hands carefully before starting.

▶ Fill a spray bottle with soapy water. Have the children take turns spraying and wiping the table surface where they are sitting. Next, the teacher should spray the disinfectant (bleach mixture or commercial product) and wipe it off.

▶ Have children wash their hands after cleaning the tables; explain that hands get dirty after touching a dirty table.

▶ Show children how to put one plate by each chair; they should only touch the outside rim of each plate.

▶ Show children how to handle silverware by touching only the handles and not the eating portion.

▶ Show children how to touch the lower part of the cup, not the rim. Have children place silverware, cups, and napkins at each place.

▶ Have children rewash their hands if they scratch their nose, cover a cough, and so on, while setting the table.

▶ Discuss how washing hands, cleaning the tables, and handling eating utensils correctly help prevent the spread of germs.

Evaluation

▶ Children will demonstrate the correct procedure for cleaning the tables.

▶ Children will set the tables correctly and touch the plates, cups, and silverware appropriately.

Additional lesson plans for grades 3–5 are available on CourseMate.

◖ Summary

▶ Food-borne illness is a significant public health threat. Factors that are contributing to an increased incidence include large-scale food production, demand for out-of-season and imported foods, consumption of more restaurant meals, and poor food handling practices followed in homes.

- Individuals at highest risk for food-borne illness are those whose immune system may be weakened by age, pregnancy, or a medical condition.

▶ Food service personnel must consistently follow basic food safety practices, including:
- Maintaining personal health and hygiene; not working around food when ill
- Practicing correct and consistent hand washing
- Purchasing and handling food items safely
- Storing and cooking foods at correct temperatures
- Sanitizing all food service areas regularly

▶ HACCP (Hazard Analysis and Critical Control Point) is a seven-step, self-administered program that aids the food handler in identifying and controlling potentially hazardous points in food production and preparation.

▶ Food-borne illnesses are most commonly caused by bacteria, viruses, parasites, and some molds. Prevention of food-related illness requires an awareness of foods typically involved, symptoms of illness, and preventive practices.

▶ The food industry currently utilizes several large-scale methods (e.g., pasteurization, steam, irradiation) to destroy harmful bacteria in foods. They are also developing and testing new techniques such as disinfectant sprays, altering animal feeding practices, and innovative packaging wrappers.

◖▶ Terms to Know

food-borne illness *p. 455*
food-borne illness outbreak *p. 455*
food infections *p. 457*
food intoxications *p. 457*

microbial *p. 469*
Hazard Analysis Critical Control
    Point (HACCP) *p. 470*
critical control point (CCP) *p. 473*

pasteurization *p. 477*
irradiation *p. 477*

◖▶ Chapter Review

A. By Yourself:

1. List three methods for maintaining food preparation areas that are clean and germ-free.
2. Describe the proper care, use, and handling of cutting boards that must be followed during food preparation.
3. How should ground meat be safely thawed if there is not time to defrost it in the refrigerator?
4. Samantha, a chef, has a cut on her hand. John, a school lunch cook, came to work with a sore throat and productive cough. Hanna, a cook's assistant, has experienced several days of unexplained diarrhea. What precautions must each of these food handlers take?

B. As a Group:

1. Describe the HACCP process. Develop your own HACCP plan that outlines the safety procedures that must be taken from the time you purchase a pound of ground beef until it shows up as a hamburger on your plate.
2. Identify and describe the personal sanitation practices that would be important to review with a newly hired cook.
3. Hold a class debate and argue the pros and cons of food irradiation.
4. Describe the audiences most likely to be sickened by food-borne illnesses and explain why they are at greater risk.

◖ Case Study

The health department recently investigated an outbreak of food poisoning at a local school. The children had been served a menu that included tacos, tossed lettuce salad, fresh melon cubes, and milk. Chris, the head cook, had forgotten to put the ground beef in the refrigerator to defrost a few days earlier, so she allowed it to thaw on the counter overnight. After dividing the partially thawed raw ground beef with her bare hands, she continued preparations for lunch and chopped the ingredients for a tossed salad. She then diced the melon into cubes for the fruit salad with the same knife that had been used to open the packages of ground beef,

1. What is the likely cause of this food-borne illness outbreak?
2. In what ways did the cook contribute to this situation?
3. How could this outbreak have been prevented?

◖ Application Activities

1. The cook at your early childhood center called in sick with strep throat. Using the emergency stock described in this chapter, plan a lunch menu that meets the CACFP meal pattern requirements outlined in Chapter 17.

2. Invite a laboratory technician to class. Ask her to make culture plates of a:
   a. hand before washing
   b. hand after washing with water only
   c. hand after washing with soap and water
   d. strand of hair
   e. classroom table (or desk); kitchen counter

   Have the technician return with the cultures after they have incubated for several days.
   a. Is bacterial growth present on any of the culture plates?
   b. Which cultures have the most bacterial growth?
   c. Discuss how these results could be best utilized in terms of:
      1. food preparation and service procedures
      2. early childhood center meal and snack times.

3. Visit a local early childhood center or public school. Use the sanitation checklist in Teacher Checklist 18-2 to assess the kitchen. Prepare a list of suggestions for correcting any problem areas noted and share your results with the program director.

◖ Helpful Web Resources

Canadian Food Inspection Agency (CFIA)	http://www.inspection.gc.ca
Centers for Disease Control and Prevention	http://www.cdc.gov
Partnership for Food Safety Education: Fight BAC!	http://www.fightbac.org
U.S. Food and Drug Administration	http://www.fda.gov
U.S. Department of Health & Human Services: Gateway to Government Food Safety Information	http://www.FoodSafety.gov
USDA Food Safety & Inspection Service (FSIS)	http://www.fsis.usda.gov

Visit the Education CourseMate for this textbook to access the eBook, Did You Get It? quizzes, Digital Downloads, TeachSource Video Cases, flashcards, and more. Go to CengageBrain.com to log in, register, or purchase access.

References

Centers for Disease Control & Prevention (CDC). (2011). Estimates of foodborne illness in the United States. Accessed on August 18, 2012 from http://www.cdc.gov/foodborneburden.

Chen, J., Ren, Y., Seow, J., Liu, T., Bang, W., & Yuk, H. (2012). Intervention technologies for ensuring microbiological safety of meat: Current and future trends, *Comprehensive Reviews in Food Science & Food Safety*, 11(2), 119–132.

Ganesh, V., Hettiarachchy, N., Griffis, C., Martin, E., & Ricke, S. (2012). Electrostatic spraying of food-grade organic and inorganic acids and plant extracts to decontaminate *Escherichia coli* O157:H7 on spinach and iceberg lettuce, *Journal of Food Science*, 77(7), M391–M396.

Griffin, E., Hallman, G., & Griffin, R. (2012). Current and potential trade in horticultural products irradiated for phytosanitary purposes, *Radiation Physics & Chemistry*, 81(8), 1203–1207.

Heaney, C., Sams, E., Dufour, A., Brenner, K., Haugland, R., Chern, E., Wing, S., Marshall, S., Love, D., Serre, M., Noble, R., & Wade, T. (2012). Fecal indicators in sand, sand contact, and risk of enteric illness among beachgoers, *Epidemiology*, 23(1), 95–106.

Hoffman, S., Batz, M., & Glenn, M. (2012). Annual cost of illness and quality-adjusted life year losses in the United States due to 14 foodborne pathogens, *Journal of Food Protection*, 75(7), 1292–1302.

Li, Y., Jiao, B., Zhao, Q., Wang, C., Gong, Y., Zhang, Y., & Chen, W. (2012). Effect of commercial processing on pesticide residues in orange products, *European Food Research & Technology*, 234(3), 449–456.

Moosekian, S., Sanghyup, J., Marks, B., & Ryser, E. (2012). X-Ray irradiation as a microbial intervention strategy for food, *Annual Review of Food Science & Technology*, 3, 493–510.

Soares, V., Pereira, J., Viana, C., Izidoro, T., Bersot, L., & Pinto, J. (2012). Transfer of *Salmonella* enteritidis to four types of surfaces after cleaning procedures and cross-contamination to tomatoes, *Food Microbiology*, 30(2), 453–456.

Soon, J., Baines, R., & Seaman, P. (2012). Meta-analysis of food safety training on hand hygiene knowledge and attitudes among food handlers, *Journal of Food Protection*, 75(4), 793–804(12).

Stinson, W., Carr, D., Nettles, M., & Johnson, J. (2011). Food safety programs based on HACCP principles in school nutrition programs: Implementation status and factors related to implementation, *Journal of Child Nutrition & Management*, 35(1), 15–24.

U.S. Food and Drug Administration (U.S. FDA). (2013). Hazard Analysis & Critical Control Points (HACCP). Accessed on May 17, 2013 from http://www.fda.gov/Food/GuidanceRegulation/HACCP/default.htm.Winter, C. (2012). Pesticide residues in imported, organic, and "suspect" fruits and vegetables, *Journal of Agricultural & Food Chemistry*, 60(18), 4425–4429.

Yamahara, K., Sassoubre, L., Goodwin, K., & Boehm, A. (2012). Occurrence and persistence of bacterial pathogens and indicator organisms in beach sand along the California coast, *Applied & Environmental Microbiology*, 78(6), 1733–1745.

chapter 19

Nutrition Education: Rationale, Concepts, and Lessons

▶ **#1 a, b, and c:** Promoting child development and learning
▶ **#2 a, b, and c:** Building family and community relationships
▶ **#3 a, c, and d:** Observing, documenting, and assessing to support young children and families
▶ **#4 a, b, c, and d:** Using developmentally effective approaches to connect with children and families
▶ **#5 a, b, and c:** Using content knowledge to build meaningful curriculum
▶ **#6 b, c, and d:** Becoming a professional
▶ Field experience

Learning Objectives

After studying this chapter, you should be able to:

LO 19-1 Explain why it is important to educate young children about nutrition and the role schools and families play in this process.

LO 19-2 Summarize the basic nutrition concepts and safety considerations that must be addressed in planning learning experiences for children.

LO 19-3 Discuss the principles of effective curriculum and lesson development.

LO 19-4 Identify several additional sources that influence children's ideas about food and nutrition.

In the simplest of terms, **nutrition education** is any activity that tells a person something about food. These activities may be structured, planned activities, or very brief, informal happenings. The primary goals of nutrition education designed for young children are to introduce them to a few basic nutrition principles and to encourage them to eat and enjoy a variety of nutritious foods.

19-1 Rationale for Teaching Children About Nutrition

Young children are in the process of forming lifelong eating habits and, thus, are more receptive to new ideas about food and food-related practices. Many everyday experiences, such as a field trip to the grocery store or farmer's market, planting a garden, or assisting with snack preparations can become valuable "teachable moments" for helping children to learn about good nutrition. When these impromptu and formal learning experiences are based on sound pedagogical principles, they can foster children's understanding, retention, and ability to relate nutrition information to their own personal well-being. Children's learning in all developmental areas can also be supported when teachers take time to thoughtfully integrate nutrition education across the curriculum:

> ▶ *Promotion of language development and listening skills*
> Children can learn and use food names, food preparation terms, and names of utensils. Children can also use language to communicate with their peers and teachers, offer explanations,

---

nutrition education – *activities that impart information about food and its use in the body.*

and respond to the teacher's questions throughout the nutrition activity. A variety of media sources, including children's literature, video clips, and music, can also be introduced to reinforce language, listening, and motor skills as well as basic nutrition concepts (Figure 19–1).

▶ *Promotion of cognitive development*
Children can learn to follow step-by-step directions in recipes. Math concepts are learned through activities that involve measurement of food (cups, ounces, teaspoons), counting, and time periods. Science concepts, such as changes in form (e.g., solids, liquids, gases), can be reinforced through activities that involve heating, mixing, cooking, or chilling of foods. Children also begin to learn respect for other cultures, different food practices, where foods come from, and the ways in which foods are grown or produced.

▶ *Promotion of sensorimotor development*
Hand-eye coordination and hand-finger dexterity are developed through measuring, cutting, mixing, spreading, and serving food. Sensory experiences involving shapes, textures, and colors

---

FIGURE 19–1 Resources for teaching children about nutrition.

Action for Healthy Kids. **http://www.actionforhealthykids.org**

Albyn, C. & Webb, L. (1993). *The multicultural cookbook for students* (ages 9–12). Phoenix, AZ: Oryx Press.

Alliance for a Healthier Generation. **http://www.healthiergeneration.org/schools.aspx**

Berman, C. & Fromer, J. (2006). *Meals without squeals: Child care feeding guide & cookbook.* Boulder CO: Bull Publishing.

Coordinated Approach to Child Health (CATCH). **http://www.catchinfo.org**

D'Amico & Drummond, K. (1996). *The science chef travels around the world: Fun food experiments and recipes for kids.* San Francisco, CA: Jossey-Bass.

Dodge, A. (2008). *Around the world cookbook.* New York: DK Publishing.

Dole Fresh Fruit & Vegetable Planner. **http://dpi.wi.gov/fns/pdf/dole_nov_09.pdf**

Eat Well and Keep Moving (interdisciplinary curriculum). **http://www.eatwellandkeepmoving.org**

Evers, C. (2006). *How to teach nutrition to kids.* Tigard, OR: 24 Carrot Press.

Food for Thought. University of Illinois Extension. **http://urbanext.illinois.edu/foodforthought/**

HeartPower Online. American Heart Association (lesson plans for preK through first grade; in English and Spanish). **http://www.americanheart.org/presenter.jhtml?identifier=3003345**

Kalich, K., Bauer, D., & McParlin, D. (2009). *Early sprouts: Cultivating healthy food choices in young children.* St. Paul, MN: Redleaf Press.

Kids Health in the Classroom. The Nemours Foundation. Weekly newsletter for educators with lesson plans. **http://classroom.kidshealth.org**

MyPyramid for Kids **http://www.MyPyramid.gov**

National Gardening Association. Kids Gardening (lesson plans and school projects) **http://www.kidsgardening.org**

National Dairy Council. *Nutrition Explorations.* **http://www.nutritionexplorations.org**

National Institute of Dental and Craniofacial Research (education resources). **http://www.nidcr.nih.gov/EducationalResources**

National Network for Child Care. Cooking with children: Kids in the kitchen. **http://www.nncc.org/Curriculum/fc46_cook.kids.html**

Nutrition Education of Texas (extensive lesson plans and resources for teaching nutrition education to children grades preK through high school) **http://netx.squaremeals.org**

---

sensorimotor – *Piaget's first stage of cognitive development, during which children learn and relate to their world primarily through motor and sensory activities.*

can be learned through the introduction of a wide variety of foods.

▶ *Promotion of social/emotional development*

Children learn to work as part of a team in either large or small groups during nutrition activities. They begin to learn respect and acceptance of cultural differences through exposure to various ethnic foods and eating customs. Children also begin to gain self-confidence and improved self-esteem when they master skills such as pouring juice into a glass, serving their own vegetables, or cutting up a sandwich by themselves. Educational activities centered on nutrition also provide opportunities for children to develop problem-solving, decision-making, cooperation, and communication skills.

▼ **Physical activity is an important component of a healthy diet.**

© Cengage Learning

19-1a The Role of Schools in Children's Nutrition Education

An effective nutrition education program involves the cooperative efforts of directors, administrators, teachers, cooks or food service personnel, and children's families. Although the size and organizational structure may vary from program to program, everyone makes important direct and indirect contributions to children's nutrition education (Prelip et al., 2012).

Administrators can play a supportive and influential role in this process. The value they place on nutrition education sends a powerful message to teachers and food service personnel. For example, a director who considers children's nutrition education a priority will make sure that financial support is available, resources are provided, and obstacles don't interfere. In contrast, a director who considers this unimportant may also care little about the nutritious quality of children's meals and snacks or whether teachers include any nutrition education in the curriculum.

Classroom teachers are usually responsible for planning and executing nutrition education experiences. For this reason, they should be familiar with the conceptual framework that validates the importance of nutrition education (McCaughtry et al., 2012). They must understand the principles of effective instruction and utilize methods that are age- and developmentally appropriate, establish achievable objectives, and evaluate the outcome of all nutrition activities. Teachers must also be knowledgeable about the nutritional value of foods, how to introduce children to new foods, and why it is important to foster children's healthy eating behaviors.

Food service personnel are responsible for preparing and serving meals that are safe, nutritious, and appealing to children. In some programs, they may also be in charge of planning the weekly menu. These roles provide valuable opportunities to contribute to children's understanding of nutritious foods and a healthy diet. Food service personnel can also be instrumental in reinforcing classroom nutrition activities by incorporating foods that children are learning about into their weekly menus. This type of successful collaboration is achieved when teachers communicate and work closely with food service personnel so they can have the necessary foods and equipment on hand.

Underlying the effectiveness of all nutrition education for young children is one very simple, basic concept: *Set a*

▼ **Family involvement in children's nutrition education is essential for positive outcomes.**

© Cengage Learning

good example. Children who observe a teacher eating and enjoying a variety of nutritious foods will begin to develop healthier eating behaviors than children who observe adults drinking soft drinks and consuming other empty-calorie junk foods.

19-1b Family Involvement in Children's Nutrition Education

Family involvement is vital to children's nutrition education. Teachers play an important role in this process by helping families to understand why a nutritious diet is necessary, how to meet children's nutrient needs, and how to encourage healthy eating and activity patterns (Lent et al., 2012; Zhen et al., 2012). By establishing open lines of communication, teachers can also support families' efforts to reinforce what children are learning in school by:

- posting weekly menus and including suggestions for foods that provide nutritional complements to each menu
- providing families with a report of, and recipes for, new foods that children have recently been introduced to and tasted
- sharing information about nutrition education learning activities and food experiences with families; requesting feedback on children's reactions to these experiences
- presenting occasional evening meetings or workshops for families (e.g., presentations or question/answer sessions with local health agency personnel, food demonstrations by a local chef, presentations by a parent who may be willing to share a food or nutrition experience). Sessions can be recorded and posted online for families who are unable to attend.
- inviting families to accompany children on food-related field trips
- encouraging families to occasionally join their children for lunch
- having a family volunteer to assist with menu planning
- asking families to share special recipes that are nutritious and family favorites
- inviting families to share ethnic or traditional foods for the class to sample
- requesting that families assist with or observe a classroom nutrition lesson
- soliciting volunteers to develop guidelines/policy for acceptable (nutritious and safe) food items that families can provide for birthday or holiday celebrations

Remember that the ultimate goal of nutrition education is to promote children's health and development. Achieving this goal requires that effective communication and cooperation be established between school and children's homes.

Did You Get It?

Young children who are in the formative stage of establishing lifelong habits and practices are considered _____ to/of new ideas related to food.
- **a.** highly resistant
- **b.** quite receptive
- **c.** skeptical
- **d.** only slightly receptive

Take the full quiz on CourseMate.

19-2 Planning a Nutrition Education Program for Children

The nutrition education program should be part of a coordinated plan that consists of well-designed activities leading to specific outcomes. Educational experiences should be planned to meet specified goals rather than simply being a hit-or-miss way to fill time or to keep children busy. Measurable objectives should be developed and guide the selection of content, instructional method, assessment process, and desired behavioral outcomes. The National Health Education Standards are one example of a comprehensive framework that includes learning materials, behavioral objectives, and evaluation criteria for grades PreK–12. (See Appendix A and the inside covers of this text.)

Nutrition education programs should be planned around some or all of the four basic nutrition education concepts described below. Learning experiences should also be age- and developmentally appropriate for children in the group. For example, most young children are able to comprehend that food promotes growth, eating a variety of foods is important for staying healthy, and foods can be prepared in different ways. However, some 3-year-olds may not yet realize that a head of lettuce at the store, a leaf of lettuce on a sandwich, and lettuce in a salad involve the same food. Tasting parties are an easy way to introduce children to new foods or to the same food prepared in different ways. Older children are able to understand the concept of food groups based on similar nutrient contributions and their relationship to health.

Ongoing evaluation enables the teacher to determine if nutrition lessons and activities have been effective in achieving the intended outcomes. Measurable objectives that describe expected behavioral changes should be developed during the initial planning stages and used for this purpose. The Centers for Disease Control and Prevention (CDC) offer a Health Education Curriculum Analysis Tool (HECAT) on their website that teachers may also find useful for developing effective lessons and evaluating instructional outcomes (CDC, 2012).

19-2a Basic Nutrition Education Concepts

Schools have a responsibility to promote children's health and nutrition knowledge. They can help children begin to make connections between healthy eating and wellness by conducting ongoing learning experiences that reflect four basic nutrition **concepts:**

1. Nutritious food is essential for children's bodies to grow and stay healthy.

    - All animals and plants need food.
    - Eating food helps children to grow, play, learn, feel happy, and stay well.
    - It is important to eat many different foods.
    - Food provides energy for play.
    - A healthy diet must be balanced with physical activity.

2. Nutrients come from foods. It is these nutrients that promote growth and health.

    - After food is eaten, nutrients are set free to work in our bodies.
    - Nutrients perform different functions in our bodies.
    - Many different nutrients are needed each day.
    - Foods are the source of all nutrients that our bodies need.

3. A variety of foods should be eaten each day because no one food provides all of the nutrients needed.

    - Different foods provide different nutrients so it is necessary to eat many kinds of food each day.
    - Nutrients work together in our bodies.
    - Foods in each food group come in a variety of different colors, textures, and flavors. Children should be encouraged to explore and at least taste a small bite.
    - Children can learn to identify and group foods into categories, such as vegetables, fruits, grains, and proteins.

4. Foods must be handled carefully before they are eaten to ensure that they are nutritious and safe.

    - Cleanliness of all foods and the people who handle foods prevents illness.
    - Hands should always be washed carefully before you eat or touch food.
    - Some foods need to be cooked properly and eaten hot.
    - Some foods must be kept refrigerated and may be served cold.
    - Involving children in food preparation teaches important lessons about how food must be handled to keep it safe.
    - Eating food that has not been handled properly can make children ill.

concepts – *combinations of basic and related factual information that represent a broader statement or idea.*

FIGURE 19–2 Sample outline for incorporating nutrition education Concept #1 into a classroom learning experience.

CONCEPT: CHILDREN NEED FOOD TO GROW AND HAVE HEALTHY BODIES

OBJECTIVES: The children should learn that:
▼ all living things need food
▼ food is important for growth and for good health

SUGGESTED ACTIVITIES
▼ caring for animals in the classroom with special attention to their diets
▼ taking field trips to the zoo or farm to learn what animals eat
▼ caring for plants in the classroom
▼ planting a vegetable garden in containers or a small plot of ground
▼ weighing and measuring the children periodically
▼ tracing outlines of each child on large sheets of paper

QUESTIONS FOR EXTENDING LEARNING EXPERIENCES
▼ What do animals eat?
▼ Do all animals eat the same foods?
▼ Do animals eat the same foods as people?
▼ Do animals grow faster or slower than people?
▼ What do plants eat?
▼ Can people see plants eating?
▼ Do plants eat the same foods as people?
▼ What does it mean to be healthy?
▼ Do people need food to be healthy?
▼ Do children need food to grow?

EVALUATION
▼ Children can name what animals and plants eat.
▼ Children can describe some effects of not feeding plants and animals.

These four conceptual points require that the adults responsible for nutrition education have a basic knowledge of nutrition, including nutrients and their food sources. Figures 19–2 and 19–3 illustrate how a nutrition concept can be outlined and translated into learning experiences for children.

19-2b Planning Guidelines

Nutrition education activities should contribute to children's improved understanding and practice of healthy lifestyle behaviors. In addition, lessons should reflect children's unique developmental needs, abilities, and interests.

1. Nutrition activities should be suited for children's developmental skills and abilities. They must be modified so all children, including those who have special needs, can fully participate.

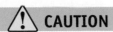

⚠ **CAUTION**

Special consideration should be given to children's chewing ability, especially when fresh fruits, peanut butter, or raw vegetables are to be used in the activity.

FIGURE 19–3 Sample outline for incorporating nutrition education Concept #4 into a classroom learning experience.

CONCEPT: FOODS MUST BE CAREFULLY HANDLED BEFORE THEY ARE EATEN

OBJECTIVES: Children should understand:
- ▼ where foods come from
- ▼ how foods are handled

SUGGESTED ACTIVITIES
- ▼ Grow, harvest, and prepare foods from a garden.
- ▼ Sprout alfalfa, radishes, or bean seeds.
- ▼ Discuss and illustrate the different parts of plants used as food (leaves, roots, fruit, seeds).
- ▼ Conduct simple experiments that show change in color or form of food.
- ▼ Play "store" or "farm."
- ▼ Take children on a field trip to a farm, dairy, bakery, or grocery store.

QUESTIONS FOR EXTENDING LEARNING EXPERIENCES
- ▼ Where does food come from?
- ▼ Where do grocery stores get food?
- ▼ Is food always eaten the way it is grown?
- ▼ Who prepares different foods?
- ▼ Does all food come from the store?

EVALUATION
- ▼ Children can name sources of specific foods.
- ▼ Children can name who handles such foods as bread, milk, etc.

2. Actual foods should be used in nutrition projects as often as possible. These may be accompanied by pictures, games, and stories to reinforce what is being learned. Special consideration must be given to food safety, funding, available equipment, and children's known food allergies when planning educational experiences that involve real food.

> ⚠️ **CAUTION**
>
> *The teacher should always check for allergies to any foods (or similar foods) that will be used in the nutrition activity.*

3. Foods used in nutrition lessons and activities should be nutritious. Only nutrient-dense foods should be chosen from the various food groups. Items such as cakes, pies, doughnuts, frostings, and cookies that are typically high in fat, sugar, and calories provide few essential nutrients and should be avoided.

4. The end products of a nutrition activity should be edible and eaten by the children on the same day to effectively reinforce learning concepts. Pasta collages, vegetable prints, and pudding finger paintings are not suitable nutrition projects because they are not edible. These activities also convey the message that it is okay to play with or to waste food; this is not an acceptable or desirable practice for children to develop.

5. Children should be involved in the actual food preparation. Hands-on experiences such as cleaning vegetables, mixing batter, rolling dough, spreading butter, and cutting

Did You Know...

the average American consumes the equivalent of 130 pounds of sugar annually? Half of this amount is in the form of high-fructose corn syrup, which is used extensively in processed foods and baked goods that are purchased.

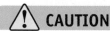

hands-on – *active involvement in a project; actually doing something.*

▶❚❚ TeachSource Video Connections

Preschool: Cooking Activities

Children are naturally curious and interested in learning about new things. Cooking activities provide a unique opportunity for children to learn about healthy eating, food safety, and different cultures. As you watch the learning video, *Preschool: Cooking Activities*, consider the following questions:

1. What skills can children learn by participating in classroom cooking activities? What others can you think of that were not mentioned in the video?

2. Why did the teacher take time to set up an example of the snack children were to prepare rather than simply giving them verbal instructions?

3. What could the teacher have substituted for the whipped cream topping on the muffins that would have improved the nutritional value for children?

Watch on CourseMate.

▼ **Involving children in nutrition activities improves their ability to learn and remember.**

biscuits reinforce learning and help children develop child's positive feelings about food (Horst, 2012). These experiences also promote children's coordination as well as their counting, problem-solving, direction-following, and motor skills. Children's involvement in food preparations is also known to increase their willingness to taste a new or an unfamiliar food.

6. Once the nutrition activity is completed, the food should be eaten within a short period of time, preferably the same day. Any delay between the time a project is completed and eventually eaten reduces the activity's educational impact.

19-2c Safety Considerations

The safety of nutrition activities must always be taken into consideration during the planning, set up, and implementation stages to ensure their success. Several areas that require special teacher attention are described here.

Basic Safety Guidelines

▶ Be aware of children's food allergies. Post a list of the children's names and the foods they must not eat. Foods that are common allergens include: wheat, milk and milk products, juices with a high acid content such as orange or grapefruit, strawberries, chocolate, eggs, soy and soy products, shellfish, and nuts.

▶ Avoid serving foods such as nuts, raw vegetables, peanut butter, and popcorn that may cause younger children to choke. These foods should also not be served to children who have problems with chewing or swallowing. Peanut butter and raw fruits and vegetables are appropriate to serve to older children under close adult supervision (AAP, 2012; Sih et al., 2012).

▶ Children should eat only when they are sitting down.

▶ Use low work tables and chairs.

▶ Use unbreakable equipment whenever possible.

▶ Supply enough tools and utensils for all children in the group to use.

▶ Provide blunt knives or **serrated** plastic knives for cutting cooked eggs, potatoes, bananas, and other soft foods. Vegetable peelers should be used under supervision and only after demonstrating their proper use to the children.

▶ Have only the necessary tools, utensils, and ingredients at the work table. All other materials should be removed as soon as they are no longer needed. Plan equipment needs carefully to avoid leaving the work area during an activity, especially when there are utensils or foods present that may potentially cause injury.

serrated – *saw-toothed or notched.*

© 2015 Cengage Learning

© Cengage Learning

▶ **Plan** each step of the cooking project before presenting it to the children. When you are ready to begin, explain to children how the activity will proceed. Children should understand what they are expected to do and what the adults will do before the cooking ingredients are presented.

▶ Long hair should be pulled back and fastened; floppy or cumbersome clothing should not be worn. Aprons are not essential, but may help protect clothing.

▶ Hands should be washed thoroughly at the start of the activity.

▶ Begin with simple recipes that require little cooking. Once children feel comfortable with basic cooking projects, move on to slightly more complex projects.

▶ Allow sufficient time for touching, tasting, looking, and comparing as well as for discussion. Use every step in the cooking project as an opportunity to expand children's learning.

▼ **Food prepared during nutrition activities should be eaten shortly after the lesson is completed.**

© Cengage Learning

Food Safety

▶ Wash hands before and after the cooking project; this also applies to teachers.

▶ Exclude any child or adult from participating in food preparation if they have a cold or other contagious illness.

▶ Bandage any cuts or open sores before beginning food preparation (use disposable gloves over bandages on hands).

▶ Keep all cooking utensils clean. Have extra utensils available in case one is dropped or a child accidentally puts one into his mouth.

▶ Teach children how to taste foods that are being prepared. Give each child a small plate and spoon for this purpose. Never allow children to taste foods directly from the bowl or pan in which the food is being prepared.

▶ Avoid using foods that spoil rapidly. Keep sauces, meats, eggs, and dairy products refrigerated.

Cooking Safety

▶ Match cooking tasks to children's developmental skills and attention spans.

▶ Take time to instruct children about the safe use of utensils.

▶ Emphasize that all cooking must be supervised by an adult.

▶ Arrange for an adult to do the cooking over a hot stove or hot plate; always turn pot handles toward the back.

▶ Use wooden or heat-resistant utensils for cooking. (Metal utensils conduct heat and can cause painful burns.

Did You Get It?

Educators responsible for planning and/or implementing a nutritional education program should possess a _____ knowledge of food, nutrients, nutrition, and food safety.

a. deep
b. professional
c. basic
d. passing

Take the full quiz on CourseMate.

preplan – *outline a method of action prior to carrying it out.*

19-3 Developing Lesson Plans for Nutrition Activities

Planning is fundamental to the success of each learning activity and its contribution to the program's comprehensive nutrition education program. Be sure to review the principles of curriculum design, including topic selection, **behavioral objectives**, instructional procedures, and **evaluation** criteria presented in Chapter 11. Additional consideration should be given to developing nutrition lesson plans and activities that:

- Contribute to children's understanding of one or more of the four basic nutrition concepts described earlier in this chapter.
- Involve hands-on experiences with actual food to improve learning and retention.
- Ensure that activities are safe and a positive learning experience for children. Most plans require a safety precautions checklist.
- Provide a sequencing of activities so each new experience reinforces and advances concepts that have already been learned.
- Incorporate improvements based on evaluation results obtained from previous lesson presentations.

Activity Plan #1: Weighing and Measuring Children

CONCEPT Weighing and measuring children

LEARNING OBJECTIVES

- Children will be able to discuss how eating healthy foods helps them to grow.
- Children can explain how growth is determined by height and weight measurements.
- Children will recognize that people come in different sizes.

SUPPLIES

- A balance-beam scale or bathroom scale
- Yardstick
- Large sheets of paper and markers or crayons
- Samples of nutritious fruits or vegetables for children to taste

LEARNING ACTIVITIES

A. Weigh and measure each child. Encourage children to assist the teacher in reading their height and weight measurements. Record the information. Older children may want to graph and compare their data. Repeat this activity every four months to monitor children's growth rate and note changes. Use this activity to reinforce the importance of healthy eating and physical activity habits.

B. Trace an outline of each child on large sheets of paper. Have children color their paper "selves."

C. Discuss individual differences among children, such as concepts of tall and short. (The discussion should be positive and focus on differences that make each child special.)

- Does everybody weigh the same?
- Is everyone the same height?
- Do children stay the same size? Do adults?
- What makes children grow?

D. Prepare samples of several nutritious fruits or vegetables for children to taste. Use this activity to reinforce the concept that nutritious foods help children to grow.

behavioral objectives – *a clear and measurable description of a specific behavior that an individual is expected to learn.*
evaluation – *a measurement of effectiveness for determining whether or not educational objectives have been achieved.*

EVALUATION

> ▶ Each child states her height and weight.
> ▶ Children name several nutritious foods that contribute to their health and growth.
> ▶ Children discuss why some people are taller or shorter than others.

Activity Plan #2: Making Hummus and Pitas

CONCEPT People from other cultures eat foods that may be different from those we typically eat.

LEARNING OBJECTIVES

> ▶ Children will learn that people from other cultures may eat different types of foods.
> ▶ Children will be able to describe correctly the ingredients used to make hummus and why hummus is considered to be a healthy food.

SUPPLIES

> ▶ Bowl
> ▶ Measuring spoons
> ▶ Spatula
> ▶ Potato masher
> ▶ Blender or food processor
> ▶ Ingredients (see recipe)
> ▶ Fresh vegetables
> ▶ Pocket pitas or flatbread cut into small wedges

LEARNING ACTIVITIES

A. Be sure teachers and children have washed their hands before proceeding. To make the hummus, assemble the equipment and all ingredients.

(For a picture recipe to use in the classroom, see Figure 19–4.)
1 15-ounce can chickpeas (garbanzo beans), drained
2–3 tablespoons warm water
2 tablespoons olive oil
2 tablespoons lemon juice
1 garlic clove, crushed
salt to flavor
2 tablespoons sesame seeds or 3 tablespoons peanut butter (optional)
an assortment of raw vegetables (carrot and celery sticks, red/orange/yellow pepper
   strips, zucchini circles, turnip, raw sweet potato sticks, broccoli pieces)
pita wedges, flatbread, or crackers for dipping

Drain chickpeas; place them in a small bowl with the water, olive oil, and lemon juice. Let children take turns mashing the beans using a potato masher. After each child has had a turn, the teacher can scrape the mixture into a blender and add the remaining ingredients, blending until smooth. Place the hummus in a small bowl and serve with raw vegetables, pita wedges, flatbread, or crackers.

 CAUTION

Be sure to check for any food allergies before beginning this project.

B. Read one or more of the following books and discuss the concept that people may eat many different kinds of foods:
Everybody Cooks Rice by Norah Dooley
Dumpling Soup by Jama Kim Rattigan

FIGURE 19–4 **Picture recipe for making hummus.**

Bee-Bim Bop! by Linda Sue Park
*Dim Sum for Every*one by Grace Lin
The Tortilla Factory by Gary Paulsen
Three Scoops and a Fig by Sara Laux Akin

C. Have each child name his favorite food. Discuss why families eat foods that may be the same or different.

EVALUATION

▶ Children name several foods that are commonly eaten by people from different cultures.
▶ Children explain why some people eat foods that may be different from those they typically eat.

Activity Plan #3: Tasting Party

CONCEPT Tasting party for dairy foods.

LEARNING OBJECTIVES

▶ Children will learn that common foods may be served in a variety of ways.
▶ Children will be able to identify foods that belong to the dairy group.
▶ Children will be able to state why it is important to drink milk or eat dairy products.

SUPPLIES

- Small pitcher of milk
- Unflavored yogurt
- Cottage cheese
- Cheddar cheese
- Ice cream
- 1 pint of whipping cream
- Small plastic jar with lid
- Plastic knives

LEARNING ACTIVITIES

A. Teachers and children should wash their hands before starting this activity. Place the pitcher of milk, unflavored yogurt, cottage cheese, cheddar cheese (cut into small cubes), and ice cream on the table. Encourage children to describe the appearance and texture of each item. Do they look alike? Is cottage cheese like cheddar cheese? How is it different? Point out that each food began as milk and has been changed as the result of different preparation methods. Have the children sample each food. Do they all taste alike? Why were these foods chilled before preparation and why should they be eaten immediately? Why is it important to drink milk and eat dairy products each day?

B. Pour the whipping cream into a small, clean plastic jar, filling it only half full. Add a few dashes of salt and tighten the jar lid. Let the jar sit until the cream reaches room temperature. Have children take turns shaking the jar until the butter separates from the milk. When it is finished, pour away the milk and remove the butter. Let children spread the butter on a small cracker to taste.

>  **CAUTION**
>
> *Check beforehand for any milk or dairy product allergies. Provide alternative foods if necessary. Stress that refrigeration and sanitation are very important when working with protein foods such as milk and milk products.*

C. Read and discuss one or more of the following books:
No Moon, No Milk! by Chris Babcock
Milk Comes from a COW? by Dan Yunk
Milk: From Cow to Carton by Aliki
From Milk to Ice Cream by Stacy Taus-Bolstad
Extra Cheese, Please!: Mozzarella's Journey from Cow to Pizza by Cris Peterson

D. Additional activities can be planned, including making yogurt or cheese from milk, preparing fruit smoothies, and making ice cream.

EVALUATION

- Children identify several foods made from milk.
- Children taste each food served.
- Children describe where milk and butter come from.

Activity Plan #4: Trip to the Grocery Store

CONCEPT Children will learn that many different types of fruits and vegetables are available.

LEARNING OBJECTIVES

- Children are encouraged to make decisions about foods and to taste a variety of foods.
- Children will select a fruit or vegetable with which they may not be familiar.
- Children will be able to name three new fruits or vegetables.

SUPPLIES

- Local newspaper with weekly food advertisements
- Paper and pencil
- Plastic foods
- Grocery bags
- Cash register and play money

LEARNING ACTIVITIES

A. Have children look at the produce section in the weekly food advertisements. Ask them to name the fruits and vegetables pictured in the paper. Find out if children have ever tasted each of the items and whether or not they liked them.

B. Plan a field trip to the grocery store. Be sure to secure parental permission in advance. Give each child a small piece of paper on which the name of a different fruit or vegetable is written. At the grocery store, help children locate their assigned fruit or vegetable. After purchasing the items and returning to the classroom, ask the children to help describe each food—its color and shape, whether or not it has seeds, how it grows, and if the skin is peeled or eaten. Finally, ask the cook to prepare the fruits or vegetables for the children to eat: a mixed fruit salad, a vegetable plate, or vegetable soup.

 CAUTION

Permission must be obtained from families before taking the field trip. Secure children in appropriate safety seats if driving to the store. If the group will be walking, review safety rules. Check for food allergies and provide alternatives if necessary.

C. Provide the children with various props—plastic foods, empty food containers, grocery bags, cash register, and play money—to create their own grocery store. Have several children act as grocers, some as clerks, and others as shoppers.

EVALUATION

- Children identify two varieties of red fruit.
- Children taste each of the prepared fruits or vegetables.
- Children name and describe three different fruits and/or vegetables.

Activity Plan #5: Safe Lunches

CONCEPT   How to pack lunches that are safe and healthy.

LEARNING OBJECTIVES

- Children will learn how to select and eat food safely.
- Children will select at least one food with which they are not familiar.
- Children will include a variety of nutritious foods in their lunch.

SUPPLIES

- Empty lunch box with thermos
- Foods that may be available in school cafeteria/kitchen and are examples of items that children can pack in a lunchbox (e.g., sandwich, milk, juice, soup, carrot sticks or other fresh vegetables, cheese cubes, tortilla, apple, banana, yogurt, salad)

LEARNING ACTIVITIES

A. Display the various food choices on a table. Have children wash their hands prior to selecting food. In groups of two, have children choose foods from those provided that they would pack in a lunchbox to bring to school. Encourage children to choose a variety of foods from each food group. After each child has packed his lunch, discuss what foods were chosen. Let children eat the foods they have packed in their lunchboxes. Extend the discussion by asking:

▶ Which foods need to be kept cold?
▶ Which foods need to be kept hot?
▶ Which foods need to be wrapped or stored in special containers to be kept safe?
▶ Which foods need to be washed before they are eaten?
▶ Are there any other foods you would choose for your lunch box that are not included here?

 CAUTION

Check for children's food allergies prior to the activity. Recommend sampling only those foods that do not require storage at extreme temperatures to avoid illness (i.e., avoid milk, yogurt, ice cream, soup).

B. Take children on an actual picnic lunch. Involve them in the preparation and safe storage of foods for this event.

EVALUATION

▶ Children participate in choosing their own food at mealtime.
▶ Children select a variety of healthful foods from each of the food groups.
▶ Children explain how foods must be handled and stored to prevent illness.

Activity Plan #6: Eating Different Fruits and Vegetables Each Day

CONCEPT It is important to eat several different fruits and vegetables each day.

LEARNING OBJECTIVES

▶ Children will learn that there are a wide variety of fruits and vegetables.
▶ Children will learn that a particular fruit or vegetable may be prepared and eaten in different ways.
▶ Children will taste different fruits and vegetables and learn about vitamins that make us healthy.

SUPPLIES

▶ Disposable plates and napkins
▶ A variety of fruits that represent different sizes, colors, and shapes (e.g., apples, bananas, oranges, kiwi, melons, star fruit, mangos)
▶ A variety of vegetables that can be prepared in multiple ways (e.g., baked potato, mashed potato, oven-baked French fries, scalloped potatoes)

▼ **Children are often more willing to taste new foods when they have helped with the preparations.**

© Cengage Learning

LEARNING ACTIVITIES

A. Be sure that adults and children wash their hands prior to handling the food. Lay out the assortment of fruits and vegetables (that have been cut into small pieces) on a table.

Give children paper plates and allow them to select a total of five fruits and vegetables. Encourage children to select and taste a variety of different items, particularly those they have never eaten before. Talk about the general nutrients (vitamins, minerals) that are in fruits and vegetables. As a group, discuss these questions:

▶ What colors are the fruits and vegetables?
▶ What are some different ways of preparing the same food? Do you know of any more?
▶ Is there a food you tried today that you have never eaten before? Will you try it again?
▶ Did you know that eating different fruits and vegetables every day can help you from becoming sick? Discuss.

> ⚠ **CAUTION**
>
> *Check beforehand for children's food allergies. Maintain foods at appropriate temperatures to avoid illness.*

B. Ask the cook to prepare some of the same vegetables on another day. Discuss how cooking affects the color, texture, and flavor of different vegetables.
C. Take the children to visit a local supermarket or farmer's market. Call ahead and make arrangements for a special tour that might include food sampling in the produce department.

EVALUATION

▶ Children explain why it is important to include a variety of fruits and vegetables in their daily diet.
▶ Children select a variety of fruits and vegetables to eat at mealtime.
▶ Children state why it is important to eat several different fruits and vegetables daily.

Did You Get It?

Experts propose that learning activities related to nutrition, nutrients, food, and safety be structured in all but which manner?
a. sequential
b. reinforcement of what children have previously learned
c. on the basis of current trends, fads, and developments
d. so they contribute to children's understanding of the four basic nutrition concepts

Take the full quiz on CourseMate.

19-4 Where Else Do Children Learn About Nutrition?

Children learn about food and nutrition from a variety of informal sources as well as from planned instructional programs. Families, teachers, peers, and various media forms (e.g., websites, television, movies, books) also contribute to children's ideas about nutrition and influence their eating habits (Gahagan, 2012; Harrison & Liechty, 2012) (Figure 19–5).

19-4a Family Influence

A family's food purchases, preferences, and **attitudes** exert a strong influence on a child's eating patterns and ideas about nutrition (Hennessy et al., 2012). Their food choices are often a reflection of cultural and regional differences, money available for food, nutrition knowledge, and specific

attitudes – *beliefs or feelings one has toward certain facts or situations.*

FIGURE 19–5 Additional factors that influence children's eating habits.

ADDITIONAL FACTORS THAT INFLUENCE CHILDREN'S EATING HABITS

▼ Families and children who have a strong preference for high-fat foods have higher BMI scores than families who tend to follow a low-fat diet.

▼ Children are more likely to eat a particular food if they observe adults eating it.

▼ There is a strong relationship between the food preferences of toddlers and their mothers, fathers, and older siblings.

▼ Children are more likely to overeat and to make unhealthy food choices when they are experiencing stress and negative feelings.

▼ Involving families in children's nutrition education programs increases the quality and diversity of student's diets.

▼ Families that share mealtimes together have children whose weight and dietary patterns are healthier.

▼ In general, the more hours women work outside the home, the fewer hours they spend preparing meals, and the more meals their children are likely to eat away from home.

▼ Food service workers' knowledge of nutrition, food handling, and preparation practices have a direct effect on the quality of food served to children (Hoffman et al., 2012; Ritchie et al., 2012).

likes and dislikes of individual members. Children growing up in these environments become familiar and comfortable with certain foods through repeated exposures (Williams et al., 2012). Because familiarity is one of the most influential factors affecting food choices, children who are more receptive to trying new foods often have families who also eat a wide variety of foods.

19-4b Teachers

Teachers also exert considerable influence on children's attitudes about food (Lynch & Batal, 2012). For this reason, it is important that teachers display a positive attitude through their actions, word choices, and willingness to try new foods.

Informed teachers are able to provide families with sound nutrition information and to correct misinformation they may have heard from friends or on television or read about in a magazine or on the Internet. Teachers are also in a position to refer families to community resources and health professionals, including dietitians, public health departments, USDA extension service offices, and health educators for additional nutrition information.

An abundance of information and educational resource materials is available on the Internet. Teachers may wish to use these resources when planning classroom nutrition activities or for distributing to children's families. However, these materials (and their sources) must be evaluated carefully to determine if they are accurate, free of bias, and appropriate for the purpose intended. Additional points that teachers must take into consideration include:

1. Is the resource known for its reliability in reporting?
2. What are the professional credentials of the author(s)?
3. Is the resource accurate and does it address nutritional facts rather than theories or biased opinion?
4. Are unsubstantiated health claims presented?
5. Is the resource trying to sell something?

CONNECTING TO EVERYDAY PRACTICE

Food Trend Predictions

Food corporations are continuously engaged in developing and marketing new items aimed at the health-conscious consumer. Marketing tactics tout the nutritional benefits of natural foods, herbal supplements, fortified waters, low- and fat-free foods, foods enhanced with phytochemicals, juice bars, energy drinks, protein shakes, and smoothies that are "natural" or can be eaten on the run. However, the nutritional quality of these food products is not always better than their traditional counterparts despite the manufacturer's health-promoting claims. Many items continue to be calorie-dense and loaded with salt, sugars, and fat.

Think About This:

▶ Do you perceive these trends to be positive or negative?

▶ In what ways might these trends influence families' ideas about what children should be eating?

▶ Why do you think the food industry continues to produce food products that are of poor nutrient quality?

▶ What can be done to improve the quality of new food products being introduced each year?

6. Is the material presented at the appropriate level or is it adaptable?
7. Are the suggested nutrition education projects healthful?
8. Are the projects safe?

As a general rule, information posted on websites with a ".gov" or ".edu" extension will usually meet these criteria and can be trusted.

19-4c Peer Groups

Children's food choices are frequently made on the basis of **peer** approval or disapproval (Frazier et al., 2012). A child with a strong personality who eats a variety of foods can be a positive influence on other children. In contrast, children who are "picky" or "selective eaters" are capable of spreading their negative influence to others at the table. A simple statement from the teacher, such as, "You don't have to eat the broccoli, Jamie, but I can't allow you to spoil it for Tara and Pablo," can be effective in limiting this negative environment. Although younger children often base their food choices on familiarity and taste, older children's (5 and up) eating patterns are more likely to be affected by peer influence.

▼ Children's food likes and dislikes are often influenced by their peers.

© Cengage Learning

19-4d Television and the Media

Television, the Internet, and print media such as magazines, newspapers, and books serve as major sources of nutrition information and misinformation for many children and their families (Harris et al., 2012). However, the lack of oversight and quality control governing the accuracy of information provided through these

peer – *one of the same rank; equal.*

channels can make it challenging for consumers to determine what is fact and what is fiction. Unfortunately, nutrient-dense foods are rarely featured in television commercials and other media formats. Rather, foods that are chocolaty, highly sugared, loaded with fat, packed with calories, are really fun, or come with a prize appear most often (Andreyeva, Kelly, & Harris, 2011). Families and teachers can be instrumental in countering television's negative influence by monitoring programs that children view and by pointing out differences between programs and commercials. Children often have difficulty understanding that a commercial's purpose is to convince people to buy a product that may not always be the most nutritious choice (Gilmore & Jordan, 2012; Graff, Kunkel, & Mermin, 2012).

Did You Know...

that in one year, a child will view approximately 20,000 to 30,000 thirty-second television commercials? The good news is that young children don't often focus on the commercial or fully understand its content.

Did You Get It?

Children are often not able to distinguish between what is educational television programming and what is commercialization and salesmanship.

a. This statement is true for children of all ages.

b. Parents can address this concern by pointing out truth from fiction.

c. Television commercials provide an excellent source of accurate nutrition information.

d. Most children have the cognitive ability to make this discrimination by the time they enter kindergarten.

Take the full quiz on CourseMate.

PARTNERING with FAMILIES

More Fruits and Vegetables Please

Dear Families,

Children are more likely to consume the daily recommended fruit and vegetable servings when they are available in your home. This is important because the nutrients in fruits and vegetables contribute to better health and reduce children's risk of developing diseases such as cancer, heart disease, hypertension, diabetes, and obesity. Try several of these activities to increase your child's interest in tasting and experimenting with new fruits and vegetables.

▶ Prepare homemade vegetable soup or a fresh fruit salad. Take your child along when you go shopping and give her a list with several items to pick out. Have your child name each vegetable or fruit in the recipe. Try different preparation and serving methods. Children will quickly learn how fruits and vegetables can be included in daily meals and snacks when you get them involved in these activities.

▶ Visit the nearest farmer's market. Not only will your child develop an appreciation for fresh produce, but the experience is likely to generate curiosity and questions that expand learning.

▶ Teach your child the importance of eating seasonal fruits and vegetables not only for the taste, but also the cost savings it can provide for your family. Below is a sampling of fruits and vegetables that are often more plentiful during certain seasons.

- Spring: apples, grapefruits, pears, strawberries, broccoli, cabbage, carrots, asparagus
- Summer: berries, cantaloupes, melons, peaches, corn, green beans, cucumbers, okra
- Fall: oranges, peaches, prunes, plums, brussels sprouts, tomatoes, peppers, zucchini
- Winter: apples, grapefruit, oranges, beets, cauliflower, potatoes, spinach, squash

▶ Plant a small garden and include some of the vegetables listed above. Vegetables can also be grown in containers set out on the deck or patio. Your child will learn about the growing process and where foods originate.

◖ Summary

▶ Nutrition education is important during the early years when children are forming many ideas about food and nutrition.

- Children's language, cognitive, sensorimotor, and social skills can be reinforced when nutrition education is integrated across the curriculum.
- An effective nutrition education program requires the involvement and support of administrators, teachers, food service personnel, and children's families.

▶ Efforts to teach children about nutrition should be part of a coordinated framework and long-range plan that continues to build children's knowledge and health-promoting behaviors.

- A sound nutrition education program is based on four basic principles: (1) food is needed for a healthy body, (2) nutrients come from foods, (3) a variety of foods must be eaten, and (4) foods must be handled carefully so they are safe to eat.
- Effective lessons are based on children's developmental abilities, the use of actual foods that are nutritious and edible, and children's involvement in food preparations.
- Safety must always be considered and addressed when conducting food-related activities and lessons.

▶ Advanced planning, including topic selection, behavioral objectives, instructional methods, and evaluation, is essential for ensuring that lessons will be effective and meaningful.

▶ Children's ideas about food and nutrition are shaped by a variety of sources including, family, teachers, peers, and the media.

◖ Terms to Know

nutrition education *p. 485*
sensorimotor *p. 486*
concepts *p. 489*
hands-on *p. 491*

serrated *p. 492*
preplan *p. 493*
behavioral objectives *p. 494*
evaluation *p. 494*

attitudes *p. 500*
peer *p. 502*

◖ Chapter Review

A. **By Yourself:**

1. Identify several factors that can influence children's ideas about food and food preferences.
2. Describe how program directors, teachers, and families collectively contribute to children's nutrition education.
3. What role do teachers play in developing and implementing nutrition education for children?
4. What fundamental principles should guide nutrition education activities conducted with children?
5. Why should food not be used for art projects?

B. **As a Group:**

1. Discuss the ways in which nutrition education experiences can promote children's knowledge and skills across all developmental areas.
2. What criteria can teachers use to identify nutrition education concepts that are appropriate for children?
3. Describe four ways that programs can involve families in children's nutrition education.
4. Why is it important to include nutrition education during children's early years?
5. What safety issues must teachers consider when conducting classroom food activities?

◖ Case Study

Jocelyn, age 3 years, has been ill several times this spring with upper respiratory infections. Her mother mentions to the classroom teacher that she is now giving Jocelyn an herbal supplement to "boost her immune system" so she won't be sick as often. She asks you, the teacher, if the supplement will be beneficial for Jocelyn and if it is safe for her to take.

1. Are you qualified to advise Jocelyn's mother on this issue?
2. What information do you need to know before responding to her questions?
3. What resources are available to help you locate information about this topic?
4. How will you determine if the information is accurate and reliable?

◖ Application Activities

1. Prepare lesson plans for a two-day nutrition education activity. Plans may be for two consecutive days or for any two days during the same week. The lesson plan for each day should follow the format presented in this unit.
2. Make arrangements to present the lessons you developed (for Activity #1) to a class in a local school or early childhood program. Did the children achieve your learning objectives? What parts of the activity went as you expected? What parts may not have gone as well, and how would you change them next time?
3. Outline an equipment list and safety plan for a class activity that involves 4- and 5-year-olds making pancakes. Cooking will be done in an electric griddle that is placed on a low table. What precautions will need to be taken? How should the room be arranged to ensure children's safety? What instructions should be given to the children beforehand?
4. Select 15 to 20 library books appropriate for young children. Note those instances where food is portrayed either in the story or pictures. What types of foods are shown? Chart these foods according to the food groups (e.g., fruits, vegetables, grains, proteins, dairy). What percentage of foods was noted within each group? Summarize the general message(s) about nutrition presented in these books?
5. Watch one hour of children's television programs on Saturday morning.
    a. Determine the percent of observed advertisements that featured "sweets" (gum, candy, soft drinks, snack cakes, and pre-sweetened cereals). Calculate the percentage of advertisements featuring fast foods or those especially high in fat.
    b. Which food groups were least represented in these commercials?
6. Review a recent article about nutrition from a popular magazine. Apply the criteria suggested in this chapter to determine if the information is reliable. Do you consider the article to be factual and accurate? Why or why not?

◖ Helpful Web Resources

Academy of Nutrition and Dietetics	http://www.eatright.org
Better Health Foundation	http://www.fruitsandveggiesmorematters.org
Let's Move	http://www.letsmove.gov
PE Central	http://www.pecentral.org
CDC: School Health (educational resources)	www.cdc.gov/healthyyouth/schoolhealth
U.S. Department of Agriculture	http://www.usda.gov

Visit the Education CourseMate for this textbook to access the eBook, Did You Get It? quizzes, Digital Downloads, TeachSource Video Cases, flashcards, and more. Go to CengageBrain.com to log in, register, or purchase access.

References

American Academy of Pediatrics (AAP). (2012). Choking prevention. Accessed on August 22, 2012 from http://www.healthychildren.org/English/health-issues/injuries-emergencies/pages/Choking-Prevention.aspx.

Andreyeva, T., Kelly, I., & Harris, J. (2011). Exposure to food advertising on television: Associations with children's fast food and soft drink consumption and obesity, *Economics & Human Biology*, 9(3), 221–233.

Centers for Disease Control and Prevention (CDC). (2012). *The Health Education Curriculum Analysis Tool (HECAT)*. Accessed on August 22, 2012 from http://www.cdc.gov/healthyyouth/HECAT.

Frazier, B., Gelman, S., Kaciroti, N., Russell, J., & Lumeng, J. (2012). I'll have what she's having: The impact of model characteristics on children's food choices, *Developmental Science*, 15(1), 87–98.

Gahagan, S. (2012). Development of eating behavior: Biology and context, *Journal of Developmental & Behavioral Pediatrics*, 33(3), 261–271.

Gilmore, J., & Jordan, A. (2012). Burgers and basketball: Race and stereotypes in food and beverage advertising aimed at children in the US, *Journal of Children & Media*, 6(3), 317–332.

Graff, S., Kunkel, D., & Mermin, S. (2012). Government can regulate food advertising to children because cognitive research shows that it is inherently misleading, *Health Affairs*, 31(2), 392–398.

Harris, J., Speers, S., Schwartz, M., & Brownell, K. (2012). US food company branded advergames on the Internet: Children's exposure and effects on snack consumption, *Journal of Children & Media*, 6(1), 51–68.

Harrison, K., & Liechty, J. (2012). US preschoolers' media exposure and dietary habits: The primacy of television and the limits of parental mediation, *Journal of Children & Media*, 6(1), 18–36.

Hennessy, E., Hughes, S., Goldberg, J., Hyatt, R., & Economos, C. (2012). Permissive parental feeding behavior is associated with an increase in intake of low-nutrient dense foods among American children living in rural communities, *Journal of the Academy of Nutrition & Dietetics*, 112(1), 142–148.

Hoffman, J., Agrawal, T., Thompson, D., Ferguson, T., Grinder, A., Carter, S., Healey, C., Bhaumik, U., & Castaneda-Sceppa, C. (2012). Increasing culturally diverse meals in Head Start using a collaborative approach: Lessons learned for school food service modifications, *NHSA Dialog*, 15(3), 246–259.

Horst, K. (2012). Overcoming picky eating. Eating enjoyment as a central aspect of children's eating behaviors, *Appetite*, 58(2), 567–574.

Lent, M., Hill, T., Dollahite, J., Wolfe, W., & Dickin, K. (2012). Healthy children, healthy families: Parents making a difference! A curriculum integrating key nutrition, physical activity, and parenting practices to help prevent childhood obesity, *Journal of Nutrition Education & Behavior*, 44(1), 90–92.

Lynch, M., & Batal, M. (2012). Child care providers' strategies for supporting health eating: A quantitative approach, *Journal of Research in Childhood Education*, 26(1), 107–121.

McCaughtry, N., Martin, J., Fahlman, & Shen, B. (2012). Urban health educators' perspectives and practices regarding school nutrition education policies, *Health Education Research*, 27(1), 69–80.

Prelip, M., Kinsler, J., Thai, C., Erausquin, J., & Slusser, W. (2012). Evaluation of a school-based multicomponent nutrition education program to improve young children's fruit and vegetable consumption, *Journal of Nutrition Education and Behavior*, 44(4), 310–318.

Ritchie, L., Boyle, M., Chandran, K., Spector, P., Whaley, S., James, P., Samuels, S., Hecht, K., & Crawford, P. (2012). Participation in the Child & Adult Care Food Program is associated with more nutritious foods and beverages in child care, *Childhood Obesity*, 8(3), 224–229.

Sih, T., Bunnag, C., Ballali, S., Lauriello, M., & Bellussi, L. (2012). Nuts and seed: A natural yet dangerous foreign body, *International Journal of Pediatric Otorhinolaryngology*, 76(1), S49–S52.

Williams, L., Campbell, K., Abbott, G., Crawford, D., & Ball, K. (2012). Is maternal nutrition knowledge more strongly associated with the diets of mothers or their school-aged children? *Public Health Nutrition*, 15(8), 1396–1401.

Zhen, C., Feng, D., Lui, Y., & Esperat, C. (2012). Sedentary behaviors among Hispanic children: Influences of parental support in a school intervention program, *American Journal of Health Promotion*, 26(5), 270–280.

Epilogue

Looking Ahead . . . Making a Difference

As promised, this book has taken you on a journey. You have had an opportunity to learn about many topics that are important to children's health, safety, and nutrition. The new skills you have developed will improve your abilities to observe children and to detect the early signs of acute and chronic health conditions and impending illness. You have become more knowledgeable about children's health problems, including childhood obesity, communicable illness, chronic medical conditions, and sensory impairments and their impact on development. You have learned about the critical importance of helping children acquire health-promoting behaviors and modifying environments to protect children from unintentional injury and unnecessary exposure to illness. Your knowledge of children's critical nutrient needs and ways to address them through thoughtful lessons and menu planning has also undoubtedly improved.

Most importantly, you have gained a better understanding of the preventive health concept, not only as it applics to the care and education of young children, but also how to implement it in your own personal life. Undoubtedly, you have also become more aware of the valuable role you play as a positive role model for children who look up to adults and often imitate their behaviors. As stated throughout the book, teachers are in an ideal position to promote children's health, safety, and nutrition and to make this a priority. Their dedicated efforts to achieving this goal through the development of meaningful learning experiences and their commitment to partnering with families can truly make a difference in children's lives.

The ultimate goal and true mark of learning is change . . . change in the way one thinks, change in one's behavior. Undoubtedly, your journey through this book has changed you in some way and caused you to question, think, or act differently. However, the journey does not end here. New discoveries continue to enhance our understanding of health promotion, chronic diseases, nutrition, and safety every day. In turn, this information shapes our ideas and best practices for promoting children's lifelong wellness. Attention is increasingly being focused on several significant aspects of children's well-being, including:

▶ Improving the quality of schools and early childhood programs.
▶ Planning and serving meals/snacks that provide essential nutrients, reduce unnecessary fat and calories, and are respectful of cultural differences.
▶ Raising awareness about childhood obesity and the importance of physical activity and outdoor play.
▶ Maintaining the safety of food and food environments.
▶ Addressing and responding to the needs of children who have chronic medical conditions and developmental challenges.
▶ Building children's resiliency to stress, bullying, and everyday environmental pressures.
▶ Improving communication with families and engaging them in children's education.
▶ Increasing awareness and sensitivity to child and family differences.
▶ Recognizing environmental contaminants and their effect on children's health.
▶ Addressing the need for more parenting education.
▶ Encouraging physical activity as a lifestyle practice.

▸ Addressing the issues of child maltreatment and domestic violence.
▸ Advocating on behalf of children's interests.
▸ Improving children's access to medical and dental care.
▸ Reducing poverty and food insecurity.

This list is not inclusive. Some issues may be of greater concern and interest to particular communities or populations. Other issues may have a more universal appeal and affect the welfare of children everywhere. In either case, the future of children's well-being offers unique opportunities for innovative solutions and teacher commitment.

Continue this journey. Keep learning about new developments as they unfold, explore topics that pique your curiosity, and become an advocate for children's health, safety, and nutrition. Accept the challenge—look ahead and make a difference for children!

APPENDICES

APPENDIX A   National Health Education Standards

NHES Standard 1: Students will comprehend concepts related to health promotion and disease prevention to enhance health.

Rationale: The acquisition of basic health concepts and functional health knowledge provides a foundation for promoting health-enhancing behaviors among youth. This standard includes essential concepts that are based on established health behavior theories and models. Concepts that focus on both health promotion and risk reduction are included in the performance indicators.

PreK–Grade 2 Performance Indicators, Standard 1
1.2.1   Identify that healthy behaviors impact personal health.
1.2.2   Recognize that there are multiple dimensions of health.
1.2.3   Describe ways to prevent communicable diseases.
1.2.4   List ways to prevent common childhood injuries.
1.2.5   Describe why it is important to seek health care.

Grades 3–5 Performance Indicators, Standard 1
1.5.1   Describe the relationship between healthy behaviors and personal health.
1.5.2   Identify examples of emotional, intellectual, physical, and social health.
1.5.3   Describe ways in which safe and healthy school and community environments can promote personal health.
1.5.4   Describe ways to prevent common childhood injuries and health problems.
1.5.5   Describe when it is important to seek health care.

NHES Standard 2: Students will analyze the influence of family, peers, culture, media, technology, and other factors on health behaviors.

Rationale: Health is affected by a variety of positive and negative influences within society. This standard focuses on identifying and understanding the diverse internal and external factors that influence health practices and behaviors among youth, including personal values, beliefs, and perceived norms.

PreK–Grade 2 Performance Indicators, Standard 2
2.2.1   Identify how the family influences personal health practices and behaviors.
2.2.2   Identify what the school can do to support personal health practices and behaviors.
2.2.3   Describe how the media can influence health behaviors.

Grades 3–5 Performance Indicators, Standard 2
2.5.1   Describe how family influences personal health practices and behaviors.
2.5.2   Identify the influence of culture on health practices and behaviors.
2.5.3   Identify how peers can influence healthy and unhealthy behaviors.
2.5.4   Describe how the school and community can support personal health practices and behaviors.
2.5.5   Explain how media influences thoughts, feelings, and health behaviors.
2.5.6   Describe ways that technology can influence personal health.

NHES Standard 3: Students will demonstrate the ability to access valid information, products, and services to enhance health.

Rationale: Access to valid health information and health-promoting products and services is critical in the prevention, early detection, and treatment of health problems. This standard focuses on how to identify and access valid health resources and to reject unproven sources. Application of the skills of analysis, comparison, and evaluation of health resources empowers students to achieve health literacy.

PreK–Grade 2 Performance Indicators, Standard 3
3.2.1   Identify trusted adults and professionals who can help promote health.
3.2.1   Identify ways to locate school and community health helpers.

Grades 3–5 Performance Indicators Standard 3
3.5.1   Identify characteristics of valid health information, products, and services.
3.5.2   Locate resources from home, school, and community that provide valid health information.

NHES Standard 4: Students will demonstrate the ability to use interpersonal communication skills to enhance health and avoid or reduce health risks.

Rationale: Effective communication enhances personal, family, and community health. This standard focuses on how responsible individuals use verbal and non-verbal skills to develop and maintain healthy personal relationships. The ability to organize and to convey information and feelings is the basis for strengthening interpersonal interactions and reducing or avoiding conflict.

PreK–Grade 2 Performance Indicators, Standard 4
4.2.1   Demonstrate healthy ways to express needs, wants, and feelings.
4.2.2   Demonstrate listening skills to enhance health.
4.2.3   Demonstrate ways to respond in an unwanted, threatening, or dangerous situation.
4.2.4   Demonstrate ways to tell a trusted adult if threatened or harmed.

Grades 3–5 Performance Indicators, Standard 4
4.5.1   Demonstrate effective verbal and nonverbal communication skills to enhance health.
4.5.2   Demonstrate refusal skills that avoid or reduce health risks.
4.5.3   Demonstrate nonviolent strategies to manage or resolve conflict.
4.5.4   Demonstrate how to ask for assistance to enhance personal health.

NHES Standard 5: Students will demonstrate the ability to use decision-making skills to enhance health.

Rationale: Decision-making skills are needed to identify, implement, and sustain health-enhancing behaviors. This standard includes the essential steps that are needed to make healthy decisions as prescribed in the performance indicators. When applied to health issues, the decision-making process enables individuals to collaborate with others to improve their quality of life.

PreK–Grade 2 Performance Indicators, Standard 5
5.2.1   Identify situations when a health-related decision is needed.
5.2.2   Differentiate between situations when a health-related decision can be made individually or when assistance is needed.

Grades 3–5 Performance Indicators, Standard 5
5.5.1   Identify health-related situations that might require a thoughtful decision.
5.5.2   Analyze when assistance is needed in making a health-related decision.
5.5.3   List healthy options to health-related issues or problems.
5.5.4   Predict the potential outcomes of each option when making a health-related decision.
5.5.5   Choose a healthy option when making a decision.
5.5.6   Describe the outcomes of a health-related decision.

NHES Standard 6: Students will demonstrate the ability to use goal-setting skills to enhance health.

Rationale: Goal-setting skills are essential to help students identify, adopt, and maintain healthy behaviors. This standard includes the critical steps that are needed to achieve both short-term and long-term health goals. These skills make it possible for individuals to have aspirations and plans for the future.

PreK–Grade 2 Performance Indicators, Standard 6
6.2.1   Identify a short-term personal health goal and take action toward achieving the goal.
6.2.2   Identify who can help when assistance is needed to achieve a personal health goal.

Grades 3–5 Performance Indicators, Standard 6

6.5.1   Set a personal health goal and track progress toward its achievement.
6.5.2   Identify resources to assist in achieving a personal health goal.

NHES Standard 7: Students will demonstrate the ability to practice health-enhancing behaviors and avoid or reduce health risks.

Rationale: Research confirms that practicing health-enhancing behaviors can contribute to a positive quality of life. In addition, many diseases and injuries can be prevented by reducing harmful and risk-taking behaviors. This standard promotes the acceptance of personal responsibility for health and encourages the practice of healthy behaviors.

PreK–Grade 2 Performance Indicators, Standard 7

7.2.1   Demonstrate healthy practices and behaviors to maintain or improve personal health.
7.2.2   Demonstrate behaviors that avoid or reduce health risks.

Grades 3–5 Performance Indicators, Standard 7

7.5.1   Identify responsible personal health behaviors.
7.5.2   Demonstrate a variety of healthy practices and behaviors to maintain or improve personal health.
7.5.3   Demonstrate a variety of behaviors to avoid or reduce health risks.

NHES Standard 8: Students will demonstrate the ability to advocate for personal, family, and community health.

Rationale: Advocacy skills help students promote healthy norms and healthy behaviors. This standard helps students develop important skills to target their health-enhancing messages and to encourage others to adopt healthy behaviors.

PreK–Grade 2 Performance Indicators, Standard 8

8.2.1   Make requests to promote personal health.
8.2.2   Encourage peers to make positive health choices.

Grades 3–5 Performance Indicators, Standard 8

8.5.1   Express opinions and give accurate information about health issues.
8.5.2   Encourage others to make positive health choices.

The revised standards and performance indicators represent the collaborative work of the Joint Committee on National Health Education Standards and are presented in the *National Health Education Standards: Achieving Excellence*. This information can also be accessed from the CDC's website (http://www.cdc.gov /healthyyouth/sher/standards).

APPENDIX B   Monthly Calendar: Health, Safety, and Nutrition Observances

Teachers may find the following list helpful for developing educational lessons and activities that focus on national observances of children's health, safety, and nutrition concerns. Additional resources and information can be accessed on many websites, including those that follow.

January

Healthy Weight Week	Healthy Weight Network http://www.healthyweightnetwork.com
Poverty Awareness Month	Children's Defense Fund http://www.childrensdefense.org

February

American Heart Month	American Heart Association http://www.heart.org
Burn Awareness	Burn Prevention Foundation http://www.burnprevention.org
Children's Dental Health Month	American Dental Association http://www.ada.org
Girls and Women in Sports Day	National Association for Girls and Women in Sports http://www.aahperd.org/nagws/programs/ngwsd National Council of Youth Sports http://www.ncys.org
National Cancer Prevention	American Cancer Society http://www.cancer.org
National Eating Disorders Awareness	National Eating Disorders Association http://www.nationaleatingdisorders.org
Random Acts of Kindness	Random Acts of Kindness Foundation http://www.actsofkindness.org

March

Brain Injury Awareness Month	Brain Injury Association of America http://www.biausa.org
Diabetes Awareness	American Diabetes Association http://www.diabetes.org
National Developmental Disabilities Awareness Month	The ARC of the U.S. http://www.thearc.org
National Nutrition Month	Academy of Nutrition & Dietetics http://www.eatright.org
Poison Prevention Month	Poison Prevention Council http://www.poisonprevention.org
Save Your Vision Month	American Optometric Association http://www.aoa.org
Sleep Awareness Week	National Sleep Awareness Foundation http://www.sleepfoundation.org
Youth Violence Prevention	National Association of SAVE http://www.nationalsave.org

April

Child Abuse Prevention Month	Prevent Child Abuse America http://www.preventchildabuse.org
National Playground Safety Week	National Program for Playground Safety http://www.playgroundsafety.org

National Safe Kids Week   Safe Kids Worldwide
                                         http://www.safekids.org
Stress Awareness Month   American Counseling Association
                                         http://www.counseling.org

May

Allergy and Asthma Awareness   Allergy & Asthma Foundation of America
Month   http://www.aafa.org or http://www.aanma.org
Better Hearing and Speech Month   American Speech-Language-Hearing Association
(ASHA)   http://www.asha.org
Bike Safety Month   League of American Bicyclists
                                         http://www.bikeleague.org
                                         Safe Kids Worldwide
                                         http://www.usa.safekids.org
Buckle Up America Week   National Highway Traffic Safety Administration
                                         http://www.nhtsa.gov
Clean Air Month   American Lung Association
                                         http://www.lungusa.org
Healthy Vision Month   National Eye Institute
                                         http://www.nei.nih.gov/hrm
Lyme Disease Awareness Month   Lyme Disease Association
                                         http://www.lymediseaseassociation.org
Mental Health Month (Children)   Mental Health America
                                         http://www.nmha.org
National Hurricane Preparedness   National Weather Service
                                         http://www.weather.gov
National Melanoma/Skin Cancer   American Academy of Dermatology
Awareness   http://www.aad.org
Physical Fitness and Sports   President's Council on Fitness, Sports, & Nutrition
                                         http://www.fitness.gov

June

Home Safety Month   Home Safety Council
                                         http://www.homesafetycouncil.org
Lightning Safety Week   National Weather Service
                                         http://www.lightningsafety.noaa.gov
National Safety Month   National Safety Council
                                         http://www.nsc.org
Sun Safety Week   Sun Safety Alliance
                                         http://www.sunsafetyalliance.org

July

Fireworks Eye Safety Month   Prevent Blindness America
                                         http://www.preventblindness.org
UV (Ultra Violet) Eye Safety Month   American Academy of Ophthalmology
                                         http://www.aao.org

August

Children's Eye Health and Safety   Prevent Blindness America
Month   http://www.preventblindness.org
Immunization Awareness Month   Centers for Disease Control and Prevention
                                         http://www.cdc.gov/vaccines

September

America on the Move   America On the Move Foundation
                                         http://www.americaonthemove.org

Baby Safety Month	U.S. Consumer Product Safety Commission
	http://www.cpsc.gov
Fruit and Vegetable Month	Fruit and Vegetable Program Office Centers for
	Disease Control and Prevention/Produce for Better
	Health Foundation
	http://www.fruitsandveggiesmatter.gov
National Childhood Obesity	President's Council on Fitness, Sports, & Nutrition
Awareness Month	http://www.fitness.gov
National Preparedness Month	American Red Cross
	http://www.redcross.org
	Federal Emergency Management Agency (FEMA)
	http://www.ready.gov
National Yoga Month	Yoga Health Foundation
	http://www.yogamonth.org
Sickle Cell Awareness Month	Sickle Cell Disease Association of America, Inc.
	http://www.sicklecelldisease.org
Sports and Home Eye Safety	Prevent Blindness America
	http://www.preventblindness.org
Whole Grains Month	Whole Grains Council
	http://www.wholegrainscouncil.org

October

Eye Injury Prevention Month	American Academy of Ophthalmology
	http://www.aao.org
Fire Prevention Week	National Fire Protection Association
	http://www.nfpa.org
Health Literacy Month	National Institutes of Health (NIH)
	http://www.nih.gov
National Health Education Week	Society for Public Health Education
	http://www.sophe.org
National School Lunch Week	School Nutrition Association
	http://www.schoolnutrition.org/nslw
School Bus Safety Week	National Association for Pupil Transportation
	http://www.naptonline.org
SIDS Awareness Month	SIDS Alliance
	http://www.sidsalliance.org

November

American Diabetes Awareness Month	American Diabetes Association
	http://www.diabetes.org
Epilepsy Awareness Month	Epilepsy Foundation
	http://www.epilepsyfoundation.org
National Healthy Skin Month	American Academy of Dermatology
	http://www.aad.org

December

National Handwashing	Henry the Hand Foundation
Awareness Week	http://www.henrythehand.com
National Safe Toys Month	Consumer Product Safety Commission
	http://www.cpsc.gov
	Kids Health
	http://www.kidshealth.org

APPENDIX C   Federal Food and Nutrition Programs

Federal food programs are funded and regulated by the U.S. Department of Agriculture (USDA) and administered at the state level by the Department of Education or the Public Health Department. These programs are intended to improve the health and wellness of the recipients. Information about the availability of food and nutrition programs in a particular community can be obtained from city or county health departments, state office of public health, or the state department of education.

Child Nutrition Programs

Child nutrition programs provide cash assistance and/or food commodities for children enrolled in public schools, nonprofit private schools, early education centers, home-based child care programs, summer day camps, and after-school programs.

National School Lunch Program (www.fns.usda.gov/cnd/Lunch)

The National School Lunch Program (NSLP) is the oldest and largest federal child food program in existence, both in terms of the number of children it reaches (more than 30 million) and dollars spent. The NSLP is administered at the national level by the USDA and at the state level by the U.S. Department of Education. Participating public and nonprofit schools are reimbursed for serving children lunches that meet specific nutrient guidelines. After-school and enrichment programs are also eligible to apply for reimbursement for the snacks they provide to children (through age 18 years). The amount of money schools receive per meal depends upon whether the student qualifies for free, reduced price, or full price meals. The families of students eligible to receive free or reduced price meals must submit financial statements and meet family size and income guidelines. These categories are adjusted periodically to reflect changes in national poverty guidelines. Families caring for foster children are exempt from proving income eligibility.

Meals served to children participating in the school lunch program must comply with the Dietary Guidelines for Americans in addition to new nutrition standards established by the Healthy, Hunger-Free Kids Act 2010. Schools are required to serve more fruits and vegetables (especially fresh), whole grains, and fat-free or 1-percent milk each day. Meals must also be planned not to exceed new levels for sodium content and calories in an effort to address childhood obesity and improve children's long-term health.

School Breakfast Program (http://www.fns.usda.gov/cnd/Breakfast)

The School Breakfast Program, authorized by the Child Nutrition Act of 1975, has also undergone changes and must comply with the nutrition mandates outlined in the Healthy, Hunger-Free Kids Act 2010. This program makes provision for free, reduced price, or full price meals based on a family's income eligibility. The School Breakfast Program is available to public and nonprofit schools (Pre-K through high school) and to licensed nonprofit residential child care institutions.

Summer Food Service Program (http://www.summerfood.usda.gov)

The purpose of the Summer Food Service Program is to address the nutrition needs of children during months when school is not in session. Schools, parks and recreation centers, playgrounds, churches, day camps, housing projects, residential summer camps, and migrant centers located in communities or on Indian reservations where at least 50 percent of children qualify for free or reduced price meals can apply to become a sponsor site. Most sites also provide supervised play and educational activities. Funding for meals is provided by the USDA's Food and Nutrition Service and administered through state education departments. Meals must meet federal nutrition guidelines and are provided free-of-charge to any child on a first-come basis.

Child and Adult Care Food Program (http://www.fns.usda.gov/cnd/care)

The Child and Adult Care Food Program (CACFP) provides cash reimbursement for meals served to children in licensed early childhood centers, home-based child care programs, children in emergency shelters, at-risk after school programs, and adults living in group homes. The program benefits children 12 years old and under, disabled persons in an institution serving a majority of persons 18 years old and under, migrant children 15 years old and younger, children 18 years or younger staying in emergency shelters, and adults with disabilities. The USDA's Food and Nutrition Service provides funding for the CACFP program, which is administered through the Department of Education in most states. The program is designed to improve the quality of children's nutrient intake.

Programs are reimbursed for a maximum of two meals and one snack or one meal and two snacks. Reimbursement rates are based on a family's income eligibility. The meal pattern follows the same guidelines required for the National School Lunch Program that are adjusted by age categories: infants, children 1–2 years, children 3–5 years, children 6–12 years, and adults.

Family Nutrition Programs

Two governmental programs that provide food assistance to eligible families are the Special Supplemental Nutrition Program for Women, Infants, and Children, better known as WIC, and the Supplemental Nutrition Assistance Program (SNAP).

Women, Infants, and Children (http://www.fns.usda.gov/wic)

WIC is administered at the federal level by the USDA Food and Nutrition Service, which provides local public health and/or nonprofit health agencies with funding to operate this program. WIC offers nutrition education, health care referrals, and checks, vouchers, or electronic cards (EBT) that recipients can use to purchase foods rich in protein, iron, and vitamin C. Women who are pregnant and/or breastfeeding, infants, and children up to 5 years of age who are identified to be at nutritional risk and income-eligible are considered for this program. Participants receive specified amounts of the following foods:

- iron-fortified infant formula and baby foods
- iron-fortified adult cereals
- fresh fruits, vegetables, and juices rich in vitamin C
- whole grain bread
- fortified milk
- proteins, including cheese, eggs, peanut butter, tofu, and canned fish
- dried beans, peas, and legumes

Supplemental Nutrition Assistance Program (http://www.fns.usda.gov/snap)

SNAP is a food-assistance program designed to improve nutrient intake in low-income families; nearly half of the recipients are children under 18 years. Eligibility is based on a combination of financial and non-financial factors. The program is typically administered by either state or local welfare agencies. Monthly benefits are deposited electronically into a credit account that recipients are able to use for food purchases. The purpose of the electronic benefits transfer (EBT) is to reduce the potential for fraud. Funds may be used to purchase *allowed foods*, such as breads and cereals, fruits and vegetables, meats, fish or poultry, and dairy or seeds that can be used to grow food for consumption. Items not allowed include soap, cigarettes, paper goods, alcoholic beverages, pet foods, vitamins, or deli foods that may be eaten on the premises.

APPENDIX D   Children's Book List

Dental Health

Civardi, A. (2010). *Going to the Dentist*. Usborne Books.

Cousins, L. (2009). *Maisy, Charley, and the Wobbly Tooth: A Maisy First Experience Book*. Candlewick.

Katz, B. (2002). *Hello Reader: Make Your Way for Tooth Decay*. Cartwheel.

Keller, L. (2000). *Open Wide: Tooth School Inside*. Henry Holt & Company.

Lewison, W. (2002). *Clifford's Loose Tooth*. Scholastic.

Mayer, M. (2001). *Just Going to the Dentist*. Golden Books.

Miller, E. (2009). *The Tooth Book: A Guide to Healthy Teeth and Gums*. Holiday House.

Minarik, E. (2002). *Little Bear's Loose Tooth*. HarperFestival.

Munsch, R. (2002). *Andrew's Loose Tooth*. Scholastic.

Murkoff, H. (2002). *What to Expect When You Go to the Dentist*. HarperFestival.

Schuh, M. (2008). *At the Dentist (Healthy Teeth series)*. Capstone Press. (Also available in Spanish).

Ziefert, H. (2012). *ABC Dentist: Healthy Teeth from A to Z*. Blue Apple Books.

Illness/Germs

Berger, M. (1995). *Germs Make Me Sick!* HarperCollins.

Berger, M. (2002). *Why I Sneeze, Shiver, Hiccup, & Yawn*. HarperCollins.

Capeci, A. (2001). *The Giant Germ*. Scholastic Paperbacks.

Cote, P. (2002). *How Do I Feel?* Houghton Mifflin. (Spanish and English).

Dealey, E. (2002). *Goldie Locks Has Chicken Pox*. Scholastic.

Harvey, R. (2005). *Caillou: Is Sick*. Chouette Publishing.

Newman, A. (2012). *How to Catch a Cold*. MiLo Ink Books.

O'Brien-Palmer, M. (1999). *Healthy Me: Fun Ways to Develop Good Health and Safety Habits: Activities for Children 5–8*. Chicago Review Press.

Oetting, J. (2006). *Germs*. Children's Press.

Rice, J. (2002). *Those Mean, Nasty, Dirty, Downright Disgusting but Invisible Germs*. Redleaf Press.

Romanek, T. (2003). *Achoo: The Most Interesting Book You'll Ever Read About Germs*. Kids Can Press.

Ross, T. (2006). *Wash Your Hands!* Kane/Miller.

Rylant, C. (2003). *Mr. Putter & Tabby Catch the Cold*. Sandpiper.

Verdick, E. (2006). *Germs Are Not for Sharing*. Free Spirit Publishing. (Also available in Spanish)

Mental Health (Feelings)

Aboff, E. (2010). *Everyone Feels Scared Sometimes*. Picture Window Books.

Agassi, M. (2000). *Hands Are Not for Hitting*. Free Spirit Publishing.

Anholt, C. (1998). *What Makes Me Happy?* Candlewick Press.

Annunziata, J., & Nemiroff, M. (2009). *Sometimes I'm Scared*. Magination Press.

Baker, L. (2001). *I Love You Because You're You*. Cartwheel Books.

Bang, M. (1999). *When Sophie Gets Angry—Really, Really Angry*. Scholastic.

Beaumont, K. (2004). *I Like Myself!* Harcourt Children's Books.

Blumenthal, D. (1999). *The Chocolate-Covered-Cookie Tantrum*. Clarion Books.

Cain, J. (2000). *The Way I Feel*. Parenting Press.

Carle, E. (1999). *The Very Lonely Firefly*. Philomel Books.

Carle, E. (2000). *The Grouchy Ladybug*. Scholastic.

Child, L. (2007). *You Can Be My Friend*. Grosset & Dunlap.

Cole, J. (2010). *I'm a Big Brother*. HarperFestival.

Cole, J. (2010). *I'm a Big Sister*. HarperFestival.

Cook, J. (2005). *A Bad Case of Tattle Tongue*. National Center for Youth Issues.

Cruz, R. (2009). *Alexander and the Terrible, Horrible, No Good, Very Bad Day*. Antheneum.

Cutis, J. L. (1998). *Today I Feel Silly: And Other Moods That Make My Day*. HarperCollins.

Cutis, J. L. (2002). *I'm Gonna Like Me: Letting off a Little Self-Esteem*. Joanna Cotler.

Hallinan, P. K. (2005). *A Rainbow of Friends*. Ideals Children's Books.

Hankinson, S. (2008). *Carrot-Walnut Pie*. AuthorHouse. (Bullying)

Henkes, K. (2007). *Chrysanthemum*. Greenwillow Books.

Hudson, C., & Ford, B. (1990). *Bright Eyes, Brown Skin*. Just Us Books.

Karst, P. (2000). *The Invisible String*. DeVorss & Co. (Death)

Ketteman, H. (2000). *Armadillo Tattletale*. Scholastic Books.

Krasny, L., & Brown, M. (2001). *How to Be a Friend: A Guide to Making Friends and Keeping Them*. Little Brown & Co.

Lalli, J. (2007). *I Like Being Me: Poems for Children, About Feeling Special, Appreciating Others, and Getting Along*. Free Spirit Publishing.

Lewis, P. (2002). *I'll Always Love You*. Tiger Tales.

Lite, L. (2007). *A Boy and a Turtle: A Children's Relaxation Story to Improve Sleep, Manage Stress, Anxiety, Anger*. Stress Free Kids.

Lite, L. (2008). *The Angry Octopus*. Stress Free Kids.

Lovell, P. (2001). *Stand Tall, Molly Lou Melon*. Scholastic.

Masurel, C. (2003). *Two Homes*. Candlewick. (Divorce)

Meiners, C. (2003). *Share and Take Turns*. Free Spirit.

O'Neill, A. (2002). *The Recess Queen*. Scholastic.

Parr, T. (2011). *The I'M NOT SCARED Book*. Little, Brown.

Parr, T. (2009). *It's Okay to be Different*. Little, Brown.

Parr, T. (2005). *The Feelings Book*. Little, Brown Books for Young Readers.

Sáenz, B. (2009). *The Dog Who Loved Tortillas/La perrita que le encantaban las tortillas*. Cinco Puntos Press.

Silver, G. (2009). *Anh's Anger*. Plum Blossom Books.

Spelman, C. (2000). *When I Feel Angry*. Albert Whitman & Co.

Tarpley, N. (2001). *I Love My Hair*. Little Brown.

Tetik, B. (2009). *If You Are Mad Say It with Words*. BookSurge Publishing.

Thomas, P. (2000). *Stop Picking on Me*. Barrons.

Vail, R. (2002). *Sometimes I'm Bombaloo*. Scholastic.

Weninger, B., & Marks, A. (1995). *Good-bye Daddy*. North-South Books.

Willems, M. (2007). *My Friend Is Sad*. Hyperion Book CH.

Personal Health & Self-Care

Baker, K. (2001). *Brave Little Monster*. HarperCollins.

Berry, J. (2010). *I Love Getting Dressed (Teach Me About)*. Joy Berry Books.

Brown, M. (2005). *Good Night Moon*. HarperFestival.

Cason, S. (2008). *The Night-Night Dance*. Tate Publishing.

Chodos-Irvine, M. (2003). *Ella Sarah Gets Dressed*. Harcourt Children's Books.

Civardi, A. (2005). Usborne First Experiences Collection: "*Going to School,*" "*Going to the Doctor,*" "*Moving House,*" "*The New Baby.*" Usborne Publishing Ltd.

Fox, L. (2010) *Ella Kazoo Will Not Brush Her Hair*. Walker Books for Young Readers.

Giles, S. (2011). *The Children's Book of Healthy Habits*. Award Publications Ltd.

Katz, A. (2001). *Take Me Out of the Bathtub*. Scholastic.

Keats, E. J. (2000). *Dreams*. Puffin.

Murkoff, H. (2000). *What to Expect at Bedtime*. HarperFestival.

Murkoff, H. (2000). *What to Expect When You Go to the Doctor*. HarperFestival.

Reidy, J. (2010). *Too Purpley!* Bloomsbury USA Children's Books.

Ricci, C. (2007). *Show Me Your Smile! A Visit to the Dentist*. Simon Spotlight Nickelodeon.

Timberlake, A. (2003). Th*e Dirty Cowboy*. Farrar, Straus, & Giroux.

Wood, A. (2009). *The Napping House*. Harcourt Children's Books.

Yolen, J. (2000). *How Do Dinosaurs Say Goodnight?* Blue Sky Press.

Safety

Boxall, E. (2002). *Francis the Scaredy Cat*. Candlewick Press.

Caviezel, G. (2007). *Policeman's Safety Hints*. Barron's Educational Series.

Committee, C. B. (2000). *Buckles Buckles Everywhere*. Palmetto Bookworks.

Cook, J. (2007). *SCOOP (Children's Life Skills)*. National Center for Youth Issues.

Cuyler, M. (2001). *Stop, Drop, Roll.* Simon & Schuster.

Federico, J. (2009). *Some Parts Are Not for Sharing.* Tate Publishing.

Feigh, A. (2008). *On Those Runaway Days.* Free Spirit Publishing.

Hayward, L. (2001). *A Day in the Life of a Firefighter.* Dorling Kindersley Publisher.

Kelman, M. (2009). *Safety First!* Disney Press.

Kurtz, J. (2005). *Do Kangaroos Wear Seatbelts?* Dutton Juvenile.

MacLean, C. K. (2002). *Even Firefighters Hug Their Moms.* Dutton.

Mattern, J. (2007). *Staying Safe in the Car.* Weekly Reader Early Learning Library.

Meiners, C. (2006). *Be Careful and Stay Safe.* Free Spirit Publishing

Mitton, T. (2001). *Down by the Cool of the Pool.* Orchard Books.

Palatini, M. (2002). *Earthquack!* Simon & Schuster.

Pendziwol, J. (2006). *Once Upon a Dragon: Stranger Safety for Kids (and Dragons).* Kids Can Press.

Prigger, M. (2002). *Aunt Minnie and the Twister.* Clarion.

Reasoner, C. (2003). *Bee Safe (The Bee Attitudes).* Price Stern Sloan Publishers.

Spelman, C., & Weidner, T. (2000). *Your Body Belongs to You.* Albert Whitman.

Tekavec, H. (2002). *Storm Is Coming!* Dial.

Thomas, P. (2003). *I Can Be Safe!* Barrand's Educational Series.

Wahman, W. (2009). *Don't Lick the Dog: Making Friends with Dogs.* Henry Holt & Co.

Weeks, S. (2002). *My Somebody Special.* Harcourt, Inc.

Special Needs

Bunnett, R. (2006). *Friends at School.* Star Bright Books.

Chirstenson, D. (2012). *Elephant on My Chest.* Peebles Publishing Co. (Asthma)

Gaynor, K., Carswell, C., & Quirke, K. (2009). *A Birthday for Ben – Children with Hearing Difficulty.* Moonbeam Children's Books.

Gosselin, K. (2004). *Taking Diabetes to School.* JayJo Books.

Heelan, J. (2000). *Rolling Along: The Story of Taylor and His Wheelchair.* Peachtree Publishers LTD.

Lang, R. (2004). *Lara Takes Charge.* MLPI Books. (Chronic illness)

Lears, L. (2005). *Nathan's Wish: A Story about Cerebral Palsy.* Albert Whitman & Co.

Lewis, B. (2007). *In Jesse's Shoes.* Bethany House Publishers.

London, J. (1997). *The Lion Who Had Asthma.* Albert Whitman & Co.

Maguire, A. (2000). *Special People, Special Ways.* Future Horizons.

Millman, I. (2000). *Moses Goes to School.* Frances Foster Books/Farrar, Straus & Giroux.

Nausau, E. (2001). *The Peanut Butter Jam.* Health Press.

Peete, H. (2010). *My Brother Charlie.* Scholastic. (Autism)

Recob, A. (2009). *The Bugabees: Friends with Food Allergies.* Beaver Pond Press.

Shriver, M. (2001). *What's Wrong with Timmy?* Little Brown & Co.

Skinner, J. (2010). *Food Allergies and Me.* Create Space.

Smith, N. (2006). *Allie the Allergic Elephant: A Children's Story of Peanut Allergies.* Allergic Child Publishing Group.

Thomas, P. (2005). *Don't Call Me Special.* Barron's Educational Series. (Disabilities)

Willis, J. (2000). *Susan Laughs.* Henry Holt & Co. (Wheelchair)

Nutrition

Appleton, J. (2001). *Do Carrots Make You See Better?* Red Leaf Press.

Brennan, G., & Brennan, E. (2004). *The Children's Kitchen Garden: A Book of Gardening, Cooking and Learning.* Ten Speed Press.

Brown, M. (1997). *D.W. The Picky Eater.* Little, Brown Books for Young Readers.

Brown, P. (2009). *The Curious Garden.* Little, Brown Books for Young Readers.

Caplan, J. (2009). *Gobey Gets Full: Good Nutrition in a Nutshell.* BookSurge Publishing.

Carle, E. (2008). *The Very Hungry Caterpillar.* Philomel.

Chamberlin, M. (2006). *Mama Panya's Pancakes.* Barefoot Books.

Charney, S., Goldbeck, D., & Larson, M. (2007). *The ABCs of Fruits and Vegetables and Beyond.* Ceres Press.

Child, L. (2003). *I Will Never Eat a Tomato.* Candelwick

Compestine, Y. (2001). *The Runaway Rice Cake.* Simon & Schuster.

Cooper, H. (2005). *Pumpkin Soup.* Farrar, Straus & Giroux (BYR).

D'Aluisio, F. (2008). *What the World Eats*. Tricycle Press.

Ehlert, L. (2006). *Eating the Alphabet: Fruits and Vegetables from A to Z*. HMH Books.

Geeslin, C. (1999). *How Nanita Learned to Make Flan*. Atheneum.

Gibbons, G. (2000). *The Honey Makers*. HarperCollins.

Gibbons, G. (2008). *The Vegetables We Eat*. Holiday House.

Hutchins, P. (2007). *Ten Red Apples*. Greenwillow Books.

Katzen, M. (1994). *Pretend Soup and Other Real Recipes: A Cookbook for Preschoolers and Up*. Tricycle Press.

Kye, J. (2011). *Jojo Eats Dim Sum*. Wonderscopic.

Krauss, R. (2004). *The Carrot Seed*. HarperCollins.

Levenson, G. (2002). *Pumpkin Circle: The Story of a Garden*. Tricycle Press.

Lin, G. (2003). *Dim Sum for Everyone*. Dragonfly Books.

Lin, G. (2009). *The Ugly Vegetables*. Charlesbridge Publishing.

Leedy, L. (2007). *The Edible Pyramid: Good Eating Every Day*. Holiday House.

Montes, G. (2012). *My Grandmother's Tortillas*. Infinity Publishing.

Rabe, T. (2001). *Oh the Things You Can Do That Are Good for You!* Random House.

Reiser, L. (1998). *Tortillas and Lullabies*. Greenwillow Books.

Richards, J. (2006). *A Fruit Is a Suitcase for Seeds*. First Avenue Editions.

Rockwell, L. (2009). *Good Enough to Eat: A Kid's Guide to Food and Nutrition*. HarperCollins.

Rubin, A. (2012). *Dragons Love Tacos*. Dial.

Russ-Ayon, A., & June, C. (2009). *We Eat Food That's Fresh*. OurRainbow Press.

Sanger, A. (2001). *First Book of Sushi*. Tricycle Press.

Sayer, A. (2012). *Go! Go! Grapes: A Fruit Chant*. Beach Lane Books.

Sayer, A. (2011). *Rah! Rah! Radishes: A Vegetable Chant*. Beach Lane Books.

Schuh, M. (2006). *Being Active (Healthy Eating With My Pyramid)*. Capstone Press.

Sears, W., Sears, M., & Kelly, C. (2002). *Eat Healthy, Feel Great*. Little, Brown Young Readers.

Schneider, J. (2011). *Tales for Very Picky Eaters*. Clarion Books.

Sharmat, M. (2009). *Gregory, the Terrible Eater*. Scholastic.

Wells, P. (2003). *Busy Bears: Breakfast with the Bears*. Sterling Publications.

Wallace, N. (2004). *Apples, Apples, Apples*. Amazon Children's Publishing.

Woods, D., & Woods, A. (2000). *The Big Hungry Bear*. Child's Play Publishers.

Woomer, L. (2009). *Cookie*. Outskirts Press.

Physical Activity

Ackerman, K., & Gammell, S. (2003). *Song and Dance Man*. Knopf Books.

Blackstone, S. (2001). *Bear About Town*. Barefoot Books.

Blackstone, S., & Harter, D. (2007). *Bear on a Bike*. Barefoot Books.

Brown, M. (1991). *D.W. Flips*. Little, Brown Books for Young Readers.

Brown, M. (1996). *D.W. Rides Again*. Little, Brown Books for Young Readers.

Cole, J., Calmenson, S., & Tiegreen, A. (1990). *Miss Mary Mack and Other Children's Street Rhymes*. HarperCollins.

Cole, J., & Tiegreen, A. (1989). *Anna Banana: 101 Jump Rope Rhymes*. HarperCollins.

Craig, L. (2010). *Dancing Feet*. Knopf.

Davis, K. (2001). *Who Hops?* Voyager Books.

Doering-Tourville, A. (2008). *Get Up and Go: Being Active (How to Be Healthy)*. Picture Window Books.

Esbensen, B., & Leffler, M. (2000). *Jumping Day*. Boyds Mills Press.

Fallon, J., & Stower, A. (2007). *Snowball Fight!* Scholastic Inc.

Flemming, D. (1995). *In the Tall, Tall Grass*. Henry Holt & Co.

Hutchins, P. (2007). *Barn Dance!* Greenwillow Books.

Isadora, R. (2000). *Isadora Dances*. Puffin.

Kann, V. (2012). *Pinkalicious Soccer Star*. HarperCollins.

London, J., & Remkiewicz, F. (2001). *Froggy Plays Soccer*. Puffin.

London, J., & Remkiewicz, F. (2008). *Froggy Rides a Bike*. Puffin.

Miller, E. (2008). *The Monster Health Book: A Guide to Eating Healthy, Being Active & Feeling Great for Monsters & Kids*. Holiday House.

Rosen, M. (2009). *We're Going on a Bear Hunt*. Helen Oxenbury.

Schuh, M. (2006). *Being Active*. Capstone Press.

Shannon, G., & Trynan, A. (2000). *Frog Legs*. Greenwillow Books.

Shields, D. (2008). *Saturday Night at the Dinosaur Stomp*. Candlewick.

Stickland, P. (2000). *Ten Terrible Dinosaurs*. Puffin.

Thomas, P., & Facklam, P. (2008). *Snow Dance*. Pelican Publishing.

Torrey, R. (2003). *Beans Baker Bounces Back*. Random House Books.

Tourville, A. (2008). *Get Up and Go: Being Active*. Picture Window Books.

Walton, R., & Gorton, J. (2000). *My Two Hands, My Two Feet*. Puffin.

Winch, J. (2000). *Keeping Up With Grandma*. Holiday House.

APPENDIX E   Nutrient Information: Fast-Food Vendor Websites

Arby's	http://www.arbys.com
A&W	http://www.awrestaurants.com
Back Yard Burgers	http://www.backyardburgers.com
Baja Fresh	http://www.bajafresh.com
Blimpie	http://www.blimpie.com
Burger King	http://www.bk.com
Carl's Jr.	http://www.carlsjr.com
Chick-fil-A	http://www.chick-fil-a.com
Chipotle Mexican Grill	http://www.chipotle.com
Church's Chicken	http://www.churchs.com
Dairy Queen (DQ)	http://www.dairyqueen.com
Domino's Pizza	http://www.dominos.com
El Pollo Loco	http://www.elpolloloco.com
Einstein Bros. Bagels	http://www.einsteinbros.com
Hardee's	http://www.hardees.com
In-and-Out Burger	http://www.in-n-out.com
KFC	http://www.kfc.com
Krystal	http://www.krystal.com
Little Caesars	http://www.littlecaesars.com
Long John Silver's	http://www.ljsilvers.com
McDonald's	http://www.mcdonalds.com
On the Border	http://www.ontheborder.com
Pizza Hut	http://www.pizzahut.com
Quiznos	http://www.quiznos.com
Sonic Drive-In	http://www.sonicdrivein.com
Steak 'n Shake	http://www.steaknshake.com
Subway	http://www.subway.com
Taco Bell	http://www.tacobell.com
Wendy's	http://www.wendys.com
White Castle	http://www.whitecastle.com

*For additional information on the nutritional value of most foods, visit the USDA National Agricultural Library, Nutrient Data Laboratory database (http://ndb.nal.usda.gov).

Glossary

A

abdomen – the portion of the body located between the diaphragm (located at the base of the lungs) and the pelvic or hip bones.

absorption – the process by which the products of digestion are transferred from the intestinal tract into the blood or lymph or by which substances are taken up by the cells.

abuse – to mistreat, attack, or cause harm to another individual.

accreditation – the process of certifying an individual or program as having met certain specified requirements.

acute – the stage of an illness or disease during which an individual is definitely sick and exhibits symptoms characteristic of a specific illness or disease.

airborne transmission – the process by which germs are expelled into the air through coughs and sneezes, and transmitted to another individual via tiny moisture drops.

alkalis – group of bases or caustic substances that are capable of neutralizing acids to form salts.

amblyopia – a condition of the eye commonly referred to as "lazy eye"; vision gradually becomes blurred or distorted due to unequal balance of the eye muscles. There are no observable abnormalities of the eyes when a child has amblyopia.

amino acids – the organic building blocks from which proteins are made.

anaphylaxis – a severe allergic reaction that may cause difficulty breathing, itching, unconsciousness, and possible death.

anecdotal – brief notes describing a person's observations.

antibodies – special substances produced by the body that help protect against disease.

apnea – momentary absence of breathing.

aseptic procedure – treatment to produce a product that is free of disease-producing bacteria.

aspiration – accidental inhalation of food, fluid, or an object into the respiratory tract.

asymptomatic – having no symptoms.

attachment – an emotional connection established between infants and their parents and/or primary caregivers.

attitudes – beliefs or feelings one has toward certain facts or situations.

atypical – unusual; different from what might commonly be expected.

audiologist – a specially prepared clinician who uses nonmedical techniques to diagnose hearing impairments.

B

basal metabolic rate (BMR) – minimum amount of energy needed to carry on the body processes vital to life.

behavioral objectives – a clear and measurable description of a specific behavior that an individual is expected to learn.

C

calcium – mineral nutrient; a major component of bones and teeth.

calories – units used to measure the energy value of foods.

coenzymes – a vitamin-containing substance required by certain enzymes before they can perform their prescribed function.

cognitive – the aspect of learning that refers to the development of skills and abilities based on knowledge and thought processes.

collagen – a protein that forms the major constituent of connective tissue, cartilage, bone, and skin.

communicable – capable of being spread or transmitted from one individual to another.

complementary proteins – proteins with offsetting missing amino acids; complementary proteins can be combined to provide complete protein.

complete protein – protein that contains all essential amino acids in amounts relative to the amounts needed to support growth.

compliance – the act of obeying or cooperating with specific requests or requirements.

concepts – combinations of basic and related factual information that represent a broader statement or idea.

conductive loss – affects the volume of word tones heard, so that loud sounds are more likely to be heard than soft sounds.

contagious – capable of being transmitted or passed from one person to another.

convalescent – the stage of recovery from an illness or disease.

cost control – reduction of expenses through portion control inventory and reduction of waste.

critical control point (CCP) – a point or procedure in a specific food system where loss of control may result in an unacceptable health risk.

cryptosporidiosis – an infectious illness caused by an intestinal parasite. May be present in water (e.g., swimming pools, hot tubs, streams) contaminated with feces or from unwashed hands. Often causes severe diarrhea in children.

cyber-bullying – sending embarrassing or threatening messages to an individual via the Internet, electronic media, or cell phone.

cycle menus – menus that are written to repeat after a set interval, such as every three to four weeks.

D

deciduous teeth – a child's initial set of teeth; these teeth are temporary and gradually begin to fall out at around 5 years of age.

dehydration – a state in which there is an excessive loss of body fluids or extremely limited fluid intake. Symptoms may include loss of skin tone, sunken eyes, and mental confusion.

dental caries – tooth decay.

development – commonly refers to the process of intellectual growth and change.

developmental or physiological readiness – growth (both physical and cognitive) and chemical processes that lead to the ability to perform a function.

developmentally appropriate practices (DAP) – learning experiences and environments that take into account children's individual abilities, interests, and diverse needs. DAP also reflects differences among families and values them as essential partners in children's education.

diagnosis – the process of identifying a disease, illness, or injury from its symptoms.

Dietary Guidelines for Americans – a report that provides recommendations for daily food choices, to be balanced with physical activity, to promote good health and reduce certain disease risks.

Dietary Reference Intake (DRI) – a plan that presents the recommended goals of nutrient intakes for various age and gender groups.

digestion – the process by which complex nutrients in foods are changed into smaller units that can be absorbed and used by the body.

direct contact – coming in direct or immediate contact with infectious material.

discipline – training or enforced obedience that corrects, shapes, or develops acceptable patterns of behavior.

disorientation – lack of awareness or ability to recognize familiar persons or objects.

distention – the state of being stretched or enlarged.

DNA – deoxyribonucleic acid; the substance in the cell nucleus that codes for genetically transmitted traits.

Down syndrome – a genetic disorder that is characterized by unique facial features, intellectual disability, and motor delays.

E

electrolytes – substances that, when in solution, become capable of conducting electricity; examples include sodium and potassium.

elevate – to raise to a higher position.

emotional abuse – repeated humiliation, ridicule, or threats directed toward another individual.

emotional or psychological neglect – failure to meet a child's psychological needs for love and attention.

endocrine – refers to glands that produce substances called hormones that are secreted directly into the bloodstream.

energy – power to perform work.

enriched – adding nutrients to grain products to replace those lost during refinement; thiamin, niacin, riboflavin, and iron are nutrients most commonly added.

environment – the sum total of physical, emotional, cultural, and behavioral features that surround and affect an individual.

enzymes – proteins that catalyze body functions.

essential amino acids – amino acids that can only be obtained from protein food sources.

essential nutrient – nutrient that must be provided in food because it cannot be synthesized by the body at a rate sufficient to meet its needs.

ethnic – pertaining to races or groups of people who share common traits or customs.

evaluation – a measurement of effectiveness for determining whether or not educational objectives have been achieved.

F

failure to thrive – a term used to describe an infant whose growth and mental development are severely slowed due to lack of nurturing or mental stimulation.

fat-soluble vitamins – vitamins that are dissolved, transported, and stored in fat.

fecal-oral transmission – the process in which germs are transferred to the mouth via hands contaminated with fecal material.

fever – an elevation of body temperature above normal; a temperature over 99.4°F or 37.4°C orally is usually considered a fever.

First-In-First-Out (FIFO) inventory method – a method of storage in which the items stored for the longest time will be retrieved first.

fluorosis – white or brown spots that form on children's teeth due to excessive fluoride intake.

food infections – illnesses resulting from the ingestion of live bacteria in food.

food insecurity – uncertain or limited access to a reliable source of food.

food intolerance – unpleasant reactions to particular foods that do not involve an immune response and are usually outgrown.

food intoxications – illnesses resulting from the ingestion of food containing residual bacterial toxins in the absence of viable (live) bacteria.

food-borne illness – a disease or illness transmitted by the ingestion of food contaminated with bacteria, viruses, some molds, or parasites.

food-borne illness outbreak – two or more persons become ill after ingesting the same food and laboratory analysis confirms that food is the source of the illness.

fruit drinks – products that contain 0–10 percent real fruit juice, added water, and sugar.

full-strength – undiluted (as in 100 percent fruit or vegetable juice).

G

gestational diabetes – a form of diabetes that occurs only during pregnancy; affects the way the mother's body utilizes sugars in foods and increases health risks for the baby.

Good Samaritan Law – legal protection afforded to an individual who renders emergency or first aid care in a reasonable manner.

gram – a metric unit of weight (g); approximately 1/28 of an ounce.

growth – increase in size of any body part or of the entire body.

H

hands-on – active involvement in a project; actually doing something.

Hazard Analysis Critical Control Point (HACCP) – a food safety and self-inspection system that highlights potentially hazardous foods and how they are handled in the food service department.

head circumference – distance around the largest part of the head; used to monitor brain growth and development.

health – a state of wellness. Complete physical, mental, social, and emotional well-being; the quality of one health element affects the state of the others.

health assessment – the process of gathering and evaluating information about an individual's state of health.

heat exhaustion – overheating that occurs when a person is exposed to high outdoor temperatures and humidity during vigorous activity.

heat stroke – failure of the body's sweating reflex to function properly during exposure to high temperatures; causes body temperature to rise.

hemoglobin – the iron-containing, oxygen-carrying pigment in red blood cells.

heredity – the transmission of certain genetic material and characteristics from biological parents to a child at the time of conception.

hormones – special chemical substances produced by endocrine glands that influence and regulate specific body functions.

hyperglycemia – a condition characterized by an abnormally high level of sugar in the blood.

hyperopia – farsightedness; a condition of the eyes in which an individual can see distant objects clearly but has poor close vision.

hypertension – elevation of blood pressure above the normally accepted values.

hyperventilation – rapid breathing often with forced inhalation; can lead to sensations of dizziness, lightheadedness, and weakness.

hypothermia – below-normal body temperature caused by overexposure to cold conditions.

I

immunized – a state of becoming resistant to a specific disease through the introduction of living or dead microorganisms into the body, which then stimulates the production of antibodies.

impairments – a condition or malfunction of a body part that interferes with optimal functioning.

incidental learning – learning that occurs in addition to the primary intent or goals of instruction.

inclusion – the practice of including and integrating children of all abilities in a classroom and individualizing instruction to meet each child's unique learning needs.

incomplete proteins – proteins that lack required amounts of one or more essential amino acids.

incubation – the interval of time between exposure to infection and the appearance of the first signs or symptoms of illness.

indirect contact – coming in contact with infectious material that is transmitted via surfaces, animals, or insects.

individualized educational plan (IEP) – a plan that identifies specific developmental and academic goals and intervention services for a child or youth 3 to 22 years of age who has special needs.

individualized family service plan (IFSP) – a plan that outlines specific goals and intervention services for children 0 to 3 years of age who have special needs and their families.

individualized health services plan (IHSP) – a plan that identifies and addresses a child's special health care needs during school hours.

infection – a condition that results when a pathogen invades and establishes itself within a susceptible host.

ingested – the process of taking food or other substances into the body through the mouth.

inservice – educational training provided by an employer.

intervention – practices or procedures implemented to modify or change a specific behavior or condition.

intestinal – pertaining to the intestines and intestinal tract.

iron-deficiency anemia – a failure in the oxygen transport system caused by too little iron.

irradiation – food preservation by short-term exposure of the food to gamma rays.

L

latch-key – a term that refers to school-age children who care for themselves without adult supervision before and after school hours.

lethargy – a state of inaction or indifference.

liability – legal responsibility or obligation for one's actions owed to another individual.

licensing – the act of granting formal permission to conduct a business or profession.

linoleic acid – a polyunsaturated fatty acid that is essential (must be provided in food) for humans; also known as omega-6 fatty acid.

linolenic acid – one of the two polyunsaturated fatty acids that are recognized as essential for humans; also known as omega-3 fatty acid.

listlessness – a state characterized by a lack of energy or interest in one's affairs.

low-birthweight (LBW) – weighing less than 5.5 pounds (2,500 grams) at birth.

Lyme disease – bacterial illness caused by the bite of infected deer ticks found in grassy or wooded areas.

lymph glands – specialized groupings of tissue that produce and store white blood cells for protection against infection and illness.

M

macrocytic anemia – a failure in the oxygen transport system characterized by abnormally large immature red blood cells.

malnutrition – prolonged inadequate or excessive intake of nutrients and/or calories required by the body.

megadose – an amount of a vitamin or mineral at least ten times that of the RDA.

metabolism – all chemical changes that occur from the time nutrients are absorbed until they are built into body tissue or are excreted.

microbial – refers to living organisms, such as bacteria, viruses, parasites, or fungi that can cause disease.

microcytic anemia – a failure in the oxygen transport system characterized by abnormally small red blood cells.

microgram (mcg or μg) – a metric unit of measurement; one microgram equals one-millionth of a gram.

milligram (mg) – a metric unit of weight (mg); approximately 1/1,000 of a gram.

minerals – inorganic chemical elements that are required in the diet to support growth, repair tissue, and regulate body functions.

misarticulations – improper pronunciations of words and word sounds.

mixed hearing loss – a disorder that involves a combination of conductive and sensorineural hearing losses.

Mongolian spots – patches of blue-grey skin located on the lower back; more common among children of Asian, Native American, and Middle Eastern ethnicities.

mottling – marked with spots of dense white or brown coloring.

MUFAs – monounsaturated fatty acids; fatty acids that have one double hydrogen bond; nuts, avocados, and olive oil are high in this form of fat.

myopia – nearsightedness; an individual has good near vision but poor distant vision.

N

neglect – failure of a parent or legal guardian to properly care for and meet the basic needs of a child under 18 years of age.

negligence – failure to practice or perform one's duties according to certain standards; carelessness.

neophobic – fear of things that are new and unfamiliar.

neurological – pertaining to the nervous system, which consists of the nerves, brain, and spinal column.

neuromuscular – pertaining to control of muscular function by the nervous system.

neurons – specialized cells that transmit electrical impulses or signals.

non-essential amino acids – amino acids that are produced in the body.

normal – average; a characteristic or quality that is common to most individuals in a defined group.

norms – an expression (e.g., weeks, months, years) of when a child is likely to demonstrate certain developmental skills.

notarized – official acknowledgment of the authenticity of a signature or document by a notary public.

nutrients – the chemical substances in food.

nutrition – the study of food and how it is used by the body.

nutrition claims – statements of reduced calories, fat, or salt on the food labels.

nutrition education – activities that impart information about food and its use in the body.

O

obese – a BMI over 30.

objectives – clear, meaningful descriptions of specific behavioral outcomes; can be observed and measured.

observation – to inspect and take note of the appearance and behavior of other individuals.

odd-day cycle menus – menus planned for a period of days other than a week that repeat after the planned period; cycles of any number of days may be used. These menus are a means of avoiding repetition of the same foods on the same day of the week.

ophthalmologist – a physician who specializes in diseases and abnormalities of the eye.

optometrist – a specialist (nonphysician) trained to examine eyes and prescribe glasses and eye exercises.

overweight – a BMI greater than 25.

P

pallor – paleness.

palmar grasp – using the entire hand to pick up objects.

paralysis – temporary or permanent loss of sensation, function, or voluntary movement of a body part.

pasteurization – the process of heating a food to a prescribed temperature for a specific amount of time necessary to destroy disease-producing bacteria.

pathogen – a microorganism capable of producing illness or infection.

peer – one of the same rank; equal.

Percent Daily Values (% DV) – measures of the nutritional values of food; used in nutrition labeling.

person first language – a manner of addressing an individual first and then their disability; e.g., a child with autism.

physical abuse – injuries, such as welts, burns, bruises, or broken bones, that are caused intentionally.

physical neglect – failure to meet children's fundamental needs for food, shelter, medical care, and education, including abandonment.

pincer grip – using the thumb and finger to pick up an object.

plasticity – the brain's ability to organize and reorganize neural pathways.

Prader-Willi syndrome – a chromosomal disorder that causes learning and behavior problems, poor muscle tone, short height, and overeating that can lead to obesity.

precipitating – factors that trigger or initiate a reaction or response.

predisposition – having an increased chance or susceptibility.

preplan – outline a method of action prior to carrying it out.

preventive health – personal and social behaviors that promote and maintain well-being.

procurement – the process of obtaining services, supplies, and equipment in conformance with applicable laws and regulations.

prodromal – the appearance of the first nonspecific signs of infection; this stage ends when the symptoms characteristic of a particular communicable illness begin to appear.

protein – class of nutrients used primarily for structural and regulatory functions.

PUFAs – polyunsaturated fatty acids; fatty acids that contain more than one bond that is not fully saturated with hydrogen.

punishment – a negative response to what the observer considers to be wrong or inappropriate behavior; may involve physical or harsh treatment.

R

recovery position – placing an individual in a side-lying position.

referrals – directing an individual to other sources, usually for additional evaluation or treatment.

registration – the act of placing the name of a child care program on a list of active providers; usually does not require on-site inspection.

regulations – standards or requirements that are set to ensure uniform and safe practices.

regurgitation – the return of partially digested food from stomach to mouth.

reprimand – to scold or discipline for unacceptable behavior.

resilience – the capacity to endure or overcome difficult conditions.

resilient – the ability to withstand or resist difficulty.

resistance – the ability to avoid infection or illness.

respiratory tract – the nose, throat, trachea, and lungs.

resuscitation – to revive from unconsciousness or death; to restore breathing and heartbeat.

retention – the ability to remember or recall previously learned material.

risk management – measures taken to avoid an event such as an injury or illness from occurring; implies the ability to anticipate circumstances and behaviors.

RNA – ribonucleic acid; the nucleic acid that serves as messenger between the nucleus and the ribosomes where proteins are synthesized.

S

safe haven – a designated place, such as a hospital or fire station, where parents can leave their infant and give up parental rights without fear of criminal charges.

salmonellosis – a bacterial infection that is spread through contaminated drinking water, food, or milk or contact with other infected persons. Symptoms include diarrhea, fever, nausea, and vomiting.

satiety – a feeling of satisfaction or fullness.

sedentary – unusually slow or sluggish; a lifestyle that implies inactivity.

seizures – a temporary interruption of consciousness sometimes accompanied by convulsive movements.

self-concept – a person's belief of who they are, how they are perceived by others, and how they fit into society.

self-esteem – an individual's sense of value or confidence in himself or herself.

sensorimotor – Piaget's first stage of cognitive development, during which children learn and relate to their world primarily through motor and sensory activities.

sensorineural loss – a type of loss that occurs when sound impulses cannot reach the brain due to damage of the auditory nerve, or cannot be interpreted because of prior brain damage.

sensory qualities – aspects that appeal to sight, sound, taste, feel, and smell.

serrated – saw-toothed or notched.

sexual abuse – any sexual involvement between an adult and child.

shaken baby syndrome – forceful shaking of a baby that causes head trauma, internal bleeding, and sometimes death.

skeletal – pertaining to the bony framework that supports the body.

skinfold – a measurement of the amount of fat under the skin; also referred to as fat-fold measurements.

sleep apnea – temporary interruptions or stoppages in breathing during sleep.

speech – the process of using words to express one's thoughts and ideas.

spina bifida – a neural tube defect that occurs during early fetal development; a malformation (gap or opening) in the spinal column that affects the nerves and spinal cord.

sterile – free from living microorganisms.

strabismus – a condition of the eyes in which one or both eyes appear to be turned inward (crossed) or outward (walleye).

submerge – to place in water.

supervision – monitoring the behaviors and actions of children and others.

supplementary proteins – a complete protein mix resulting from combining a small amount of a complete protein with an incomplete protein to provide all essential amino acids.

susceptible host – an individual who is capable of being infected by a pathogen.

symptomatic control – treatment that controls symptoms but does not cure the condition.

symptoms – changes in the body or its functions that are experienced by the affected individual.

T

temperature – a measurement of body heat; varies with the time of day, activity, and method of measurement.

thermal – caused by heat.

thermic energy of food – energy required to digest, absorb, transport, and metabolize nutrients in food.

toxic stress – stress over which children have no control or adult support; it is intense, frequent, and often prolonged.

trans-fats – unsaturated fats that have been converted to a solid by a process called hydrogenation.

tympanic – referring to the ear canal.

U

undernutrition – an inadequate intake of one or more required or essential nutrients.

underweight – a BMI of less than 18.5.

unintentional injury – an unexpected or unplanned event that may result in physical harm or injury.

universal infection control precautions – special measures taken when handling bodily fluids, including careful hand washing, wearing disposable gloves, disinfecting surfaces, and proper disposal of contaminated objects.

urination – the act of emptying the bladder of urine.

V

values – the beliefs, traditions, and customs an individual incorporates and utilizes to guide behavior and judgments.

verbal abuse – to attack another individual with words.

W

water-soluble vitamins – vitamins that are dissolved and transported in water/fluids; cannot be stored.

weekly menus – menus that are written to be served on a weekly basis.

well child – a child who enjoys a positive state of physical, mental, social, and emotional health.

whole grains – grain products that have not been refined; they contain all parts of the kernel of grain.

Index